THE ENCYCLOPÆDIA OF BRIGHTON

by

Timothy Carder

ISBN: 086 147 3159

East Sussex County Libraries

CONTENTS

Preface and Acknowledgments
List of Entries
List of Figures
Encyclopaedia
Sources and Bibliography
General Index
Index to People

ISBN 086 147 3159

Written, designed and typeset by Timothy Carder, November 1990

Published by East Sussex County Libraries, Southdown House, 44 St Anne's Crescent, Lewes, BN7 1SQ

Printed by East Sussex County Council Printing Department

PREFACE AND ACKNOWLEDGMENTS

BRIGHTON! The very name conjures images of happy holidaymakers, cosmopolitan high life and outstanding architecture. A town so popular is naturally the subject of a multitude of guide-books pointing both visitor and resident in the direction of the tourist haunts, smart shops, ***haute cuisine*** and fashionable nightspots. Other works cover the history of the town from its origins as a small sea-faring town to the present day, highlighting the glorious 'reign' of the Prince of Wales, the sophistication of the Regency and the splendour of the Royal Pavilion.

But what history lies behind the buildings that we pass every day without a second thought? What of the streets and parks, the railways and utilities, the theatres and cinemas? It was to answer such questions as 'When was the first electricity supply provided?', 'Where did the trams and trolley-buses run?', 'What was the name of the cinema in Lewes Road?', and even 'When was my house built?' that this work was conceived, compiled and edited as a reference book on Brighton.

Arranged as an encyclopaedia of 216 entries, it brings together for the first time in one publication a wealth of information covering the people, events and buildings that have shaped the town from prehistory to the 1990s. The book is intended as a comprehensive introduction to all aspects of the town which will satisfy most users; for more in-depth study this work acts as a guide to sources and further reading. It would be impossible not to make errors and omissions in a work of this size, and I apologise in advance for such mistakes.

In writing this note I must thank the patient staffs of Brighton Reference Library, Hove Reference Library, and East Sussex County Record Office; Brighton Borough Council Planning Department; Brighton Borough Council Estates Department; Brighton Borough Council Tourism and Resorts Services Department; Brighton Borough Council Secretary's Department; Brighton Borough Council Technical Services Department; and the Department of Transport for the help that all have given in providing information. Thanks also to Eschmann Equipment Ltd of Lancing, Cooke Technology Ltd of Portslade, Martin Oakley and David Carder for the use of equipment. Finally, many thanks to Stephanie Green of Brighton Reference Library and Chris Smith of East Sussex County Libraries, without whose assistance this publication would not have been possible.

Tim Carder

November 1990

LIST OF ENTRIES

1 Albion Hill
2 Ancient Customs
3 Aquarium and Dolphinarium
4 Architecture
5 Balsdean
6 Banks
7 Bathing
8 Batteries and Fortifications
9 Bear Road and East Preston
10 Bedford Hotel
11 Bevendean
12 Black Rock
13 Boundaries
14 Breweries
15 Brighton - Location and functions
16 Brighton - The name
17 Brighton - Early history
18 Brighton Centre
19 Brighton College
20 Brighton and Hove Albion F.C.
21 Brighton and Hove Stadium
22 Brighton, Hove and Sussex Sixth-Form College
23 Bristol Road
24 Broadcasting
25 Brunswick Town
26 Buses
27 Bypass
28 Cannon Cinema
29 Sir Herbert Carden
30 Carlton Hill
31 Castle Inn
32 Castle Square
33 Cemeteries
34 Chain Pier
35 King Charles II
36 Church Street
37 Churchill Square
38 Cinemas
39 Clifton Hill
40 Climate
41 Clock Tower
42 Coaching
43 Coastline
44 Coldean
45 Conservation
46 Co-operatives
47 Corporation and Council
48 Courts
49 Development
50 Devil's Dyke
51 Ditchling Road
52 Dome and Corn Exchange
53 Downs
54 Duke of York's Cinema
55 Dyke Road
56 East Cliff
57 East Street
58 Eastern Road
59 King Edward VII
60 Edward Street
61 Elections - Parliamentary
62 Electricity Supply
63 Elm Grove
64 Fairs
65 Falmer
66 Fire-Brigade
67 Fishing Industry
68 Freedom of the Borough
69 Gas Supply
70 General Hospital
71 King George IV
72 Grand Hotel
73 Grand Junction Road
74 Hanover
75 Hollingbury
76 Hollingdean
77 Hospitality Inn
78 Hospitals and Dispensaries
79 Hove
80 Thomas Read Kemp
81 Kemp Town
82 Kemp Town Railway
83 King's Road
84 Kingswest Boulevard
85 Ladies Mile
86 Level
87 Lewes Road
88 Library - Brighton Public Library
89 Libraries - Proprietary
90 Lifeboats
91 London Road
92 London Road, Patcham
93 Lower Esplanade
94 Lower Town
95 Madeira Drive
96 Manors
97 Manor Farm
98 Marina
99 Marine Parade
100 Markets
101 Master of Ceremonies
102 Mayors
103 Hotel Metropole
104 Mods and Rockers
105 Moulsecoomb
106 Museum and Art Gallery
107 New Road
108 Newspapers
109 Norfolk Resort Hotel
110 North Laine
111 North Road
112 North Street
113 Old Ship Hotel
114 Old Steine
115 Old Town
116 Ovingdean
117 Palace Pier
118 Parishes
119 Parks
120 Park Crescent
121 Patcham
122 Patcham Village
123 Police
124 Polytechnic
125 Pool Valley
126 The Poor
127 Population
128 Port of Brighton
129 Postal Services
130 Preston (including Preston Park Conservation Area)
131 Preston Village
132 Preston Park
133 Preston Road
134 Prestonville

135 Public Houses
136 Queen Square
137 Queen's Hotel
138 Queen's Park
139 Queen's Road
140 Race-Course
141 Railways
142 Railways - London main line
143 Railways - West Coastway
144 Railways - East Coastway
145 Railways - Brighton Station
146 Railways - Engineering Works
147 Refuse
148 Regency Square
149 Regency Square Conservation Area
150 Religion
151 Roads
152 Roedean
153 Roedean School
154 Rottingdean
155 Rottingdean Green
156 Rottingdean High Street
157 Rottingdean Railway
158 Rottingdean Windmill
159 Round Hill
160 Royal Albion Hotel
161 Royal Pavilion
162 Royal Sussex County Hospital
163 Royal York Buildings
164 Dr Richard Russell
165 St Dunstan's Institute for the Blind
166 St George's Road
167 St James's Street
168 St Mary's Hall
169 St Nicholas's Church
170 St Peter's Church
171 Saltdean
172 Schools
173 Sewers and Drains
174 Shoreham Airport
175 Stanmer
176 Street-Lighting
177 Sussex County Cricket Club
178 College of Technology
179 Telegraphs and Telephones
180 Telscombe
181 Theatres
182 Theatre Royal
183 Town Commissioners and Town Acts
184 Town Halls
185 Tramways
186 Trunk Murders
187 Undercliff Walk
188 University of Sussex
189 Valley Gardens
190 Veteran Car Run
191 Viaduct Road
192 Vicars
193 Queen Victoria
194 Victoria Gardens
195 Magnus Volk
196 Volk's Railway
197 Revd Arthur Wagner
198 Revd Henry Wagner
199 Waterhall
200 Water Supply
201 Wellesbourne
202 West Blatchington
203 West Hill
204 West Pier
205 West Street
206 Westdene
207 Western Road
208 Whitehawk
209 Amon and Amon Henry Wilds
210 King William IV
211 Windmills
212 Withdean
213 Withdean Stadium
214 Woodingdean
215 Workhouses
216 World Wars

LIST OF FIGURES

1 Albion Hill and Carlton Hill before redevelopment (map)
2 Albion Hill and Carlton Hill now (map)
3 Brighton Aquarium
4 Garden Cottage, North Road, Preston
5 44-46 Old Steine
6 Montpelier Crescent
7 Location of Balsdean hamlet (map)
8 Martha Gunn
9 Bathing-machines
10 Dr Awsiter's baths
11 Sake Dene Mahomed's baths
12 The ruined blockhouse in 1761
13 Dentsply factory, Coombe Road
14 Bedford Hotel
15 Boundary changes (map)
16 Commemorative pylon on A23
17 Meeting House Lane
18 Sheridan Hotel, King's Road
19 Brighton under attack in 1514
20 Black Lion Lane
21 Brighton College
22 238 Dyke Road
23 St John the Baptist R.C. Church
24 Trolley-bus routes (map)
25 Brighton Buses depot, Lewes Road
26 Tower in Tarner Recreation Ground
27 South Lodge of the Royal Pavilion
28 Extra-Mural Cemetery
29 Woodvale Cemetery chapel
30 Royal Suspension Chain Pier
31 Pier-head of the Chain Pier
32 Central National School
33 Church Street (map)
34 'Spirit of Brighton' in Churchill Square
35 Churchill Square area before redevelopment (map)
36 Churchill Square area now (map)
37 53 Montpelier Road
38 Montpelier Villas
39 T.R.Kemp's residence, The Temple
40 Jubilee Clock Tower
41 Beach and crumbly cliffs below the Old Town
42 Patcham Court Farm dovecote
43 Conservation in Brighton (map)
44 Constituencies and wards (map)
45 Property owned by Brighton Council (map)
46 Arms of the Borough of Brighton
47 Dyke Hotel
48 Royal Pavilion estate in about 1845
49 Parish of Brighton in 1792 showing the tenantry laines (map)
50 Dyke Road (map)
51 Port Hall
52 Charles Street
53 Portland Place
54 East Street
55 Eastern Road and Upper Bedford Street area before redevelopment (map)
56 Eastern Road and Upper Bedford Street area now (map)
57 Hustings at the Town Hall in 1841
58 St Wilfrid's Church, Elm Grove
59 Hauling boats onto the beach
60 Fishermen mending nets
61 Selling the catch by Dutch auction
62 Brighton Fish Market
63 Gas lamp-standard in the Pavilion Grounds
64 Statue of King George IV
65 Grand Hotel
66 Hanover Crescent
67 Brighton Dispensary, Queen's Road
68 View of Kemp Town in the 1840s
69 View of Kemp Town from the beach
70 Kemp Town esplanades in about 1845
71 King's Road by the Old Ship in about 1845
72 King's Road (map)
73 Embassy Court, Peace Statue and Norfolk Resort Hotel
74 Percy Almshouses
75 Lewes Road (map)
76 Library and museum, Church Street
77 Regency-style façades in London Road
78 London Road area before redevelopment (map)
79 London Road area now (map)
80 Queen's Place
81 London Road, Patcham (map)
82 King's Road Bandstand
83 Detail of Madeira Lift
84 Marine Parade and the Chain Pier toll-house
85 Marine Parade (map)
86 Selling produce in Market Street
87 Cottage behind Moulsecoomb Place
88 Royal Colonnade, New Road
89 Frederick Gardens
90 Leeds Permanent Building Society, North Street
91 North Street and Castle Square (map)
92 Old Steine (map)
93 View of the Old Steine in about 1850
94 Western side of the Old Steine in 1840
95 A view of the town in 1765
96 Brighton in 1779 (map)
97 Old Town (map)
98 Bartholomews
99 Black Lion public house
100 37a Duke Street
101 Market Inn and Hanningtons, Market Street
102 Pump House, Market Street

103 Meeting House Lane
104 15 Prince Albert Street
105 62-63 Ship Street
106 St Wulfran's Church, Ovingdean
107 Ovingdean village (map)
108 Ovingdean Hall
109 Chain Pier toll-house now on Palace Pier
110 Fred Ginnett's tomb, Woodvale
111 Patcham Court Farmhouse
112 Patcham village (map)
113 Patcham Place
114 23-25 Church Hill
115 Mill Cottages, Highview Avenue South
116 Pool Valley in storm of 17 July 1850
117 Blind beggar in Brighton
118 Disabled beggar in Brighton
119 Model Dwellings, Church Street
120 Growth of Brighton's population
121 Preston village (map)
122 Preston Old Church
123 19-27 North Road
124 Entrance to Preston Park
125 199 Preston Road
126 Queen's Hotel
127 Queen's Park in about 1880
128 Royal Spa building in 1841
129 Thomas Attree's villa
130 Queen's Road (map)
131 Western side of Queen's Road
132 Brighton races in 1790
133 New race stand of 1851
134 View of New England Viaduct and Brighton Station
135 London Road Viaduct
136 Brighton Station in 1842
137 The impressive roof of Brighton Station
138 Royal Sussex Regiment War Memorial
139 Oriental Place
140 Royal Newburgh Rooms
141 Former coastguard cottages at Roedean Terrace
142 Rottingdean Gap
143 The Elms
144 Wishing stone in garden wall of The Elms
145 Tudor Close
146 Rottingdean village (map)
147 Royal Albion Hotel
148 Original Marine Pavilion in 1813
149 Transitional view of Pavilion in 1818
150 Royal Pavilion from the Steine in 1829
151 Sussex County Hospital
152 Royal York Buildings
153 Dr Richard Russell, F.R S.
154 Dr Russell's house
155 St George's Church
156 East Mill in 1840
157 St James's Place
158 High Street Chapel
159 Former synagogue in Devonshire Place
160 St Mary's Hall
161 St Nicholas's Church in 1842
162 Cross in St Nicholas's Churchyard
163 Dyke Road Rest Garden
164 St Peter's Chapel in about 1850
165 Royal British Schools, Eastern Road
166 Stanmer village (map)
167 Stanmer House and Park
168 Lower Lodges of Stanmer Park
169 Lamp-standards in King's Road
170 Theatres and cinemas in Brighton (map)
171 Brighton Town Hall
172 Brighton Corporation Tramways (map)
173 Tram shelter in Queen's Park Road
174 St George's Place, St Peter's Chapel, and northern end of North Steine
175 Richmond Terrace
176 Richmond Gardens
177 Parochial Offices, Prince's Street
178 Brighton Business Centre, Viaduct Road
179 Victoria Fountain, Old Steine
180 Magnus Volk's last home in Dyke Road
181 Christ Church, Montpelier Road
182 Waterhall Mill
183 West Pier
184 West Street before widening
185 77 West Street
186 Western Road before widening
187 Western Road (map)
188 Western Pavilion
189 Borough Street
190 Tomb of Amon Wilds
191 Ammonite capitals by Amon Henry Wilds at 23 Montpelier Crescent
192 North Gate of the Royal Pavilion
193 View from Race Hill in about 1850 showing seven windmills
194 Home Farmhouse, Peacock Lane, Withdean
195 St Patrick's R.C. Church, Woodingdean

ENCYCLOPAEDIA

The encyclopaedia is mainly topgraphical in nature. Buildings and other features are generally included in the entry for a road or district, but the more important public buildings have separate entries. Other more general topics also have their own entries. Much emphasis has been placed on conservation areas, and also on buildings listed by the Department of the Environment as being of 'special architectural or historic interest'; all 'listed buildings are mentioned. The whole of the present borough, including Bevendean, Coldean, Patcham, Rottingdean, Saltdean, Stanmer and Woodingdean, is covered but features outside the borough are included only for their relevance to Brighton. Note that the maps of areas before redevelopment do not depict that area at any particular date, but rather show an amalgam of features from previous eras.

In ***all*** cases the reader is advised to consult the comprehensive index which cross-refers entries and lists all relevant references. Numbers in small type within angular brackets refer to sources and bibliography.

1. ALBION HILL

a) *HISTORY:* The steep slopes rising eastward from Grand Parade and Richmond Place reach 230 feet above sea-level near Windmill Terrace and make up the area known as Albion Hill. Developed with dense, poor quality housing as the town's population soared in the first thirty years of the nineteenth century, much of the district degenerated into appalling slums and the many back streets, such as Nelson Row and Carlton Row where herrings were smoked on 'dees' by the fishermen, were notorious for the deprivation of their inhabitants.

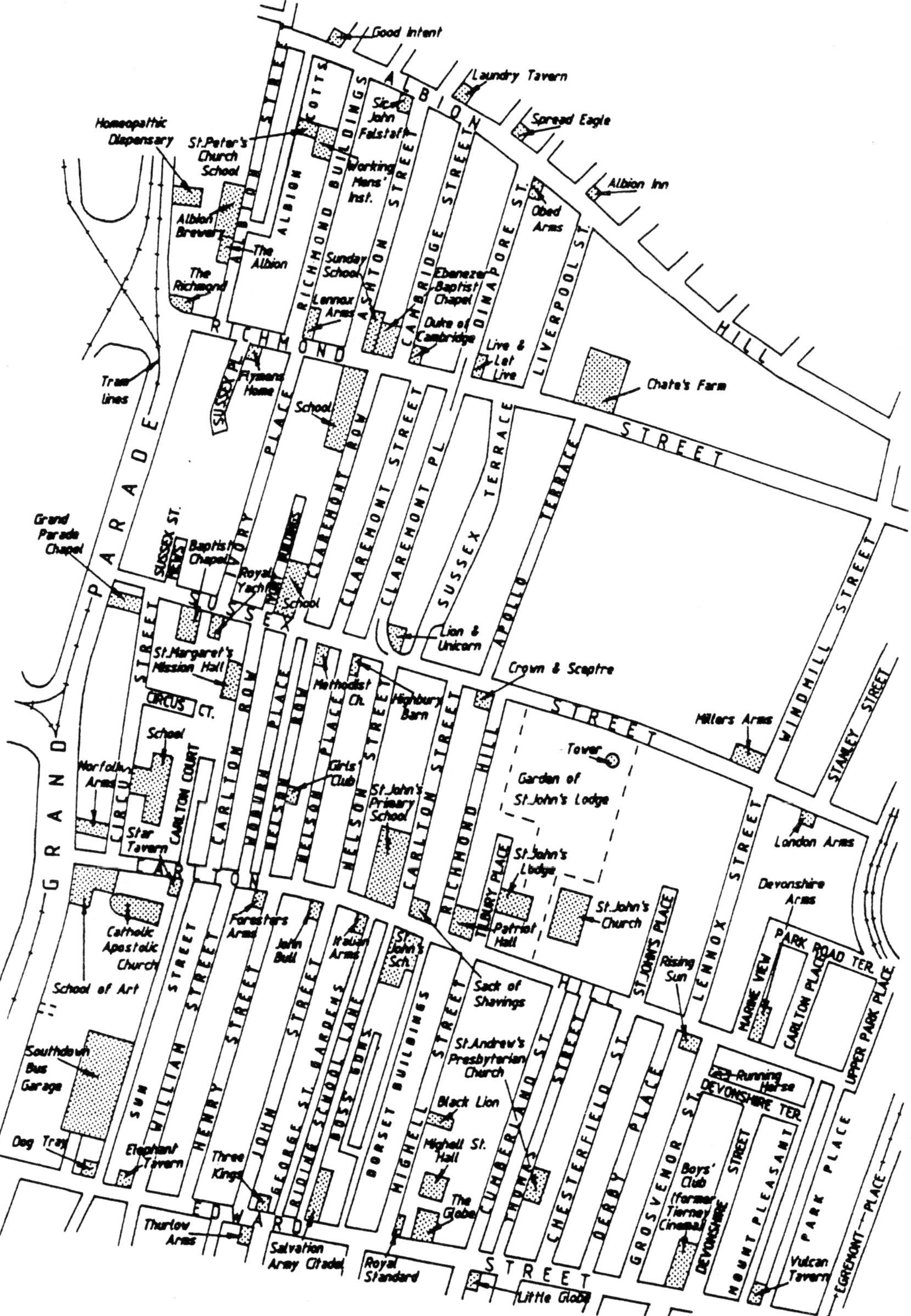

Figure 1: The Albion Hill and Carlton Hill areas before redevelopment

The worst slums persisted until the 1930s when the corporation embarked upon a large-scale redevelopment scheme in the Morley Street (formerly Sussex Street) area which resulted in the removal of many small houses and the opening of the Chest Clinic in 1936 (closed 1989), the new municipal market in 1937, and the School Clinic and Infant Welfare Centre in 1938. (During the war the latter received a direct hit in an air-raid, causing the death of three children.) Many residents were rehoused in the corporation's first block of flats, the four-storey Milner Flats which were erected on the site of Woburn Place in 1934 and named after Alderman Hugh Milner Black, a champion of corporation housing. The adjacent Kingswood Flats, named

Figure 2: The Albion Hill and Carlton Hill areas now

for Minister of Health Sir Kingsley Wood, were built in 1938 on the sites of Nelson Place and a Primitive Methodist chapel of 1856 in Sussex Street. The nearby Tarnerland council estate was developed on vacant land in 1931.

The war prevented any further redevelopment and the Albion Hill area suffered from a number of air-raids, especially in Dinapore Street, Sussex Terrace, the roads to the north of Edward Street, and at the School Clinic as noted above.

Clearances on the slopes to the north of Morley Street commenced in 1959, the narrow streets and courtyards being replaced by flats and grassed open spaces. The town's first 'tower-block' flats were erected on Albion Hill in 1961 and the area is now dominated by seven 11-storey blocks; Highleigh was the first, opened by the mayor, Alan Johnson, on 16 May 1961.

One of the principal thoroughfares of Albion Hill was Richmond Street, once the steepest road in the town (gradient 1:5) with a wall across its width at Dinapore Street to stop runaway carts<109>. Formerly lined with shops and public houses, it is now restricted to its upper reaches only, the lowest part having been rebuilt as Richmond Parade. Chates Farm Court, opened on 26 February 1980 in an unusual and attractive tiered style, does indeed stand on the site of the Chate family's 1860s dairy farm on the northern side of Richmond Street; no.34a appears to have been connected with it <83,108>. Lower down at the corner with Cambridge Street, where the bottom of the zig-zag path now lies, stood the Ebenezer Baptist Chapel, a Renaissance-style building opened on 13 April 1825. It was demolished in 1966 and the replacement, by C.J.Wood, now stands in Richmond Parade <62>. Nearby, on the site of the Albion Brewery in Albion Street, is the Elim Church of the Four Square Tabernacle, opened in September 1988 when the congregation moved from Union Street <123>.
<48a,48b,62,116,123>

b) *WINDMILLS:* The summit of Albion Hill has been the site of several windmills. The Albion Hill Mill, also known as Brighton Park Mill, stood on a site on the south-eastern side of Toronto Terrace from around 1822 until it was removed to the Race Hill in December 1861 (see "Bear Road and East Preston"). However, Windmill Street and the Millers Arms in Sussex Street are probably named after Taylor's Mill, the former East Mill which was removed from Kemp Town to the top of Lennox Street in the mid 1840s. Unfortunately this mill collapsed in 1862 when it was about to be moved for a second time to the Industrial Schools at Warren Farm, Woodingdean. A third mill, on the eastern side of Windmill Street, was known as Clifton Mill as it was removed from Clifton Gardens in around 1837; it was demolished in about 1862. It is also thought that a fourth mill stood on the site of Park Road Terrace from the 1820s until the 1840s. <249a>

2. ANCIENT CUSTOMS

<1,6,18,273>

a) *BACKGROUND:* By the late sixteenth century the inhabitants of Brighton were principally divided into those dependent on the fisheries, and those supported by crafts and farming; the latter were known as 'landsmen'. Both groups had grievances: the fishermen were unhappy that the landsmen paid no contribution to church maintenance or town defences, nor to the relief of the poor who were said to be 'a great burden increasing daily'. On the other hand the landsmen, who paid a rental only for the windmills, were unrepresented on the 'Society of the Twelve', a self-perpetuating ancient body probably derived from the jury of the hundred court which was regulating some of the town's affairs and assisting the constable. (The Society of the Twelve probably died out around 1641, the last known reference.) Both sides petitioned Parliament in 1575 and again in 1579 for an inquiry.

On 12 February 1579 the Privy Council established a commission of inquiry comprising four local worthies: Thomas Sackville, the Lord Buckhurst, one of the lords of the Manor of Brighton and joint Lord Lieutenant of Sussex; the Earl of Arundel, the other lord of the manor; Sir Thomas Shirley of Wiston; and Richard Shelley of Patcham Place. Any two commissioners were authorised to act and so it was that Buckhurst and Shirley ordered the fishermen to meet and set down in writing their ancient customs and orders on the contribution and use of profits from the fisheries.

b) *The BOOK:* The result was *The Book Of All The Auncient Customs heretofore used amonge the fishermen of the Toune of Brighthelmston* (sic). Two copies were made in black ink on parchment, dated 23 July 1580, and are described below.

An introduction and explanation is followed by a detailed section on customs relating to the fishing 'fares' or seasonal voyages, the payments due to the men, and the 'quarter-share' contribution to the church-wardens' funds (see "Fishing Industry"). There is a passage of regulations on the sizes of nets and hooks to be used, and further orders on payments. Then follow orders for the three church-wardens, who were to be two fishermen and one landsman, and for the composition of the Twelve who were to be 'the ancientest, gravest and wisest inhabitants, eight fishermen and four landsmen, to assist the constable as required'. A list of 103 'husbandmen and artificers' is given, with each ordered to pay annually on St Stephen's Day an individually specified rate of between three farthings and four pence.

The last order concerns the books themselves. One was to be kept by the Lords Arundel and Buckhurst, the other was to remain in the town in a chest secured by three locks and was to be read annually in public by the vicar or parish clerk. Alterations to the orders or rates could be made by the vicar, constable and twenty inhabitants, subject to ratification by the two lords. Any doubts or ambiguities were to be settled by any two of the commissioners, although this practice appears to have ceased with the death of Lord Buckhurst in 1608.

The book concludes with notes on the town's ordnance and property which included one windmill, the

Blockhouse and the Townhouse. It is finally endorsed with seven signatures and eighty-three marks of the town's principal inhabitants. The Arundel and Buckhurst copy of the book is now in the British Museum, but the town's copy eventually found its way into the offices of solicitor William Attree at 8 Ship Street where it is still preserved by his successors, Howlett Clarke Cushman.

c) *The SECOND TOWN BOOK:* The book was revised on 2 February 1618 by the mutual agreement of fishermen and landsmen as the 'Second Town Book' or 'Costumal' of Brighton. It included more detailed orders on the expenditure of the quarter-share contributions, while the landsmen were ordered to pay one-half of the fishermen's contributions. The church-wardens and any six of the Society of the Twelve were empowered to raise a tax if required. No building was to be erected to the annoyance of the market place on the cliff or the Blockhouse.

The customs and orders set down in the two books were legally binding and could only be repealed by Parliament. One order remains effective to this day as, unusually, three church-wardens are still chosen for the Parish of Brighton (St Peter's).

3. AQUARIUM and DOLPHINARIUM, Madeira Drive

<24,123,256>

a) *ORIGIN:* Brighton Aquarium was the brainchild of Eugenius Birch, the famous pier engineer and designer of Brighton's West Pier, who conceived the idea following a visit to Boulogne Aquarium. Erected on the approach roadway to the Chain Pier, the Aquarium necessitated the construction of a new sea-wall and promenade, the Madeira Road, which was commenced in 1869. The whole project was completed in 1872 at a cost of £130,000, and the Aquarium was inaugurated by Prince Arthur at Easter although there were no exhibits at the time. It was formally opened to the public on 10 August 1872 by the mayor, Cordy Burrows.

b) *DESCRIPTION:* The new Italianate building extended for about 700 feet along the base of the cliff. The entrance was at the western end, on the site of the Chain Pier's toll-house, where a wide flight of steps descended into a large courtyard formed by five red-brick arches and terracotta columns. Inside the building a large entrance hall led into the main aquarium corridor, 224 feet long and lined with large tanks lit from behind to add to the air of mystery. This impressive corridor, with its vaulted ceiling supported by columns of granite and marble decorated with marine capitals, remains the main aquarium hall and is now listed as being of special architectural and historic interest. The visitor then entered a central hall, now the Dolphin Lounge, which housed a hundred-foot tank to Birch's unique design; holding 110,000 gallons, it was the largest display tank in the world at that time. Marine exhibits were not the only attraction however, as a reading room, restaurant and a conservatory with fernery, rockery and cascade were also provided.

The roof terrace was completed in the summer of 1874 and a distinctive clock tower, gateway and toll-houses were added by T.Boxall in the October of

Figure 3: The Brighton Aquarium

that year. In June 1876 the terrace was extended by 180 feet and a roller-skating rink, terrace garden, smoking room, café and music conservatory were all added on the roof.

c) *NINETEENTH-CENTURY DEVELOPMENTS:* The Aquarium proved to be an instant success with the town's fashionable society and received many royal visitors. Among the early attractions was a large octopus, and in 1877 the first sea-lions arrived; the exhibition of a live Norway lobster in 1874 caused a furore! By 1880 organ recitals were being given twice daily in the hall, while concerts under the direction of William Kuhe were performed in the conservatory. In 1883 lectures and exhibitions were introduced to further stimulate public interest, and in 1889 a dramatic licence for the production of plays was obtained.

d) *CORPORATION PURCHASE:* The initial success was not sustained however, and by the turn of the century the Aquarium was in financial difficulty. In October 1901 the building and business were purchased by the corporation for just £30,000, and Brighton Aquarium was henceforth managed as a municipal enterprise, apart from a brief private letting in 1905 and 1906. The Aquarium's popularity then rose again as Brighton's fortunes in general revived. From 1907 until 1918 a municipal orchestra played in the conservatory which was renamed the Winter Garden. There were also occasional film shows from before 1900, and in the First World War the Winter Garden was briefly known as the Aquarium Kinema; film shows continued until 1939. <68,68a>

In July 1922 Brighton Council gave the Southdown bus company permission to convert the building into a bus and coach station, but the plan was unexpectedly withdrawn at a public inquiry.

e) *RECONSTRUCTION and POST-WAR DEVELOPMENTS:* In 1927 the Aquarium closed for a £117,000 modernisation to the plans of borough engineer David Edwards. When it was reopened by the Duke of York on 12 June 1929, the exterior had been rebuilt in white Empire stonework, the entrance was replaced by two square kiosks with pagoda-style roofs, and the distinctive clock tower had been demolished. A new entrance hall had been built with an adjoining restaurant, while the Winter Garden had been transformed into the Prince's Hall, a modern concert hall seating some 1,250 people. A ballroom, bandstand and other small buildings were added to the Sun Terrace which was extended eastwards above a colonnade and shops to meet the Madeira Terrace. A lift was also installed from Marine Parade down into the Aquarium, while the subway to the Lower Esplanade was opened in 1935. Both slipper and shower baths, which closed in about 1979, and a miniature rifle-range were also provided.

During the war the Aquarium was requisitioned by the RAF. When it reopened, chimpanzee tea-parties and other small animal attractions were introduced, but in 1955 the building was privately leased again, to Aquarium Entertainments Ltd. The Prince's Hall, which had been used nightly as a ballroom, later became the Florida Rooms night-club but was transformed in 1961 into the Montagu Motor Museum.

The first pair of dolphins were exhibited in a pool at the western end of the Aquarium in 1968 and proved so popular that the motor museum was converted into a permanent dolphin attraction. Opening at Easter 1969, the dolphinarium has seating for a thousand visitors around an oval pool holding 210,000 gallons of sea-water. However, serious concern about the effect of permanent enclosure on these intelligent mammals has led to a considerable movement to close the dolphinarium, which attracts about 290,000 people each year. In November 1990 it was announced it would be replaced in 1991 by a Sea Life Centre.

Pirates Deep, an indoor adventure playcentre for children, has opened in another part of the building while the most recent addition is the shark pool of April 1987. The Sun Terrace has been converted into a popular small-scale funfair, Holiday World.

4. ARCHITECTURE

A detailed account of the many different architectural styles found in the town is beyond the scope of this text, but a brief description of the principal styles and materials used is given below, together with the best examples <1,45,45a>. For more information on individual locations and architects, consult the index. See also "Conservation" and "Wilds, Amon and Amon Henry".

a) *WEATHER-BOARDING:* A few examples are to be found in the centre of Brighton: e.g. 29-30 and 43 Meeting House Lane; 37a Duke Street; and 179 Edward Street. There are also weather-boarded houses at 8-9 The Square, Patcham; and barns at Patcham and Stanmer.

b) *FLINTS:* The most common local building stone, closely associated with chalk, is flint, either rough stones picked up from the fields or smoothed, round flint cobbles (known locally as 'pitchers') from the beaches. In many cases the flints have been 'knapped' to present a flat face to the exterior, and on some of the larger houses the flints are also 'squared' to give a regular coursing; the random joints formed when knapped flints are not squared are known as 'snail-creep' <296a>. Good examples of knapped flint buildings can be seen at Ovingdean, Patcham, Rottingdean and Stanmer villages; at St Nicholas's Church; the Druid's Head, Brighton Place; and 8 Ship Street. Knapped and squared flints may be seen at Court House and Down House, Rottingdean; Southdown House, Patcham; Home Farmhouse, Withdean; and in Preston at 36 North Road, 199 Preston Road, and in South Road.

Flint-cobble buildings, often coated with tar to improve weather-proofing, are common and mostly date from the early nineteenth century. Good examples in the town may be found at Bartholomews; Church Street; the Cricketers Arms, Black Lion Street; Dorset Gardens; Kemp Town Place; Marlborough Place; Middle Street; Mighell Street; New Road; Pavilion Parade; Queen's Place; Richmond Gardens; St James's Place; Ship Street; Southover Street; Union Street; and York Place.

Figure 4: Garden Cottage, no.26 North Road, Preston. A fine example of an eighteenth-century façade of knapped and squared flints.

c) *MATHEMATICAL TILES:* These were hung on timber-framed buildings to give the appearance of higher quality brick walls, and it is usually difficult to distinguish them from the real thing. Black, glazed mathematical tiles are easy to discern, however, and may be seen at many locations including Grand Parade; Manchester Street; Market Street; Old Steine; Pool Valley; Royal Crescent; and York Place; also at Patcham Place and Wootton House, Patcham; and at North End House, Rottingdean. No.8 Wentworth Street is a good example of a house faced in cream-coloured mathematical tiles; many other late-eigtheenth- and early-nineteenth-century houses in the East Cliff area are also faced with these tiles.

d) *GEORGIAN:* The streets of the East Cliff contain numerous examples of small-scale, Georgian-style housing, many with bows to allow visitors and lodgers a view down the road to the sea. Other good examples may be found at Bartholomews; 15 Prince Albert Street; Ship Street; and a terrace at Tilbury Place reminiscent of Georgian London.

e) *REGENCY:* The great expansion of Brighton in the late eighteenth and early nineteenth centuries produced most of the town's outstanding examples of architecture, and although the Prince of Wales's regency

Figure 5: Nos.44-46 Old Steine, faced with black, glazed mathematical tiles

Figure 6: Grand Regency-style façades of 1843-7 at Montpelier Crescent

lasted only from 1811 until 1820, the term 'Regency-style' has come to be applied to many of the buildings of the period from around 1810 until the 1840s. Typical are the classical crescents, squares and terraces, adorned with pilasters, ironwork balconies, verandahs and bows. Most are covered in a painted plaster known as 'stucco' which resembles stone and gives the town its traditional white and cream appearance; those that remained unstuccoed were usually faced with flint, or with yellow bricks from the former brickfields around the Hove boundary. (The use of stucco was, for many years, considered sham, and it was not until Sitwell and Barton wrote appreciatively of the Regency style in 1935 that general opinion changed <129>.)

Outstanding examples of the Regency style are the classical terraces of the Kemp Town and Brunswick estates; Cavendish Place; Marine Parade; Marine Square; Montpelier Crescent; New Road; Old Steine; Oriental Place; Portland Place; Regency Square; Russell Square; Sillwood Place; and Western Terrace. Excellent examples on a smaller scale may be seen, among others, at the Cricketers Arms, Black Lion Street; Montpelier Street; 79 Preston Street; and 87 London Road.

From the late 1820s until the 1860s a later style was in evidence which retained some elements of the Regency period. Many houses were refronted with newly fashionable wide bows while new houses in this style were erected at Belvedere Terrace; Chesham Place; Chichester Place; Clarendon Terrace; Eastern Terrace; Eaton Place; Grand Parade; Montpelier Road; Norfolk Square; Percival Terrace; Powis Square; and St George's Place. Attractive Italianate villas were built at Buckingham Place; Clifton Terrace; 128-130 Dyke Road; Montpelier Road; Montpelier Villas; Powis Villas; and Russell Crescent. Less impressive but still attractive contemporary cottages may be found at Blenheim Place; Camden Terrace; Clarence Gardens; Crown Gardens; Crown Street; Dean Street; Frederick Gardens; Hanover Street; Marlborough Street; Norfolk Street; North Gardens; Regent Hill; Spring Street; and Trafalgar Terrace.

f) *GOTHIC:* Despite the many Victorian churches and chapels, there are few examples of domestic Gothic-revival architecture in the town. The Percy and Wagner Almshouses; Debenhams store, Western Road; and Wykeham Terrace are the best examples.

g) *VICTORIAN:* Angular window bays and decorative details are the typical features of mid- to late-nineteenth-century Brighton houses and public buildings; indeed, some previously bowed buildings were refronted at this time. Houses of the period may be found in many parts of the town, especially in the Hanover, St Saviour's and Prestonville areas, while good examples of grander Victorian terracing may be found at Buckingham Road; Denmark Terrace; Gladstone Terrace; Park Crescent; Round Hill Crescent; St Michael's Place; and Vernon Terrace. Many large villa residences were also erected, especially in the Buckingham Road/Dyke Road area; the Clermont Estate at Preston; Florence Road; London Road, Withdean; Old Shoreham Road; Preston Road; Richmond Road; Springfield Road; Stanford Avenue; Walpole Road; Wellington Road; and York Villas.

h) *RED BRICK:* From the 1890s to the 1920s large areas of red-brick housing were erected, particularly in Preston. Fine examples, often with decorated gables, may be seen at Beaconsfield Villas; Compton Road; Ditchling Road; Edburton Avenue; Hollingbury Park Avenue; Inwood Crescent; Queen's Park Rise; Queen's Park Terrace; St James's Avenue; St Luke's Road; St Luke's Terrace; and Southdown Avenue. Much larger red-brick residences are found in Beaconsfield Villas; Dyke Road; Harrington Road; and Preston Park Avenue.

j) *PRE-WAR STYLES:* The 1920s and '30s saw dramatic changes in the Brighton townscape as the main shopping streets were widened and the slums of

Carlton Hill and Upper Russell Street were swept away. Art Deco and International Modern styles began to appear, and the first high-rise blocks were erected on the sea-front. The most notable buildings from this period are the Cannon Cinema; the Co-operative Society store, London Road; the former Dog Hospital in Robertson Road, Preston; Electric House (now Royal Bank of Scotland), Castle Square; Embassy Court, King's Road; Marine Gate, Black Rock; the Ocean Hotel, Saltdean; St Dunstan's, Ovingdean Gap; St Wilfrid's Church, Elm Grove; Saltdean Lido; Varndean Sixth Form College, Surrenden Road; the White House, Saltdean Drive; and the stores on the northern side of Western Road.

Council housing of the period includes the early 'model' estate of South Moulsecoomb; North Moulsecoomb; the Queen's Park estate; Manor Farm and Whitehawk; and the Milner and Kingswood flats. Private housing ranged from the 'Tudorbethan' style of Braybons Ltd in the Valley Drive area and the brown brick of the Brangwyn Estate, to the numerous bungalows of the Ladies Mile, Ovingdean, Patcham, Saltdean and Woodingdean.

k) *POST-WAR DEVELOPMENT:* The immediate post-war need was for housing and large estates were rapidly erected by the council at Bevendean, Coldean and Hollingbury. A little of the pre-war style lingered on into the 1950s, however, with buildings such as the Western Bathing Pavilion; Barclays Bank, North Street; and some of the factories on the Hollingbury and Moulsecoomb Way industrial estates.

From the late 1950s until the early 1970s the townscape was radically changed by the widespread replacement of many small, terraced houses with numerous blocks of both high- and low-rise flats. The predominant use of concrete, the harshness of line, the brutal disregard for location, and the pure functionalism of designs in this period have resulted in many buildings which can only be described as 'ugly': within this category must fall the Albion Hill redevelopment; the Bedford Hotel; Churchill Square; the Law Courts, Edward Street; New England House; Osprey House, Sillwood Place; the Police Station, John Street; the eastern side of Queen's Road; St James's House, High Street; Sussex Heights; Sussex University; and Wellesley House, Waterloo Place. Other less objectionable buildings of the era include the Brighton Centre; Brighton Square; Church of Jesus Christ of Latter Day Saints, Coldean; Church of the Holy Cross, Woodingdean; Church of the Holy Nativity, Bevendean; Kingswest Boulevard; Polytechnic Art Faculty, Grand Parade; and the Spiritualist Church, Edward Street.

l) *'POST-WILSON':* On 22 March 1973 Brighton Council unanimously rejected the 'Wilson report', a town-centre plan by Sir Hugh Wilson and Lewis Womersley which proposed large-scale road construction in the vicinity of Preston Circus and a 'spine road' through the North Laine to a car-park in Church Street, both involving the demolition of over five hundred houses as an interim measure preluding even more extensive new road construction. (The essential aim of the plan, to restrict town centre traffic and introduce extensive pedestrianisation, was, however, laudable.) Five town-centre conservation areas were designated that year (with five more in 1977, notably North Laine), and so 1973 marked something of a watershed in civic attitudes towards the inherited townscape. Many new buildings erected since that time, while still often controversial and merely echoing past styles, have escaped the drab concrete mania of the 1960s and reflect a little of the style of the nineteenth-century town, buildings such as Amex House; the Boots store, North Street; Castle Square House; Chates Farm Court, John Street; Dukes Lane; no.1 Edward Street; the Hospitality Inn; the Marina village development; Nile Pavilions; Queen Square House; Sainsburys store, Lewes Road; St Peter's House, Richmond Place; Security Pacific House, Dyke Road; Trustcard House; the Whitehawk redevelopment; and the Y.M.C.A. in North Road. Too many individual and distinguished buildings of all eras continue to be demolished, however.

m) *COUNCIL PLANNING AWARDS:* Since 1983 Brighton Council has given awards for the design of new buildings and for the restoration of old ones. The winners have been <123,306>:

1983 132 Queen's Road (design);
14 Montpelier Terrace (restoration).
1984 27 Old Steine (restoration).
1985 Sainsburys store, Lewes Road (design).
1986 124 King's Road (restoration);
164-165 Marine Parade (restoration).
1987 36-37 Frederick Place (design);
St Peter's House, Richmond Place (design).
1988 Beach Hotel, 3-4 Regency Square (restoration);
Kipling Garden, Rottingdean (environmental enhancement).
1989 Asda superstore, Crowhurst Road (design);
20 New Road (design);
Libertys store, East Street and Bartholomews (design).
1990 No award.

5. BALSDEAN

<1,193,305>

Balsdean, 'Beald's valley', was an isolated hamlet in the northernmost part of the Saltdean valley to the east of Woodingdean. Although it was part of the parish of Rottingdean, Balsdean formed a separate chapelry covering 1,559 acres <107> which joined the rest of the parish only at a single point on High Hill. The 792-acre manor of Balsdean, which also included the manor of Bazehill by the eighteenth century, was acquired in July 1925 by Brighton Corporation, and the entire area was annexed by the county borough on 1 April 1928.

The hamlet had become somewhat depopulated by this time and consisted of two farms: Norton Farm, and the manorial Sutton Farm which had a charming farmhouse of about 1790. There were also two cottages, a few outbuildings, and a Norman chapel which was

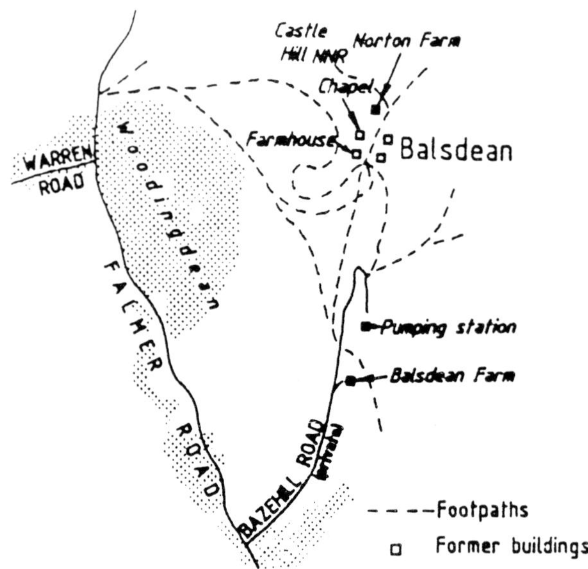

Figure 7: Location of Balsdean hamlet

being used as a barn. During the Second World War however, the valley was occupied by the military and the buildings were used for target practice, resulting in the complete destruction of Sutton Farm and outbuildings; the rubble was cleared at the end of the conflict and a new Balsdean Farm was erected on High Hill to the south. (Pickers Hill Farm near Saltdean was also destroyed and rebuilt.) The Balsdean valley is now peacefully deserted apart from the three ruined barns of Norton Farm and the water-pumping station of 1936.

The medieval chapel of Balsdean was probably erected between 1121 and 1147, a small, flint building about 35 feet long and 20 feet wide with a window and door in the northern wall. The chancel, which extended for another 17 feet, was destroyed at an unknown date to leave only the nave standing with the chancel arch bricked up. As late as 1579 the Vicar of Rottingdean was required to conduct a service at Balsdean Chapel four times a year, but by 1780 it was in use as a barn or stable. It may also have been used as a cottage at some stage as extra doors and windows were added at a later date and the roof was thatched. It was partially rebuilt in the latter eighteenth century and was still in use as a farm outbuilding until it was destroyed during the military occupation. The site was excavated after the war when three graves and some pottery were found, but the chapel is now marked only by a plaque set in a boulder on a grass bank on the western side of the bridleway leading south from Norton Farm.

To the north of Balsdean lies Castle Hill, the site of an earthwork enclosure which is now a protected ancient monument. Castle Hill is also home to an area of uncultivated downland stretching westwards to include Falmer and Newmarket Bottoms; this area has been designated a site of special scientific interest and a national nature reserve in order to preserve the natural downland grasses, flowers, and other flora and associated fauna which are typical of the increasingly rare unpastured and uncultivated land of the South Downs. The site is accessed by permission only from the bridleway from Balsdean to Newmarket Hill via Falmer Bottom. <306,311>

6. BANKS

<15,18,263a>

Until 1787 Brighton townsfolk and visitors used banking facilities at the county town of Lewes, but in that year Thomas Harben and associates opened a banking office at 103 North Street, an establishment that failed in 1793; it was then restarted by Shergold Michell Mills and Company and came to be known as the Old Bank.

Several other private banks opened around the turn of the nineteenth century. These included the Brighthelmstone Bank, established in 1794 by Rickman and Wigney at Steine Lane before moving in 1819 to the corner of Castle Square and later to Avenue; the Brighton Union Bank, opened 1 August 1805 at 6 North Street by Messrs Golding, Browne, Hall, Lashmar and West; and the Brighton and Sussex Bank, founded in 1818 in St James's Street. In fact seven private banks were established in the town in the period from 1787 to 1842, but only two survived the financial panic of 1825 and were still trading in 1836. The Brighthelmstone Bank, known also as Wigneys Bank, absorbed the Old Bank, but it too was forced to close in March 1842, ruining many people and forcing the resignation of Isaac Wigney as a Member of Parliament for Brighton.

The lone survivor was the Brighton Union Bank which increased its trade following the failure of Wigneys. It expanded into adjacent buildings, occupying nos.6-9 North Street, and its partners were treasurers of several local institutions including the town commissioners and borough council. In the 1860s, '70s and '80s the Union Bank opened several branch offices in Sussex, but it was one of several taken over by Barclay Bevan Tritton Ransom Bouverie and Company of London as they expanded into provincial banking; Barclays Bank took over the Union Bank on 22 August 1894. The local head office remained at 6-9 North Street until 1959 when it moved to the new building at 139-142 North Street; the old building was then absorbed by Hanningtons department store where it is distinguished by angular bays.

The banks of the late twentieth century are, naturally, wealthy institutions and occupy some interesting buildings. Indeed, the Barclays Banks at Rottingdean High Street and St Peter's Place; the National Westminster Bank in St James's Street; and the Lloyds Bank at the corner of Norfolk Road and Western Road are listed buildings. Five banks in North Street, one at Pavilion Buildings and two in Western Road utilise classical stone designs mainly of the early twentieth century (the Midland in Western Road is particularly impressive), while other interesting bank buildings include the Royal Bank of Scotland in Castle Square, formerly Electric House; the Co-operative Bank in Ship Street, formerly the Robertson Hall of Holy Trinity

Church; Lloyds Bank in Rottingdean High Street, a cobble-fronted building that once housed a National Telephone Company exchange; the Allied Irish Bank in an elegant 1930s design in Marlborough Place; and the National Westminster Bank in London Road, a noble Victorian red-brick building.

7. BATHING

<2,3,10,14,15,112,115>

a) *HISTORY:* Sea-bathing was a popular recreation long before the establishment of the resort function at mid-eighteenth-century Brighton <19a>. In 1641 a certain Mary Askell is recorded as coming to Brighton for 'the cure', possibly by sea-bathing, but the first specific reference to bathing at Brighton was in 1736 when the Revd William Clarke of Buxted wrote in a letter of his daily practices of 'sunning himself upon the beach', 'bathing in the sea' and 'riding out for air'. Sea-bathing was also common practice at this time in the north of the country at the spa town of Scarborough. <2>

By the 1740s, and perhaps even before, Dr Russell (q.v.) of Lewes was prescribing bathing and even the drinking of sea-water for many ailments, and the popularity of sea-bathing rapidly increased. Bathing-machines (see below) appeared on the beach by 1750, and although bathing was mixed initially, separate beaches for the sexes were later established, the ladies' beach being just east of the Steine with the gentlemen's to the west. In 1776 Dr Samuel Johnson bathed at Brighton, and when the Prince of Wales expressed his pleasure at the practice during his first visit in 1783 the future of sea-bathing was assured. In the early nineteenth century some doctors advocated bathing in cold water throughout the winter, but this practice did not apparently last long!

By the end of the nineteenth century bathing was extremely popular as the masses flocked to the seaside, but the sexes were still confined to designated bathing beaches and specified times. Mixed bathing, from machines only, was first sanctioned by the corporation in July 1901, and restrictions on bathing remained for many years into the 1930s <27>.

In 1807 the parish vestry prohibited bathing without a machine between Royal Crescent and the brick kilns at the Hove boundary; one John Crunden was consequently fined for bathing naked in 1809. However, nude bathing by men continued on the beaches until the introduction of mixed bathing in 1901. On 1 April 1980 a controversial naturist beach sanctioned by the council was opened at the Cliff bathing beach below Duke's Mound, the first on a prime beach at a British resort.

b) *DIPPERS and BATHERS:* As the popularity of sea-bathing grew so a new profession developed, with some of the town's fishermen and their families turning to bathing visitors for a living. Ladies were bathed by so-called 'dippers' and gentlemen by 'bathers'; in both cases the subject was plunged vigourously into and out of the water by the bather or dipper. By 1790 there were about twenty dippers and bathers at Brighton and they continued in business until about the 1850s.

The 'queen' of the Brighton dippers was the famous Martha Gunn. Born in 1726, she was a large, rotund woman and 'dipped' from around 1750 until she was forced to retire through ill health in about 1814. She was a great favourite of the Prince of Wales who granted her free access to his kitchen; an amusing story relates how she was given some butter on one of her visits, but was cornered by the Prince who continued talking to her while edging her nearer the fire until the butter was running out of the poor lady's clothes. Martha died on 2 May 1815 and is buried by the south-eastern corner of St Nicholas's Church; her portrait, painted in 1796 by John Russell, hangs in the tea-room of the Royal Pavilion and her house still stands at 36 East Street.

Martha Gunn's male equivalent was John 'Smoaker' Miles, who also became a devoted friend of the Prince of Wales. He is said to have pulled the Prince back by the ear when he thought he was straying too far from the shore, and once even walked to London to enquire about His Royal Highness's illness. He was a frequent visitor to the Marine Pavilion, and the Prince named a racehorse after him and also introduced the Smoaker Stakes to Brighton Races in 1806. Miles died at the age of 74 in February 1794 and was buried by the west wall of St Nicholas's Churchyard, but the grave is now unidentifiable. His portrait, painted by John Russell in

Figure 8: Martha Gunn, queen of the Brighton dippers in the late eighteenth century

Figure 9: Bathing-machines on the beach below the Old Steine c. 1845

1791, hangs in the King's Apartments of the Royal Pavilion.

c) *BATHING-MACHINES:* Bathing-machines were individual, wooden changing-rooms on wheels, usually drawn into the water by horse, from which the bather could step directly into the sea; modesty hoods could be fitted so that the naked bather could not be seen until covered by water. First appearing in the mid seventeenth century, there were six for men and six for women by 1786. By 1880 the numbers had grown to 150 ladies' and 100 gentlemen's machines, but they fell out of favour in the early twentieth century.

d) *PROPRIETARY BATHING ESTABLISHMENTS:* Proprietary baths were popular in the late eighteenth century and throughout the nineteenth as a means of enjoying the benefits of sea-bathing but avoiding exposure both to the elements and prying eyes. The more famous establishments in the town are described below in chronological order.

e) *AWSITER'S BATHS, Pool Valley:* In 1768 Dr John Awsiter published a pamphlet entitled 'Thoughts on Brighthelmston concerning sea-bathing and drinking sea-water with some directions for their use' in which he advocated the use of individual indoor sea-water baths to protect infirm and fragile bathers from the elements. He also advocated the drinking of sea-water mixed with milk and cream of tartar for the cure of several afflictions including infertility.

Awsiter himself opened the first baths in the town, in a building on the south-western side of Pool Valley designed by Robert Golden. The foundation stone of the small, single-storey, classical building was laid on 4 October 1769, and there were six cold baths, a hot bath, a showering bath and a sweating bath. Sea-water was supplied from the 'Old Pump House' that stood on a groyne in front of the baths until Grand Junction Road was constructed in 1829. The baths eventually passed into the hands of a Mr Wood who added another storey and extended the building southwards, and then to a Mr Creak. They were demolished when Brill's Baths were extended in 1861 (see "Brill's Baths" below).

f) *MAHOMED'S BATHS, King's Road:* Opened in 1786 by 'Sake' (Sheikh) Dene Mahomed, they provided

Figure 10: Dr John Awsiter's original Brighton baths in 1803

Figure 11: Sake Dene Mahomed's baths in 1826; the site is now occupied by the Queen's Hotel. The road shown is the King's Road heading for East Street. Note the proximity of the sea.

vapour or Turkish baths, the first in the country, and a 'shampooing' (massaging) service performed by an attendant through flannel sleeves in a tent-like cover. They became popular after several successful cures, especially of rheumatic problems, and the walls were hung with the discarded crutches of cured patients. Mahomed published several books and pamphlets on his methods and was eventually appointed 'Shampooing Surgeon' to King George IV, an appointment continued by William IV. Mahomed died in 1851 aged 102, and is buried just to the west of the northern entrance of St Nicholas's Church. Mahomed's Baths were taken by a Mr Knight in 1841 but were later acquired by Charles Brill. The three-storey building was demolished in 1870 to make way for Markwell's Hotel (later absorbed by the Queen's Hotel).

g) *WILLIAMS'S ROYAL HOT AND COLD BATHS, Old Steine:* Opened in 1803 at the southern end of the Steine, Williams's Baths became very popular and were later taken over by a Mr Bannister and then Mr Knight. The popularity did not last, however, and the buildings became dilapidated. They were demolished in 1856 to make way for the Lion Mansion Hotel.

h) *ARTILLERY or BATTERY BATHS, Artillery Place, King's Road:* Established in 1813 by Nathan Smith, these baths achieved widespread fame for the treatment of gout by the use of a vacuum pump which was passed over the afflicted area. In 1824 the baths were taken over by a Mr Hobden, and they were carried on after his death in 1861 by his widow. In 1864 they were rebuilt at the same time as the Grand Hotel was completed adjacently and a direct access was made between the two buildings. A magnificent swimming-bath was added in 1865, but the baths were demolished in 1908 when the hotel's ballroom was built on the site. They are now commemorated by Hobdens Health Hydro at the Grand.

j) *BRILL'S BATHS, East Street:* These were originally opened by a Mr Lamprell in 1823, at the south-eastern corner of East Street in a circular domed building 53 feet across nicknamed 'the bunion'; it projected into Grand Junction Road somewhat when that road opened in 1829. Inside was the first communal swimming-bath in the town, as opposed to baths for personal bathing.

In the 1840s Lamprell's nephew Charles Brill inherited the baths. The bunion was removed in 1858, and in 1861 he opened a new ladies-only sea-water bath in a handsome Gothic building on the west side of Pool Valley, on the site of Creak's, formerly Awsiter's, Baths. In 1869 Brill erected a new gentlemen's bath in a red-brick building between East Street and Pool Valley. Designed by Sir George Gilbert Scott at a cost of £90,000, it had a circular swimming-bath 65 feet in diameter, the largest in Europe at that time, holding about 80,000 gallons of sea-water which was brought in from Hove as Brighton's was considered polluted. The building also had cold water baths, vapour baths, medical douche baths, a barber, and reading and billiard rooms.

The popularity of bathing establishments in general declined in the early twentieth century and Brill's Baths were demolished in January 1929 for the erection of the Savoy Cinema (now the Cannon), but the name lives on in 'Brill's Lane' which runs between East Street and Grand Junction Road.

8. BATTERIES and OTHER FORTIFICATIONS

<1,10,15,18,285b>

The earliest known fortification of the town was possibly the 'werke', probably a bulwark, which was referred to in 1497 together with a 'sea-gate'. Neither is depicted in the 1545 drawing of the town under attack, however. The first major fortification was:

a) *The BLOCKHOUSE:* Erected in 1559 on the cliff top between Ship Street and Black Lion Street, it was a circular fort 50 feet in diameter with flint walls 18 feet high and about 7 feet thick; it was financed out of both town and government funds. Inside were arched recesses for storing ammunition with a dungeon below, while a battery of four large cannons from the Tower of London stood on the cliff in front; ten small guns were also provided by the town. A turret on the top housed the town clock.

The small fort was maintained from the 'quarter-share' claimed by the church-wardens from each fishing trip and also by the landsmen's rates in accord with the Book of Ancient Customs (see "Ancient Customs"), but the foundations were gradually undermined by erosion and the fort was badly damaged by the great storms of 1703 and 1705. The clock was taken down in 1726, the walls were partly washed away by another storm in January 1749, and by 1761 the blockhouse was completely ruined. It was eventually dismantled for an improvement to the cliff-top road in 1775.

b) *'CLIFF WALL':* It is also possible that a wall of flint with embrasures for guns was built along the cliff top from the Blockhouse eastward to East Street. Said to have been 15 feet high and 3 feet thick, with a smaller 3-foot-high parapet wall extending to West Street, there were four gates giving access to the beach known as the 'East Gate'; the 'Portall Gate' almost adjacent to the East Gate; the 'Middle Gate' or 'Gate of All Nations'; and the 'West Gate'. It should be noted, however, that the only evidence for the existence of this wall is a description of the town in former times published in 1730; the 'gates', which are mentioned in 1665, may have been merely paths to the beach. What appears to be a wall is visible at the western end of the town in Lamprière's 1743 view, though, together with an East Gate providing an entrance to the Pool (Pool Valley) from East Street; this was an authentic gateway but was removed for the construction of the new battery in 1760 (see below). <10>

The Blockhouse was replaced by:

c) *The BATTERY:* Built by the Board of Ordnance in 1760 at the bottom of East Street, it was equipped with twelve old and dangerous guns; during a salute to Princess Amelia in August 1782 a gunner had both hands blown off, and when the Prince of Wales visited the town for the first time in September 1783 another gunner was killed; it was not subsequently used again. The battery was severely damaged during a storm on 7

Figure 12: The ruined Blockhouse in 1761

August 1786 and fell down completely on 3 November 1786. Part of the battery wall was later used in the foundations of Markwell's Hotel.

Two other batteries were built:

d) *EAST CLIFF BATTERY:* Built in 1793 on the cliff top opposite Camelford Street, it was equipped with four 36-pounders and, together with the West Battery, provided some defence for the town at a time of unrest across the Channel. It was dismantled in about 1803 however, as vibration from the guns and encroachment by the sea had made the walls dangerous.

e) *WEST BATTERY:* Erected in 1793 on the cliff top at Artillery Place, where the Grand Hotel's access road now lies. The guns, eight 36-pounders, were never fired in anger but were used for saluting royalty, often causing nearby windows to shatter. The battery was removed in 1858 or 1859 for the widening of King's Road, but Artillery Street and Cannon Place were named from it.

9. BEAR ROAD and EAST PRESTON

Bear Road has an average gradient of 1:11 and a maximum of 1:8, and formed part of the boundary between Brighton and Preston until 1928; it took its name from the Bear Inn, a centre for bear- and badger-baiting in the late eighteenth century for the 'entertainment' of visitors. (Bear-baiting was legal until 1835.) On Bear Hill to the north of Bear Road, at a site approximating to 89 Ladysmith Road, once stood the Bear Mill, a white post-mill with a round house and cloth sails; it was erected in around 1810 and stood until about 1903. Near the police aerial mast at the top of Bear Road stood the Race Hill Mill. Also a white post-mill, it was moved to the site over three weeks in December 1861 and January 1862 from Albion Hill where it had been known as the Park Mill. However, it collapsed on the morning of 16 May 1913 after being disused for several years. <15,109,249a,249b>

The area to the north of Bear Road, sometimes known as East Preston as it formed the easternmost part of that parish, was developed from the early 1900s and many of the road names have Boer War connections. The parish church of the area, St Alban's in Coombe Road, was built in 1910-14 by Lacy W.Ridge in Early English style; on 15 May 1974 the parish was merged into the new parish of the Resurrection. The parish room at the corner of Bear Road and Riley Road was built in 1902-3 and is now a polytechnic annexe. The lower part of Coombe Road is dominated by two large factories on either side of the road. The southern one (Tyreco Ltd) was erected in 1917 for Oppenheimer diamond merchants but was taken by Allen West and Schweppes in 1927 and later by CVA Tools. The impressive factory opposite was erected in 1918 as another diamond factory but is now the home of Dentsply, one of Europe's largest false teeth manufacturers. <1,83,311>

The buildings of the former Bevendean Hospital still stand in Bear Road and Bevendean Road, and originally opened in 1881 as a smallpox sanatorium. The main buildings were erected in 1898, and the institution continued as the Brighton Borough Hospital until taken over by the National Health Service in 1948. Bevendean Hospital closed to in-patients in April 1989 and is scheduled for redevelopment as housing. See "Hospitals and Dispensaries" for full details.

The land to the south of Bear Road is mostly taken up by three cemeteries, fully described under "Cemeteries".

Figure 13: Dentsply factory, Coombe Road, erected in 1918

10. BEDFORD HOTEL, 137 King's Road

<2,3,46,123>

Opened on 16 September 1967 on the site of the old Bedford Hotel, it was the first major new hotel development in the town for over half a century. Designed by R.Seifert and Partners, the 17-storey block includes a 127-room hotel and the flats of Bedford Towers, and at 168 feet tall is one of four modern blocks that unfortunately dominate the western sea-front vista.

The old Bedford Hotel was opened in October 1829 for William Manfield who, in 1835, leased it to the designer, Thomas Cooper, but bought the lease back the following year and ran the hotel himself until 1844 when he leased it to Joseph Ellis. In 1855 Ellis purchased the Bedford outright, and established for it a reputation as the town's leading hotel for the accommodation of royalty, the fashionable and the famous; the guests included Charles Dickens who wrote *Dombey and Son* while staying there.

The Bedford was also considered the most distinguished late-Georgian building in the town after the Royal Pavilion. It had five storeys with two recessed, Ionic porticoes facing south and west above the entrances, while the west wing, which was the first part to open, was erected back from the road and was decorated with giant pilasters. The interior had a splendid Grecian hall with Ionic columns and a glazed dome. In 1963 there was considerable debate over whether permission should be given to the owners, AVP Industries, to replace the hotel with a 14-storey block, but it proved academic as the building was destroyed by a fire on 1 April 1964 with the death of two people.

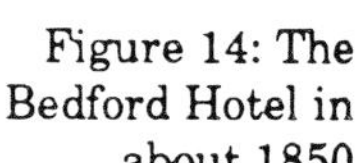

Figure 14: The Bedford Hotel in about 1850

11. BEVENDEAN.

The Domesday Book of 1086 recorded the manor of Bevendean, 'Beofa's valley', to be worth £6 and held by one Walter from William de Warrenne. It was eventually divided between two estates, Lower and Upper Bevendean, which were acquired by the corporation in November 1913 and January 1940 respectively; the whole Bevendean area was annexed by the county borough from Falmer parish on 1 April 1928. Lower Bevendean Farm was originally accessed from Bear Road by a trackway now known as Bevendean Road and had an eighteenth-century farmhouse, but the buildings were demolished to provide the open space known as Farm Green between Auckland Drive and Bevendean School. Upper Bevendean Farm survives however, and has a late-nineteenth-century farmhouse approached from Warren Avenue, Woodingdean. <1,282,289,305>

The first development of the Lower Bevendean estate came in the early 1930s when the corporation extended its housing from South Moulsecoomb up the valley on Bevendean land: thus 85-123 and 110-120 The Avenue (eastwards from the cross roads at the western end of Manton Road), plus Lower Bevendean Avenue, Upper Bevendean Avenue and Manton Road, are part of Bevendean. At about the same time, the Widdicombe Way/ Bevendean Crescent area was developed privately and was also known as part of the Bevendean estate, but it is now normally counted as part of the Moulsecoomb district. <83>

With a pressing need for new homes in the post-war period, the greater part of the Bevendean housing estate was rapidly developed higher up the valley from 1948 by the corporation, which named the roads after English castles. The population of Bevendean is now around the 4,000 mark <277>. Bevendean Barn, at the corner of Auckland Drive and Heath Hill Avenue, was used as a chapel for the estate from 1953, but it was replaced in

1963 by the Church of the Holy Nativity, a Modern-style building in brick, mottled knapped-flint and cobbles by Richard Melhuish Ariba. The industrial estate at The Hyde was developed from 1955; the first factory was Elizabeth English shoes, followed by Hibberd furniture, Brighton Sheet Metal works, Redifon, Canada Dry and Gulton Europe. <83,123,124,311>

12. BLACK ROCK

Probably named after a large rock or cave that once lay at the foot of the cliffs, Black Rock, at Boundary Road, marked the eastern limit of Brighton until 1928, a boundary which was fixed by an inquiry in 1606 after an argument over wrecker's rights <1>.

Black Rock also marks the point where the white chalk of the South Downs meets the sea, and there are some unusual geological formations in the vicinity. Visible in the fawn-coloured cliffs behind the Asda superstore, about 15 feet above the Undercliff Walk, is a 'raised beach' of rounded, flint pebbles and sandy gravels up to 10 feet thick, resting on chalk. This beach was laid down around 100,000 years ago during a warm interval in the Ice Age and has yielded sea-shells and the remains of whales. Above lies a 45-foot-thick layer of 'Coombe Rock', a chalky rubble eroded by freeze-thaw action during the colder periods and 'sludged' down into the valleys by the spring and summer rains. This layer has produced fossil remains of mammoths, wooly rhinos and hippopotamuses. The strata here may be seen to curve upwards where the solid chalk of the South Downs becomes exposed as cliffs; the prehistoric coastline was once at an oblique angle to the present cliffs. This area is protected as a site of special scientific interest. <283a,306,311>

About 350 yards offshore to the west of the Marina breakwater is the site of an historic wreck, protected from interference by statute. On the sea-bed lies a large, timber framework from which a cannon ball, an anchor and other metal objects have been recovered. The origin of the wreck is uncertain but it may be a French ship from one of the sixteenth-century raids on Brighton (see "Brighton - Early History"), or even a Spanish galleon from the 1588 Armada <304>.

The first development at Black Rock was the gas-works, established in 1818-19 by the Brighton Gas Light and Coke Company (see "Gas Supply"). This was soon followed by some terraced housing to the east, and by 1828 the Abergavenny Arms had also opened. However, constant erosion claimed the cliff top for 75 feet inland in the fifty years to 1897, causing the closure of the road to Rottingdean and the opening of Roedean Road as an alternative; large landslips continued into the 1920s. On 22 July 1932, with the cliffs now protected by the Undercliff Walk, a new 60-foot-wide highway, the Marine Drive, was opened between Black Rock and Rottingdean; the old inn was demolished at this time. The small community at Black Rock centred on Rifle Butt Road was eventually demolished for the construction of the Marina road interchange which opened in 1976. <107,112,115,116,123>

In 1824 a tunnel was constructed from the eastern end of the Kemp Town esplanade to the gas-works to facilitate the carting of coal, but it fell into disuse once coal started to be landed at Aldrington Basin, and was blocked at both ends by the town commissioners in 1850 after it had collapsed in the middle. In January 1906 Magnus Volk rented the southern entrance and, describing it falsely as a smugglers' cave, used it briefly as a tourist attraction for his railway extension to Black Rock. The entrance disappeared completely when the corporation constructed public conveniences in the 1930s. <46,189>

Black Rock was perhaps best known for its swimming-pool, formally opened on the site of a terrace garden on 8 August 1936 and necessitating a slight shortening of Volk's Railway. The pool, 165 feet by 60 feet, closed in 1978 and the handsome changing room and café building was demolished, but the site still awaits a water 'theme-park' development. The most prominent building on the cliff top is Marine Gate, a large, eight-storey block of 105 flats erected around an open quadrangle in 1937-9 to the design of Maurice Bloom. There was a large public restaurant until it was converted for further residential accommodation in about 1955, but the block's proximity to the gas-works resulted in a good deal of bombing during the war and it received a direct hit in 1944. Courcels is a seven-storey block of 1971, while the nearby French Convalescent Home opened in 1896 (see "Marine Parade"). The undercliff at Black Rock is dominated by the Marina (q.v.). <3,45a,116,123>

13. BOUNDARIES

The boundary of the ancient ecclesiastical and civil parish of Brighton, which was also the area incorporated as a borough on 1 April 1854, followed the present boundary with Hove from the sea-front via Little Western Street and Boundary Passage to Goldsmid Road. It then went directly to the junctions of Russell Crescent and Dyke Road, and Prestonville Road and Old Shoreham Road, to follow the line of Old Shoreham Road, New England Road, Viaduct Road, Ditchling Road, Florence Place, Hollingdean Road and Bear Road to the Race Hill reservoir. The boundary line then ran south across the race-course to follow generally the course of Whitehawk Road (before realignment, now including Haybourne Road) to Roedean Road, and finally along the eastern side of Boundary Road to the sea. This area amounted to approximately 1,640 acres, although reclaimed beaches added to the total over the years. <109>

The Brighton borough boundary has been extended on several occasions in order to accommodate development outside the original area. The alterations have been:

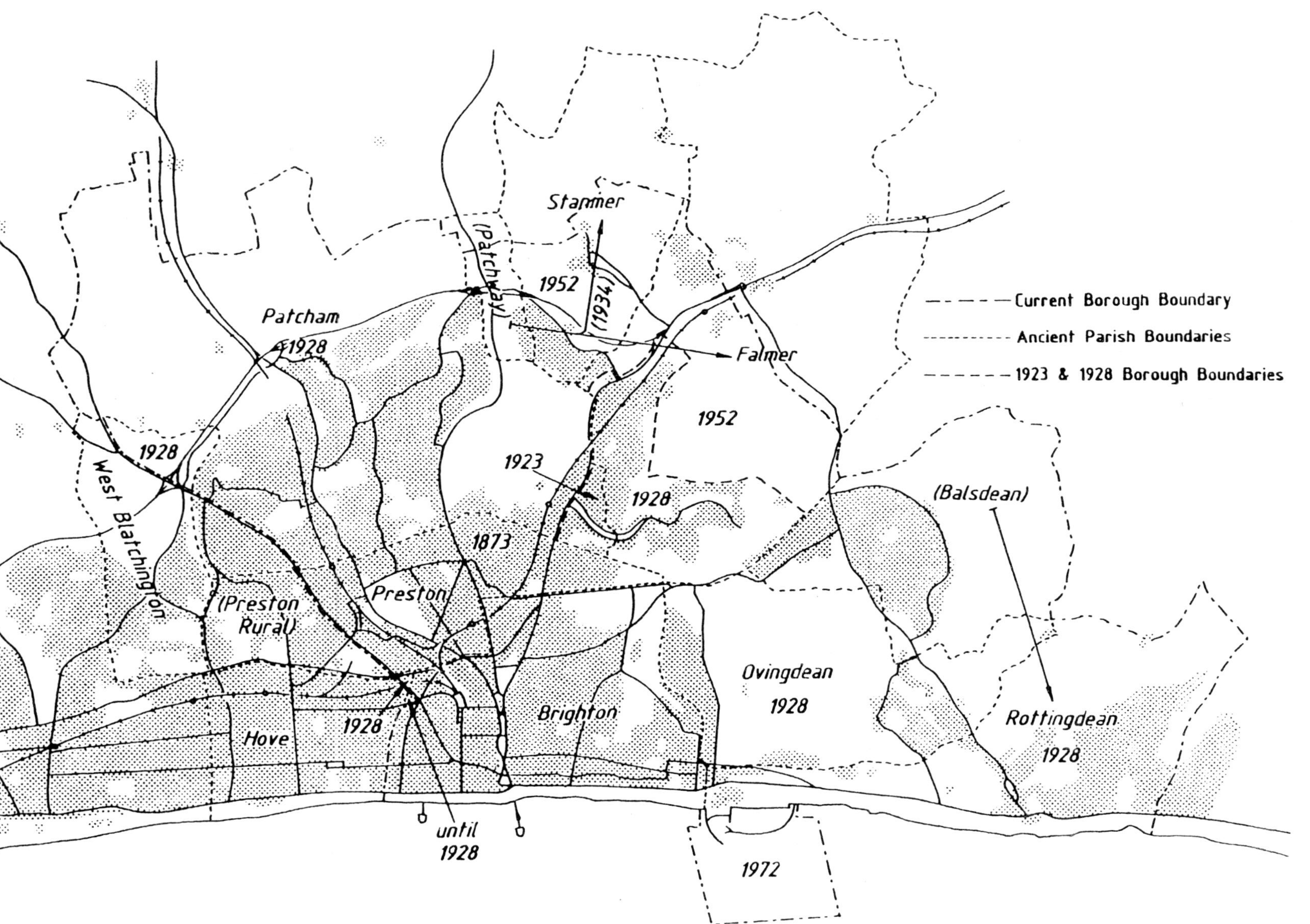

Figure 15: Changes to boundaries in the Brighton area

i) *31 OCTOBER 1873 ('1873 Brighton Borough Extension Act'):* That part of Preston parish to the east of Dyke Road, an area of about 905 acres, was added to the borough for municipal purposes only; the boundaries remained unaltered for parochial purposes (see "Parishes") until 1894 when that part of Preston parish outside the borough, i.e. to the west of Dyke Road, was constituted as the parish of Preston Rural; and that part within the borough was constituted as the new parish of Preston. Preston remained a separate parish within the county borough of Brighton until 1928 (see below). <33,279>

ii) *1 OCTOBER 1923 ('1923 Ministry of Housing Provisional Order Confirmation (Brighton Extension) Act'):* That part of Patcham parish to the east of Lewes Road, an area of 94 acres already developed by the corporation as the original Moulsecoomb housing estate, was added to the county borough of Brighton and to the parish of Preston. <38,279>

iii) *1 APRIL 1928 ('1927 Brighton Corporation Act'):* The whole of the parishes of Ovingdean and Rottingdean, a large part of Falmer parish (including the rest of the Moulsecoomb estate, the Falmer School area and Bevendean), and those parts of Patcham and West Blatchington parishes to the east of Dyke Road Avenue and Devil's Dyke Road, were added to the county borough. In addition, a small exchange of land was made with Hove to the north of Seven Dials to simplify the boundary; the new line ran along Goldsmid Road and Dyke Road, such that Goldsmid Road and parts of Addison, Davigdor, Julian and Melville Roads were transferred to Hove while Belmont and parts of Dyke Road and Old Shoreham Road were added to Brighton .

This enormous expansion created what was popularly known as 'Greater Brighton', with the area of the county borough, which was also constituted as a single parish of Brighton (thus also absorbing Preston parish), increasing nearly five-fold to 12,503 acres. A week-long celebration culminated in the unveiling of the Pylons by the Duke and Duchess of York to mark the new northern boundary of the town. <39,115,279>

iv) *1 APRIL 1952 ('1951 Brighton Extension Act'):* Substantial areas of Falmer and Stanmer parishes, including Old Boat Corner, Stanmer Park, Stanmer village, Coldean and the downland to the west of Falmer Road, were added to the county borough and parish of Brighton to bring the total area up to 14,347 acres. Those parts of Falmer and Stanmer not annexed combined to form the present parish of Falmer. <41,279>

v) *31 MARCH 1972 ('1968 Brighton Marina Act'):* Land reclaimed for the Marina development, plus a substantial area of sea defined by national grid references, was added to the parish and county borough. The added area was about 694 acres, making the total borough area 15,041 acres. <42,307>

a) *BOUNDARY STONES:* There are not many places where the Brighton boundary is obvious to the observer. The Peace Memorial on the seafront was built on the Brighton/Hove boundary, while the well-known Pylons on the London Road are actually some 35 yards inside the borough. As mentioned above, the boundary also runs along the western side of Dyke Road to the north of Seven Dials and then along the eastern side of Dyke Road Avenue. There are, however, a number of boundary stones remaining which mark both current and former boundaries. Among those most easily seen are:

Figure 16: Commemorative pylon on the A23 at the northern limit of Brighton

i) Brighton/Hove: in the Western Road pavement at Boundary Passage; at the mid-point and northern end of Boundary Passage; the southern side of Temple Gardens; either side of Windlesham Avenue; and at Dyke Road/Old Shoreham Road. (This last stone marked the former Hove/Preston boundary to 1928 and although the present borough boundary does not run along the same line it is mered to the stone.)

ii) Brighton/Preston (to 1928): in the north-eastern pier of the New England Viaduct.

iii) Brighton/Stanmer (1928-52): at Highfields, Coldean.

iv) Brighton/Falmer/Preston/Ovingdean (to 1928): at the south-eastern corner of the Race Hill Reservoir in Bear Road.

v) Brighton/Ovingdean (to 1928): two between the Race Hill Reservoir and Haybourne Road, and two on the western side of Haybourne Road where there are also a number of Race Ground boundary stones; on the eastern side of Whitehawk Road at Roedean Road.

vi) Brighton/Telscombe (from 1928): either side of Marine Drive to the east of Longridge Avenue, Saltdean.

<109>

14. BREWERIES

<83,123,275>

The apparently insatiable thirst for beer and the large number of public houses and beer-houses opening in the nineteenth and early twentieth centuries led to the establishment of many breweries in the town. Some of the better known breweries are detailed below.

a) *ALBION BREWERY, Albion Street:* Acquired by the Phoenix Brewery in 1892, it was used only as a store from 1924 and then as a builder's yard until demolished in the 1970s. The site is now occupied by the Elim Church. The adjacent Stable public house is named from the brewery's stable that stood opposite.

b) *AMBER ALE BREWERY, Preston Circus:* Once dominating Preston Circus with a very large clock tower and a domed roof, it was probably established in the 1820s by Smithers. The brewery was later acquired by Longhursts but was demolished in 1901 to allow tram lines to be laid on a curve between Beaconsfield Road and Viaduct Road. Part of the building was adapted as a fire station, since rebuilt, but the malting was incorporated into the Duke of York's Cinema and may still be seen behind the present fire station.

c) *BLACK LION BREWERY:* Said to have been the oldest brewery building in the world. See "Old Town (Black Lion Street)".

d) *CANNON BREWERY, Russell Street:* Established in the early nineteenth century by a Mr Barnett, it was acquired by Tamplins in 1926 but was demolished in 1969 for the extension of Churchill Square. It was latterly used as a bottling plant only.

e) *KEMP TOWN BREWERY, Seymour Street:* Founded by William Hallett as the Bristol Brewery in about the 1840s, it was later taken over by the Abbey family and became the Kemp Town Brewery in 1933. In 1963 it was taken over by Charringtons, but brewing ceased in April 1964 and it became empty in 1966. The main buildings were sold in January 1970 for the development of Seymour Square. There was also a malting at the corner of Eastern Road and Sutherland Road, a site now used by Brighton College.

In 1989 a new Kemp Town Brewery opened at the Hand in Hand public house in Upper St James's Street.

f) *NORTH STREET BREWERY:* Established in the first half of the nineteenth century by William Smithers. When Imperial Arcade was built on the site in 1923 the brewery continued trading from premises in Regent Hill until it was acquired by Tamplins in 1929. A malt-house belonging to this brewery remains on the southern side of Blenheim Place.

g) *PHOENIX BREWERY, Albion Street:* Built in 1821 to replace Richard Tamplin's Southwick Brewery following its destruction by fire in August 1820, the brewery thus rising up from the ashes like the fabulous Arabian phoenix. Part of the Watney empire since 1953, it occupies a large site behind Richmond Terrace. One old, flint malting remains in Southover Street, while the decorated former brewery office of 1893 stands in Phoenix Place near the brewery's own public house, the Free Butts. The surrounding roads also retain their original setts. Since 1973 it has been used as a bottling plant and depot only, the beer being brought in from the Watney brewery at Mortlake, but the whole site is scheduled for closure in early 1991 as the distribution depot moves to Lewes. A 1990 plan for the redevelopment of the site with offices and housing also involves the demolition of Wellesley House in Waterloo Place, but retains the Free Butts and the 1893 offices.

h) *PRESTON BREWERY, South Road:* Stood at the rear of the Preston Brewery Tap. Its flint-walled malting still stands in South Road.

j) *ROCK BREWERY, St James's Street:* Stood at the corner of Mount Street with premises also in Warwick Street and St Mary's Place. It was established in about 1809 and continued brewing until about 1928.

k) *WEST STREET BREWERY:* Dating from at least the mid eighteenth century, it became the first Brighton brewery to employ steam in about 1800. In 1824 it was taken over by Vallance and Son, and later became Vallance and Catt's brewery. Standing behind the King's Head near the south-western corner of West Street, it was taken over by Smithers in 1913 but was closed by Tamplins in 1929.

15. BRIGHTON - Location and functions

<2,11,123,277>

Brighton is an important residential, commercial, educational, entertainment, tourist and conference centre on the Sussex coast, forty-six miles due south of London and just east of the head of a wide bay formed by Selsey Bill and Beachy Head, at 50° 49' N latitude, 00° 08' W longitude.

The settlement, which was well established by the time of the Domesday Book in 1086, grew up at the point where the Downs meet the sea to provide easy hill or valley routes to Lewes and beyond, and was probably originally situated on an extensive foreshore protected from the force of the Channel by an offshore submarine bar of shale; there may have also have been a small inlet, while flat ground behind the beach provided a convenient shelter for boats in time of storm. In medieval times the village grew with the success of the fisheries into a small town, but fell into an economic depression in the late seventeenth century.

Figure 17: Brighton's attractive shops bring thousands of visitors to the town. This is Meeting House Lane early in the morning before the crowds arrive.

Around 1750 though, the wind of fortune turned again as the health resort function became established, chiefly at the prerogative of Dr Richard Russell (q.v.) of Lewes. As first the county and then London society flocked to the town, so the facilities for their amusement were developed, the libraries, theatre and assembly rooms which were modelled on those provided by the older inland spa towns. The town grew once more, the first authentic seaside resort in the country, and was eventually transformed into the largest and most fashionable resort of the era, the haunt of royalty and nobility, the rich and the famous. The population doubled in the ten years from 1811 to 1821, and the coming of the railway in the 1840 brought further rapid urban and industrial development; the first hoards of summer day-trippers from London also arrived, a new phenomenon that led to the development of a separate fashionable season in the winter. Suburban development on the slopes of the Downs followed from the 1870s until the 1960s to complete the town as we know it today.

Now, in the last years of the twentieth century, the resort function has diminished somewhat as the masses turn to Europe for guaranteed sunshine holidays, and more emphasis has been placed on short-stay holidays and also on the conference and exhibition trade which was worth £53 million to the town's economy in 1988. The opening of the Brighton Centre in 1977 has stimulated a widespread hotel improvement programme, culminating in the new Ramada Renaissance (now the Hospitality Inn) in 1987, and further facilities will be provided in West Street and at the completed Marina project. The number of day-trippers has declined from up to ten million in the pre- and post-war eras to some two million per year, with another 670,000 staying for longer periods. The tourist, hotel and catering trade is still vital to the town and provides employment for around 8,000 people.

As a shopping centre, Brighton, with some 2,000 shops, has a variety matched only by the largest cities; nearly half these shops are located in the main centre around Western Road and the outdated Churchill Square, but the specialist shops of the Old Town and North Laine areas provide a great attraction for many, while the district centres of London Road, St James's Street and Lewes Road fulfil the everyday needs of residents. The construction of large 'superstores' at Lewes Road, Nevill Road, Hollingbury and the Marina in 1985-7, and the provision of retail warehouses may well produce marked changes in the nature of town centre shopping, however.

Some 65,000 people are employed in the town, chiefly in the service, administrative and distributive sectors. Around 25,000 commute daily into Brighton while 15,000 travel out each day. Heavy industry virtually disappeared with the closure of the railway works in the 1950s, while light engineering, chiefly on the industrial estates, has declined since the 1970s although many new small businesses have opened since 1980. Widespread office construction means that a large proportion of employees now work in financial, administrative and corporate areas.

In the education sector, Brighton, with a university, polytechnic and college of technology, provides tuition for 10,000 or so full-time higher education students. There are also around thirty summer language schools with an annual turnover of some 25,000 foreign students. Indeed, education is so important that it is now the largest single employment sector.

Entertainment is provided by the usual seaside facilities plus a multitude of concert halls, night-clubs, public houses, theatres and cinemas, while the range of restaurants is said to be second only to that of London itself. The Brighton Festival, first staged in 1967, is now the second largest arts festival in the country after

Figure 18: The Sheridan Hotel, King's Road. Sea-front hotels and splendid architecture attract both holidaymakers and conference delegates to the town in large numbers.

Edinburgh's. Spectator sport facilities are provided throughout the twin towns, but public sporting and recreational facilities are woefully lacking and a number of new sports centres are required as leisure time increases; facilities to be provided at the Marina and Moulsecoomb will improve the situation.

Now that the widespread destruction of the Regency and Victorian heritage has ceased, the bane of Brighton's life must surely be the traffic congestion experienced every day in the town centre. The combination of narrow and hilly streets and the sheer volume of traffic generated by commercial activity makes public transport unreliable and brings the town almost to a standstill. The long-promised bypass is unlikely to ease the congestion in the heart of the town, and only radical policies such as the prohibition of town-centre through traffic envisaged in the 'Breeze into Brighton' plan of September 1988 will improve the situation.

Finally, the population of Brighton is surely as diverse as that of anywhere in the country. The centre of a conurbation of some 280,000 people from Saltdean to Shoreham, the town has extensive council estates and thousands living on poverty levels, and yet it is one of the most expensive in the country and extremely attractive to the 'professional classes'. The south coast is renowned for its retired population, but at the same time Brighton has some 10,000 students and numerous other young people in its many bed-sitters. The gay community is second in size only to London's. The diversity of the population contributes greatly to cultural life and adds to the rather attractive eccentricities of the town. Politically, Brighton has provided the only Sussex Labour M.P., and is probably unique for so large a resort in having a Labour-controlled council.

Today's Brighton is therefore primarily a service town, a function it has performed for the last two-hundred years or more, and is rightfully the capital of Sussex in all but name. It remains distinct from other British seaside resorts and towns because of its unique fashionable past and splendid architecture, its liberal and cosmopolitan culture, and the enduring contrast between the town's two faces: the rich and fashionable; and the poor and shabby.

16. BRIGHTON - The name

a) *ETYMOLOGY:* Although the first known use of the name 'Brighton' was in 1660, it did not come into general use until the late eighteenth century and its official use dates only from 1810 when it was adopted by the town commissioners <3>. 'Brighton' is in fact a contraction of the older 'Brighthelmston' which lasted into the 1850s and of which there are at least 44 known variations. In the Domesday Book Brighton was 'Bristelmestune', and other variations included 'Bredhemston', 'Brichelmston', 'Brighthampstead', 'Brighthelmsted', 'Brighthelnisted', 'Brighthempston', 'Brithelmeston', and 'Brogholmestune'. <63>

It has been suggested that the original name could have been derived from two Saxon words, one meaning 'division' or 'valley', the other meaning 'stones': 'the stony valley', perhaps a reference to the large sarsen stones found in the Steine. However, the most widely accepted etymology is from 'Beorthelm' or 'Brithelm', a personal name not unusual among Anglo-Saxons, and 'tun', or homestead: thus 'Beorthelm's homestead' or possibly 'Beothelm's village'. This derivation has also been assigned to other villages, viz: Bricklehampton, Worcestershire; Brighthampton, Oxfordshire; and Brislington, Somerset. <18,20,289,301a>

b) *OTHER 'BRIGHTONS':* At least 48 settlements in 11 different countries are known as 'Brighton', together with numerous variations such as 'New Brighton', 'Brighton Beach', 'Brighton Hills', 'Brightons', etc. In the United Kingdom, the hamlet of Brighton lies south-east of Newquay in Cornwall, while a Brighton farm stands one mile south of Hartington in Derbyshire, and another lies to the south-west of Cupar in Fife. The largest Brighton other than our own is situated six miles south of Melbourne, Australia, on the eastern side of Port Philip Bay, and has a population of about 40,000.

Settlements are to be found in the following countries <303a>:

i) Australia (4 instances): near Adelaide, Brisbane, Hobart and Melbourne;

ii) Barbados (1);

iii) Canada (4): in New Brunswick, Newfoundland, Nova Scotia and Ontario provinces;

iv) Guyana (1): east-south-east of Georgetown;

v) Jamaica (2): both south of Montego Bay;

vi) New Zealand (2): west-south-west of Dunedin, and north of Greymouth (but now known as Tiromoana);

vii) St Kitts (1);

viii) South Africa (2): near Cape Town, and in the Orange Free State;

ix) Trinidad (1): forty miles south-south-west of Port of Spain;

x) United States of America (27): in the states of Alabama, Arkansas, Colorado, Florida, Illinois, Iowa, Kentucky, Maine, Maryland, Massachusetts, Michigan, Minnesota, Missouri, Montana, New Jersey, New York (2), Ohio (2), Oregon, South Carolina, Tennessee, Texas, Utah, Vermont, Virginia and West Virginia.

c) *NICKNAMES:* Brighton has acquired several nicknames over the years, the most popular being 'The Queen of Watering Places', first used by Horace Smith who also coined the description 'Old Ocean's Bauble'. At the time of the so-called 'Trunk Murders' (q.v.), the former phrase was popularly corrupted to 'The Queen of Slaughtering Places'! William Thackeray in *The Newcombes* states, 'One of the best of Physicians is kind, cheerful, merry Doctor Brighton'. Other nicknames have included 'London-by-the-Sea' and 'London-super-Mare'. <2,3>

17. BRIGHTON - Early history

<1-3b,10-14,17,262>

A necessarily very brief outline of the main events in the history of the town up to the establishment of the resort function in the mid eighteenth century. See also "Ancient Customs", "Batteries and Fortifications", "Charles II", "Coastline", "Fishing Industry", "Lower Town", "Manors" and "Population".

a) *EARLY SETTLEMENTS:* The earliest known settlement in the Brighton area is the Neolithic encampment of around 2700 B.C. on Whitehawk Hill, although flint implements of a much earlier date have been found in cliffs at Black Rock and Saltdean. A Bronze Age settlement was discovered north of Coldean in 1990, while Hollingbury Castle Camp followed in the third and second centuries B.C. The area was also populated in Roman times as a small villa has been found at Preston; numerous Roman coins have been found throughout the district, and a Roman road, still traceable around Burgess Hill and Haywards Heath, came south from London to the coast near Brighton.

b) *SAXONS:* Probably in the early Saxon period the settlement of Brighton was founded, possibly just a farm as the older name, 'Brighthelmston', is believed to derive from 'Brithelm's Tun'; 'tun' is the Old English word for a homestead and is generally associated with villages of that period. The settlement grew up at the point where the Downs meet the sea, providing easy hill or valley routes to Lewes and beyond, with perhaps a small inlet (at Pool Valley) and a large, flat, sheltered area (Old Steine) nearby to accommodate boats and encourage the growth of an embryo fishing industry. The fishing village probably developed on an extensive chalk foreshore below the cliff and above the high-water mark, protected from the force of the Channel by an offshore submarine bar of shale.

It is known that in the eleventh century the manors in the Brighton area were under the lordship of Wolnuth, a nobleman of Sussex who commanded a fleet against the Danes in 1008. His son Godwin was created Earl of Kent, Surrey and Sussex by King Canute in 1019, but after helping defeat the Danes in 1046, Godwin was banished by Edward the Confessor and his estates, including forty-four manors in Sussex, were seized. Threatening to retaliate with force, he regained his possessions and found favour with the King once again. On the death of Godwin in 1053 one of the manors of Brighton was passed to Brictric, the son-in-law of Ethelred, but the other two became the possessions of Godwin's son Harold, who was later to become King Harold II.

c) *NORMANS:* Following the Norman Conquest, King William I conferred the barony of Lewes, including most of the local manors, on his son-in-law William de Warrenne whom he created Earl of Surrey. The Domesday Book of 1086, the earliest documentary mention of Brighton, records the following local manors: 'Bristelmestune' (Brighton) which had three manors, 'Hovingedene' (Ovingdean) and 'Rotingedene' (Rottingdean), all in 'Welesmere' hundred; in 'Falemere' (Falmer) hundred were 'Bevedene' (Bevendean) and 'Stamere' (Stanmer); and counted in 'Prestetune' hundred were 'Prestetone' (Preston) and 'Piceha' (Patcham). These manors were leased to Norman tenants by William de Warrenne, except for Stanmer and Preston which belonged to the Archbishop of Canterbury and the Bishop of Chichester respectively. Churches are mentioned at Brighton, Ovingdean, Patcham and Preston.

The fishing industry was well established at Brighton by this time as a tribute of 4,000 herrings was paid to one of the local manors. The information provided by the Domesday Book would also indicate a sizeable population at Brighton, something in of the order of 400.

d) *MEDIEVAL TIMES and FRENCH ATTACKS:* The early settlement of 'Bristelmestune', which eventually developed into Brighton, was probably a fishing village concentrated below the cliffs, the so-called 'Lower Town', with some farming on the hills above. A small priory was established between 1120 and 1147 on the site now known as the Bartholomews by the great Cluniac Priory of St Pancras at Lewes, possibly as a monastic farm.

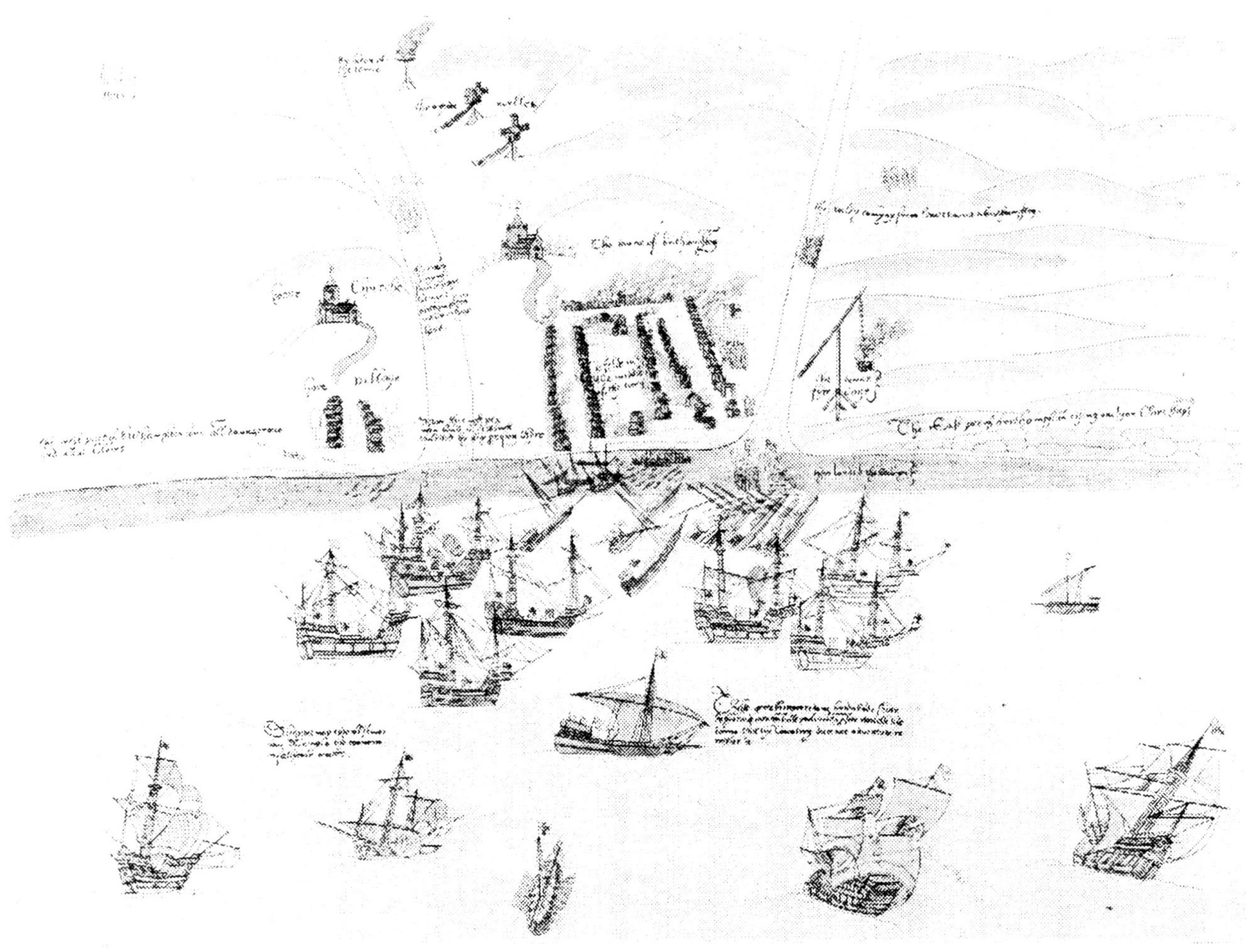

Figure 19: An Elizabethan drawing of a French raid on the town of Brighton or 'Brithampton'. Although dated 1545, it is believed to depict an attack of 1514. Note the church, fire-beacons and windmills; also the tenements of the 'Lower Town' and the single street of Hove village.

From certain names and customs it has been suggested that a colony of Flemings settled in Brighton in about the thirteenth century, contributing greatly to the success of the fisheries. Certainly the village grew into a town of size and importance, one of the largest in Sussex, and it probably spread onto the cliff top around this time, either through population growth or because of the ravages of the Lower Town by the sea. In 1313 a weekly market and annual fair were granted by Edward II, and the old parish church of St Nicholas appears to have been built, or perhaps rebuilt, at around this time. The townsfolk struggled to make a living, however. It is recorded that forty acres of land were lost to the sea in the fifty years from 1290 until 1340, and in 1341 the parish claimed relief from the 'Nonae' taxes on the grounds of poverty and crop failure.

During the sixteenth century the inhabitants of Brighton also had to contend with French raiders, whose attacks culminated in the burning of the town in June 1514 (England and France were at war from 1511 to 1514). This is probably the scene depicted in a drawing dated 1545 and held by the British Museum (figure 19): it shows a rectangular pattern of streets with the houses ablaze. <278>. The French, led by Admiral Prégent (known also as Prior John), destroyed most of the town except the church but were eventually driven off by archers from across the county who were attracted by the warning beacon on the East Cliff. A retaliatory raid on Normandy by Sir John Wallop resulted in the burning of twenty-one towns and villages. At Brighton virtually all buildings in the Old Town were destroyed at this time so that only St Nicholas's Church and the rectangular pattern of the streets now survive from medieval times.

There were further raids along the south coast in 1545, but at Brighton the French were driven off by the large numbers gathered on the cliff who had once again been attracted by the beacons. (The wreck of a ship from around this time lies offshore at Black Rock, q.v.) The town's defences were considerably improved with the erection of a circular fort known as the Blockhouse on the cliff top in 1559, but problems for the fishermen continued. They were involved in a local dispute with the farming community over the cost of town defences and church maintenance, a quarrel that led to the compilation of the Book of All the Auncient Customs (sic) (see "Ancient Customs"), and then in 1609 they petitioned Parliament over the harassment of men and seizure of boats, both by fishermen from Great Yarmouth and by pirates from Dunkirk. In February 1630 a Dunkirker warship was chased onto the beach where it was broken up and its ten guns were installed in the Blockhouse.

e) *SEVENTEENTH-CENTURY PROSPERITY and DECLINE:* Despite these difficulties, the town was relatively prosperous with the success of the fisheries. The small town grew despite plagues and epidemics in 1563, 1587-8 and 1608-10, and by the beginning of the seventeenth century the population had risen to around 1,500, with East Street, North Street, West Street, Middle Street, the Market Place, the Steine and the Hempshares all established. By the 1640s Brighton was the largest and one of the most important towns in Sussex, with about 4,000 inhabitants and an economy dominated by the fisheries; the inner area known as the Hempshares was developed around this time with streets leading northwards from the cliff. Brighton also figured briefly in national affairs in 1651 as King Charles II stayed overnight in the town before escaping to France via Shoreham (see "Charles II").

From that zenith, however, the town went into a long decline, the main factors being a slump in the demand for fish, increased erosion from around the 1640s of the foreshore so vital to the fishing industry, and attacks by foreign powers on English ships; Parliament was again petitioned over attacks by French and Dunkirker ships which had resulted in a loss to the town amounting to £30,000, while the fishermen deserted the North Sea and turned instead to coastal trading for a living. In 1676 William Jeffrey went before the Lewes Justices to ask for the provision a pier or some other defence against the sea, without which it was feared that the whole town would eventually be inundated. In 1687 customs officers were removed from the town because of the decline in trade, and three years later the church-wardens and overseers were forced to appeal to the Lewes Justices for help in the relief and maintenance of the large numbers of poor in the town. This resulted in the levy of a sixpenny rate in Aldrington, Hangleton, Ovingdean, Patcham and West Blatchington; however, several of these parishes themselves pleaded poverty and in 1708 a general three-halfpenny rate to assist Brighton was levied throughout eastern Sussex.

The start of the eighteenth century saw the remaining tenements and workshops of the Lower Town and most of the foreshore destroyed by the great storms of 1703 and 1705. The cliff-top town itself was now seriously under threat, and Daniel Defoe described Brighton as an old and poor fishing town in imminent danger of being completely swallowed by the sea; the proposed expense of £8,000 on groynes was, in Defoe's opinion, more than the whole town was worth! Two groynes were constructed as a defence against further encroachment in about 1723 with funds raised in churches throughout the country, but the decline of the fishing industry resulted in much unemployment, and when the population had fallen to around 2,000 by the mid eighteenth century the fortunes of the town had reached their nadir.

Figure 20: Seventeenth-century houses in Black Lion Lane, probably the oldest in the Old Town of Brighton

f) *EIGHTEENTH-CENTURY REVIVAL:* The impoverished town was in the right place at the right time to take advantage of the rising popularity of sea-water cures, advocated principally at Lewes by Dr Richard Russell (q.v.); perhaps in the 1730s, and certainly by the 1740s, Russell was sending his patients to Brighton. Only eight miles from the county town, with an unemployed workforce and the facilities of a small town, Brighton was a natural choice; with its proximity to London and the arrival of fashionable society, it has not looked back.

18. BRIGHTON CENTRE, King's Road

<123,277>

Schemes for a conference centre and winter garden on the site of Russell Street were proposed both before and after the last war, and in 1958 the area was cleared in readiness. As part of the 15-acre Churchill Square/ West Street redevelopment scheme, the site of the Brighton Centre was scheduled for a public building topped by a 30-storey block of flats that would have dominated the sea-front. Fortunately the plan was 'watered down' and the site remained vacant while the Top Rank Centre (Kingswest) and Churchill Square phases of the redevelopment were completed. However, the need for a new conference and entertainment centre to compete with facilities offered by Blackpool was brought to a head by the Rank Organisation's 1971 decision to refurbish the Top Rank Centre, thereby severely restricting conference accommodation in the town. The new conference centre was approved by the council in January 1972 at an estimated cost of £3 million, funded mainly by the sale of council-owned land including the Varndean Park estate to developers. Construction commenced in 1974.

The Brighton Centre, which eventually cost £9 million, was formally opened on 19 September 1977 by the Prime Minister, James Callaghan, although the first event, a folk-music festival, was held at the beginning of the month. Designed by Russell Diplock, the building was unique when it was erected although Bournemouth and Harrogate now have similar venues. The main auditorium has gallery seating for 2,100, with retractable seating for another 2,900 or an exhibition space of 1,925 square metres; a small adjacent hall, the Hewison Hall, can accommodate 800 people in 597 square metres. A banqueting suite has room for 1,200, and facilities also include 4 camera rooms, 8 interpreting rooms, and 650 telephone lines. The exterior grey façade is relieved by first-floor windows and upper storeys in brown brick, decorated with the borough arms and a BC motif, the overall appearance being an improvement on that of its eastern neighbour.

The Centre has been in almost continuous use since it opened, playing host to international singing stars, party-political and other conferences, exhibitions, ice shows, and major sporting events such as Brighton Bears National League basketball, the annual women's tennis tournament, and Davis Cup tennis in March 1981. It has given the conference and exhibition trade a significant boost, stimulating the hotel improvement schemes of the 1980s, and has provided much entertainment for residents. In 1990 a scheme was commenced to provide additional exhibition space at the rear of the Centre, linked to the new Oak Hotel in West Street.

Brighton has been a major conference centre since the 1853 annual meeting of the British Association for the Advancement of Science was held at the Royal Pavilion and Town Hall <7>. The first party-political conference was held by the Conservatives in 1875, while Labour first came in 1921 and the Liberals in 1963 <123>. By 1988 the conference trade brought an estimated 350,000 delegates and visitors to the town, and £53 million, spent mainly on accommodation and food, was injected into the local economy.

19. BRIGHTON COLLEGE, Eastern Road

<123,203a,204,204a>

a) *HISTORY:* The town's public school for boys opened as Portland House boarding school on 26 January 1847 at 13 Portland Place (now part of Pearson House) under principal Revd Arthur MacLeane; the school had forty-seven boys and included a junior department. Its aim was to provide 'a thoroughly liberal and practical education in conformity with the principles of the Established Church'. Plans were soon made for a new permanent building on the northern side of Eastern Road, a Gothic design in flint by Sir George Gilbert Scott; the foundation stone was laid on 27 June 1848 by the Bishop of Chichester, and the new school building was opened in about June 1849 by the Earl of Chichester.

At first the boys were boarded in nearby lodgings and the present library was used as a chapel, but School

Figure 21: Brighton College in about 1860

House, for the accommodation of boys, was added in 1854 together with the headmaster's house. The school grew steadily: a new chapel, also by Scott, was added in September 1859, and by 1863 there were 200 pupils. The south-western blocks were erected in 1885 (Chichester House) and 1887 by Sir Thomas Jackson who, in 1922, greatly enlarged the chapel as a memorial to old boys lost in the Great War. The junior school occupied part of the south-western block from 1895 until 1918 before moving to 16 Lewes Crescent; it returned during the Second World War, but in 1945 moved across Eastern Road to the former Deaf and Dumb School (erected 1848) before moving to Walpole Lodge, formerly the Convent of the Blessed Sacrament, in 1971. In 1942 the engineering workshops were given over to the war effort as a munitions factory.

Other prominent buildings in the school complex include the school hall (opened 1914); the swimming-pool and gymnasium (1923); the south-eastern block (1930); the science block (1958); the workshops and day-boy houses (1959); the Woolton Building (1972); the sports hall (1973); a new classroom block and pavilion (1980); computing/electronics/maths block (1986); and the day-girls house (1989). In July 1962 Queen Elizabeth II unveiled a plaque on the chapel wall. The main school building is now listed as being of special architectural and historic importance.

The school currently has about 460 pupils; girls were first admitted in 1973 to the sixth form, but in 1988 the school went completely coeducational. It is divided into five day houses (Aldrich, Durnford, Hampden, Leconfield, and Ryle), and two boarding houses (Chichester and School); the girls are in Fenwick House. Gordon, Stenning, Walpole and Wilson houses were disbanded during the financial crises of the 1930s and 1940s, and Bristol in 1983. The large playing field has been called the best cricket ground in the county after the County Ground; the school has also used playing fields at East Brighton Park since 1925 when it moved from the fields at Manor Farm used since the 1910s.

b) *HEADMASTERS:*

1847 Revd Arthur MacLeane
1851 Revd Henry Cotterill
1856 Revd John Griffith
1871 Revd Charles Bigg
1881 Revd Thomas Belcher
1892 Revd Robert Chambers
1895 Revd Arthur Titherington
1906 Revd William Dawson
1933 Revd Arthur Belcher
1937 Christopher Scott
1939 Walter Hett
1944 Arthur Clark
1950 William Stewart
1963 Henry Christie
1971 William Blackshaw
1987 John Leach

c) *CONSERVATION AREA:* The school grounds and the attractive residential area around Brighton College, including the impressive late-nineteenth-century houses of College Terrace (1880s), Walpole Road (1860s) and Walpole Terrace (1870s), were designated as the College conservation area in 1988.

Just outside the conservation area at the corner of Sutherland Road and College Terrace stands St Matthew's Court, built on the site of St Matthew's Church. Erected with a small tower in 1881-3, the building was designed in Early English style by John Horton and faced in knapped flint with stone dressings. The church had a wide nave and narrow aisles, but was demolished in 1967 and the parish merged with St Mark's. Connected with the church was the Bute Mission Hall, now the Rainbow Nursery at the corner of Sutherland Road and Rochester Street. This building, which has foundation stones laid 'on behalf of Sunday Scholars' by the mayor and mayoress, Sir Joseph and Lady Ewart, on 28 July 1892, served the surrounding densely-populated area which was developed in the 1870s. <1,45,62,83,331>

20. BRIGHTON and HOVE ALBION F.C., Goldstone Ground, Hove

<123,124,214,215,312>

a) *HISTORY:* The first professional football team in the area was Brighton United, a Southern League team which played at the County Ground from 1898 until 1900 but was forced to disband towards the end of its second season owing to financial difficulties. An amateur team including some former United players, Brighton and Hove Rangers, was formed in 1900 and played on the site of Surrenden Field at Home Farm, Withdean. The new club did well enough in its first season to be accepted into the Southern League's second division, and so the Rangers turned professional, signed up more players, and changed name to Brighton and Hove Albion. Matches were played at the County Ground in 1901-2, but they moved to the Goldstone Ground for the following season and won promotion to the first division. The 'Albion' then struggled somewhat, but in 1909-10 they won the Southern League championship, and, on 5 September 1910, defeated Football League champions Aston Villa 1-0 at Stamford Bridge to win the F.A. Charity Shield and be dubbed 'Champions of All England'.

The club closed down from 1915 until 1919 but became founder members of the Football League Third Division (South) in 1920. Although consistently in the upper half of the table, the Albion's chief successes during the 1920s and '30s were in the F.A. Cup where there were a number of giant-killing successes, notably on 2 February 1924 when Everton were beaten 5-2 and in 1932-3 when they progressed from the first qualifying round (because of a forgotten application) to the fifth round proper, a total of eleven matches. During the Second World War Albion competed in the Football League (South), Regional League (South) and London War League. The Football League recommenced in 1946, but in 1948 Albion were forced to apply for re-election for the only time.

Figure 22: The gable of no.238 Dyke Road. Once owned by Mr Noah Clark, a director of the Albion, it has a replica of the Football Association's Charity Shield, won by the team in 1910.

After several near misses in the 1950s, promotion to the second division finally came in 1958. Five years later, however, the club found itself in the fourth division. The championship was won in 1965, and in 1972 the second division was regained but this success was short lived. In 1977 promotion to the second division was achieved for the third time, and, on 5 May 1979, an historic victory at Newcastle ensured promotion to the first division, a status that was maintained for four years. Although the team was relegated in 1983, the greatest day in the club's history came on 21 May 1983 when they drew 2-2 with Manchester United in the F.A. Cup final at Wembley, watched by 100,000 spectators and an estimated 600 million people on television worldwide. The replay was lost 0-4, and the club has since had to rise once again from the third division.

The Goldstone Ground itself dates from 7 September 1901 when it was first used by Hove F.C.; the field was previously part of Goldstone Farm. The Albion first played there on 22 February 1902, and it became their permanent home the following season. The West Stand dates from 1958, although the southern section was added a little later. The North Stand was built in 1984, and the South Stand dates from 1949 when an older structure was raised to accommodate more spectators; it became all-seated in 1980. The ground's floodlights were inaugurated on 10 April 1961. <123>

b) *HONOURS:*

1901 Sussex Senior Cup runners-up
Brighton Challenge Shield runners-up
1902 Southern League Division Two joint champions
1909 Western League Section A champions
1910 Southern League champions
Southern Charity Cup winners
F.A. Charity Shield winners
1914 Southern Alliance champions
1941 Football League South champions
1958 Football League Division Three (South) champions
1965 Football League Division Four champions
1972 Football League Division Three runners-up
1977 Football League Division Three runners-up
1979 Football League Division Two runners-up
1983 F.A. Cup runners-up.
1988 Football League Division Three runners-up
Sussex Senior Cup Winners

c) *MANAGERS:*

1900 John Jackson
1905 Frank Scott-Walford
1908 John Robson
1919 Charles Webb
1947 Tommy Cook
1947 Don Welsh
1951 Billy Lane
1961 George Curtis
1963 Archie Macaulay
1968 Freddie Goodwin
1970 Pat Saward
1973 Brian Clough
1974 Peter Taylor
1976 Alan Mullery
1981 Mike Bailey
1982 Jimmy Melia
1983 Chris Cattlin
1986 Alan Mullery
1987 Barry Lloyd

d) *LEAGUE and CUP PERFORMANCES (showing the league position and round reached in cups for each season):*

Season	Div.	Pos.	FA Cup	FL Cup
1900-1	-	-	3Q	-
1901-2	SL2	3	3Q	-
1902-3	SL2	1=	4Q	-
1903-4	SL1	17	3Q	-
1904-5	SL1	12	Int	-
1905-6	SL1	16	2	-
1906-7	SL1	3	1	-
1907-8	SL1	17	2	-
1908-9	SL1	18	1	-
1909-10	SL1	1	1	-
1910-1	SL1	3	2	-
1911-2	SL1	5	1	-
1912-3	SL1	9	2	-
1913-4	SL1	7	3	-
1914-5	SL1	10	2	-
1915-9	-	-	-	-
1919-20	SL1	16	6Q	-
1920-1	FL3s	18	2	-
1921-2	FL3s	19	2	-
1922-3	FL3s	4	2	-
1923-4	FL3s	5	3	-
1924-5	FL3s	8	2	-
1925-6	FL3s	5	1	-
1926-7	FL3s	4	3	-
1927-8	FL3s	4	2	-
1928-9	FL3s	15	1	-
1929-30	FL3s	5	5	-
1930-1	FL3s	4	4	-
1931-2	FL3s	8	3	-
1932-3	FL3s	12	5	-
1933-4	FL3s	10	4	-
1934-5	FL3s	9	3	-
1935-6	FL3s	7	3	-
1936-7	FL3s	3	1	-
1937-8	FL3s	5	3	-
1938-9	FL3s	3	1	-
1939-45	War Leagues		-	-
1945-6	"	"	5	-
1946-7	FL3s	17	1	-
1947-8	FL3s	22	3	-
1948-9	FL3s	6	1	-
1949-50	FL3s	8	1	-
1950-1	FL3s	13	4	-
1951-2	FL3s	5	1	-
1952-3	FL3s	7	3	-
1953-4	FL3s	2	2	-
1954-5	FL3s	6	3	-
1955-6	FL3s	2	2	-
1956-7	FL3s	6	1	-
1957-8	FL3s	1	2	-
1958-9	FL2	12	3	-
1959-60	FL2	14	5	-
1960-1	FL2	16	4	3
1961-2	FL2	22	3	1
1962-3	FL3	22	1	2
1963-4	FL4	8	1	2
1964-5	FL4	1	1	1
1965-6	FL3	15	2	2
1966-7	FL3	19	4	4
1967-8	FL3	10	2	2
1968-9	FL3	12	2	2
1969-70	FL3	5	2	3
1970-1	FL3	14	3	1
1971-2	FL3	2	2	2
1972-3	FL2	22	3	2
1973-4	FL3	19	1	1
1974-5	FL3	19	3	1
1975-6	FL3	4	3	1
1976-7	FL3	2	1	4
1977-8	FL2	4	4	2
1978-9	FL2	2	3	5
1979-80	FL1	16	4	4
1980-1	FL1	19	3	3
1981-2	FL1	13	4	3
1982-3	FL1	22	Final	2
1983-4	FL2	9	5	3
1984-5	FL2	6	4	2
1985-6	FL2	11	6	3
1986-7	FL2	22	3	2
1987-8	FL3	2	4	1
1988-9	FL2	19	3	1
1989-90	FL2	18	4	1
1990-1	FL2			1

N.B. Prior to 1925-6, the F.A. Cup first round was equivalent to the third round from that season.

e) *RECORDS:*

Biggest home victories:
14-2 v. Brighton Amateurs, FA Cup Q1, 4 October 1902.
10-1 v. Wisbech, FA Cup R1, 13 November 1965.
9-1 v. Newport, FL D3s, 18 April 1951.
9-1 v. Southend, FL D3s, 27 November 1965.

Biggest away victories:
12-0 v. Shoreham, FA Cup Q2, 18 October 1902.
8-2 v. Merthyr, FL D3s, 1 February 1930.

Biggest home defeats:
0-6 v. Plymouth, FL D3s, 18 November 1950.
2-8 v. Bristol Rovers, FL D3s, 1 December 1973.

Biggest away defeats:
0-18 v. Norwich, Regional League South, 25 December 1940.
0-9 v. Middlesbrough, FL D2, 23 August 1958.

Largest Home Crowd:
36,747 v. Fulham, FL D2, 27 December 1958.

Smallest Home Football League Crowd:
2,093 v. Norwich City, FL D3s, 2 February 1929.

Largest Away Crowds:
100,000 v. Manchester Utd, FA Cup Final, Wembley, 21 May 1983.
52,641 v Manchester Utd, FL D1, 6 October 1979.

Most Appearances:
566 by Ernie Wilson 1922-36 (509 FL + 49 FA Cup + 8 D3s Cup).

Most Goals:
123 by Tommy Cook 1922-9 (114 FL + 9 FA Cup).

Most Goals in one season:
36 by Peter Ward 1976-7 (32 FL + 1 FA Cup + 3 FL Cup).

Most Goals in one match:
6 by Arthur Attwood v. Shoreham, FA Cup Q1, 1 October 1932.
5 by Frank Scott v. Southall, SL D2, 28 February 1903.
5 by Jack Doran v. Northampton, FL D3s, 5 November 1921.
5 by Adrian Thorne v. Watford, FL D3s, 30 April 1958.

Most capped player:
Stephen Penney (N. Ireland), 17 caps 1984-8.

21. BRIGHTON and HOVE STADIUM, Nevill Road, Hove

<100,123,299>

Brighton's greyhound stadium opened on 2 June 1928, just two years after the first greyhound meeting in the country. Costing £40,000, the arena was built on the site of Messrs Clark's market garden, and was furnished with redundant fittings and materials from the old Brighton Aquarium; in June 1939 the grandstands were extended. In 1976 the track was purchased by the leisure group Corals and considerable improvements have been made, including the addition of a computerised tote, and a squash and badminton centre in October 1978. There are now two grandstands; the Orchard Road Stand is the popular enclosure, while the Main Stand fronts Nevill Road and houses a 400-seat restaurant. Up to 5,000 race-goers can now be accommodated.

The track is now one of the country's leading greyhound stadia, but it has hosted many other events in addition to racing. Many first division football teams (and the England team) used the stadium for training prior to important cup-ties in the 1930s, '40s and '50s, and athletics, football, horse shows, military tattoos, boxing matches, American football and rugby have all been staged; All Black, Wallaby and Springbok rugby tourists have all played here. Speedway was rejected following noise tests in September 1976 and May 1977, however. In July 1962 the stadium was visited by Queen Elizabeth II. The adjacent Brighton Co-operative Society superstore opened on 11 June 1986.

The track holds the world speed record for a greyhound on a four-corner course, set on 4 May 1982 by 'Glen Miner' over a 563-yard race at an average 38.89 m.p.h. In front of a crowd of over 8,000 on 9 December 1986, 'Ballyregan Bob' set a new world record of thirty-two successive victories. The record attendance at the stadium was approximately 20,000 for the Canadian Army Athletic Championships during World War Two.

22. BRIGHTON, HOVE and SUSSEX SIXTH-FORM COLLEGE, Dyke Rd, Hove

<100>

This large school, which actually stands within the borough of Hove, has its origins in the Brighton Proprietary Grammar and Commercial School, founded in July 1859 at Lancaster House, 47 Grand Parade. Pupils were nominated and elected to the proprietary school by shareholders, to be transferred later to the higher school on approval. There they were instructed in the classics, arithmetic, bookkeeping, accounting, etc., and also received a non-sectarian religious education. Non-proprietary pupils paid an entrance fee of one guinea and a quarterly fee of £2 10s. The boys had one week's holiday at Christmas and one month in the summer.

On 27 May 1868 the 180 pupils of the Brighton Grammar School marched in procession to a new, plain, three-storey school building in Buckingham Road. The headmaster from 1861 until 1899 was E.J.Marshall, to whom a plaque has been erected on the adjacent 79 Buckingham Road. Due to the increasing number of pupils, the Grammar School moved for a second time in September 1913 to a site off Dyke Road then in the parish of Preston Rural; the Buckingham Road building at the corner of Upper Gloucester Road then became the Sussex Maternity Hospital and has now been replaced by a county council social education centre.

The new school, designed by S.B.Russell and known as the Brighton, Hove and Sussex Grammar School, was requisitioned for use as a military hospital soon after it opened in 1914. It continued after the Great War as a grammar school until 1975 when it became a sixth-form college, commonly known by the acronym 'BHASVIC'; there are now around 675 students. Especially notable is the panelled hall, decorated with murals, while the large library was added in 1935. The playing fields occupy 15 acres.

23. BRISTOL ROAD

<44,56,62>

On the northern side of Bristol Road stands the Roman Catholic Church of St John the Baptist. Consecrated on 9 July 1835, it replaced a small chapel in High Street, and was only the fourth Catholic church to be erected in England since the Reformation. Built and probably designed by William Hallett, the Corinthian-style church was altered in 1866, 1875 and 1888, and in 1890 became the first Catholic church in England to have electric lighting installed. It was completely redecorated in 1976 when the Calvary Chapel was converted into a porch on the western side, and is now a listed building. The interior contains the tomb, by John Carew, of Maria Fitzherbert who was buried there on 6 April 1837.

Adjacent to the church is St Joseph's Convent of Mercy, now a listed building used as an old people's home by the Sisters of Mercy. Founded in June 1852 at Egremont Place, the convent moved initially to a house opposite the church and then in 1858 to the adjacent Bristol Lodge, a yellow-brick house of about 1835. A cell block and refectory were added in 1864-6 by Charles Buckler around an internal courtyard, and the convent was physically linked to the church. The convent chapel was also added by Buckler in 1892.

Marine Terrace Mews, entered through an archway off Bristol Road, dates from the 1820s when it serviced Marine Terrace, now 84-89 Marine Parade. A group of contemporary, cobble-fronted mews cottages stands adjacently in Bristol Road itself. <108>

Figure 23: The Roman Catholic Church of St John the Baptist, Bristol Road

Bristol Road Methodist Church is a red-brick, Romanesque building in St George's Terrace at the corner of Montague Place, built in 1873 by Thomas Lainson with a three-arch portico and small spire. In 1989 the congregation moved to nearby St Mary's Church, and the old church was converted into the Advision recording studios.

24. BROADCASTING

<123,124,309>

a) *AM RADIO:* The BBC's first AM (medium wave) radio broadcast in the Brighton area was made in 1927 from a mast at the Dyke Road reservoir, but a permanent transmitter station was later opened south of Stoney Lane at Kingston-by-Sea, Shoreham. It now broadcasts Radio One (1053 kHz), Radio Three (1215 kHz), Radio Five (693 kHz), Radio Sussex (1485 kHz) and Southern Sound (1323 kHz), fed in all cases by land-line. Radio 4 AM is received in Brighton from the Droitwich transmitter in Worcestershire (198 kHz).

b) *BBC RADIO SUSSEX, 1 Marlborough Place:* Opened as Radio Brighton on 14 February 1968 under manager Bob Gunnell in the former Blenheim Hotel, it was only the fifth local radio station in the country and actually went on air two months earlier with an emergency blizzard service on 8-9 December 1967. The station initially covered the coastal area from Shoreham to Peacehaven with 75 watts on 88.1 MHz from Whitehawk Hill. The frequency changed to 95.8 MHz in May 1971 and then to 95.3 MHz on 27 June 1973, supplemented by an AM frequency on 2 September 1972 from Shoreham, now 1485 kHz. The editorial area was extended to Worthing in March 1970, Seaford (July 1971), Lewes and Ringmer (March 1978), to Haywards Heath (April 1979), and to the whole of East Sussex in 1983. On 22 October 1983 Radio Brighton became BBC Radio Sussex and now broadcasts in stereo VHF-FM from six transmitters, and on AM from three; a secondary studio has been established at Eastbourne.

c) *SOUTHERN SOUND RADIO, Radio House, Franklin Road, Portslade-by-Sea:* Opened on 29 August 1983 in the former Rothbury Cinema, the station initially covered the area between Chichester, Haywards Heath and Eastbourne, but since February 1989 has had a twin station covering Hastings and eastern Sussex as well. Locally it transmits from Whitehawk Hill on 103.5 MHz stereo VHF-FM and from Shoreham on 1323 kHz AM. The programme output is more music based than that of Radio Sussex.

d) *RADIO FALMER:* Covers the campus of the university on a frequency of 999 kHz from an inductive loop aerial around the perimeter. It has been operating since February 1976 and is specially licensed by the Department of Trade and Industry.

e) *FESTIVAL RADIO:* A temporary radio station broadcast on 97.7 MHz VHF-FM for the duration of the 1990 Brighton Festival. It used a studio off London Road and a transmitter in Kemp Town.

f) *TELEVISION:* The BBC's television service reached the town just in time for the coronation when, on 9 May 1953, the country's first relay transmitter opened at the old radar station on Truleigh Hill to the north of Shoreham. (Some viewers were already receiving programmes via a cable relay from Devil's Dyke, while viewers on high ground could receive other transmissions.) However, following the opening of the Rowridge station on the Isle of Wight in November 1954, Truleigh Hill operated on reduced power until a new transmitter at Whitehawk Hill opened in 1959. Brighton now lies at the edge of the BBC's South Region which, for some years, operated a news studio in one of the upper rooms of the Royal Pavilion.

Independent Television commenced in 1955; Southern Television started broadcasting from the Isle of Wight on 20 August 1958, but was replaced by Television South (TVS) on New Year's Day 1982. There is a small TVS news studio at the Brighton Centre with a direct link to Southampton which was inaugurated in April 1988.

g) *WHITEHAWK HILL and RELAYS:* Built on +he site of a wartime radar station, the town's main transmitting station first broadcast the BBC's VHF television service on 5 April 1959, relaying Crystal Palace before switching to Rowridge on 14 April 1962. BBC1 (ch. 57) and BBC2 (ch. 63) colour UHF television were broadcast from 21 September 1970, ITV (ch. 60) from 28 April 1972, and Channel 4 (ch. 53) from 17 May 1983. VHF-FM radio services commenced on 13 March 1967 and in stereo from 4 November 1972, relaying the broadcasts from Wrotham in Kent; the frequencies are: Radio Two 90.1 MHz, Radio Three 92.3 MHz, and Radio Four 94.5 MHz. Radio One is scheduled for December 1990 on 99.7 MHz.

The mast, 148 feet high with a total height of 182 feet to the top of the UHF aerial, stands on a ground site 396 feet above sea-level and replaced the original mast of similar size in 1983 when the two stood side by side for a time. It serves around 400,000 people, but gaps in its coverage have been filled by smaller relay stations at Ladies Mile, Patcham, serving 3,800 people (September 1982); at Mount Pleasant, Ovingdean, serving 2,100 people (March 1983); and north-east of Looes Barn, Saltdean, for 1,750 viewers (March 1983). Relays at The Meads, serving parts of Coldean and Moulsecoomb, and at Theobald House, serving parts of central Brighton and Moulsecoomb, were due on the air in 1990 but have been delayed.

h) *CABLE TELEVISION:* Rediffusion has provided a limited cable service for many years in the Brighton area, but a franchise for mass coverage has been awarded to Southdown Cable Vision to transmit eighty channels to 160,000 homes from Brighton to Worthing by 1996. The first service will be provided in 1991, and the channels will include community programmes made at the company's own studio. <123>

25. BRUNSWICK TOWN, Hove

<46,100-103>

The Brunswick area was developed as an estate of very high-class housing, the western equivalent of Kemp Town, and although it has always lain just within the parish of Hove, that village was nearly a mile away and the estate was considered very much a part of Brighton. It is now an outstanding conservation area and contains many impressive buildings.

In 1824 builder Amon Wilds and architect Charles Busby commenced work on the original estate to the south of Western Road and east of Lansdowne Road for the freeholder, Revd Thomas Scutt. Brunswick Terrace and Brunswick Square, both now listed grade I and decorated with Corinthian pilasters, were finished by 1830, while less expensive housing was provided in Lansdowne Road and Waterloo Street where there are also many listed buildings. The estate church, the grade B St Andrew's in Waterloo Street, was designed by Charles Barry in 1828 and was the first Italianate church in England. There was also a school in Farman Street and a large market building, now listed; in fact the estate was much more complete and self-contained than Kemp Town ever was.

In 1830 the grade II* Adelaide Crescent was begun to the west of Brunswick Terrace by Decimus Burton on behalf of Sir Isaac Goldsmid, but it was not completed until the 1850s when the design was altered somewhat to include Palmeira Square. This square was built on the site of a giant cast-iron and glass conservatory, the Anthaeum, which unfortunately collapsed on 29 August 1833, the eve of its opening day. Less expensive housing was erected to the north of Western Road in the 1850s at Lansdowne Road, Brunswick Place and Brunswick Road, all bow-fronted and now listed. St John's Church was erected in 1852-4.

From 1830 the estate was managed under an Act of Parliament by the Brunswick Square Commissioners. Their regulatory area was extended westwards and northwards in 1851, and in 1875 they became the Hove Commissioners, the forerunners of the Hove Corporation which was established in 1898. The Brunswick Town Hall of 1856 still stands at 64 Brunswick Street West but was replaced in 1882 by a new town hall in Church Road by Alfred Waterhouse. This building burnt down in January 1966 and the present Hove Town Hall opened on the site in 1973.

By the mid twentieth century most of the large houses of Brunswick Town had been divided into flats, many lacking basic amenities, and the area has become one of the most deprived in the south-east despite the grandeur of the architecture. Hove Council discussed the demolition of the whole area in 1945, a proposal that led to a massive public outcry, and also to the formation of the Regency Society which is dedicated to the preservation of Brighton. The Brunswick area remains a fascinating, contrasting area of magnificent architecture, interesting mews, and small side streets.

26. BUSES

<51,53,123>

a) *HORSE-BUSES:* The town's first regular horse-bus service connected the Kemp Town estate to Brighton Station from 11 May 1840, the first day of operation of the railway in Brighton. This route was later extended to the Cliftonville Inn in Hove, and by the 1870s several other east-west routes were operating. Services then expanded considerably with additional routes to Preston village, Preston Barracks, Stanford Avenue and Port Hall Road.

On 12 September 1884 most companies in the area amalgamated to form the Brighton, Hove and Preston United Omnibus Company (the 'United Company') which operated with 30 buses and 150 horses from stables and garages in Conway Street, Hove; from additional stables in Belfast Street, Hove, and Gloucester Place; and from a stable and coach works in Upper St James's Street. The double-decked vehicles, which usually had seating for twenty-six passengers, were pulled by two horses and ran at five- or ten-minute intervals. <50>

b) *INTRODUCTION of MOTOR-BUSES:* The withdrawal of horse-buses commenced in the early 1900s with the advent of the new motor-buses. Tilley's horse-buses ceased operating on the introduction of the corporation's tram service in 1901, and the United Company, which ran the first motor-bus on 24 December 1903 from Hove Town Hall to Castle Square, replaced horses on the Kemp Town route in April 1904. By 1913 the United Company was operating six motor routes with both single- and double-decked vehicles, but still ran four horse routes until 8 December 1916 when the last horse-bus ran from Carlisle Road, Hove, to Brighton Station. (In 1976 a Brighton double-decker motor-bus of 1905, the oldest known in existence, was being restored. <123>)

c) *ELECTRIC TRACTION EXPERIMENTS:* In 1909 the United Company successfully experimented with four battery-driven buses. Although some difficulties were experienced on hills, twelve vehicles were operated the following year from a garage in Montague Place.

In November 1910 the United Company also made plans to use trolley-buses and promoted a Bill in Parliament for routes from Worthing to Rottingdean, but the corporations of both Brighton and Hove responded by promoting their own Bills for municipal operations and these were passed in 1912 as the Brighton and Hove Corporation Acts. Brighton Corporation borrowed a trolley-vehicle from Leeds and a ran a test route firstly along the length of London Road at the end of December 1913, and then on the Ditchling Road, Preston Drove and Beaconsfield Villas tramway route the following month. The bus, which also underwent trials with Hove Corporation, proved a success and negotiated the hills quite easily, but further plans for trolley-bus operation were dropped because of the First World War. <56>

d) *FORMATION of SOUTHDOWN:* On 1 January 1915, the Worthing Motor Services Company, the London and South Coast Haulage Company, and the excursion services of the Brighton, Hove and Preston United Omnibus Company were amalgamated into a single undertaking which was formally established as Southdown Motor Services Ltd on 2 June 1915. The new company, which was formed as a reaction to government policy during World War One, operated out of the Steine Street garage which had been used since 1909 by the Worthing company. It also acquired eleven buses from the United Company on the condition that the Brighton and Hove areas would not be worked.

Southdown grew steadily, building a new garage at Freshfield Road in 1916 and another at the bottom of Edward Street in 1925. The green-liveried buses used Madeira Drive as a terminus until July 1929 when the corporation provided Pool Valley as a more convenient bus station. The Steine Street premises were used as a coach station from 1920 until about 1970 but the site is now occupied by Dolphin Mews. <52>

e) *ARRIVAL of TILLINGS and GENERAL EXPANSION:* In 1915 the long-established Thomas Tilling Ltd of London entered the local omnibus scene by operating a route from Portslade Station to Castle Square, although no local fares were permitted within Brighton. The following year, on 22 November 1916, the newcomer acquired the United Company together with its aging fleet for £44,000, and Tilling's Brighton and Hove omnibus section was formed. The forty-one petrol, twelve electric and eight horse vehicles of the United Company were duly replaced by modern motor vehicles in a red and cream livery, each open-topped and carrying forty-three passengers. The Southdown agreement was renegotiated with a new allocation of routes; Tillings were granted service nos.1-7, several of which still partly operate over their original routes.

Services expanded in the 1920s and '30s as new suburbs were developed, and Tillings acquired the Brighton Downs Company in October 1926 to provide a service to the new Woodingdean estate. In 1930 they introduced a fleet of covered double-deck buses, and two years later opened a new garage in Whitehawk Road, selling off the premises in Montague Place. A new regulatory body, the South-East Traffic Commissioners, was established on 1 April 1931 with responsibility for the issue of route licences, at which time Tillings ceased making their annual contribution of about £3,000 to the corporation for road maintenance.

f) *BRIGHTON, HOVE AND DISTRICT OMNIBUS COMPANY:* On 2 November 1935 Tillings established the Brighton, Hove and District Omnibus Company (hereinafter 'B.H.D.') to run their Brighton services, although it was still managed from London. Initially some buses changed to an all-cream livery but they soon reverted to red and cream except for the no.17 open-top sea-front service which first ran on 10 April 1936.

g) *BRIGHTON CORPORATION BUSES and POOLING:* In 1938 the Brighton Corporation (Transport) Act was passed, authorising a corporation trolley-bus operation (see below) and requiring the pooling of the various undertakings from 1 April 1939 in order to improve the service to the town. The corporation's own motor-bus service started on that date, but their routes were restricted to the county borough only while Southdown were given permission to work those parts of 'Greater Brighton' added in 1928, including Patcham and Rottingdean. The corporation buses also adopted a red and cream livery, although with the borough arms to distinguish them. All buses bore the title 'Brighton, Hove and District Transport'.

h) *TROLLEY-BUSES:* The idea of operating trolley-buses, experimented with before the First World War, was revived when two vehicles were borrowed and run experimentally around the Level for a brief period in December 1935 and January 1936. Following this successful trial the corporation promoted a Bill to replace the aging tramway system; it was rejected by the House of Lords, but an amended Bill requiring greater co-ordination between rival companies was accepted by a town poll and became the Brighton Corporation (Transport) Act of 1938. The first public trolley-buses ran on the no.48 route on 1 May 1939, replacing tram route L from Old Steine to Preston Barracks, and the whole system was formally inaugurated on 1 June 1939 when service nos.26 and 46 were introduced along Ditchling Road, Preston Drove and Beaconsfield Villas, and the no.40A route via New England Road to Brighton Station.

Operating cleanly, quietly and efficiently, the trolley-buses proved to be very popular with the public. Where the routes diverged the points of the overhead lines were operated electrically from the driver's cab, the setting being indicated by advance warning arrows. Buses also carried long poles for reconnecting the lines when necessary. <54,55>

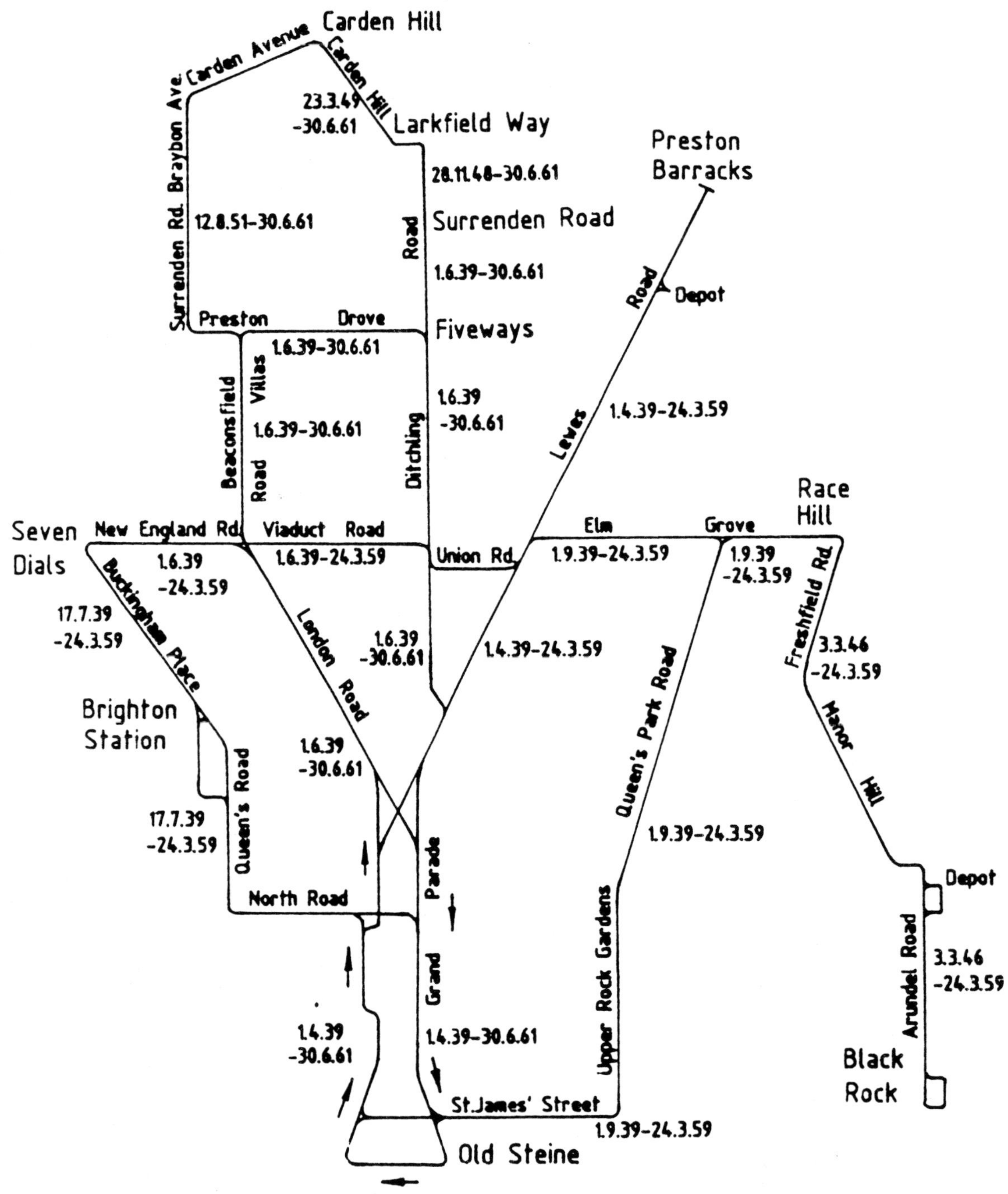

Figure 24: Trolley-bus routes in Brighton 1939-61

j) *WARTIME OPERATION:* The Second World War brought many restrictions to bus operations in the town. Some vehicles were lent to other towns, while others were commandeered for transporting evacuees; those that remained had their interior and exterior lighting severely restricted, resulting in many accidents, and the livery was changed to 'battleship grey' from October 1942. In order to save fuel a coal-burning gas-turbine and petrol bus was introduced in November 1939 but it partially exploded at Patcham in November 1940; nevertheless, several buses operated with trailing gas producers from 1943.

k) *POST-WAR TROLLEY-BUS EXPANSION and DEMISE:* The war brought a halt to trolley-bus expansion plans and B.H.D.'s trolley-vehicles were mothballed until 1945 when they entered service under the auspices of the corporation. Trolley routes were then expanded from 1946 until the route mileage reached 14.54 miles in 1951. However, following the 1948 nationalisation of electricity supplies Brighton's trolley-buses no longer operated from the corporation's own supply, and as operating costs rose the council's transport committee recommended the withdrawal of the trolley operation in 1954. By 1955-6 the system was operating at a loss and the council decided to run down its trolley operation. Services were halved on 25 March 1959 when routes along Lewes Road and those to the east were replaced by motor-buses. The last Brighton trolley-buses, on the Patcham and Fiveways routes, ran on 30 June 1961.

Eight of Brighton's trolley-buses were purchased by other operators with the others sold for scrap, but now only one survives, owned by a private enthusiast in Kent. <54,55>

l) *POST-WAR MOTOR-BUS EXPANSION and NATIONALISATION:* Under the terms of the 1947 Transport Act the B.H.D. company was nationalised following the purchase of Tillings by the British Transport Commissioners. Services and buses were unaffected, but a local general manager was appointed to run the operation.

Services continued to expand throughout the suburbs, and in July 1948 the traffic commissioners allowed the corporation to operate outside the borough boundary for the first time. Peak Southdown annual mileage of 142,000,000 miles was reached in 1956 and they opened a new garage at Moulsecoomb Way in 1957. A new seven-storey headquarters, Southdown House, opened at Freshfield Road in 1964.

m) *'BATS' AGREEMENT:* With the withdrawal of trolley-bus services it was obvious that a new agreement was required between the respective undertakings, and on 1 January 1961 the Brighton Area Transport Services ('BATS') agreement came into operation, covering the area from Shoreham Beach to Telscombe Tye. The three undertakings were permitted to work any part of the area and routes were reorganised over a period of three-and-a-half years. An open-top circular tour of the borough ran from 10 July 1964, and the first one-man double-deck buses were introduced in 1966 on the 26A route.

n) *NATIONAL BUS COMPANY:* The 1968 Transport Act created the National Bus Company, thereby bringing Southdown and B.H.D. into common ownership for the first time. In the interests of efficiency Southdown took over B.H.D. on 1 January 1969, although the red and cream livery and name remained. Southdown now ran 80%, and the corporation 20%, of the BATS routes.

The new Southdown operation introduced one-man working from 1970 for economic reasons, and changed the B.H.D. livery to green and cream with the name 'Southdown-BHD' from October 1971. In 1972 National Bus introduced standard liveries and all Southdown buses were painted entirely green from September 1972 until the last red and cream bus ran in March 1975. The

Figure 25: The Brighton Buses depot in Lewes Road, built originally for Brighton Corporation Tramways, as the etched windows show

late 1970s saw further rationalisation of routes, and more single-deck and one-man buses. Frequent 'shuttle' buses were introduced on some routes from April 1983.

p) *DEREGULATION OF SERVICES and OTHER DEVELOPMENTS:* On 1 January 1986 the town services of Southdown were re-established as an independent company, the Brighton and Hove Bus and Coach Company, with the old red and cream livery, and in May 1987 the new company was acquired by its senior management. Southdown then concentrated solely on its country routes and vacated Southdown House in 1987 when the company moved to a Lewes base; the building was then taken by BUPA. In August 1989 Southdown was sold to the Scottish-based Stagecoach Holdings Ltd for around £10 million.

The corporation services, which had opted for a blue and white livery in June 1970, were renamed simply 'Brighton Buses' in 1986, a private subsidiary of Brighton Borough Transport with no rates support. The 25-year-old BATS agreement ended at the start of 1986, and routes were opened up to all operators upon the national deregulation of services in October 1986. While profitable routes were naturally continued by the main companies, loss-making services were opened to tender and paid for by the county and district councils.

For many years now since the 1960s the town's buses have been caught in a vicious circle of competition from private transport, increasing fares, poor time-keeping and the consequent further increases in private traffic. Traffic management measures and radical fare policies are surely necessary if the bus services vital to so many people are to survive into the next century.

27. BYPASS

A ring road 'to assist in the distribution of traffic and to relieve congestion in the town centre' was first suggested by a planning committee in 1932, and was proposed again in the town's 1958 development plan to include Mill Road and Coldean Lane.

In 1973 six routes for a new east-west road, including downland and urban options, were identified for public consultation; the following year the Department of the Environment effected planning protection on a downland route. It was not until 1980, however, that the Department published a draft bypass route. A 97-day public inquiry into both the need for the new road and its route commenced in March 1983 (one week at the Hotel Metropole and then at the Wagner Hall), and was followed by a 10-day inquiry in January 1987 at Dorset Gardens Methodist Church.

The route of the new 8.5 mile road, which will cost at least £60 million and consume some 500 acres of land, was fixed to run along the fringe of the urban area from the Shoreham bypass, just west of the Kingston roundabout, to the Lewes Road at Stanmer Park; junctions will be provided with a new Benfield Valley link road; at the Devil's Dyke Road/Mill Road crossroads; at London Road/Mill Road/Vale Avenue; and at Old Boat Corner. Twin 400-yard tunnels will carry the carriageways beneath Southwick Hill. The bypass, to be part of the A27 Folkestone to Honiton trunk-road, will be an all-purpose road with dual two-lane carriageways, except for the section between Devil's Dyke Road and London Road which will have three lanes either way. Another inquiry is still required for the change of route at Southwick Hill.

On 2 April 1989, Brighton Pavilion M.P. Julian Amery formally cut the first turf of the Brighton and Hove Bypass in the Waterhall Valley. The first section, from London Road to Devil's Dyke Road, is scheduled to be completed in mid 1991, with the whole route finished in 1995; construction of the second section, from Devil's Dyke Road to Hangleton, commenced in June 1990.
<123>

28. CANNON CINEMA, East Street and Grand Junction Road

<68,68a,123>

The Cannon Cinema was originally opened on 1 August 1930, on the site of Brill's Baths, by Associated British Cinemas as the Savoy Cinema-Theatre, a massive building faced with glazed cream terracotta tiles and decorated with Corinthian pilasters; the façades in Grand Junction Road and East Street, with their emphasis on geometric forms, are typical of the Art Deco style of the era. Seating 2,300 people and costing £200,000, it was the first serious rival to the Regent and included two restaurants, two cafés, and a large basement car-park for 300 cars among its facilities. The magnificent interior was fitted out in Japanese style by architect William Glen. The name was changed to the ABC in 1963, but with a significant change in cinema-going habits it was divided into four smaller auditoria from November 1975, the former circle becoming the ABC 1. Reopened by the mayor, William Clarke, on 3 April 1976, the ABC lost much of its elaborate decoration in the conversion. In 1986 the ABC chain was acquired by Cannon Cinemas Ltd, and Brighton's ABC was subsequently renamed the Cannon. From 21 to 25 May 1987 the Cannon played host, jointly with the Odeon, to the first Brighton Film Festival; the second was held on 8-10 September 1989.

Cannon Cinemas have also purchased the eight-screen complex due to open at the Marina in March 1991, leaving the older cinema's future in some doubt.

29. Sir Herbert CARDEN

<2,3,19>

Perhaps the greatest figure in Brighton's civic history since incorporation, Alderman Sir Herbert Carden was a visionary of Brighton Council for over forty years and was known as the 'maker of modern Brighton'. Born in 1867 of an old Brighton family, he was educated at the old Brighton Grammar School in Buckingham Road and was admitted as a solicitor in 1889. In 1895 Carden was elected as a socialist councillor and became an alderman within eight years. He was mayor for three years from 1916 and also sat on Hove Council from 1902 until 1905.

It was chiefly due to Carden that Brighton Corporation embarked upon many of its municipal enterprises such as the telephone and tramway systems. He also saw the need to preserve the surrounding downland, both to protect the water supply, and to provide recreational facilities and beautiful countryside for the inhabitants of the town. A wealthy man, he bought large areas of downland himself which he resold to the corporation for the same amount to defeat unfair pricing. For his contribution to the town Carden was made an honorary freeman of the borough on 28 October 1926, and was knighted in 1930; he died in 1941. Several roads and a park in the Hollingbury area have been named after him, and a plaque has been erected at his home, 103 Marine Parade; his portrait may be found in Brighton Museum. Fortunately not all Carden's proposals won favour, though. At one time he advocated the rebuilding of the entire sea-front from Kemp Town to Hove in the 1930s style first represented by Embassy Court; the demolition of the Royal Pavilion to build a conference and entertainment centre; and the redevelopment of the Lanes area.

30. CARLTON HILL

A steep road that formerly ran through one of the poorest areas of the town, Carlton Hill has now been redeveloped for most of its length, principally in the 1930s and '60s, except for some red-brick terraces which remain either side of Blaker Street. The lowest part is now known as Kingswood Street; the area to the north, including the flats and market, is dealt with under "Albion Hill". See also figures 1 and 2.

On the southern side of Kingswood Street once stood the Catholic Apostolic Church. This Early English, red-brick chapel was built in 1865, but after closing in 1954 it was used as a student centre by the adjacent art college until it was demolished in 1964 when the college was rebuilt. <48a,62,76>

Higher up Carlton Hill, on the northern side, is the:

a) *GREEK ORTHODOX CHURCH of the HOLY TRINITY:* Built for the Revd Henry Wagner by George Cheeseman, and designed in Doric-style by George Cheeseman junior, this church was consecrated on 28 January 1840 by the Bishop of Worcester and former Vicar of Brighton, Dr James Carr, as the Anglican Church of St John the Evangelist. The façade was altered in 1957 by L.A.Mackintosh whose monogram, topped by a crown, lies to the left of centre; the eagle motif to the right is the emblem of St John. The church, which seats 1,200 worshippers and has large galleries, never attracted a large congregation and closed in 1980, but plans to convert it into a detoxification centre were rejected after a public inquiry and it remained empty until March 1986 when the listed building was taken over by the Greek community. The adjacent Edward Riley Memorial Hall opened in 1938, but has been used as the Diocesan Centre for the Deaf (Sussex Deaf Association) since St John's Church closed. <44,62,64a,65,123>

To the west of the church is:

b) *TILBURY PLACE:* No.1 Tilbury Place is a large, three-storey house, formerly St John's Lodge. Erected in the 1810s, it was occupied for many years by merchant Edwin Tarner and his wife Laetitia (née Tilbury), and was inherited by his son, Edwin Tilbury Tarner. It was left to Brighton Corporation in 1933 by Miss Laetitia Tilbury Tarner, who had devoted her life to the parish,

Figure 26: Edwin Tarner's tower in the recreation ground named after him

and it became the Tarner Home, a charitable home under Miss Blanche Fair to provide skilled nursing for the desperately ill who could not themselves otherwise afford it. St John's Lodge is now a listed building, as are the attractive houses of Tilbury Place adjoining, nos.2-5, which are also part of the Tarner Home. This is an excellent example of a Georgian-style terrace, faced in yellow brick and fitted with excellent fanlight doorways.

The garden of St John's Lodge is now the Tarner Recreation Ground in Sussex Street, 1.24 acres acquired in January 1934 and remodelled in 1987-8. An old flint garden wall remains on the eastern side with a blocked-up archway and figurehead. Nearby stands a small tower which is now a listed building. Faced in knapped and squared flint with seventy or so steps, it is closed to the public but is said to have been built in the mid nineteenth century by Edwin Tarner to enable him to sight his ships in the Channel in time to meet them at London docks. Tarnerland Nursery School opened in 1933. <44,64a,83,123,126>

At the end of Tilbury Place is Prior House, now the Brighton Unemployed Centre, but built in 1936 as the Brighton Girls' Club which was originally founded in 1928 at 17 Nelson Row. It was named after the club's secretary, Peggy Prior, but became a remedial education centre in 1970. <48a,115,123,311>

Opposite Tilbury Place is the remaining length of:

c) *MIGHELL STREET:* Mighell Street was demolished in the early 1970s for the Amex House development and only nos.34-35 now remain, an early-nineteenth-century listed farmhouse now divided into two dwellings; its cobbled façade and Doric doorway are unfortunately obscured by fences and trees <44>. Mighell Street Hall stood on a site now occupied by the Amex House forecourt in Edward Street. It was built in 1878 as a Strict Baptist chapel by T.Boxall on the site of the Globe music hall, and was used as St John's Church Hall from 1910 until 1927, and then a spiritualist church until it was demolished in about 1965 <62,83>.

31. CASTLE INN, Castle Square

<3,10,14,15,64a,194>

a) *The NEW INN and ASSEMBLY ROOMS:* The Castle Inn, one of the town's two principal meeting places at a time when fashionable society had just started to arrive in numbers, stood on the northern side of the square to which it gave its name. It was originally built as a private house in the 1740s, the first new resort development in the town, but in 1752 it was acquired by Samuel Shergold and converted into an inn; it had its own water supply from a well. Fashionable balls, assemblies and other functions were held at the Castle which was rivalled only by the Old Ship.

To cater for ever-increasing numbers of visitors, the inn was rebuilt in 1766 by John Crunden who added the impressive assembly rooms at the rear in a tall, red-brick building facing west into what later became Palace Place. The ballroom, which was considered one of the most elegant rooms in the country, was designed in Adam-style with a brilliantly decorated ceiling, plaster relief walls, colonnaded recesses, and a musicians' gallery. It measured 80 feet by 40 feet by 40 feet high.

b) *RISE and FALL:* The inn became very popular and held regular assemblies and dances. In 1776 Shergold passed control to a Mr Stuckey, but soon resumed control himself in partnership with Messrs Best and Tilt. When Shergold finally retired in February 1791 the inn was run by Thomas Tilt, and by Tilt's widow after his death in 1809. In 1814 Messrs Gilburd and Haryett took over, improving the buildings and adding a fine organ to the assembly rooms, but by this time the attraction of the Castle was waning, owing mainly to the hostility of the Master of Ceremonies and the availability of other facilities in the expanding town. Indeed, in August 1815 the assembly rooms were closed for the season because of a lack of subscribers.

c) *ROYAL PURCHASE and DEMOLITION:* In July 1815 the Prince Regent purchased one-quarter of the Castle business with an eye to enlarging his Pavilion estate; he bought another quarter in December 1816 and completed the purchase in 1821 at a total cost of £11,000. The inn was consequently demolished in October 1823 and replaced by a four-storey row of houses later known as 'Needham's Corner', while Castle Square and Old Steine were widened.

The assembly rooms were spared however, and were converted into a Royal Chapel with the musicians' gallery converted into the King's personal gallery; a connecting covered passageway was made to the Royal Pavilion. The chapel held over 400 people, with admission by private ticket, and was consecrated on 1 January 1822; George IV, William IV and Victoria all worshipped there. In 1850, when the Royal Pavilion estate was purchased by the town commissioners, the Church Commissioners claimed the Royal Chapel as a consecrated building. The interior was subsequently dismantled and reassembled in a new building in Montpelier Place to form St Stephen's Church, now a grade II*-listed building (see "Clifton Hill (Montpelier Place)").

32. CASTLE SQUARE

Castle Square became the commercial hub of the town in the late eighteenth century when the Castle Inn (q.v.), after which the square is named, became established. When the inn was demolished in October 1823 the square was opened up into a broad thoroughfare which became the main coaching centre of the town and later the terminus of the many horse-bus routes. A number of early banks were also established in the square and its immediate vicinity. <14>

Nos.1-8 on the south side are all listed buildings. No.1a faces the Steine and was probably designed by

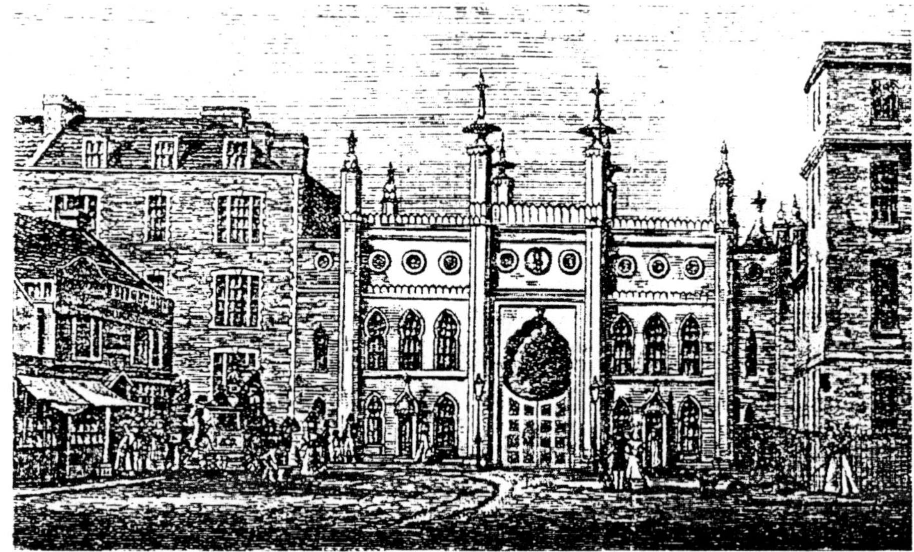

Figure 27: The South Lodge of the Royal Pavilion in about 1831, now the site of Pavilion Buildings. To the right is Castle Square; on the left a coach waits outside no.1 North Street, the town's first coaching office.

Wilds and Busby in the 1820s, as was no.4, a narrow four-storey building with balcony and pilasters; nos.2-3, with bows, date from slightly earlier, while nos.5-6 were probably erected in the late eighteenth century. At the corner with East Street is Castle Square House, a five-storey development completed in 1985 in an interesting style by Fitzroy Robinson Miller Bourne. <44>

The Royal Pavilion Tavern, nos.7-8, was established in about 1816, but was altered somewhat in 1820 by A.H.Wilds; it has a shallow bow-front and an ironwork balcony adorned with dolphins. In Steine Lane at the rear of the tavern are the Pavilion Vaults Wine Bar and the Shades Bar. It was upon the latter that former proprietor Edmund Savage erected a sign referring to a 'Gin Palace'. Mrs Fitzherbert, residing opposite in Steine House, objected to this and so Savage substituted the word 'shades' which subsequently became a local word for a bar. Whether it was used because it was in the shade of Steine House, or because of the shady nature of the business is not clear! No.1 Steine Lane, also part of the tavern, is a four-storey listed building with a good doorway of the late eighteenth or early nineteenth century. <15,18,44>

Standing on the northern side of the square is the Royal Bank of Scotland, an elegant Art Deco building decorated with the borough arms. Originally known as Electric House, it was opened on 20 January 1933 as offices and showrooms for the corporation's electricity department (see "Electricity Supply"). It was built on the site of Needham's Stores and some four-storey houses which were themselves erected on the site of the Castle Inn. <26>

To the west of Palace Place are the Pavilion Buildings, erected in 1852-3 on the site of some four-storey offices of the Royal Pavilion. Nos.4-7, which are listed, and nos.12-14 are decorated with urns, lions and other figureheads; interrupting these two ranges is the National Westminster Bank of 1911. On the western side of Pavilion Buildings are the elegant neo-Georgian offices of the Royal Insurance Company. Formerly the offices of the *Brighton and Hove Herald*, the building was designed in 1934 by John Denman and is decorated with the arms of the two boroughs. At the rear are vestiges of the cobble and brick walls of the guest dormitories of the Royal Pavilion, built westwards to Prince's Place at the southern end of the Royal Pavilion estate in 1831 for William IV. <26,194>

33. CEMETERIES

Some seventy acres of land between Bear Road and Hartington Road are used by the town for cemeteries and crematoria. The area was formerly the open arable field of Scabe's Castle, a late-eighteenth-century farm with buildings in Hartington Road which were demolished in the 1900s when Hartington Place and Hartington Terrace were developed. <106,107,83>

(For details of other cemeteries in the town, consult the index entry on "cemeteries".)

The oldest of the three cemeteries is the:

a) *EXTRA-MURAL CEMETERY:* Originally a private burial ground, laid out on 28 acres in 1850 by the Brighton Extra-Mural Company, 6 acres being the gift of the Marquess of Bristol. The entrance was a castellated gateway with a round tower in Lewes Road, and there were two mortuary chapels designed by A.H.Wilds of which only the Anglican chapel remains, a large building in knapped flint with a turret spire; the Dissenting chapel to the south-west was a smaller building with a thin spire.

The cemetery was a favourite resort in the nineteenth century and even had a guide book published, but in 1956 the now redundant cemetery was purchased by the corporation and restored as an interesting and picturesque garden of remembrance which contains many impressive Victorian tombs, including those of several important figures in Brighton's history. In the driveway is the borough mortuary which opened in August 1962 and has between 600 and 700 admissions a year. <24,83,126,257>

Figure 28: Tombs in the Extra-Mural Cemetery

The drive through the Extra-Mural Cemetery eventually leads into the council's own cemetery, which is also approached from Lewes Road and Bear Road. Since about 1955 it has been known as:

b) *WOODVALE:* Following the rapid expansion of the town in the early nineteenth century, the churchyard and cemetery extensions of St Nicholas's Church became severely overcrowded causing the Home Secretary to prohibit further interments there from 1 June 1853, although the deadline was later extended until 1 October. The vestry approached the Extra-Mural Company but they refused to sell land and demanded too high a charge for parochial burials. After the Home Secretary had refused to extend the deadline further, the Marquess of Bristol 'came to the rescue' by offering the parish 20 acres of land to the east of Lewes Road in April 1856 which were gratefully accepted. A burial board was formed the following month, and the new parochial cemetery was laid out in 1857. On 1 April 1902 it became the Brighton Borough Cemetery when the corporation took over the functions of the parochial burial board.

The original area is approached by a long drive from Lewes Road with two knapped flint lodges about

Figure 29: The impressive Decorated Gothic chapel of Woodvale Cemetery

halfway up; a memorial gateway to the Marquess of Bristol with two crocketed spires formerly stood between them. The cemetery contains several impressive tombs of important figures in Brighton's history, and the large mortuary chapel is one of Brighton's most impressive Gothic chapels. Built in the Decorated style, it is faced in knapped flint and has a large tower and spire with an octagonal lantern tower at the rear. The chapel also houses the Brighton Borough Crematorium which opened in 1930, the first crematorium in Sussex. The cemetery grounds have been beautifully laid out with rock gardens and cascades and provide interesting sylvan walks.

An extension of 23 acres to the north of Bear Road was added in 1868, an area which now includes the Commonwealth war graves and St Dunstan's plots. In 1919 3.5 acres off Bevendean Road were sold to the Jewish community as a burial ground. <24,83,112,126>

The third cemetery in the area is the:

c) *BRIGHTON AND PRESTON CEMETERY:* Opened in 1885 on 27 acres of ground, this cemetery has a pinnacled archway entrance in Hartington Road and a mortuary chapel in knapped flint with an octagonal spire. The adjoining Downs Crematorium in Bear Road was established in 1941 by the cemetery company with a separate chapel. <83,123>

d) *LAWN MEMORIAL PARK, Warren Road, Woodingdean:* Developed on 9.5 acres of Warren Farm land in 1962, the Lawn Memorial Park has gravestones laid flat to preserve the external appearance as a park and to allow for easy mowing. The park opened on 1 January 1963 and is now the principal cemetery in Brighton for new burials. It includes 311 interments removed from the Quaker's burial ground in Rifle Butt Road in 1972. <123,126>

34. CHAIN PIER

<3,142,144,145>

a) *ORIGIN and CONSTRUCTION:* The growth of cross-channel traffic via Brighton and Dieppe in the years following the Napoleonic Wars necessitated a more suitable means of embarkation and disembarkation than the small boats which were launched from the beach to meet the larger vessels. It was principally for this purpose that the construction of a pier opposite the Steine was proposed, although the site was later moved to below the New Steine following objections from fishermen and bathers.

Construction commenced on 18 September 1822 under the direction of Captain Samuel Brown, who had designed the Union suspension bridge over the Tweed and a smaller chain pier at Newhaven near Edinburgh in 1821. Although construction was hampered by a series of storms, rapid progress was made following a change in the workforce by Brown who brought in ex-naval men. The first piles were completed in January 1823 and by July the chains were in position. The pier was completed in September 1823 at a cost of £30,000.

The deck of the pier was 1,154 feet long and 13 feet wide, supported by chains suspended from four cast-iron towers spaced at 260 feet intervals on wooden piles driven into the seabed. The chains themselves were carried 54 feet into the cliff through a bazaar, and affixed to 3-ton steel plates set in cement. The pier-head, used as the landing stage, was a platform of Purbeck stone 80 feet wide. Access to the pier was either via a new esplanade along the foot of the cliff from a toll-house at the Old Steine, or down a flight of steps from New Steine.

b) *OPENING and EVENTS:* The Royal Suspension Chain Pier was opened on 25 November 1823 with a procession and firework display, but, to the disappointment of the town, without royalty being present. It proved an immediate success with both cross-channel travellers and also with promenaders who were charged an admission of two pence or one guinea annually. Although embarkation piers had already been constructed at Ryde in 1813-14 and at Newhaven (near Edinburgh), the Brighton Chain Pier did have attrac-

Figure 30: The Royal Suspension Chain Pier from the east. Note the bazaar below the cliff, also the steamer and sailing ships at the pier-head.

Figure 31: The pier-head

tions which were designed purely for the pleasure of promenaders and therefore may claim to have been the first pleasure pier. Kiosks were opened in the towers and several other attractions opened in the following years included a bazaar, saloon lounge, reading room and camera obscura at the shore end. The pier also attracted many artists with its graceful outline, including Constable and Turner.

Nevertheless, the Chain Pier proved to be an important point of embarkation. and with several steam-ships operating daily to Dieppe, Brighton became the busiest cross-Channel port in England for a time as it was on the quickest route between London and Paris (as overland speeds were roughly the same as those at sea). Facilities were never as good as a natural harbour though, and the opening of the railway to Newhaven in December 1847 brought an end to most of the passenger traffic from Brighton. On 15 October 1829 the Duke and Duchess of Clarence, who enjoyed daily walks along the pier, disembarked from Dieppe. In 1843 Queen Victoria was received from France in the royal yacht by the now Sir Samuel Brown before embarking for Ostend a few days later.

The weather was not so kind to the pier, though. On 24 November 1824 the toll-house was swept away during a storm, but worse was to follow on 15 October 1833 when the pier itself was struck by lightning resulting in a disastrous fire; the second and third bridges were destroyed, but a public subscription raised £1,300 to repair and strengthen the structure. Another storm on 29 November 1836 caused the centre bridges to oscillate and the third bridge eventually fell into the sea, but the pier was once again repaired.

c) *DECLINE and DESTRUCTION:* In 1872 the Aquarium was opened on the site of the Chain Pier's esplanade and toll-house, so two new toll-houses were erected at the shore end of the pier by the new Madeira Road. A plan was then devised by that supreme pier engineer Eugenius Birch for the addition of a marine kursaal; parliamentary sanction was obtained, but Birch died in 1884 before any progress could be made.

Throughout the remaining years of the century the Chain Pier, with its modest attractions, continued to lose custom to the newer facilities at the Aquarium and West Pier. In 1891 the Marine Palace and Pier Company obtained permission to erect a new pier opposite the Steine provided that the old pier was removed. The Chain Pier remained open until 9 October 1896 when it was declared unsafe, the pier-head being some way out of vertical, but a great storm just two months later, on 4 December 1896, completely destroyed the structure at about 10 p.m. The wreckage caused considerable damage to the new Palace Pier which was then under construction, and also to the West Pier and Volk's Electric Railway.

Although the pier foundations remained visible at low tide until 1949, there is now no sign of the former Brighton Chain Pier, but its position is marked by a plaque in the sea-wall above the eastern end of the Aquarium Sun Terrace. The bazaar remained under the cliff until 1927 when it was demolished during the reconstruction of the Aquarium and its arcade. However, the two entrance kiosks on the shore were saved, and were later added to the Palace Pier where they remain, flanking the entrance to the main Palace of Fun amusement arcade (see figure 109) <131>. Samuel Brown's house at 48 Marine Parade, now known as Chain Pier House, bears a plaque to the pier's engineer, and a silver urn presented to Brown by the town may be seen in Brighton Museum along with a model of the pier.

35. King CHARLES II

<1,3>

Probably the first monarch to come to Brighton, but his visit was very brief! Following the defeat at Worcester on 3 September 1651, Charles travelled to Sussex with Lord Wilmot in the hope of escaping to France. Wilmot approached Colonel Gounter of Racton, who in turn approached a merchant who traded with France, Francis Mansell. Through him, Gounter was introduced to Nicholas Tettersell of Brighton, who agreed to take two passengers to France for £60 in his small coal brig, the *Surprise*.

Charles and Wilmot stayed at the George Inn in West Street <3> on 14 October 1651 where the landlord, Anthony Smith, recognised the King even though he had shorn his locks, but swore his loyalty. Tettersell also recognised the King and demanded a fee of £200 for the passage. In the early hours of 15 October 1651, Charles, Wilmot, Gounter and Mansell rode to Shoreham where the boat was moored, and Charles, Wilmot, Tettersell and a crew of four sailed for Fécamp where they arrived the next morning; the King was carried ashore on the shoulders of one Thomas Carver.

Charles, of course, returned to England at the Restoration of 1660. Tettersell, having renamed his boat the *Royal Escape*, was granted the rank of captain in the navy and was given command of the *Monk* from 1661 until he was dismissed. In December 1663, Tettersell, his wife, son and daughter were granted a pension of £100 per annum for 99 years, and he was given a ring as a memento. In 1671 he became landlord of the Old Ship Inn, but his year as high constable was noted for his persecution of non-conformists. Tettersell is buried in St Nicholas's Churchyard.

Some years later Thomas Carver returned from the West Indies and, finding many of his Quaker friends imprisoned, personally approached the King to ask for their release. Charles, surprised that Carver had not presented himself sooner, agreed to release six Quakers; Carver did not consider this a fair recompense for saving a king's life, apparently to the King's delight! In return, 471 Quakers and 20 other Dissenters, including John Bunyan, were eventually pardoned in 1672.

The flight of Charles II is remembered annually by the Royal Escape yacht race, and by the Royal Escape public house on Marine Parade.

36. CHURCH STREET

Originally known as North Back Side and then as Spring Walk, Church Street was a track at the rear of the crofts and gardens stretching northwards from North Street. This area began to be developed in the 1780s and '90s, and buildings then started to appear in Church Street itself, which was given its new name by the town commissioners in 1792; several side streets and small courtyards leading off the main street have since been removed in slum clearance programmes. The roadway was extended through to Grand Parade in about 1816 when a road just to the north of the Pavilion was stopped up. Church Street was made one-way to traffic in June 1976.
<10,14,48a,112,123,194>.

See also "Dome and Corn Exchange", "Library", "Museum and Art Gallery", "Royal Pavilion" and "St Nicholas's Church".

a) *NORTH-WESTERN END:* At the end of the eighteenth century, at a time of great unrest across the Channel, infantry barracks were established at the bottom of Church Street backing onto the rear of the King and Queen Inn in Marlborough Place. They eventually became the headquarters of the 1st Sussex Rifles and the 1st Sussex Artillery Volunteers, commemorated by the Volunteer public house at the corner of New Road and by Barrack Yard off North Road, but they finally closed in 1870 when the volunteers moved to large drill halls in Gloucester Road, and at the corner of Church Street and Spring Gardens (see below). The barrack site was then acquired by the corporation for the erection of the North Road Slipper Baths, and for a new county court building in Church Street which opened in 1869; the court remained in use until 1967, but the red-brick building, adorned by a lion and unicorn, is now a library store. The large range of buildings to Marlborough Place was also erected at about this time and later became the Blenheim Hotel.

A pathway leads north from Church Street to the Prince Regent Swimming Complex, opened on 22 April 1981 at a cost of £2.5 million. Its main 33-metre pool replaced the former North Road pool on the same site, and the building also houses diving and learning pools, a solarium and a cafeteria. <123>

The building now in use as the Music Library was erected in about 1925 as an office and showroom for the Brighton and Hove General Gas Company, on the site of the Pavilion Baptist Chapel. This chapel was designed by Thomas Cooper in Ionic style and opened as the Trinity Independent Presbyterian Chapel in about 1825, but in about 1896 it was converted into a bazaar and then a warehouse.

No.111 is a small cobble-fronted cottage restored in 1986 as the Brighton Arts Information Centre. The Waggon and Horses was built in 1848 by Frederick Mahomed as a gymnasium, but became a public house in 1852 when the gymnasium was removed to Paston Place. <24,62,83,115,268>

b) *CENTRAL SCHOOL and JUBILEE STREET:* The vacant site opposite New Road was occupied from 1829 until 1971 by the prominent Central National School, one of the town's earliest schools, which was designed in a Regency Gothic style with oriel windows and pinnacles by Stroud and Mew. The three-storey building had two shops on the ground floor and the master's residence on the second. Later the Central Church of England School and eventually the Central

Figure 32: The Central National School

Voluntary Primary School, it closed in March 1967 and was shamefully demolished by the corporation in 1971 before a protection order was received during a postal dispute. To quote from the Department of the Environment's Statutory List: 'The building forms the terminal feature of the view down New Road and forms an important group with Christ Church and 23-24 New Road'. See also "Schools".

The adjacent nos.107-108 at the corner of Jubilee Street, also listed and decorated with oriel windows, were demolished the following year. The large Jubilee Street site itself has been empty since the mid 1970s, an eyesore in the centre of the town. Demolition of the small houses, shops and workshops of the area, which is now scheduled for an ice-rink and office development, originally commenced as long ago as the mid 1950s. <44,45,48b,83,123>

c) *BUILDINGS FROM NEW ROAD TO QUEEN'S ROAD:* Several interesting buildings remain on the south side of Church Street and the roads leading thereof.

No.2 Church Street is a listed, cobble-fronted building of about 1807, forming part of no.24 New Road which was originally the Regent Hotel <44>. At the corner of Jew Street are the Model Dwellings, a five-storey block of flats originally built as housing for the poor of the town in about 1852 by a charitable trust under Dr William Kebbell (see figure 119). Another block was erected in Clarence Yard in 1854, but was removed when the Head Post Office was extended in 1892 <15,83>. Jew Street itself is named from Brighton's first synagogue which was probably sited at the southern end from about 1792 and is said to have also had a school. The synagogue had moved to Poune's Court off West Street by 1808 before finding a permanent home in Devonshire Place <66>. The adjacent multi-storey car-park has 600 spaces and opened in 1984 <123>.

Some late-eighteenth- or early-nineteenth-century cobble-fronted houses may still be found at 21-22 Church Street, also in the remaining length of King Street (no.27), and at Portland Street where nos.3-4 are included on the council's local list of buildings of special interest <306>; no.10 also has a cobbled façade. Windsor Street was developed from the 1780s, but only a few houses now remain. In the mid nineteenth century this small street had three chapels. Adullam Chapel was built in 1836 and stood on the south side of Windsor Buildings, now Windsor Court; in about 1840 the notorious sect of Revd Henry Prince, who declared himself to be immortal and preached 'free love', took the chapel. Known also as Windsor Street Chapel, it became a furniture store in the 1870s but was destroyed by fire in 1880. On the east side were the Bethsaida Hall Chapel, and the barn-like Zoar Chapel which was rented by independent ministers but converted into a provision store in 1853 <3,62,62a>.

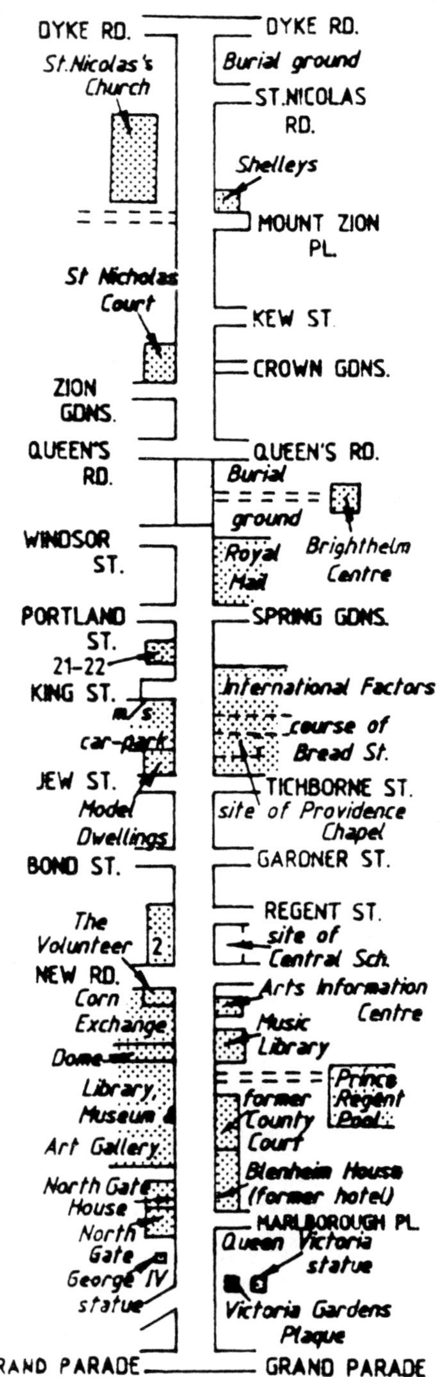

Figure 33: Church Street

On the northern side of Church Street, at the corner of Spring Gardens, stands a large Seeboard building; the land at the rear to North Road was formerly occupied by a power station (see "Electricity Supply"). The former drill hall of the Royal Sussex Regiment, built in 1889-90 by Edmund Scott, stands on the opposite corner but has been used since 1967 as the Royal Mail's parcel-sorting office <45,123>.

d) *TICHBORNE STREET and BREAD STREET:* Mid-nineteenth-century Church Street was the haunt of beggars, brawlers, drunkards, prostitutes and thieves, the Canterbury music hall being particularly notorious. Some of the worst housing in the town lay to the north between Gardner Street and Bread Street, in the alleys and courtyards of Pimlico, Orange Row, and Pym's Gardens where the thousand or so inhabitants, mainly fishermen and labourers together with their pigs and other livestock, lived in appalling conditions in 175 dwellings. In the 1870s this area was the subject of the corporation's first slum clearance scheme, resulting in the construction of Tichborne Street. The notorious slum tenements were swept away and replaced by new artisan houses which have now been demolished for further redevelopment, although nos.1-10 remain an attractive terrace on the eastern side of Tichborne Street. <2,23,76,114,275a>

The most famous son of the area was the famous prize-fighter Tom Sayers. Born in Pimlico, Sayers was a bricklayer by trade and worked on the London Road Viaduct, but he became champion of All-England, the last before the introduction of the Queensberry Rules. In 1860 Sayers contested the first international bout with American John Heenan; it was declared a draw after thirty-seven rounds! He often used the Plough Inn at Rottingdean as his training headquarters in the 1850s, and was presented with a dog by the Earl of Derby, the three-times prime minister. His burial at Highgate Cemetery, Middlesex, in 1865 was attended by ten thousand people. <17,24,26,28,296>

A large headquarters designed by APP for International Factors, Sovreign House, was opened in 1989 on the site of Bread Street between Tichborne Street and Spring Gardens. At the corner of Church Street and the former Bread Street once stood the Providence Chapel, built in 1805 by the Calvinistic followers of William Huntingdon. A plain building in chequered brick with a vestigial pediment, it was considerably altered over the years and was demolished in 1965 when the congregation moved to West Hill Road. On the eastern side of Bread Street itself was the Church of St Mary and St Mary Magdalene, opened in 1862, the first church built for Revd Arthur Wagner (q.v.). A simple building by George Bodley, it was built in brick with a timber roof on wooden pillars, while the simple interior had a sanctuary at the southern end. The church was never consecrated and closed in about 1922 except for services for the deaf and dumb. It reopened in November 1928, but it closed again in 1948 and was then used by the electricity board until it was demolished in 1965. The northern end of Bread Street now leads to the flats of Belbourne Court. <62,65>

e) *BRIGHTHELM CENTRE:* The Brighthelm United Reformed Church and Community Centre is approached from Church Street through the Queen's Road Rest Garden, and backs onto North Road where there is a sculpture by John Skelton depicting the loaves and fishes story. Built as a new home for the Central Free Church, it incorporates the former Hanover Chapel, built in 1825 as an Independent chapel for the Revd M.Edwards and then used by the Presbyterian Church from 1844 until 1972 when the congregation combined with that of the Union Church. The chapel was then used as a Greek church until 1978, but the church hall in North Road was gutted by fire in 1980 when in use as a resource centre. The southern façade of the listed building, with twin porches, Tuscan columns and giant pilasters, has been preserved and restored, however. Designed by Wells-Thorpe and Suppel Ltd, the Brighthelm Centre has a stage and several halls for community use, and was opened on 10 October 1987.

In 1845 Queen's Road was constructed over the western edge of the Hanover Chapel's burial ground, but the cemetery's boundary wall and railing remain on the western side of Queen's Road as a raised pavement <140>. The churchyard became the corporation's responsibility following the 1884 Brighton Improvement Act and was laid out as a public garden, the Queen's Road Rest Garden, in 1949 when the gravestones were removed to line the perimeter walls. In 1989 the churchyard was remodelled with access from Queen's Road. An obelisk monument in the garden has a very faint inscription to Dr Struve of the Royal Spa in Queen's Park <312>. <24,44,62,64a,123,126>

f) *WEST of QUEEN'S ROAD:* Church Street crosses over Queen's Road towards the former Brighton parish church of St Nicholas. The flats of St Nicholas Court, inaugurated in July 1990 by Princess Helen of Romania, stand on the site of the Sussex Throat and Ear Hospital, closed in 1986; see "Hospitals and Dispensaries". Higher up on the northern side, at 2 Mount Zion Place, is Shelleys, a listed yellow-brick house of 1821 with a small front garden and a cobbled garden wall. It was once the home of William Shelley, parish beadle and for more than fifty years the parish sexton; there is a now blocked-up tunnel connecting it with the church. <15,24,44,83,123>

37. CHURCHILL SQUARE

<123,124>

A new shopping and entertainment heart for the town was first conceived in 1935, and the dilapidated buildings of Blucher Place and Upper Russell Street were cleared in 1938; the war prevented any further progress, however, and the vacant site was used largely used as a car-park. Further clearances followed at Artillery Street, Cannon Street and Russell Street in 1957-8.

In 1959 the council decided to redevelop the whole site for shopping and entertainment. Following a public inquiry, ministerial approval was given in January 1963 for a fifteen-acre redevelopment from Western Road to King's Road, including the Kingswest and Brighton Centre sites but excluding the Grand Hotel which the council had hoped to include. The Top Rank Centre (Kingswest) and the Russell car-park were the first of the new developments to open, and in 1965 work on the main part of the site, Churchill Square, commenced. The first shop of the development, Blackburns menswear, opened in June 1967 but the rest of the sixty-one shops of this phase, on one level only and including two supermarkets, did not open until the autumn of 1968. Churchill Square was formally opened, at a cost of £9 million, by mayor Thomas Taylor on 11 October 1968. The additional multi-level development to the south of the main square opened in late 1971 and 1972.

The complete precinct has some seventy shop premises, and there are 105,000 square feet of offices for British Telecom and the south-eastern headquarters of the Post Office. The offices are known as Grenville House and the underground service road is known as Grenville Street, both reminders of the early-nineteenth-century, cobble-fronted houses of the former Grenville Place which stood on the site. The development also includes Chartwell Court, an eighteen-storey block 298 feet tall completed in 1971 above the Cannon car-park and one of the four modern blocks which unfortunately dominate the sea-front vista. (The original plan had a second block of similar height and a third, thirty-storey, block on the sea-front.) The three multi-storey car-parks, Cannon, Churchill and Russell, provide 1,450 parking spaces; in 1990 construction of a new 572-space car-park was commenced behind the Grand Hotel.

The open area alongside Western Road has become a popular meeting place and street entertainment area, but the whole square and adjacent development, designed by Russell Diplock for contractors Taylor Woodrow, is drab and has dated badly; plans have been made for its improvement. The central square is adorned by a 30-foot concrete sculpture by William Mitchell, the 'Spirit of Brighton', which is intended purely as a 'piece

Figure 34: The concrete edifice known as the 'Spirit of Brighton'. In the background is Chartwell Court.

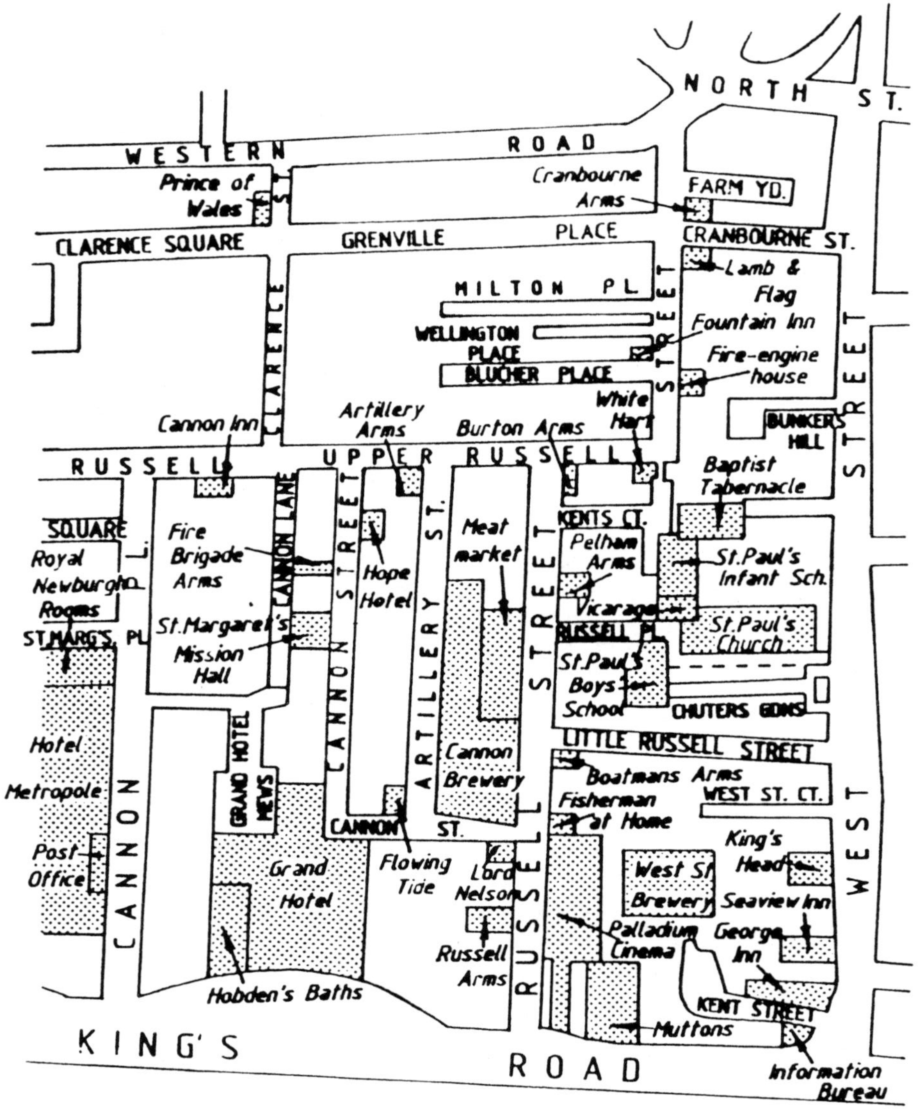

Figure 35: Churchill Square area before redevelopment

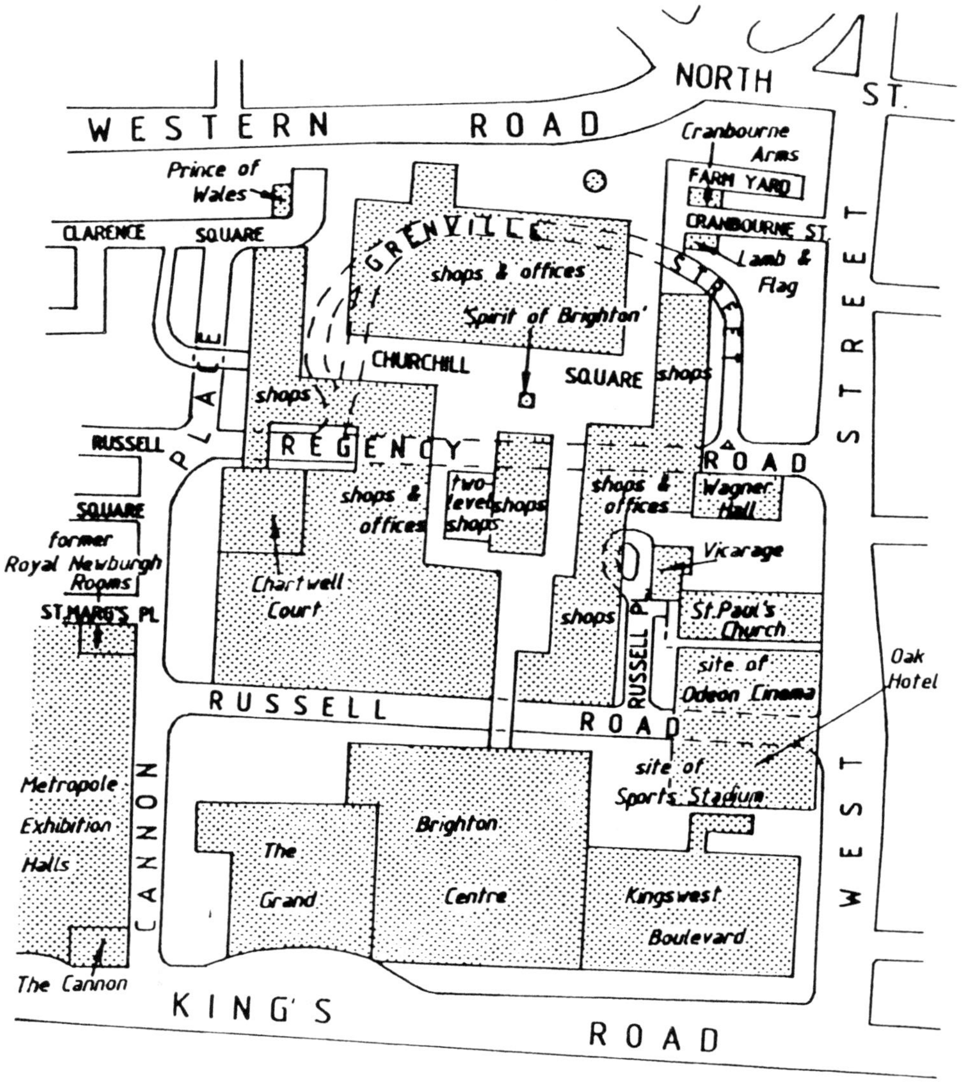

Figure 36: Churchill Square area now

of fun'; it originally had a cascade of water to encourage plant growth, but in reality it epitomises the dreadful concrete redevelopment of Brighton in the 1960s and '70s. In the adjacent pavement is the square's inaugural plaque. At the north-eastern corner of Churchill Square, the cul-de-sac Farm Yard is a reminder of more rural days in the eighteenth century when there was indeed a farm yard on the site <18>.

38. CINEMAS

<68-68b,123>

Several pioneers of the motion picture industry lived and worked in Brighton and Hove in the late nineteenth and early twentieth centuries. Particularly notable are William Friese-Greene at Middle Street (see "Old Town"), George Albert Smith at St Anne's Well Gardens (see "Hove"), and the first film-maker in Brighton, Esme Collings of Alexandra Villas (see "West Hill").

Regular film shows were given at Hove Town Hall as early as 1895 by these pioneers, while the first demonstration of the 'Celebrated Animatographe' in Brighton was given at the Victoria Hall in King's Road (possibly no.132) on 1 July 1896. The first authentic cinema in Brighton, the Queen's Electric, opened in 1910 in Western Road; the Duke of York's, now the oldest cinema in the town, opened the same year.

The era of the giant cinema lasted from the 1920s until the '50s and led to the building of the Regent, Savoy, Astoria, Odeon and Essoldo cinemas with smaller auditoria in the suburbs. Rationalisation of facilities in the 1970s led to the multi-screen venues concentrated in the town centre. Although there are now only three cinemas (eleven screens) in Brighton, many others have operated over the years with a maximum of seventeen from 1937 until 1939 when there were also five more in Hove and Portslade; several former cinema buildings still remain. An eight-screen Cannon cinema is planned for the Marina, due to open in March 1991.

From 21 until 25 May 1987 the Cannon and Odeon cinemas played host to the first Brighton Film Festival; the second was held on 8-10 September 1989.

For details of all individual cinemas consult the index entry on "cinemas". See also figure 170.

39. CLIFTON HILL

The western part of Church Hill was developed from the 1820s to the 1860s. As it was considered to be the most salubrious part of the town, particularly the Montpelier area, much of the housing was of a high-class nature with many fine examples of Regency and Victorian architecture. Known as Clifton Hill, the area is now an outstanding conservation area stretching northward from Western Road between Dyke Road and the borough boundary, and has about 4,500 residents <277>. Roads of particular interest in Clifton Hill are detailed below in alphabetical order (although those leading northward from Western Road are dealt with under "Western Road"). See also "Dyke Road" and "Western Road".

a) *BELVEDERE TERRACE:* A listed terrace with bow fronts and balconies, built in about 1852 for Mary Wagner, sister of Revd Henry Wagner, on her land at the rear of Belvedere House. Norfolk Terrace opposite also has six bays of four-storey bows. <44,65>

b) *CLIFTON HILL:* Has several listed buildings. Nos.1-3 are semi-detached Italianate villas of about 1850; no.7 with its verandah dates from about 1840; nos.10-11 also date from around 1840 and have iron-work balconies and verandahs; and nos.24-25 have bows and glazing bars. <44>

The car-park between Clifton Hill and Powis Grove was the site of Vine's Mill from around 1810 until about 1850 (see "Vine Place" below). The adjacent flint building, richly decorated with lion heads, classical busts and other figurines, may have been connected with this mill, but it is generally believed to have been erected in the early nineteenth century as a coach house; it was restored in 1989. <108,249a,249b>

c) *CLIFTON ROAD:* Lining the eastern side near Clifton Hill are some three-storey houses dating from about 1830, nos.1-4 and 7-8, listed buildings with good doorways, bows, balconies and verandahs. Nos.9-10 are also listed, together with no.26 on the opposite side which has Ionic pilasters and was probably designed by Wilds and Busby in the 1820s. <44>

d) *CLIFTON TERRACE:* A very attractive composition completed in 1847. The whole terrace, which has the three-storey nos.12-15 as a centre-piece, is listed along with the detached no.25 and nos.27-31 which form the terminal view from the east; no.17 was the home of playwright Alan Melville until 1973. The Clifton Gardens in front of the terrace remain for the exclusive use of the residents, but were once the site of the Clifton Windmill. Probably erected in the 1810s or '20s, this mill was moved in around 1837 to Windmill Street where it was still known as the Clifton Mill (see "Albion Hill"). It is thought that the nearby Windmill public house was named from Vine's Mill, however (see "Vine Place" below). <44,83a,249a,249b>

e) *DENMARK TERRACE:* An 1860s terrace of four-storey houses with wide angular bays, ironwork balconies and interesting doorways. <83>

f) *MONTPELIER CRESCENT:* In the 1830s and '40s the site of Montpelier Crescent was a cricket ground known as Lillywhite's, Lee's Trap or the Temple Fields Ground; on 29-30 August 1842 Sussex played All-England there. The crescent was erected in 1843-7 by A.H.Wilds, the grandest of his many works, and these original houses, nos.7-31, are decorated with giant fluted pilasters and either Corinthian or ammonite capitals (see figures 6 and 191). The wings at nos.1-6 and 32-38 were added in the 1850s, but all the houses are listed and form a magnificent sweeping crescent. <15,44,46>

g) *MONTPELIER PLACE:* Nos.20-24 are large, bow-fronted, listed houses of about 1855 with balconies. Listed also are no.14, bow-fronted and dating from about 1830, and the Montpelier Inn, a three-storey building of about 1849 with three bows. <44>

The principal building of Montpelier Place is the former St Stephen's Church, now a grade II*-listed building. Dedicated on 25 July 1851, the interior was reconstructed from the Royal Chapel in Palace Place which itself had been, until 1822, the ballroom of the Castle Inn, constructed originally in 1766 by John Crunden. Following the town's purchase of the Royal Pavilion estate in 1850, the chapel was claimed by the Church Commissioners as a consecrated building and removed to a new classical building by Cheesemans with pilasters, pediment, and an octagonal lantern with orb and cross. The magnificent ballroom interior, which has a shallow vaulted ceiling and urn frieze supported by columns with foliated capitals, formed a wide rectangular nave with a railed-off sanctuary. Opening on 25 July 1851, the first incumbent was Revd George Wagner whose aunt Mary Wagner provided the land. In 1889 the church was remodelled by Arthur Blomfield, and it was restored in 1908. However, St Stephen's closed in 1939 and was then used by the Diocesan Association for the Deaf and Dumb, but since 1974 has been the First Base Day Centre for the homeless. In March 1988 the interior was badly damaged by fire, but the centre reopened a year later with the interior splendidly restored. <44,45,64a,65,123,194>

Standing on the boundary between Brighton and Hove is the Baptist Tabernacle, opened on 1 April 1967 on the site of the Emmanuel Church, a Reformed Episcopal church of 1867-8 which was built in Early English style with a south-eastern tower. In the Tabernacle wall is a foundation stone laid by the Revd C.Brake on 1 May 1834 at the original Baptist Tabernacle, an Ionic-style building that stood off West Street but was demolished in 1965 with the Wagner Hall later erected on the site. <62,123>

Figure 37: Façade by A.H.Wilds at no.53 Montpelier Road

h) *MONTPELIER ROAD:* Montpelier Road once ran all the way from King's Road to Ditchling Road, but the name is now restricted to the section south of Denmark Villas. It was developed from the 1820s in what was considered the most salubrious area of the town and the houses were consequently of a high-class nature with many now listed. The most distinctive are nos.53-56, designed by A.H.Wilds with fluted ammonite pilasters and shell decorations, and nos.91-96, small villas of about 1830 with Ionic doorways, possibly by A.Wilds and Busby. No.90 is notable on account of its cast-iron and stained-glass porch. Other listed houses north of Western Road include nos.51-52, 58-65, 70-74, 76-80, and the unstuccoed nos.36-42; all have late-Regency, wide bow-fronted façades of around 1840. Nos.48-50, with narrow bows, are also listed. No.60 was the home of Revd F.W.Robertson (see "Montpelier Terrace" below) from 1850 until 1853. <44,46,64a,75>

Park Royal, once a private block of flats but purchased by the council in about 1974, stands on the site of Belvedere, a Jacobean-style house erected in about 1840 for Mary Wagner who lived in the adjacent vicarage with her brother Revd Henry Wagner. Now only the garden walls of Belvedere remain, at Belvedere Terrace and in Montpelier Road where the wall is a listed structure. The house was let as a girls' school, but on Mary Wagner's death it passed to her nephew Arthur Wagner who lived there from 1870 until 1902. It was later converted into the Park Royal Court Hotel, but was demolished in 1965. <65,123>

The unlisted First Church of Christ Scientist, to the south of Montpelier Terrace, has an elaborately decorated pediment but was originally a private house, obviously so from the rear. It was built in about 1850 and converted into a church in 1921 when the sect moved from the Athenaeum Hall in North Street. <62,83>

For the section of Montpelier Road to the south of Western Road, see "Regency Square Conservation Area".

j) *MONTPELIER STREET:* An attractive listed terrace of small, mostly bow-fronted houses of about 1845 lines the western side. No.40, with a wide bow on the eastern side of the road, is also listed. <44>

k) *MONTPELIER TERRACE:* Nos.1-7, together with no.89 Montpelier Road, form a listed three-storey terrace dating from about 1830 with balconies and Ionic pilasters, although nos.6-7 were added in about 1850. No.1 has a plaque to Ray Noble, the former bandleader and composer who was born there in 1903. Nos.8-13 are a terrace of listed villas with balconies and verandahs of about 1840; the Revd F.W.Robertson, famed for his preaching at Holy Trinity and for founding the Brighton Working Men's Institute, lived at no.9 from 1847 until 1850. No.14 won a council award in 1983 for its restoration. On the southern side of the road, the red-brick no.16 dates from about 1830, has a fanlight doorway, and is listed along with the late-Regency no.17, Montpellier Hall, of about 1850. <44>

l) *MONTPELIER VILLAS:* A road lined with delightful, semi-detached Italianate villas, all listed buildings with ironwork balconies and verandahs. Dating from about 1845, they are said to have been built on the site of a bluebell wood and many bluebells still grow in the gardens. No.20 was the home of television personality Gilbert Harding in the 1950s. <3,44,83>

1840s Regency style in Montpelier Villas

m) *POWIS SQUARE:* Built about 1850, the attractive three-storey houses have bow fronts with ironwork balconies and are all listed except nos.12-13 which lie to the east and have angular bays. The garden came under the control of the corporation in 1887 following the 1884 Brighton Improvement Act. The two K6-type telephone kiosks are also listed buildings. <44,126>

n) *POWIS VILLAS:* Built in the early 1850s, all the houses are listed buildings. No.1 is plain but has a good Doric porch. Nos.10-13 are semi-detached villas with ironwork balconies and verandahs. There is also a good view over the town to the sea. <44>

p) *ST MICHAEL'S PLACE:* An impressive street of three and four-storey terraced housing dating from the late 1860s, all with angular bays and black ironwork balconies. <83>

q) *TEMPLE GARDENS:* This road derives its name from the large building on the northern side now occupied by the Brighton and Hove High School for Girls. The Temple was erected in 1819, probably by A. and A.H.Wilds, as a residence for Thomas Read Kemp in a then quite isolated location. It is said to be based on the Temple of Solomon, and has an unusual ground floor colonnade with Egyptian pilasters, but the exterior was significantly altered in 1911-12 when the domed roof and corner chimneys were removed along with an unusual winding staircase enclosed in a cylindrical compartment. Surrounding the house is a flint garden wall with huge gateposts and lion heads. The Temple is now listed mainly on account of its historical association with Kemp, the founder of Kemp Town who lived in the house until 1827, rather than for any remaining architectural merit.

In the 1830s the building became a young gentlemen's academy, and since 1880 has been the home of the Brighton and Hove High School for Girls. This school was founded in 1876 at 75 Montpelier Road by the Girls' Public Day School Trust with the intention of providing more than the superficial education received by girls at that period. In 1891-2 a new south wing was added, and the main building was altered radically in 1911-12 as mentioned above. In more recent years a science wing (1961) and a gymnasium/hall have been added. Still run

Figure 39: Thomas Read Kemp's residence, The Temple, in an isolated position in about 1827

by the G.P.D.S.T., the High School has about 550 day-girls and boarders, and uses playing fields at the Droveway, Hove.

In 1904 the junior school was removed to 8 Norfolk Terrace, to Montpelier Crescent in 1917, and finally to the Old Vicarage on the southern side of Temple Gardens in 1922. This listed building was built in 1834 for the Revd Henry Wagner and was designed in Tudor-style by a Mr Mew with three gables and a cement rendering. The junior school has around 180 girls.
<44,45,46,203a,205>

r) *UPPER NORTH STREET:* Nos.77-89 on the northern side form an attractive listed terrace of about the 1830s, three-storey houses with fluted Ionic pilasters; nos.73-76 also have Ionic pilasters and there are other examples of impressive, small-scale terraced housing. The bow-fronted no.64 is also listed. The Windmill public house dates from about 1828 and is probably named from Vine's Mill (see "Vine Place" below); the K6-type telephone kiosk outside is a listed building. The southern side has a mixture of two- and three-storey houses including several antique shops, and nos.42-43, decorated with Ionic pilasters, are listed. The Roman Catholic Church of St Mary Magdalene was erected in 1861-4 to the Early English and Decorated design of Gilbert Blount, a listed red-brick building with elaborately carved stone dressings and a tall spire. The listed red-brick presbytery of around 1890 adjoins to the east with the former St Mary Magdalene School to the west. <44,62>

s) *VERNON TERRACE:* An impressive terrace of thirty-seven houses built in about 1850 in five distinct compositions, but all with ironwork balconies. Nos.1-6, plain, three-storey houses, and nos.7-16, four-storey bow-fronted houses, are listed buildings. <44<

t) *VICTORIA PLACE:* Small cottages on the northern side face Victoria House, an elegant three-storey listed house of about the 1840s with bay windows and a good doorway with wreath decorations and lamps. <44>

u) *VICTORIA ROAD:* No.1 is listed as the end house of Montpelier Street, but nos.14-15, with fluted Ionic pilasters, are also listed. The adjacent no.16 has an ironwork balcony and verandah.

The red-brick Church of St Michael and All Angels was originally built in 1858-62 for the Misses Windle by George Bodley in Italian Gothic style, but almost immediately plans were made for its enlargement by William Burges. The alterations were not carried out until after Burges's death, however, by John Chapple in 1895 when the original church was incorporated as the south aisle and side chapel of the much larger new church. The elaborately decorated interior has a reredos by Romaine Walker and stained glass by William Morris, and there is a fifteenth-century triptych above the altar. The parish was formed in 1925 and the church is now a listed building. In the late nineteenth century St Michael's was one of several churches involved in the ritualism controversy. <1,44,45,62>

v) *VICTORIA STREET:* Lined with attractive terraced houses of about 1840, most now with angular bays, but nos.12, 13-14, 16-17, 19, 21-22 on the western side, and nos.23-25 and 30 on the eastern side all have narrow bows and are listed buildings. No.28 was the home of playwright Alan Melville for some years from 1973. <44,83a>

w) *VINE PLACE:* Several attractive one- and two-storey cottages lie along this narrow twitten behind Clifton Terrace, and no.9, Vine's Cottage, retains a cobbled façade. The old cottages at the Dyke Road end probably date from about 1810 when the lane was known as Mill Place after William Vine's post-mill. This stood slightly to the north-west, on the land between Powis Grove and Clifton Hill now used as a car-park, from around 1810 until about 1850 and probably gave the Windmill Inn in Upper North Street its name; it is possible that Clifton Place was originally the approach road to this mill. <108,249a,249b>

x) *WINDLESHAM ROAD:* The New Sussex Hospital occupies Windlesham House, a building of 1843-4 which is unfortunately rendered in a coarse pebble-dash and cement, and several other more recent buildings which straddle the Brighton/Hove border. The hospital has its origins in the Lewes Road Dispensary for Women and Children which opened on 31 October 1899 at 145 Islingword Road under the patronage of the Countess of Chichester. In March 1905 it was replaced by a proper hospital, the Lewes Road Hospital for Women and Children, which opened at 101 Round Hill Crescent to deal with the early treatment of nervous and mental cases in women and children, the first hospital of its kind; it had twelve beds and a cot. In 1910 it moved to 8 Ditchling Road as the Lady Chichester Hospital, and in 1912 also took over 4-6 Ditchling Road. Later that year the hospital for nervous diseases was removed to 70 Brunswick Place, Hove, and was moved again in 1920 to 35 New Church Road where the Lady Chichester Hospital remained as a psychiatric facility until converted into a day centre, Aldrington House, in late 1988.

In 1921 the remaining facility at Ditchling Road moved to Windlesham House, a former school, as the New Sussex Hospital for Women. Principally dealing with the treatment of gynaecological disorders, it was staffed entirely by women. In March 1928 the Sir John Howard wing was opened by Lady Leconfield, and other enlargements were made in 1931, 1932 and 1936 so that it now has forty beds. In 1964, however, the first male specialist was appointed, and by 1969 there were no women surgeons remaining. The New Sussex is now used principally as a community mental health hospital. <94,96,115,123>

40. CLIMATE

The virtues of Brighton's climate were first specifically expounded in the 1761 guide book of Dr Anthony Relhan where he suggested that the air was healthy and free from perspiration due to the then lack of trees and rivers, and to the town's situation on a bed of absorbent chalk. The healthy bracing air and above average sunshine, with cooling sea breezes in the summer, played a large part in the establishment of the town as a health resort in the late eighteenth century. <2,71-73>

Meteorological figures have been recorded by the corporation since 1877, principally by the water department. Unfortunately, because of vandalism the town's weather station was shut down from April 1981 until August 1983 and has had to be re-sited. In the period from 1958 to 1990 the following mean figures (the most important for the tourist trade) have been recorded (but note that average annual rainfall varies from around 740 mm. by the coast to 1,000 mm. at Ditchling Beacon) <308>:

	Mean daily max. temp.		Rainfall		Days with rain	Daily sun
Month	°C	°F	mm.	in.	(>0.2 mm.)	hours
January	6.8	44	76	3.0	16	2.0
February	6.9	44	47	1.9	12	2.9
March	8.8	48	56	2.2	13	4.1
April	11.5	53	50	2.0	12	5.5
May	15.1	59	45	1.8	11	7.1
June	17.7	64	49	1.9	9	7.5
July	19.5	67	49	1.9	10	7.0
August	19.7	68	59	2.3	10	6.6
September	17.8	64	60	2.4	10	5.5
October	15.0	59	75	2.9	12	4.0
November	10.5	51	86	3.4	15	2.7
December	8.3	47	80	3.2	15	1.8
Year	13.1	56	736	29.0	147 or 40%	1719 or 4.7 per day

a) *STORMS:* Although Brighton generally has a mild climate without extremes, it has long suffered from the severity of occasional gales and storms. On the other hand, ships and cargoes washed up onto the Brighton beaches during storms provided a valuable source of income for the town's wreckers.

The great storm of October 1987 caused damage on a scale which had not been seen for over 250 years. Unsettled weather had prevailed for over a week, and torrential rain over 7-9 October twice caused the New Barn area of Rottingdean to be inundated by up to three feet of mud and slime washed from nearby fields. However the progress of a deepening depression over the Channel took everyone by surprise and in the early hours of Friday 16 October the whole of the south of England was subjected to continuous force ten winds with gusts of up to 113 m.p.h. Thousands of houses suffered considerable structural damage particularly to fences, roofs and chimney pots, and many shop-windows were destroyed. Lorries and cars were overturned on the sea-front and a stone minaret was sent crashing through the ceiling of the recently restored Royal Pavilion Music Room. The situation was made more critical by lengthy electrical power cuts, blocked roads, and the withdrawal of buses and trains. The greatest legacy, however, was the considerable change in the landscape caused by the uprooting of over 2,500 mature urban trees, some 15% of the total, particularly in the Valley Gardens and the town's numerous parks. Since the mid 1970s Brighton Council has operated a strict Dutch Elm disease control policy in the town and the 20,000 or so elm trees were the only large concentration remaining in the country, but overnight the woodland in many areas, which had stood for 150 years or more, was decimated. A succession of severe storms followed just over two years later at the beginning of 1990, especially on 25 January when winds blew up to 104 m.p.h. These caused severe damage to the Undercliff Walk and other sea-defences. <123>

The worst storm in recorded history was probably the Great Channel Storm of 26 November 1703 which is estimated to have killed 8,000 people in England <299>. Over a period of eight hours at Brighton a number of houses were demolished or lost their roofs, the town windmills were flattened, several boats and crews were lost, and the lead was ripped from the roof of the parish church. Less than two years later a storm of only slightly less intensity, on 11 August 1705, again stripped the church roof and buried the remaining tenements of the Lower Town beneath a bank of shingle.

Other destructive storms have included 15 December 1806 when much of the Marine Parade cliff top was washed away from Lower Rock Gardens to Royal Crescent; 23 November 1824 when Pool Valley was inundated; 29 November 1836 when the Chain Pier was wrecked; 5 August 1848 when a whirlwind and water-spout passed over the town, scattering bathing machines and uprooting everything in its path; 17 July 1850 when a thunderstorm inundated the Valley Gardens and Pool Valley was flooded to a depth of nearly six feet; 18 January 1881 when a snowstorm produced drifts of up to eight feet in the town; 4 December 1896 when the Chain Pier and Rottingdean Railway were wrecked; June 1910 when an eight-hour thunderstorm produced a state of shock in many people; and 8 December 1967 when continuous heavy snow in the morning brought the whole town to a standstill with drifts several feet deep. <6,8,15,115,123>

41. CLOCK TOWER, North Street and Queen's Road

<3,189>

Brighton's Jubilee Clock Tower, designed by John Johnson, was built in 1888 to commemorate Queen Victoria's golden jubilee of the previous year. The foundation stone was laid by Sir Arthur Otway on 20 January 1888, the seventieth birthday of John Willing, a local advertising contractor whose gift to the town the Clock Tower was at a cost of £2,000. Despite being described as 'worthless' by Sir Nikolaus Pevsner <45>, the Brighton public has retained a nostalgic affection for the Clock Tower and it remains at what is probably the hub of modern Brighton despite proposals to remove it.

The tower stands 75 feet high on a red granite base with four seated female statuettes. Above are portraits of Queen Victoria; her late husband Prince Albert; her son Edward, Prince of Wales; and his wife Princess Alexandra. They are flanked by columns and topped by pediments with four projecting hulls giving directions to Hove, the sea, Kemp Town and the station. Above the 5-foot clock faces and cupola is a 16-foot mast, at the base of which lies a gilt-copper sphere. This was a time ball, designed by Magnus Volk and controlled by land-line from Greenwich Observatory, which rose hydraulically up the mast and fell on the hour, but it functioned for a few years only after complaints about the noise. An excellent model of the Clock Tower may be found in Brighton Museum.

Figure 40: Brighton's Jubilee Clock Tower

42. COACHING

<2,15,69,70>

a) *EARLY CARRIERS:* The first record of a regular carrier to Brighton dates from 1681 when Thomas Blewman conveyed goods and passengers from London to Lewes, Newhaven, Brighton and Shoreham. By 1732 there was a regular coach service from Brighton to London, and in 1745 the *Flying Machine* was leaving the Old Ship at 5.30 a.m. and reaching London the same day. As the number of visitors increased so did the coaching traffic, then the only means of long-distance transport, and the first separate coaching office (i.e. not based at an inn) was opened at 1 North Street in about 1794.

The main route from London was via Henfield, Saddlescombe and along the Dyke Road into North Street, but this changed in 1810 when the new turnpike opened between Pyecombe and Bolney. Journey times were eight hours or more with stops made at almost every inn en route, and passengers had to walk up some of the steeper hills. Those who could not afford such luxury were carried in open carriers' wagons taking up to two days.

b) *IMPROVEMENTS IN SPEED:* By June 1811 there were twenty-eight coaches daily between London and Brighton taking six hours, with the first coach journey from London to Brighton and back in the same day coming in 1813. In 1815 there were fifty-two coaches daily but, as rival companies attempted to better journey times, the authorities intervened to restrict the continuous galloping of horses following a week in 1816 in which fifteen horses died.

The 'golden age' of coaching lasted from 1820 until the arrival of the railway from London in 1841, with coaches leaving from the six offices in Castle Square for London, Portsmouth, Southampton, Tunbridge Wells, Maidstone, Oxford, Windsor and other Sussex destinations. Times were improved by the macadamisation of roads, by the use of lighter coaches and shorter stages, although the higher speeds resulted in many accidents. The improvement in times also gave rise to the first London commuters, stock-jobbers being recorded in 1823 as spending two-and-a-half hours in the city daily <2>. In 1832 steam coaches were introduced but were never a serious rival to horse power. On 25 October 1833 a record 480 visitors arrived in the town by coach, and in February 1834 the all-time speed record was set when the *Criterion* brought the King's speech to Brighton in just 3 hours 40 minutes.

c) *COMING OF THE RAILWAY:* The rapid demise of horse-coaching came in 1841 when the railway from London opened, such that by 1843 only one coach was still operating to the City and none at all after 1845. A few years later the *Age* started running again until 1862 as a romantic alternative and a coaching revival followed from 1867 until 1887, but the last coach to run regularly was the *Vigilant* from 1901 until 1905.

d) *MOTOR-COACHES:* The first regular London-to-Brighton motor-coach, the *Vanguard,* was run by the London Motor Omnibus Company from August 1905 <2>. The number of coaches coming to the town rose rapidly, necessitating restrictions along Madeira Drive by 1927, and in August 1928 a record 623 coaches arrived in the town in one day. There was a proposal in 1929 to turn the Level into a coach-park but this was fortunately rejected. The post-war peak was reached in June 1952 when 530 coaches arrived in one day. <164>

43. COASTLINE

a) *BACKGROUND:* Both the nature and the size of the beaches at Brighton have changed over the last 400 years or so as the sea has first eroded the foreshore and cliff, and then retreated with the development of sea-defences. The solid chalk foreshore, protected by an offshore submarine bar, was once very extensive and the fishing community of Brighton developed the so-called 'Lower Town' (q.v.) upon it. It is recorded that forty acres were lost at Brighton between 1290 and 1340, but the fisheries prospered and the town grew. By the 1640s however, following a general rise in sea-level, the sea was once more threatening the foreshore and also the town on the cliff top above. By 1676 the situation was considered so serious that William Jeffrey went before the Justices of the Peace at Lewes to ask for a pier or other defensive structure to be built before the town disappeared completely. The great storms of 1703 and 1705 destroyed the remainder of the Lower Town and most of the foreshore, but in 1713 and 1722 the town was granted 'Church Briefs' which allowed money to be collected in churches throughout the country for the purposes of erecting a sea-defence at Brighton. At about this time Daniel Defoe described Brighton: 'The sea is very unkind ... (and the inhabitants) might reasonably expect it would eat up the whole town, above one hundred houses having been devoured by the water in a few years past'. He continued by saying that the anticipated expense of £8,000 for the groynes appeared to be more than the whole town was worth! <2,10>

The first groynes were constructed in 1723-4. The construction of larger groynes throughout the nineteenth century has halted erosion and accumulated shingle on the foreshore to a depth of 15 feet or so, greatly increasing the size of the beaches and protecting the fragile cliffs at the same time. At one time, for instance, the sea came right up to the base of the East Cliff below Marine Parade, but the construction of groynes and sea-walls has extended the beach a hundred yards or so from the cliff. However, large landslips occurred at the unprotected Black Rock as recently as the 1920s.

The beaches and foreshore were commercially important to the fisheries, and also to the growing passenger and cargo trade of the eighteenth and early nineteenth centuries. Until the construction of the Chain Pier in

Figure 41: The beach and crumbly cliffs below the Old Town in 1822

1823, passengers and other cargoes were landed on the beaches and carried up the several gaps that existed in front of the town, but since the development of the ports of Newhaven and Shoreham, and also with the arrival of the railway in the 1840s, the beaches have been used principally by bathers and fisherman. During the Second World War the government closed all beaches at 5 p.m. on 2 July 1940; at Brighton they were protected by barbed wire and mines, but were cleared and reopened in July 1945.
<1,2,10,14,123>

b) *GROYNES:* The first effective sea-defences to be constructed at Brighton were the 'groynes', walls projecting into the sea at right angles to the shore. They are effective due to the accumulation of shingle on the western side, the 'longshore drift' in the area being from west to east. The banks of shingle thus build up around the base of the cliffs to a depth of fifteen feet or more and prevent any further erosion of the cliff by the sea. They therefore utilise one of the sea's deadliest weapons, the shingle, to neutralise its destructive action.

The first groynes, funded by Church Briefs, were started in September 1723 and completed in 1724, two wooden structures in front of the Old Town each of five piles planked with timber. By 1743 there were five groynes. Maintenance was spasmodic though and the groynes decayed badly, necessitating a second Church Brief in 1757, but the responsibility for sea-defences was one of the main provisions of the 1773 Brighton Town Act. It gave that responsibility to the town commissioners and established a coal-tax to provide funds for 'building and repairing groyns, to render the coast safe and commodious' (sic). Duty was charged on 'sea-coal, culm or other coal landed on the beach' at Brighton at the rate of sixpence per chaldron (36 bushels), but was increased by the 1810 Town Act to three shillings per chaldron. Tollgates were established at the parish boundaries following the 1825 Town Act which extended the tax to all coal brought into the town, and by the 1840s coal-tax was bringing in about £6,000 to £8,000 annually. Although the town commissioners were dissolved in 1855, coal-tax at Brighton continued until 1887.

By 1808 there were also four groynes below the East Cliff, and in about 1813 a groyne 120 feet long was constructed behind Russell House. Many more wooden groynes were built in the nineteenth century, but the first concrete groyne was constructed in 1867 at East Street; it also proved very successful as a free promenade pier 195 feet long. A second concrete groyne, 275 feet long, was constructed in 1876; initially known as the Aquarium Promenade Groyne, it later became the Albion Groyne and was doubled in width in 1896 when the storm water outfall was enlarged. Both groynes were lit by gas to aid the fishermen at sea. The Banjo Groyne was built in 1877 and derives its name from its shape; officially it is the Paston Place Groyne. It provides a promenade about 270 feet long and 14 feet wide, has walls over 3 feet thick, and by 1884 had reclaimed several acres of land enabling the Madeira Lawns to be laid out. The other concrete promenade groynes are the Norfolk Groyne of 1894, and the Black Rock Groyne which was completed in 1895.
<1,10,14,112,115>

c) *SEA-WALLS:* The first sea-wall, to protect the base of the cliffs directly, was built by the proprietors of the New Steine and other East Cliff residents in about 1795, a simple flint structure along the foot of the cliff. The sea came right up to the bottom of the cliffs at this time, and the town commissioners built a similar wall for some distance along the same cliff in 1809. The construction of the Chain Pier in 1822-3 involved a mortar sea-wall some yards in front of the cliff to carry the new promenade, but the greatest improvement came in 1830-3 when a huge cement wall was built along the face of the East Cliff from Old Steine to Royal Crescent, further protected by large amounts of rubble which were tipped over the cliff top until they rose to half the height of the cliff. By 1838 the new wall had been completed to join the wall of the Kemp Town estate. Constructed by William Lambert at a total cost of £100,000, the massive structure is 23 feet thick at the base and up to 60 feet high, and has a large commemorative plaque above the Madeira Terrace to the west of the Madeira Lift. The rubble mounds were levelled for the construction of the Madeira Drive in 1872 when a smaller esplanade sea-wall was constructed to the south. In the 1930s a sea-wall over three miles in length, the Undercliff Walk (q.v.), was constructed from Black Rock to Saltdean.

The western cliffs in front of the Old Town were first protected by a wall in 1811 when a flint and limestone structure was built between Black Lion Street and Ship Street. This was extended to West Street when the King's Road was constructed in 1821-2, and to East Street in 1825-7; by 1829 the build-up of shingle by the groynes enabled the construction of the Grand Junction Road and the extension of the sea-wall to meet the Chain Pier promenade. It was extended further westwards in 1853 to the West Battery (in front of the Grand Hotel), and to the Brunswick Town sea-wall at the Hove boundary in 1894.
<24,26,112,115>

d) *DESCRIPTION:* The sea-front at Brighton has long been dominated by its cliffs. To the west of Pool Valley, which is the natural drainage point for most of Brighton, they rise to a height of about 40 feet in front of the Old Ship before tailing off towards Hove, but have become obscured by the accumulation of shingle and the extension of the King's Road promenade above the King's Road Arches; the actual cliff edge roughly follows the building line of King's Road. These cliffs are composed of 'Head' (or 'Coombe') drift, an easily eroded deposit of chalk rubble and flint with a proportion of clay and sand which outcrops in all the valleys of Brighton and westwards along the coastal plain to Shoreham. In front of the Old Town the cliffs were known as Middle Street Cliff, Ship Street Cliff, Black Lion Street Cliff and the East Cliff, and were separated by gaps with steep paths to the beach along which cargoes were conveyed.

To the east of Pool Valley the Coombe deposits rise again to form what is now known as the East or King's Cliff, which reaches 80 feet at Eaton Place. Since the 1830s the whole length of the East Cliff from the Aquarium to Kemp Town has been protected by a wall. At Black Rock, where the deposits are still exposed, the solid chalk of the South Downs meets the sea and a long line of white cliffs then stretches to Newhaven with gaps at Roedean, Ovingdean, the deepest at Rottingdean, and at Saltdean. Averaging roughly 100 feet, these cliffs rise to about 135 feet between Rottingdean and Saltdean, and to 200 feet to the west of Newhaven. At Black Rock (q.v.) and Saltdean they have been designated sites of special scientific interest for their geological formations.

Brighton's coastline, just 2.2 miles long before 1928, now stretches 5.4 miles from the Hove boundary to Saltdean, and is protected for its entire length by groynes and walls. All the town's beaches are owned by the council, and since 1979 have been known as (west to east) Boundary, Norfolk, Bedford, Metropole, Grand, Centre, King's, Old Ship, Volk's, Albion, Palace Pier, Aquarium, Athina, Paston, Banjo, Duke's, Cliff (naturist), Crescent, and Black Rock beaches. Although predominantly composed of shingle accumulated by groynes, the beaches do have sizeable stretches of sand between the Palace Pier and Black Rock, especially at low tide. To the east of the Marina the tide retreats further than in front of the town and the solid chalk foreshore is exposed beyond the small accumulations of shingle which protect the Undercliff Walk, a feature that allows visitors to explore the many delightful rock pools. There are also small bathing beaches at Ovingdean, Rottingdean and Saltdean Gaps.
<1,2,14,24,109,305,306>

44. COLDEAN

<123,228,276,277>

This area was originally 'Cold Dean', a deep valley between Hollingbury and Stanmer which had a few farm buildings and some cottages near the Lewes Road. Only one of these buildings now remains, the late-eighteenth-century flint barn of Coldean Farm (also known as the Menagerie) which was restored and converted into St Mary Magdalene's Church, Selham Drive, in 1955 <108,311>. In 1990 the largest site of Bronze Age huts in the county was found on the southern-western side of Coldean Lane where the bypass is due to be constructed.

The first housing development in Coldean was the Parkside estate of the late 1930s around Park Road, which was completed in 1948 when it was still part of Falmer parish. The rest of the estate, which was then part of Stanmer parish, was developed by Brighton Corporation from 1950. On 1 April 1952 the whole area of Coldean became part of the county borough. By 1981 the population of Coldean had grown to over 3,500.

Coldean Library was opened on 8 March 1975 in Beatty Avenue. The Church of Jesus Christ of Latter-Day Saints in Park Road (the Mormon Church) was erected in 1963. George Humphrey Park, a children's playground in Wolseley Road, was opened in April 1989. The Brighton bypass, scheduled for completion in 1995, will skirt the northern edge of the estate, crossing over Coldean Lane and requiring the demolition of Downsview Special School in 1990.

See also "Moulsecoomb (Wild Park)".

45. CONSERVATION

<44,70a,277,306>

a) *CONSERVATION AREAS:* Areas of 'special architectural or historical interest, the character or quality of which it is desirable to preserve or enhance' may be designated 'conservation areas' under the 1967 Civic Amenities Act and the 1971 Town and Country Planning Act. The borough council as planning authority may exercise special controls within such areas and can require owners to repair properties. The council may also apply 'Article 4 Directions' to certain designated roads to ensure that houses are uniformly painted and that inappropriate alterations are brought under control. All trees within a conservation area are protected.

Brighton has eight conservation areas which are recognised by the Department of the Environment as 'outstanding'. They are: Old Town (designated 1973), the former fishing town; the Regency areas of Clifton Hill (1973, extended 1977), East Cliff (1973, extended 1989), Kemp Town (1970), Regency Square (1973), and Valley Gardens (1973, extended 1988 and 1989); and the two villages of Rottingdean (1970) and Stanmer (1970, extended to include park 1988). The nine other conservation areas include the Victorian suburban developments at College (1988); North Laine (1977, extended 1989); Preston Park (1988, area originally designated 1977 as extension to Preston); Queen's Park (1977); Round Hill (1977); West Hill (1977, extended 1988 to include Brighton Station); and the suburban villages of Ovingdean (1970); Patcham (1970); and Preston Village (1988, originally 1970 as Preston, extended 1977). Several areas were also extended in 1977 to include the beaches.

The advantages of a conservation area are typified by the North Laine, an area of dense Victorian terraced housing which has greatly increased in prosperity since the removal of planning blight and its designation. (All these conservation areas have individual entries in this text - see "Brighton College" for College, and "Preston" for Preston Park).

b) *SCHEDULED ANCIENT MONUMENTS and SITES OF SPECIAL SCIENTIFIC INTEREST:* There are nine scheduled ancient monuments within the borough, protected against damage by statute. They are:

- i) Beacon Hill long barrow, Rottingdean
- ii) Castle Hill earthworks, Balsdean
- iii) Eastwick earthworks and lynchets, Patcham
- iv) Ewe Bottom entrenchment, Patcham
- v) Hollingbury Castle Camp
- vi) Patcham Court Farm dovecote, Church Hill (which is also a listed building)
- vii) Pudding Bag Wood round barrow, Stanmer
- viii) Tegdown Hill tumuli, Patcham
- ix) Whitehawk Hill Camp

Only the Beacon Hill, Hollingbury and Whitehawk Hill sites have public access. It will be noted that eight of the nine are archaeological sites, the other being Patcham Court Farm dovecote.

Brighton also has three sites of special scientific interest (SSSIs):

- i) Castle Hill, Balsdean (also a National Nature Reserve; see "Balsdean");
- ii) Cliffs from Saltdean to Newhaven (most important exposures of the offaster pilula zone in Britain);
- iii) Black Rock Cliffs (see "Black Rock").

Figure 42: The dovecote at Patcham Court Farm, the only building in Brighton to be designated an Ancient Monument

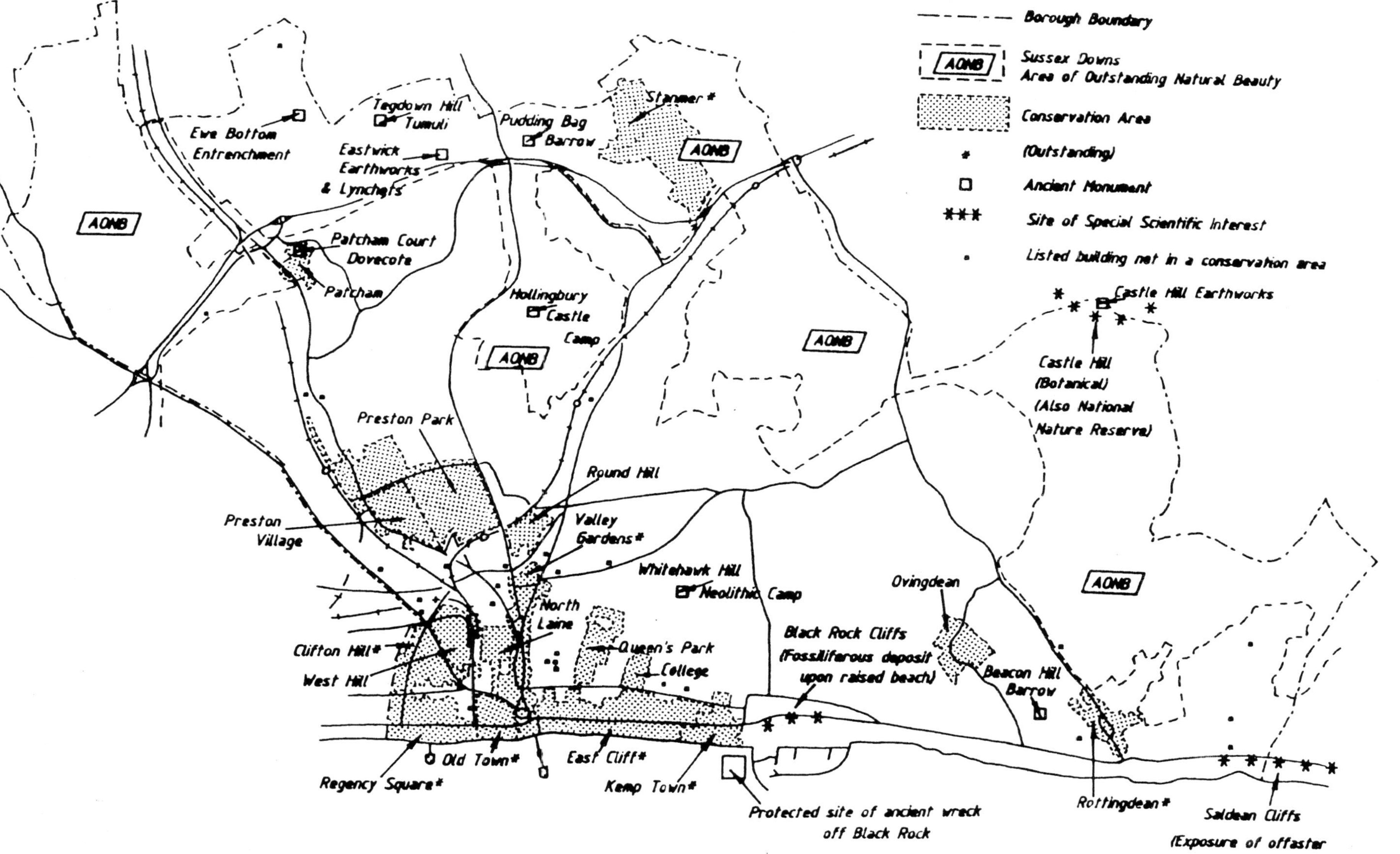

Borough Boundary
AONB
Sussex Downs
Area of Outstanding Natural Beauty
Conservation Area
(Outstanding)
Ancient Monument
Site of Special Scientific Interest
Listed building not in a conservation area
Castle Hill Earthworks
Castle Hill
(Botanical)
(Also National
Nature Reserve)
Ewe Bottom
Entrenchment
Tegdown Hill
Tumuli
Pudding Bag
Barrow
Stanmer*
Eastwick
Earthworks
& Lynchets
Patcham Court
Dovecote
Patcham
Hollingbury
Castle
Camp
Preston Park
Preston
Village
Round Hill
Valley
Gardens*
Whitehawk Hill
Neolithic Camp
Ovingdean
Black Rock Cliffs
(Fossiliferous deposit
upon raised beach)
Beacon Hill
Barrow
North
Laine
Queen's Park
College
Clifton Hill*
West Hill
Old Town*
Regency Square*
East Cliff*
Kemp Town*
Protected site of ancient wreck
off Black Rock
Rottingdean*
Saltdean Cliffs
(Exposure of offaster
pilula zone)

Figure 43: Conservation in the Borough of Brighton

c) *LISTED BUILDINGS:* Individual buildings have been protected in Brighton since October 1952 by being placed on the Department of the Environment's 'Statutory List of Buildings of Special Historic or Architectural Interest', a process commonly known as 'listing'. Such buildings may not be demolished nor materially altered without the consent of the borough council as planning authority, and only then after a thorough examination of the case; cases involving important buildings are referred to the Department. Special grants for repairs are also available. Grade I-listed buildings are considered to be of outstanding interest and national importance while those listed grade II warrant every effort to preserve them; particularly important grade II buildings are listed grade II*. Churches are listed grade A, B or C, although they are being regraded as for other buildings. Most buildings built before 1840 and those of 1840-1914 of definite quality are listed, while selected buildings of 1914-39 are now being designated as well; outstanding post-war buildings more than thirty years old may also be listed.

Grade I-listed buildings in Brighton are the Royal Pavilion, Dome and Corn Exchange; the original Kemp Town estate; Stanmer House; and the West Pier; St Bartholomew's is a grade A church. The newest building to be listed is Saltdean Lido which dates from 1937. In 1990 there are around 1,900 listed buildings in the borough including houses, hotels, public houses, churches, schools, barns, windmills, walls, lamp-posts, archways, stables, well-houses, statues, fountains, war memorials, a former fire station, a block of flats, a railway station, a railway viaduct, telephone kiosks and a pillar box. All listed buildings are referred to in the text and, unless otherwise stated, are grade II or, in the case of churches, grade B. A number of other buildings not considered sufficiently important for statutory protection by the Department are included on the council's own local list of buildings of special interest and are subject to similar planning considerations on a voluntary basis by the borough council.

d) *GARDENS AND TREES:* The grounds of both Preston Manor and the Royal Pavilion have been designated as gardens of special historic interest by English Heritage, and special care will be taken to preserve their original layout and features. A number of other historic parks and gardens are treated similarly by Brighton Council on a voluntary basis; they are: the Kemp Town enclosures; Kipling Garden, Rottingdean; Park Crescent; Preston Park; Preston Rockery; Queen's Park; Stanmer Park; and the Victoria Gardens.

Individual trees may have preservation orders placed upon them, and, as mentioned above, all trees within a conservation area are protected.

46. CO-OPERATIVES

<74,75,123>

a) *EARLY SOCIETIES:* The Brighton Co-operative Benevolent Fund Association, based on the communal ideas of social pioneer Robert Owen, was formed on 1 January 1828 and opened a shop at 31 West Street, the first co-operative retail shop in the country. Among its supporters were Lady Byron, and also Dr William King who wrote articles for a monthly journal, *The Co-operator*, of which twenty-eight issues were published from May 1828 until August 1830; they were one of the inspirations for the Rochdale pioneers. The society's store later moved to 37 West Street and then to Upper North Street. The Sussex General Co-operative Trading Association, formed at about the same time, operated a store at 10 Queen's Place, but both these early ventures had ceased trading by 1830.

In 1846 the Sussex Joint Stock Co-operative Friendly Society was founded by trade union pioneer George Henderson with a store at 100 Trafalgar Street which continued trading until 1857. It was followed by the Working Men's Co-operative Industrial Society in 1860 with a shop in London Street.

b) *BRIGHTON CO-OPERATIVE SOCIETY:* The Brighton 'Co-op' was founded at a meeting at the Coffee Palace, 29 Duke Street, on 26 November 1887. With George Holyoake as president, the society was formally established on 1 January 1888 with 200 members, and the first store was opened at 32 North Road on 16 May 1888. Membership increased slowly with only 932 members by 1900, but by 1914 it had risen to 4,414 and after the war increased rapidly to 10,000 by 1921 when other Sussex societies had been absorbed. In 1900, 96 London Road was purchased as a main office, and nos.97-101 were also acquired by 1909. These premises were converted into a single store in about 1919 when the Lewes Road store was also enlarged and branches had opened in several Sussex towns.

The 1920s and '30s saw a large expansion in operations, and the 'Co-op' played a very important part in the lives of many of the poorer inhabitants of the town, organising social and sporting events as well as providing dividends for its members and value-for-money shopping. Many new shops were opened across the county and a new bakery was established in 1920 at Portland Road, Hove, which was joined by a large laundry in 1934; the dairy operation was also expanded greatly behind Hanover Place. The culmination of the society's early success was the opening of the large central store in London Road on 12 September 1931, now the largest department store in Brighton. Designed by Bethell and Swannell, it has four storeys and a 180-foot frontage relieved only by two giant fluted Doric columns above the entrance. The total floor area now amounts to some 70,000 square feet with the additions of 1962, 1975 and 1980.

In 1978 the first large Brighton Co-op 'superstore' was opened at Peacehaven; a second opened on 11 June 1986 in Nevill Road, Hove, and there are others at Worthing and Hailsham.

47. CORPORATION and COUNCIL

a) *INCORPORATION:* The earliest known attempt to incorporate Brighton as a borough was in 1684 when Charles II apparently favoured a petition and referred it to the Attorney General, but it was not heard of again. By the start of the nineteenth century the town had grown sufficiently for the Prince of Wales to suggest incorporation, but the idea was rejected at a town meeting in July 1806 due to the probable expense. The 'Great Reform Act' of 1832 created the Parliamentary Borough of Brighton but municipal government continued in the hands of the town commissioners and the vestry. In April 1848 a town poll again rejected incorporation, but petitions for and against were sent to the Privy Council in 1852 which, after an eleven-day public inquiry, found in favour of the 'non-incorporationists'.

The supporters of incorporation, who included the parish vestry, maintained that the town commissioners were extravagant, too many in number, unrepresentative, and limited in certain powers (see "Town Commissioners and Town Acts"), and that only an elected and fully representative council could effectively govern the town on behalf of its 70,000 inhabitants. Another petition and Privy Council inquiry in August 1853 was successful and resulted in the award of a charter of incorporation on 19 January 1854; the Municipal Borough of Brighton, governed in virtually all matters by a newly-elected council under the Municipal Corporations Act of 1835, was officially created on 1 April 1854, the charter arriving in the town two days later. <1,112>

The first elections to the new council were held on 30 May 1854 when thirty-six councillors were returned for three years from the six wards. At their first meeting on 7 June 1854, Lieutenant-Colonel John Fawcett was elected as the first mayor of Brighton and the two councillors who had polled the highest vote in each ward were elected as aldermen to serve for six years. A second election was then held to return twelve more councillors, making a total of thirty-six councillors and twelve aldermen.

Initially, the town commissioners retained a few functions and buildings including the Town Hall and Royal Pavilion, but the 1855 Brighton Commissioners Transfer Act completed the handover of property, powers, privileges and liabilities, and dissolved the town commissioners from 29 May 1855. Incorporation also put an end to parish vestry meetings in their previous form except to discuss specific parochial items such as cemeteries, church maintenance, etc. <7,112>

b) *DEVELOPMENT of BRIGHTON CORPORATION and BOROUGH COUNCIL:* The 1873 addition of part of Preston parish increased the borough council to thirteen aldermen and thirty-nine councillors, but Preston's representation was made equal to other wards by the 1884 Brighton Improvement Act, resulting in a council of fourteen alderman and forty-two councillors. On 1 April 1889, under the 1888 Local Government Act, Brighton became a county borough with all-embracing responsibilities, completely independent of any county council. Note that the first woman councillor was a Mrs Blatch who was elected in 1918.

At the creation of 'Greater Brighton' in 1928, the borough was divided into nineteen wards with a council of nineteen aldermen and fifty-seven councillors. Two years later the local boards of guardians of the poor were abolished, and the county borough council had by then assumed responsibility for virtually all municipal affairs including education, libraries, police, fire-brigades, health, sewers, water, electricity, burials and public assistance. Although several of these functions were later administered by national boards, ministries or joint local boards, the county borough council continued to run the town until 1 April 1974 when Brighton, with boundaries unaltered, became one of seven district councils within the Shire County of East Sussex, under the terms of the 1972 Local Government Act, and was stripped of many of its responsibilities. A second charter came into effect on the same date to incorporate the new district as a borough with any previous privileges as a borough maintained; in effect this charter is for ceremonial purposes only, the chairman of the council being designated mayor and the council being known as a borough council. (Both the 1854 and 1974 charters may be seen in the town museum.) The 1972 Act also abolished the office of alderman, and the borough council then consisted of fifty-nine councillors only. This number was reduced to fifty-six in 1979 and to forty-eight councillors in sixteen wards in 1983.

East Sussex County Council took control of education, fire services, libraries, refuse disposal, social services and overall structure planning, but Brighton Borough Council retains responsibility for housing, planning, refuse collection, environmental health, parks and recreation, and, on an agency basis for the county council, highways. Brighton was initially represented by twenty-one county councillors, but since 1983 it has had sixteen councillors on a county council of seventy members. <1,33-36,39,43,115,300>

c) *ARMS and MOTTO:* The arms of Brighton Corporation were officially granted by the College of Heralds on 14 April 1897, but a simplified and updated version with modern-style dolphins, a simplified wreath and a forward facing helmet has been used by the new borough council since April 1974. They are described as: 'Argent, two dolphins naiant sable, a bordure azure, charged with six martlets or. And for the crest, on a wreath of the colours, two dolphins in saltire, heads downwards, sable, between as many branches of coral gules'. This may be interpreted as 'a silver shield with two black dolphins swimming horizontally, one above the other, within a blue border containing six gold, legless swallows; the crest has a wreath and mantling of silver and black with two black dolphins, heads downward and crossing, between two branches of red coral'. The wreath rests upon a silver helmet which in turn sits atop the shield. Beneath the shield is the town's motto *In Deo Fidemus*, meaning 'In God we trust'; it was chosen by Alderman Cordy Burrows.

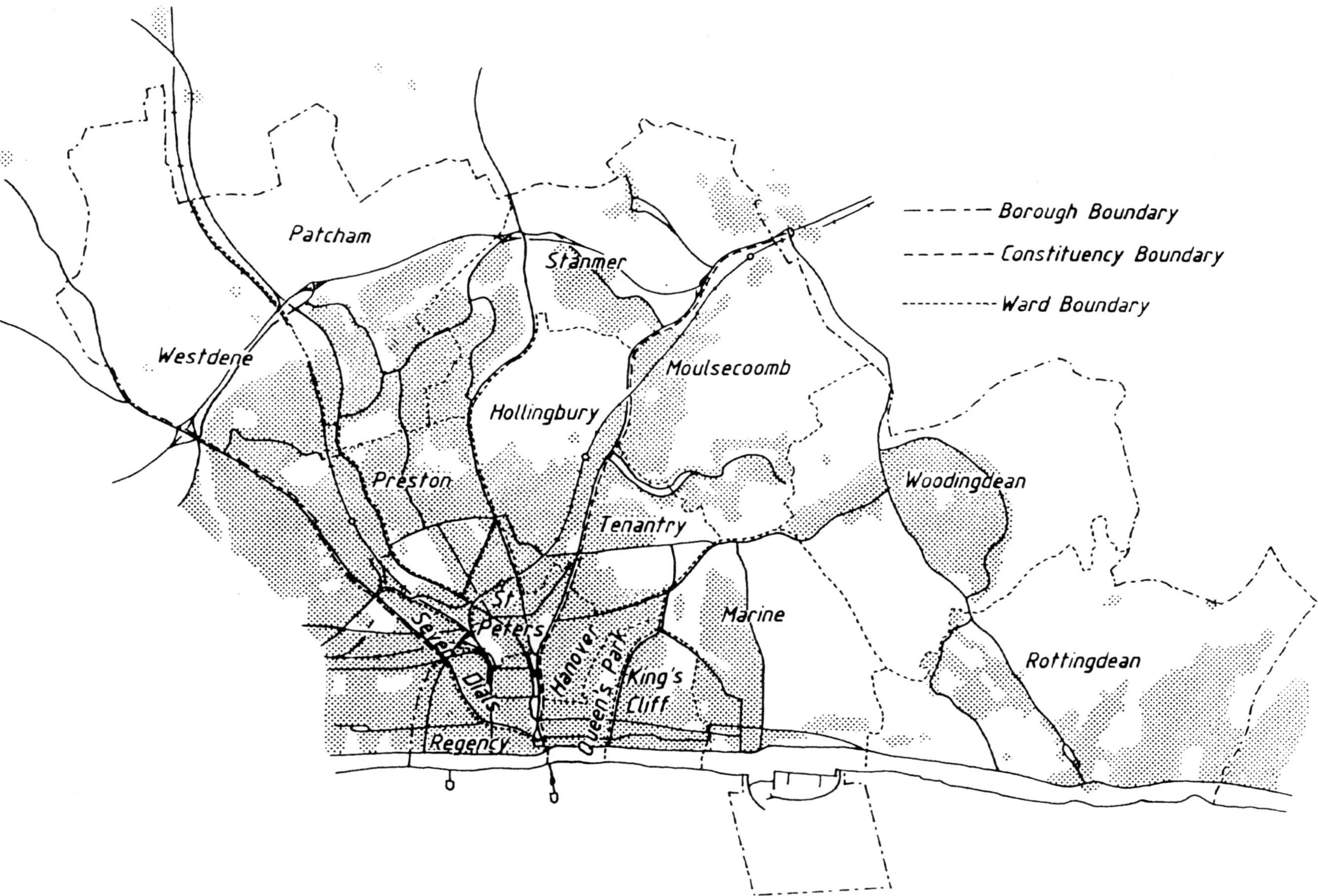

Figure 44: Constituencies and wards

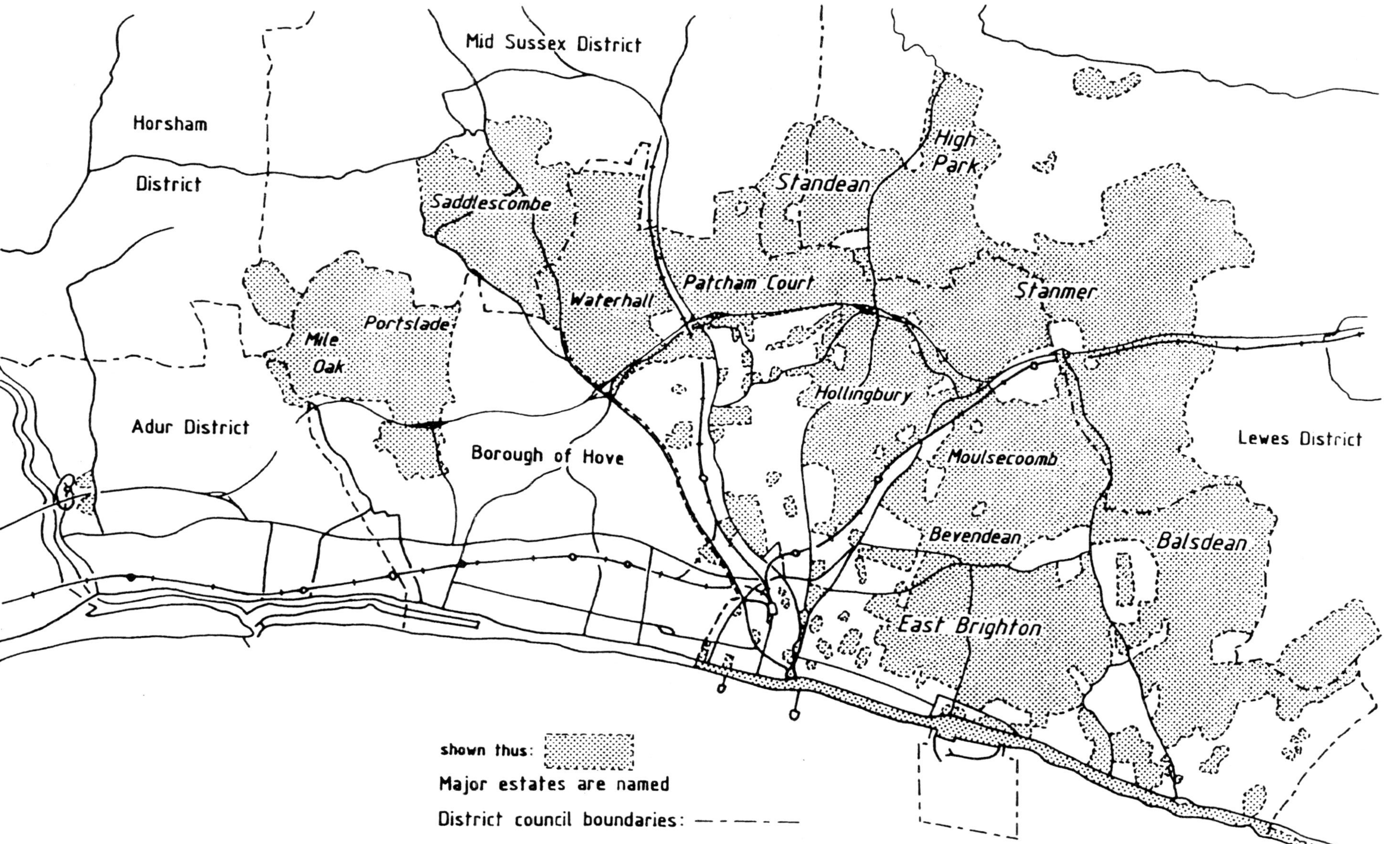

Figure: 45: Land owned by Brighton Borough Council

Figure 46: Arms of Brighton Borough Council

Dolphins were used as a symbol of the town long before the official granting of arms, and reflect the town's dependence on the sea (possibly derived from the arms of the Scrase family, former lords of the manor). The martlets are taken from the arms of Sussex. <17,18,123>

d) *POLITICAL COMPOSITION:* Ruled for many years by the Conservative Party, Brighton Council had no party with an absolute majority from 1983 until 1988, but the Conservatives continued to govern until 1986 when the Labour Party gained control on the casting vote of the mayor. Since 1951 the political composition of Brighton Council has been as follows <123,303>:

	Con	Lab	Lib/ SLD	SDP	Ind	Vacant
1951	59	12	-	-	5	-
1952	54	16	-	-	4	2
1953	52	20	-	-	4	-
1954	51	22	-	-	3	-
1955	51	22	-	-	3	-
1956	46	26	-	-	3	1
1957	47	25	-	-	4	-
1958	45	27	-	-	4	-
1959	52	22	1	-	1	-
1960	53	22	-	-	1	-
1961	52	22	-	-	2	-
1962	49	24	1	-	2	-
1963	49	23	2	-	2	-
1964	50	22	2	-	2	-
1965	52	22	1	-	1	-
1966	54	22	-	-	-	-
1967	57	19	-	-	-	-
1968	62	14	-	-	-	-
1969	68	8	-	-	-	-
1970	65	11	-	-	-	-
1971	56	20	-	-	-	-
1972	50	26	-	-	-	-
1973	50	26	-	-	-	-
1974	31	28	-	-	-	-
1975	31	28	-	-	-	-
1976	44	15	-	-	-	-
1977	44	15	-	-	-	-
1978	44	15	-	-	-	-
1979	37	16	3	-	-	-
1980	37	16	3	-	-	-
1981	37	16	3	-	-	-
1982	37	16	3	-	-	-
1983	24	20	3	1	-	-
1984	23	21	3	1	-	-
1985	22	22	3	1	-	-
1986	19	24	3	1	1	-
1987	20	24	3	-	1	-
1988	19	27	2	-	-	-
1989	19	26	2	-	1	-
1990	17	29	1	-	1	-

e) *WARDS:* In 1854 Brighton was divided into six wards for municipal elections, namely Park, Pavilion, Pier, St Nicholas, St Peter, and West. Preston ward was created in the 1873 extensions of the borough, and in 1894 the town was redivided into fourteen wards, viz.: Hanover, Kemp Town, Lewes Road, Montpelier, Pavilion, Pier, Preston, Preston Park, Queen's Park, Regency, St John, St Nicholas, St Peter, and West. Kemp Town ward was renamed King's Cliff in 1908 in honour of Edward VII, and in 1923 the new Moulsecoomb estate annexed by Brighton was added to Preston ward.

On the creation of 'Greater Brighton' in 1928 the former Preston parish was divided into four wards while two more wards were created to cover the additional areas outside the old borough. With the creation of an Elm Grove ward, the total number was brought to nineteen, viz: Elm Grove, Hanover, Hollingbury, King's Cliff, Lewes Road, Montpelier, Moulsecoomb, Pavilion, Pier, Patcham, Preston, Preston Park, Queen's Park, Regency, Rottingdean, St John, St Nicholas, St Peter, and West.

In 1952 the county borough was extended again to include parts of Falmer and Stanmer which were added to Patcham and Rottingdean wards. With much development in the suburbs, wards were redistributed in 1955 but remained at nineteen, viz: Elm Grove, Falmer, Hanover, Hollingbury, King's Cliff, Lewes Road, Montpelier, Moulsecoomb, Patcham, Pier, Preston, Preston Park, Queen's Park, Regency, Rottingdean, St Nicholas, St Peter, Stanmer, and Warren wards. The most recent redistribution of seats was in 1983, resulting in the following sixteen wards: Hanover, Hollingbury, King's Cliff, Marine, Moulsecoomb, Patcham, Preston, Queen's Park, Regency, Rottingdean, St Peter, Seven Dials, Stanmer, Tenantry, Westdene, and Woodingdean. <83,108,109,109a,307>

f) *COUNCIL PROPERTY:* Brighton Council owns some 9,000 acres of land within the borough boundary and another 7,500 outside, mostly purchased between 1900 and 1940. Agricultural estates account for about 11,000 acres and most of the rest is open downland surrounding the town, but the council also owns many valuable sites within the urban area, generating considerable income in the form of leases; the northern side of Western Road is one example. <306>

48. COURTS

{15,24,112,115,123}

For centuries petty offenders were dealt with by the hundred courts, the Court of Whalesbone in the case of Brighton, but when this practice died out they were taken before the bench at Lewes. The first magistrates' court in the town, still under the county bench, was established at the New Inn in North Street (now Clarence House) in 1808 with sessions held three days a week, but it was briefly transferred to the old Town Hall before moving to the Old Ship in 1814. In 1821-3 the sessions were held again at the New Inn, but then remained at the Old Ship until about 1832 when they were removed to the new Town Hall in Bartholomews.

In 1847 the petty sessions were joined at the Town Hall by a county court which was soon removed to 151 North Street and then to Prince's Street. In 1869 a new county court building opened at the bottom of Church Street with two court rooms. Built in red brick with stone dressings and a royal coat of arms over the western entrance, the building was used until 1967 and is now a library store. Borough quarter sessions commenced on 26 March 1855, two months after the first borough bench of magistrates sat with the mayor as chief magistrate. During the reconstruction of the Town Hall in 1897-9 the bench sat at the building now occupied by the public library.

On 3 November 1967 the Lord Chancellor, Lord Gardiner, opened a new court building at Edward Street and John Street. Costing £665,000 and designed by Percy Billington, it housed magistrate, juvenile, coroner, county and quarter session (later crown) courts. On 23 October 1985 an extension to the high court and county court was opened in William Street by senior circuit judge Granville Wingate. Between 1986 and 1989 the former parochial offices in Prince's Street were used by magistrates as the Edward Street building was refurbished. The latter was formally reopened by the Lord Chief Justice, Lord Lane, on 27 April 1989, the new facilities including three crown courts and eight magistrate courts.

49. DEVELOPMENT

The following tables list the roads and streets of the borough of Brighton with the approximate dates of their first significant development. This information has been derived from contemporary plans and directories in periods of approximately five or ten years, and the town has been divided into convenient districts for ease of use. It should be noted that many roads, particularly in the Patcham, Rottingdean, Saltdean and Woodingdean areas, were developed piecemeal over many years, while other roads, mainly in the town centre, have been rebuilt since their initial development. Current road names are used in all cases, but streets no longer in existence are shown in *italics*. The reader is advised to use these tables in conjunction with a street-plan. <10,83,107,108,109>

i) OLD TOWN area (bounded by West Street, North Street and Old Steine):

pre-1665: Bartholomews; Black Lion, Boyces, East, Little East, Market (north), Middle (south), North, Ship (south), Union & West Streets; Brighton Place; King's Road; Meeting House Lane; *the lower town below the cliff.*

1665-1744: Market (south) & Middle (north) Streets; Pool Valley; Steine Lane.

1745-79 Castle Square; Duke, Nile & Ship (north) Streets; Old Steine (south & west).

1827-30: Grand Junction Road.

1842-7: Prince Albert Street.

1963: Regent Arcade.

1966: Brighton Square.

1979: Dukes Lane.

ii) REGENCY SQUARE area (bounded by West Street, Western Road and Hove boundary):

1780-8: King's Road (east of Russell Street); *Little Russell*, *Russell* & *Upper Russell* (north) Streets.

1788-99: King's Road (Russell Street-Regency Square).

1800-8: Clarence Square (north side); *Grenville Place*; King's Road (west of Regency Square).

1808-21: Bedford, Regency & Russell Squares; *Blucher Place*; Cannon Place & *Street*; Norfolk, *Upper Russell* (west) & Western Streets; Western Road (south side to Castle Street).

1822-9: Castle, *Clarence*, Little Preston, Little Western, Preston & Sillwood Streets; Cavendish, Oriental, St Margaret's & Sillwood Places; Montpelier Road (east side); Norfolk Square; Sillwood Road (east side); Western Road (south side west of Castle Street); Western Terrace.

1831-5: Bedford Place; Cranbourne Street; Montpelier Road (west side).

1842-7: *Artillery Street*; Clarence Square (south side).

1869-75: Sillwood Road (west side).

1969-72: Churchill Square.

iii) CLIFTON HILL area (bounded by Western Road, Dyke Road and Hove boundary):

1665-1744: Dyke Road (south of Upper North Street).

1809-21: Western Road (north side to Hampton Place).

1822-30: Crown, Dean, Marlborough & Spring Streets; Montpelier Road (west side) & Terrace; Norfolk Square (north

side); Regent Hill & Row; Vine Place; Western Road (north side west of Hampton Place).
1831-5: Borough & Temple Streets; Hampton Place; Montpelier (west side) & Norfolk Roads.
1837-41: Victoria Street.
1842-7: Clifton Hill, Road & Terrace; Goldsmid Road; Montpelier Crescent, Place, Street & Villas; Upper North Street; Victoria Place.
1848-53: Belvedere, Norfolk & Vernon Terraces; Clifton Place; Dyke Road (Clifton Road to Seven Dials); Powis Grove, Square & Villas; Victoria Road.
1865-9: Denmark Terrace; Dyke Road (Upper North Street to Clifton Road); Powis Road; St Michael's Place.
1900-9: Temple Gardens; Windlesham Avenue, Gardens & Road.
1987: Marlborough Mews.

iv) WEST HILL area (bounded by Dyke Road, Queen's Road, railway, New England Road, and Chatham Place):
1665-1744: Air Street; Dyke Road (south of Upper North Street).
1800-8: Zion Gardens.
1809-21: Mount Zion Place; New Dorset Street; North Gardens.
1821-30: Church Street; Crown Gardens.
1831-5: Queen's Road (west side Church Street to North Road).
1836-41: Kew Street; Surrey Street.
1842-7: Camden Terrace; Guildford Street; Queen's Road (except west side Church Street to North Road); Terminus Place, Road & Street; Upper Gloucester Road.
1848-53: Bath, Clifton & Railway Streets; Buckingham, Chatham & Howard Places; Dyke Road (Clifton Road to Seven Dials); Queen Square; Russell Crescent.
1854-8: Buckingham (north), Centurion & Guildford Roads; Compton Avenue; West Hill Place, Road & Street.
1865-9: Albert, Buckingham (south), Dyke (Upper North Street to West Hill Road) & St Nicholas Roads; Buckingham Street.
1870-4: Alfred & Leopold Roads; Alexandra Villas.

v) NORTH LAINE area (bounded by North Street, Valley Gardens, Trafalgar Street and Queen's Road):
1745-1779: Bond Street (south); King, Marlborough & Prince's Places.
1780-9: Bond (north), Jew, Portland & Windsor Streets.
1789-99: Church Street (east of Spring Gardens); King Street; Spring Gardens.
1800-8: Gloucester Place.
1809-22: *Bread*, Gardner, *Jubilee* & Regent Streets; Frederick Place; Kensington Gardens; New Road; North Road (south side); Orange Row; *Pimlico*.
1823-30: Church (west of Spring Gardens), Gloucester, Kensington, Upper Gardner & Vine Streets; Frederick Gardens & Street; Kensington Place (west side); North Road (north side); St George's Place.
1836-41: Robert & Tidy Streets; Kensington Place (east side); Trafalgar Terrace.
1842-7: Blenheim & Cheltenham Places; Foundry, Kemp & Trafalgar (south side) Streets; Gloucester & Queen's Roads; Pelham Square (west side); Queen's Gardens.
1848-53: Over & Sydney Streets.
1859-64: Pelham Square (south & east sides).
1870-4: North Place.
1875-9: Tichborne Street.

vi) LONDON ROAD area (bounded by Trafalgar Street, railway, New England, Viaduct and Ditchling Roads):
1809-21: roads from St Peter's Place to Marshalls Row; Belmont Street; *Cavendish Place North*; Ditchling Road (south of Baker Street); London Road (south of Baker Street); York Place.
1822-30: Elder Place; London Road (north of Baker Street); Pelham Street (south); Rosehill Close; Trafalgar Street (north side); *Wood Street*.
1836-41: Blackman, Redcross & Whitecross Streets.
1842-7: Ann, Baker, Pelham (north), St Peter's, Station & Trafalgar (south side) Streets; Cheapside; Providence Place; York Hill.
1848-53: *Elder*, *London*, New England, *Peel* & *Queen* Streets.
1854-8: Ditchling Road (Baker Street to Viaduct Road); Kingsbury Road & Street.
1859-64: Boston Street; *Peel Place*; Rosehill & London Terraces; Viaduct Road.
1870-4: New England Road.

vii) ST JAMES'S STREET area (bounded by Old Steine, Edward Street, Eastern Road, Upper Bedford & Bedford Streets):
1779-88: Charles. Manchester, Prince's & Steine Streets; Madeira Place; Old Steine (east side).
1788-99: Broad, Camelford, George, Margaret & Wentworth Streets; Dorset, Lower Rock (west side) & Steine Gardens; Marine Parade (west of Lower Rock Gardens); New Steine; Pavilion Parade; St James's Place & Street (west of Dorset Gardens).
1800-8: Bedford, Cavendish, Chapel, Edward (west of Chapel Street), High, *Little St James's*, St James's (east of Dorset Gardens) & Upper St James's Streets; Lower Rock Gardens (east side); Rock Place.
1809-21: Devonshire Place; Charlotte, Edward (east of Chapel Street), Essex, Grafton, Hereford, Lavender, *Mount*, *Warwick* & Wyndham Streets; Marine & Upper Rock (west side) Gardens; Marine Parade (Lower Rock Gardens to Bedford Street).
1822-30: Eastern Road (west of Upper Bedford Street); Upper Bedford Street.
1830-6: Atlingworth Street.
1870-4: Madeira Drive.
1880-4: Upper Rock Gardens (east side).
1895-9: St James's Avenue.
1970-3: Ardingly Street.
1984-5: Dolphin Mews.

viii) KEMP TOWN area (east of Bedford & Upper Bedford Streets, including Eastern Road, Bristol Gardens and associated roads, to Black Rock):
1788-99: Royal Crescent.
1800-8: Bedford Street
1809-21: Bloomsbury & Crescent Places; Burlington & Telegraph Streets.
1822-30: Arundel Place & Terrace; Eastern Place & Terrace; Kemp Town Place; Lewes Crescent; Marine Parade (Bedford Street to Paston Place) & Square; Montague, Somerset & Upper

Bedford Streets; Portland Place; Rock Grove & Street; Sussex Square.
1830-6: Chichester Terrace; College Place; Millfield Cottages; St George's Road (west of Portland Place).
1837-41: Bloomsbury Street.
1842-7: Belgrave, Chichester & Eaton Places; Marine Parade (east of Paston Place); Percival Terrace; St George's Road (east of Portland Place) & Terrace; St Mark's Street; *Seymour Street*.
1848-53: Church Place; College Gardens; Eastern Road (Upper Bedford Street to College Place); Sussex Mews.
1854-8: Chesham Place; Clarendon Place & Terrace; College & Great College Streets; Montague Place.
1859-64: Bristol, Chesham & Eastern (College Place to Paston Place) Roads; Paston Place.
1865-9: Chapel Terrace; College Road; Prince's Terrace; *Rifle Butt Road*; Sudeley Place & Street; Upper Sudeley Street.
1870-4: Abbey Road; Arundel Street; Duke's Mound; Madeira Drive (west of Duke's Mound).
1875-9: Chesham Street; Eastern Road (Paston Place to St Mark's Street); Sudeley Terrace.
1880-4: Eastern Road (east of Sussex Square); Rugby Place; Whitehawk Road (west side south of Marlow Road).
1895-99: Madeira Drive (east of Duke's Mound).
1900-4: Bennett Road.
1905-9: Arundel Road.
1920-4: Bristol Street.
1925-9: Bristol Gate.
1963: Prince Regent's Close.
1976-7: Seymour Square.

ix) ALBION HILL area (bounded by Edward Street, Egremont Place, Queen's Park Road, Albion Hill and Valley Gardens):
1789-99: Grand Parade (south of Kingswood Street).
1800-8: Albion, *Carlton*, Circus, Edward (west of Grosvenor Street), John (south of Sussex Street), *Sun* & *Thomas* Streets; *Carlton Row*; Grand Parade (Kingswood Street to Morley Street); Mount Pleasant; Richmond *Hill* & Place.
1809-21: Albion Hill (west of Grove Hill); *Apollo Terrace*; *Ashton*, *Chesterfield*, *Claremont*, Edward (east of Grosvenor Street), Grosvenor, *Henry*, Kingswood, Mighell, Morley, Richmond (west of John Street) & William Streets; Carlton Hill (west of Tilbury Place); *Claremont*, *Cumberland*, Devonshire, Egremont (west side), Ivory, *Nelson*, Phoenix, Tilbury & Waterloo Places; Grand Parade (north of Morley Street); *Nelson Row*; *Richmond Buildings*.
1821-30: *Cambridge Street*; Carlton Hill (south side east of Mighell Street); *Claremont Row*; Marine View; Richmond Gardens; St John's Place.
1836-41: Carlton Hill (north side east of Tilbury Place).
1842-7: Lennox Street.
1854-8: Carlton & Upper Park Places; Windmill Street.
1859-64: Albion Hill (Grove Hill to Chate's Farm Court); *Dinapore*, *Liverpool* & Sussex (east of St John's Place) Streets.
1870-4: Queen's Park Road (west side); Stanley Street.
1880-4: Park Road Terrace.
1890-4: Albion Hill (south side east of Chate's Farm Court); Richmond Street (north side east of John Street; south side east of Windmill Street); Windmill Terrace.
1895-9: Blaker & White Streets.
1905-9: Sussex Terrace.
1931: Elmore & Tarner Roads; Richmond (south side Elmore Road to Windmill Street) & Sussex (Elmore Road to Windmill Street) Streets; Tilbury Way.
1934: Milner Flats.
1938: Kingswood Flats.
1960-5: Ashton Rise; Grove Hill; Richmond Parade.

x) HANOVER area (bounded by Lewes Road, Elm Grove, Queen's Park Road and Albion Hill):
1795: Hanover Place (almshouses).
1809-21: Albion Hill (west of Lewes Street); Hanover Crescent; Phoenix Place; Richmond Terrace; Waterloo Place.
1822: Hanover Street
1822-30: Southover Street (west of Hanover Street).
1831-6: Hanover Terrace.
1848-53: Lewes & Newhaven Streets.
1854-8: Milton Road.
1859-64: Albion Hill (Lewes Street to Scotland Street); Belgrave, Coleman, Holland, Jersey, Scotland, Southover (Hanover Terrace to Southampton Street) & Washington Streets; Cobden, Hampden, Howard & Islingword (west of Cobden Road) Roads; Elm Grove (west of Luther Street).
1865-9: Albion Hill (north side east of Scotland Street); Finsbury Road; Islingword Place & Road (east of Cobden Road); Montreal, Quebec, Southampton & Southover (east of Southampton Street) Streets; Toronto Terrace; Whichelo Place.
1870-4: Islingword Street; Newark Place; Queen's Park Road (west side south of Islingword Road).
1875-9: Beaufort Terrace.
1880-4: roads from Luther Street to Cromwell Street; Elm Grove (Luther Street to Queen's Park Road); Grant, Jackson & Lincoln Streets; Queen's Park Road (west side north of Islingword Road).
1890-9: Ewart & Grove Streets.

xi) QUEEN'S PARK area (bounded by Egremont Place, Queen's Park Road, Elm Grove, Whitehawk Hill Road and Eastern Road):
1809-21: Edward, *Egremont*, Leicester & *Spa* Streets; Eastern Road (west of Freshfield Road).
1822-30: *Coalbrook Road*; Egremont Place (east side); Park & *Sloane* Streets.
1848-53: Eastern Road (Freshfield Road to Walpole Road).
1859-64: Canning Street.
1865-9: Walpole Road.
1870-4: Hendon Street; Sutherland Road; Walpole Terrace.
1875-9: Bute Street; Cuthbert Road; Park Hill.
1880-4: College Terrace; Evelyn Terrace (north side); Freshfield Road (south Queen's Park Terrace); Rochester Street.
1885-9: Queen's Park Road (east side south of Tower Road).
1890-4: Queen's Park Terrace.
1895-9: Down Terrace (south side); Freshfield Place & Street; St Luke's Road & Terrace; South Avenue.
1900-4: Belle Vue Gardens; East & West Drives; Elm Grove (east of Queen's Park Road); Tillstone Street; Upper Abbey Road.
1905-9: Dawson Terrace; Freshfield Road (Queen's Park Terrace to

Down Terrace); Queen's Park Rise.

1915-9: Queen's Park Road (east side Queen's Park Terrace to Down Terrace).

1920-4: Down Terrace (north side); Evelyn Terrace (south side); Firle, Freshfield (north of Down Terrace), Glynde, Plumpton, Queen's Park (east side north of Down Terrace) & Tower Roads; Pankhurst Avenue.

1925-9: Hallett Road.

1930-4: Clayton Road.

1951-5: Craven Vale estate.

1956-9: Hadlow & Southwater Closes.

1970-3: Attree Drive; Barnfield Gardens; Barry Walk.

1974-5: Freshfield Way; Stevenson Road.

xii) ELM GROVE area (between Elm Grove and Bear Road):

1854-8: Melbourne Street; Wellington Road.

1859-64: Elm Grove (west of Wellington Street); Wellington Street.

1865-9: Franklin, Hastings & Lewes (east side) Roads; Gladstone Place & Terrace.

1870-4: Agnes & Franklin Streets; De Montfort Road; Fairlight & St Martin's Places.

1875-9: Pevensey & St Leonards Roads; Picton Street.

1880-4: Bonchurch, Brading, Newmarket & Upper Wellington Roads; Elm Grove (Wellington Street to Totland Road); Normanton Street.

1885-9: Hartington Road (north side west of Whippingham Street); Whippingham Road.

1895-9: Hartington Road (south side west of Whippingham Road); Shanklin Road.

1900-4: roads from Bernard Road to St Helens Road; Bembridge, Seville & Whippingham Streets; Elm Grove (east of Totland Road).

1905-9: Coronation Street; Hartington Place, Road (north side east of Whippingham Street) & Terrace; May Road.

1915-9: Hartington Road (south side east of Whippingham Road).

xiii) ROUND HILL area (bounded by Lewes, Hollingdean, Ditchling and Union Roads):

1822-30: Rosehill; Union Road.

1848-53: Park Crescent.

1854-8: Ditchling Road (east side Union Road to Prince's Crescent); Lewes Road (west side).

1859-64: Caledonian, Ditchling (east side Prince's Crescent to Florence Place), Edinburgh & Wakefield Roads; Park Crescent Terrace; Roundhill Crescent.

1865-9: Aberdeen, Inverness & Richmond Roads; St Mary Magdalene & St Paul's Streets.

1870-4: Park Crescent Place & Road; St Martin's Street; Upper Lewes Road.

1880-4: Ashdown, Crescent, D'Aubigny & Mayo Roads; Brewer & Trinity Streets; Prince's Crescent & Road; Round Hill Road & Street.

1890-4: Belton Road.

1895-9: Newport Street.

1951-5: Sylvan Hall estate.

xiv) EAST PRESTON area (north of Bear Road to Natal Road and Jevington Drive):

1885-9: Belle Vue Cottages.

1895-9: Bear Road; Coombe Terrace.

1900-9: Buller, Coombe (west end), Dewe, Ewhurst, Ladysmith, Milner (west end), Natal (south side), Nesbitt, Redvers & Riley Roads.

1910-5: Kimberley & Mafeking Roads.

1920-4: Baden, Canfield, Coombe (east end), Crayford, Eastbourne, Milner (east end) & Natal (north side) Roads; Carlyle Avenue.

1956-9: Canfield Close.

1960-5: Birling & Willingdon Closes; Jevington Drive.

xv) PRESTON (SOUTH) area (bounded by New England, Viaduct & Ditchling Roads, Stanford Avenue, Preston Road, Lovers Walk and railway):

pre-1850: Lovers Walk Cottages.

1859-64: Viaduct Road.

1870-4: Argyle, Beaconsfield (south of viaduct), Campbell, New England, Preston (south of viaduct) & Stanley Roads.

1875-9: Clyde, Preston (viaduct to Preston village), Shaftesbury, Springfield & Warleigh Roads; Ditchling Rise; Gerard, Winchester & Yardley Streets; Lovers Walk.

1880-4: Beaconsfield Road (north of viaduct); Parkmore Terrace; Ditchling (west side south of Rugby Road), Florence (west), Grantham & Vere Roads; Dyke Road Drive; Stanford Avenue (south-west of Chester Terrace).

1885-9: Florence Road (east).

1890-4: Edburton Avenue.

1895-9: Ditchling (Rugby Road to Fiveways), Rugby & Semley Roads; Southdown & Stanford (north-west of Chester Terrace) Avenues.

1900-4: St Andrew's Road.

1970-3: Ditchling Gardens.

xvi) PRESTON (NORTH) area (bounded by Stanford Avenue, Hollingbury Park Avenue, Balfour, Loder, Harrington & Preston Roads):

1859-64: Harrington Road (western end).

1880-4: Beaconsfield Villas (south); Chester Terrace; Havelock (south) & Waldegrave Roads; Preston Park Avenue; Stanford Avenue (south-west of Chester Terrace).

1885-9: Cleveland & Havelock (north) Roads.

1890-4: Southdown Road; Edburton Avenue.

1895-9: Bates, Ditchling (Fiveways to Hythe Road), Herbert, Hythe & Lucerne Roads; Preston Drove (west of Surrenden Road); Stanford Avenue (north-west of Chester Terrace).

1900-4: Ashford, Balfour (south of Loder Road), Ditchling (Hythe Road to Osborne Road), Dover, Gordon, Knoyle, Loder, Lowther, Osborne, Sandgate & Surrenden (south of Surrenden Crescent) Roads; Beaconsfield Villas (north); Harrington Road (east) & Villas; Hollingbury Park Avenue & Terrace; Preston Drove (east of Surrenden Road).

1905-9: Cornwall Gardens (east side).

1925-9: Bavant Road.

1930-4: Balfour Road (north).

1935-9: Ditchling Road (north of Osborne Road).

1956-9: Beacon Close.

1960-5: Poplar Close.

xvii) PRESTON (WEST) area (bounded by Dyke Road, Millers Road, Grange Close, Preston Road, Clermont Road and Tivoli Crescent North):

pre-1850: Preston village.

1865-9: Clermont, Cumberland, Preston (north of village) & Station Roads; Lorne Villas; Clermont Terrace.

1880-4: Scarborough Road.
1885-9: Reigate & Robertson Roads.
1890-4: Hampstead, Kingsley & Maldon Roads; The Drove.
1895-9: Compton, Lauriston, Matlock & Millers (north) Roads; Woodside Avenue; Tivoli Crescent South.
1900-4: Inwood Crescent.
1905-9: Dyke Road (north of Highcroft Villas); Tivoli Crescent North; Wincombe Road.
1910-4: Millers Road (south).
1915-9: Tivoli Road.
1966-9: Grange Close.

xviii) PRESTONVILLE area (bounded by Dyke Road, Chatham Place, New England Road, railway and Highcroft Villas):

1848-53: Chatham Place; Dyke Road (Seven Dials to Russell Crescent); Howard Terrace; Russell Crescent.
1854-8: Belmont; Prestonville (south) Road.
1859-64: York Grove.
1865-9: Brigden Street; Hamilton, Old Shoreham, Prestonville (north) & Stanford (south) Roads; Lancaster & York Villas; Prestonville Terrace.
1870-4: New England Road.
1875-9: Dyke Road (Old Shoreham Road to Highcroft Villas).
1880-4: Coventry & Exeter Streets; Upper Hamilton Road; Highcroft Villas; Port Hall Avenue, Place, Road & Street; Stanford Road (north).
1890-4: Buxton, Lancaster & Stafford Roads.
1895-9: Chatsworth Road.

xix) HOLLINGDEAN (between Lewes and Ditchling Roads, north of Hollingdean Road):

1865-9: Freehold Terrace.
1870-4: Hollingdean Road (north side).
1875-9: Hollingdean Road (south side); Pope's Folly.
1895-9: Hollingbury (west side), Roedale & Upper Hollingdean Roads.
1900-4: Hollingbury Park Avenue & Terrace; Hollingdean Terrace (south).
1905-9: Hollingbury Place & Road (east side); Stanmer Park Road (south).
1910-4: Hollingbury Crescent.
1925-9: Barnett, Dudley, Hertford & Quarry Bank Roads; Hollingbury Rise & Rise West; Hollingdean Terrace (north); Stanmer Villas.
1935-9: Harrington Place; Stanmer Park Road (north).
1951-5: most of east Hollingdean estate.
1956-9: Thompson Road.
1960-5: most of north-east Hollingdean estate; Tavistock Down.
1966-9: Barrow & Lambourne Closes; Brentwood Close, Crescent & Road (except east end); Shenfield Way.
1970-3: Burstead Close.
1975-80: Adams Close; Hutton Road; Lynchet Close, Down & Walk.
1984-5: Hughes Road.

xx) WITHDEAN (EAST) area (bounded by Harrington Road, Loder Road, Balfour Road, Ditchling Road, Surrenden Road, Peacock Lane and London Road):

1859-64: London Road (Preston Road to Withdean Park).
1900-4: Surrenden Road (south of Surrenden Crescent).
1905-9: Cornwall Gardens (east side).
1925-9: Cornwall Gardens (west side); Friar Road (east); Surrenden Crescent (north side) & Road (Surrenden Crescent to Braybon Avenue).
1930-4: Peacock Lane; Surrenden Close, Crescent (south side) & Road (east of Braybon Avenue); Varndean Gardens; Withdean Crescent.
1935-9: Ditchling Road (north of Osborne Road); Friar Crescent, Road (west) & Walk.
1946-50: Hollingbury Copse.
1956-9: Varndean Road.
1960-5: Cliveden Close; Surrenden Holt & Park.
1966-9: Varndean Close; Whittinghame Gardens.
1970-4: Draxmont Way; Fairlie Gardens; Mulberry Close; Varndean Park estate.
1978-84: Kingsmere.

xxi) WITHDEAN (WEST) area (bounded by Dyke Road Avenue, Woodside Avenue, Clermont Road, London Road, The Deneway, and including Redhill Drive, Glen Rise and Green Ridge):

1859-64: London Road (Preston Road to Withdean Park).
1890-4: Dyke Road Avenue.
1925-9: Croft & Hillbrow Roads; Tongdean Lane; Valley Drive (east of Hillside Way).
1930-4: Cedars Gardens; Colebrook Road; Hillside Way; Valley Close; Withdean Road.
1935-9: Eldred (west side), Elms Lea, Gableson & Withdean Court Avenues; Redhill Drive; Valley Drive (Hillside Way to Redhill Drive).
1946-50: The Deneway; Glen Rise; Green Ridge; Redhill Close; Wayland Avenue.
1951-5: Eldred Avenue (east side); Tongdean Rise; Valley Drive (west of Redhill Drive).
1956-9: Curwen Place; Glen Rise Close; Shepherds Croft.
1960-5: Leahurst Court; Whitethorn Drive; Withdean Close.
1966-9: The Beeches; Hazeldene Meads; Withdean Rise.
1978-84: Blackthorn Close; Lion Gardens.

xxii) WESTDENE (bounded by Eldred Avenue, Windmill Drive, Millcroft and Hillcrest):

1935-9: Barn Rise; Copse Hill; Dene Vale; Eldred Avenue (west side).
1951-5: Downside; Eldred Avenue (east side); Fernwood Rise; Highbank; Hillcrest.
1956-9: Bramble Rise; Deneside; Fairview Rise; Millcroft; Mill Rise.
1960-5: Bankside; Westdene Drive; Windmill Drive.
1966-9: Wayside.

xxiii) PATCHAM (north of Carden Avenue, south of Ladies Mile Road, Vale Avenue plus Brangwyn Estate):

pre-1800: Church Hill; Old London Road (north).
1925-9: Patchdean.
1930-9: Brangwyn Estate; Carden Avenue (north side to Carden Crescent; rest of area not included under other dates.
1946-50: The Deneway; Highview Avenue South; The Woodlands.
1951-5: Grangeways; Highview Road & Way; Sunnydale Close.
1956-9: Ladies Mile Close.
1960-5: Audrey & Carol Closes.
1966-9: Brompton, Stoneleigh & Winfield Closes; Overhill Gardens; South Woodlands.
1970-3: Ashley Close.

xxiv) SOUTH PATCHAM (bounded by Carden Avenue, Wilmington Way, Westfield Crescent, Northfield Way, Larkfield Way, Surrenden Road, Peacock Lane and London Road):

1930-9: All roads in area not mentioned under other dates.
1946-50: Old Court Close.
1960-5: Beechwood Close.

xxv) LADIES MILE ESTATE (bounded by Ladies Mile Road and Vale Avenue):

1930-9: All roads in area not mentioned under other dates.
1956-9: Ladies Mile Close.

xxvi) HOLLINGBURY (including Petworth Road, Carden Avenue (part), Denton Drive, Lyminster Avenue and Woodbourne Avenue):

1946-50: All roads on council estate not mentioned under other dates.
1951-5: Elsted Crescent; Rotherfield Close.
1956-9: Chelwood Close; Rudgwick, Rustington & Sedgewick Roads.
1960-5: Ditchling Crescent; Youngsmere Close.

xxvii) MOULSECOOMB (including The Avenue to Manton Road (western end) and Southall Avenue):

1920-4: The Avenue (to western end of Manton Road); The Crescent; The Highway; Colbourne & Southall Avenues; Hillside.
1925-9: Barcombe, Chailey, Newick & Ringmer Roads.
1930-4: East Moulsecoomb (Widdicombe Way to Bevendean Crescent).
1935-9: East Moulsecoomb (Hodshrove & Birdham Roads to Shortgate Road).
1946-50: Ashurst, Bolney, Halland & Stonecross Roads; Friston Close; Moulsecoomb Way (north of Shortgate Road).
1951-5: Bates estate; Staplefield Drive.
1956-9: Eggington Road.
1960-9: Lucraft Road; Selba Drive; Sullington Close; Wheatfield Way.
1970-3: Broadfields Road.
1975-8: Eggington Close.

xxviii) BEVENDEAN (east of the western end of Manton Road):

1930-4: The Avenue (east of the western end of Manton Road); Lower & Upper Bevendean Avenues; Manton Road.
1948-53: All roads in area not mentioned under other dates.
1956-9: The Hyde.
1960-5: Durham & Leybourne Closes.
1970-4: Dartmouth Close & Crescent; Fitch Drive.

xxix) COLDEAN:

1935-9: Coldean Lane (east end); Park Road; Ridge View; Rushlake Road (east of Forest Road).
1946-8: Arlington Crescent; Coldean Lane (west); Forest Road; Middleton Rise; Park Close; Roundway.
1951-5: All roads in area not mentioned under other dates.
1960-5: Ashburnham Close; The Byway; Walton Bank; Woburn Place.
1966-9: The Meads; Rushlake, Standean & Woodview Closes.

xxx) WHITEHAWK & MANOR FARM area (including Bristol Estate):

1880-4: Whitehawk Road (west side south of Marlow Road).
1925-9: *Hervey Road*; Whitehawk Road (west side north of Marlow Road).
1930-4: All roads in Whitehawk council estate not mentioned under other dates; Marlow, Peel & Reading Roads; Wilson Avenue (south of Piltdown Road).
1935-9: All roads on Manor Farm estate not mentioned under other dates; Henley Road; Whitehawk Close.
1946-50: Alan Way; Albourne Close; Danehill Road; Manor Green; Nuthurst Place; Ticehurst Road; Wadhurst Rise.
1951-5: Manor Gardens.
1956-9: Bristol estate; Desmond Way; Manor Paddock.
1960-5: Aldrich Close; The Meadway; Sadler Way; Swanborough Drive; Vines Cross Road; Wilson Avenue (north of Piltdown Road).
1966-9: Robin Dene; Swanborough Place.
1974: Madehurst & Slinfold Closes.
post-1976: Whitehawk estate redevelopment.

xxxi) ROEDEAN (east of Cliff Road):

1900-5: Roedean Terrace.
1925-9: The Cliff; Cliff Road; Roedean Road.
1935-9: Roedean Crescent & Way.

xxxii) OVINGDEAN (excluding Eley Drive area):

pre-1850: Ovingdean Road; Greenways (north).
1925-30: Ainsworth Avenue; Greenways (south); Longhill Road.
1935-9: Beacon Hill.
1946-50: The Vale.
1956-9: Ovingdean Close.
1966-9: Ainsworth & Martyns Closes.
1970-5: Dower Close; Wanderdown Road.
1978-84: Longhill Close; Wanderdown Close, Drive & Way.

xxxiii) ROTTINGDEAN (west of Cranleigh Avenue, including Eley Drive area):

pre-1800: The Green; High Street.
1820-50: Marine Drive (west of High Street); West Street.
1900-20: Nevill Road.
1920-30: Bazehill, Knole, Newlands, Romney & Steyning Roads; Chailey & Cranleigh Avenues; Marine Drive (east of Newlands Road); The Park; Park Crescent & Road.
1930-4: Court Farm, Dean Court, Falmer & New Barn Roads; Grand & Little Crescent.
1935-9: Court Ord Road; Eley Crescent & Drive; Lenham Road East & West.
1951-5: Meadow Close.
1956-9: Challoners Close; Elvin Crescent; Gorham Avenue; Rowan Way; Welesmere Road.
1960-5: Northfield Rise; Royles Close.
1970-3: The Rotyngs.
1977: Challoners Mews.
1978-84: Northgate Close; St Aubyn's Mead.
1989: Caspian Square.

xxxiv) WOODINGDEAN:

1925-9: Channel View, Downland, Falmer, McWilliam, Seaview & Warren Roads; The Ridgway.
1930-4: roads from Roseberry Avenue to Vernon Avenue; Balsdean, Helena & Hillview Roads; Warren Rise.
1935-9: Downsway; Crescent Drive; Downs Valley Road (west side); Holt View; Ivor Road; Warren Way.
1946-50: Kipling Avenue; Lockwood Crescent; Rudyard Road.
1951-5: Abinger, Brownleaf, Downs Valley (east side), Foxdown, Selhurst & Shipley Roads; Broad Green; Chalkland Rise;

Cowley, Ravenswood & Stanstead Drives; Deans, Downland, Hylden & Littleworth Closes; Millyard Crescent.
1956-9: Bexhill, Briarcroft, Donnington, Heronsdale & Laughton Roads; Burnham, Crescent, Hunston, Maple, Marden, Merston, Newells, Pinfold, Rosedene, Sutton, Treyford & Truleigh Closes; The Brow; Falmer Gardens; Langley Crescent; Netherfield Green; Sandhurst Avenue.
1960-5: Frimley, Heyworth & Sycamore Closes; Sherrington Road.
1966-9: Batemans, Connell & Dudwell Roads; Bush, Lockwood, Ridgway, Rudyard & Warren Close; Holton Hill; Kevin & Pitt Gardens.
1970-5: Briar Close; Nolan Road; Villiers Close.
1976-8: Catherine Vale; Larch Close.

xxxv) SALTDEAN (Cranleigh Avenue to Longridge Avenue):
1930-4: Ashdown Avenue; Founthill & Hill Roads; Marine Drive.
1935-9: roads from Saltdean Drive to Longridge & Rodmell Avenues; Mount estate (Westfield Avenue South to Hilgrove Road & Saltdean Vale); Founthill & Westmeston Avenues; Tumulus Road; Lenham Road East.
1946-50: Arlington Gardens; Berwick & Hempstead Roads; Greenbank (north of Mount Drive), Heathfield & Tremola Avenues; Mount Drive.
1951-5: Bishopstone Drive; Eileen & Lenham Avenues.
1956-9: Chorley, Falmer, Greenbank (south of Mount Drive), Ridgewood & Shepham Avenues; Coombe Vale; Lustrells Crescent & Vale; Marine Close; Perry Hill; Saltdean Vale (Lustrells Crescent to Hempstead Road); Wivelsfield Road.
1960-5: Chiltington Way; Coombe Rise; Glynde, Glyndebourne & Winton Avenues; Lindfield & Lustrells Close; Westfield Avenue North; Westfield Rise.
1970-5: Chiltington, Effingham, Hawthorn & Saxon Closes.

50. DEVIL'S DYKE

a) *HISTORY:* The Devil's Dyke is a deep valley in the Downs to the west of Saddlescombe and five miles north-west of Brighton in the parish of Poynings. The adjacent hill has no particular name of its own, but is crowned by an Iron Age hill fort and, at 711 feet above sea-level, has magnificent views over the Weald. The legend of the Dyke is widely known: it is said that the Devil dug the chasm to allow the sea to inundate the churches and pious inhabitants of the Weald, but an old lady, on hearing the noise, lit a candle and Ol' Nick, believing it to be the rising sun, left his terrible work unfinished. In reality the 300-foot-deep valley was carved by tremendous amounts of water running off the Downs during the last Ice Age when large amounts of snow thawed and the frozen chalk prevented any further absorption; erosion was aided by the freeze-thaw cycle and the valley was deepened by the 'sludging' of the saturated chalk.

In April 1928 Brighton Corporation, through the initiative of Herbert Carden, purchased 190 acres of downland in the area for £9,000. It was dedicated for public use by the Duke and Duchess of York on 30 May 1928 when a commemorative seat was unveiled; the inscription reads 'God gave all men all earth to love'. The Dyke has always been a popular resort for Brightonians and there has been a refreshment building of some sort there since 1818. The first hotel building, designed by George Cheeseman, was erected in 1831 but replaced in 1871; the second hotel was burnt down in 1945 and the present structure built in 1955. Tourist attractions at the Dyke since the late nineteenth century have also included a funfair, bandstand, observatory, camera obscura and coffee rooms. Both William IV and Queen Victoria visited the Dyke while staying at Brighton.

From 24 July 1897 until 1908 a steep-grade railway (maximum gradient 1:1.5) ran down the northern slope of the hill to a point west of Poynings village; the two cars carried fourteen passengers each, some 275,000 a

Figure 47: The Dyke Hotel in the nineteenth century

year. The course of the railway may still be seen from the underhill lane together with the concrete base of the hill-top terminus. Across the Dyke itself ran a cable railway, suspended from two pylons 650 feet apart and providing an exhilarating trip 230 feet above the bottom of the defile. This latter attraction operated from 13 October 1894 until about 1909, but the concrete pylon bases may still be seen. A short 'switchback railway' or 'roller-coaster' also operated near the hotel. All these attractions were launched by the hotel landlord, a Mr Hubbard, but proved so successful that they took trade away from the hotel itself and he was eventually forced to close them. <79-82,109>

b) *The DYKE RAILWAY:* A conventional railway also operated from Brighton to the Devil's Dyke. Opened on 1 September 1887 by the Brighton and Dyke Railway Company, it left the Shoreham line at Aldrington and ran alongside Amherst Crescent, Rowan Avenue and Poplar Avenue (which were, of course, built later), past Brighton and Hove Golf Course, to a station at Devil's Dyke Farm, some 200 feet below and over half a mile from the hotel; the total length from Aldrington was about 3.5 miles at an average gradient of 1:45. However, as the popularity of motoring increased and the masses were able to drive all the way to the hotel, the line lost its attraction and eventually closed on 31 December 1938. Dyke Junction Halt, later Aldrington Halt, had opened on 3 September 1905, and there was another stop at Rowan Halt in Rowan Avenue from 12 January 1934. From 1891 trains also stopped on request at Golf Club Halt for the Brighton and Hove golf-course; an automatic bell in the clubhouse would warn members that a train was about to leave the Dyke Station. The platform at the Dyke Station and the site of Golf Club Halt may still be seen. The course of the railway itself now forms a pleasant walk from Hangleton Way (near The Downsman public house) to the Golf Club Halt. There was also a bogus 'Hangleton Halt' which was marked on maps by an unscrupulous developer! <81,82>

c) *GOLF-COURSES:* The Dyke golf-course was laid out in 1908 and is considered the best of the local courses with the greatest variety of holes. It has a length of 6,519 yards and was a Brighton municipal course until 1966 when it was leased to the Dyke Golf Club by the corporation.

The oldest club in the Brighton area is the Brighton and Hove Golf Club off Devil's Dyke Road, which opened in October 1887 with nine holes. It was later extended to eighteen holes, but sixty acres were sold following persistent trespass and nuisance, and the course was reduced to nine holes again in 1960; an eighteen-hole 'equivalent' course is now provided by two tees at each hole giving a course length of 2758+2777 yards. A bell remains in the clubhouse which rang when a train was about to leave the Dyke Station, giving golfers time to down their drinks and hurry to the club's own private railway platform (see "Dyke Railway" above). A separate Brighton and Hove Ladies' Golf Club was run from 1891 until 1939 on a nine-hole course to the south-west of the Dyke Hotel.

A new course for the West Hove Golf Club was laid out to the west of the old railway line in 1989-90 to replace their course in Benfield Valley which will be lost to the bypass link road; it will be ready early in 1991. <123,218,219,221,305>

d) *SADDLESCOMBE:* This small hamlet, just a farm and a few cottages around a pond, lies in Newtimber parish just to the east of the Devil's Dyke. It was mentioned in the Domesday Book as 'Salescome', and from the fourteenth century until the sixteenth the manor was a preceptory of the Knights Templar and Knights Hospitaller. The present farmhouse dates mainly from the 1700s, but nearby is a sixteenth- or seventeenth-century weather-boarded well-house enclosing a donkey-wheel and a 150-foot shaft; the well was in use until around 1910. In October 1926 the manorial estate of Saddlescombe was acquired for £10,215 by Brighton Corporation. <1,45,305>

51. DITCHLING ROAD

Reaching 525 feet above sea-level over Hollingbury, and with extensive views to east and west, Ditchling Road is the highest road in Brighton outside the Woodingdean area, and was established as a turnpike road to Lindfield and Cuckfield in 1770 with a tollgate at the Patcham/Preston boundary near Osborne Road <112>.

Alongside the Level (q.v.) Ditchling Road was originally known as Brunswick Place North and retains several interesting buildings from the 1810s; no.3, probably by A.H.Wilds, and the adjacent composition, nos.5-13 which are adorned with balconies, verandahs, bow windows and a pediment on the centre-piece, are listed buildings. The Open Market opened on its present site in 1926, but was rebuilt in 1960 (see "Markets"). No.93 Ditchling Road housed corporation slipper baths from 1891 until about 1932. Facing the northern side of the Level, no.2 is an attractive yellow-brick house with a Doric doorway, while the adjacent nos.4-8 were once home to the Lady Chichester Hospital (see "Clifton Hill (Windlesham Road)"). Back along the main length of Ditchling Road, ascending the hill, are nos.12-24, attractive cottages formerly known as Ditchling Terrace. No.26 was built as a branch of the Brighton and Hove Dispensary in 1885. <44,83,94>

The Brighton Business Centre at the corner of Viaduct Road opened in 1987 in the former Chichester Diocesan Training College for Schoolmistresses, erected in 1854 (see "Viaduct Road").

The borough boundary ran along the western side of Ditchling Road from Viaduct Road to Florence Place until 1873. In the mid nineteenth century several large residences were built on the eastern, or Brighton, side; these included Sylvan Hall, the home of Henry Infield, which gave its name to the estate of council flats developed on the site from 1949. The attractive nos.68-82 Ditchling Road are a row of 1850s semi-detached villas originally known as Round Hill Park; they are now included in the Round Hill conservation area along with the former Ranelagh Terrace to the north. The western, or Preston, side of Ditchling Road was developed from the 1880s; large, semi-detached houses with Corinthian doorways line the road to the south, impressive red-brick housing was erected to the north. <83,109>

Opposite Round Hill Road stood St Saviour's Church, built in 1886 by Edmund Scott and F.T.Cawthorn. Faced in flint with brick dressings, the church was dominated by a very large reredos by W.Slater and R.H.Carpenter which was removed from Chichester Cathedral in 1904-5. A chapel was added in 1889, but the church closed in 1981 and was demolished in 1983 to be replaced by the flats of St Saviour's Court. A red-brick archway remains in Vere Road, and the parish has merged with St Augustine's. The area of attractive terraced housing to the south of the railway and west of Ditchling Road came to be known as St Saviour's in the late 1980s following the formation of a residents' association of that name.

At the end of Florence Place is the Freehold Burial Ground, given to the Brighton Synagogue congregation in 1826 by T.R.Kemp for use as a cemetery; it has an unusual octagonal, red-brick mortuary chapel with a turret roof <112>. St Matthias's Church to the north of Fiveways was built in 1906-7 by Lacy W.Ridge in Early English style, a red-brick building with a wooden hammer-beam roof, a small spire, and an apsidal chancel. It was consecrated in 1912. <1,45,123>

Ditchling Road then continues over the slopes of Hollingbury (q.v.) to Old Boat Corner, the junction with Carden Avenue and Coldean Lane. Lying about 475 feet above sea-level, this crossroads is named from an upturned boat that was once used as a shepherd's hovel <128>, and lay within a detached part of Falmer parish until 1934; it was then transferred to Stanmer, but was annexed by Brighton in 1952. The old crossroads signpost is now exhibited at Stanmer Rural Museum. The Brighton bypass will run through a cutting underneath Ditchling Road to the south of the crossroads; there will be an interchange with Carden Avenue to the west and an eastbound slip road from Coldean Lane to the east.

The road then leads out of the borough to Ditchling Beacon which, at 813 feet above sea-level, is the highest hill in East Sussex and the fourth highest point on the South Downs; only Butser Hill, Littleton Down and Linch Down are higher. The summit area, which has an Iron Age entrenchment, is owned jointly by the National Trust and Brighton Council which purchased 386 acres of High Park Farm in October 1928. <1,305>

52. DOME and CORN EXCHANGE, Church Street

a) *ROYAL STABLES:* The Dome was originally built as a stable for the Prince of Wales in 1803-8 by William Porden who based his design on the Paris Corn Market. Owing to slow finance and a shortage of materials the building took several years to complete and the contractor, Edward Saunders, died in 1805 heavily in debt because of the delays. Faced in yellow brick, the Indian-style building cost £55,000 together with the adjacent riding school.

The great domed roof, 80 feet in diameter and 65 feet high, was one of the largest in the world at the time and was finished by the end of 1804. The exterior was not finished until April 1808, but the interior was in use by August 1806 and could accommodate forty-four horses with ostlers' and grooms' quarters in the circular galleries. With entrances on four sides, the stable opened out into a courtyard surrounded by coach houses and servants' quarters, a site now occupied by the public library, and thence by a wide archway into Church Street. A frontage was erected along Church Street in front of the courtyard, but a proposed indoor tennis court was never built and in 1832 the space was filled by stables for Queen Adelaide and other buildings now occupied by the museum and art gallery. The west wing housed the riding school, now the Corn Exchange (see below). An underground passage was constructed in about 1822 from the stables to the northern end of the Royal Pavilion.
<45,194>

b) *CONVERSION TO CONCERT HALL:* Following the purchase of the Royal Pavilion estate in 1850, the stables and riding house were let as cavalry barracks from 1856 until about 1864; the name 'Dome' was used officially for the first time in this period. The interior was then reconstructed by Cheesemans Ltd as a concert hall, to the Moorish design of borough surveyor Philip Lockwood, at a cost of £10,000. The Dome reopened on 24 June 1867 as a magnificent assembly hall for some 2,500 people, and was adorned with a beautiful gas chandelier 30 feet high and 16 feet in diameter with 1,300 gas jets. The present Church Street entrance and the eastern portico were added in 1901, but the First

Figure 48: The Royal Pavilion estate in about 1845

World War saw the Dome in use as an Indian Hospital along with the rest of the estate (see "Royal Pavilion"). <45,194>

c) *REFURBISHMENT:* In 1934-5 the Dome interior was redesigned by Robert Atkinson at a cost of £50,000 to give a total of 2,100 seats. An interior ceiling, electric organ and a new balcony were added, while the road by the portico was made and the access road was extended through to New Road. The Dome was reopened by the mayor, Sidney Gibson, on 14 September 1935.

Now a grade I-listed building, the Dome Theatre was the principal concert, conference and entertainment hall of the town until the opening of the Brighton Centre in 1977; it remains important and there are plans for further refurbishment and improvement. Perhaps the most famous event held there was the Eurovision Song Contest, seen by an estimated television audience of some 200 million on 6 April 1974. The U.K. was represented by Olivia Newton-John, but the contest was won by the Swedish group Abba singing 'Waterloo'. <45,123,194>

d) *CORN EXCHANGE:* Built in 1803-8 by William Porden, the Corn Exchange was erected for the Prince of Wales as a riding school, and forms the western wing of the Prince's stables now known as the Dome. The splendid interior measures 178 feet by 58 feet with an unsupported roof 34 feet high, and is now used for exhibitions, receptions and other functions. The exterior is in yellow brick and the building has very large Oriental windows. As part of the original Royal Pavilion estate the Corn Exchange is now a grade I-listed building.

In 1856 the riding school, which was purchased by the town in 1850 as part of the Pavilion estate, was let as a cavalry barracks along with the Dome. It acquired its present name on 1 October 1868 when the corn market was transferred from the King and Queen Inn and was then held every Thursday until the building was given over to a military hospital in December 1914. After the war it became an exhibition and function room, and in 1934 alterations were made by Robert Atkinson at a cost of £34,000; the royal box was removed, and a new entrance was made in Church Street with a large figure of Ceres, the goddess of corn, by James Woodford in a recess above the canopy. The interior, which had been divided at the northern end, was restored to a single grand room with new windows in Church Street similar to the originals.

At the same time the Pavilion Theatre was erected in New Road as a supper room for the Corn Exchange with a kitchen below. It stands on the site of a corporation yard and derelict stabling erected in 1806 for Mrs Fitzherbert, but its oriental façade sadly lacks the style of the original estate. The Pavilion Theatre seats 250 people. <194>

53. DOWNS

a) *BACKGROUND:* The South Downs are a range of chalk hills seventy miles long from Beachy Head to Winchester, reaching 888 feet at Butser Hill, Hampshire, and 837 feet at Littleton Down near Petworth. Sloping gently southwards with a steep scarp to the north, the Downs are up to seven miles wide east of Brighton and represent the southern remnant of a prehistoric ridge that once stretched across the Weald to the North Downs, layers of chalk up to 1,400 feet thick laid over millions of years in some primeval sea. In April 1966 the Sussex Downs were designated a 379-square mile 'Area of Outstanding Natural Beauty', including all the open downland in Brighton except the area between Bevendean, Whitehawk, Ovingdean and Woodingdean; they have also been designated an 'Environmentally Sensitive Area'. The many dry valleys in the hills were cut by surface running water in the last Ice Age when snow and rainfall were higher, and water frozen in the permafrost prevented any further percolation through the chalk; 'sludging' of saturated chalk also played a large part in their formation. These valleys are composed chiefly of 'Head' drift (often known as 'Coombe' deposits), a mixture of eroded chalk sludge and flint with some clay and sands. There are also small outcrops of sand and clay in the district, but most of Brighton stands on the porous bed of chalk that is the Downs and which provides a giant natural reservoir for the town's water supply. <2,123,283a,306>

b) *LAINES:* Until the early nineteenth century the downland surrounding the Old Town of Brighton was used mainly for agricultural purposes and was divided into five 'laines'. Laine, a word of Anglo-Saxon origin meaning 'loan' or 'lease', was the local term for the open arable fields common in medieval agriculture before enclosure, the freeholds of which belonged to several people but which were let in small portions to tenant husbandmen. Each field was divided into 'furlongs' which varied greatly in size and were known either by numbers or by individual names; these were further subdivided into many 'paul-pieces', the basic land unit of about one-eighth of an acre and often rented in groups known as 'yardlands'. The furlongs themselves were separated by paths known as 'leakways'. This feudal system lasted many years longer in Brighton than the surrounding parishes, due mainly to the number of landowners involved and to the town's principal interests in fishing and coastal trading, agriculture playing a lesser role.

The pattern of laines, furlongs and paul-pieces greatly influenced the development of the town in the late-eighteenth and nineteenth centuries as land was usually sold and developed in blocks of paul-pieces. Main through routes such as St James's Street, Edward Street, Eastern Road, Carlton Hill, Sussex Street, Cheapside, Ann Street, York Hill, etc. were developed in a direction away from the central valley and along the leakways between the furlongs as the smaller side streets were built up in the perpendicular paul-pieces. Thus a very regular pattern of streets was established in the laines to the east and west of the central valley. In the West Laine however, land was acquired in larger blocks before being developed and the streets do not follow the same pattern.

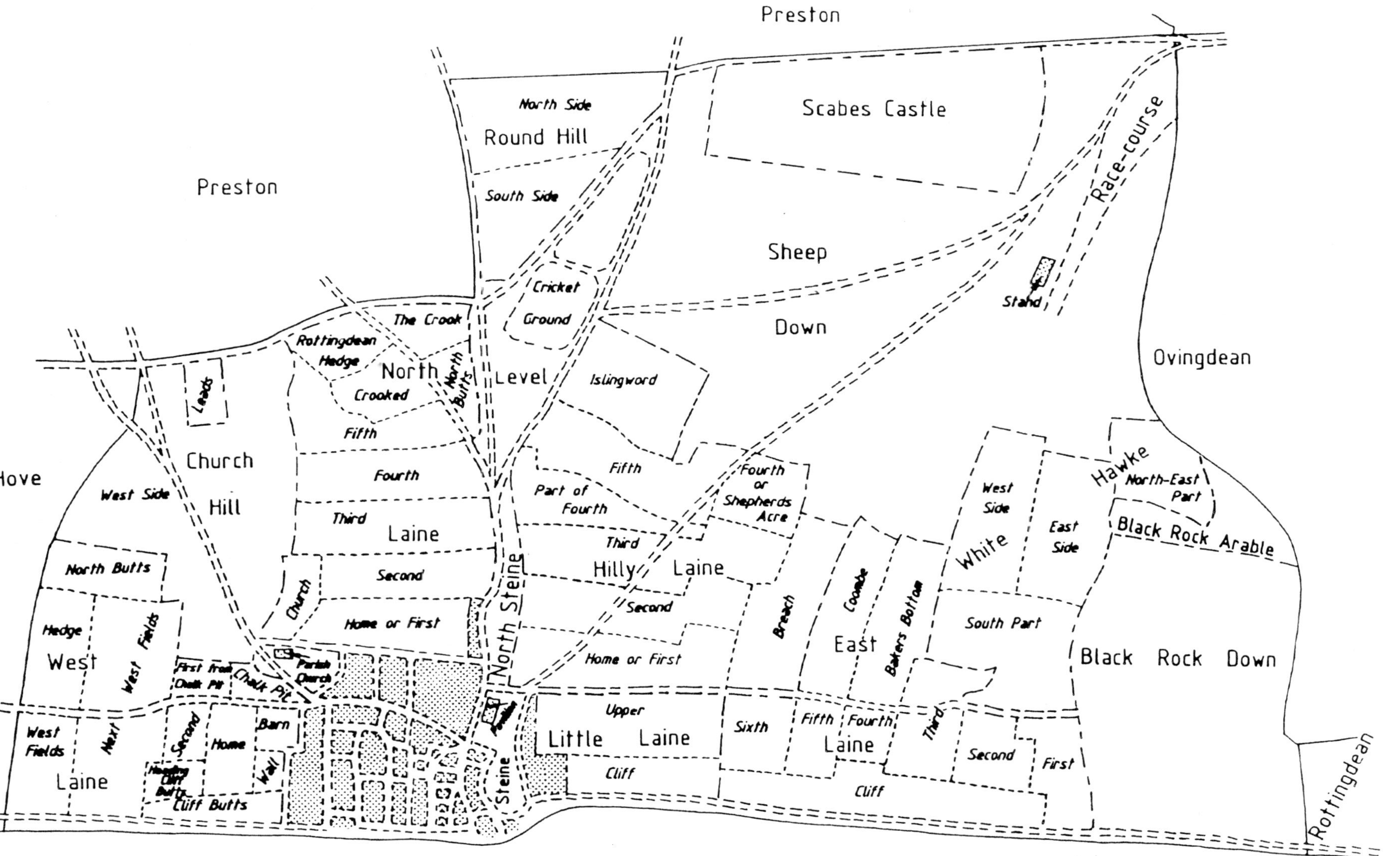

Figure 49: Parish of Brighton in 1792 showing the tenantry laines

There were five laines in the parish of Brighton, viz.: the East, Hilly, Little, North and West Laines. Surrounding parishes also had named laines. Other downland was ploughed up in the period 1739-92 at Scabe's Castle, White Hawke, Round Hill and Black Rock, but most of the rest of the downland was given over to sheep (see below). The name 'North Laine' (q.v.) has been revived for the conservation area which lies between Trafalgar Street and North Street.
<1,2,10,14,18,106>

c) *TENANTRY DOWNLAND:* Until the nineteenth century the pasture rights to most of the downland in the parish of Brighton which was not arable belonged to the several landowners of the laines (see above), but it was leased to tenants as sheep pasture (commemorated by Tenantry Down Road and Tenantry ward). By the 1820s development of the town was rapid and the landowners, who included Thomas Read Kemp, Charles Scrase Dickins, John Wickels and Nathaniel Kemp, agreed in 1822 to divide the remaining downland that had not been cultivated in proportion to their holdings in the laines for easier disposal. <2>

Virtually all the remaining open downland in the borough is now the property of Brighton Council which has made many purchases since the 1890s, and especially in the 1920s and '30s, in order to protect the beautiful downland itself, to safeguard the water supply, and to provide some building land. Large estates at Mile Oak, Devil's Dyke, Saddlescombe, Waterhall, Patcham Court, High Park, Hollingbury, Stanmer, Moulsecoomb, Bevendean, East Brighton and Balsdean have been acquired, and the council now owns some 16,000 acres of land, most of which is let to tenant farmers. (See figure 45.) <305>

d) *HILLS:* The highest hill in the borough of Brighton is Bullock Hill which reaches 645 feet above sea-level to the north-east of Woodingdean, although a point of similar height is reached in the extreme north-west of the borough where the boundary crosses a shoulder of West Hill. Prior to the boundary extension of 1928, Race Hill, by the top of Bear Road, was the highest point at approximately 463 feet. The main hills within the borough, with approximate heights in feet above sea-level, are:

645 Bullock Hill, Woodingdean
584 Hollingbury, Patcham
580 Holt Hill, Patcham
534 Falmer Hill, off Falmer Road
531 near Pudding Bag Wood, Stanmer Park
510 Varncombe Hill, Patcham
509 The Bostle, Woodingdean
503 Heath Hill, Woodingdean
485 Tegdown Hill, Patcham
476 on Ditchling Road south of Old Boat Corner
463 Race Hill, by Bear Road
435 Scare Hill, Patcham
430 in Stanmer Great Wood
430 Red Hill, Westdene
427 Sweet Hill, Patcham
417 Race Hill, by the Race Stands
417 Telscombe Tye, Saltdean
411 at Balsdean Reservoir
410 Ewebottom Hill, Patcham
398 High Hill, Balsdean
396 Whitehawk Hill, Brighton
387 Coney Hill, Westdene
367 Mount Pleasant, Woodingdean
355 on Dyke Road Ave, near Dyke Road Place
352 Red Hill, Roedean
334 Tenant Hill, Saltdean
330 Richmond Hill, Stanmer
304 Cattle Hill, Ovingdean
276 East Hill, Rottingdean Heights
270 Long Hill, Ovingdean
230 Albion Hill, Brighton
223 Round Hill, Brighton
220 Church Hill, Brighton
216 Beacon Hill, Rottingdean
213 near Overhill Way, Patcham

In addition, the following approximate heights are reached on the borough boundary, but are not hill summits:

645 on West Hill, Patcham
545 on Castle Hill, Balsdean
515 west of Saddlescombe Road
512 at Millbank Wood, Stanmer
453 on Swanborough Hill, Balsdean

The highest road in the borough is Laughton Road, Woodingdean, which reaches about 575 feet above sea-level; nos.13-15 are the highest houses in Brighton. Falmer Road is the highest main road, reaching 535 feet north of Bexhill Road, while the highest road outside the Woodingdean area is Ditchling Road which reaches 525 feet at Hollingbury.
<83,109>

54. DUKE OF YORK'S CINEMA, Preston Circus

<68,68a,286>

Formally opened by the mayor, Charles Thomas-Stanford, on 22 September 1910, the 'Duke's' was built on part of the site of the Amber Ale Brewery for Mrs Violet Melnotte-Wyatt, the lessor and later manager of the Duke of York's Theatre in London. Designed by theatre architect C.E.Clayton, the new cinema seated 800 and was considered very luxurious with Wilton carpets, tip-up seats, electric fans and an electric projector. Sound equipment was installed in May 1930, and the whole building was redecorated in June 1937. Following a brief period of wrestling bouts and bingo in the 1970s, the Duke's took over the mantle of the Brighton Film Theatre in 1979 by presenting a varied programme of 'art' and 'cult' films. The building itself, one of the oldest purpose-built cinemas in the country, retains a largely unaltered façade in Edwardian baroque style, but once had two small domes at the corners of the roof. Behind the fire station the cinema may be seen to have incorporated part of the brewery's flint malting.

55. DYKE ROAD

Until the late eighteenth and early nineteenth centuries, when the London Road via Cuckfield route was developed, the Dyke Road was the main route into the town from the north, coach traffic travelling via Henfield and Saddlescombe down the length of Dyke Road to the inns of North Street and Castle Square. From 1777 the road was managed by a turnpike trust.

Dyke Road itself now extends from Western Road to Tivoli Crescent North where it becomes Dyke Road Avenue, but until the early 1950s that part below Upper North Street was a continuation of North Street, while

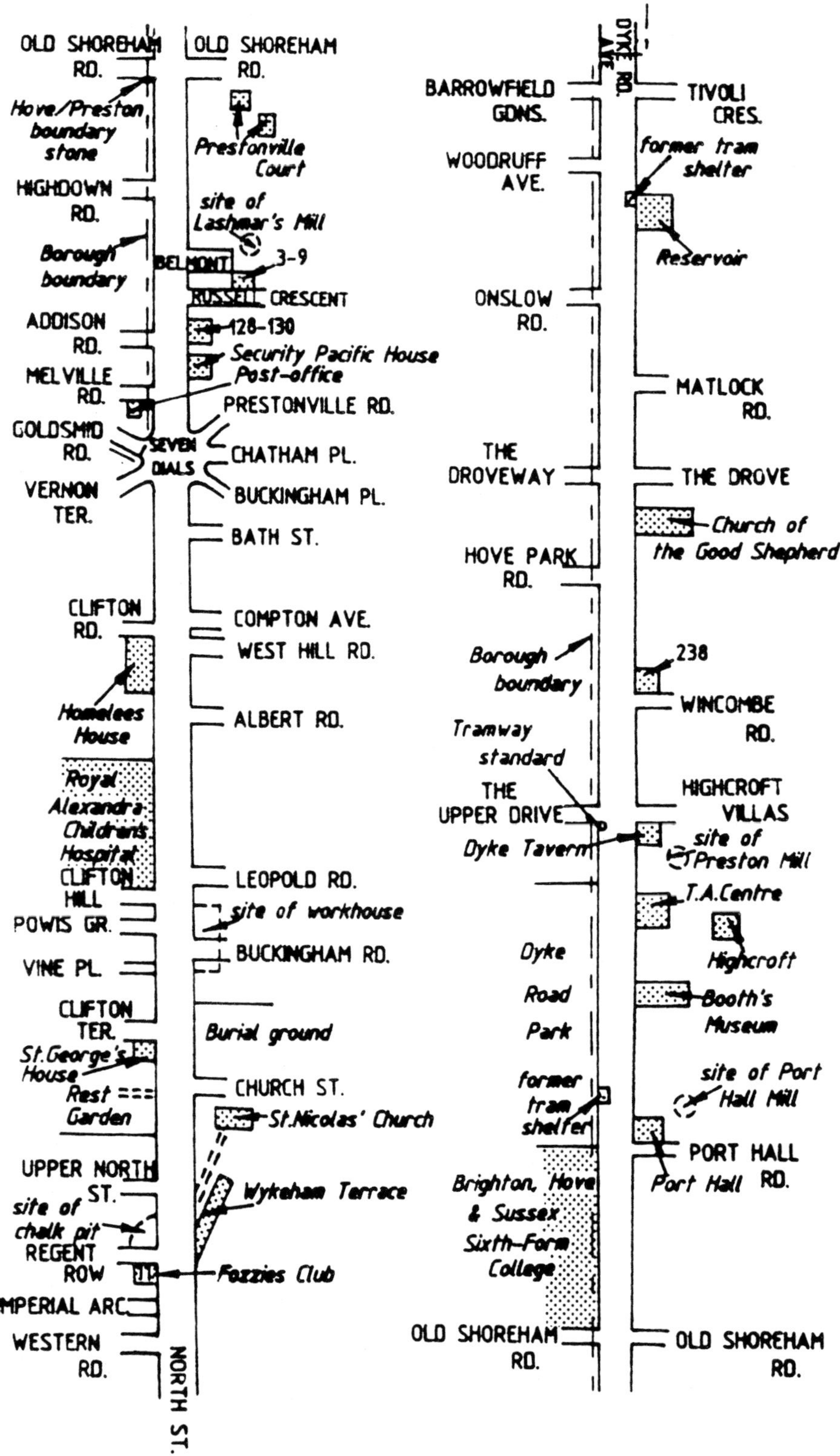

Figure 50: Dyke Road

in earlier times the length south from Seven Dials was known as Church Hill. Since 1873 the borough boundary has run along the western line of walls and fences to the north of Old Shoreham Road, and, since 1928, from Old Shoreham Road to Seven Dials; the section from Russell Crescent to Old Shoreham Road was previously part of the borough of Hove. The boundary then continues along the eastern side of Dyke Road Avenue. <2,33,39,83>

a) *SOUTH of SEVEN DIALS:* Climbing up Dyke Road from Western Road, the first building of note is no.11, Fozzies club. Now a listed building and adorned with an oriel window and foliated capitals, it was built in German Gothic style by George Somers Clarke in 1867 as the Swan Downer School, a charitable school for the education of twenty poor girls founded in 1816 from the bequest of a Brighton merchant. Originally at 12 Gardner Street, the school moved to Windsor Street in 1859 and then to Dyke Road, but closed in 1939. The building has had a variety of uses since, including a chapel and Sloopys discotheque. <44,209>

The lie of the land around no.11 and Regent Row gives a clue to the existence of a large chalk pit from which building materials were extracted in the seventeenth, eighteenth and early nineteenth centuries. The pit, which was partially filled when Upper North Street was constructed in the 1820s, used to have a forge at its entrance and a cave in the chalk face where once lived the eccentric Corporal Staines. To the north is the Dyke Road Rest Garden, the 1841 extension to St Nicholas's churchyard; the adjacent K6-style telephone kiosk is a listed building. See also "St Nicholas's Church". <18,44>

On the opposite side of Dyke Road is Wykeham Terrace, an attractive, listed terrace completed between 1827 and 1830 <108> in Regency Gothic style with dormer windows, projecting bays and unusual diagonal glazing bars. Nos.1-5 and 8-11 formed part of St Mary's Home for prostitutes (see "Queen Square") from the 1850s. The whole block was restored in 1970 having been occupied for some time by squatters, and an excellent model of it may be found in Brighton Museum. No.7 was the home of actress Dame Flora Robson until her death in July 1984. <44,83a,123>

Development along Dyke Road took place throughout the Victorian era, including the large, semi-detached villas erected above Buckingham Road in about 1870 in the grounds of the former workhouse. On the western side the large St George's House, an Italianate villa at the corner of Clifton Terrace, was built in about 1840 as the Norman Villa and was later known as Clifton Lodge. Used as a secretarial college after the Second World War until 1974, it is now used by the county council. The most prominent building was the Dials Congregational Church at the corner of Clifton Road, a Romanesque building of 1871 by Thomas Simpson with a horseshoe-shaped auditorium and a 150-foot Rhenish clock tower which was a considerable landmark across the town. The church was demolished in April 1972 and Homelees House was erected on the vacant site in 1985-6. <44,83,123>

b) *ROYAL ALEXANDRA HOSPITAL for SICK CHILDREN:* The Brighton Hospital for Sick Children was founded at 178 Western Road on 3 August 1868 by Dr R.P.B.Taafe. It expanded into an adjacent building in 1870, but in the same year the hospital moved to the disused Church Hill School in Dyke Road where it was reopened with twenty beds on 14 July 1871 by the Bishop of Chichester. The present hospital building was erected on the site in 1880-1, a three-storey red-brick building which was opened on 21 July 1881 by Princess Alexandra. Decorated with terracotta mouldings, it was designed in Queen Anne style by Thomas Lainson at a cost of £10,500. The girls' ward was named the Taafe Ward in honour of the founder.

The Royal Alexandra has now been enlarged to 114 beds. A two-storey out-patient and isolation ward opened in 1904; the east wing was opened by the Duke and Duchess of York on 30 May 1928; and the Gillespie Wing was opened on 4 December 1945 by Princess Elizabeth, who also attended a concert at the Dome in aid of hospital funds. The Cawthorne Ward was converted in 1966 from the 1896 nurses' home. Since 1954 the patron has been the present Princess Alexandra. <24,98,115>

c) *SEVEN DIALS to OLD SHOREHAM ROAD:* This area was developed initially in the late 1840s and '50s, and a number of interesting buildings remain from that period. Security Pacific House, an office block completed in 1985 in classical style, blends nicely with the adjacent nos.128-130, attractive, mid-nineteenth-century listed houses with iron balconies and verandahs, part of what was once Peel Terrace; no.128 was the home of Magnus Volk from 1914 until his death in 1937 (see figure 180). Just off Dyke Road in Russell Crescent are some more attractive listed villas, nos.3-7, of around 1845; no.7 has a single-storey, five-sided coachman's cottage, no.9. <44>

The six large houses of Belmont, faced in knapped flint, were erected in the 1850s on the site of Lashmar's Windmill, also known as Hove Mill. There was certainly a mill on the site by 1780, and it was replaced once or possibly twice by 1821, but in 1852 or 1853 the mill was removed by sledge to the Downs above Clayton where it still stands, the white, square, post-mill known as 'Jill' with the tower mill known as 'Jack' nearby; the pair are now grade I-listed buildings. Prestonville Court, two eight-storey blocks of flats, were built in 1972 on the site of the former Hove Villa, a large house of about 1840 which was used as a private mental hospital from 1899, and as Prestonville School from 1954. Both Belmont and Hove Villa stood within the borough of Hove until 1928. <44,123,249-253>

d) *OLD SHOREHAM ROAD to HIGHCROFT VILLAS:* The Brighton, Hove and Sussex Sixth Form College ('BHASVIC') was erected in 1913 as a grammar school and has its own entry in this text. The adjacent Dyke Road Park, although situated in Hove since 1928, is owned and managed by Brighton Council which purchased the land, then in Preston Rural parish, in November 1914. The north-western part was initially intended for a hostel for the Municipal Training College, but the whole area of about ten acres was laid out as a park which was opened to the public on 17 September 1924 by the mayor, Hugh Milner Black <126>.

At the corner of Port Hall Road stands Port Hall itself, a small listed house of about 1800. The unusual

Figure 51: Port Hall

building, which was the residence of Sir Page-Dyck in the early nineteenth century when it was quite isolated, has a sham ecclesiastical window with the statuette of a monk, a castellated roof, and the prominent figure of a knight above the doorway; it is said to be haunted by the ghost of a red crusader. Port Hall post-mill stood on Port Hall Mews behind the house and was built by 1795, but it was demolished in 1887. <44,107,108,123,249>

Beyond the Booth Museum of Natural History (see below), the Territorial Army Headquarters has a drill hall erected at the time of the Second World War for the volunteers previously based in Church Street and Gloucester Road. Behind the hall is a large red-brick villa of 1876, Highcroft, which has a south lodge in Dyke Road and a north lodge in Highcroft Villas. <83,306>

Lambourne's Old Mill Works at the top of Highcroft Villas are named from the former Preston Mill which stood on the site. It was originally erected in Belle Vue Field, now Regency Square, as the West Mill, but following complaints from nearby residents it was carried on a sled pulled by thirty-six yoke of oxen on 28 March 1797, an event depicted in a pair of paintings now hanging in Preston Manor. The mill gave Millers Road and the Windmill Inn, now the Dyke Tavern, their names, but it was also known as Streeter's Mill, the Black Mill, and Trusler's Mill. When it was demolished in 1881, parts of the machinery were included in the new Waterhall Mill. <249a>

e) *BOOTH MUSEUM OF NATURAL HISTORY:* This building was erected in a quite isolated position in 1874 by Thomas Booth to house his collection of stuffed British birds displayed in their natural habitats. Following Booth's death in 1890 the collection was offered to the Natural History Museum at South Kensington which declined owing to a lack of space, but his widow then presented the museum and its 308 exhibits to the town in October 1890 on condition that the display cases should not be altered. The museum was formally opened to the public the following year, and the bird collections have since been augmented by several other private collections.

In 1973 Booth's was redesignated a museum of natural history, and the town's zoological, geological and natural history collections were transferred from Church Street; the new galleries were formally opened on 13 February 1976 by Dr Desmond Morris. Booth's Museum now houses the second largest regional natural history collection in the country with 621,000 items, and contains displays of butterflies, moths and other insects; skeletons; reptiles; mammals; geological exhibits; and, of course, Thomas Booth's birds in their original cases. It attracts around 50,000 visitors a year and maintains free admission.

Thomas Booth himself was born at Chalfont St Giles, Buckinghamshire, in 1840 and lived adjacently to his museum in Bleak House, demolished in about 1939 for the erection of Fairways and Elm Court. <83,118-122a,123>

f) *NORTH of HIGHCROFT VILLAS:* No.238 Dyke Road, at the corner of Wincombe Road, has a plaster decoration of the Southern League Championship Shield in its western gable, and a replica of the F.A. Charity Shield in its southern gable, both painted in blue and white. The house was built in about 1910 for Noah Clark, a director of Brighton and Hove Albion F.C. which won both trophies in that year. (See figure 22.) <214>

The Church of the Good Shepherd, built by E.P.Warren in 1920-2, has a prominent tower with additions at the rear of 1927; the foundation stone was laid by Mrs Alice Moor in memory of her late husband Gerald, Vicar of Preston. There is a small war memorial chapel to the north-east of the nave. The adjacent church hall was opened on 15 July 1936 by Major George Tryon, M.P. <45,311>

The road continues northwards from Tivoli Crescent North as Dyke Road Avenue, a road lined with large, late-Victorian and Edwardian villas together with more recent suburban development. Tongdean Farm once stood at the junction of Dyke Road Avenue and Hill Brow, but some old farm cottages remain at The

Spinney. The former Dyke crossroads on Red Hill is now the site of an interchange on the Brighton bypass, the Devil's Dyke Road bridging the new highway which will run through a deep cutting. The road then continues towards Saddlescombe and Devil's Dyke (q.v.). <83,123>

56. EAST CLIFF

Brighton's East Cliff rises to around eighty feet above the sea at Eaton Place on 'Head' or 'Coombe' deposits, an easily eroded chalk rubble mixed with clay and flints. Protected from the 1830s for the whole of its length by a massive sea-wall, the East Cliff presents, in its Marine Parade frontage, a sea-front façade unsurpassed anywhere in Britain. Since 1908 it has also been known as the King's Cliff in honour of Edward VII (q.v.) who had associations with Kemp Town.

Developed from the 1780s until the 1870s, the East Cliff is now an outstanding conservation area and includes also the many roads leading northwards from Marine Parade, delightful streets lined with small-scale lodging houses, and middle-class and artisan housing. It also covers the small streets to the north of St James's Street and the attractive Victorian terraces around College Place and Sudeley Place.

To make an exploration of the area easier, the streets of principal interest leading northwards from Marine Parade are detailed below in topographical order from the Steine eastwards, but see also "Bristol Road", "Marine Parade", "St George's Road" and "St James's Street".

a) *MANCHESTER STREET:* The two listed buildings are no.9, the Star public house which has narrow bows and a good doorway, and no.10, the Golden Girl Restaurant, a three-storey, late-eighteenth-century building with a pair of bows and faced in mathematical tiles. No.17, included on the council's local list, is also faced with mathematical tiles and has a bow. Dolphin Mews was completed in 1985 in Georgian style on the site of the Southdown Coach Station. <44>

b) *CHARLES STREET:* A delightful street of small, late-eighteenth-century cottages. Nos.9-12 are bow-fronted listed buildings, nos.10-11 being faced with mathematical tiles. Nos.20-23, which were saved by the Environment Minister after a public inquiry in December 1968 from demolition by Southdown Motors Ltd, are also faced with the distinctive black glazed tiles and are listed. No.8 has a cobbled façade. <44,123>

c) *BROAD STREET:* Developed in the 1790s by Thomas Howell with small lodging houses. Nos.4, 7, 9, 21, 23, 25 and 26, mostly with bows and fanlight doorways, are included on the council's local list of buildings of special interest. No.14 is faced with black mathematical tiles. <14>

d) *MADEIRA PLACE:* A wide road of attractive, four-storey lodging houses developed from the late 1780s and known as German Place until 1914 after the proprietor's nationality. No.18 is an early-nineteenth-century listed house with mathematical tiles and a bow, while nos.11, 13 and 14 are included on the council's local list; all have narrow bows. Nos.20-23 were restored in 1985 as part of Olivier House. <14,48>

e) *CAMELFORD STREET:* A street lined with attractive, late-eighteenth-century cottages, many faced with mathematical tiles. Nos.8-19 on the western side are listed, with nos.10-12 having narrow bows. On the eastern side nos.33-36 are also listed; no.34 has a bow and cobbled façade, while no.36 has a plaque to George Jacob Holyoake (1817-1906), the social reformer and first president of the Brighton Equitable Co-operative

Figure 52: Mathematical tiles and bows at 20-23 Charles Street

Society who lived in the house from 1881 until his death. A devout socialist, Holyoake founded Secularism, a sect of religious disbelief, and was the last man to be gaoled for atheism, in 1841. <3,44,75>

f) *WENTWORTH STREET:* Formerly a service road for the houses of New Steine. No.8 is an excellent example of a small cottage faced with cream-painted mathematical tiles.

g) *NEW STEINE:* The development of the New Steine in the 1790s led to the original Steine being prefixed 'Old', and its large garden was probably intended to be a similarly fashionable promenade. It is lined with four-storey, balconied houses with bows or angular bays, mostly hotels, but there is no sense of unity despite the use of decorated double doorways. Nos.1, 3, 8, 10-12a, 14, 15, 28, 29 and 31 are listed buildings, mostly with bows; nos.12-14 have fluted Corinthian pilasters. The garden was taken over by the corporation following the 1884 Brighton Improvement Act. Facing the northern side of the New Steine are Devonshire Mansions and New Steine Mansions (originally the New Steine Hotel), which are included on the council's local list of buildings of special interest. These early-nineteenth-century buildings have been drastically refaced, but were once a symmetric pair adorned with Ionic pilasters. <44,126,306>

h) *LOWER ROCK GARDENS:* In 1788 Rock House was erected in a fairly isolated position on the East Cliff and named from a large rock on the beach below now submerged in shingle. In the 1790s it was joined by Rock Buildings, a row of houses stretching northwards, and as the development proceeded a garden was laid out along the middle of the road, thus giving it the name of Rock Gardens. The top of the garden was at a level about six feet lower than St James's Street, but in 1879 the garden was cleared and a gradual slope was introduced. Rock House itself was rebuilt in the 1970s, but some Gothic windows and part of the castellated roof still face eastwards. Most of the remaining houses date from the early nineteenth century and have four storeys with balconies and angular bays. Nos.8-9, with double bow-fronts, are listed buildings while nos.11 and 12 are included on the council's local list. <2,15,123>

j) *ATLINGWORTH STREET:* Named after the former manor of Atlingworth, it is lined with four-storey houses with iron balconies. Nos.1-5 and 17-24 are early-nineteenth-century, bow-fronted listed buildings. No.11 retains a humbler façade of flint cobbles and weather-boarding. <16>

k) *GRAFTON STREET:* Nos.2-4 and 12-13 are early-nineteenth-century listed buildings with narrow bows. The shallow bow-fronted no.14 was probably designed by Charles Barry and is also listed, while nos.6 and 7 are included on the council's local list for their doorways. <44>

l) *WYNDHAM STREET:* On the western side, no.1 was built in 1807 and has a good doorway. The adjacent nos.1a-2, in red brick with a central archway, were built in 1866 as a fire station. Now used as flats and a workshop, they are listed buildings. No.5, set back slightly from the road, is a cobble-fronted cottage with a good doorway and is included on the council's local list, as are nos.7-19 which form an attractive Regency terrace on the eastern side; several are faced with mathematical tiles. Notice the Royal Insurance firemark on no.15. <44>

m) *CHARLOTTE STREET:* Lined with four-storey buildings of about the 1810s with balconies, now mostly hotels and guest houses. Nos.16-17, with wide bow-fronts, and nos.18-20 and 23-24, also with bows, are listed. <44>

n) *MARINE GARDENS:* Formerly a service road for the grand houses of Charlotte Street. No.12 is a good example of an early-nineteenth-century, cobble-fronted house. No.14 was the home of actress Dame Flora Robson in the 1960s and '70s.

p) *BEDFORD STREET:* The eastern side is lined with three- and four-storey houses; the narrow bowed no.17, probably by Wilds and Busby from the 1820s, and no.18 are listed. The road has a number of antique shops. <44>

q) *BURLINGTON STREET:* A road of two- and three-storey houses, some erected in red brick and flint in 1891. The bow-fronted nos.1, 4-7 and 23 are all listed and were probably built by Wilds and Busby in the 1820s <44>. No.25 has a plaque to 'cheeky chappie' comedian Max Miller. Born at 43 Hereford Street in 1895 as Thomas Sargent, Miller joined Billy Smart's Circus and then went solo during the First World War. He lived in this house from 1948 until his death in 1963 <19,123,311>.

On the western side stood St Anne's Church, built in the Decorated style in roughened stone by Benjamin Ferrey for Mrs Maria Cook, in memory of her son Revd James Churchill. Consecrated on 13 June 1863 by the Bishop of Chichester, the interior had a clerestoried nave and chancel with another chapel in the western aisle. The parish was combined with St George's in 1979, and the church was closed in 1983 and demolished in March 1986 to be replaced by sheltered housing, St Anne's Court. The church hall in St George's Road was built in 1912 as a memorial to John Nixon, and is now used as a community centre known as 'Kemptown Pier'. <1,45,65>

r) *CRESCENT PLACE:* Developed in the 1810s and '20s, the eastern side is lined with three-storey houses. Nos.1-2, probably by Wilds and Busby, and nos.11-12 are listed buildings with bows and balconies. <44>

s) *BLOOMSBURY PLACE:* A road of four-storey houses, many with bows and ironwork balconies, developed in the 1810s and '20s. Nos.1-13 and nos.16-31 are listed buildings, nos.16-18 forming the terminal view. <44>

t) *PORTLAND PLACE:* Built on land owned by Major Villeroy Russell in 1824-8, Portland Place was the first development between Royal Crescent and Kemp Town, and allowed a broad vista from the Major's Portland House at the top. Unfortunately this classical mansion was burnt down on 12 September 1825, before it was even completed, but three houses were built on the site in 1847 known as West House, Portland House

Figure 53: Portland Place. The large mansion at the top was destroyed before completion.

and Portland Lodge, nos.12-14 Portland Place although they stood on the northern side of St George's Road. All three were later merged into one, West House, which was acquired at the end of the First World War by the St Dunstan's Institute (q.v.) and later renamed Pearson House. A listed building, it was rebuilt in 1971 with the façade preserved.

The two elegant terraces of Portland Place are symmetric compositions by Charles Busby, his last work in Brighton. All the houses are listed and every third one has Corinthian pilasters; some remain unstuccoed in yellow brick, and all have balconies. <44,46,123>

u) *PASTON PLACE:* No.1 Paston Place was the home of the novelist William Black (1841-98) from 1879 until his death. At the corner with St George's Road stands the Bombay Bar, a low, square, listed building with oriental details and a pagoda roof. It was built in 1892 as a mausoleum for Sir Albert Sassoon, who lived at 1 Eastern Terrace and was buried in this building in 1896, to be followed by his son Sir Edward in 1912. Their remains were removed to London by the grandson, Sir Philip, when he sold it in 1933. During the war the building was used as an air-raid shelter, and it became part of the adjacent Hanbury Arms public house in 1953. <3,44,45>

At the corner of Sudeley Street is a two-storey building with Doric pilasters and large pediment. It was erected in 1864 by Frederick Mahomed, the second son of Sake Dene Mahomed, as the Royal Gymnasium and fencing rooms, these having been removed from what is now the Waggon and Horses public house in Church Street. Now used as an office, it became St George's Church Hall in 1889, but the gymnastic fittings remained in situ until 1962. <268>

v) *BELGRAVE PLACE:* The first development on the land conveyed by Thomas Read Kemp to Thomas Cubitt, who was connected with Belgrave Square in London, in lieu of payment for work on the Kemp Town estate. Belgrave Place has the date of construction, 1846, in the pediment above the centre-piece, no.9. All the houses are listed and have either three or four storeys with iron balconies. <44,46>

w) *EATON PLACE:* Started in about 1846 by Thomas Cubitt on his own land, and completed by about 1855. The lower part is lined with impressive, four-storey houses with wide bows and iron balconies, all listed buildings. <44,46>

x) *CHESHAM PLACE:* A wide road of four-storey houses with ironwork balconies, initially called Lyall Street. Nos.1-6 are late-Regency-style listed houses of the 1850s with wide bow fronts. <44,46,83>

y) *CHICHESTER PLACE:* Nos.23, 25, 27 and 29 are listed buildings, built in late-Regency style by Thomas Cubitt in the late 1840s; nos.23 and 25 have wide bow fronts. Three adjacent houses were destroyed by a bomb in the war and have been replaced by the flats of Chichester Close. St Mary's Square is a development of 1989 in a Regency pastiche, built on a playing field of St Mary's Hall. Another new development along the south-eastern side of the road is known as Cubitt Terrace after the well-known builder of many houses in the Kemp Town area. <44,46,242,243,244>

57. EAST STREET

Forming the eastern limit of the built-up area until the late eighteenth century, East Street was possibly developed from the fourteenth century as the town spread onto the cliff top. By the mid eighteenth century it was the most densely populated part of Brighton, and had a gateway, the East Gate, which led down into Pool Valley; this was removed for the construction of the battery in 1760. Further growth was stimulated by the opening of the Castle Inn in 1755, causing infilling of spaces on both sides of the road, and by the turn of the nineteenth century, East Street was a commercial thoroughfare servicing the large houses of the Steine. Formerly known as Great East Street, the roadway continued past the Prince of Wales's Marine Pavilion as far as Church Street to form the principal approach to Brighton from Lewes, but that part to the north of Castle Square was closed in 1805 at the Prince's request when New Road was constructed. Still one of the principal shopping streets of the town, and one of the more select, East Street retains several interesting buildings, although many on the eastern side were rebuilt in the 1880s. On 5 March 1990 cars were prohibited in East Street between Steine Lane and Avenue; the attractive pedestrianisation was formally inaugurated on 28 April 1990. <10,14,123>

In front of the Sussex Tavern the street widens out to form an area which it has been suggested was once a wharf alongside a small inlet from the sea; there is no evidence for this, but the area is surrounded by a group of attractive listed buildings, nos.26-31 and 33-36, which date from the late eighteenth or early nineteenth centuries. The Sussex itself has a bow window on the western (Market Street) façade while the East Street frontage has one more floor and a wide bow. Known as the Spread Eagle until 1816, it is said to have been used by smugglers. No.36, Al Forno Restaurant, is a three-storey house of the late eighteenth century, with a cobbled front and bow window, which was the home of the famous bathing woman Martha Gunn. <15,16,44>

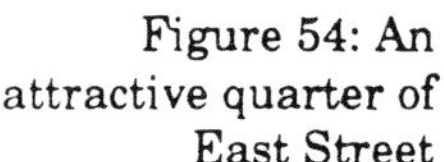

Figure 54: An attractive quarter of East Street

The bow-fronted nos.15 and 22-23 are included on the council's local list of buildings of special interest; nos.16-19, Libertys store, are facsimiles rebuilt in 1989 and won a council planning award. Other interesting buildings include the cobble-fronted nos.5-6; nos.8 and 12, faced with mathematical tiles; Hanningtons store of 1883, with a bridge to the North Street building constructed in 1989; the tall, decorated no.63 (The Reject Shop) of 1888; and no.68, which has fluted Corinthian columns and pilasters.

The Greyhound is an attractive building at the corner of Pool Valley with first-floor bow windows. The original inn probably dated from at least 1658 when it was the Blue Anchor, but it was known as the Greyhound by the end of the eighteenth century <15>. At the end of the road is the former Restoration public house and the elegant Clarendon Mansions, formerly the Clarendon Hotel. Built in 1870 by Charles Brill on the site of his domed baths (originally Lamprell's), the building is listed and has a scrolled doorway, but the balconettes have been removed in its current state of disrepair <26>.

Between Pool Valley and the sea-front once stood the Rising Sun, one of several inns demolished for the erection of Brill's new bathing establishment in the late 1860s. It was reputedly haunted by 'Old Strike-a-Light', a seven-foot high figure with a black cloak, conical white hat, and flint lighter which would illuminate the whole building with its spectral glow. In the sixteenth century a Brighton fisherman, Swan Jervoise, investigated the light and was literally frightened to death by the apparition. However, before he passed away, Jervoise was able to relate to Father Anselm of St Bartholomew's Chapel how the apparition had pointed to the hearth of the inn. The monk found some treasure under the floor which was quickly conveyed to the mother priory at Lewes, and also some human bones which were reburied in the churchyard; Old Strike-a-Light was then never seen again. <6,15,89,91>

See also "Cannon Cinema" and "Queen's Hotel".

58. EASTERN ROAD

(See figures 55 and 56.)

Originally a trackway leading to Black Rock, Eastern Road developed into a main road to Kemp Town, and in the mid nineteenth century came to be lined with a number of important institutions together with some large villas and small but elegant terraces. The two surviving villas are Walpole Lodge, now Brighton College Junior School, and Fair Lee, now 17-19 Abbey Road and once the home of Henry Abbey, the mayor of 1875. Belle Vue Court was erected in Belle Vue Gardens in about 1968 on the site of the early-nineteenth-century Belle Vue Hall, once the home of William Percival Boxall, the developer of Percival Terrace; the Hall's flint garden wall still remains, as does the gardener's cottage behind 22 Walpole Road. <83,123>

In the 1960s it was planned to construct a dual carriageway along the line of Eastern Road as far as Chichester Place, before diverting along Bristol Gardens to Roedean Road; only the western part was ever completed, in 1971, but both sides of the road from Park Street to Sutherland Road have been cleared and partially rebuilt. Redevelopment of the slum housing around the Eastern Road and Upper Bedford Street areas started in 1926-8 with the rebuilding of Hereford Street, and continued into the 1930s before being halted by the war; the area was severely damaged in war-time air-raids. Clearances recommenced in the mid 1950s however, and were completed in the late '60s and early '70s with the erection of five council 'tower blocks'. Still standing is the extended Stag public house, and, between Montague Street and St George's Terrace, the former Pelham Institute, now used as a warehouse and by the Mid-Sussex Judo Club. Built in 1877 on the site of the 1829 Zion Chapel, it provided cheap accommodation, refreshment and recreational facilities for the working people of the eastern town. There was a large hall where services, lectures and concerts were held, but the institute closed in about 1959. <24,62,83,123,124>

The church serving this poor area was All Souls', designed in plain classical style by Messrs Mew on the Eastern Road site now occupied by the Miles Court Church Army home. It was the first of several churches to be erected for Revd Henry Wagner, who laid the foundation stone on 29 July 1833, and was consecrated by the Bishop of Chichester on 4 April 1834. It was hemmed in on three sides by houses and had a clock tower over the western entrance; the interior had galleries on three sides supported on thin columns, and nearly all the 1,000 sittings were free. All Souls' was enlarged and gothicised in 1858, and again in 1879 by Edmund Scott; it became a parish church in 1883 and had stained glass added by Charles Kempe in 1903 and 1906. In 1967 the parish was merged with St Mary and St James, and the building was demolished the following January. In connection with the church, the Countess de Noailles provided a workmen's library and lecture room at 43 Essex Street in 1856 with room for 500 to 600 persons. <45,65,83>

a) *INSTITUTIONS:* The Female Orphan Asylum was founded in Western Road in 1822 by Francois de Rosaz, and later moved to the top of Gloucester Street where it now meets Sydney Street. In 1853 a new building was erected in Eastern Road which was used until 1936; no.2 Bristol Gate, Rosaz House, was then used as the Brighton and Hove Girls Orphanage, and is still used as a holiday home for deprived and handicapped children, although it is scheduled to close. The former asylum building still stands in Eastern Road however, and is now the Latilla Building of the Royal Sussex County Hospital. <6,24,83,123>

The Blind Asylum originally opened at St James's Sunday school-room in October 1839, but moved to the Central National Schools in 1842. A new Blind School in Eastern Road, designed by George Somers Clarke, was opened on 22 October 1861, a four-storey, red-brick building in Venetian Gothic style. It closed in about 1952, but was needlessly demolished in 1958; the Royal Sussex County Hospital's Charles Hunnisett Building now stands on the site. <6,24,123>

The Deaf and Dumb School was established in 1840, also at St James's Sunday school-room. It moved to 12 Egremont Place in 1842, and to a new building built and designed by Cheesemans in Eastern Road in 1848, with a new wing added in 1854. From 1945 the building was used by Brighton College Junior School until it was demolished in 1971, initially for road widening but later replaced by Danny Sheldon House. <6,24,123,204>

See also "Brighton College", "Kemp Town", "Royal Sussex County Hospital" and "St Mary's Hall".

59. King EDWARD VII

<3,48,115,261>

The young Prince Edward first visited Brighton with his parents, Victoria and Albert, in 1842, aged less than one year. Edward came to the town many more times as Prince of Wales, and after he had succeeded his mother on 22 January 1901 at the age of fifty-nine, he convalesced in Brighton on several occasions in an attempt to improve his health; he suffered from bronchitis. He stayed with his daughter, Princess Louise, at her house, 1 Lewes Crescent, for a week in February 1908 and was afforded exclusive use of the Kemp Town enclosures. He was also a friend of the Sassoon family, and often stayed with Arthur Sassoon at 8 King's Gardens, Hove.

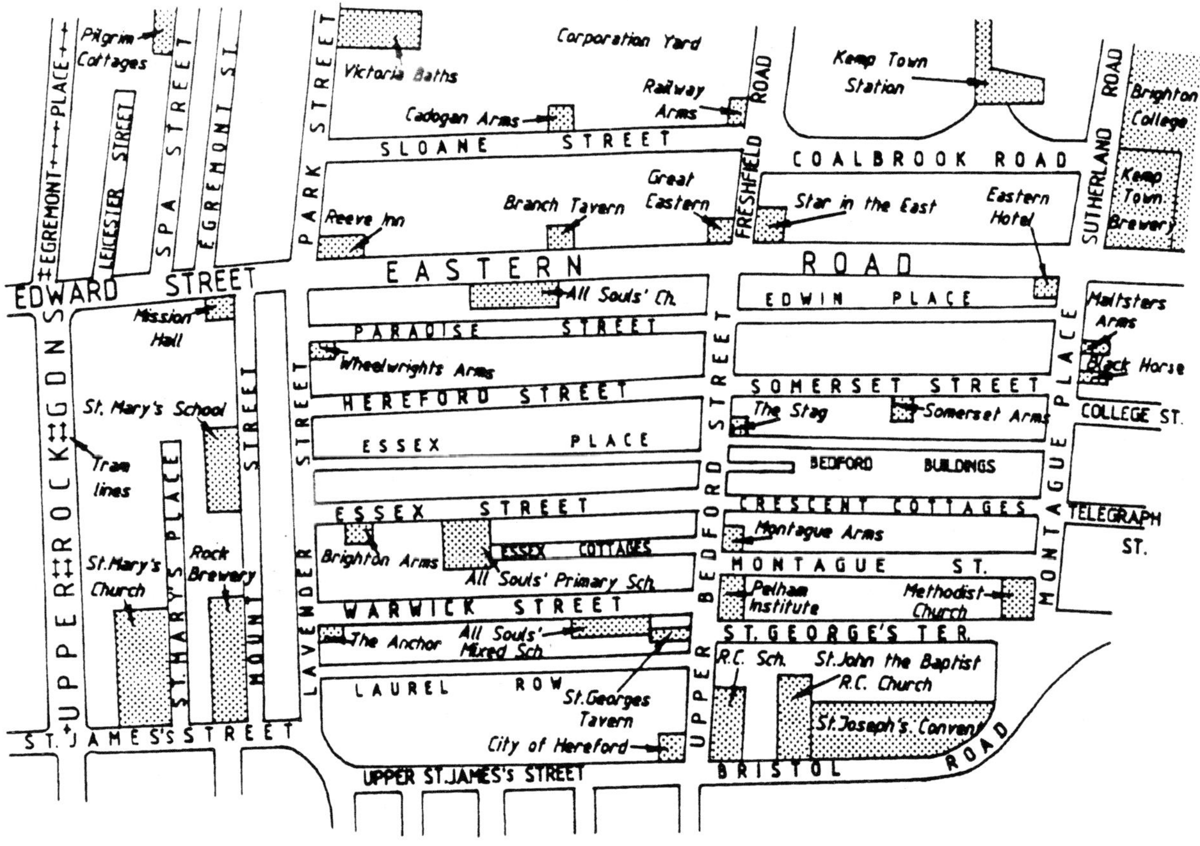

Figure 55: Eastern Road and Upper Bedford Street area before redevelopment

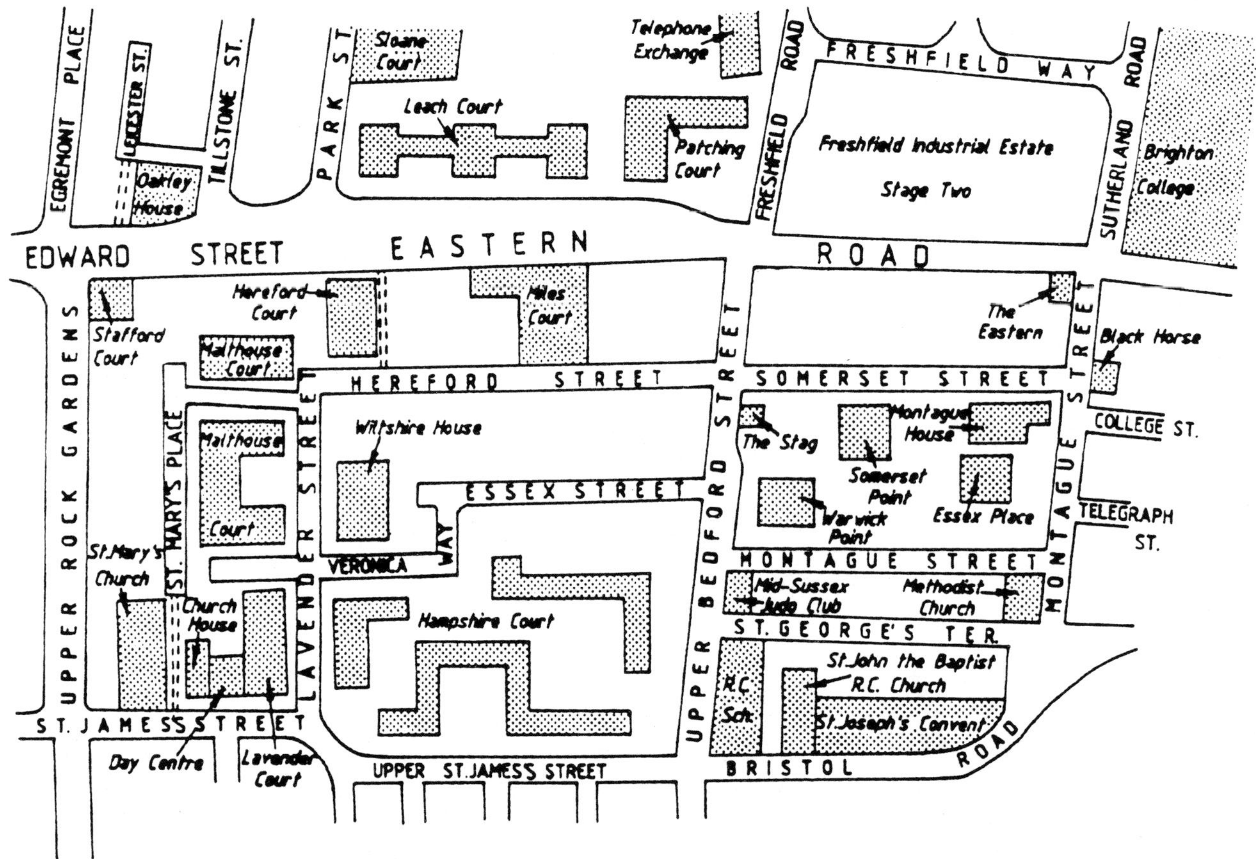

Figure 56: Eastern Road and Upper Bedford Street area now

The return of the sovereign to Brighton after some sixty years helped to re-establish Brighton's fashionable reputation and winter society season, and brought about a general revival in the town's fortunes. In 1908, in honour of the King, the corporation renamed the Kemp Town ward (and also tried, unsuccessfully, to rename the whole area) 'King's Cliff', and also appended that title to Marine Parade. The Peace Statue on the Hove boundary is also a memorial to King Edward VII (see "King's Road"), while Hove renamed its coast road 'Kingsway'.

60. EDWARD STREET

See also figures 1 and 2.

Stretching from Pavilion Parade to Park Street, Edward Street was once very narrow, only twenty-five-feet wide in places, and lined both sides with shops; indeed, Edward Street and St James's Street were the two principal shopping streets of the eastern town. Serving the area of poor housing to the north, it was a tough district where the police were said to patrol in pairs only. Several of the roads leading northwards were badly affected by war-time bombing. However, the face of Edward Street was completely altered by large-scale clearances in the 1950s together with road widening in 1961-4, resulting in a completely rebuilt northern side with only a few old houses remaining on the southern side around Chapel Street, Devonshire Place and below George Street. The road was widened beyond Upper Rock Gardens to Park Street (and, as Eastern Road, to Freshfield Road) in 1971; the dual carriageway was once intended to stretch all the way to Black Rock.

Edward Street is now dominated by Amex House, a nine-storey, 300,000 square foot office block in a tiered design by the Gollins Melvin Ward Partnership which has been nicknamed 'the wedding cake'. Costing a reported £10 million, the tiers are highlighted in white reinforced plastic while the windows have a blue tint to create a pleasing impression. Built over part of Mighell Street, it was officially opened on 15 September 1977 as the European operations centre of the American Express Corporation, Brighton's largest private-sector employer, and houses some 1,800 workers. The adjacent Windsor House of the Department of Social Security was opened in 1973.

The town's new law courts were opened on 3 November 1967 by Lord Gardiner, the Lord Chancellor. Designed by Percy Billington, the building cost £665,000 and was remodelled in 1986-9 to include three crown courts and eight magistrate courts, plus juvenile and coroner's courts. On 23 October 1985 a new high court and county court building was opened adjacently in William Street. <123> (See also "Courts".)

No.1 Edward Street is an office block of 1990 with a pleasant, bay-windowed design.

Clearances of some of the slum housing to the north of Edward Street were made in the 1890s when Blaker Street and White Street were erected on the site of Chesterfield Street, Cumberland Place, Derby Place and Thomas Street; the new roads contain good red-brick housing designed by borough surveyor Francis May, but the houses were erected privately <115.306>.

The nearby Brighton National Spiritualist Church was built in 1964-5 in an unusual figure-of-eight design by Overton and Partners, replacing a church in Mighell Street <83.123>. To the east is the Brighton Youth Centre, formerly the Brighton Boys' Club which was founded in John Street in 1917. It later moved to 14-16 Manchester Street, but on 23 March 1927 a new building was opened by the Prince of Wales in the remodelled Tierney cinema in Edward Street. On 29 October 1930, the Duke of York opened a Boys' Club Week there, and it was visited in 1938 by the Duke of Gloucester, president of the National Association of Boys' Clubs. The present building was opened in a new position on 28 October 1957 to allow for road widening. The Tierney Royal Picture Theatre itself opened in 1911 on the site of the Tierney Arms, and was known briefly as the Pictured-rome in 1916, the Majestic in 1919 and the Devonshire in 1920 before closing in 1922 <19,48a,68,68a,76,115,275a>.

On the opposite side of Edward Street, at the corner of Dorset Place, is the former Little Globe public house. Lower down stands the Thurlow Arms, an early-nineteenth-century listed building with two first-floor bows and mathematical tiles. Steine Gardens retains a few late-eighteenth-century cottages, while at the very foot of the street may be seen the premises of the Brighton Charity Organisation Society, formed in 1872 to 'improve the condition of the poor, to administer relief, and to suppress begging'; the name may still be made out on the plain wall on the southern side of the street near the traffic lights. <83>

61. ELECTIONS - Parliamentary

Until 1832, Brighton was represented only by the two Members of Parliament elected for the whole of the county of Sussex, but in that year the Representation of the People Act (the 'Great Reform Act') created the Parliamentary Borough of Brighton, entitled to send its own two Members to Westminster. The new borough consisted of the parishes of Brighton and Hove, and had a population of about 41,000 although only 1,649 were eligible to vote at the 1832 general election. Preston was added in 1868, and Aldrington in 1918 when Preston Rural (that part of Preston to the west of Dyke Road) was removed.

The parliamentary borough remained unaltered even though municipal boundaries were greatly extended in 1928; the peak electorate was reached at the general election of 14 November 1935 when 129,356 voters were registered. In 1949 the whole county borough was

Figure 57: Hustings at the Town Hall for the 1841 general election

divided into two borough constituencies, Kemptown and Pavilion each returning one Member, and Hove became a separate constituency; Stanmer was added to Pavilion constituency by 1955. The Round Hill area, together with Preston Barracks and the Parkway, Coldean, was transferred from Kemptown to Pavilion prior to the election of 1983, such that the dividing line now runs along the eastern side of Old Steine, Grand Parade and Lewes Road (see figure 44). <1,109>

There have been forty general elections and seventeen by-elections in the period from 1832 until 1987, although nine of the by-elections were uncontested. The highest majority ever achieved at a British parliamentary election was 62,253 by Sir Cooper Rawson (Conservative) over his nearest opponent on 27 October 1931 <299>. The longest serving M.P. was Captain George Tryon (Conservative) for thirty years from 1910 until 1940. Having been defeated in 1906, he won nine elections, also the most. The shortest serving was David Smith (Conservative), who won the seat at the general election of 25 November 1885 but died after eleven months. Only Isaac Wigney (Liberal), elected in 1832 and 1841, but defeated in 1837, has ever regained his seat.

Brighton's representatives were mostly Liberal until the 1880s, but have been virtually all Conservative since. In 1905 a Liberal won a sensational by-election victory, a success that was repeated in the 1906 general election, and in 1964 Dennis Hobden took Kemptown, the only Sussex seat ever won by Labour; having proved victorious by just seven votes after seven recounts, Hobden held the seat in 1966 but lost it in 1970.

The successful Brighton candidates 1832-1987 have been <298>:

(Note: Con.-Conservative, Lib.-Liberal, Lab.-Labour.)

11-12 December 1832: Isaac Wigney (Lib.)
George Faithfull (Lib.)

8-9 January 1835: Capt. George Pechell (Lib.)
Isaac Wigney (Lib.)

25 August 1837: Capt. George Pechell (Lib.)
Sir Adolphus Dalrymple (Con.)

1 July 1841: Capt. George Pechell (Lib.)
Isaac Wigney (Lib.)

(By-election on resignation of Wigney)

5 May 1842: Lord Alfred Hervey (Lib.-Con.)

30 July 1847: Sir George Pechell (Lib.)
Lord Alfred Hervey (Lib.-Con.)

8 July 1852: Sir George Pechell (Lib.)
Lord Alfred Hervey (Lib.-Con.)

(By-election on appointment of Lord Hervey as Lord of Treasury)

4 January 1853: Lord Alfred Hervey (Lib.-Con.) returned unopposed

28 March 1857: Sir George Pechell (Lib.)
William Coningham(Lib.)

30 April 1859: Sir George Pechell (Lib.)
William Coningham (Lib.)

(By-election on death of Pechell)

16 July 1860: James White (Lib.)

(By-election on resignation of Coningham)

16 February 1864: Henry Moore (Lib.-Con.)

13 July 1865: James White (Lib.)
Henry Fawcett (Lib.)

18 November 1868: Henry Fawcett (Lib.)
James White (Lib.)

5 February 1874: James Ashbury (Lib.-Con.)
Major-General Charles Shute (Con.)

3 April 1880: John Hollond (Lib.)
William Marriott (Lib.)

(By-election on resignation of Marriott)

1 March 1884: William Marriott (Con.)

(By-election on appointment of Marriott as Judge Advocate-General)

10 July 1885: William Marriott (Con.) returned unopposed
25 November 1885: Rt Hon. William Marriott (Con.)
David Smith (Con.)
3 July 1886: David Smith (Con.)
Rt Hon. William Marriott (Con.)

(By-election on appointment of Marriott as Judge Advocate-General)

11 August 1886: Rt Hon. William Marriott (Con.) returned unopposed

(By-election on death of Smith)

29 November 1886: William Robertson (Con.) returned unopposed

(By-election on death of Robertson)

25 October 1889: Gerald Loder (Con.)
6 July 1892: Gerald Loder (Con.)
Sir William Marriott (Con.)

(By-election on resignation of Marriott)

14 December 1893: Bruce Wentworth (Con.) returned unopposed
16 July 1895: Gerald Loder (Con.)
Bruce Wentworth (Con.)
3 October 1900: Gerald Loder (Con.)
Bruce Wentworth (Con.)

(By-election on appointment of Loder as Lord of Treasury)

5 April 1905: Ernest Villiers (Lib.)
16 January 1906: Ernest Villiers (Lib.)
Edward Ridsdale (Lib.)
18 January 1910: Capt.George Tryon (Con.)
Hon. Walter Rice (Con.)
6 December 1910: Capt.George Tryon (Con.)
Hon. Walter Rice (Con.)

(By-election on elevation of Rice to peerage)

26 June 1911: Hon. John Gordon (Con.) returned unopposed

(By-election on resignation of Gordon)

29 June 1914: Charles Thomas-Stanford (Con.) returned unopposed
14 December 1918: Capt. George Tryon (Con.)
Charles Thomas-Stanford (Con.)
15 November 1922: Rt Hon. George Tryon (Con.)
Cooper Rawson (Con.)
6 December 1923: Rt Hon. George Tryon (Con.)
Cooper Rawson (Con.)
29 October 1924: Rt Hon. George Tryon (Con.)
Cooper Rawson (Con.)
30 May 1929: Sir Cooper Rawson (Con.)
Rt Hon. George Tryon (Con.)
27 October 1931: Sir Cooper Rawson (Con.)
Rt Hon. George Tryon (Con.)
14 November 1935: Rt Hon. George Tryon (Con.)
Sir Cooper Rawson (Con.)

(By-election on elevation of Tryon to peerage)

9 May 1940: Lord James Erskine (Con.) returned unopposed

(By-election on resignation of Lord Erskine)

15 November 1941: Anthony Marlowe (Con.) returned unopposed

(By-election on resignation of Rawson)

3 February 1944: William Teeling (Con.)
5 August 1945: William Teeling (Con.)
Anthony Marlowe (Con.)

The results in the two single-member constituencies (K - Kemptown, P - Pavilion) have been:

23 February 1950: K - Howard Johnson (Con.)
P - William Teeling (Con.)
25 October 1951: K - Howard Johnson (Con.)
P - William Teeling (Con.)
26 May 1955: K - Howard Johnson (Con.)
P - William Teeling (Con.)
8 October 1959: K - David James (Con.)
P - William Teeling (Con.)
15 October 1964: K - Dennis Hobden (Lab.)
P - Sir William Teeling (Con.)
31 March 1966: K -Dennis Hobden (Lab.)
P - Sir William Teeling (Con.)

(By-election on resignation of Teeling)

27 March 1969: P - Rt Hon. Julian Amery (Con.)
18 June 1970: K - Andrew Bowden (Con.)
P - Rt Hon. Julian Amery (Con.)
28 February 1974: K - Andrew Bowden (Con.)
P - Rt Hon. Julian Amery (Con.)
10 October 1974: K - Andrew Bowden (Con.)
P - Rt Hon. Julian Amery (Con.)
3 May 1979: K - Andrew Bowden (Con.)
P - Rt Hon. Julian Amery (Con.)
9 June 1983: K - Andrew Bowden (Con.)
P - Rt Hon. Julian Amery (Con.)
11 June 1987: K - Andrew Bowden (Con.)
P - Rt Hon. Julian Amery (Con.)

62. ELECTRICITY SUPPLY

<115,123,153,154,155>

a) *The HAMMOND COMPANY:* In 1881 Robert Hammond demonstrated the brush arc-lighting system in the town, and was employed by shopkeepers to light their premises along a 1.75 mile ring in Queen's Road and Western Road. The Hammond Electric Light and Power Company started supplying power on 21 January 1882 with sixteen arc-lamps in the series circuit at 800 volts d.c.; a permanent system was inaugurated on 27 February 1882. The generator, which was sited at the Regent Iron Foundry in North Road (a site now occupied by the Post Office sorting office), was initially regulated by a boy operating a variable shunt resistance, but it soon changed to automatic operation. It was in the charge of Arthur Wright, who designed the first supply meter in 1884. With an unbroken supply since January 1882, Brighton can probably claim the oldest continuous public electricity supply in the world.

b) *BRIGHTON ELECTRIC LIGHT COMPANY:* In January 1885, Hammond sold out to the newly formed Brighton Electric Light Company. As demand grew, a new power-house was erected in the Regent Foundry yard with three generators which, by 1886, were supplying 1,000 lamps on an eight-mile circuit. The new company became the Brighton and Hove Electric Light Company in 1888, and then established a continuous supply at 100 volts a.c., transformed locally from a 2,000 volt distribution.

c) *CORPORATION SUPPLY and NORTH ROAD:* In 1883 Brighton Corporation was sanctioned to supply the Old Town, but no action was taken until 1890 when, prompted by the Electric Light Company's expansion plans, the corporation built a power station in North Road almost opposite the foundry. Opened on 14 September 1891 by the mayoress, Mrs Soper, it produced a supply of 115 volts d.c. The municipal system was extended in 1893 when a three-wire 115 and 230 volt system was introduced. In April 1894 the corporation acquired the rival Electric Light Company and appointed Arthur Wright as engineer-in-charge. A rapid increase in demand led to further extensions at North Road, and by 1904 there were fifteen generating units with supplies at 115, 230, 460 and 550 volts, a total capacity of 5.935 MW. (A d.c. supply was in fact retained until 14 September 1965 and was latterly used by the Post Office Sorting Office and Telephone Exchange <123>.)

The North Road building, which stood to the east of Spring Gardens, had a red-brick façade with the borough arms in a pediment, but was demolished in September 1986 to be replaced by the Y.M.C.A.'s William Collier House.

d) *SOUTHWICK POWER STATION:* It was soon obvious that a larger station was required to meet future demand, and in May 1902 construction of the Southwick power station was begun. Opened on 16 June 1906 by R.Burns, President of the Local Government Board, at a cost of £350,000, Southwick initially operated with three turbines producing 4.895 MW; another was added in 1907, and, as capacity increased, North Road was run down and ceased generating in 1908 to become the principal substation for the town. In 1911 a single generator of 5.25 MW was installed at Southwick, and a large plant extension opened in September 1924. In 1924 also, large substations were opened at Roedean Road, Hollingdean Road and behind the Rookery in Preston Road, all of which still stand. Southwick was connected to the new national grid in 1926 when the supply was made standard, and had further plant extensions in the following years. The corporation's first collier, the *Arthur Wright*, made its maiden voyage in 1936, and was soon followed by the *Henry Moon* which was sunk in the war. By 1946 Southwick's capacity had increased to 190 MW.

e) *ELECTRIC HOUSE, Castle Square:* New offices and showrooms for the corporation's undertaking, which covered the parishes of Falmer, Hangleton, Portslade-by-Sea, Southwick, Telscombe and West Blatchington in addition to the county borough, were opened in Castle Square on 20 January 1933 by Sir John Reeve Brooker. Known as Electric House, the building is decorated with the borough arms and regularly hosted exhibitions of the latest electrical appliances. Electric House was later used by the South-Eastern Electricity Board, and since 1989 has been the Royal Bank of Scotland.

f) *NATIONALISATION and BRIGHTON 'B':* In 1946 the C.E.G.B. authorised the corporation to construct a second power station at Southwick. The first pile was driven on 25 November 1947, but the corporation's undertaking was transferred to the South-Eastern Electricity Board on 1 April 1948 when electricity supplies were nationalised. The new station, known as Brighton 'B', opened in 1952 in a massive building with 360-foot chimneys to the west of Brighton 'A', the older Southwick station. In March 1969 however, the aging 'A' station was run down with a partial plant closure, and with a further closure in July 1973, generation ceased completely on 15 March 1976; the building was demolished in May 1980. By June 1987 Brighton 'B' itself had also come to the end of its useful life and had ceased production. The eastern chimney was blown up before a large crowd on 16 July 1988 at the start of the demolition of the building.

63. ELM GROVE

The main road from the town to the race-course was given its name in 1852 when it was planted with trees, many of which were uprooted in the storm of October 1987; it increased in importance with the opening of the new workhouse in 1867, now the General Hospital (q.v.). The lower part of Elm Grove was developed principally around 1860 and the higher part in the 1880s, while the small roads leading northwards, in one of the mostly densely populated parts of the town, were built in the 1860s and '70s around Franklin Road, and in the 1880s, '90s and 1900s around Hartington Road and east of Bonchurch Road. Wellington Road, however, was developed in the mid 1850s with several large villa residences. Only one detached villa now remains, no.18, a Church of England home with a Doric porch. Nos.12-14 Wellington Road are the home of the Queen's Nurses, opened on 12 October 1912 in memory of the late King Edward VII, in conjunction with the Peace Statue on the sea-front; the home was extended in 1936. <83,108,112,311>

At the bottom of Elm Grove stands the Roman Catholic Church of St Joseph, a tall, grade II*-listed building in Early English style. The nave and transepts were built from rough Kentish ragstone by W.K.Brodo in 1866-9, and the three polygonal apses at the eastern end were added by J.S.Hansom in 1881-3. The church was completed by F.A.Walters with the addition of the west front in 1900 and the northern transept and chapel in 1906, but it was not dedicated until 8 May 1979 because of a long-standing debt. It has an impressive vaulted interior. The building bearing a cross at the corner of Milton Road was formerly St Joseph's School. <44,45,83,123>

The chapel in De Montfort Road was erected in 1932 as the Emmanuel Full Gospel Church. <83>

Higher up Elm Grove stands the now redundant St Wilfrid's Church, erected in 1932-4 to the design of H.S.Goodhart-Rendel on the site of a temporary iron church of 1901. A large, brick edifice, it 'does not imitate any style of the past, nor indeed the modern style of 1930' according to Pevsner <45>. With a tall northern bell tower and a saddleback roof, it has been described by Sir John Betjeman as 'about the best 1930s church there is'. To reflect this architectural merit it has now been listed grade II*. The interior is spacious and sparsely ornamented, but was greatly enriched when the Lady Chapel was decorated with a large mural by German refugee artist Hans Feibusch in 1940. The church was closed in 1980 when blue asbestos was discovered in the ceiling and a public inquiry was held over its future; the Church Commissioners dropped a plan to demolish it following the inspector's recommendation, and it is now being converted into sheltered housing for the elderly. The parish, created in 1922, merged with St Martin's, but the 1926 church hall still stands in Whippingham Road. <44,45,123>

The Hanover Mill, a tall post-mill erected in about 1838 but demolished in the late 1890s, stood on a site approximating to 39 Bernard Road; see figure 193. <109,249,249b>

Figure 58: St Wilfrid's Church

64. FAIRS

<1,15,17,18>

Fairs were once important annual events in the commercial life of a town and provided trade on a larger scale than the weekly markets. By a charter of 1313, John de Warrenne, Earl of Surrey and lord of the manors of Brighton, was granted a weekly market and a three-day fair to be held in the town on the 'eve, day and morrow of St Bartholomew' (3, 4 and 5 September), a profitable concession for the Earl as he was empowered to collect tolls. It was slightly unusual that the fair was not granted on St Nicholas's Day as it was the custom to use the dedication of the parish church, but this may have been due to the proximity of a fair on that day at Portslade; the dedication of the small priory in the centre of Brighton was used instead.

At the start of the nineteenth century the traditional Brighton St Bartholomew's Day Fair was still being held as a toy and pedlary fair with menageries, exhibitions, theatrical performances, etc., first on the cliff top in front of the Old Town, and then at a variety of locations including Belle Vue Field, the Level, the North Steine and Race Hill. By the mid nineteenth century however, it was the resort of ruffians, thieves and other undesirables and became 'an excuse for drunkenness and debauchery'; it consequently petered out in about the 1870s. There was also a Spring Fair held on Holy Thursday, and a large September sheep fair in 1807-13 when some 20,000 sheep were penned on the Level. The White Hawk Fair was held at the race-course during the annual race meeting from 1791 for several years.

As the weekly and daily markets took over much of the trading function, fairs became primarily sources of entertainment for the townsfolk and now take the form of travelling funfairs which encamp upon the Level at various times of the year, including the Brighton Festival period and carnival week. Although carnivals have been held from at least 1922, the present Brighton Lions Carnival commenced in 1964 and is now probably the nearest embodiment to the traditional Brighton fair. It includes a colourful procession of floats from Hove to

Preston Park where many other displays and side-shows assemble, and several other events held throughout the week including the funfair on the Level. The proceeds from the week now go to charity rather than into the pocket of the lord of the manor, however!

A fair at Preston was granted to the Bishop of Chichester in 1225, to be held on the eve, day and morrow of SS Peter and Paul; a second was granted in 1307 at St Edward's Day, but probably neither lasted for many years.

65. FALMER

<1,84,123,279,305>

In 1086 the manor of Falmer was held by the Priory of St Pancras at Lewes, but in 1776 it was sold to Thomas Pelham, later the Earl of Chichester, and was part of the Stanmer estate of 4,958 acres acquired by Brighton Corporation in 1947. Therefore, although Falmer lies just outside the borough boundary, much of the village and parish, including the pond, the green and many of the old cottages, is now the property of Brighton Council. Domesday also records a population of around 300 and a church at Falmer, but the present Church of St Laurence was rebuilt in about 1850 in Norman style. The inappropriately named 'Falmer Diversion' A27 road scheme was completed in 1981, splitting the village in two, but it was in fact the second diversion of the main road which originally ran on the northern side of the village along Mill Street until the late eighteenth century.

The parish of Falmer, a member of the Newhaven Union and later Newhaven Rural District, covered a large area to the east and south-west of the village, with a detached portion of 242 acres known as Patchway in the Old Boat Corner area. On 1 April 1928 Brighton annexed 781 acres of Falmer, including the areas around East and North Moulsecoomb, Bevendean and Falmer School. In 1934 Patchway was transferred to Stanmer, and on 1 April 1952 a further 1,028 acres were annexed by Brighton, including the lower part of Stanmer Park, the sites of the university and polytechnic campuses, and a large area of downland on Falmer Hill. At the same time Falmer, by then in Chailey rural district, absorbed that part of Stanmer parish not similarly transferred. It is now a parish of 3,122 acres under Lewes District Council.

66. FIRE-BRIGADE

<83,156-157a>

In the early years of the nineteenth century fire-fighting in Brighton was principally in the hands of individual fire insurance companies which employed groups of fire-fighters to attend blazes only on premises insured by that company; the Parish of Brighton also possessed a single primitive fire-engine <112>. To improve the situation, the 1825 Brighton Town Act authorised the town commissioners to provide further fire-engines, and in 1831 they established the town's first fire service.

a) *BRIGHTON FIRE ESTABLISHMENT:* Established on 5 January 1831, with one salaried and uniformed engineer, twenty-eight men paid for attendance at fires, three fire-engines, and a fire escape ladder which was kept at the Town Hall. In the 1850s arrangements were made with the Brighton, Hove and Preston Constant Service Water Company to use mains water, and by the 1860s an engine and escape were being kept at Grafton Street police station, a reel at the Level police station, a reel at the Western Road toll-house, and a reel at the Elm Grove workhouse. However, the Fire Establishment was disbanded when the police fire-brigade was formed in 1881.

b) *BRIGHTON VOLUNTEER FIRE-BRIGADE:* Inaugurated on 14 October 1867 at the Town Hall, the volunteer brigade moved soon after to New Road (where the Pavilion Theatre now stands), then to Upper Russell Street in 1869, and finally to 4 Duke Street (now Browns Restaurant) in 1875. The brigade was funded by subscriptions from insurance companies, and was initially loaned two fire-engines, while the forty-six volunteers provided their own uniforms. They engaged in a friendly rivalry with the police brigade from 1881, but in 1902 the corporation purchased the Duke Street premises and the volunteers were placed under the overall control of Inspector La Croix of the police fire-brigade. On 9 June 1921 the volunteer brigade attended its last fire and was then disbanded following the formation of the county borough fire-brigade.

c) *BRIGHTON POLICE FIRE-BRIGADE:* The police turned out with the town's fire escapes as well as the volunteer brigade and the fire establishment, but after a serious fire in Queen's Road in 1880, an official police fire-brigade was formed at the Town Hall in 1881 under Superintendent Thomas Gibbs. Following several bad fires over a number of years, the brigade was reorganised under Inspector Victor La Croix, formerly of the volunteer brigade, who remained in charge until 1921. (La Croix was, incidentally, the first holder of the mayoral car number plate, CD 1.)

By 1897 there were twelve police fire stations throughout the town, all connected to the headquarters at the Town Hall by telephone. In 1898 the headquarters were moved to the site of the present Corn Exchange entrance in Church Street, but in 1901 a new headquarters was established on the site of the Amber Ale brewery at Preston Circus. The police fire-brigade was disbanded in 1921 when the county borough fire-brigade was formed.

d) *BRIGHTON COUNTY BOROUGH FIRE-BRIGADE:* Following a bad fire in December 1920 at the corner of Duke Street and West Street, much criticism was levelled at the arrangement of police and volunteer brigades. Consequently, a full-time, fully trained corporation brigade was established at Preston Circus in

May 1921 under chief officer Stanley Thorpe, with the police and volunteer fire-brigades disbanded.

Following the creation of 'Greater Brighton' in 1928, when the brigade had forty-five men and six vehicles, the branch police and fire stations were closed, but an eastern fire station was established in an adapted building on the northern side of West Street, Rottingdean. On 21 May 1938 a new headquarters building at Preston Circus, designed by Graeme Highet in Portland stone and brick, was opened by Earl Winterton. During the war fire services were nationalised from August 1941; the National Fire Service, which used the Ocean Hotel at Saltdean as a training college, continued until 1 April 1948 when the county borough council resumed control. In February 1957 Roedean (Brighton no.2) fire station was first used, replacing the Rottingdean station, and in the following year the public street fire-alarms, installed in 1904, were deemed unnecessary and were removed.

The four Chief Officers of the Brighton County Borough Fire Brigade were:

1921-29 Stanley Thorpe
1929-55 Charles Birch
1955-73 Edmund Calvert
1973-74 Frank Furlong

On 1 April 1974, following the 1972 Local Government Act, the fire-brigade became the responsibility of East Sussex County Council. The Preston Circus station is now the headquarters of 'A' Division, covering the coast from Hove to Seaford and inland to Lewes and Barcombe; it answers about 2,500 calls each year with up to six appliances.

67. FISHING INDUSTRY

Brighton's economy and early prosperity was based upon the success of its fisheries for many centuries. A brief history of the industry now follows. (See also "Brighton - Early History".)

a) *EARLIEST TIMES:* Brighton's fishery was already established by 1086 when the Domesday Book recorded one of the manors being paid a tribute of 4,000 herrings (a custom continued to some extent as late as the nineteenth century when the manor of Brighton-Lewes could claim six mackerel from each trip). This early fishing settlement was probably a collection of cottages, workshops, netshops, capstans and stake places on the extensive foreshore below the cliff and above the high-water mark (the 'Lower Town', q.v.) but, as the industry prospered, the fishermen's numbers grew and they started to develop the cliff top area, now the Old Town, together with the landsmen; the ancient parish church of St Nicholas was built, or perhaps rebuilt, at this time. Flax was grown in neighbouring Hove to make linen for the sails, and hemp was probably either grown or processed for rope on the 'Hempshares', an open area in the Old Town between West Street and the Bartholomews on which Middle Street and later the Lanes, Black Lion Street and Ship Street were developed in the fifteenth to the eighteenth centuries. From certain customs and names, it is quite probable that a colony of Flemings settled in the town in about the thirteenth century, contributing greatly to the success of the fisheries. <1,2,6,10,18>

Figure 59: Hauling boats onto the beach

b) *ELIZABETHAN TIMES:* A great insight on Brighton's fishing industry in the sixteenth century is provided by the 1580 Book of Auncient Customs (sic) which laid down strict rules and procedures for the fleets and the distribution of the catches, and detailed the seasonal voyages or 'fares' that were undertaken by the Brighton boats. There were 80 boats, 400 men, 10,000 nets, and four inshore fares were fished:

'Tucknett', with boats up to three tons, fishing for plaice, from February to April;
'Drawnet', three tons, mackerel, May-June;
'Harbour', eight tons, conger, summer;
'Cok', two to six tons, herring, October-December.

The English Channel fares were:

'Shotnett', six to twenty-six tons, mackerel, April-June;
'Flew', eight to twenty tons, herring, November-December.

The furthest trips were to the North Sea where the fares were:

'Yarmouth', fifteen to forty-five tons, herring, September-November;
'Skarborow', eighteen to forty tons, cod, June-September.

With the fisheries run on a co-operative basis, each catch was divided into a number of 'shares' to be divided amongst the men. Tucknett fare, for instance, was divided into thirteen shares per boat, and each man took at least one share, more if he contributed nets. Always, one share was divided with a quarter going to the churchwardens for church maintenance and town defences, one-half to the vicar as a tithe payment, and one-quarter to the master of the ship.

Figure 60: Fishermen mending nets. Note the shape of the 'hoggies'.

The men were kept away from the town for several months during the important Yarmouth fare in the North Sea. Out of season, or during the less important Scarborough fare, the fishing boats were usually used for conveying cargoes along the coast. <3a,10,11,12,17,273,296a>

See also "Ancient Customs".

c) *PROSPERITY and DECLINE:* In Tudor and Stuart times the fishing industry prospered at Brighton, and in 1601 the largest ever fleet of sixty-six boats sailed for the Yarmouth fare. However, restrictive practices operated by the Yarmouth fishing community caused the Brighton fishermen to present a petition to Parliament in 1609. In 1626 the fishermen again petitioned Parliament, this time for protection from French and 'Dunkirker' pirate ships after fourteen boats had been seized. Erosion of the foreshore, where the fishing workshops were concentrated and onto which the boats were hauled, continued unabated from around the 1640s. Together with a general slump in the demand for fish, these adverse factors contributed to a marked decline from about 1650 onwards and many Brighton fishermen took to coastal cargo trading. No more boats were sent to Yarmouth after 1697, and the fifty mackerel boats at the end of the seventeenth century were reduced to half that number over the next thirty years. The Lower Town was completely destroyed by 1705, and by the mid eighteenth century the fortunes of the town in general had reached rock bottom. <11,12,17>

A 1770 description of the town reported that 300 men and 100 boats were still involved in the Brighton fishery. Oysters were dredged in the spring; May, June and July were spent catching mackerel at night, together with red mullet in May and lobsters and prawns in July; flat fish were trawled in August; whiting were caught with hooks in September and October; and herring were caught in November. Dealers from London purchased the catch at the fish market on the beach, while some herring were dried or pickled for foreign markets. <282a>

Employment connected with the new health resort function resulted in increasing numbers of fishermen leaving the sea in the latter eighteenth century. Nevertheless, great disputes arose in 1776 and 1822 over the use of the Steine, where nets had been dried and boats hauled to safety for centuries; the fishermen tried to invoke their ancient rights to these practices but were defeated by the town commissioners. Most of the Brighton fishermen were said to live in the poor Russell

Figure 61: Selling the catch by 'Dutch' auction

Street area in the nineteenth century, and a Bethel chapel was opened in West Street in 1830; a Sunday School for their children was later established in the King's Road Arches. <6,7,15>

The decline of Brighton's fishing industry continued throughout the nineteenth and twentieth centuries, especially when refrigeration enabled fish to be brought into the town by rail after the First World War. In 1862 it was reported that there were 150 fishing boats but the manor of Brighton-Lewes could still claim six mackerel from each trip. In 1902 there were still eight-eight fishing boats operating from Brighton, with the fishermen living mainly in the Russell Street and Carlton Hill areas; herrings were smoked on 'dees' in Carlton Row. By 1948 the number of boats had declined to forty-eight, and by 1963 the weight of fish actually landed on the beach at Brighton was less than one ton per annum <123>. Today only a handful of fishermen operate from Brighton beach, principally from the area below Royal Crescent, but several larger fishing vessels use a special berth near the eastern end of the Marina, while other boats now operate out of Shoreham or Newhaven, selling their catch at the Circus Street market. The Brighton Fishermen's and Boatmen's Protection Society still operates at 200 King's Road Arches, below the Old Ship, and a boat winch, named after the bathing woman Martha Gunn, was recommissioned nearby in 1984. <1,2,48b,123>

d) *HOGBOATS and CUSTOMS:* Brighton fishermen used their own type of vessel known as a 'hogboat' or 'hoggie' which was especially suited to the particular local conditions; they had a very wide beam making them stable in rough seas and were easily hauled onto the shingle beaches. Some were even cut in half and used as homes on the beach by the poorest fishermen. The last one was burnt on a Bonfire Night in the late 1880s, but an excellent model of a Brighton hoggie may be found in the town's museum. <18,31,296a>

There were also a number of traditions and customs practised by the fishing community. At the beginning of the mackerel season in the spring parties would be held on the beach and the nets and boats would be blessed by a clergyman, a custom known as 'bending in' (short for benediction); this practice has been revived at the beginning of the Brighton Festival. On Good Friday fishermen and their families could be seen skipping with ropes at the Fish Market and on the Level until the 1920s, a custom also performed in some villages. At the fish market, the catch was, unusually, sold by Dutch auction (see below). Two arches on the Lower Esplanade by the Grand Hotel steps were decorated with scenes depicting Brighton's fishing heritage for the 1984 Brighton Festival. <123,296a>

e) *The FISH MARKET:* Brighton's fish market was, from time immemorial, situated on the beach below the low cliffs near the end of East Street, a site now built over by the Grand Junction Road. The catch was sold by Dutch auction, possibly due to the influence of Flemish immigration in the thirteenth century, and the sale stopped at the cry of 'Has 'em!'. When the King's Road Arches were formed in the 1880s, nos.216-224 (below the Hospitality Inn) were set aside for the use of the fish market with a hard provided in front for stalls. The colourful and lively scene attracted many visitors who watched the proceedings from the promenade above. Although the fisheries diminished in importance at Brighton, the market continued for the wholesale of 'imported' fish until it was closed by the council on hygiene grounds in 1960. The fish market was then removed to a £10,000 extension at Circus Street which was officially opened by the Duke of Norfolk in January 1960, but the traders have always sought to return to their traditional site. The arches have since been used for other attractions such as Railwayland, and are now occupied by the National Museum of Penny Slot Machines and an amusement arcade, but the Fish Market Hard continues to be used as a traditional venue for political meetings and public speaking. <1,14,15,24,123>

Figure 62: Brighton Fish Market in about 1847

68. FREEDOM of the BOROUGH

<123,126,310>

The following 'persons of distinction, and persons who have, in the opinion of the council, rendered eminent service to the borough', have been awarded the Honorary Freedom of the Borough of Brighton by Brighton Council:

i) *Field Marshal Rt Hon. Viscount Wolseley (19 November 1898):* commander-in-chief of the British Army, and leader of the Nile River Expedition of 1884-5.

ii) *General Sir John French (14 January 1903):* later the Earl of Ypres; cavalry commander in the Boer War.

iii) *Field Marshal Rt Hon. Earl Haig (30 November 1920):* commander-in-chief on the western front 1915-8, to whom a statue has been erected in Whitehall, London.

iv) *Admiral of the Fleet Rt Hon. Earl Beatty (7 October 1922):* commander-in-chief of the Grand Fleet and First Sea Lord, to whom there is a bust in Trafalgar Square, London; the Admiral inaugurated the Brighton War Memorial on the same day.

v) *Alderman Sir Charles Thomas-Stanford, J.P. (30 July 1925):* former mayor and M.P. for Brighton, who bequeathed Preston Manor to the town.

vi) *Lady Ellen Thomas-Stanford (30 July 1925):* wife of Sir Charles above.

vii) *Alderman Herbert Carden, J.P. (28 October 1926):* former mayor and municipal visionary who was much involved in corporation land purchase and housing (see "Carden, Sir Herbert").

viii) *Benjamin James Saunders, C.B.E., J.P. (23 September 1937):* did much to promote children's sport and was chairman of the local employment committee; also presented land at Hollingbury to the town, and financially contributed to the development of the Preston Park cycling track.

ix) *The Royal Sussex Regiment (27 October 1944):* formed in 1804, much involved in the Egyptian and Nile River campaigns, the Boer War, and the two World Wars; on 31 December 1966 the Royal Sussex was absorbed by the Queen's Regiment which has been allowed to continue the 'Freedom of Entry to the Borough'; they may march through the town with bayonets fixed, drums beating, and colours flying <123>.

x) *Rt Hon. Sir Winston Spencer Churchill, M.P. (3 October 1947):* statesman for many years and prime minister during the Second World War, to whom a statue has been erected in Parliament Square, London.

xi) *Alderman Hugh Milner Black (30 September 1948):* councillor since 1902 and former mayor; a council visionary who was much involved in corporation housing and education.

xii) *Alderman Miss Dorothy Stringer (19 December 1968):* former mayor; councillor since 1933; member of the education committee since the 1920s.

xiii) *William Dodd (27 July 1972):* deputy town clerk from 1938 until 1953; town clerk from 1953 until 1972.

69. GAS SUPPLY

<83,112,115,158,159,170>

a) *The FIRST SUPPLY:* The first gas supply in the town was established in 1818-19 by the Brighton Gas Light and Coke Company which built a coal-gas production works at Black Rock. (These works were deliberately sited just outside the Brighton parish boundary to avoid the payment of the local coal-tax (see "Coastline (Groynes)"), and were the first portent of the new industrial age in Brighton.) The Pavilion Grounds were the first area to be lit and gas lighting was installed throughout the principal rooms of the Royal Pavilion itself, but many townsfolk feared explosions from the new energy source and petitioned Parliament against the new development. In order to reassure the public the company illuminated a prince of Wales's feathers sign on Mr Stone's shoe-shop at the corner of East Street and Steine Lane on 12 August 1819; it seemed to have the desired effect as gas lighting was then taken up by the residents.

Figure 63: Gas lamp-standard in the Royal Pavilion Grounds, one of several erected in the reign of William IV

b) *The RIVAL COMPANY:* In 1825 a second concern, the Brighton and Hove General Gas Company, established a works adjacent to St Andrew's Church, Hove, and continued manufacturing gas there until 1871 when a large new works was opened on the southern arm of Shoreham Harbour at Portslade-by-Sea.

On 1 January 1882 the Brighton and Hove General Gas Company absorbed its older rival, and in 1885 all manufacture was transferred to the Portslade works; the Hove and Black Rock sites were then used for storage only. Following many initial complaints the luminosity and pressure were also improved. In the sixty-five years from 1860 to 1925, annual gas demand rose from 100 million cubic feet to 2,230 million cubic feet, necessitating the rebuilding and enlargement of the Portslade works in the 1920s. In 1931 the company absorbed the Worthing Gas Company to become the Brighton, Hove and Worthing Gas Company; the Littlehampton company was absorbed in 1934. During the war the Portslade works were a target for German bombers, as was the Black Rock depot where a direct hit resulted in a spectacular flame some 300 feet high.

In 1882, the Brighton and Hove Gas Company opened offices and showrooms in the large, bow-fronted building at 77 West Street, now Swifts cocktail bar; from 1925, the present music library in Church Street was also used.

c) *NATIONALISATION and NATURAL GAS:* The gas supply industry was nationalised on 1 May 1949, and the Brighton, Hove and Worthing Gas Company was absorbed into the South-Eastern Gas Board (SEGAS). The Portslade works were rebuilt in 1949-54, and the local offices were removed from West Street to Black Rock in 1964. During the 1960s a massive operation was undertaken to change all fittings for natural gas consumption, supplied from fields under the North Sea. This resulted in the closure of the Portslade works, and they were eventually demolished in about 1970, much to the relief of the nearby residents who complained about the permanent smell. In 1989 the Hove gas-holder was also demolished.

70. GENERAL HOSPITAL, Elm Grove

<95>

Built by George Maynard in 1865-7, the buildings now occupied by the Brighton General Hospital were administered by the Board of Guardians for the Parish of Brighton as a workhouse and infirmary until 1 April 1930 when their responsibilities passed to the public assistance committee of the county borough council. (They had been used as a hospital during the First World War, however.) The former Poor Law Institution became known as the Elm Grove Home, and on 1 November 1935 the Brighton Municipal Hospital was established in most of the buildings. (For details of the building's life prior to this time see "Workhouses".) More buildings were taken over in 1937, and in 1939-40 the new hospital took over the whole site, with the remaining occupants of the home evacuated to various establishments throughout the county. In May 1948 the establishment was renamed Brighton General Hospital, and was taken over the following month by the Ministry of Health following the National Health Service Act. It now has 495 beds, and is also the local teaching hospital with a post-graduate medical centre added in 1966. There are, however, plans to close the aging building if a new hospital is built at Hove.

The principal building, facing north-west above Elm Grove, is an impressive four-storey edifice with four gables and dolphin decorations, and has a frontage of 318 feet; the central clock tower has a cupola and weather-vane, and bears the date 1866. The large blocks facing Pankhurst Avenue were added in the 1890s.

The adjacent ambulance station in Elm Grove was erected in 1951-2 on the site of the former workhouse vegetable garden. The Brighton County Borough Ambulance Service took over from the police accident ambulance service on 1 October 1948, but was itself taken over by East Sussex County Council in April 1974.

71. King GEORGE IV

<1,2,3,48,85-88,152,152a,296>

a) *PRINCE OF WALES:* George, Prince of Wales (or 'Prinny'), was born at St James's Palace on 12 August 1762, the eldest son of King George III. He grew to be a cultural and artistic man, the leader of fashionable society, and his patronage of Brighton in the late eighteenth and early nineteenth centuries did much to ensure the town's success. He was also, however, headstrong and disrespectful, prone to lying and keeping bad company, a drinker and gambler, and he ran up large debts much to his father's dismay.

b) *EARLY VISITS TO BRIGHTON:* The Prince's first visit to the town was on 7 September 1783 to visit his uncle, the Duke of Cumberland, at Grove House. It was the Duke's marriage to an Irish widow in 1771 which led to the 1772 Royal Marriage Act, and the feud between the Duke and his brother the King appeared to encourage a rebellious attitude in the young Prince of Wales.

The first royal visitor to the town (apart from Charles II, q.v.) was the Duke of Gloucester on 11 July 1765, and he was followed by the Duke of York in August 1766, and by the Duke of Cumberland. Brighton townsfolk were therefore accustomed to the visits of royalty, but were naturally excited at the prospect of receiving the heir to the throne. A salute was fired from the battery (which unfortunately killed the gunner), and in the evening the Prince promenaded on the Steine, which was illuminated for the occasion, to watch a firework display. The following day he rode out with stag hounds, attended a ball at the Castle Inn in the evening. and later in his visit attended a performance at the theatre in North Street. Staying for a total of eleven days, the Prince declared himself highly delighted with the little town.

His second visit commenced on 23 July 1784 on the advice of his physicians, possibly for the sea-water cure as he had swollen throat glands. George stayed for ten weeks, again staying at Grove House, but there was considerable criticism in the town over his choice of disreputable companions. His third visit was in the following season, June 1785.

c) *MARRIAGE TO MRS FITZHERBERT:* Maria Anne Smythe was born on 26 July 1756 at Bramsbridge, Hampshire. A devout Roman Catholic, she married Edmund Weld at the age of eighteen, but was widowed within a year; she then married Thomas Fitzherbert who died of a chill three years later.

Twice-widowed but still young, Mrs Fitzherbert now had a modest fortune of her own and took up residence at Richmond Hill near London. The Prince of Wales is said to have first met her at the opera and was immediately smitten, but he knew that marriage was impossible because of her Catholic faith. Mrs Fitzherbert then went abroad for some time, but the Prince continued to pursue her, and on her return from France she agreed to marriage with a secret but illegal wedding service being held on 15 December 1785 at her home in Park Street, London. (It was illegal due to the Royal Marriage Act of 1772 which forbade unapproved marriages by members of the Royal Family.) Following the wedding, Maria first came to Brighton in July 1786 and probably stayed at Marlborough Row; the Prince had arrived two weeks earlier and was probably staying at Thomas Kemp's farmhouse on the Steine. The couple were popular visitors to the town over the next few years, but they never stayed in the same house.

Later in 1786 Louis Weltje obtained a lease on Kemp's house on behalf of the Prince, and it was subsequently replaced by the Marine Pavilion which was ready for occupation by the summer of 1787 (see "Royal Pavilion").

d) *MARRIAGE TO PRINCESS CAROLINE:* After several years of contentment, George started to take an interest in other ladies of the court; the couple separated and the Prince ended the relationship in June 1794, but granted Mrs Fitzherbert an annuity of £6,000. The Prince's debts were rapidly increasing however, and his father agreed to settle them only if he married and secured the Protestant succession. Consequently he married his cousin, the Princess Caroline of Brunswick, on 8 April 1795 and they arrived in Brighton about two months later, staying at Gerald Hamilton's house on the Steine (now Marlborough House) as the Marine Pavilion was being decorated. A daughter, Princess Charlotte, was born on 7 January 1796 in London, but soon afterwards the Prince, who was never fond of his wife, separated from her and in fact spent the 1796 season at Bognor rather than Brighton because of public sympathy for his new wife. Their daughter and heir Charlotte was later to die in childbirth on 6 November 1817.

Figure 64: The statue of King George IV near tthe North Gate of the Royal Pavilion

George proved to be still obsessed with Maria Fitzherbert however, and declared to his brother William that she was his only true love; he made out a will leaving all his possessions to her in 1796, and then begged her for a reunion. In 1800 Maria received the Pope's declaration that she was George's only true wife in the eyes of God, and the couple were duly reunited. Steine House (now the Y.M.C.A.) was built for Maria in 1804, and the couple lived a devoted life again for several years.

e) *The REGENCY:* By 1811, with the King severely ill, the Prince was fearful that his liaison with Mrs Fitzherbert, a Catholic, would adversely affect his position as probable Regent; he finally ended their relationship in June 1811 when he snubbed her at a dinner. Having been created Regent on 5 February 1811 (he also acted briefly as Regent in 1788), the Prince then planned the transformation of his Marine Pavilion into a splendid palace, the Royal Pavilion, to befit his new status.

Maria never again entered the Pavilion while George was alive, but her annuity was raised to £10,000 in 1820. Indeed, she was only reconciled after his death when his brother, William IV, learned of her secret marriage; he insisted that her servants should wear the royal livery. Maria Fitzherbert died at Steine House on 27 March 1837 aged eighty and is buried near the altar of St John the Baptist's Catholic Church in Bristol Road. Her memorial, designed by John Carew, shows her kneeling with three rings on her wedding finger.

The question of whether Maria had any children remains unanswered. She lived for a long time with two adopted daughters, one of whom, Minnie Spencer, the Prince was certainly very fond of; it has been suggested that they were the children of her marriage to the Prince.

f) *ACCESSION:* The Prince Regent succeeded to the throne on 29 January 1820 at the age of fifty-seven, and made his first visit to Brighton as King George IV on 26 October 1820, staying at Marlborough Row while the Pavilion was being transformed. He was crowned on 19 July 1821 with huge celebrations held in Brighton, but he refused his legal wife, Princess Caroline, access to the coronation ceremony. After the Royal Pavilion was finished in 1821 however, George IV visited the town at less frequent intervals as he became annoyed with the ever-increasing crowds and an insult to one of his lady friends; indeed, he made his last visit to Brighton in 1828. He died at Windsor on 26 June 1830 aged sixty-seven, and was buried at Windsor together with a locket of his one true love, Maria Fitzherbert. A statue of George IV, erected in 1828, may be found adjacent to the North Gate of the Royal Pavilion. A BBC drama series starring Peter Egan and Susannah York, *The Prince Regent*, was shown in 1979.

72. The GRAND HOTEL, King's Road

<2,3,44,45,123>

Designed in Italian style by J.H.Whichcord, the Grand Hotel was built in 1862-4 at a cost of about £100,000 on the site of the houses of Artillery Place; the West Battery formerly stood directly in front of the service road. Opening on 23 July 1864, it was by far the largest hotel in Brighton with over 150 bedrooms, and, with eight storeys, was also the tallest building in the town. The Grand was kept up-to-date with all the modern conveniences, and was among the first hotels in the country to include electric lighting and lifts, or 'ascending omnibuses' as they were initially known. Many famous guests have stayed at the hotel over the years including Napoleon III, President Kennedy, the Duke of Windsor, Ronald Reagan, and the Russians Malenkov and Bulganin. In the 1960s Prime Minister Harold Wilson held a full cabinet meeting in the banqueting room during a Labour Party conference.

In November 1961 the hotel came under the threat of redevelopment by Brighton Council which decided to compulsorily purchase it as part of the Churchill Square project, but it was listed by the government and demolition thereby prevented; it would have been replaced by an amusement centre.

The Grand achieved world fame, or rather notoriety, on the morning of 12 October 1984 when, at 2.54 a.m., a twenty-five pound gelignite bomb planted by the Provisional Irish Republican Army exploded in room 629 in an attempt to assassinate Prime Minister Margaret Thatcher and her cabinet, who were attending the Conservative Party conference in the adjacent Brighton Centre. Five people were killed and thirty-four injured, and by the light of day a gaping chasm could be seen in the centre of the building. On 10 June 1986 Patrick Magee was convicted at the Old Bailey and given a life sentence for murder in the event which has become known as the 'Brighton Bombing'.

The hotel's owners, De Vere Hotels, decided to rebuild and refurbish the whole building in its original style at a cost of £10 million. The decorative details, the two wide bows topped by roof pavilions, and the intricate ironwork were all restored, and a new conservatory was added along the length of the ground floor. The magnificently reconstructed hotel was formally reopened on 28 August 1986 by Margaret Thatcher, and now has 162 bedrooms and many other new facilities, including Hobdens Health Hydro which commemorate the former baths that stood on the site. In 1988 the Grand became the first five-star hotel in Brighton.

Figure 65: The Grand Hotel shortly after its opening in 1864

73. GRAND JUNCTION ROAD

Built on a newly-constructed sea-wall, this important road opened as Grand Junction Parade on 10 December 1829 to provide a through route from Marine Parade to King's Road for the first time. Traffic had previously been forced to travel via King's Road, Pool Valley and Old Steine, but the new thoroughfare greatly eased the passage and quickly led to the establishment of a daily fashionable horse parade from Kemp Town to the Brunswick Estate. In 1929-30 the Grand Junction Road and Madeira Drive promenades were extended over pillars to form a colonnaded walk on the Lower Esplanade below, an improvement inaugurated by the mayor, Horace Aldrich, on 27 June 1930. The ornate lamp-standards were also originally erected in the 1930s. <15,116>

At the corner with East Street is the former Restoration public house with the elegant Clarendon Mansions above. Formerly the Clarendon Hotel, this listed building was erected in 1870 by Charles Brill on the site of his domed baths (originally Lamprell's). It has a scrolled doorway, but the balconettes have been removed in its current state of disrepair. <26,44>

The 28-bedroom Prince's Hotel, nos.10-12, is a listed building of around 1840 with five storeys, two bows and first-floor balconies. It was Waite's Hotel until 1938 and then the Palace Pier Hotel, but was refitted and renamed in 1985-6 by Cheffik Ltd. No.14, now rebuilt as part of the Royal Albion Hotel, housed Tussaud's Waxworks from 1937 until 1979. <44,83,123>

See also "Cannon Cinema", "Lower Esplanade", "Palace Pier", "Queen's Hotel" and "Royal Albion Hotel".

74. HANOVER

a) *HISTORY:* The Percy Almshouses at the bottom of Elm Grove were erected in 1795 (see "Lewes Road"), but they remained in a quite isolated position until the construction of Hanover Crescent and Hanover Street in about 1822. However, most of the densely-populated district which has become known as Hanover was developed from about 1860, typically small terraces with angular window bays. Hanover ward was first designated in 1894, covering the area between Lewes Road, Southover Street, Queen's Park Road and Elm Grove, but it has been expanded since to include the area between Lewes Road, Grand Parade, Carlton Hill, Queen's Park Road, Pankhurst Road, Freshfield Road, Elm Grove and Franklin Road. Since being designated a 'general improvement area' in 1969-76, Hanover has become a more attractive residential district and has escaped the massive redevelopment of the adjacent Albion Hill area. Together with Albion Hill, Hanover has a population of around 7,500. <83,123,277>

b) *HANOVER CRESCENT and HANOVER STREET:* Hanover Crescent itself consists of twenty-four grand, listed houses which were completed by A.H.Wilds for one Henry Brooker in about 1822, the year in which the Level was laid out. Despite the use of bow fronts, shell motifs, and Corinthian and ammonite pilasters, they do not, however, form a unified composition. In 1844-6 11 Hanover Crescent was the home of Sir Rowland Hill, the originator of the penny post and the chairman of the London and Brighton Railway Company from 1843, while novelist Horace Smith lived at no.10 from 1826 until 1840 before moving to Cavendish Place. The two lodges, single-storey buildings with Tuscan columns and pediments, are also listed, as is the garden

Figure 66: Hanover Crescent

wall; the small garden itself was taken over by the corporation in 1884 following the Brighton Improvement Act.

Hanover Street, behind the crescent, is an attractive road of small cottages with front gardens, and bears the date 1822 on no.1. In 1988 Hanover Street and Hanover Terrace were added to the Valley Gardens conservation area. The nearby nos.1-4 Southover Street also form an attractive group of early-nineteenth-century, cobble-fronted cottages. <44,45,126,259,311>

c) *CHURCH OF THE ANNUNCIATION:* The Anglican Church of the Hanover area is the Annunciation of our Lady, Washington Street, which was built for Revd Arthur Wagner to a modest Early English design by William Dancy. Opening on 15 August 1864, the flint and red-brick church was partially rebuilt in 1881 by Edmund Scott who added the aisles and the south chapel in memory of John Keble and Edward Pusey, two leaders of the ritualist movement. In 1892 a tower and short spire were added by F.T.Cawthorn who also added the vestry and installed the large east window; this has stained glass by Sir Edward Burne-Jones and was originally installed at St Nicholas's Church in 1853. The Annunciation was served by curates from St Paul's until the parish was formed in 1881, and in 1884 it was consecrated. The adjacent vicarage was built in 1897 in memory of Revd Reginald Fison, the second vicar of the parish.

The Church of the Annunciation became heavily involved in the arguments over ritualism that centred around Arthur Wagner (see "Religion" and "Wagner, Arthur"). Following lengthy hearings by the Church Association a number of crucifixes, statues and other ornaments were removed on 1 September 1903, but they were almost immediately returned as the more acute phase of anti-ritualism passed. Further ornamentation was added in 1924-34. <1,45,62,64a,65,311>

d) *OTHER BUILDINGS:* Cobden Road public slipper baths were opened in April 1894 by the mayor, Sir Joseph Ewart, in a red-brick building with shell and dolphin decorations at the corner of Islingword Road. Closing in 1976, the building was used as the Hanover Community Centre until 1982 and then as a resource centre, but it was converted into flats in 1985-6 with the inaugural tablet remaining in the entrance hall. The community centre itself moved to 33 Southover Street. Built in 1872 as St Mary's School for Boys, this building became the Annunciation School in about 1900 and the corporation's handicraft school in 1924, but was used as an education supply store after the war. Harry Cowley (1890-1971), a hero to the downtrodden poor of the town, was born at 33 Lincoln Street. No.145 Islingword Road was the Lewes Road Dispensary for Women and Children from 1899 until 1905 (see "Clifton Hill (Windlesham Road)"). <83,94,96,123,281>

Belgrave Street Congregational Church was built in Early English style by Thomas Simpson, rendered, with a pitched roof and large windows. It opened on 1 January 1863, but closed in 1942 and became an annexe of the technical college. Islingword Road Mission opened in 1881 as a Primitive Methodist chapel, but became a mission hall in 1893; it is now an Evangelical Free Church. The building between nos.21 and 22 Islingword Road was a Baptist Chapel for many years. Bentham Road Congregational Mission Hall opened in 1882 and became a Free Church in the late 1950s; it closed in the late 1980s. <62,83>

Hanover Mill, a tall post-mill erected in about 1838 but demolished in the late 1890s, stood on a site approximating to 39 Bernard Road. (See figure 193.) <109,249,249b>

75. HOLLINGBURY

a) *HOLLINGBURY HILL and CASTLE:* The hill which lies to the north of the town between the London Road and Lewes Road valleys is known as Hollingbury. Reaching 584 feet above sea-level, it enjoys the widest panorama in the town, and the walker will be rewarded on a very clear day with views that extend to the New Forest, the Isle of Wight, Chanctonbury Ring, the North Downs, Hastings, and of course the spectacular Brighton townscape below. Visitors should be aware, however, that there are only two rights-of-way over the golf-course: one leads from Lynchet Close, Hollingdean, due north via the Iron Age camp to the '39-acre field' car-park in Ditchling Road; the second leads from Ditchling Road, to the north of Woodbourne Avenue, to the camp. Most of the downland estate, then in the parish of Patcham, was purchased by the corporation in March 1901 for £25,000 <305>.

The summit of the hill is crowned by Hollingbury Castle Camp, an early Iron Age hill fort dating from the sixth century to about the middle of the second century B.C.; it has been the property of the corporation since June 1903. Although commonly referred to as such, it certainly never was a castle. It is, however, a scheduled ancient monument and covers approximately nine acres in a rough square about 600 feet across, with gateways to east and west through the still-evident ramparts. The camp was excavated by Herbert Toms in 1908, Cecil Curwen and the Brighton and Hove Archaeological Society in 1931, and by John Holmes in 1967; they have shown that the ramparts were defended by wooden barricades, and have also discovered the sites of wooden huts. <260>

b) *HOLLINGBURY PARK:* Hollingbury golf-course covers most of the area of Hollingbury Park, about 240 acres. This municipal course was laid out with nine holes in 1907 for £460, and was formally opened by the mayor, John Roberts, on 11 September 1908. The first two holes were made where the football pitches now lie alongside Ditchling Road, with the present tennis pavilion as the clubhouse, but the course was extended to eighteen holes in 1910 and was completely remodelled in 1936 by Charles Hawtree; the length is now 6,502 yards. The second clubhouse, a wooden building at Lower Roedale, was originally presented to the town by Queen Mary as a workshop for the disabled during the First World War and stood in the Royal Pavilion grounds; it was later purchased by Arthur and Benjamin Saunders and presented to the golf club. A new clubhouse opened at Upper Roedale in April 1987. Much of the adjacent woodland, planted in the first half of the nineteenth century, was destroyed in the storm of October 1987. <76,123,126,218,221>

c) *HOLLINGBURY HOUSING ESTATE:* The southern slopes of Hollingbury were developed principally in the 1890s and 1900s, and several roads in the Fiveways and Hollingdean areas, a public house in Roedale Road, and the borough ward for the Hollingdean area are named 'Hollingbury'. The Hollingbury housing estate, however, was developed on the north-western slopes of the hill post-war, and the two areas are sometimes confused. It is the town's largest post-war council estate, and was developed on land principally acquired in November 1909. The first houses were erected in 1946 at Midhurst Rise and Petworth Road, and building continued until 1964. <83,276,305>

Hollingbury Methodist Church, Lyminster Avenue, was opened in September 1952. The branch library opened on 27 April 1962 in a small, pre-fabricated building which originally opened in September 1950 as the County Oak public house; the new County Oak opened in March 1961 <123>. Carden Park occupies about twelve acres and was laid out in the 1950s, but tennis courts and swings were lost when the KTM (now FMT) factory was extended in 1968. The corporation then added part of the adjoining downland to compensate, but part was again taken for the construction of the £350,000 Carden Community Centre which was paid for by the Asda company; it was officially opened on 28 April 1988 <123,126>.

d) *HOLLINGBURY INDUSTRIAL ESTATE:* The Hollingbury Industrial Estate was developed by the corporation on eighteen acres around Crowhurst Road from 1950; the first factories were occupied by Ogdens bakery and Underwood Elliott Fletcher typewriters. By 1956, several other engineerings firms were established including CVA tools (later Kearney and Trecker Marwin (KTM) and now Flexible Manufacturing Technology). Underwoods were subsequently taken over by Creeds, ITT and STC, but their factories closed in the mid 1980s, part of a recession that saw employment on the estate fall from 8,000 to under 1,000 by 1980. However, the Enterprise Estate, a collection of small factory units, opened in October 1985. The Asda superstore, with its attractive entrance hall reminiscent of the Crystal Palace, was designed by APP Brighton and opened on 9 November 1987 on the site of an STC factory; it won a council planning award in 1989. An MFI superstore, also designed by APP, opened nearby on 28 September 1989. The Brighton bypass, scheduled for completion in 1995, will have an interchange with Carden Avenue and Crowhurst Road. <83,123>

76. HOLLINGDEAN

<83,93,107,109,115,123,126>

A large housing estate which lies between Round Hill and Hollingbury, and Ditchling Road and the Lewes railway. The name belonged to one of the large open fields or 'laines' of the parish of Preston in the early nineteenth century, but there was no housing development until the 1890s when the Hollingbury Road/Roedale Road area was built; the Hertford Road area followed in the 1920s. The council estate to the east was built mainly in the early 1950s, but the Brentwood and Uplands Road areas were added in the 1960s, while the tower-block flats off Upper Hollingdean Road opened in 1966. In 1981 the Hollingdean area had a population of about 8,000 <277>.

Much of the land was associated with Harrington Farm, which stood on a site between Hollingdean Terrace and the southern end of Hertford Road from the mid nineteenth century until the 1920s; in 1931 Hertford Road School was built on the site of the farmhouse. The only buildings in the area now surviving from before 1890 are Lower Roedale cottages and stores in Stanmer Villas, which were actually situated in the parish of Patcham. Once part of the Roedale Model Dairy Farm, the remaining flint buildings and cottages date from the early nineteenth century and are used by the council's Parks and Recreation Department; the corporation's Roedale Nursery lay to the east until the 1950s, and an associated mid-nineteenth-century house stands nearby.

St Richard of Chichester's Church and Hall, The Crossway, is a single-storey chapel of ease to St Matthias's Church, and was built in 1954 to a design by Clayton, Black and Daviel <311>. Hollingbury Gospel Hall, Hollingdean Terrace, opened as the Hollingbury Hall in 1932 and is now used by the Christian Fellowship. Hollingdean Community Centre, Thompson Road, opened in December 1985.

Hollingdean Road was originally known as Dog Kennel Road from the Union Hunt's kennels which were on the site of the abattoir. It ran from the Lewes Road straight through to the Jolly Brewers at Florence Place to form the Brighton/Preston boundary until 1928 <112>, but the western part is now a private access road to the borough council's technical services depot (once the site of the town's dust destructor - see "Refuse"), wholesale meat market (see "Markets"), and to the former municipal abattoir. This latter facility opened on 30 June 1894 and put an end to many of the forty or so insanitary slaughterhouses that were to be found in the more densely populated areas of the town. Nearly 7,000 animals were handled in the first year, and by 1928 the figure had risen to some 34,400 animals with only eleven other slaughterhouses remaining. However, after several years of private leasing the abattoir was closed in 1986 on hygiene grounds. No.84 Hollingdean Road, a knapped-flint and brick house, was the home of the abattoir superintendent. A siding from the Lewes railway line formerly served both the abattoir and the depot.

77. HOSPITALITY INN, King's Road

<123>

Built in 1984-7 as the Ramada Renaissance Hotel, the 204-bedroom Hospitality Inn was the first major hotel to be built in Brighton since the new Bedford twenty years before, and was the culmination of the upsurge in the town's conference and tourist trade since the opening of the Brighton Centre in 1977. Designed by Michael Lyell and Associates, the Hospitality Inn stands on the site of Harrison's Hotel, several other buildings in King's Road, and parts of Market Street and Little East Street. The obliteration of Market Street has destroyed part of the ancient street pattern of the Old Town and, although much of the site had been vacant for many years, the new building, like the Top Rank Centre some twenty years earlier, has been heavily criticised for its design in a prime sea-front location; the rather plain façade is relieved only by green glass bays which are intended to echo this characteristic feature of Victorian Brighton. It does have a little style, however, and certainly adds to the marine façade in a way in which the Bedford and other developments of the 1960s could never do; it does not, for instance, break the roof line of its neighbours.

Opening in July 1987 at a cost of some £25 million, the hotel has an extremely spacious and lofty atrium foyer, accessible from both King's Road and from Bartholomew Square. This civic square was created at the same time as the hotel, together with the surrounding municipal offices and an underground car-park. The Ramada was formally opened by the Marquess of Abergavenny, Lord Lieutenant of East Sussex, on 18 September 1987 and was awarded five stars for its facilities; Le Pavillon Café in Bartholomew Square opened slightly later. In April 1989 the hotel was sold to the Mount Charlotte group and was subsequently renamed.

78. HOSPITALS and DISPENSARIES

The forerunners of the town's hospitals were the benevolent and charitable institutions, and the public dispensaries established in the early nineteenth century, mainly for the benefit of the poor. The two principal dispensaries in Brighton are described below.

a) *BRIGHTON, HOVE AND PRESTON DISPENSARY, 113 Queen's Road:* Founded as the Brighthelmston Dispensary with the patronage of the Prince of Wales, this institution opened on 1 January 1810 at the eastern end of Nile Street. Advice and medicine were given free, and the sick were attended in their own homes upon the recommendation of a subscriber. In July 1811 it moved to North Street, opposite Ship Street, and was joined there by the Sussex General Infirmary in November 1812. Both establishments moved to 25 Middle Street in 1819, but the infirmary closed when the Sussex County Hospital opened in 1828.

In 1849 the dispensary moved to a new building in Queen's Road, at the south-eastern corner with North Road. Designed by Herbert Williams in Gothic style, it was faced in knapped flint with a Dutch gable and oriel window, and continued as a dispensary until 1930 when it was converted to offices. After the Second World War, the building was used as an ex-servicemen's hall, Churchill House, but was eventually acquired by Eagle Star Insurance before being demolished in the 1960s for the erection of new offices.

In 1859 a western branch opened at 4 Farm Road, Hove, and the name was changed to the Brighton and Hove Dispensary. The branch started to take in-patients, and in 1888 moved to Sackville Road where it became Hove Cottage Hospital in 1902 and then Hove General Hospital. A second branch opened in 1885 at 26 Ditchling Road, a large red-brick building at the corner

Figure 67: The Brighton Dispensary, Queen's Road, in about 1849

of Upper Lewes Road. The dispensary became the Brighton, Hove and Preston Dispensary in 1918, and continued to function from Sackville Road and Ditchling Road until 1948 when the National Health Service was established. The Ditchling Road building then became a mass radiography unit and is still used by the health authority.
<24,83,94>

b) *BRIGHTON, HOVE AND PRESTON PROVIDENT DISPENSARY, 117 Queen's Road:* Established as the Brighton Provident and Self-Supporting Dispensary to promote a spirit of independence amongst the poor, it opened in 1837 at 32 Middle Street, a few doors from the Brighthelmston Dispensary with Dr William King as physician. The dispensary was supported by voluntary contributions, and for one penny per week per person, and one halfpenny per child, it gave medical aid to those who could not obtain the services of the Brighthelmston Dispensary, although aid was given gratis when necessary. In 1878 it moved to 117 Queen's Road, again just a few doors from the Brighton and Hove Dispensary, and continued to function with branches at 110 Springfield Road; 2 Whitehawk Avenue; 27 Rifle Butt Road; 23 Chailey Road; 2 Westbourne Street, Hove; and at 33 Elm Road, Portslade, until the National Health Service was established in 1948.
<24,83,94,100>

c) *DEVELOPMENT of HOSPITALS:* The Sussex General Infirmary was established in November 1812 in the North Street building of the Brighthelmston Dispensary, and continued until the opening of the town's first hospital, the Sussex County Hospital and General Sea-Bathing Infirmary, in Eastern Road in 1828. Patients at the hospital were treated upon the recommendation of a subscriber.

Several other voluntarily-supported hospitals opened in the latter nineteenth century for specialist treatment. In 1881 Brighton Corporation opened a borough sanatorium at Bevendean Road, and converted the Elm Grove workhouse into the General Hospital (originally Brighton Municipal Hospital) from 1935. The corporation also maintained a smallpox isolation hospital from 1901 at Fulking Grange on the Downs above Fulking, and a lunatic asylum at St Francis's Hospital, Haywards Heath, from 1858 <83,115>. However, following the 1947 Health Act, all hospitals in the area were taken over by the Ministry of Health on 5 July 1948.

For details of individual hospitals, consult the index entry on "hospitals".

The following four hospitals are no longer in existence.

d) *BEVENDEAN HOSPITAL:* The former Bevendean Hospital originated as a wooden sanatorium for infectious diseases. Known as the Brighton Borough Hospital, it was erected on the eastern side of Bevendean Road in 1881 during an outbreak of smallpox. The first section of the permanent borough sanatorium, a three-storey building with the borough arms on turreted corners which latterly served as the main reception and administrative block, was designed by borough engineer Francis May and opened on 27 October 1898 by the mayor, Sir John Blaker. The sanatorium entrance was flanked by two red-brick lodges. An isolation pavilion was opened at the same time to the north-west with a scarlet fever pavilion to the north; two further pavilions were added in 1903. The sanatorium operated principally as an isolation hospital for infectious diseases under municipal control until 1948 when, having been taken over by the Ministry of Health, it became Bevendean Hospital. Three years later the buildings were quarantined for thirty-four days during an infamous outbreak of smallpox. A diagnostic theatre and x-ray unit were added in 1967. Latterly used for the care of psychiatric and geriatric patients as well as the treatment of infectious diseases, the 127-bed hospital was closed to in-patients on 24 April 1989 because of budget cuts, and the last day-ward shut on 26 September 1990. The buildings are said to be haunted by former patients. An AIDS hospice and housing is to be built on the site.
<97,115,123>

e) *BRIGHTON, HOVE AND PRESTON DENTAL HOSPITAL:* Opening in 1886 at 39 Marlborough Place, it moved to 116 Queen's Road in 1889. In 1917 the hospital moved to 27 Queen's Road, and then to 7 Buckingham Road in 1931 where it remained until the formation of the National Health Service in 1948. <83,115>

f) *SUSSEX MATERNITY HOSPITAL:* Established in 1830 by Dr Lyons at 69 High Street, it was originally known as the Lying-in Institution and Dispensary for Women and Children, and gave assistance and comfort to poor women during confinement. In about 1854 it moved to 76 West Street and became the Women's Lying-in Institution and Hospital. Other branches were opened at 9 Portland Road, Hove, and 10 Richmond Terrace, and in 1912 it became Brighton and Hove Women's Hospital.

In 1922 the hospital moved to the former Brighton Grammar School building at 76-80 Buckingham Road where it was renamed the Sussex Maternity Hospital. The square, three-storey building was extended in about 1929, but with the transfer of maternity cases to the the new Tower Block of the Royal Sussex in 1969-70, the hospital became redundant and was acquired by the corporation for social services purposes; it was demolished in September 1976 and an East Sussex social education centre now occupies the site. There were also branches of the maternity hospital at 16 Wellington Road, and at the former clinic in Whitehawk Avenue.
<6,24,83,115,123>

g) *SUSSEX THROAT AND EAR HOSPITAL:* Founded in 1879 at 17 Grenville Place, it moved to 23 Queen's Road in 1882, with beds for in-patients from 1889. A new red-brick building opened in Church Street in 1897, to the west of Queen's Road, with a two-storey extension added in 1931, but the 23-bed hospital closed on 1 August 1986 when it was replaced by a new unit at the Royal Sussex County Hospital. It was demolished in September 1988 and replaced by St Nicholas Court.
<24,83,123>

79. HOVE

<1,2,45a,100-101a>

Brighton's western neighbour was first mentioned in a record of 1288, a small medieval fishing village which grew up almost on the foreshore itself. Over the centuries much land was washed away by the sea, just as at Brighton, and Hove remained impoverished such that until 1825 only some 300 people lived in the parish, principally in the old village which then stretched along Hove Street, with a few scattered farms in the rest of the parish's 778 acres.

a) *ST ANNE'S WELL:* There was one eighteenth-century location in Hove which was of real significance to Brighton, however. The 'chalybeate' (iron-bearing) waters of St Anne's Well were known before the development of Brighton as a resort, but it was Dr Richard Russell who developed the spring as a small spa when he had a basin erected there in about 1750 and recommended it to his patients. St Anne's Well therefore contributed to the successful establishment of Brighton as a health resort. In about 1830 an Ionic-style pump-room was erected at the spa to cater for the fashionable visitors who included Queen Adelaide, but its popularity declined from the mid nineteenth century and the estate was laid out as a private pleasure garden in 1850 by Sir Isaac Goldsmid. It was later acquired by Hove Corporation and opened as a public park on 24 May 1908. The pump room itself was sadly demolished in 1935, but the spring still issues its brown waters which now run as a stream into an ornamental pond. The gardens were also the home of one of the world's first film studios, that of local pioneer George Albert Smith in the 1890s and 1900s.

b) *DEVELOPMENT of HOVE:* In 1825 construction of the Brunswick Town estate (q.v.) commenced within the parish of Hove, but it was governed by a local Act of Parliament from 1830 and was generally considered part of Brighton anyway. The first real development of Hove to the west of Adelaide Crescent came in 1851-2 with the construction of Albany, Medina, Osborne and Ventnor Villas on the Stanford family's estate, the district known as Cliftonville. Later that decade came the development of the Goldsmid family's Wick estate around the Avenues, an area which came to be known as West Brighton; indeed, Cliftonville Railway Station was renamed West Brighton in 1879 before becoming Hove Station in 1895. During the latter nineteenth century the rest of the Stanford estate was developed, mostly with very large villas and terraces in a dull yellow brick, a characteristic of Victorian Hove contrasting with the white and cream stucco of Regency Brunswick Town and Brighton.

Municipally, the Brunswick Town Commissioners became the Hove Commissioners in 1873, an urban district authority was created in 1894, and a municipal borough corporation was chartered in 1898. Aldrington was annexed for municipal purposes in 1893, and on 1 April 1928 the borough of Hove was extended to include Hangleton, Preston Rural, most of West Blatchington (q.v) and part of Patcham, bringing the total area to 3,953 acres; Aldrington, Hangleton, Hove and West Blatchington maintained their separate parochial status, however. (There was also a small transfer of land with Brighton in the Seven Dials area to produce an easier boundary.) Vast areas of middle-class housing were developed in Aldrington, Hangleton and West Blatchington, with more expensive housing in the Preston Rural and Patcham (Tongdean) areas. On 1 April 1974, under the 1972 Local Government Act, the urban district of Portslade-by-Sea was merged into the new borough of Hove with the urban parishes abolished.

c) *HOVE TODAY:* Very few buildings in the borough of Hove date from before 1825. No pre-nineteenth-century buildings at all remain of the former village of Hove as the thirteenth-century Church of St Andrew was almost wholly rebuilt by George Basevi in 1836. Hangleton and Portslade churches are medieval, but there are scant remains at the other ancient parish churches of Aldrington and West Blatchington. Hangleton Manor is a grade II*-listed building of the sixteenth century with the eighteenth-century Benfield Barn standing nearby, and there are also a number of pre-nineteenth-century houses in Portslade village. Conservation areas have now been designated at The Avenues, Benfield Barn, Brunswick Town, Cliftonville, Denmark Villas, The Drive, Goldstone Pumping Station, Hangleton, Pembroke and Princes, Portslade Village, Tongdean Avenue and Tongdean Road, and the Willett Estate.

Since the early nineteenth century the Hove authorities have always strongly resisted Brighton's several attempts at annexation, and, although the two towns are always thought of as one by outsiders, 'Hove actually' maintains its independence as a quiet and genteel town, a 'distinguished resort', in contrast to its brash, cosmopolitan neighbour. The difference is obvious when one looks at the respective sea-fronts, the Brunswick and Western Lawns of Hove providing a complementary facility to the mainly commercialised promenades of Brighton. Note, however, that Hove was a part of the Brighton parliamentary borough from 1832 until 1949.

80. Thomas Read KEMP

<46>

This important local figure was born on 23 December 1782 at Lewes, the son of Thomas Kemp who, in 1774, was left a moiety of the manor of Brighton by his uncle, Thomas Friend. Kemp's farmhouse was rented by the Prince of Wales in 1786, and was later demolished when the Marine Pavilion was erected <3>.

T.R.Kemp graduated in theology at Cambridge in 1805, and married Frances Baring in 1806 by whom he had four sons and six daughters, but she died in childbirth in 1825 and is buried in St Nicholas's Church. In 1811 he succeeded to his late father's moiety of the manor, and also became Member of Parliament for Lewes when he won his father's former seat. In March 1816 however, he resigned his seat and founded a dissenting religious sect at St James's Chapel, Brighton, which moved the following year to his newly-built Trinity Chapel in Ship Street; Kemp preached there for six years.

The Kemps lived at Herstmonceux Place from 1807 until 1819, but in that year they moved to a new house known as the Temple off Montpelier Road (see "Clifton Hill (Temple Gardens)"). By 1823 Kemp had returned to the established church, and also to Parliament as Member firstly for Arundel and then for Lewes again in 1826-37. It was in 1823 that he conceived the idea of the fashionable estate east of Brighton that was to bear his name, principally as a speculation to improve his finances. The project was not initially successful though, and as Kemp fell into greater financial difficulty he was forced to convey about £10,000 worth of land to the west of the estate to builder Thomas Cubitt in lieu of payment. He sold Trinity Chapel in 1825, but then purchased much of the Wick estate in Hove which he resold to Isaac Goldsmid in 1830.

Kemp was very prominent in local affairs as he was lord of the manor (and therefore a large property owner), an ex-officio town commissioner until 1825, a trustee of the Steine, and a magistrate; his generosity in gifts of land for worthy causes such as schools and hospitals is particularly noteworthy. In October 1827 he moved to 22 Sussex Square, and in 1832 married Frances Harvey by whom he had a son, Frederick, who was eventually to inherit his moeity of the manor and the freehold of the Kemp Town enclosures. In 1834 Kemp had a house completed at 24 Belgrave Square, London, but just three years later he was forced to leave England in order to escape his creditors; he returned only once, in September 1840. In January 1842 much of his land was auctioned, and on 10 January 1844 a proclamation of outlawry against Kemp was pinned on the door of St Peter's Church following his failure to surrender to a suit brought by Sir William Pilkington.

Thomas Read Kemp died on 20 December 1844 at 64 Rue de Fauborg Saint-Honore in Paris, and is buried at Père-la-Chaise cemetery in that city. A tablet was erected to his memory at St Nicholas's Church by his widow.

81. KEMP TOWN

<44,46,83,126,261>

The name Kemp Town is now applied generally to the area east of Rock Gardens, and has also been given to the parliamentary constituency which includes that half of the borough to the east of Old Steine, Grand Parade and Lewes Road. The original Kemp Town estate, however, consists of the grand houses of Arundel Terrace, Chichester Terrace, Lewes Crescent, Sussex Square, and their associated service roads; the history of that estate is now detailed below. Note that in 1908 the Kemp Town ward was renamed 'King's Cliff' in honour of Edward VII and the council also tried to encourage the use of the new name for the whole district. (The Churches of St George and St Mark were also associated with the estate; see "St George's Road" and "St Mary's Hall" respectively.)

a) *DEVELOPMENT of the ESTATE:* The grade I-listed estate, an outstanding conservation area, was built in an isolated position for Thomas Read Kemp in an attempt to improve his finances by providing high-class housing for the growing town. Architect Charles Busby and his building partner Amon Wilds were commissioned to develop the estate, and work commenced in May 1823. Busby's original plan called for two more squares and a total of 250 houses; however, the final plan included only 106 houses.

Figure 68: A view of Kemp Town in the 1840s

Construction was initially slow because of a lack of finance. The first houses were occupied in 1826, and the façades of the square and crescent were finished in 1827 but most were mere skeletons to be fitted out by the purchasers. The houses sold slowly, mainly owing to their then isolated position, and only eleven were occupied in 1828, and thirty-six by 1834. A horse-bus service to the railway station from 1840 helped to end the isolation and sales picked up, although the estate was not completed until about 1855.

The Kemp Town estate was governed by deeds and covenants, rather than by a local Act of Parliament as at the Brunswick estate. A management committee was established in 1828 including Kemp himself and builder Thomas Cubitt; the Revd James Anderson, curate of the estate's Chapel of St George, was honorary secretary from 1832 to 1853. From 1865, two members were voted onto the committee annually.

In 1903 Lord Rendel acquired about twenty of the houses and converted them into flats, a trend that continued until nearly all the houses had been converted by the 1960s.

b) *ARUNDEL TERRACE:* The first part of the estate to be finished, and the only part to be designed and built as a whole, was Arundel Terrace; the first houses were completed in 1828, and by 1834 ten of the thirteen houses were in occupation. They have Doric porches and ironwork balconies, but a number have been altered and the unity of the composition has been destroyed somewhat. The centre-piece, no.7, has a large portico and, along with nos.1, 5-6, 8-9 and 13, is adorned with giant Corinthian columns, although those of no.8 are now unfortunately obscured.

No.13, Arundel House, was probably the first on the estate to be finished, in 1826, and was opened as the Bush Hotel by William Bush; he was followed as proprietor by Henry Bell from 1828 until 1847. In about 1850 the hotel was removed to its present location on the northern side of Arundel Place, and no.13 became a private house and later a girls' school; in about 1910 it became a rest home and then a guest house in the 1950s.

Figure 69: Another view of Kemp Town, from the beach

No.5 was the home of novelist William Harrison Ainsworth from 1853 until 1867. Born in Manchester in 1805, he first visited Brighton in 1827, and while residing at Arundel Terrace wrote *Star Chamber*; *The Flitch of Bacon*; *Spendthrift*; *Mervyn Clitheroe*; and *Ovingdean Grange, a tale of the South Downs*, which includes a romantic account of the escape of King Charles II to France, and also the legend of the Devil's Dyke. Ainsworth later moved to Hurstpierpoint and then to Reigate where he died on 3 January 1882.

c) *CHICHESTER TERRACE:* This was the last piece of the estate to be completed. No.14 was finished by 1828, nos.12-13 were completed in 1835, and no.11 a few years later, but the gap between no.11 and Chichester House was not filled until about 1850 when Thomas Cubitt, a nationally famous builder who erected about thirty-seven of the estate's houses, built nos.1-3 and then nos.4-10 to complete the terrace in about 1855. It does not, however, follow Busby's original plan of Corinthian pilasters on every third house as only nos.1 and 14 have them. All the houses have Doric porches surmounted by verandahs, but the terrace lacks a centre-piece.

Chichester House at the western end, which was not originally considered to be part of either the terrace or estate, was built and let by 1832, and stood on its own before the rest of the terrace was completed. It was initially used as a young gentlemen's academy, but from 1938 until 1944 it was the home of historic novelist D.L.Murray, the 'leader' of the town's literary community. It has a broad frontage with a wide bow, a fluted Doric porch, and an extraordinary thirteen Corinthian pilasters.

At the rear of Chichester Terrace is Kemp Town Place, an attractive, wide mews of contemporary, cobble-fronted cottages. The roadway retains its original setts and is entered through large gateways. All the cottages are grade II listed together with nos.2-3 Rock Grove which form part of the mews; no.1 Rock Grove, on its own, is also listed.

d) *LEWES CRESCENT:* This magnificent crescent, with a span of 840 feet, has twenty-eight four-storey houses which follow Busby's original plan of every third house bearing giant Corinthian pilasters and iron balconies; those on the eastern side also have Doric porches and verandahs. The façades were completed by 1827, but most houses remained shells for several years.

Builder Thomas Cubitt lived at no.13 from 1846 until 1855. Nos.15-16 were used as a military hospital during the First World War. Fife House, 1 Lewes Crescent together with 14 Chichester Terrace, was the residence of the sixth Duke of Devonshire from 1828 until 1858; the embankment down to Madeira Drive in front of his house is named Duke's Mound after him. From 1896 until 1924 this house was the home of Princess Louise, daughter of Edward VII, and her husband the Duke of Fife; the King himself stayed here during his convalescence in 1908. No.18 was the home of actress Anna Neagle and her producer husband Herbert Wilcox from 1953 until 1969. Their neighbour at no.17 for a number of years was Lord Frederick Elwyn-Jones (1909-89), a Labour M.P for nearly thirty years, a prosecutor at Nuremburg, and Lord Chancellor in the 1970s.

e) *SUSSEX SQUARE:* Measuring about 300 feet wide by 550 feet long, Sussex Square was commenced in 1823 and the façades were complete by 1827, but most of the fifty houses were mere skeletons which were let or sold for completion. No.25 was the first private house on the estate to be occupied, in 1826 by Philip Storey, Kemp's brother-in-law. Kemp himself lived at no.22 from 1827 until 1837. All the houses have four storeys, Doric or Ionic porches, and ironwork balconies; every third house has pilasters, mostly with Corinthian capitals, but several houses remain unstuccoed and are faced with yellow brick. The centre-piece of the square is the pedimented nos.24-27, all decorated with Corinthian pilasters. No.32 Sussex Square even has giant, fluted Ionic pilasters on its rear façade in Bristol Place.

The square naturally became the residence of the rich and famous. Perhaps most famous was Revd Charles Dodgson, better known as the author Lewis Carroll, who lived at no.11 from 1874 until 1887. Nos.19-20 were the home of the first Marquess and fifth Earl of Bristol between 1831 and 1859. Formerly Under-Secretary for Foreign Affairs in the Addington government of 1801-4, he was created Marquess in 1826, and was an important local landowner who contributed land and finance to many local institutions. The Marquess died on 15 March 1859 and was buried in the Lewes Road Parochial Cemetery (now Woodvale). He is commemorated by several streets in the Kemp Town area, by the Bristol public house, and by the Bristol estate.

f) *The ENCLOSURES:* The estate gardens are still privately owned, used and maintained by the residents under the management of estate agents Bernard Thorpe; the keys are held by the residents along with twelve selected 'outsiders'. The principal gardens, occupying about four acres, were enclosed with iron railings in 1823, and until 1828 were three in number as Lewes Crescent was then a continuous roadway. In that latter year they were laid out by landscape gardener Henry Phillips, with the tunnel to the esplanade added in about 1830. William IV and Queen Adelaide, and later Victoria and Albert, enjoyed walking in the gardens on their visits to Brighton. They were set aside exclusively for the pleasure of Edward VII in 1908 when staying with his daughter at 1 Lewes Crescent.

The gardens were extensively replanted in 1878. In 1886 four tennis courts were provided in the southern enclosure, and a croquet lawn, which remained until about 1935, was laid out in 1890 in the northern garden. In 1940 the gardens were taken over by the military, with the tunnel bricked up and the iron railings removed for scrap. They inevitably suffered and were not formally released until May 1946, but restoration took place in 1947, a new fence was erected in August 1949, and the tunnel opened again in 1952. In 1969 the gardens were one of several Brighton locations used for filming *On a clear day you can see for ever*, starring Barbra Streisand. The small Arundel and Chichester Terrace lawns have been maintained by the borough council since 1952.

Figure 70: The Kemp Town Esplanades in about 1845. Note the gap between Chichester House and the rest of Chichester Terrace.

g) *SLOPES AND ESPLANADES, Madeira Drive:* The attractive slopes to the beach in front of the cliffs were begun in September 1828, and were completed in August 1830 to the design of William Kendall. Two esplanades were built below the cliff top connected to the Lewes Crescent gardens by a tunnel beneath the road; the tunnel's esplanade entrance is flanked by two small cottages, one of which was occupied by the head gardener, the other by the estate constable. The cliff-top esplanade and the sea-wall were built in two sections in 1833 and 1835, and in February 1835 Kendall added a reading-room on the lower esplanade which was used for many years for committee meetings.

The slopes were not enclosed and remained open to the public. In 1865 though, the committee erected a fence along the western boundary, an action which initiated a long argument with the corporation which insisted that the land belonged to the town. The extension of Madeira Drive to Black Rock in 1895 led to further fences and hedges, and the committee decided to exclude the public completely in February 1896. Eventually agreement was reached and an exchange of land took place which allowed the slopes to be extended to the west and the Madeira Drive ramp to Marine Parade to be constructed at Black Rock. The slopes were planted with shrubs in 1900.

The slopes suffered badly during the military occupation of the Second World War when the tunnel was blocked off, and the War Department later paid £2,245 in compensation. In 1952 the Kemp Town slopes, which are an excellent example of 1820s landscaping, were purchased by the corporation for just £750 under the terms of the 1949 Brighton Corporation Act which laid down strict conditions on their use, and they have been restored to their original appearance. The tunnel cottages, one of which has been bricked up and the other now used as a store, were not part of the purchase but are leased to the council. The cottages, tunnel entrance, reading-room, and the shelter known as the 'Temple' at the eastern end of the esplanade are all listed buildings.

82. KEMP TOWN RAILWAY

<7,123,126,176,179,180,187a>

Built in 1866-9 by the London, Brighton and South Coast Railway Company under an Act of May 1864, the Kemp Town branch line was opened principally to fend off a possible rival line into eastern Brighton. The first turf was cut by the mayor, Henry Martin, on 17 February 1866, and the line opened on 2 August 1869. It was a single track, 1 mile 726 yards long, leaving the Lewes line 1,606 yards from Brighton at Kemp Town Junction; the short section from the junction to Lewes Road Station was doubled in July 1895. The journey from Brighton was therefore over 2.3 miles long, about twice the distance by road.

Services were temporarily withdrawn from 1 January 1917 until 10 August 1919, but after attracting some 70,000 to 80,000 passengers annually in the late 1920s, passenger services were permanently withdrawn on 31 December 1932 having been badly affected by competition from buses. The line was then used by goods traffic only and Kemp Town became the Brighton East goods-depot, but in August 1971 the line finally closed and the goods traffic was transferred to Hove; a final, commemorative, diesel passenger service was run on 26 June 1971.

Despite its short length, the line was heavily engineered. The Lewes Road Viaduct, about 180 yards long, carried the track fifty feet above Lewes Road and Melbourne Street, but was demolished in April 1976; the western arches were removed later in 1983 for the new Vogue gyratory road layout and the erection of the Sainsburys superstore. Hartington Road was crossed on a three-arch viaduct (demolished 2 December 1973), and the line then ran through a cutting, now partially filled and levelled as a large recreation ground behind Picton Street, William Clarke Park. Beneath Elm Grove Junior School the line entered the 946-yard Kemp Town Tunnel, to emerge from the chalk cliffs at the northern end of Kemp Town Station yard. From October 1941 until May 1944 the tunnel was used as a store for rail stock and was also made available for use as an air-raid shelter <123>. Part of the tunnel is now used as a mushroom farm, and the almost circular southern portal may still be seen behind the Booker warehouse in Stevenson Road.

Kemp Town Station stood in the former Coalbrook Road, and opened in 1869 with four sidings and one platform, but by 1880 a large goods-yard and coal depot with seventeen sidings had opened. The station building was similar to those at Hove, London Road and Portslade, but nothing now remains of it; the large Freshfield Industrial Estate was opened on the site in June 1974, and by 1987 over 500 people were employed there. Lewes Road Station opened on 1 September 1873 on a site behind the Rediffusion factory in D'Aubigny Road, with another approach via a footpath from Lewes Road. There was a small station building and two platforms connected by a footbridge, but it closed to passengers along with the rest of the line at the end of 1932 and became first a pickle factory and then a builder's store. The area to the west was used as a goods yard, but the whole site is now occupied by the Centenary Industrial Estate of 1986. Hartington Road Halt was a single platform on the western side of the track just to the south of Hartington Road, and was accessed by a cinder path between Hartington Road and Upper Wellington Road. It opened on 1 January 1906 but closed on 1 June 1911.

83. KING'S ROAD

a) *HISTORY:* The King's Road was laid out as a carriage road and promenade in 1821-2 to replace a rough track which had run along the cliff top from Little East Street to Middle Street; traffic previously had to turn inland at these points. The new road and promenade was extended seaward on supports in conjunction with a new sea-wall, and enabled traffic to travel directly from East Street to West Street. A.H.Wilds supervised the construction, and King George IV, who had contributed £200 to the project, opened the road on 29 January 1822 in the presence of 10,000 residents; the King was bestrewn with sugar plums, an old local custom. The track westwards from West Street to the Hove boundary, which had been developed with large villas by the beginning of the nineteenth century, was also named King's Road and continued through Hove to New Shoreham. Wilds extended the promenade to Brunswick Town in 1834. <15,46>

With the opening of the Grand Junction Road in 1829, King's Road became part of *the* most fashionable equestrian and carriage drive <24>; every day, the titled, the rich and the famous would ride from Kemp Town via Marine Parade, Grand Junction Parade and the King's Road to Brunswick Town. In the 1850s and '60s the road and promenade were widened, resulting in the removal of the West Battery, while further widening and improvements in 1883-7 involved extensions seawards above the King's Road Arches; the bandstand, the rotunda and shelter hall at the bottom of West Street, and ten sheltered promenade seats, seven of which remain, all date from this time (the date of the improvement, 1886, is marked on the railings in places). That part of the road to the west of the West Pier was widened in 1894. Electric street-lighting was inaugurated in 1893, but the present ornate lamp-posts were added in the 1930s (see "Street-lighting"). The tarmacadam surface of King's Road and Grand Junction Road was inaugurated on 22 July 1910, and the roadway itself was 'dualled' for part of its length in 1969. The large iron railings that once ran along the kerb were removed in 1924.

King's Road remains one of the principal promenades of the town, and is lined with large hotels, guest houses, shops, restaurants and entertainments. Following a great deal of redevelopment, however, it lacks much of the architectural style for which Brighton is famous. Separate entries are given for the following buildings in King's Road: "Bedford Hotel", "Brighton Centre", "Grand Hotel", "Hospitality Inn", "Kingswest Boulevard", "Lower Esplanade", "Metropole, Hotel", "Norfolk Resort Hotel", "Old Ship Hotel", "Queen's Hotel", and "West Pier".

b) *OTHER BUILDINGS OF INTEREST:* The King's Road actually begins behind the Queen's Hotel at East Street, where no.6, Dolphin Cottage, is an unusual early survivor in this part of the town, but is accessible only via a private passage. At the corner of Little East Street stands Dr Brightons. Formerly the Star and Garter Hotel, it was dubbed Dr Brightons in the nineteenth century and the name has stuck; the proprietor posted a notice on the wall giving the 'consulting hours' and listing the 'prescriptions of the finest quality' which were available inside. The hotel has played host to many famous people, including Winston Churchill, Jack Dempsey, Charlie Chaplin, Richard Burton, and the Prince of Wales (later Edward VIII), and dates back to at least 1785 when twin Irish giants were exhibited there. In front of the original bow-fronted building stood a capstan which was removed in 1827 to make way for the construction of the Grand Junction Road. This action provoked the last major argument between the town's fishermen and other inhabitants <15,123>.

Between the Old Ship and West Street stand some impressive but mixed five- and six-storey buildings of the early to mid nineteenth century. No.39, for instance,

Figure 71: King's Road by the Old Ship in about 1845

on the Ship Street corner, has much decoration in the form of shell motifs, urns and composite capitals. Nos.42-43, faced with black glazed mathematical tiles, date from 1813. No.50, the Argyle public house, has a number of figurehead decorations.

At the corner of West Street is the Sheridan Hotel, a highly attractive, six-storey building with much terra-cotta decoration on both façades. It was built in 1882 as the fashionable Orleans residential club, and in 1898 became the Victoria Hotel (see figure 18) <24,83>. On the opposite promenade stands the former summer tourist information bureau, a delicate ironwork rotunda built as a promenade shelter in 1887; a shelter hall was constructed on the Lower Esplanade below at the same time <24,115>.

One of the most famous establishments of King's Road was Muttons Hotel and Restaurant, opened by William Sexton Mutton between West Street and Russell Street in the 1840s. Almost an institution of Brighton society, it closed in 1929 and Kingswest was later built on the site, but it is remembered in Cuthbert Bede's novel, *Matins and Muttons* <3>. At the corner of the former Russell Street once stood the Palladium Cinema. Built on the site of the Whitehall Livery Stables, it opened on 29 October 1888 as the Alhambra Opera House and Music Hall, and films were shown on the bill from 1897. On 6 April 1912 it reopened as the Grand Cinema de Luxe or Palladium Cinema, and a year later the last variety performance was given. Holding 1,200 people, the cinema was designed by Frank Matcham and had a lavish interior, a highly decorated exterior with balustrades, cupolas, statues and ironwork canopy, and a roof which could be opened in hot weather. Sound equipment was installed in July 1929, and in 1936 it was given a new Art Deco façade and became known briefly as the Odeon until the West Street Odeon opened the following year. The Palladium closed in May 1956 and the site now lies under the Brighton Centre <68,68a>.

Beyond the Metropole, the bow-fronted 125-126 and 128 King's Road are listed buildings of the 1820s by Wilds and Busby; no.127 has been completely ruined. The Royal Sussex Regiment's War Memorial stands alongside King's Road at Regency Square, a Portland stone cenotaph erected to the 152 men of the regiment who perished in the South African or Boer War of 1900-2. It was unveiled on 29 October 1904 by the Marquess of Abergavenny, and is surmounted by a bronze bugler and four artillery shells. Now a listed structure, it also commemorates the men lost at Louisberg and Quebec in 1759, in Egypt in the 1880s, and in the two World Wars. <44,311>

No.131 King's Road is a grade II*-listed building which, with 1 Regency Square, was once the home of the Duke and Duchess of St Alban's (see "Regency Square"). The seventy-bedroom King's Hotel is decorated with giant fluted Corinthian pillars and pilasters, and was erected as part of a proposed Oriental Terrace in the 1820s; the buildings were converted into a hotel in about 1864 by T.H.King, but were badly damaged by fire in 1967. Further west still, nos.146-148 are also listed buildings, with fluted Ionic pilasters and columns supporting delicate ironwork balconies and verandahs; they were originally nos.1-3 Bedford Square and date from around 1810. <44>

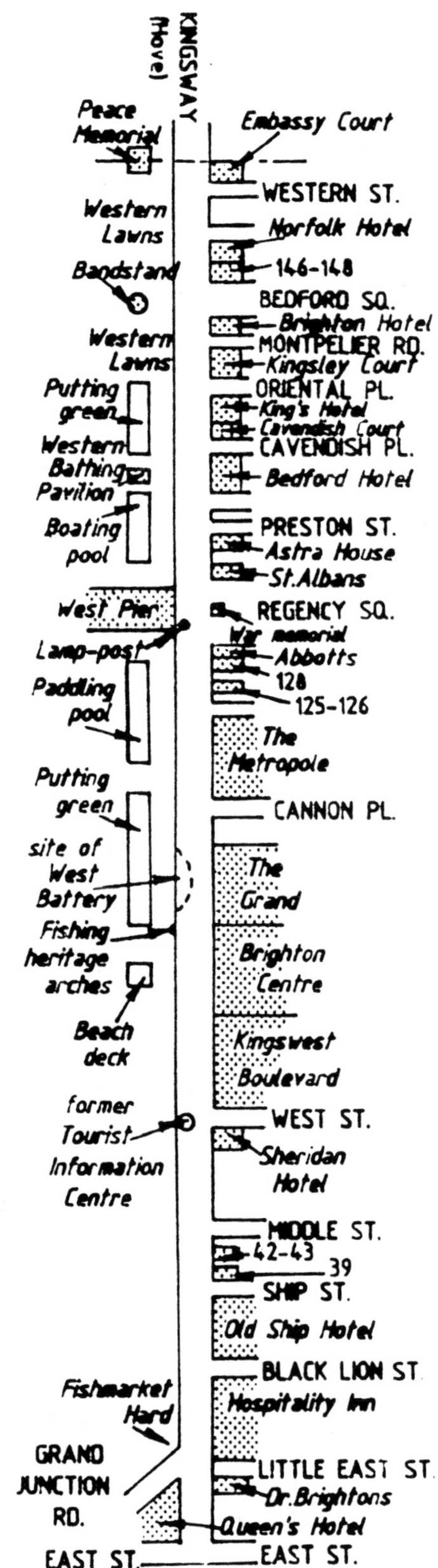

Figure 72: King's Road

The King's Road Bandstand stands on the Lower Esplanade opposite, but is raised to the level of King's Road. Nicknamed the 'birdcage' bandstand, it is a light ironwork, listed building which was erected in 1884 with a public convenience in the base. Topped by an oriental dome, the roof is supported by eight delicate ironwork pillars, and there were originally shutters to shelter the performers from the breeze. In 1986 it was brought into use again. (See figure 82.) <24,44,123>

The boundary with Hove is reached at the Peace Memorial, which bears a portrait of Edward VII (q.v.), the arms of the two boroughs, and the following inscription: 'In the year 1912 the inhabitants of Brighton and Hove provided a home for the Queen's Nurses, and erected this monument in memory of Edward VII and as a testimony of their enduring loyalty'. Standing thirty feet tall, the listed memorial is surmounted by an angel of peace bearing an orb and olive branch, standing on a sphere supported by four dolphins. Designed by Newbury Trent in a competition, it was unveiled by the Duke of Norfolk on 12 October 1912, the same day as the nurses' home was opened at 12-14 Wellington Road. <44,311>

c) *FLATS:* There are now several large blocks of flats in King's Road, most of which have been erected on the sites of large villas. The most distinctive is Embassy Court, an eleven-storey block of 104 flats at the very western end of the borough. Erected in 1934-5 to the design of Wells Coates on the site of the former Brunswick Baths, Embassy Court was the first modern high-rise block in the town and was an especially controversial development as it stands adjacent to Hove's Brunswick Terrace. However, it does possess some architectural merit of its own and is a fine example of the architect's work. The 110-foot tall building has distinctive, continuous horizontal balconies of concrete which taper towards the top, and in 1984 it was listed as being of special architectural interest. <44,45>

Kingsley Court was erected in 1985-7 on the site of the neo-Georgian Abinger Hotel, which itself opened in May 1956 on the site of the mid-nineteenth-century Abinger House; the latter was the last private mansion on the sea-front and was demolished in 1948 <45,83,311>. Cavendish House, a fourteen-storey block in black brick, justifiably provoked intense criticism because of its colour when it was erected in 1966-7 on the site of the Union Club, a large bow-fronted house of 1865 <83,123>. Astra House is a ten-storey block of sixty-two flats and shops in yellow brick, erected in 1938 on the site of the New Club, a tall Palladian-style building of 1876. Abbotts, a plain eight-storey block, was built in 1961-2 at the corner of Regency Square on the site of the mid-Victorian Abbott's Hotel. <45,83>

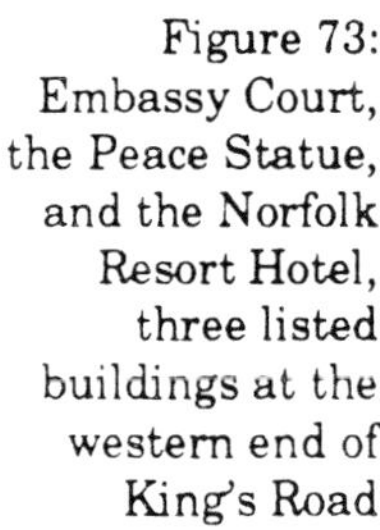

Figure 73: Embassy Court, the Peace Statue, and the Norfolk Resort Hotel, three listed buildings at the western end of King's Road

84. KINGSWEST BOULEVARD, King's Road and West Street

<123>

The site of the Kingswest complex was partially cleared pre-war for a proposed winter garden, but the buildings fronting King's Road, Kent Street and West Street were not demolished until 1963. Designed by Russell Diplock, the new building was the first phase of the massive West Street/Churchill Square redevelopment area, and opened as the Brighton Top Rank Suite on 10 November 1965; the original plans also included a banqueting hall, restaurant, cinema and car-park on the adjacent Sports Stadium site. The initial facilities included only bars and a large dance hall, but in December 1966 a tenpin bowling centre and an ice-rink, which was convertible into a conference hall for 6,000 delegates, were opened to compensate to some extent for the loss of the S.S.Brighton (see "West Street").

After only four years operation though, the bowling lanes closed in November 1970 and the ice-rink was closed the following September after financial losses; no more conferences were then held. In the summer of 1972 the building was renamed the 'Kingswest', and underwent a £500,000 conversion; the lower floors were converted into several separate dance halls and bars, and the upper floor, the former ice-rink, was converted into a triple-screen Odeon cinema complex. Opening on 18 April 1973, the cinema replaced the nearby Odeon in West Street, and also the Academy and the Regent cinemas.

Further changes were completed in May 1987 when an arcade from King's Road to West Street was opened, adding café-bars and shops to the facilities of the Odeon, Busbys discotheque, and the Top Rank Suite. The building was renamed the 'Kingswest Boulevard', and two more cinema screens, on the ground and basement levels, were added; the changes coincided with the first Brighton Film Festival. In August 1989, a sixth screen was opened for 103 viewers in the former Boulevard restaurant in time for the second film festival on 8-10 September 1989. The Odeon can now accommodate 2,397 film-goers. On 22 March 1990 Busbys reopened as Oriana's, while the Top Rank Suite was renamed The Event.

The Kingswest building is probably the most heavily criticised in the town for its appearance in such a prime location. The pale cream southern façade is topped by an unusual faceted roof of gold-coloured aluminium which was intended to glitter in the sun and to give the impression of floating as a band of reflected light at night. To many, however, the Kingswest is a plain, bulky, shapeless edifice. The appearance of the building has been improved since it opened though, and at least the site was spared the grey concrete drabness of many other buildings of the 1960s.

85. LADIES MILE, Patcham

The Ladies Mile Road is an old drove road from Patcham to Stanmer Park which became popular with horsewomen in the late nineteenth century, part of a pleasant circular ride from Preston Park via London Road, the Ladies Mile, Ditchling Road and Surrenden Road. Developed mainly with bungalow housing in the 1930s, the Ladies Mile ridge extends eastwards to Old Boat Corner where forty acres of open downland have been preserved by the corporation as an open space, although some of this will disappear beneath the Brighton bypass. <107,126,127a>

Near the western end of Ladies Mile Road, Mile End Cottages are an attractive Victorian terrace in a light brick. Nearby Place Farm House at the corner of Highview Avenue North is modern, but Drove Cottages, 36-44 Ladies Mile Road, are heavily-restored flint cottages built in 1815 for the poor of the parish <48b>. Patcham Methodist Church, designed by Peter Gibbs, was built in 1968 on the site of Drove Barn, a flint and timber building which was restored as a church in 1935; it was said to date from 1595 and to have used timbers from an Armada ship wrecked at Rottingdean. <107,108,124,311>

Ladies Mile Road continues eastwards past the White House Nursery School, once the home of George Ferguson who developed the Ladies Mile estate in the valley below, Eastwick Bottom. This area belonged to Place Farm and was once deserted apart from the early-nineteenth-century Eastwick Barn, although the name dates from at least the thirteenth century <108,289>. The flint barn still stands in Eastwick Close, but has been heavily restored and converted into a home, and with the addition of window bays is barely recognisable as a barn at all. The housing estate was developed in the 1930s; Patcham Clock Tower was erected as an advertising aid, while the nearby Ladies Mile Hotel, a superb example of a 1930s estate public house, opened in 1935. The Mackie Hall opened in 1937 in connection with All Saints' Church, Patcham, and in about the same year George Ferguson presented the Mackie Avenue Recreation Ground, the Plainfields open space, and the two Vale Avenue open spaces to the corporation. Also in Vale Avenue is the Horsdean Recreation Ground, eighteen acres levelled in the 1930s and extended in the 1960s; part of this is also to be taken for construction of the bypass, however. <83,124,126,128>

86. The LEVEL

<3,15,24,112,115,126>

Now the principal public open space of the Valley Gardens and covering 8.05 acres, the Level was once a marshy area of open land which stretched north to include the present Park Crescent and south to embrace the Victoria Gardens (q.v.), although these were also known as the North Steine. The intermittent streams from the London Road and Lewes Road valleys converged at the Level, and it was probably the swampy nature of the land that prevented any building upon it. It has always been a popular venue for circuses, fairs, celebrations and other events, and when the North Steine was enclosed in 1817 it became the only remaining recreational area in the town. Cricket was played on the Level from at least the mid eighteenth century, and the northern part was laid out as a cricket ground for the Prince of Wales in 1791; both the Prince and his brother the Duke of York were keen players and spectators of the game. On 7-8 August 1792 Brighton beat Hampshire there, and followed it by a three-wicket win against Marylebone (M.C.C.) on 23 August 1792; the last grand match on the Prince's ground was in August 1822 when Brighton played Dorking. These early matches are now commemorated by the Bat and Ball public house in Ditchling Road.

On 22 April 1822 the present area of the Level was vested by Thomas Read Kemp and the other landowners in trustees on behalf of the town, and it was formally laid out in the same year by A.H.Wilds and Henry

Phillips. Union Road was constructed to link the Ditchling and Lewes Roads, while that part to the north was sold to James Ireland who laid out the Royal Gardens (see "Park Crescent"). Under the terms of the 1873 Brighton Borough Extension Act, the trustees' powers and responsibilities were vested in the corporation.

In November 1844 the fine avenues of elm trees were planted, a gift of the Earl of Chichester, but many were uprooted in the great storm of October 1987. Further alterations were made in 1877 when a low wall was built along the inside of the avenues and the low fence was replaced by six-foot iron railings; these were themselves replaced by dwarf fences in about 1922. The northern part is still a level grassed area (with a hard floodlit football pitch) frequented by visiting fairs, festivals, exhibitions and rallies. It is separated from the playground by a fine rose-walk which was the site of the Open Market in the 1920s. The children's playground itself was laid out in 1927 with a boating pool, bridges and pergola, but the pool has now been paved over with a much smaller paddling pool installed, and one of the two shelters is now a café. A large skateboard park was added in the late 1980s. The formal southern entrance to the Level is decorated with ornamental dolphin-shaped lamps, and is flanked by a small building on the western side which was a branch police station from about 1865 until 1919; it later became the main office of the Brighton Parks and Gardens Department. The materials of a similar building opposite were used to construct the thatched shelter at Preston Rockery.

The Level has traditionally been a place for meeting, speaking and demonstrating, and was the venue of annual May Day workers' rallies for many years. Large public dinners were held on it to celebrate the coronations of George IV and Victoria, and also at the end of the Napoleonic and Crimean Wars.

87. LEWES ROAD

a) *HISTORY:* With a length of 3.46 miles from Waterloo Place to the Falmer boundary, Lewes Road is the longest continuously-named road in Brighton, and replaced the downland Drove Road and Juggs Road over Newmarket Hill in medieval times. (A 'jug' was a Brighton fisherman; their wives took the catch along this route by donkey for sale at Lewes. <296a>)

Lewes, the county town of Sussex, lies seven-and-a-half miles to the north-east of Brighton, and has always been important to the town. Lewes Castle was built by the Norman son-in-law of William the Conqueror, William de Warrenne, who was Lord of the Rape of Lewes and thereby lord of the manors of Brighton. De Warrenne also founded the great Cluniac Priory of St Pancras at Southover in 1077, the mother church of the medieval Priory of St Bartholomew at Brighton. The ruins of both the castle and the priory may be visited. It was probably the proximity of the markets at Lewes and their easy access via the Downs that helped to establish the medieval fishing town of Brighton, and in the mid eighteenth century it was once again the proximity of the county town that helped to transform Brighton from an economically depressed fishing town into a fashionable resort.

From 1770 the road to Lewes was maintained by a turnpike trust, with a tollgate to the north of the Bear Inn and a toll-house at Kingston which still survives. The modern road was 'dualled' to the south of The Avenue and alongside Stanmer Park in 1963-4, and the length in between in 1967-8, a project that won a Civic Trust design award in 1970. The dual carriageway from Brighton to Lewes was completed at Falmer in 1981,

Figure 74: The Percy Almshouses, the earliest Gothic revival buildings in the town

while the Brighton bypass, scheduled for completion in 1995, will leave the Lewes Road at the Southern Water offices. <1,2,123,313>

The first developments along Lewes Road, both in 1795, were the almshouses and the barracks (see below). The Level was laid out in 1822, and in the 1820s Richmond Terrace and Hanover Crescent were developed (see "Valley Gardens" and "Hanover" respectively). The road north from the Level to the borough boundary at Bear Road was developed from the 1860s, and then northwards in Preston parish to Natal Road in the

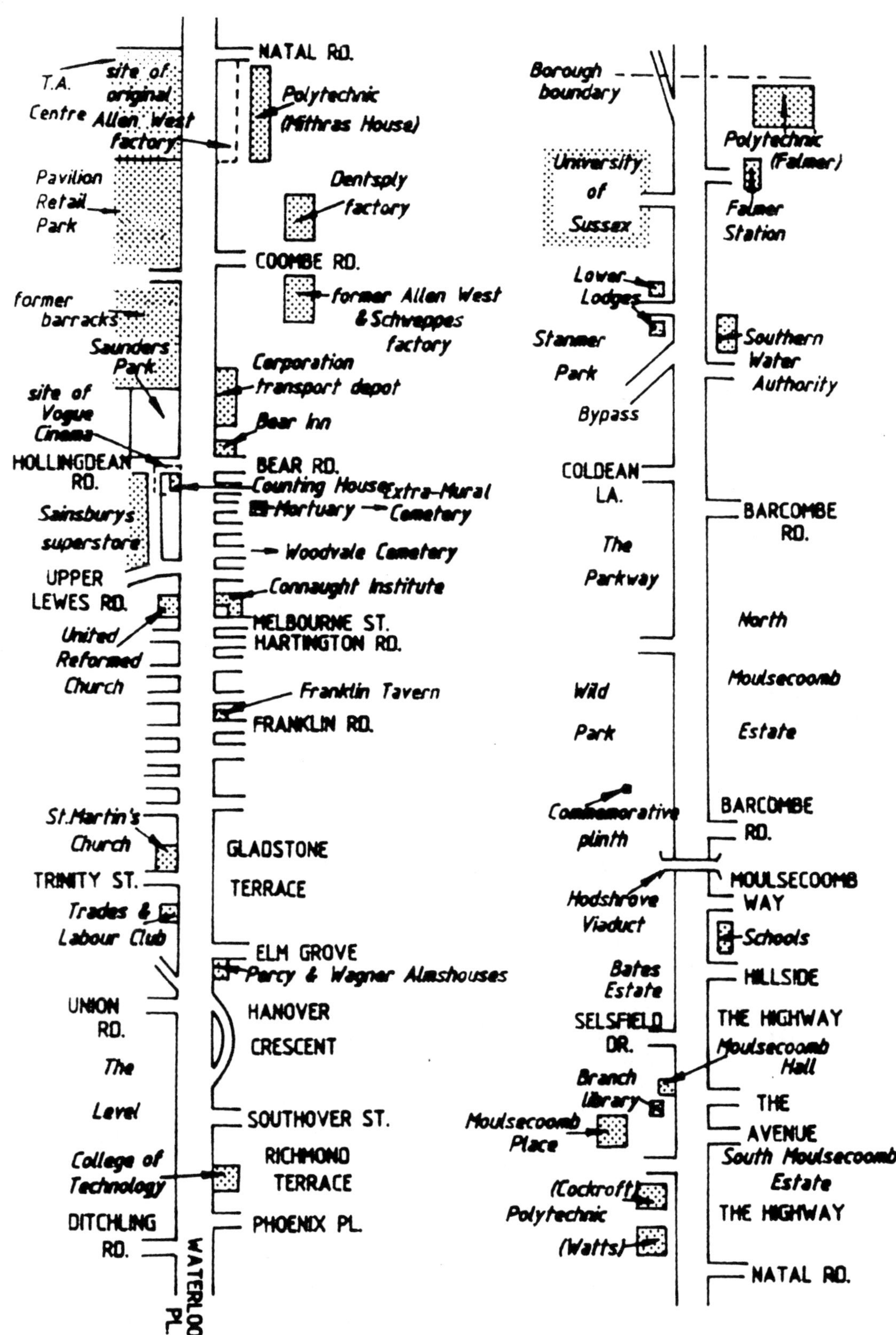

Figure 75: Lewes Road

1890s and 1900s. During the 1910s a small industrial area of diamond and engineering factories was established on the eastern side of Lewes Road around Coombe Road (see "Bear Road and East Preston"), and further development came in the 1920s with the Moulsecoomb estates. The section from Elm Grove to Upper Lewes Road is now a shopping area of considerable importance to the surrounding area, augmented by the Sainsbury store. <83>

Places of interest in Lewes Road are detailed below, but the following have separate entries: "Cemeteries", "Level", "Moulsecoomb", "Polytechnic", "Stanmer" and "University of Sussex". See also "Tramways" for information concerning the Brighton Buses depot north of Bear Road.

b) *PERCY AND WAGNER ALMSHOUSES:* The town's only remaining almshouses stand by the bottom of Elm Grove, but when they were built in 1795 it was in a then quite isolated position. They were erected to the memory of the late Dorothy and Philadelphia Percy, the daughters of the Duke of Northumberland, and were provided for six poor widows of the Church of England who, having received no parish relief, were also given £48 per annum and a new gown and cloak every second year; this was later increased to £96 and two gowns and bonnets each year, and a duffel coat every third year. The original houses, nos.4-9, were the first Gothic revival buildings in Brighton; they were added to in 1859 at the expense of Revd Henry Wagner and his sister Mary in memory of the Marquess of Bristol. The yellow-brick houses, now amongst the oldest in the town, were to be demolished in the 1960s, but happily they were listed in March 1971 and restored in 1975-6. <3,44,65,123>

c) *ST MARTIN'S CHURCH:* The congregation of St Martin's originally used the former school building (now flats) of 1867 in St Martin's Street, but the permanent church was built in 1872-5 by George Somers Clarke for the three sons of Revd Henry Wagner in memory of their late father. Consecrated on 1 May 1875, the listed building is in Early English style with pinnacled buttresses at both ends and a large pitched roof. The entrance is a large, ribbed Gothic arch with a bas-relief of St Martin and the Beggar, and on the southern exterior wall is a memorial to the men of the parish who fell in the Great War. The interior, also designed by Clarke, is very large and spacious, with a clerestoried nave sixty-nine feet high, aisles, chancel, and an eastern chapel. Its decoration has been called the most beautiful in Brighton; the roof panels are painted with representations of colonial and American sees, while the altar, dating from 1949, is adorned by a large reredos by H.Ellis Wooldridge of twenty pictures and sixty-nine statuettes. The church seats a congregation of 1,500, and due to its proximity to Preston Barracks was Brighton's 'military' church for many years. The adjacent Wagner Memorial Hall was erected in 1905. The parish, which was created in October 1875, has now merged into the parish of the Resurrection. <1,44,45,65>

d) *OTHER BUILDINGS to BEAR ROAD:* The Trades and Labour Club, 16 Lewes Road, stands on the site of the Arcadia Cinema. In about 1907 Tilleys horse-bus stables, with an entrance in Park Crescent Place, were let to a fairground animated-picture operator as the Arcadia Theatre of Varieties; both film-shows and variety acts were presented, and the famous escapologist Harry Houdini performed on the stage. In 1910 a permanent 478-seat cinema, the People's Picture Palace, opened on the site, soon changing its name to the Arcadia Cinema, and an entrance was made in Lewes Road. It closed in 1957. On the opposite side of the road is the impressive Gladstone Terrace, erected in the late 1860s and faced in an attractive brick. <68,68a,83,123>

Lewes Road United Reformed Church was built as a Congregational chapel in 1878 by A.Harford in Italian Gothic style, and has an adjacent church hall of 1892 <62>. On the eastern side of the road, the Franklin Tavern was rebuilt after receiving a direct hit during an air-raid in which several people were killed <242>.

At 131 Lewes Road, with another entrance in Melbourne Street, stands the New Life Centre. Formerly the Connaught Institute, the two-storey, red-brick building opened in 1879 as a soldiers' home and mechanics' institute. It housed a temperance bar, reading-rooms, lecture-rooms, etc., and also a branch of the Medical Mission which administered to the sick in their own homes. The hall seats 1,000 and is now used by the Connaught Christian Fellowship. <24,83>

Alfred Edgar Coppard (1878-1957), short-story writer and poet, was born just off Lewes Road at the now demolished 28 Melbourne Street, but had moved to 27 Gladstone Place by 1905. <83a,296>

The junction of Lewes, Bear, Hollingdean and Upper Lewes Roads is known as the 'Vogue gyratory system' after the former Vogue Cinema. Built as the Gaiety in 1937 in the grounds of the Allen Arms (now the Counting House), the cinema had a fifty-foot high neon-lit façade. In November 1965 it was renamed the Ace, and in January 1968 became a full-time bingo hall, but films were presented again from December 1969 and in 1971 the name was changed to the Vogue. It later became a pornographic film club with regular strip-tease acts, but in 1979 the 1,500-seat Vogue was renamed the Classic after that cinema in Western Road had closed, and it then closed itself in October 1980. The new road layout opened in the summer of 1984. The Sainsburys superstore opened on 23 April 1985 on the site of the railway viaduct and Arthur H.Cox's pill factory, and won the 1985 Brighton Council design award with its 'warehouse' style, the arches of its walls echoing those of the former viaduct. <68,68a,123>

e) *SAUNDERS PARK:* Saunders Park covers 4.2 acres to the north of Hollingdean Road, and was laid out in 1924 on the site of the Lewes Road waterworks which had latterly been used by the Parks Department as a nursery. Unemployed labour was used to construct the park, and it was formally opened by the mayor, Hugh Milner Black, on 17 September 1924. In the same year Arthur and Benjamin Saunders offered an area of their land behind the pumping station to the corporation for about £1,000 and the park is named after them; this land was in the occupation of, and subsequently sold to, the War Office for £2,000, the proceeds going towards the cost of the Preston Park cycling track stand. Several old flint walls of the waterworks remain, while the large, brick building was an electricity substation erected in 1924. <83,115,126>

f) *PRESTON BARRACKS and the PAVILION CENTRE RETAIL PARK:* In 1795, at a time when Europe was on the brink of war, a cavalry barracks was established alongside the Lewes Road in the parish of Preston. The site included a hospital, smithy and riding school, and a small community grew up on the opposite side of the road to service them. Now, nearly 200 years later, the barracks are largely redundant and the seventeen-acre site will provide land for about 200 houses in addition to the retail park known as the Pavilion Centre. This latter site houses Halfords (opened 30 September 1989), Harveys/Lounge House (3 November 1989, Comet September 1990), and B & Q (19 October 1989) superstores. Five acres have been retained for Territorial Army use, and the new T.A. Somme Centre opened in October 1988. Some of the service houses were taken over by the council at Christmas 1987. Two early barracks blocks, formerly the married men's quarters, survive at the southern end of the site. <17,107,109,123>

88. LIBRARIES - Brighton Public Library

<3,15,115,123,194,311>

a) *REFERENCE LIBRARY:* Brighton's public library was established when the Royal Literary and Scientific Institution closed in 1869 and presented its large collection of books to the town. Together with some other collections which had been bequeathed to the corporation, the institution's books formed the basis of a reference library which opened in some of the upper rooms of the Royal Pavilion in 1869.

This accommodation soon proved inadequate and so the former royal servants' quarters, coach houses and stables, which were built in 1832 to the east of the Dome, were remodelled as a library, museum and art gallery by borough surveyor Philip Lockwood; the exterior was unaltered but the interior was fitted out in Moorish style. The new free public library, which was for reference use only, was opened on 12 September 1873 by Dr Carpenter of the British Association. The entrance to the building, which may still be seen from the outside, led directly into the large central hall which is still used by the art gallery and museum; the library occupied two large rooms overlooking the Pavilion grounds to the east of the entrance. By 1885 the stock had reached 15,000 volumes, and opening times were from 10 a.m. to 5 p.m., and again from 7 p.m. until 10 p.m.

b) *LENDING LIBRARY:* Approval for a free public lending library was given by the council in July 1888, and a chief librarian, Mr F.W.Madden, was appointed for the first time. The Victoria Lending Library was opened by the mayor, William Sendall, on 16 October 1889 with a stock of over 17,000 volumes.

c) *REBUILDING:* As the public library grew ever more cramped, so plans were made to use the parish guardians' rooms to the west. However, this area was not released until 1895 when the new Parochial Offices opened in Prince's Street, and it was then used for a time as a magistrates' court while the Town Hall was remodelled. Reconstruction as a library eventually commenced in April 1901, and the new lending and reference libraries were opened to the public in their present positions on 5 November 1902. The exterior was considerably altered with the construction of a new entrance and the addition of Indian ornamentation and minarets; the old entrance lies below the clock, but the later exterior can be seen to have a different style from the original façade. A newspaper reading-room was provided in the present ticket area, while the rooms previously occupied by the library were taken over by the museum and art gallery which were enlarged at the same time; the total cost of the alterations was £50,000. The library, museum and art gallery are now listed as buildings of special architectural interest.

Figure 76: The Library and Museum building in Church Street in the early years of the century

d) *FURTHER DEVELOPMENTS:* The children's library was established in 1928 and moved to the adjacent North Gate House in 1930, but it has since returned to the main building. The music library was established in 1964 at the former gas company showrooms on the opposite side of Church Street. The newspaper reading-room, which had occupied the present library ticket area, moved to the first floor of the music library, but has since been incorporated with the reference library. The ticket-issue system was computerised in November 1969, one of the first systems in the country.

In 1974 East Sussex County Council assumed control of the library service, and there has been a marked decline as cut-backs in stock and opening hours have taken effect. The central library, little changed from the time of its opening in 1902, has been extremely cramped for many years, but nothing has yet come of plans for its replacement. The reference library is particularly rich in local material and has received many collections as gifts and bequests; it now has in the order of 130,000 books and over 100,000 illustrations. However, a desperate lack of space prevents it from becoming one of the finest in the country.

For details on branch libraries refer to the entries on those localities.

89. LIBRARIES - Proprietary

<2,3,14,15,165,166>

The subscription libraries of the late eighteenth century provided one of the earliest amusements for visitors to Brighton other than promenading and riding, and were therefore important establishments where visitors would sign the Master of Ceremonies' book to announce their arrival in the town. They could also converse, listen to music, buy frippery, gamble at 'Pam' or 'Loo', or even read books! Two of the leading establishments are now described below.

a) *BAKER'S LIBRARY, Old Steine:* The town's first library was established in 1760 by Mr E.Baker, a Tunbridge Wells bookseller. It was a single-storey timber building with an arched verandah, and stood at the southern corner of what was to become St James's Street; it was in fact the first building on the eastern side of the Steine. The library initially opened only until the end of October, and was more like a club than a modern-day library with a billiards room and a wooden rotunda for musicians.

Following Baker's death in May 1774 it was taken by R.Thomas who kept it open all year round as the Brighthelmston Circulating Library. From 1781 until about 1784 the town's post-office was situated at Thomas's Library. It then passed to a Mr Dudlow, to Messrs Dulot and Gregory, and finally to a Mr Donaldson who opened a new library on the site in June 1806. The Prince of Wales appointed Donaldson as his bookseller and librarian, but the library was later run by Thomas Luccombe and was modernised in the mid nineteenth century. In 1856 the building was taken by the Electric Telegraph Company, and the site is now occupied by St James's Mansions.

b) *WOODGATE'S LIBRARY, Old Steine:* Opened in about 1767 on the southern side of the Steine, to the west of Dr Russell's house. It was a two-storey wooden building with a Doric colonnade, and was later taken by A.Crawford. From about 1784 until 1803 it included the town's post-office, and was run at various times by a Miss Widgett, Mr Bowen, F.Fisher and a Mr Shaw.

90. LIFEBOATS

<160-161>

Brighton's first lifeboat, paid for by the town, was established in January 1825 in a cave by the Chain Pier; it was soon moved to a boathouse below Middle Street and was operated until 1837, but unfortunately records of its launches have been lost. A replacement boat was installed the same year, but in 1854 it was sold to pleasure boat operator John Wright who used it as a private lifeboat for at least five years. By 1857 though, there was another replacement town boat and also a vessel of the Royal Humane Society, making a total of three lifeboats on station at Brighton.

Following a dramatic rescue from the *Pilgrim* in October 1857 which involved all three boats, the first Royal National Lifeboat Institute (R.N.L.I.) boat in the town, of unknown name, was installed in 1858, but it was replaced on 1 October 1867 by a larger boat, the *Robert Raikes*, in a new boathouse below the Bedford Hotel. Named after the founder of the Sunday School movement (because Sunday school children in Brighton and London had collected £580 in pennies towards it), the *Robert Raikes* was itself replaced by the *Robert Raikes II* in 1874. In 1879 a new town boat was installed, the *John Whittingham*, and in February 1888 a new R.N.L.I. boat, the *Sunlight No.2*, was donated by Lever Brothers Ltd and operated from a new boathouse at arch no.109 (below Cannon Place) until December 1904 when it too was replaced by the *William Wallis*. This last Brighton offshore lifeboat of the R.N.L.I. was launched thirty-four times and saved twenty-two lives before the station was officially closed on 7 July 1931. The town's *John Whittingham* continued from arch no.111 until August 1932. Plaques at arches 109 and 110 now record the gift of the *Robert Raikes* and the location of the R.N.L.I. station.

Brighton is now covered by offshore boats at Newhaven and Shoreham, but in 1965 the R.N.L.I. stationed an inflatable Atlantic 21-type inshore rescue boat just to the east of the Palace Pier; it was removed to a pontoon at the western end of the Marina in 1976. The boat covers the area from Peacehaven to Hove Lagoon, and by 1988 had saved 144 lives.

91. LONDON ROAD, Brighton

a) *HISTORY and BUILDINGS:* Now one of the principal shopping streets of the town, London Road was a comparatively recent trackway through the North Laine when it was first developed in the 1810s and '20s as a middle-class residential area known as Queen's Road until about 1826. The first shops had appeared on both sides of the road to the south of Francis Street by 1840, and the conversion to shops was virtually complete when the road was widened in 1903 <83,114>. Although not particularly impressive from an architectural point of view, London Road has not been redeveloped as much as some streets and retains a number of original buildings on the western side. Several bow-fronted buildings still stand between Ann Street and York Hill, while a number of other grand residences may be seen above the projecting shop-fronts which were built on their front gardens. Nos.9-17, 32-37, 54, 56-57 and 68-72 are all decorated with pilasters, nos.56-57 have petal and wreath decorations as well. The eastern side of London Road retains only two early buildings, no.87 (see below), and one at the Open Market corner, no.109.

In the 1930s several large stores were opened, in 1931 for the Brighton Equitable Co-operative Society (see below), in 1935 for Marks and Spencer (now Peacocks, etc.), and in about 1936 for Roslings drapers (now Woolworths). The other large stores, Sainsburys, Gateway (as Bellmans) and Boots, adopted their present form in the early '70s. <306>

The finest building, and the only remaining residential house in the road, is no.87, an elegant, listed house of about 1825 with fluted Ionic pilasters and an ironwork porch, which was probably designed by Charles Busby. In 1882 it became St Bartholomew's vicarage, but it has recently become the home of the vicar of Brighton (St Peter's) <44,46>. The adjacent Methodist church was built in 1894 for the Viaduct Road congregation, by James Weir in red brick with terracotta dressings; it was extended forward to the present line in 1910 in Renaissance style, but was remodelled in 1938 with the present rendered façade <62>. No.36a on the opposite side of London Road was once the Gem Electric Cinema, opened in 1910 by a Mr Thompson and operated with sixty seats until 1914 <68,68a>.

The Hare and Hounds at Preston Circus dates originally from about the 1820s, but was rebuilt in 1905; in the early nineteenth century the annual Brewsters' Sessions were held on the upper floor <15,311>. Preston Circus itself was once dominated by the Amber Ale Brewery, but today's wide junction was created in 1901 when the large brewery building was demolished to allow tram lines to be laid on a curve between Beaconsfield Road and Viaduct Road. The south-western range of buildings were erected in the 1930s along with the fire-station which dates from 1938. See also "Duke of York's Cinema".

b) *CO-OPERATIVE SOCIETY STORE:* The largest building in London Road is the Brighton Co-operative Society store. In 1906 the 'Co-op' acquired no.96 and gradually took over the adjoining premises which were united into a single store in about 1919. The present store, designed by Bethell and Swannell, was opened on 12 September 1931 with four storeys and a 180-foot frontage relieved only by two giant, fluted Doric columns above the entrance. Now the largest department store in Brighton, it is rivalled in size only by Hanningtons; the Baker Street supermarket originally opened in 1962, and further additions in 1975 and 1980 have brought the total floor area to some 70,000 square feet. <74,75,123>

Figure 77: Regency-style façades may be seen above and behind the shop-fronts that were built in the front gardens. In the background looms New England House.

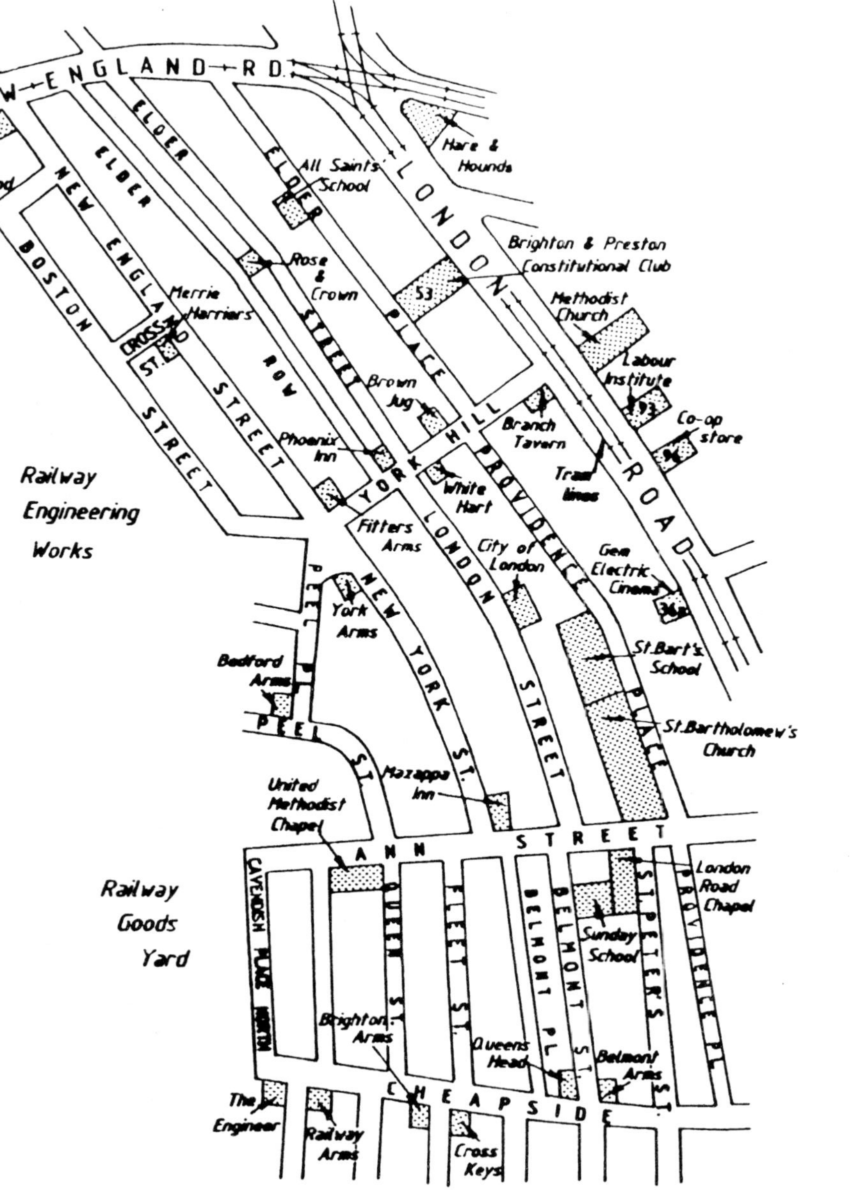

Figure 78: London Road area before redevelopment

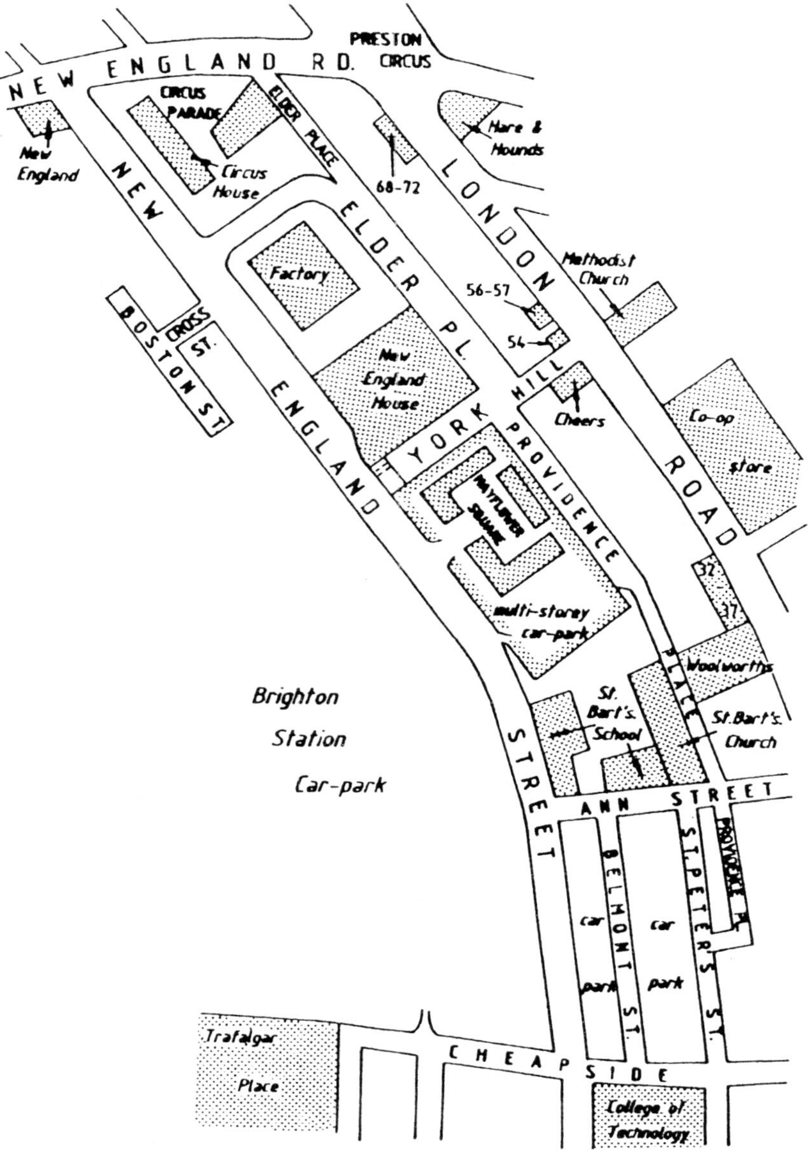

Figure 79: London Road area now

c) *SIDE STREETS and the OPEN MARKET:* The initial development of the London Road area came in the 1810s, generally to the south of the Open Market, but further development occurred in the 1840s and '50s following the arrival of the railway; the busy shopping thoroughfare of Baker Street was developed at this later time <83>. Queen's Place retains a row of listed, cobble-fronted houses of the 1810s, nos.4-9; several have figureheads above the doorways, and no.9 has a royal coat of arms in plaster at the side.

Oxford Street was the original site of the Open Market which began in 1919 as an unorganised collection of barrows mainly owned by ex-servicemen. They were soon moved to the central rose-walk of the Level, but following a campaign by their 'leader', Harry Cowley, a permanent site for the mobile barrows opened on the gardens of the cobble-fronted cottages of Marshall's Row on 19 November 1926. The cottages were demolished in 1938, and the present permanent retail market with forty-two stalls was opened on 7 January 1960 by the Duke of Norfolk. No.26 Oxford Street, which forms an attractive row with the adjacent nos.27-29, was built in 1815 and is also cobble-fronted with a bow window. The small alleyway beside no.25 formerly led to the small houses of Brunswick Court, while the site of the twenty or so houses of Oxford Court, once known as the 'black spot of Brighton', is now a car-park; a slaughterhouse once stood on the western side. Oxford Street Chapel, built in 1890 by Parker Anscombe in Renaissance style, has been the Church of Christ since about 1918. The main post-office was relocated in 1967; since 1929 it had stood near the corner of London Road. <44,48a,62,83,291,311>

Development of the hillside to the west of London Road with dense terraced housing was also stimulated from the 1840s by the railway. Clearances commenced in 1962 in Blackman, Whitecross and Wood Streets, and further areas were swept away in 1968 when three blocks of flats opened in Wellington Road to accommodate many of the residents who had to be rehoused. Several of the cleared sites still await redevelopment after twenty years, and the only dwellings between Trafalgar Street and New England Road are now the flats of Theobald House and Mayflower Square. The 530-space London Road car-park opened in December 1976, and the nearby New England House, an eight-storey block of factory units which overlooks London Road, opened on 17 January 1963 with eighteen firms in residence. In 1989 plans were announced for the vacant sites together with the adjacent railway land, to include housing, offices, shops, a superstore, a public square (New England Square) in front of St Bartholomew's Church, and a relief road for London Road and Preston Circus, running from Cheapside to Preston Road. <123>

Nearby, on the northern side of New England Road, stands Christ Church Evangelical Chapel, built in 1871 by J.G.Gibbins in Early English style. From 1920 it was a mission hall of St Saviour's Church, and from 1963 an Elim Free Church and Evangelical centre before closing in August 1988. <62,83,275a>

At the western corner of Ann Street and St Peter's Street stood London Road Chapel, opened on 25 July 1830 for the Countess of Huntingdon's Connexion. A small, classical building by William Simpson, it was enlarged in 1857 by Thomas Simpson, and in 1881 became a Congregational chapel, but it closed in about 1961 and became a warehouse. The building was demolished in March 1976. <62>

In Ann Street stands the dominant building of the whole London Road area:

d) *ST BARTHOLOMEW'S CHURCH:* This huge church was built for the Revd Arthur Wagner by local architect Edmund Scott, the pinnacle of his career. Costing about £18,000, it replaced a small mission church of 1866 and has a foundation stone laid in

Figure 80: Cobble-fronted cottages in Queen's Place

February 1872. St Bartholomew's opened on 8 September 1874, became a parish church in July 1881 and was consecrated on 15 June 1887, but the size of the church and the fact that the 1,500 seats were all free led to it being dubbed 'Wagner's Folly'. The vast building, in Italian Gothic style with a large rose window and a statue of St Bartholomew in a niche below, completely dominated the surrounding houses and was built to the supposed dimensions of Noah's Ark, 180 feet long, 58 feet wide and 140 feet to the top of the gilt metal cross. The building is particularly impressive when viewed from the other side of the valley on Albion Hill.

Even more impressive is the immense interior which has no aisles or chancel, but nine shallow bays are formed along the nave by the internal buttressing. St Bartholomew's has the tallest nave of any parish church in the country, the walls being 90 feet high, and the lack of aisles tends to emphasise the height even further. A towering cross lies above the altar, and there are also several mosaics and paintings, part of the beautiful decoration scheme of Henry Wilson in 1897-1908 which included the 1902 Lady Altar. The church's immense size and superb decoration have led to its listing as the only grade A church in Brighton. A parish hall was opened in Providence Place in 1893, but a new hall has been provided in New England Street as part of the school redevelopment.
<1,44,45,62,64a,65,123>

92. LONDON ROAD, Patcham

a) *HISTORY:* London Road runs the length of the former parish of Patcham from the Preston boundary near Clermont Road, through Withdean and Patcham village to the Pylons. In 1770 it became the Cuckfield Turnpike, with tollgates at South Road and Mill Road, and increased in importance as the Bolney to Pyecombe section of the present A23 road to London opened on 28 June 1810, establishing it as the main coaching route in preference to the Saddlescombe and Dyke Roads; the Redhill to Povey Cross section was opened in 1816.

Further improvements were made in 1922-7 when the road was widened from Preston to Newtimber, with the Patcham bypass constructed in 1926, and again between the wars when the Handcross to Warninglid and Crawley bypass sections of the A23 were opened. The latest improvements have been the construction of the Gatwick bypass in the 1950s, and the M23 motorway which opened on 17 December 1974 bypassing Crawley and Redhill. Upgradings and diversions between Patcham and Warninglid crossroads are under construction in 1990. The new A27 Brighton bypass will cross the road just north of Mill Road by 1991, with a major interchange on the hillside to the east; a six-lane dual-carriageway, to be completed in 1993, will lead northwards to Pyecombe, with a four-lane highway running the rest of the way to the M23.

Together with Preston Road, London Road forms an attractive, tree-lined approach to the town centre of Brighton. <1,2,115,123>

b) *TOWERGATE and the TIVOLI GARDENS:* At the start of the London Road, just north of Clermont Road on the western side, stands the imposing and richly detailed Tower House, built in 1902 for John James Savage, a London jeweller, and now converted to flats; the adjacent Edwardian Tivoli House was demolished in September 1988 for the Towergate development. The two houses were built on the site of the Tivoli Gardens, a nineteenth-century pleasure ground. Originally opened as the Strawberry Gardens in the 1830s, they were improved and renamed in 1851-2, increasing immensely in popularity with the removal of the Preston tollgate to Withdean Farm in 1854. The lower half was laid out with tree-lined walks, arbours, shrubberies and flower gardens, while the upper part had a large field and swings; a bridge over the railway connected the two.

The gardens closed in 1888 when the land was bought by R.C.Gazeley, owner of the adjacent Elms Lea House, but the upper part is still known as Tivoli Copse, a small wooded area to the north of Woodside Avenue; the Tivoli housing estate was developed from 1891 nearby. Two buildings contemporary with the gardens still survive in Station Road. Woodpeckers is a flint-walled cottage, while the adjacent Dene's Close was rebuilt in 1930 but retains a flint ground floor; they probably date from the early nineteenth century <107,109>.
<15,24,254>

c) *OTHER VILLAS:* From the 1850s onwards, about seventeen large, detached residences were built between Preston and Withdean Farm on both sides of the road, again encouraged by the removal of the tollgate to the north of Tongdean Lane in May 1854. Since the 1930s most have been replaced by flats and smaller houses, and only three now remain, including the Edwardian Tower House mentioned above.

On the eastern side of the road, at the bottom of Varndean Gardens, stands Withdean Hall, a two-storey building of 1861 which was once used as a girls' school but has now been remodelled as flats; there are two lodges at the rear. The other remaining villa, from the 1860s, is Grove Lodge, now St Bernadette's Primary School, which has a lodge opposite Clermont Road; the school opened when the adjacent Lourdes Convent (founded 1903) was demolished in 1972 and replaced by the Kingsmere flats. The lodges of Springfield or Hartford Villa (at Cliveden Court), Hatch Beauchamp or Withdean House (at Withdean Court), Laine House (at Varndean Park), and Miramichi (now Cedars Lodge) also remain. The octagonal Round House was the lodge to Withdean Lodge, the coach house of which remains in Varndean Road. <109,254>

d) *WITHDEAN:* The small hamlet and farmstead of Withdean stood beside the London Road to the north of Tongdean Lane, and three original buildings remain. (For further details of the hamlet, estate and park see "Withdean".) On the western side of the road stands a large, listed farmhouse of about 1800, faced in flint and pebble dash and now divided into two cottages, Karibu and Tabora. The adjacent Tabora Forge is a single-storey flint building now converted into a dwelling. The roadway alongside Tabora and Tabora Forge was the road to Tongdean Farm until Tongdean Lane was

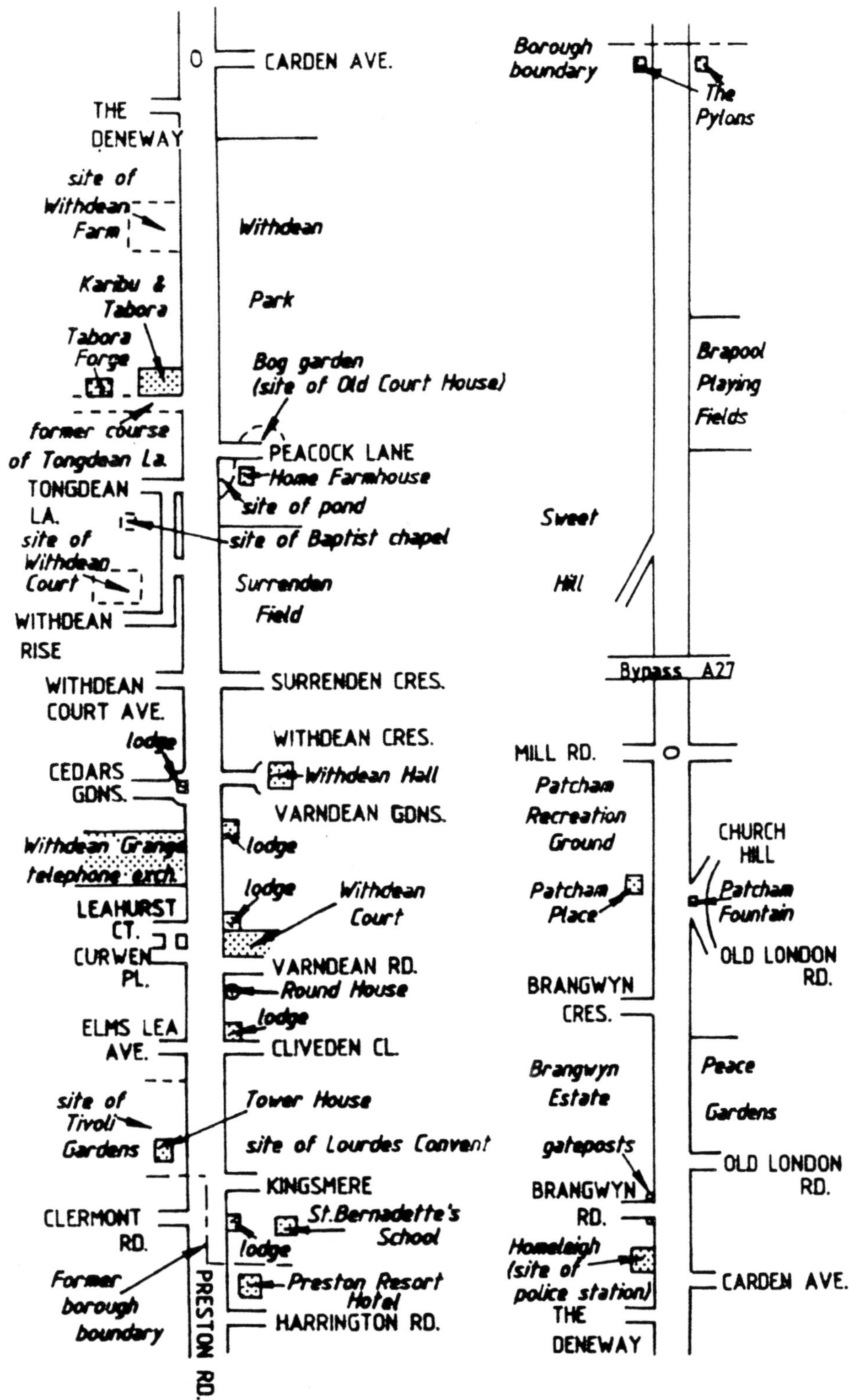

Figure 81: London Road, Patcham

diverted by the construction of the railway in 1840. Nearly opposite in Peacock Lane is Home Farmhouse, an early-nineteenth-century listed building faced in knapped and squared flint; a pond once lay between it and London Road <44,107>. The nearby open space at the bottom of Surrenden Crescent covers 5.65 acres and is known as Surrenden Field. It once belonged to Home Farm, and in 1900-1 was the home ground of Brighton and Hove Rangers, the forerunners of Brighton and Hove Albion F.C. <126,215>.

The Withdean area has been developed since the 1850s, firstly with the large villas mentioned above, then with suburban housing. Since the 1930s, and especially in the 1960s and '70s, many large blocks of flats have replaced the villas and farm buildings. See also the entry on "Withdean" itself.

e) *NORTH of WITHDEAN:* The entrance to the Brangwyn Estate is marked by two tall, square, brick lamp-posts at Brangwyn Drive. They were designed by artist Sir Frank Brangwyn of Ditchling who had initially threatened legal action against developer W.H.Lee on the use of his name in 1936 <76>. On the opposite side are the Peace Gardens, 3.12 acres of land purchased from the Abergavenny estate in June 1928, chiefly through the efforts of Herbert Carden (see "Patcham Village (Old London Road)"). A drinking fountain at the southern end dates from 1897 and originally stood in the London Road at Home Farm, Withdean, until the road was widened. <26a,126>

The road then passes Patcham village and the eighteenth-century façade of Patcham Place (see "Patcham Village") to reach the junction with Mill Road, now the site of a large roundabout as part of the interchange with the Brighton bypass. London Road will pass under the bypass itself to run alongside the Brapool playing fields. This area of 13.56 acres was levelled by unemployed labour and was formally opened by the mayor, Herbert Hone, on 20 May 1938 <126>. The name Brapool dates from at least the thirteenth century and signifies the springs and former marshy nature of the valley which is still prone to flooding in this area <289>.

Further north still, the Pylons were erected to mark the northern limit of 'Greater Brighton' which was created on 1 April 1928 (see "Boundaries"); the borough boundary had previously been at the southern end of London Road near Clermont Road. Actually standing about thirty-five yards inside the boundary, the Pylons were designed by John L.Denman and have foundation stones laid by the Duke and Duchess of York on 30 May 1928. Buried inside are coins, copies of the *Brighton and Hove Herald* and *Sussex Daily News*, and also a bound book recording the laying of the foundation stones. The cost was born by a public subscription of £993 and a contribution from Herbert Carden of £2,555. The western Pylon bears the message 'Hail guest, we ask not what thou art. If friend we greet thee hand and heart. If stranger such no longer be. If foe our love shall conquer thee.' (See figure 16.) <115,126,311>

93. LOWER ESPLANADE

<24,115,123,126>

The Lower Esplanade runs below Madeira Drive, Grand Junction Road and King's Road from beyond the Aquarium to Western Street, and for many years was a ramshackle area frequented by stall-holders and street entertainers. It was improved in 1864-7, and again in 1882-7 when the main road was widened over top of the King's Road Arches. It is now a mixture of private beach chalets and commercial enterprises including amusement arcades, cafés and public houses. The Lower Esplanade now epitomises the day-tripper, slot-machine, fish'n'chip side of Brighton's appeal as a resort, but remains somewhat ramshackle.

It now begins about a quarter-mile to the east of the Palace Pier, where a small path crosses Volk's Railway and then runs past the railway station and a crazy golf-course before widening out opposite the Aquarium. On 27 June 1930 the mayor, Horace Aldrich, inaugurated an extension to the roadway and promenade of both Madeira Drive and Grand Junction Road, and from this point to beyond the East Street Groyne the widened upper promenade forms a colonnaded walkway on the Lower Esplanade lined with commercial premises. The subway under Madeira Drive to the Aquarium opened in 1935.

Figure 82: The King's Road Bandstand

The path rises to road level at the East Street Groyne, but then descends again to the former Fish Market, arches 216-224, and the Fish Market Hard, an area traditionally used for meetings and entertainments (see "Fishing Industry"). No.217 is now occupied by the fascinating Old Fashioned Penny Palace, the National Museum of Penny Slot Machines. A little further, on the beach below the Old Ship, stands the Martha Gunn Winch, recommissioned in 1984 as a reminder of the past importance of the fishing industry.

The café and amusement arcade below West Street opened in August 1887 as a public shelter hall with a handsome interior holding 500 people in inclement weather; the exterior is decorated with many figure-heads of Neptune. Beyond the West Street subway the Lower Esplanade widens out considerably and part is set aside for the Beach Deck, a seaside entertainment area. Two arches by the Grand Hotel steps were decorated with the story of Brighton's fishing heritage for the 1984 Brighton Festival. At arches nos.109 and 110 below the Metropole are two plaques to the former lifeboat stations at this point (see "Lifeboats"). The adjacent paddling pool and putting green were laid out in 1935-8.

The putting green and boating pool beyond the West Pier were added in 1925. Between the two stands a Modern-style café and amusement arcade, built in 1953 as a contribution to the Festival of Britain. It opened as the Western Bathing Pavilion and provided changing room for 2,000 bathers, but it proved unpopular and became a café in 1957. The area of formal gardens, walks and flower beds beyond are known as the Western Lawns and were laid out in the 1884 improvements. The King's Road Bandstand is a light ironwork listed building with a public convenience in the base. Topped by an oriental dome, the roof is supported by eight delicate ironwork pillars and there were originally shutters to shelter the performers from the breeze. A special area for the disabled was added nearby in 1981 to celebrate the wedding of the Prince and Princess of Wales.

The Lower Esplanade then joins the King's Road promenade beyond the Western Lawns as it stretches past the Peace Memorial into Hove as the Brunswick Esplanade.

94. LOWER TOWN

<1,2,4,6,10>

The original fishing village of Brighton was probably situated on an extensive chalk foreshore below the cliffs and above the high-water mark, protected from the force of the Channel by an offshore bar below the surface of the sea. This so-called 'Lower Town' may have been the site of the church mentioned in the Domesday Book, but as the fisheries prospered and the population grew so an upper town on the cliff top, now the Old Town, was developed, perhaps from around the thirteenth century; it is possible that the Lower Town was destroyed by the ravages of the sea, necessitating the development of a safer residential area with the undercliff used by the fisheries mainly as a working area.

The Lower Town was burnt in the French raid of 1514, probably the event depicted in a British Museum drawing of 1545 which shows the town under attack and a row of tenements alight below the cliff (see figure 19). From around the 1640s the foreshore itself was constantly threatened by the sea following a general rise in sea-level; in the latter seventeenth century it was recorded that 22 tenements had recently been lost from below the cliff, including 12 workshops and 3 cottages, but that 113 tenements remained, including about 75 workshops and netshops, 25 cottages, a salt-house, a stable, 22 capstans, and a number of stake places. Most were grouped below the cliff between Ship Street and Black Lion Street, and also at the bottom of East Street.

Most of the remaining workshops, capstans and cottages were washed away in the great storm of November 1703, and the rest were probably demolished by the storm of 11 August 1705 which covered the site with shingle. The last record of any Lower Town buildings occurs in 1704, but in around 1710 a visitor reported seeing the remains of many flint or brick walls on the beach, the inference being that the buildings had had timber superstructures, probably tile hung or weather-boarded. The mouth of a well, the last relic of the Lower Town, remained visible until 1781 when it too was lost under the shingle. In March 1818 some walls said to be from the Lower Town were discovered under fifteen feet of shingle when the foundations of a new building between Ship Street and Middle Street were being dug.

The Lower Town of Brighton was the heartland of the fishing industry so vital to the town, and its loss was a contributory factor to the decline of that industry. It has been compared to the fishing community at Hastings, where the tall, wooden netshops are similarly grouped on an extensive foreshore below the cliff (although, unlike Brighton, Hastings Old Town is not situated on the cliff top).

95. MADEIRA DRIVE

a) *HISTORY:* The first road along the base of the East Cliff was the carriage road constructed on top of a new sea-wall to the Chain Pier in 1822-3. In 1872 however, the Aquarium was erected on the site of this road, and a new promenade and carriage drive from the Old Steine were constructed on a new sea-wall. The new road, known as Madeira Road until the First World War, continued past the Chain Pier and up a ramp to meet Marine Parade at the Duke's Mound. With its sheltered situation it quickly became a popular promenade, especially with invalids, and was improved in 1890-7 with the addition of the Madeira Terrace.

In 1895 the roadway was extended past the Kemp Town slopes and esplanades to meet Marine Parade at Black Rock, but this section has been a 'no through road' since the construction of the Marina interchange in the 1970s. In 1927-9 the Aquarium Sun Terrace was extended eastwards above a new colonnade of shops in Madeira Drive, while the western end of the road was widened in 1929-30 by extending the promenade seawards over a colonnade on the Lower Esplanade, an improvement inaugurated by the mayor, Horace Aldrich, on 27 June 1930. The distinctive lamp-standards date originally from the 1930s. Once the terminus for Southdown buses and coaches, Madeira Drive is still lined with coaches on sunny Sundays, and has overtaken the King's Road as the principal sea-front promenade. <115,116,261a>

See also "Aquarium", "Kemp Town (Slopes and Esplanades)", "Lower Esplanade", "Marina", "Palace Pier" and "Volk's Electric Railway".

b) *MADEIRA TERRACE and LIFT:* The great sea-wall stretching along the face of the East Cliff from Old Steine to Kemp Town was constructed in 1830-8 by William Lambert at a cost of £100,000 (see "Coastline (Sea-Walls)"). A plaque recording this massive construction may be seen above the Madeira Terrace, to the west of the cliff lift, two further improvements that were added in 1890 under the terms of the 1884 Brighton Improvement Act. The terrace has a length of 2,837 feet from the Aquarium to Duke's Mound, a width of 25 feet, and is listed as being of special architectural interest. Designed by borough surveyor Philip Lockwood, it is supported by cast-iron columns and delicate latticed arches adorned with alternate figurines of Neptune and Aphrodite; the sheltered promenade below is known as the Madeira Walk. The terrace opened to the east of Royal Crescent in 1890, but it was somewhat controversial and its completion was delayed until 1897 at a total cost of £29,000; in 1927-9 it was extended above a colonnade to meet the Aquarium Sun Terrace.

The Madeira Lift and Shelter Hall, both listed buildings, were constructed at the same time as the terrace. The lift, which was initially powered by hydraulics, has an iron building on Marine Parade decorated with four griffins and an ornate dolphin weather-vane. It descends into the shelter hall, now Clown's Café, which was intended to accommodate visitors during inclement weather. The two were inaugurated on 24 May 1890. By the roadway to the west of the Shelter Hall stands the marble base of a drinking-fountain, erected in 1896 through the munificence of Mrs Bryan of Portland Lodge.

The Madeira Terrace, which looks particularly impressive when viewed from the Palace Pier, provides a magnificent promenade and also the middle tier of a three-tiered 'grandstand' for the regular events that take place in Madeira Drive. These include the well-known National Speed Trials, organised annually in September by the Brighton and Hove Motor Club. The first Motor Race Week was held on 19-22 July 1905 to inaugurate the new tarmacadam surface of Madeira Drive, with J.T.C.Brabazon, C.S.Rolls and T.Schneider competing. <3,26,44,115,261a,311>

c) *PETER PAN'S LEISURE PARK:* Standing alongside Madeira Drive opposite the shelter hall, Peter Pan's Playground was developed on a site reclaimed from the sea by the Banjo Groyne from 1877. By 1889 enough shingle had been accumulated to allow some bowling greens and gardens known as the Madeira Lawns to be laid out, and there was also a bandstand from 1898 until the Second World War when the beaches were closed. The present leisure centre was developed after the war with funfair rides, slot-machines, roller-skating, miniature coaches, a children's theatre, etc., along with the more traditional swings and roundabouts. It suffered a serious fire in January 1987, but there are plans to enlarge it considerably over Volk's Railway and onto the beach. <27,115>

d) *ATHINA B:* On the promenade between Peter Pan's and the Aquarium stands the anchor of the *Athina B*, a Greek cargo ship which ran aground on the beach below. On 11 December 1979 she sailed from the Azores for Shoreham loaded with 3,000 tons of pumice,

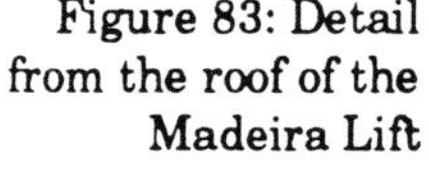

Figure 83: Detail from the roof of the Madeira Lift

but on arrival at Shoreham she remained outside the harbour and drifted eastwards as the weather deteriorated. Most of the crew of twenty-five were taken off by the Shoreham lifeboat in the morning of 21 January 1980, but the ship continued to drift, and the captain and the remainder of the crew were rescued at 9.15 p.m. Later that night the *Athina B* ran aground on the beach below Lower Rock Gardens and remained for nearly a month, providing a great tourist attraction as crowds flocked to the town, especially on the sunny weekend that followed; Volk's Electric Railway ran an out-of-season service to provide a good view.

The ship was immediately declared a write-off, and was salvaged by Eurosalve Ltd. The pumice was off-loaded on 14 February, and the ship was eventually hauled off the beach at noon on Sunday 17 February on an unfortunately foggy day. With buoyancy tanks fitted to the sides, the *Athina B* was towed to Chatham and scrapped, but the anchor was returned to the town and is now exhibited on the Madeira Drive promenade with the beach below now known as the Athina bathing beach.

The *Athina B* was only one of many ships that have been driven onto Brighton beaches in the past. Especially notable was the *Atlantique*, which was wrecked on the Albion groyne on the night of 2 June 1860 with the death of one man. <141,160,274>

96. MANORS

<1,3a,10>

Eleventh-century Brighton was divided between three estates or 'manors' which held virtually all land and property between them. Once the possessions of Wolnuth, a Saxon nobleman, they passed to his son, the Earl Godwin, but two of the three eventually came into the hands of King Edward the Confessor. The King's successor, Harold II, was Godwin's son, but following the Norman Conquest in 1066 William I granted the manors of Brighton, and indeed the whole of the Rape of Lewes, to his son-in-law, William de Warrenne, whom he created Earl of Surrey. These estates then remained the possessions of the earls of Surrey, under Norman tenants, until 1347, since when they have descended through many different families.

The Domesday Book of 1086 gives a great deal of information about the manors of the time. One was held by 'Ralph' and paid a rent of 4,000 herrings per annum to de Warrenne. It became known as the manor of Brighton-Lewes, and in 1483 was divided into several parts or 'moieties'. By the late eighteenth century, when manorial land had started to be sold for development, the moieties had passed into the hands of the Scrase-Dickins and Kemp families. As late as 1862 though, the manor could still claim a tribute of six mackerel from each fishing trip. The second largest manor, first named in 1296, was Atlingworth, now commemorated by the street of that name off Marine Parade; it was acquired by solicitor William Attree in the late eighteenth century.

There were a number of other, smaller manors by the Middle Ages, including Erlyes (probably absorbed by the Kemp's holding of Brighton-Lewes), Harecourts (or Seyntclere), and Pekes. The manor of Raddingdean, a name often confused with Rottingdean, had evolved by the sixteenth century, and in the 1700s Rusper (or Old Shoreham) and Portslade manors also had property in Brighton. Raddingdean is commemorated by Radinden Manor Road, Hove, and also by the southern entrance pylon of Preston Park; it possessed land in the Stanford Avenue area from at least 1234, and may have had a manor house at the Prince of Wales's dairy where Argyle Road now stands, but it was probably absorbed by the manor of Preston. The manor of Brighton-Michelham was the possession of the Sackville family for several centuries until auctioned in July 1988; it was subsequently given away as a competition prize in the *Evening Standard*.

The manors of the surrounding parishes included:

Falmer:	Bevendean, Falmer, Patchway.
Ovingdean:	Ovingdean.
Patcham:	Moulsecoomb, Patcham Court, Patcham Place, Withdean Court, Withdean Kayliffe.
Preston:	Preston.
Rottingdean:	Balsdean, Bazehill, Challoners, Rottingdean.
Stanmer:	Stanmer.

Manors were once very important in the local community because they held virtually all land, buildings and property between them, thereby governing the lives of most people; they summoned private 'court-barons' to pass bye-laws and enforce customs, or 'court-leets' to try petty offenders; they claimed wrecker's rights from shipwrecks and received other payments and rentals such as those from the fishermen mentioned above; and they formed the basis of medieval administration. Although they lost importance with the division of the moieties, the local manors remained prominent until the nineteenth century in Brighton, and into the twentieth century in the rural parishes when many of the manorial estates were acquired by Brighton Corporation and much of their land was sold off for development. Most of the manorial titles still exist, and a number are now held by Brighton Borough Council.

97. MANOR FARM

The original Manor Farm, together with Manor House, stood on the site of the present Manor Gardens and Manor Green until the 1950s, and was well-known for the quality of its produce. The farm was erected on the site in about 1850, while the house was added a perhaps a little later, in around 1855, for William Hallett, founder of the Kemp Town Brewery and the town's second mayor. In April 1936 the corporation purchased forty-one acres at Manor Farm and erected some 422 houses there, principally to rehouse people from the slum clearance areas around Carlton Hill. A few flats and houses were added post-war on the site of the farm buildings, while the adjacent Bristol Estate was developed in the late 1950s. <2,83,108,109>

At the southern end of Manor Road stand two large detached houses. No.1, a convent and nursing home of the Augustinian Sisters, was built in 1906 and has a small chapel to the south. Adjacent is Robindene, a large, three-storey, late-Victorian house with a Doric porch.

On the night of 6-7 January 1973 at 119 Maresfield Road, seven-year-old Maria Colwell, weighing just thirty-six pounds, was beaten to death by her stepfather William Kepple. Maria had been happy with foster parents but was returned to her mother by the authorities despite warnings from neighbours. She was buried at Trafalgar Road Cemetery, Portslade, and Kepple was jailed for manslaughter, but her death led to unprecedented anger in the town and press, and the government was forced to hold a 41-day public inquiry, the first into child battering, at Crown Street. The authorities and voluntary organisations were severely criticised by the inspector's report, and on 2 November 1974 a 'Maria Day' rally was attended by over a thousand people in Trafalgar Square, London, to call for reforms in the law. The result was the passing of the 1975 Children Act and reforms to social services departments. <19,123>

98. MARINA, Black Rock

<123>

a) *ORIGINAL SCHEME:* Schemes for harbours at Brighton have been proposed since at least the early nineteenth century (see "Port of Brighton"), but the only one to come to fruition is the Brighton Marina. It was conceived by garage proprietor Henry Cohen whose group commissioned a plan from architects Overton and Partners which was put to the council in October 1963. Costing £9 million, the development was to be sited to the west of Duke's Mound, and was to include 3,000 yacht berths, helicopter and hovercraft stations, flats, hotel, restaurant, shops, clubs, conference hall, swimming-pool, bowling alley, theatre, cinemas, casino and car-parks. The plan was given approval in principle in November 1963, but it aroused much opposition, especially from the residents of Kemp Town.

b) *BLACK ROCK and the ROADS BILL:* Following numerous complaints about the site, a new location was chosen to the east at Black Rock, and in September 1965 revised £11 million plans were approved provided that no building projected above the cliffs. A public inquiry was held at the Dome the following January, and ministerial approval was given in September 1966. The Brighton Marina Act, authorising the harbour construction and associated works, was given royal assent in April 1968 despite vigourous opposition in Parliament.

In March 1968 the council promoted a Bill for the construction of a large, gyratory access road system, considered vital to the whole project. This provoked a fierce debate as opposition to the marina was still strong, and a town meeting at the Dome on 20 December 1968 rejected the council's decision; a town poll was then held in January 1969, resulting in a vote of 15,042 for the Bill against 9,022. However, the Bill itself was defeated in Parliament in March 1969. A second town poll in November 1969 resulted in 9,461 votes for and 5,422 against an amended Bill which was eventually passed as the Brighton Corporation Act in July 1970. The road interchange, which involved the demolition of Rifle Butt Road and other houses of the small Black Rock community, was completed in 1976 although not to the original gyratory plan.

c) *MORE INQUIRIES and CONSTRUCTION:* The marina plans were altered again in July 1970 by architect David Hodges of Overton and Partners, and received planning permission in January 1971. Site construction by Taylor Woodrow Ltd commenced in March 1971 with the reclamation of a large area of land below the cliff, and on 1 March 1972 the Marina Company formally signed a 125-year lease with the corporation which had purchased the foreshore from the Crown Estates Commissioners for £50,000.

The proposed 'city-by-the-sea' remained a stumbling block, though. The council had given its approval in September 1974, but the Environment Secretary decided that a public inquiry should be held. In May 1975 he gave his approval on condition that the buildings should not now exceed half the cliff height, and that the numbers of houses and flats were reduced. This final ministerial approval brought an end to twelve years of meetings, inquiries and polls to approve the whole marina scheme.

d) *HARBOUR COMPLETION:* The wall of the inner harbour was finished in June 1975, and on 24 May 1976 the last concrete 'caisson' of the massive outer breakwaters was put in position, enclosing seventy-seven acres of sheltered water. The breakwaters are formed by 110 caissons, each 38 feet high, 40 feet in diameter and weighing 600 tons, which were lowered into position by an immense gantry crane; each one was then filled with a further 1,000 tons of concrete. On 2 May 1977 the mayor, Peter Best, formally opened the lock-gates between the inner and outer harbours, and the public were admitted from 25 July 1978. The harbour was completed in January 1979, and the whole £41 million complex was formally opened on 31 May 1979 by Queen Elizabeth II. A jetfoil service to Dieppe commenced in April 1979, but was withdrawn in August 1980.

e) *TAKEOVER and DEVELOPMENT:* Mainly because of a lack of finance, the 'city-by-the-sea' was never realised. However, in November 1985 the marina was purchased by the Brent Walker Company for just £13 million, and a new £120 million development programme began in January 1986, mainly on the partly-reclaimed inner harbour. The first phase to open was the Gateway superstore on 16 November 1987 (becoming Asda early 1990), and was followed by an 875-home 'Marina Village'. Built in a pleasing Georgian pastiche, the flats and houses have been erected on promontories around an attractive inner harbour, and also around the Octagon, a public shopping piazza. The development also includes a public house by the waterside, the Master Mariner, which has been constructed in a weather-boarded style echoing the taverns of older harbours. A modification to Marine Drive was opened in 1989 to cater for the newly-generated traffic travelling from Brighton.

The foundation stone of the next stage of the development, a four-star hotel and leisure centre including an eight-screen 2,200-seat multiplex Cannon cinema, health hydro, night-club and car-park, was laid on 25 May 1988 by John Lee, Minister of Tourism. Another development will include a banqueting suite, offices and car-park, while Brent Walker will erect a water 'theme-park' on the adjacent site of Black Rock swimming-pool.

Brighton Marina covers an area of about 127 acres, extending for about 1,100 yards along the bottom of the cliffs and for 600 yards seaward, one of the largest artificial yacht marinas in the world. The Brent Walker development leaves around 1,500 moorings for boats; there are also special berths for the town's inshore lifeboat, and for a small fishing fleet beyond the eastern pontoon.

99. MARINE PARADE

a) *HISTORY:* Marine Parade forms the country's most impressive marine façade, the major feature of the East Cliff outstanding conservation area; it is especially impressive when viewed from afar, for instance from the Palace Pier. Commencing in about 1790, development continued eastwards from the Steine until about 1850 when Kemp Town had been reached, and was protected against coastal erosion by a huge sea-wall constructed along the length of the cliff in 1830-8 (see "Coastline (Sea-Walls)"). With its magnificent setting, all the development was of a high-class nature, and it constitutes much of the Regency architectural splendour of the town. There are many listed buildings, which are detailed below. The many interesting side streets leading north from Marine Parade are dealt with under "East Cliff". See also "Kemp Town", which forms part of the Marine Parade façade.

The roadway itself, which runs from the Steine to the former borough boundary at Boundary Road, was widened, and the promenade constructed, in 1827-38 when the sea-wall was built below. The Marine Parade then became part of a very fashionable equestrian and carriage drive from Kemp Town to Brunswick Town, with society gathering every day to see and be seen <24>. In 1880 the old wooden railings were replaced by the present cast-iron rails with their dolphin motifs, and the old shelters on the promenade opposite Lower Rock Gardens, Marine Square and Eaton Place were erected in about 1883. The ornate lamp standards date originally from the 1930s. The Madeira Lift, a listed building decorated with four dragons and an ornate dolphin weather-vane, was inaugurated on 24 May 1890 and descends into the Madeira Drive shelter hall, now Clown's Café (see "Madeira Drive").

In 1908 the name of the road was officially changed to Marine Parade King's Cliff in honour of King Edward VII who stayed with his daughter at 1 Lewes Crescent. <115>

Figure 84: Marine Parade and the Chain Pier toll-house

From 1824 the road was continued along the cliff top to Rottingdean as the Newhaven Turnpike with a tollgate at Roedean, but in 1897 this road was closed due to erosion of the cliff and Roedean Road was constructed further inland as an alternative route. On 22 July 1932, with the cliffs protected by the new Undercliff Walk, a 60-foot-wide highway, Marine Drive, was opened to Rottingdean by P.J.Pybus, Minister of Transport, at a cost of £105,000. <112,115,116>

b) *LISTED BUILDINGS:* There are many listed buildings in Marine Parade, but particularly impressive are the bow-fronted nos.18 (Olivier House), 41-45 and 102-104 (with giant, fluted Ionic pilasters), all designed by Wilds and Busby in the 1820s. They also probably designed nos.37, 50-51, 73, 78, 113-119, 124-127 and 137-141.

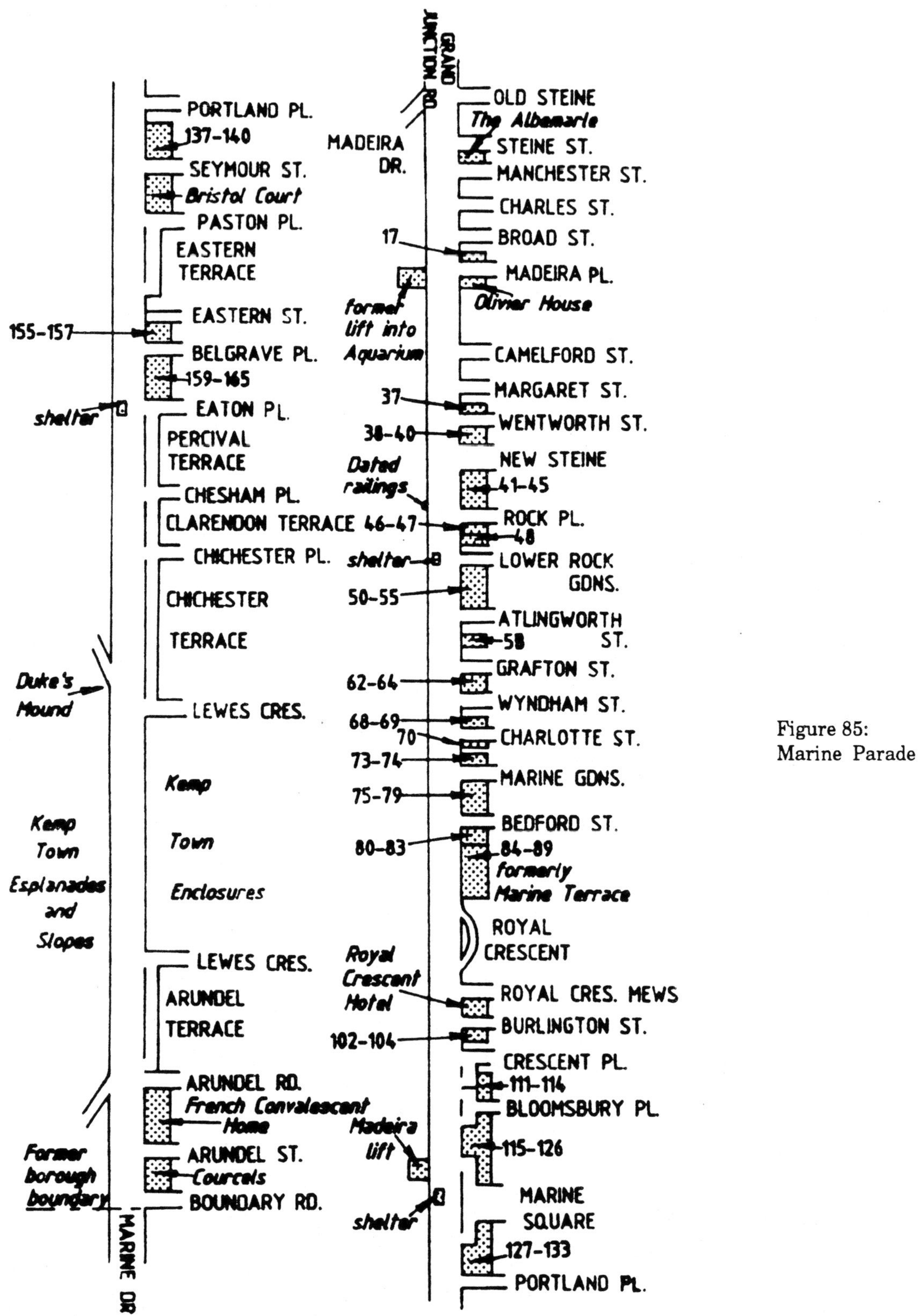

Figure 85:
Marine Parade

Other impressive houses include nos.48 (Chain Pier House, with delicate ironwork porch, home of Captain Samuel Brown, designer of the Chain Pier); 54-55 (wide bow, fluted Corinthian pilasters, verandah); 80-83 (wide bows, porches, pilasters with unusual chevron capitals); 84-89 (a composition once known as Marine Terrace, with a mews at the rear approached through a large archway off Bristol Road); 127-133a (Corinthian pilasters); and nos.142-143 (now Bristol Court flats, but built as the Bristol Hotel in 1835 by proprietor William Hallett and named after the first Marquess of Bristol, a local landowner; it was converted in 1935 and has delicate ironwork balconies).

Also listed are nos.17, 38-40, 52-53, 58, 62-64, 68 (Princess Charlotte's House), 69, 70 (Lanes Hotel in red brick and knapped flint), 74-77, 100-101, 111-112, 120-123 and 155-165.

Nos.100-101 are the Royal Crescent Hotel, opened in 1857. The building was radically altered in 1848 with the addition of three storeys, but the original house was once the home of George Canning, Prime Minister of 1827.

Nos.12, 13, 14, 46 and 47 Marine Parade are included on the council's local list of buildings of special interest. <44,45,46,306>

A number of terraces, a crescent and a square also form part of the Marine Parade façade, as does the Kemp Town estate which has its own entry. They are now described below.

c) *ROYAL CRESCENT:* This is a particularly notable resort development in the town as it was both the first unified composition, and also the first development to face the sea. Construction commenced in 1798 in a then quite isolated position on the East Cliff for a West Indian merchant and speculator named J.B.Otto; the architect is unknown. However, Otto left the country after only three houses at either end had been erected and did not return to complete the crescent until 1807. The fourteen houses, which are listed grade II*, are timber-framed but faced with black glazed 'mathematical' tiles to resemble brick. They have four storeys, balconies, verandahs and angular bays, except no.1 which has lost its verandah and nos.12 and 14 which have narrow bows. At the top of the central houses is the name of the crescent, originally painted by a Mr Leggatt who, while leaning back to admire his handiwork, unfortunately fell and was killed on the railings below. Royal Crescent Mews at the rear has a row of small cottages.

In 1802 Otto erected a statue of the Prince of Wales in the garden in an attempt to curry favour with H.R.H. It stood seven feet high on an eleven-foot pedestal and was designed in artificial Coade stone by Rossi. However, the stone did not wear well; the left fingers were broken off in November 1807, and when the right arm broke off a little later, the statue was said to have borne more of a resemblance to Nelson. The Prince was evidently not amused, refusing even to allow Otto's name to be mentioned in his presence, and the statue was eventually removed in November 1819. The garden was vested in the corporation following the 1884 Brighton Improvement Act.

No.4 Royal Crescent (and later no.5 as well) was the home of the actor Lord Olivier of Brighton from 1961 until 1979, while another knight of the stage, Sir John Clements, lived at no.7.
<3,44,46,83,123,126>

d) *MARINE SQUARE:* Built in 1823-5 for Thomas Attree, probably by Wilds and Busby. The houses, all listed, have balconies and verandahs, and some yellow-brick houses remain unstuccoed. In the early nineteenth century no.11 was the home of Cardinal John Newman (1801-90), a leading member of the Oxford Movement. The gardens were taken over by the corporation following the 1884 Brighton Improvement Act. <46,123,126>

e) *EASTERN TERRACE:* This imposing terrace has nine large, four-storey, listed houses of about 1827-8, some of the finest in the town. Nos.1-2 and 9 have wide bow fronts, while no.8 has a concave façade. Most have Doric porches, and nos.5-7 have unstuccoed first floors faced in yellow brick. No.1 was occupied from 1836 until 1858 by the first Lord Sudeley, and then by Sir Albert Sassoon in 1876-96; the Bombay Bar in St George's Road (q.v.) behind the house was constructed as his private mausoleum. The house became the Court Royal Hotel in 1914, and was converted into Court Royal Mansions in the early 1950s. No.2 was the home of the famous journalist George Augustus Sala in the 1890s, while no.9 was occupied for some time by King Manoel II of Portugal during his exile; it later became the Royal Sussex Hotel and then part of the Municipal Training College until the 1970s. <44,46,83>

Behind the terrace are the small cottages of Eastern Terrace Mews which were rebuilt in 1989. The mews is entered through an archway from St George's Road.

f) *CLARENDON and PERCIVAL TERRACES:* Both terraces were developed for W.Percival Boxall of Belle Vue House, who had purchased the land from Thomas Cubitt. The five-storey bow-fronted houses were built by Cheesemans, and George Cheeseman junior may also have been the architect.

The ten listed houses of Percival Terrace were erected in 1845-50. No.5 was the home of philosopher Herbert Spencer for several years, while no.4 was occupied by architect and writer Sir James Knowles from 1903 until 1908. However, on 13 November 1987, the front of no.10 completely collapsed as a large crater opened up in front of the house, and no.9 has also now been demolished. Clarendon Terrace has six listed houses with Doric porches, two of which were occupied by 1856 and five by 1859. <44,46,311>

g) *FRENCH CONVALESCENT HOME:* Standing at the Black Rock end of Marine Parade, with an entrance in De Courcel Road, this large building was designed by Clayton and Black for the French Government and opened in 1896 as a convalescent home in connection with the French Hospital in Shaftesbury Avenue, London, to give accommodation to poor and aged Frenchmen and women resident in Britain. The foundation stone was laid by Baron de Courcel, the French ambassador, and the home is run by the Sisters of St Paul of Chartres. <83,311>

h) *FLATS:* The Albemarle, an eight-storey block between Steine Street and Manchester Street, was completed in 1970 on the site of the early-nineteenth-century Albemarle Hotel, which had been demolished ten years earlier. At Arundel Street, Courcels is a seven-storey block built in 1971 on the site of some late-nineteenth-century houses known as Madeira Mansions. No.19 Courcels was the home of actor Wilfred Pickles for about ten years until his death in March 1978. <83,83a,123>

Marine Gate is a very large, eight-storey block of 105 flats just beyond the end of Marine Parade at Black Rock. It was erected around an open quadrangle in 1937-9 to the design of Maurice Bloom, and included a large public restaurant until it was converted for further residential accommodation in about 1955. The block's proximity to the gas-works prompted a good deal of bombing during the war, and it received a direct hit in 1944. <3,45a>

100. MARKETS

a) *MEDIEVAL MARKETS:* The tolls charged from markets and fairs were once an important source of income for manorial lords. The first Brighton market was a weekly Thursday market granted to the lord of the manor, John de Warrenne, Earl of Surrey, by Edward II in a charter dated 23 July 1313, and was probably held on the cliff top between Black Lion Street and Ship Street, just east of the Townhouse. By 1665 though, following erosion of the cliff, the Market Place had moved to the Hempshares in the middle of the town, and in about 1730 the Thursday market was re-established at the Bartholomews in front of the old Town Hall. <1,10,14,18>

An earlier Tuesday market was granted to the Bishop of Chichester at Preston in 1226 by Henry III. In 1307 the day was changed to Monday, but it probably died out in the fifteenth century, if not before. <1>

b) *FIRST DAILY MARKET:* The 1773 Brighton Town Act authorised the newly-established town commissioners to erect and regulate a market building for the daily sale of meat, fish, poultry, butter, and garden produce. The new market hall was erected in 1774 in the Bartholomews, on the site of the present Town Hall, and from 1797 the tolls were leased to private individuals for collection. In 1802 the market house was enlarged on both east and west sides, and further additions were made in June 1806, principally for the fish traders. In 1823 it expanded into the former workhouse building, that establishment having moved to Church Hill, but the whole building was removed in 1829 for the erection of the new Town Hall. <1,14,18,112>

c) *NEW MARKET BUILDING:* In 1828-30 a new market house was erected on the site of the old Town Hall on the western side of Market Street, backing onto the Thatched House in Black Lion Street. Designed by Thomas Simpson, it was a 'T'-shaped building with a classical façade of pediment supported on four square pillars, and had entrances in Market Street and Black Lion Street; another entrance was made from Little Castle Square to the south in about 1842 when new facilities were added for fish traders. The market was open daily, but the principal days were Tuesday, Thursday and Saturday when it remained open until 10 p.m. <24,112>

d) *RECONSTRUCTION:* In 1900-1 the market was rebuilt by borough engineer Francis May in a red-brick and terracotta design in three sections, each with arched glass and iron roofs. Two of the sections dealt in fruit and vegetables, while the southern part was used for selling flowers, the Floral Hall. This market building itself closed in 1938 after the Circus Street building opened, and was demolished and converted into a car-park in 1940, although the Market Street façade remained until the construction of Bartholomew Square in 1984-7. <114,130>

e) *MUNICIPAL MARKET:* The present municipal wholesale market in Circus Street was opened in January 1937 on a slum clearance site which included St Margaret's Mission Hall and the small houses of Circus Street and Circus Court. A new fish market was opened in the building in January 1960 by the Duke of Norfolk, replacing the Victorian facility on the Lower Esplanade. This market building is now scheduled for redevelopment. <83,116>

f) *SATURDAY MORNING MARKET, Upper Gardner Street:* In the last years of the nineteenth century, street-traders ('barrow-boys') began to congregate in Bond Street and Gardner Street. The police and the county borough council, tired of moving the traders on, set aside Upper Gardner Street for their use on Saturday mornings just after the turn of the century. The antiques, bric-a-brac and junk now sold between 7 a.m. and 1 p.m. every Saturday are a great attraction.

The 'leader' of Brighton's barrow-boys was Harry Cowley (1890-1971), a chimney-sweep by trade but a champion of the traders, the poor, the elderly and the homeless. Born at 33 Lincoln Street, his campaigns won fixed pitches for street-traders in both Upper Gardner Street and the Open Market, and he also started a movement of 'vigilantes' ('squatters' in modern parlance) after both wars to provide roofs over the heads of the homeless in empty properties. He was one of the best-known and best-loved men in the town for many years. <281,291>

g) *OPEN MARKET, Marshall's Row:* Started in Oxford Street in 1919 as an unorganised collection of barrows, mainly owned by ex-servicemen. They were soon moved to the central rose-walk of the Level, but following a campaign by Harry Cowley (see "Saturday Morning Market" above), a permanent site for the mobile barrows opened on the gardens of the cobble-fronted cottages of Marshall's Row on 19 November 1926. The cottages were demolished in 1938, and the present permanent retail market with forty-two stalls was opened on 7 January 1960 by the Duke of Norfolk. <291,311>

Figure 86: Selling produce in Market Street in about 1832. The new Town Hall is on the left, the new Market Hall on the right.

h) *CATTLE MARKET:* A cattle market was established in the workhouse grounds on Church Hill in 1831, but was soon discontinued due to a lack of pasturage <7>.

j) *CORN MARKET:* A corn market was held at the Old Ship from around the turn of the nineteenth century, but was transferred to the King and Queen in Marlborough Place by 1822. In October 1868 the market, which was held on Thursdays, was removed to the former Royal Pavilion riding school in Church Street which was renamed the Corn Exchange. It continued until the First World War when the building was used as part of a military hospital <24,194>.

k) *FISH MARKET:* see "Fishing Industry".

l) *MEAT MARKET:* The town's wholesale meat market was formerly situated in Russell Street, in a building originally erected in 1876-7 as the Church of the Resurrection. Built for the Revd Arthur Wagner, it was intended as a simple chapel of ease to St Paul's for the fishermen of the area. The adjacent Cannon Brewery objected to the proposed height of the building, so the architect, R.H.Carpenter, built it partly below ground; it was reached by thirty-two steps. The red-brick exterior was extremely plain, while the interior had a north aisle and a very tall nave. The church was consecrated in 1878 but closed in about 1912, and it was then used as a meat market until it was demolished in 1968 for the Churchill Square scheme. The market was replaced by a new facility adjacent to the abattoir at Upper Hollingdean Road. <62,64a,65,83,123>

101.MASTER OF CEREMONIES

<3,15>

An important figure at fashionable health resorts and spas in the eighteenth and nineteenth centuries was the Master of Ceremonies. He regulated and organised events, maintained registers of visitors in the libraries, and effected introductions. Brighton had three Masters of Ceremonies in its early years as a resort.

a) *CAPTAIN WILLIAM WADE:* Appointed in about 1767, Wade also officiated at Bath until 1777 when he was forced to leave for publicly ridiculing an admirer. He regulated the principal assemblies at the Castle and Old Ship, and promulgated rules within the town, even, in 1787, prohibiting the playing of games on the Steine on penalty of a fine. By 1806 though, his influence was waning and he was attending functions at the Castle Inn only following a dispute with the Old Ship. Wade's last season was 1807, and he probably died the following year.

b) *WILLIAM FORTH:* Chosen by a committee in 1808, William Forth proved to be unpopular, and the Old Ship even appointed its own master of ceremonies until 1819; he also had a series of disputes with the Castle. On 25 November 1823 Forth became the first toll-paying visitor to the Chain Pier, but ill health and increasing unpopularity led to his resignation in March 1828 from a job which at that time paid over £1,000 per annum, a very considerable sum.

c) *LIEUTENANT-COLONEL JOHN ELD:* The third and last Master of Ceremonies was elected at a meeting of prominent inhabitants at the Old Ship in 1828. Eld attended balls and made introductions as usual, but with the advent of the railway from London in 1841 his functions largely died out as many times more visitors arrived by train than ever did by coach. The Master's Ball continued until 1854 though, and Russian officers from Lewes Gaol (at the time of the Crimean War) were invited to the last one. Eld died on 22 December 1855 at the age of 76, and the office was then discontinued.

102. MAYORS

<7,310>

Since 1854 Brighton has been a chartered borough with a council chaired by a mayor, who, in the absence of royalty or the lord lieutenant, is also the sovereign's representative in the town. Brighton's first mayor was Lieutenant-Colonel John Fawcett who was elected at the first council meeting on 7 June 1854. The only person to have been mayor four times was John Brigden, in 1863, 1864, 1873 and 1874, but John Cordy Burrows was the first to be mayor both twice and three times. The first woman to become mayor was Miss Margaret Hardy in 1933.

A complete list of Brighton's mayors is given below; many names will be familiar with streets, roads, parks and flats named after them. Note that the dates shown refer to the year in which the mayors took office.

1854 John Fawcett
1855 William Hallett
1856 Isaac Bass
1857 Cordy Burrows
1858 " " " " "
1859 William Alger
1860 " " " "
1861 Henry Smithers
1862 Richard Wilson
1863 John Brigden
1864 " " " "
1865 Henry Martin
1866 William Henry Hallett
1867 " " " " " " " " "
1868 Thomas Lester
1869 Arthur Cox
1870 Richard Webb
1871 Cordy Burrows
1872 James Ireland
1873 John Brigden
1874 " " " "
1875 Henry Abbey
1876 Charles Lamb
1877 John Mayall
1878 Henry Davey
1879 " " " "
1880 David Smith
1881 William H.Hallett
1882 Arthur Cox
1883 " " " "
1884 Edward Reeves
1885 " " " " "
1886 " " " " "
1887 Edward Martin
1888 William Sendall
1889 George Manwaring
1890 Samuel Soper
1891 Sir Joseph Ewart
1892 " " " " " "
1893 " " " " " "
1894 William Botting
1895 Sir John Blaker
1896 " " " " "
1897 " " " " "
1898 Alfred Hawkes
1899 John Stafford
1900 " " " "
1901 " " " "
1902 John Buckwell
1903 Emile Marx
1904 Frederick Blaker
1905 James Colbourne
1906 Henry Gervis
1907 John Roberts
1908 " " " "
1909 Edward Geere
1910 Charles Thomas-Stanford
1911 " " " " " " " " " "
1912 " " " " " " " " " "
1913 John Otter
1914 " " "
1915 " " "
1916 Herbert Carden
1917 " " " " "
1918 " " " " "
1919 William Wellman
1920 Bertram Southall
1921 Edward Pankhurst
1922 " " " " " " "
1923 Hugh Milner Black
1924 Charles Teasdale
1925 John Thompson
1926 Richard Major
1927 Charles Kingston
1928 Herbert Galliers
1929 Horace Aldrich
1930 Sidney Thompson
1931 Thomas Braybon
1932 Frank Beal
1933 Miss Margaret Hardy
1934 Sidney Gibson
1935 Edward Deane
1936 John Routley
1937 Herbert Hone
1938 John Nanson
1939 " " " "
1940 " " " "
1941 Martin Huggett
1942 Bernard Dutton Briant
1943 " " " " " " " "
1944 Arthur Nicholls
1945 Walter Clout
1946 Thomas Morris
1947 Percy Friend-James
1948 " " " " " " "
1949 Ernest Marsh
1950 Samuel Davey
1951 Eric Simms
1952 Miss Dorothy Stringer
1953 John Hay
1954 Walter Dudeney
1955 Jasper Leek
1956 Lewis Cohen
1957 Charles Tyson
1958 Alfred Sadler
1959 Ernest Kippin
1960 Alan Johnson
1961 George Baldwin
1962 William Button
1963 Stanley Deason
1964 Walter Clout
1965 Dudley Baker
1966 Mrs Dorothea Watson-Miller
1967 Ronald Bates
1968 Thomas Taylor
1969 Frank Masefield-Baker
1970 Herbert Nettleton
1971 Stanley Theobald
1972 Gordon Packham

1973	George Lucraft	1979	Dennis Hobden	1985	Robert Cristofoli
1974	Danny Sheldon	1980	John Leach	1986	Mrs Jackie Lythell
1975	William Clarke	1981	Joseph Wakefield	1987	Ray Blackwood
1976	Peter Best	1982	Geoffrey Theobald	1988	Ms Pat Hawkes
1977	Mrs Hilary Somerville	1983	Charles Jermy	1989	Brian Fitch
1978	Alfred Feld	1984	John Blackman	1990	Mrs Christine Simpson

103. Hotel METROPOLE, King's Road

<3,45,45a,123>

Brighton's largest hotel, with 328 bedrooms of various sizes, was opened by the Gordon Hotels Company in July 1890 on the site of several houses and shops in King's Road and Westfield Gardens. The architect was Alfred Waterhouse, but the building, which cost £57,000 to build, was at the time called the ugliest in Brighton, especially as the seven-storey hotel was erected in red brick and terracotta, the first building to break with the traditional cream colour of the sea-front. The rather plain edifice has some decorative details at fourth- and fifth-floor levels, and is adorned with ironwork balconies. The construction itself was delayed by continual labour disputes that led, in 1890, to the establishment of the Brighton Trades Council at the Eagle Hotel (now the George Beard) in Gloucester Road, uniting the many unions in the town <104,105>.

The Metropole, which was then the largest hotel in the country outside London, naturally became a focus for social and other events in the town, and has played host to many important guests. During the Second World War it was used by the Australian and New Zealand armed forces. In 1959 the hotel was purchased by AVP Industries which almost immediately made major alterations. Extra bedrooms and flats were added on the roof, resulting in the removal of the distinctive bronze spire and several turrets, cupolas and pinnacles. The interior was also considerably altered with the addition of a winter garden, but the original marble arches, barrel-vaulted ceilings and panelled walls remain. The roof-top Starlit Room restaurant, opened in October 1961, became famous for its superb view, but closed in August 1975. A casino, the first in the country, was established in 1962 following the revision of the gaming laws.

Following these improvements, architects R.Seifert and Partners designed the 85,000-square-foot Metropole Exhibition Halls, the Sussex Heights 'tower-block', and a 250-space underground car-park at the rear of the hotel; the site was previously occupied by a large courtyard and ornamental garden, some houses in Cannon Place and Queensbury Mews, and St Margaret's Church. The development was completed in 1966, but the exhibition halls were extended to 110,000 square feet in 1972, and have proved a great benefit both to the hotel and to the town as a whole. Sussex Heights have not proved so popular, however. At a height of 336 feet, the 24-storey block is the tallest building in Brighton and has been severely criticised for dominating the sea-front vista.

Further major improvements to the hotel facilities were made with the opening of the Cannon public house in 1981, and with the addition of a swimming-pool and health club a few years later. The modern east wing though, while utilising features of the original hotel, has destroyed the building's symmetry somewhat.

104. MODS and ROCKERS

<123,287>

Two rival youth cultures that clashed several times at Brighton in the 1960s, the most infamous occasion being the so-called 'Battle of Brighton' at the Whitsun holiday, 17-18 May 1964. The Brighton police were prepared for trouble as there had been clashes at Clacton and Hastings at Easter, but the town was invaded by up to 3,000 youths. The leather-jacketed 'Rockers' arrived on their motor-bikes on the Sunday morning, but were challenged in the afternoon by a much larger number of the neatly-dressed 'Mods' on their motor-scooters.

Several small scuffles broke out, but the most serious trouble was around the Palace Pier where hundreds of deckchairs were broken, pebbles were used as missiles, and the Savoy (now Cannon) Cinema windows were smashed. Eventually 150 police and a police horse quelled the disturbance, but the violence was repeated the following morning with several thousand spectators watching the confrontations from the Aquarium Sun Terrace and Marine Parade; the sea-front traders, however, rapidly boarded up their properties. Twenty-six youths appeared in the juvenile court the following week and were handed stiff sentences, but fortunately no-one was seriously injured.

The events of the Whitsun holiday of 1964 were never repeated again in such magnitude, but trouble amongst youths has flared on several Bank Holiday weekends since, notably in 1969, 1970, 1974, 1977, 1980 and 1981. However, the worst violence seen in the town in recent years occurred after the English football team's World Cup semi-final defeat on 4 July 1990 when mobs of youths ran through the town centre smashing windows and looting shops.

105. MOULSECOOMB

a) *MOULSECOOMB PLACE:* Moulsecoomb, as a manor, dates from at least the eleventh century, but the present façade of the manor house, Moulsecoomb Place, was constructed in 1790 for Benjamin Tillstone on a building which includes much work from the early eighteenth century. Faced in yellow brick, the house has a central pediment, a south wing which was added in 1906, a single bow and a recent conservatory. The listed building was acquired by the corporation in February 1925 as part of the 315-acre, £30,000 Moulsecoomb estate of Mr B.T.Rogers-Tillstone, and has since been used at various times as a school annexe and a branch library; it is currently the headquarters of the Parks and Recreation Department.

Attached to the rear of the house is a listed cottage said to be the oldest secular building within the borough, and also reputedly haunted by a mistress of James II. Dating from around 1500 or earlier (some references say 1350-1400), it has recently been restored and has a projecting, timber-framed upper storey which may be viewed from Queensdown School Road. It is the only surviving portion of a larger building which was perhaps the medieval manor house. Nearby is a large, weather-boarded tithe barn of the sixteenth century with timbers said to have come from the Spanish Armada, and a single-storey flint extension. A dovecote, known as the Prince's Tower from visits made by the Prince of Wales (later George IV), was destroyed by vandals in 1942.

Upper Moulsecoomb or Home Farm stood on the other side of the railway line until the 1960s, a site now occupied by Queensdown (formerly Woodside) Special School; in 1989-91 land to the north-east is being developed as a light industrial estate, the Home Farm Business Centre. The site of Lower Moulsecoomb Farm is now covered by the houses around 68 The Highway. <1,8,44,45a,109,110a,305>

b) *HISTORY AND DEVELOPMENT OF MOULSECOOMB HOUSING ESTATE:* Now the borough's largest housing estate, Moulsecoomb was also the corporation's first large-scale estate, the initial development at South Moulsecoomb commencing in the early 1920s. This original estate, which included The Avenue, Colbourne Avenue, The Crescent, The Highway, Hillside, Southall Avenue and some houses in Natal Road, was erected on ninety-four acres of land to the east of the Lewes Road acquired in November 1920 which were annexed by the county borough from the parish of Patcham on 1 October 1923. A fierce debate raged over the spelling of the name for many years, but 'Moulsecoomb' was generally agreed upon in the 1960s. It probably derives from the personal name 'Mul', and dates from at least the twelfth century. <123,289>

South Moulsecoomb was considered something of a model garden estate with its large open spaces and two-storey, semi-detached houses with large gardens, described as 'homes fit for heroes' by one alderman in the post-Great War era; there were even tennis-courts provided in The Avenue. The 478 houses were meant to provide new homes for people in the proposed slum clearance areas on Albion Hill, but the rents charged by the council were prohibitive for most of the intended residents, and tenants were brought in from other towns, especially London, following an advertising campaign. Little was therefore done to relieve the appalling conditions in central Brighton. <2,110a,123>

The North Moulsecoomb estate of 390 houses followed in 1926-30, on forty-six acres acquired in October 1925, but was developed to a higher density than South Moulsecoomb, a factor which has perhaps contributed to the social problems experienced there. Originally part of Falmer parish, the area was annexed by Brighton on 1 April 1928. Redevelopment of the estate, which has also suffered from a lack of facilities and maintenance,

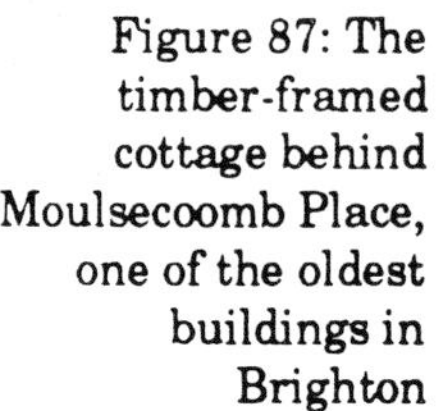

Figure 87: The timber-framed cottage behind Moulsecoomb Place, one of the oldest buildings in Brighton

commenced in 1979 but has been restricted by financial restraints.

In the early 1930s the corporation extended its housing up the Bevendean valley with 85-123 and 110-120 The Avenue, Manton Road, and Upper and Lower Bevendean Avenues. As this was on land previously belonging to Lower Bevendean Farm, these new houses were known as the Bevendean estate; Moulsecoomb therefore ends at the western end of Manton Road, the limit of the original estate. There was also some private development at this time in the Bevendean Crescent/Widdicombe Way area similarly on Bevendean land, but this area is now generally regarded as part of Moulsecoomb.

The East Moulsecoomb housing estate from Hodshrove Road and Birdham Road to Moulsecoomb Way was built by the corporation on part of a 300-acre estate which was purchased in December 1935. Moulsecoomb was completed in the 1940s and '50s with the Halland Road area and the flats of the West Moulsecoomb or Bates Estate, on the site of the Bates Nursery. In 1981 the population of the Moulsecoomb district was around 8,500. A light industrial area was developed on the slopes north-east of the railway line in 1989-91, the Home Farm Business Centre. <83,110a,277>

c) *BUILDINGS:* The estate church of St Andrew, Hillside, was consecrated on 23 June 1934 and replaced an earlier temporary church removed from Lewes in 1922. Built with a squat tower, tiny spire and transepts, the church has a roof which was intended to resemble an upturned fishing boat (St Andrew was a fisherman), and contains some modern murals. The parish was united with Stanmer and Falmer from 1956 until 1976. St George's Hall, a chapel of ease in Ringmer Road for North Moulsecoomb, opened in May 1930 but was rebuilt as a community centre in 1989. The R.C. Church of St Francis of Assissi in Moulsecoomb Way was converted from an Anglican chapel in 1953, the same year as the nearby Moulsecoomb Baptist Church opened. The latter was derelict and acquired by the council in 1988 for the erection of the Moulsecoomb Community Leisure Centre, scheduled to open late in 1990. Moulsecoomb Hall, a community centre in Lewes Road, opened in 1946. Moulsecoomb Library originally opened in a room at Moulsecoomb Place in December 1929, but the permanent library was opened on 13 March 1964 by the mayor, Stanley Deason, on the site of a lodge. <83,110a,123>

The estate's most famous resident was William Havergal Brian (1896-1972) who lived at 130 Hillside in the 1920s. Largely self-taught, he found initial success with his music, but his later work was neglected and he descended into obscurity. While living at Moulsecoomb in 1927, Brian wrote the *Gothic Symphony* which, requiring 200 players, was the biggest symphony ever written. However, the work was not performed until 1961 and it was only then that he was recognised as one of the greatest of British composers. In all, Brian composed thirty-two symphonies, five operas and many other works, and a plaque has been erected on his former house. <123,255a>

d) *ALLEN WEST LTD:* Employment for many of the estate's inhabitants was provided by the small industrial estates along Lewes Road to the south and in Moulsecoomb Way. The leading industrial concern was Allen West Ltd, a firm of electrical engineers founded in April 1910 by Mr Allen West at a shared factory in Lewes Road to the south of Natal Road. The firm soon took over its co-occupiers, Reasons, and in 1927, jointly with Schweppes, took over the large Oppenheimer diamond factory on the southern side of Coombe Road. As the company expanded so several overseas subsidiaries were established, and by 1939 more space was required at Brighton. The first Moulsecoomb Way factory opened in 1939, followed by a second in 1940, and the firm made a great contribution to the war effort, building thousands of radar sets and sections for the Mulberry harbour. Up to 3,000 people were employed by Allen West after the war, and further factories were opened in Moulsecoomb Way in 1953, 1956 and 1957. A new administrative and design office was opened in 1966 at Dewe Road above the original factory.

However, the following year saw a number of redundancies, and all production and offices were transferred to Moulsecoomb Way. The almost new Dewe Road building was put up for sale in 1968, but the corporation declined to buy it and it was sold to a property company in March 1972; it was then renamed Mithras House and since 1977 has been used by the polytechnic. The original Lewes Road factory was demolished in October 1972, and in early 1973 Allen West Ltd was acquired jointly by Tube Investments and General Electric of America. By December 1984, Allenwest Electrical Ltd had been acquired by its own management for £27.5 million. Now most of the Moulsecoomb Way sites have been sold, with just one factory operated by Allen West Electrical. The Moulsecoomb Way sites are destined to become the Fairway Retail Park; the first warehouse, Texas Homecare, opened at Christmas 1985. <83,123,272>

e) *HODSHROVE:* Only one flint outbuilding and a small wall now remain of Hodshrove, a farm that stood on the western side of Hodshrove Road from at least the thirteenth century until that part of the estate was developed in the 1930s. The timber and flint farmhouse, which showed traces of medieval work, was probably rebuilt in the sixteenth and nineteenth centuries, and was approached from Lewes Road along Hodshrove Lane; in the mid eighteenth century it was the property of John Friend, one of the lords of the manor of Brighton. Some mid-nineteenth-century cottages also remain adjacent to the railway viaduct. Hodshrove Woods cover 4.36 acres between Hodshrove Road and Birdham Road. <1,10,109,126,298>

f) *WILD PARK:* Moulsecoomb Wild Park was purchased by the corporation as part of the Moulsecoomb estate in February 1925. Over 200 acres are now leased as farm land, but the 90-acre park, apart from the playing fields in the valley, has been left as open downland and therefore in its wild state. It was formally opened by the mayor, Charles Teasdale, on 30 June 1925, an inauguration recorded on a commemorative plinth which was removed from the Victoria Gardens.

An interesting nature trail starts at the steps adjacent to the pavilion, while the access road extends nearly half a mile up the valley known as Moulsecoomb Pit towards the summer dry ski-slope. Two young trees and a commemorative seat in the northern woodland by the pavilion mark the spot where the so-called 'Wild Park Murders' were committed on 9 October 1986, when two nine-year-old girls from North Moulsecoomb were brutally killed.

The ornamental area of about five acres alongside Lewes Road to the north is known simply as the Park or the Parkway, and was laid out in 1955 on the site of Woollard's nursery. It received a Civic Trust Award in 1960, but some land was lost when the Lewes Road was 'dualled' in the late 1960s. The northern edge formed part of the county borough boundary from 1928 until 1952.
<123,126>

106. MUSEUM and ART GALLERY, Church Street

<15,24,115,117>

a) *HISTORY:* Using the proceeds from several exhibitions which were held at the Royal Pavilion in the 1850s, a municipal art collection was established in some of the first-floor rooms of the Pavilion in about 1860; in 1862 the display was joined by various museum collections that had been presented to the corporation. In 1869 the museum collection was augmented by that of the Royal Scientific and Literary Institution which also left the town a collection of books to enable a reference library to be established at the Pavilion.

The space available in the Royal Pavilion soon proved inadequate, and so borough surveyor Philip Lockwood remodelled the former servants' quarters, coach houses and stables connected with the Dome in Church Street as a new art gallery, library and museum, fitted out in Moorish style. The new art gallery opened on 20 January 1873 in the large central hall, into which the entrance led directly, and the new museum was opened on 12 September 1873 at the same time as the library by Dr Carpenter of the British Association; rooms were devoted to archaeology, botany, geology and zoology. Several important private collections were added during the next few years, and rooms were kept in the Royal Pavilion as an annexe. The exhibition galleries were enlarged in 1894, and further alterations were made in 1901 when the refurbishment of the Town Hall had been completed, thereby releasing rooms previously used for other purposes. On 5 November 1902 the Victoria Public Library opened in its present position, allowing the museum and art gallery to expand to their present size; a new entrance hall was also made, and the façade was altered somewhat with the addition of oriental ornamentation. The museum, art gallery and library buildings are now listed as being of special architectural interest. (See figure 76.)

b) *MUSEUM EXHIBITS:* Brighton Museum has one of the richest collections in the country, but due to a chronic lack of space many pieces are kept stored away from public gaze. It is particularly strong in ceramics, and includes the important Willett collection of 1,715 pieces of decorated porcelain and pottery which was first loaned in the 1880s and then presented in 1901 to celebrate the remodelling of the building. There is a large collection of costume and fashion, the Spencer collection of musical instruments, and the Alldridge and Lucas collections of ethnographica. A well-presented gallery of Brighton's heritage from the mid eighteenth century contains many important and interesting exhibits, and some excellent models, but this collection will be rehoused in the new Museum of Brighton at the former Holy Trinity Church in Ship Street.

Perhaps the greatest treasure is the unique 'Hove Cup' displayed in the excellent archaeological galleries. One of the most important Bronze Age artifacts in the country, it is a drinking cup of circa 1240 B.C. made from a solid block of amber, and was found in 1857 at a barrow in the garden of 13 Palmeira Avenue. There is also a Bronze Age hoard of metal 'loops' from Black Rock, and a second-century copper-alloy figurine of a stag, found in 1985.

The museum is not strong on furniture as many pieces are housed in the Royal Pavilion and Preston Manor, while the natural history collection has been removed to Booth's Museum in Dyke Road. Brighton also owns the National Toy Museum collection, part of which is housed at The Grange in Rottingdean, but it is hoped to house it in the adjacent North Gate House in Church Street. Unfortunately, Brighton Museum can only expand further if and when another site is found for the public library.

c) *ART GALLERY EXHIBITS:* The large municipal art collection is particularly strong in Dutch oil paintings, principally the Willett collection presented in 1901; in twentieth-century paintings; and the Simpkins collection of Victorian English paintings. There is also a large collection of drawings and watercolours of local scenes, principally the Pocock, Furner and Blaber collections. Many paintings are also displayed in the Royal Pavilion, Preston Manor and The Grange, while several portraits of important local figures may be seen in the museum's Brighton Heritage gallery.

107. NEW ROAD

In August 1803 the town commissioners allowed the Prince of Wales to close off that part of Great East Street that ran past his Marine Pavilion, provided that a parallel road was constructed as a replacement. The New Road was subsequently laid out in 1805, by soldiers under the supervision of William Porden, along Furner's Garden which the Prince had acquired the previous year. The new thoroughfare was developed with buildings over the next ten years or so, and by 1818 fifteen houses were in use. Trees were planted in 1812. <112,194>

There are a number of interesting buildings in the road. The attractive nos.3-8 are listed houses faced in yellow brick, jointed with giant pilasters and embellished with wide bow windows. No.10, the Colonnade public house, stands within the frontage of the Theatre Royal and opened as a hotel in the early 1850s. In 1923 it was purchased by the theatre, resold in 1935, and purchased again by the theatre in 1953 for £5,900. (The Theatre Royal itself, built in 1806-7 but refaced in 1894, has a separate entry.)

The colonnade itself, once known as the Royal Colonnade, is a listed structure and was originally built in 1806-7 on Doric columns in front of the Theatre Royal only. In 1823 it was extended on Ionic columns by Cooper and Lynn around the corner to 157 North Street, now part of the National Westminster Bank. The section outside the theatre from no.9 to no.12 was replaced in 1894 when the theatre was reconstructed, and now has terracotta columns with Corinthian capitals; the height was also increased by two feet and it does not therefore match the adjacent section. Portions of the colonnade were removed in 1912, 1922, and finally in June 1929 as part of the North Street widening scheme such that now only that section at nos.6-12 New Road remains. In the nineteenth century the colonnade was notorious as the haunt of prostitutes at theatre and music hall closing times.

The Family Assurance offices at 16-17 New Road stands on the site of a second theatre. Erected on the site of the New Oxford Music Hall which was destroyed by fire in 1892, it was a four-storey, Louis XVI-style building with a decorated façade and an elaborate plaster-work interior. Opening as the Empire Theatre, its name was changed in 1905 to the Coliseum Theatre of Varieties, and again in 1907 to the Court Theatre. In 1909 the building was converted to a cinema, sound equipment being installed in 1929. Following the war the Court was taken over by J.Baxter Somerville, manager of the nearby Theatre Royal, and it reopened on 24 May 1947 as the Dolphin Theatre, presenting fortnightly repertory productions. In 1952 it was renamed Her Majesty's Theatre, and changed its name for the last time in April 1955 when it was converted into the Paris Continental Cinema, specialising in foreign films. After reverting to repertory in 1957, the Paris Theatre closed in March 1963 and was demolished in 1967. <68,68a,123>

The offices at no.20, designed by Miller Bourne, won a 1989 council planning award. <123>

Three more listed buildings stand at the northern end of the road. The Unitarian Church, more properly known as Christ Church, was built in 1820 by A.H.Wilds. With its portico and giant fluted Doric columns, the building was modelled on the Temple of Theseus at Athens; internal alterations were made in 1938 and 1966. No.23 New Road is an elegant red-brick building, probably by Amon Wilds, and is adorned with a bow, iron balcony, and Ionic open-work pilasters. No.24, an attractive bow-fronted building in flint cobbles, opened as the Regent Hotel but was used by Crabb's Wine Merchants from 1808 until the 1980s.

Some early 19th century buildings also stand on the eastern side of New Road, but the Pavilion Theatre was added in 1934 and is dealt with under "Dome and Corn Exchange". The two K6-style telephone boxes are listed as being of special architectural interest as British Telecom replaces this type of kiosk. <44,64a,235>

Figure 88: The Royal Colonnade in New Road. The original section is at the left-hand end.

108. NEWSPAPERS

<83,123,301>

The principal local newspaper of Brighton and Sussex is the:

a) *EVENING ARGUS:* Originally known simply as *The Argus*, after the hundred-eyed, all-seeing giant of Greek mythology. The first edition sold for one halfpenny and was published on 30 March 1880 at 130 North Street, where a loft on the roof housed the pigeons that brought in stories from the far corners of the county. From 7 November 1889 an East Sussex edition was printed at Hastings, and on 1 January 1897 the newspaper was renamed the *Evening Argus*; a *Morning Argus* was also published from 2 September 1897 until 3 May 1926. The price was increased to one penny in March 1918, and in February 1926 the first photograph was included, of a fire at the Court Theatre in New Road. The printing works eventually moved to Spring Gardens with type still set in North Street, but in 1926 Southern Publishing acquired Robinson's printing works and adjoining premises at the southern end of Robert Street, enabling all departments to be housed in the same building.

The *Evening Argus* reached a crisis in the Second World War when circulation fell to just 19,000. The Hastings plant was closed, but after the war the paper was reorganised and re-equipped, and the circulation gradually rose again. The 'magic' figure of 100,000 copies per day was reached in October 1964, and total readership is now around 250,000. In 1972 paper type replaced hot metal, the first photo-set front page was produced on 28 October 1977, and in July 1987 the paper went completely 'electronic'. In 1990 a £20 million newspaper printing investment at the Hollingbury industrial estate was announced, but the offices and journalists will remain in Robert Street. (See also "Southern Publishing Company" below.) <19,123>

Many newspapers and 'visitors lists' (which recorded the arrival of fashionable visitors) were published in Brighton in the nineteenth and early twentieth centuries. Many were short-lived, but the best known are detailed below.

b) *BRIGHTON GAZETTE:* A weekly paper, first published as the ***Brighton Gazette, Sussex and General Advertiser or Worthing, Eastbourne and Hastings Fashionable Chronicle*** on 22 February 1821 by E.H.Creasy, in premises beneath Donaldson's Library at the corner of Old Steine and St James's Street. The offices later moved to 168 North Street, and from 1835 it was printed in a building adjoining the Central National Schools in Church Street. From 1852 it was published at the Pavilion Dormitories behind North Street, but the *Gazette* was later acquired by the Southern Publishing Company. On 2 April 1938 it became the ***Brighton and Hove Gazette***. The paper incorporated the ***Southern Weekly News*** from 19 November 1965, and continued as the ***Brighton and Hove Gazette and Herald*** in 1971, having incorporated the ***Herald***. The last edition was published on 9 March 1985 when the *Gazette* was itself absorbed by the ***Brighton and Hove Leader***, launched as a free weekly on 25 June 1981. (See also "Southern Publishing Company" below.) <6,19,24>

c) *BRIGHTON HERALD:* The first newspaper to become established in Brighton was first published on 6 September 1806 at 8 Middle Street by H.Robertson Attree and Matthew Philips, with Robert Sicklemore as editor. From May 1808 Attree carried on the business alone and the offices were moved to the top of North Street, but in January 1810 Attree took the manager William Fleet into partnership, and then left the business himself the following April. Fleet moved the *Herald* offices to Prince's Place, and took his son Charles into partnership in 1843, retiring in 1864. Charles Fleet then took John Bishop, with the paper since 1839 and later to become a well-known local historian, into partnership, and left him as sole proprietor when he himself retired in June 1880.

The *Herald* rapidly established itself as a leading provincial weekly, and was the first newspaper to report the escape of Napoleon from Elba in 1815, the start of the French Revolution of 1830, and the arrival of Louis Phillipe at Newhaven in 1848. In 1934 an elegant new office building was opened on the western side of Pavilion Buildings; it was decorated with the arms of Brighton and Hove and is now occupied by the Royal Insurance Company. The name of the paper changed to the *Brighton Herald and Hove Chronicle* on 19 July 1902, and to the *Brighton and Hove Herald* on 4 November 1922. The final edition, no.8621 after 165 years, was produced on 30 September 1971 when the *Herald* was absorbed by the ***Brighton and Hove Gazette***. <6,15,24>

d) *BRIGHTON STANDARD AND FASHIONABLE VISITORS LIST:* Published on Tuesdays, Thursdays and Saturdays, the *Standard* first appeared on 4 July 1865 as the *Brighton Fashionable Visitors List* and changed its name on 7 May 1878. It continued until 4 March 1953, a total of 13,249 editions. (See also "Southern Publishing Company" below.)

e) *SOUTHERN WEEKLY NEWS:* A weekly from the Southern Publishing Company on Saturdays. The first issue appeared on 16 December 1876, and it continued until 11 June 1965 when it was incorporated into the *Gazette*. (See also "Southern Publishing Company" below.) <19>

f) *SUSSEX ADVERTISER:* Originally the ***Sussex Weekly Advertiser or Lewes Journal***, it was the first Sussex newspaper and was published from 1749 until the early 1900s. From 24 June 1822 until 12 April 1842, it was known as the ***Sussex Advertiser, or Lewes and Brighthelmston Journal***.

g) *SUSSEX DAILY NEWS:* The first halfpenny daily in the country, founded in November 1868 by Henry John Infield at a small printing works in Lewes Road. By the 1950s it was the only morning daily published in the south of England outside London, but the last copy was produced on 3 March 1956 when it was incorporated into the ***Evening Argus***. (See also "Southern Publishing Company" below.) <19>

h) *OTHER NEWSPAPERS:* Some of the other longer lasting newspapers were:

Brighton Advertiser, weekly 1880-1925;
Brighton Daily News, 1868-80;
Brighton Examiner, twice-weekly 1853-95;
Brighton Guardian, a radical paper published weekly at 34 North Street by Levi Emmanuel Cohen 1827-1901;
Brighton Observer, weekly 1856-76;
Brighton Programme, weekly entertainment programme 1906-36;
Brighton Society, weekly 1887-1927;
Brighton Times, weekly 1860-1915;
Sussex Evening Times, 1880-1915;

j) *SOUTHERN PUBLISHING COMPANY:* The Southern Publishing Company was founded in 1888 by Henry John Infield, who had published the *Sussex Daily News* since 1868. He was succeeded by his son Jonathan as chairman and managing director in 1921, but Jonathan himself died in 1942 and his nephew, Edward Infield Willis, took over. Offices were acquired at 50 North Street which were reconstructed in 1951 as the stylish Argus House, now Refuge Assurance House. In 1926 the printing works were removed to Robert Street.

Eventually the *Southern Weekly News* and *Sussex Daily News* were both dropped in favour of the *Gazette* and *Argus*, and in 1965 70% of the company was sold to Westminster Press Ltd, with Willis continuing as chairman; the parent company took complete control when Willis retired. Argus House was sold at the end of 1976, with all the offices of the company moving to expanded premises in Robert Street. A free weekly, *The Advertiser*, was succeeded by the *Brighton and Hove Leader* on 25 June 1981, and this incorporated the *Gazette* in March 1985. <6,19,24>

109. NORFOLK RESORT HOTEL, 149 King's Road

<2,44,123>

The Norfolk, one of Brighton's leading hotels, was built in 1824 as the Norfolk Arms, a three-storey inn rising to four floors in the centre, with a balcony and verandah on Ionic columns. In 1864-6 however, it was entirely rebuilt by Horatio Goulty in a Renaissance style with five storeys and iron balconies; note the Norfolk lion head figurines on the second floor balconies.

In 1969 AVP Industries, having been refused permission to replace it with a block of flats, sold the Norfolk to the Feld family. Now known as the Norfolk Resort, and a listed building, the hotel underwent a £2 million refurbishment in the early 1980s and has 117 rooms plus the Rafters night-club in the superstructure. An indoor swimming-pool opened in November 1985, the first hotel pool in the town centre, while at the rear a development of rooms around an ornamental lake opened in September 1985 on the site of the hotel garage. This site was originally occupied by Young's Livery Stables, and leads to Norfolk Buildings via an arched gateway with a horse-head figure and the inscription 'Rebuilt 1875'.

110. NORTH LAINE

The North Laine was one of five open, arable fields in Brighton farmed by tenant husbandmen (see "Downs (Laines)"), and covered the area from Church Street northwards to New England Road and Viaduct Road, and from Buckingham Road and the railway eastwards to Ditchling Road. It was mainly developed in small plots as an area of low-cost terraced housing and Brighton's 'industrial heartland', principally in the 1820s and again in the 1840s with the railway boom, but for a number of years in the 1960s and early '70s the area was under the threat of wholesale demolition and redevelopment; indeed, the northern part of the North Laine, to the west of London Road, has been almost completely obliterated.

In March 1973 however, Brighton Council rejected the 'Wilson report' which, although recommending a general improvement policy for the North Laine area to the south of Trafalgar Street, also called for an elevated 'spine road' from Preston Circus through the area to a car-park in Church Street. With a new awareness for traditional townscapes, the council followed up by designating a North Laine conservation area in 1977, covering most of the area between Queen's Road, North Road, Gloucester Place, St George's Place and Trafalgar Street, plus Gardner Street and Bond Street; it is this district which is now known as the North Laine although, as mentioned above, it originally covered a much larger area. (The conservation area was extended in 1989 to include the 1870s houses of North Place.) With the removal of planning blight, the North Laine has now become a desirable residential and commercial district connecting the London Road and North Street areas, a fascinating area with many specialist shops and small industrial premises. The resident population of the area is over 1,500.
<78,83,123,262a,277>

The streets of greatest interest in the North Laine conservation area are detailed below in alphabetical order (see also "Church Street" and "North Road").

a) *BOND STREET:* Developed in the second half of the eighteenth century, Bond Street was the first road built northwards from North Street. The town commissioners renamed it New Street in May 1794, but it reverted to its original name when the New Road opened nearby in 1805.

Now a busy shopping street, there are a number of buildings of interest and several are faced with mathematical tiles. Nos.2-3, plain brick buildings, and nos.4-7, grander buildings with bows, date from the early nineteenth century and are all listed. No.27 was the Wheatsheaf Inn from the mid eighteenth century until 1970. Nos.35-38 are small, eighteenth-century cottages with no.35 converted into the stage door of the Theatre

Royal in 1894. No.42 Bond Street stands on the site of the Salem Baptist Chapel, built in 1787 and enlarged in 1825 to hold 800 worshippers. It was completely rebuilt in 1861 by Thomas Simpson with a Doric entrance and gable, but was demolished in 1974. <14,15,44,62,112,123,235>

b) *BLENHEIM PLACE:* Has an attractive row of gaily painted cottages of the 1840s. On the southern side is a former flint and brick malt-house of the North Street Brewery. <83,275>

c) *CHELTENHAM PLACE:* An attractive street of small terraced cottages of the 1840s. On the eastern side is the frontage of the former malt-house of the North Street Brewery.

d) *FREDERICK GARDENS:* A narrow twitten, lined with very small but attractive bow-windowed cottages of the 1820s behind tiny gardens. They are, unfortunately, completely overshadowed by the Post Office sorting office.

e) *GARDNER STREET:* A busy shopping street developed in the first years of the nineteenth century by John Furner on the site of his market garden, but now spoilt by the oppressive Jubilee Shopping Hall, formerly Tesco. No.12, formerly the Sussex Arms, was erected as the Swan Downer School in 1816, a fact which is borne out by a barely readable inscription above the ground floor, and it is now a listed building. The school was founded by the bequest of a wealthy London merchant for the education of twenty or more poor girls; it moved to Windsor Street in 1859, and to Dyke Road in 1867. No.51 Gardner Street was formerly Beall's Cork Shop. Opened in 1883, it was the last such shop in the country when it closed on 1 October 1983; the building itself dated from the 1820s, and the shop façade has been removed and reconstructed in the town museum with the original fittings. <44,123,209,262a>

f) *GLOUCESTER ROAD:* The castellated Surridge Dawson warehouse on the northern side was built around 1870 as the headquarters of the Royal Artillery Volunteers who had moved from Church Street. It stands on the site of the Eagle Iron Foundry, where much of the town's ironwork was produced in the nineteenth century; the Eagle Hotel, now the George Beard, still stands nearby. Near the top of the road is the Galeed Strict Baptist Chapel, a plain, classical building built by Benjamin Nunn and opened on 15 October 1868. Gloucester Road is now lined with a number of antique and collector shops, and has become a much more attractive shopping street since the roadway was closed off in 1986 in an attempt to remove the menace of traffic through the area. <62,114>

g) *GLOUCESTER STREET:* A street of small terraced houses of the 1820s; a number of small courtyards have been demolished at the eastern end around St George's Mews. Approached through an archway at no.28 are the Gloucester Rooms, used as a chapel by the Plymouth Brethren until the 1960s when they became an auction room. <83>

h) *KEMP STREET:* Lined with attractive terraced houses, many with glazing bars and window shutters. In 1934 the body in one of the famous 'Trunk Murders' (q.v.) was discovered at no.52. <124>

j) *KENSINGTON GARDENS:* Developed from about 1808 onwards, the first street northwards from North Road, Kensington Gardens forms an attractive pedestrian precinct at the heart of the North Laine and retains its setts in the pathway. Originally the houses did indeed have gardens, and some of the shops on the eastern side can be seen to be single-storey extensions in the gardens of larger two- and three-storey houses behind. No.5, which was the Kensington Gardens Institute for working men from 1865 until 1920, retains its early-nineteenth-century bowed front of mathematical tiles, while several others, notably nos.7-11, retain original façades above the shop-fronts. It must be hoped that any future rebuilding will not affect the character of this charming street. <14,83>

k) *KENSINGTON PLACE:* Lined with small terraced houses and cottages of the 1820s with gardens on

Figure 89: 1820s cottages at Frederick Gardens

the western side. Nos.30-52, a neat, rusticated terrace on the eastern side, were added in the 1830s and, being decorated with Ionic pilasters, are included on the council's local list of buildings of special interest. <108>

l) *OVER STREET:* Both sides have attractive three-storey houses of around 1850.

m) *PELHAM SQUARE:* The two-storey houses on the southern and western sides of this attractive enclave were erected in the 1840s as Pelham Terrace; the three-storey houses with small front gardens on the eastern side were added in about 1860 to complete the square. Nos.1-12 and 15-24 are all listed buildings. The garden was used by the York Place schools as a recreational area at one time. Now known as the Queen Mother's Garden, it was landscaped in 1980 to celebrate Her Majesty's eightieth birthday. The two K6-type telephone boxes have been designated buildings of special architectural interest as British Telecom replaces this style of kiosk. <44,83,123,126>

n) *QUEEN'S GARDENS:* Has attractive terraces of the 1840s on both sides.

p) *ROBERT STREET:* Now dominated by the premises of the Evening Argus, but there remains an impressive terrace on the opposite side. Breaking the line of the terrace at nos.16-17 is the former Jireh Chapel, opened in 1846 as a Calvinistic chapel. The second floor was added at a later date, but it closed in about 1902 and became a furniture warehouse; it is due to be converted to flats. <62,123>

q) *SYDNEY STREET:* A busy shopping street, developed around 1850. No.36 has Ionic pilasters.

r) *TIDY STREET:* Dating from around 1840, the terraced nos.1-27 and 31-52 are included on the council's local list; nos.7-27, 30-33 and 38-46 have Ionic pilasters and fanlight doorways. <83>

s) *TRAFALGAR STREET:* This thoroughfare has a few buildings of the early 1800s at its lower end, but was principally developed in the 1840s following the arrival of the railway. In 1989 much of the northern side above Whitecross Street was demolished for the erection of Trafalgar Place, an office complex with shops fronting Trafalgar Street; it also occupies the site of the railway goods shed. The Prince Albert public house is an attractive, listed building of the 1840s with three storeys, round-headed windows, and Corinthian and Ionic pilasters, the capitals being highlighted in gold paint <44>. No.26 Trafalgar Street, at the corner of Tidy Street, is included on the council's local list as it has Ionic pilasters on its eastern side. <83>

t) *TRAFALGAR TERRACE:* A narrow twitten of small terraced houses with their gardens on the other side of the path. They were erected in the late 1830s. <108>

u) *UPPER GARDNER STREET:* In the last years of the nineteenth century street-traders ('barrow-boys') began to congregate in Bond Street and Gardner Street. The police and the county borough council, tired of moving the traders on, set aside Upper Gardner Street for their use on Saturday mornings just after the turn of the century, and the antiques, bric-a-brac and junk now sold between 7 a.m. and 1 p.m. every Saturday are a great attraction.

The street itself dates from the 1820s and a few cottages of that period remain. There are also a number of workshops and warehouses. The former Central National infant school, opened in 1887 and later the Central Boys Club, stands on the western side. <83,281,291,311>

111. NORTH ROAD, Brighton

Originally a very narrow road known as North Lane, North Road was first developed on the edge of the town in the 1810s, with the northern side built in the following decade. It was doubled in width by the corporation in 1870, and was made one-way to traffic in June 1976. North Road was once a much more important shopping street for the small terraced streets of the North Laine than now, and in 1931 it had ten public houses along its length. <24,83,115,123>

Near the bottom of the road, approached either through an archway proclaiming 'Public Baths' or via North Place, is the Prince Regent Swimming Complex. Costing £2.5 million, it has a 33-metre pool, diving and learning pools, solarium, cafeteria and gallery, and opened to the public on 22 April 1981. It was erected on the site of the corporation's first swimming-pool, the North Road pool which opened in 1895. The old pool, 120 feet by 33 feet, was initially open to men and women on separate days only; it closed in November 1979. Still standing to the north-east of the new pool is the former slipper bath building, opened by the corporation in 1870 on former barracks land; it closed in April 1976 and is now a nursery. (A slipper bath is similar to a domestic bath, and the building was used by many poor people of the town who had no bath of their own.) The roadway is now called Barrack Yard after the former infantry barracks (see "Church Street"). <24,115,123,263>

Standing almost opposite the baths entrance, 104 North Road, now a motor-cycle shop, was formerly the Coronation Cinema. Opening in 1911, it became the New Coronation in 1928, the Troxy in 1934 and the Rex News Theatre in 1938, but it closed in June 1939 having been the last Brighton cinema to install sound equipment, in 1932. It seated 350 people. <68,68a,123>

No.32 North Road was the original store of the Brighton Equitable Co-operative Society, opened on 16 May 1888.

Higher up the road, William Collier House was built in 1986-8 for the Y.M.C.A. to the design of Stuart Hunter and Malcolm Robertson, on the site of the former power station (see "Electricity Supply"). The Brighton Y.M.C.A. was originally founded at 25 Middle

Street (formerly the premises of the Brighthelmstone Dispensary) in 1854. It moved to Prince Albert Street in about 1872, and took over Mrs Fitzherbert's house at 55 Old Steine in 1884. The Old Steine premises are now used as an emergency hostel for sixty-five people; George Williams House at Portslade is used as a second-stage centre, and William Collier House, with ninety-three bed-sits, is for the final stages of rehabilitation. <24,115,123>

Near the top of North Road, Gresham House and the North Road car-park were built on the site of the Grand Theatre which was originally opened as the Hippodrome Circus in 1891 by Fred Ginnett. In 1894 it was converted into the Eden Theatre by Frank Matcham and architects Clayton and Black, and presented a high standard of productions of all types, even challenging the reputation of the Theatre Royal. In 1904 it became the Grand Theatre, the most popular theatre in the town before 1914 presenting mainly variety shows, but on 22 January 1931 the Grand was converted into a 'talkie' cinema seating 1,140. Films were presented until late 1940, but it reopened in July 1941 as a theatre once more. The Grand closed in 1955 and was converted into a furniture factory, but it was destroyed by fire in 1961. <3,68,68a,123>

The adjacent Brighthelm United Reformed Church and Community Centre opened on 10 October 1987 and has its main façade, that of the 1825 Hanover Chapel, facing Church Street, but the North Street frontage, by Wells-Thorpe and Suppel Ltd, bears a sculpture by John Skelton depicting the loaves and fishes story. (See "Church Street" for more details.)

The Post Office sorting office and former telephone exchange opposite was built in 1926 on the site of the Regent Iron Foundry, an important concern that produced much of the town's ironwork from the 1810s until 1912; it is commemorated by the adjoining Foundry Street. <83,115>

112.NORTH STREET

a) *HISTORY and BUILDINGS:* North Street has always been one of the town's main commercial thoroughfares, and is lined with many shops, banks and offices. It represents the northern limit of the medieval town, and was probably developed in the fourteenth century by the landsmen whose barns stood on the northern side of the street with fields and crofts stretching northwards to Church Street. With most coaches from London entering the town via Dyke Road as Brighton first grew as a resort, North Street developed rapidly in the eighteenth century, and by 1770 there were eighty-eight buildings in the street. From about 1780 shops also began to spread up North Street from Castle Square, and it gradually became the principal commercial street of the town. A number of squalid courtyards were built off North Street in the early nineteenth century, and by the 1840s names such as Durham, Petty France and Air Street were counted amongst the worst slums in the town; most were cleared for the construction of Queen's Road in 1845. Until the 1950s North Street extended up what is now Dyke Road as far as Upper North Street. <10,15,18,76,83>

Development of North Street itself was haphazard and the buildings projected into the narrow roadway somewhat, but it was widened in 1874-9 below Windsor Street, again in 1927-36, and finally in the early 1960s. Only a few buildings therefore survive from before the mid nineteenth century, mainly to the west of Ship Street and to the west of New Road. Large-scale redevelopment of the northern side has resulted in many large bank and office buildings, the most impressive of which is the pink-granite Leeds Permanent on the corner of New Road. Built in 1904 by Clayton and Black for the Royal Insurance Company, it was designed in Edwardian baroque style with Ionic columns on the first and second floors, and has a large clock, a cupola and a weather-vane on the roof. <114,116,123,311>

Norwich Union House was built in 1935-6 by H.S.Goodhart-Rendel, originally as a head office (Prince's House) for the Brighton and Sussex Equitable Permanent Benefit Building Society. This society, which was founded in 1863, became the Alliance in 1945 and the Alliance and Leicester in 1985, now the fifth largest in the country with assets of some £13,552 million <19,45,303>. The adjacent Prince's Place once formed the approach to the Promenade Grove (see "Royal Pavilion (Pavilion Grounds)"), and had a colonnade along both

Figure 90: The Edwardian baroque offices of the Leeds Permanent Building Society

sides with a shrubbery in the centre; the latter was removed in about 1834. A volunteer soldiers' headquarters was later erected on the site of the grove entrance, but was itself removed in 1891 to provide access to the Pavilion grounds <15,115>. Regent House, on the western side of Prince's Place, was built in about 1934 on the site of the *Brighton Herald* offices <83>.

Higher up North Street, at the corner of King Street, once stood the Prudential Buildings, a red-brick block of 1906 by Alfred Waterhouse. It was demolished in 1967 and replaced by the second stage of the present Prudential House, which also stands on the site of the Cinema-de-Luxe and Athenaeum Hall (see below). <45,123>

Other important buildings include the 1920s National Westminster and Midland Banks, and the 1959 Barclays Bank.

See also "Clock Tower".

b) *STORES:* North Street also has three of the largest stores in Brighton. The Vokins family firm was founded as Leeson and Vokins in 1882, but the present department store in North Street was built in 1935. The Boots store is one of their largest in the country; it was built in 1979 on the site of the Regent Cinema to the modernistic design of Derek Sharp, contrasting sharply with the other corners at the Clock Tower. <123,124>

Hanningtons Ltd has premises in North Street, East Street and Market Street, and is surpassed in size only by the Brighton Co-operative Society's store in London Road. The first shop was opened at 2 North Street by Smith Hannington on 25 July 1808, selling linen, drapery, mercery, haberdashery and hosiery. Six years later the shop was extended along North Street, and it received a royal warrant from Queen Victoria. Smith Hannington died in 1855, but by 1885 several other premises had been purchased and 300 persons were employed. 'Hanningtons Corner' at East Street and North Street was acquired in 1924, but was damaged by a bomb in the last war. Property purchases in 1960 and 1976 now give the store a continuous frontage along North Street from East Street to Huntingdon House; this main façade is rather attractive in its pale blue colours, and has many small decorative details. Nos.6-9, with decorated angular bays, were originally the Brighton Union Bank, later Barclays, and were taken over in about 1959. A bridge over Market Street linking the North Street and East Street (1883) premises was added in 1989. The last family owner of the business, Dorothy Hannington, died in 1969 and the shares, which were bequeathed to the Royal Sussex and London Hospitals, were then acquired by a commercial organisation with the store valued at over £1 million. <15,123,258,263a>

Burtons, at the corner of West Street, has pilasters, unusual capitals, and the name of the store emblazoned in the stonework; it was built in the 1930s in conjunction with the widening of West Street. Another interesting store is Dunns, 63-66 North Street, which overlooks Churchill Square and Western Road. It was built in 1858 as the Brighton Drapery Establishment of Joseph Smith, and is adorned with cupolas and the arms of other towns in stained glass. <83>

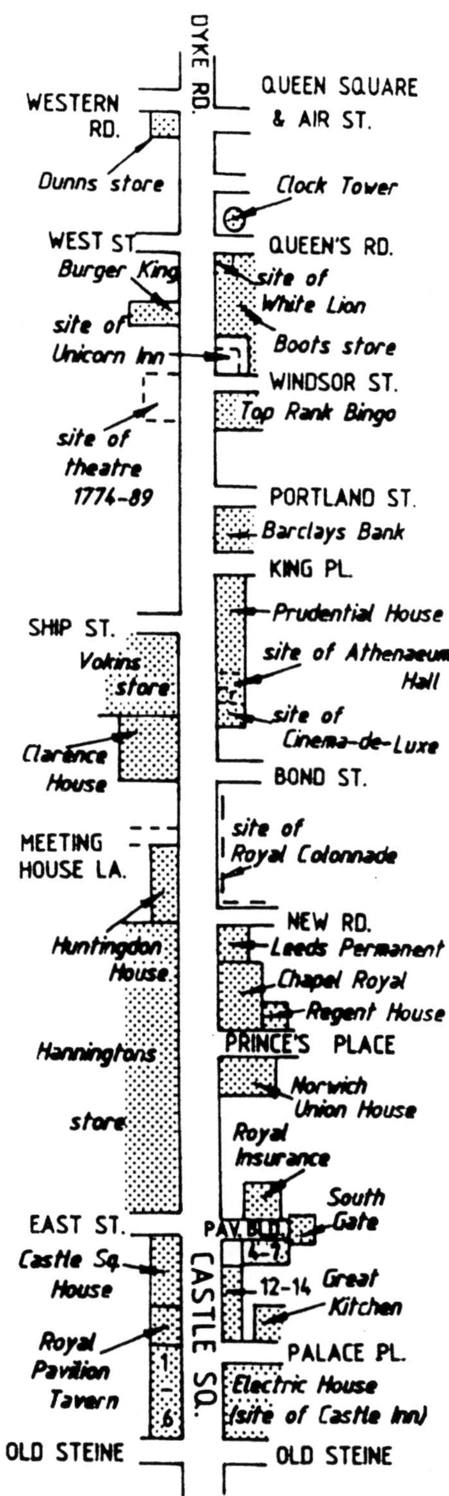

Figure 91: North Street

c) *INNS:* As the principal route into the town from London was via Dyke Road until the early nineteenth century, North Street naturally had a number of important coaching inns. The only one remaining is the former Clarence Hotel, nos.30-31, which was built in 1785 as the New Inn and run by a brewer, Mr Whichelo. By 1812 it had a large coffee room, billiards room, ten sitting rooms, twenty-six bedrooms and two kitchens. There were also two stable yards added by William Henwood with room for nearly fifty horses and six coaches, but the music room at the rear was demolished in the 1850s for the erection of Model Dwellings. In 1808 the magistrates' court was established here, and it returned in 1821-3. In 1830 the name was changed to the Clarence in honour of William IV, formerly the Duke of Clarence, and it continued as a hotel until September 1972. Although initially occupied by squatters, the building remained empty until it was reopened on 25 June 1979 by Lord Rupert Nevill as Clarence House, the head office of the Citizens Regency (now part of the Portman) Building Society. Clarence House is now a listed building, and is faced with cream-coloured mathematical tiles with a Doric porch and elegant lamp. In May 1990 North Street was closed to traffic as Clarence House was in danger of collapse during its conversion to offices. <15,123>

The Unicorn Inn stood on the western corner with Windsor Street and bore the date 1597, but it did not open as an inn until the mid eighteenth century. When it was rebuilt in red brick in 1892, the old town well was discovered, but the inn was again demolished in 1919 to make way for the Regent Cinema. The White Lion stood opposite West Street (before Queen's Road was constructed), and also dated from at least the sixteenth century. In 1757 it became the property of brewer Richard Tidy who probably turned it into an inn soon after, but the first definite record was in 1790, and it was referred to by name in 1798. It was a notable centre for cock-fighting at one time. The White Lion was rebuilt in 1821-2, but was acquired by the corporation in July 1872 and demolished in May 1874 for road widening. A new hotel was then erected, but it was again demolished in 1900 and replaced by a bank. A smaller public house was built at the corner of Queen's Road, now replaced by the Boots store. <15,83>

d) *CINEMAS and the ATHENAEUM HALL:* There were once three cinemas in North Street (along with an entrance to a fourth, the Regent - see "Queen's Road"). The Essoldo, now the Top Rank bingo hall, opened as the 1,877-seat Imperial Theatre on 9 April 1940, staging both plays and variety shows, but by 1943 film shows were alternating with stage shows. In 1947 impresario Jack Hylton presented plays and musicals, and the building was also used occasionally for conferences and wrestling bouts, but it then reverted to movies only as the Imperial Cinema and became the Essoldo in 1950. The cinema closed and became a bingo hall in May 1964.

Higher up on the other side, The Bijou Electric Empire opened in 1911 at no.63a, the former printing works of the Southern Publishing Company. In 1915 it became the Prince's Electric Theatre, the Bijou Select Palace in 1918, and the Prince's Cinema the following year. Sound equipment was installed in late 1929, and the building was transformed with a new foyer and neon-lit façade in 1933. In 1947 the cinema became the Prince's News Theatre and then the Jacey in 1967, but was taken over in association with the British Film Institute in February 1969 and showed specialist films as the Brighton Film Theatre. This venture closed in late 1978 following financial difficulties, but the building was reopened as the Cinescene on 10 September 1979 by Myles Byrne, and continued until June 1983. In 1988 the building was refronted as a Burger King restaurant.

The Cinema-de-Luxe or Theatre-de-Luxe opened in about 1910 <83> at 150 North Street, the former printing works of the Brighton Gazette. It held 529 people, unusually with no circle or balcony, but was burnt out by a fire in 1942. At 148 North Street, approached via a narrow passage, stood the Athenaeum Recreation Hall which opened in 1890. Seating 500 and with smaller lecture rooms, it was used by the Brighton School of Music from 1892, and later accommodated a billiard hall, the First Church of Christ Scientist, and the Central Spiritualist Church in 1925. Both the hall and former cinema building were demolished for road widening and the erection of Prudential House in 1962. <68,68a,83,123>

e) *CHAPEL ROYAL:* Designed in classical style by Thomas Saunders, the Chapel Royal was built in Prince's Place in 1793-5 for Revd Thomas Hudson, Vicar of Brighton, as an alternative to the very cramped St Nicholas's Church. Hudson hoped to attract the Prince of Wales to the new chapel, and it was His Royal Highness who laid the corner stone on 25 November 1793. The Prince and Princess of Wales were also present at the first service on 3 August 1795, but he attended irregularly, and after an objectionable sermon by Hudson never worshipped there again. During the resort season, services were conducted by court clergymen for the first few years, with all seats rented. In 1803 the Chapel Royal became a chapel of ease to St Nicholas's and was consecrated by the Bishop of Chichester. Hudson resigned the curacy in 1808.

The building remained largely unaltered until 1876 when the Revd C.S.Childer started a fund to buy out the proprietary rights and to reconstruct the building. The interior was remodelled in the same year with a nave, aisles, a small chancel at the western end, and galleries on three sides. The classical exterior, with its colonnade, was rebuilt by Arthur Blomfield in Renaissance style, in red brick with round-headed doors and windows. The chapel reopened on 6 February 1877, but following the demolition of buildings for the widening of North Street, the newly exposed south front was also rebuilt by Blomfield in 1879 and the clock tower and new entrances were added in 1882. The eastern façade still bears the original date of 1795 though, together with the royal arms.

The Chapel Royal became a parish church in 1897, but the parish was merged into St Peter's once again in 1978. There are extensive vaults, probably intended as a burial chamber, but used in the past as a store for adjacent wine merchants and booksellers; in 1978 they were converted into a church hall, replacing 20 New Road which was rebuilt in 1986-7. The south aisle is now an S.P.C.K. bookshop. <60,64a,123>

Between Hanningtons and the entrance to the Lanes is Huntingdon House, which stands on the site of the:

f) *COUNTESS OF HUNTINGDON'S CHURCH:* This, the original church of the Countess of Huntingdon's Connexion, was founded in 1761 by Selina Shirley who took a house in North Street in 1755 to improve her son's health. Returning in 1760, the Countess sent for the Calvinistic Methodist preacher George Whitefield who gave a first sermon on 8 September 1760 behind the White Lion Inn. The congregation quickly grew, and to accommodate her new followers the Countess sold her jewellery for £698 and opened a small chapel at the rear of her house in the autumn of 1761. It was enlarged in 1767, 1774 and 1788, and by the time the Countess died in 1791, several other chapels had also opened throughout the country. The original chapel was enlarged again in 1810, in 1822 when the Countess's former residence was converted into a long gallery and a Doric entrance was made from North Street, and in 1842.

In 1870-1 the church was entirely rebuilt by John Wimble in Early English style in flint and grey stone. There was a graceful north-eastern spire, and a triple-arched entrance supported by granite pillars with elaborate capitals, while the interior had galleries on all sides, excellent stained glass windows, a marble pulpit, and room for about 900 worshippers. The new church opened on 20 March 1871 and was initially well-attended, but eventually congregations dwindled and it proved impossible to keep the building in good repair. The church closed in September 1966 and was demolished in February 1972, although the spire had been taken down in November 1969. The proceeds from the sale of the site went towards the upkeep of other Huntingdon chapels. <15,24,62,123>

113. OLD SHIP HOTEL, 31-38 King's Road and 73 Ship Street.

<9,15,18,44,123,264>

a) *ORIGINS:* The Old Ship is the oldest inn in Brighton. The earliest known record dates from 1665 when it was owned by Richard Gilham, but it may date from the previous century as an unnamed house was owned by a Richard and John Gilham in 1559. It probably derived its name from being partly constructed from ship's timbers, and for many years the entrance to the stable included a ship's stern-piece. It serviced the market place on the nearby cliff top, while the street in which it was situated took its name from the inn, Ship Street.

In 1671 the Ship (as it was known until the New Ship opened almost opposite) was purchased by Nicholas Tettersell, the owner of the boat which carried Charles II to France (see "Charles II"); in the Tettersell Bar now hangs a painting of the *Surprise,* also Tettersell's annuity document.

b) *EXPANSION:* By 1750 the Old Ship was the property of William Hicks who, investing in Brighton's newly-found prosperity as a health resort, built a splendid new public function room by 1759. Hick died in 1765 but was succeeded as proprietor by his grandson, John.

The Old Ship hosted many of the important functions in the town for many years, and was used for town meetings, petty sessions, and meetings of the town commissioners in the late eighteenth and early nineteenth centuries. Until 1777 it also included the town's post-office, and was the original site of the Brighton corn market. Rivalled only by the Castle Inn until the opening of the Royal York in 1823, it was the most important establishment for some time and was frequented by the nobility, but was rarely used by royalty.

In order to compete with the rooms which opened in 1766 at the Castle, John Hicks commissioned Robert Golden to build the impressive assembly rooms in Ship Street in 1767. Fitted out in Adam style, they included a ball-room ninety feet long with spectators' and musicians' galleries, and also a card-room with plaster decoration and a vaulted ceiling. The popularity of grand balls waned in the mid nineteenth century however, and more informal dances and concerts were held, but by 1885 the assembly rooms had been converted to auction rooms. The façade was altered in 1895, but the Old Ship Rooms remain in Ship Street at the rear of the hotel and are listed grade II* due to their splendid interior, now restored. There is a plaque to the famous violinist Niccolo Paganini who played in the ballroom in 1831. <45a>

In 1794 the hotel gained a frontage overlooking the sea for the first time when two sea-front houses were incorporated, but by 1803, when it was purchased by Leonard Schuckard, the inn still had only eight of its sixty-eight bedrooms facing the sea. The section at the corner of Ship Street was added by the new owners, Cuff and Strachan, in 1838, and in 1895 the hotel was enlarged again with the Ship Street frontage modernised. In 1927-8 an extension was added along King's Road and a garage for 400 cars was built at the rear; the eastern corner wing was erected in 1962-4. (See figure 71.)

c) *DESCRIPTION:* The Old Ship frontage along King's Road dates only from the nineteenth and twentieth centuries, but the hotel remains one of Brighton's most historic buildings and includes a number of plaques and mementoes to historic occasions. The oldest section now is the assembly rooms, although the Ship Street corner bears a stone dated 1782.

The Old Ship was for many years the town's best known hotel, and is described by William Thackeray in *Vanity Fair* and Harrison Ainsworth in *Old Court.* Since 1979 the hotel has been owned by the engineering consultancy company Ewbank Preece, and there are plans for its future expansion. There are currently 153 bedrooms.

114. OLD STEINE

a) *EARLY HISTORY:* Known simply as 'The Steine' to locals, this natural focal point of the town became the Old Steine in the 1790s when the New Steine was developed on the East Cliff. The name has been used since at least the sixteenth century, and may well have been derived from a Flemish word meaning 'stone' as a number of large sarsen stones have been recovered from the area. For centuries it was an ill-drained area of grassland, devoid of trees, with the intermittent Wellesbourne flowing down the western side; indeed it was probably its swampy nature that prevented any development upon it. From time immemorial the fishermen of Brighton used the Steine for drying nets and storing boats in bad weather, and in 1665 it was said to extend beyond East Street to the cliff top and included a bowling-green. The area now occupied by the Victoria Gardens was also known as the North Steine. <10,15,289>

b) *FASHIONABLE PROMENADE:* The arrival of fashionable society in the latter eighteenth century brought considerable change to the Steine as it was the one area which could provide a flat, sheltered promenade for visitors. Dr Russell's house faced the Steine on the southern side, and several large houses were erected along the western edge around 1770. In 1760 a Mr Baker opened the town's first library on the eastern side of the Steine as it became the centre of the resort's attractions. In 1776 the turf itself was improved and wooden railings were erected to enclose the grassland, much to the anger of the fishermen. The North and South Parades were erected along the eastern side in 1786, and the following year the Master of Ceremonies prohibited all ball-games on the grass.

The Steine was further improved in 1792-3 when the Prince of Wales and the Duke of Marlborough constructed a sewer along the western side to channel the Wellesbourne and improve the drainage, thereby removing the stagnant pool that lay along the north-western edge in front of the Prince's Marine Pavilion; the lords of the manor granted them a portion of the Steine to enclose in front of their houses in return. A brick path was constructed around the inside of the railings in 1806, and horses were prohibited in the winter in order to preserve the turf. A superb model of the area at around the turn of the nineteenth century may be found in the Royal Pavilion.

Two large hotels, the Royal York and the Albion, opened on the southern side in 1823 and 1826 respectively, still facing inland rather than towards the sea, but the pre-eminence of the Steine as a promenade declined following the opening of the King's Road in 1822 and the Chain Pier in 1823.

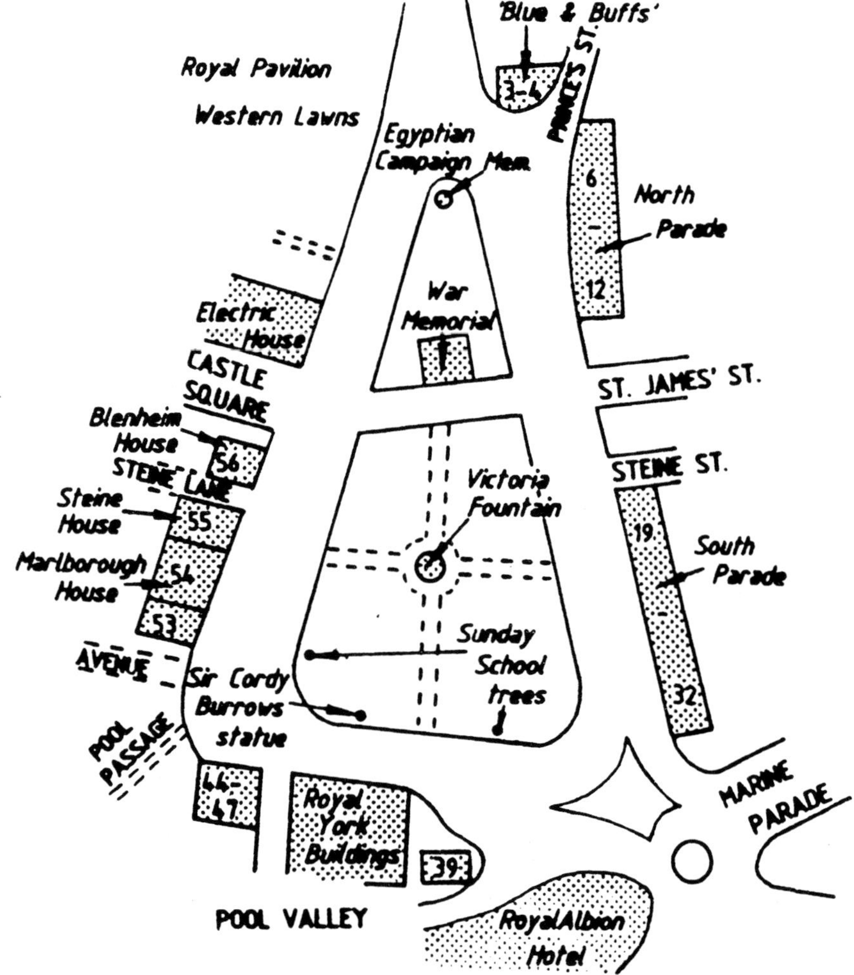

Figure 92:
Old Steine

Figure 93: View of the Old Steine in about 1850. Note the small trees, planted in 1846.

On 8 September 1823 the town commissioners enclosed the Steine with iron fencing, but this was only after an extremely vociferous protest by the fishermen who were effectively prevented from making any further use of the Steine for drying nets and sheltering boats despite their claim of inalienable rights. Gas lighting was installed in May 1824, and in the same year the road along the southern side in front of the Royal York was constructed; in March 1834 the road across the centre was opened. Around the turn of the twentieth century a bandstand stood in the south-western corner of the gardens, which had been planted with trees in 1846. In 1921 the tall iron railings were replaced with the present dwarf fences.

Although it was the freehold property of the lords of the manor (which was proved in the case against the fishermen, who had anciently paid a rental), the Steine was always considered to be a public open space and this situation was formalised on 22 April 1822 when T.R.Kemp and the other landowners vested the Steine in trustees on behalf of the town. Under the terms of the 1873 Brighton Borough Extension Act, the powers of the trustees were vested in the borough council. <2,3,14,15,33,48,126,170>

c) *THE STEINE TODAY:* The Old Steine is, topographically, the natural centre of the town, and has been a public transport terminus since 1904 when the tramways were extended from Victoria Gardens. Motor traffic was made to flow one-way from 1926. The gardens now cover 1.44 acres. At their south-western corner stands an oak tree planted on 21 July 1880 by the mayor, Henry Davey, to commemorate the centenary of the founding of Sunday schools in the town. The bicentenary was marked with a tree planted in the south-eastern section by mayor John Leach on 13 December 1980, but this was one of the victims of the great storm of October 1987 which uprooted many of the fine trees that had stood 141 years since 1846. <115,126,311>

d) *SIR JOHN CORDY BURROWS:* The statue of Sir John Cordy Burrows looks out from the Steine towards Royal York Buildings. Born in 1813 at Ipswich, he was apprenticed as a surgeon in Suffolk, studied in London, and came to Brighton in 1837 to practice. He co-founded the Royal Literary and Scientific Institution in 1841, and was elected as an alderman to the first borough council in 1854. Burrows was mayor of the town in 1857, 1858 and 1871, the first to achieve the position both twice and three times; he also chose the town's motto, *In Deo Fidemus*, and was nicknamed 'King Cordy' because of his influence. Knighted in 1873, he died on 25 March 1876 and his funeral was attended by thousands; shops and businesses closed for the procession of 2,500 people, and an estimated 25,000 to 30,000 mourners lined the streets. The marble statue, designed by E.B.Stephens, was erected 'by his fellow townsmen as a mark of their esteem' at the southern end of the Royal Pavilion grounds, and was unveiled on 14 February 1878; it was moved to its present position in about 1984 when the Pavilion grounds were remodelled. <115,296>

e) *VICTORIA FOUNTAIN:* Standing at the centre of the southern enclosure, this listed fountain was inaugurated on 25 May 1846 for the Queen's twenty-seventh birthday. Designed by A.H.Wilds, it was financed jointly by John Cordy Burrows and a public subscription, and was cast at the Eagle Foundry in Gloucester Road. It stands thirty-two feet high, with two shallow basins supported by three cast-iron dolphins above a large pool, and has a base of sarsen stones which were found in the Steine by workmen in 1823. To commemorate the inauguration, local musician Charles Coote composed the *Fountain Quadrilles*. In 1990 the top of the fountain was removed for restoration. (See figure 179.) <44,49,123,141>

f) *WAR MEMORIALS:* The Brighton War Memorial stands within the northern enclosure of the Steine. Unveiled on 7 October 1922 by Earl Beatty, it was designed in the form of a Roman water garden by Sir John Simpson. The pylons record the names of 2,597 men and 3 women of Brighton who fell in the First World War. The statue of George IV had originally stood on the site, but it was removed to the North Gate of the Royal Pavilion. At the northern end of the Steine is the Egyptian Campaign Memorial of the Royal Sussex Regiment, a plain obelisk with a list of officers and men who fell in the Egyptian Campaign of 1882, and the Nile River Expedition of 1884-5 to relieve Gordon at Khartoum. The base states simply 'Egypt' and 'Abu Klea', a battle fought in the Sudan on 17 January 1885. The memorial was erected in 1888 and is now listed. <115,295,311>

g) *BUILDINGS EAST SIDE:* As discussed above, many interesting buildings of the late eighteenth and early nineteenth centuries surround the Steine.

Nos.3-4, at the northernmost end facing south, are the remaining pair of a group once known as the 'Blue and Buffs'. Together with nos.1-2 which were demolished in 1928 for road widening, the houses were painted in those colours of the Whig Party to please the Prince of Wales, who was then a supporter of the Whigs. They were built in 1790 and are listed buildings.

The buildings to the north of St James's Street were erected in 1786 as the North Parade. Although most were refronted in the nineteenth century, nos.6-12 are listed buildings with distinctive doorways; some also have balconies and verandahs. No.9 has a plaque to Charles Talleyrand, the French statesman and ambassador who stayed there in 1831.

The South Parade faces the Steine to the south of Steine Street, and was also erected in 1786. The buildings, which are all listed except the red-brick no.19, have either four or five storeys with balconies and some verandahs, but again most have been refronted. In the 1830s no.20 was the home of Dr Gideon Mantell, a celebrated Sussex geologist and founder of the Mantellian Institution. Born in 1790, he practiced medicine in Lewes and moved to Brighton in 1833. The institution held lectures and meetings in the house, but he moved to London in 1838 when he was unable to set up a medical practice, and most of the institution's collections were donated to the Brighton Royal Literary and Scientific Institution in 1842. The house was probably altered by the partnership of Amon Wilds and Charles Busby, as were nos.23 and 30. No.26 was refaced by Amon Henry Wilds and has the fluted pilasters, shell motifs and ammonite capitals so distinctive of his work. No.28 has mathematical tiles. No.30 has a plaque to lawyer Sir Edward Marshall Hall, the 'Great Defender', who was born there in 1858. <3,15,44,47,48,311>

h) *BUILDINGS SOUTH SIDE:* The southern side of Old Steine is dominated by the Royal Albion Hotel (q.v.) and the Royal York Buildings (q.v.). No.39 stands completely isolated between the two with four storeys, Doric doorway, and a balcony above; it dates from around 1860. The late-eighteenth-century nos.44-46 at the corner of Pool Valley are distinctive, three-storey listed buildings faced with black mathematical tiles; they have excellent doorways and bay windows which retain their glazing bars (see figure 5). No.47 is also listed. <44,108>

j) *BUILDINGS WEST SIDE:* Nos.52-53 have early-nineteenth-century façades with balconies and verandahs, and are listed buildings; no.53 was at one time the home of Major-General Sir Arthur Clifton, a veteran of the Battle of Waterloo. At no.54 stands Marlborough House, and at no.55 Steine House (see below for both buildings). No.56, Blenheim House, is a large, elegant, four-storey listed building which was restored in the 1980s. It was formerly the home of the Brighton and Sussex Club, but the fabric of the building is somewhat older than its 1875 façade. The Royal Bank of Scotland building has an attractive Art Deco façade and is decorated with the borough arms. It opened on 20 January 1933 as offices and showrooms for the corporation's electricity supply undertaking (see "Electricity Supply"). <44,83>

Figure 94: A view of the western side of the Old Steine in 1840. Mrs Fitzherbert's house is visible above the bystanders at the corner. The building to the left of the Royal Pavilion was erected on the site of the Castle Inn.

k) *MARLBOROUGH HOUSE:* This, the oldest remaining house on the Steine, is a grade II*-listed building which is considered by most authorities to be architecturally the best house in Brighton. It was built in about 1765 for Samuel Shergold of the Castle Inn who let it to fashionable visitors, and was originally a three-storey, red-brick building with a steeply pitched tiled roof, dormer windows, and a small pedimented classical doorway. In September 1771 the house was acquired by the fourth Duke of Marlborough after whom it is now named, but in 1786 he sold it to William 'Single Speech' Hamilton, M.P., who employed the most prominent architect of the day, Robert Adam, to remodel the house both inside and out; it is Adam's only work in Brighton and a plaque has been erected to him. The façade has two slightly projecting bays topped by pediments, two large round-headed windows, and a pedimented fanlight doorway with fluted Doric columns. The recently restored interior retains some of Adam's original features, and the principal rooms have good ceilings and fireplaces.

The Prince of Wales stayed with Hamilton for three days in April 1789, and in June 1795 stayed there again for nearly three weeks, this time with his (legal) wife, Princess Caroline of Brunswick. Hamilton died the following year however, and the house was auctioned for 4,000 guineas. In about 1870 it was purchased by John Beal, the publisher and stationer of East Street who used the basement as a store, but he leased the ground floor and upper storeys to the Brighton School Board for use as offices. The school board purchased the property outright in September 1891 for £7,000, and the building remained in use as education offices, first for the school board and then for the county borough council, until the county council took over responsibility for education in 1974. Marlborough House then became the offices of the Tourism and Resort Services Department of Brighton Borough Council, and now houses the town's main tourist information centre. <10,15,44,48>

l) *STEINE HOUSE:* This house was built in 1804 by William Porden, the Prince of Wales's architect, for Mrs Fitzherbert (see "George IV") who lived here until her death in 1837. It originally had an Egyptian-style colonnade, but this was blown down in 1805 and the façade was rebuilt in Italian style with a trellised verandah and balcony supported by pillars. Later in the century however, the interior was substantially altered when the house was taken by the Civil and United Services Club, and in 1927 the building was entirely refaced and brought forward by the Young Men's Christian Association which had taken over the building in 1884; a new floor of bedrooms was also added. Although it still has a verandah entrance, there have been so many alterations that the building is now listed for its historical associations rather than its architectural qualities, but an imitation bamboo iron staircase remains; Lord Barrymore once rode a horse up it for a bet. Fortunately a 1964 scheme to replace the house with an office block was defeated, and it is now used by the Y.M.C.A. as an emergency hostel for sixty-five people. <3,15,44,48,123>

115. OLD TOWN

The Old Town is the area bounded by East Street, North Street, West Street and the sea which forms the historic heart of Brighton. It was probably developed from about the thirteenth or fourteenth centuries around East Street, Middle Street and West Street as the result of expansion onto the cliff top by the fishermen of the 'Lower Town' (q.v.) below the cliffs. However, the whole town was burnt by the French in 1514 (see figure 19) and now only the street pattern remains in the Old Town from this period, although altered since by the construction of Prince Albert Street and the obliteration of the southern half of Market Street. More streets were developed northward from the cliff top on the open space in the middle of the town from the late seventeenth century and some building also occurred on the 'Knab', but most of the remaining

Figure 95: A view of the town in 1765 by James Lambert from what is now the Carlton Hill area. Note the church on the hill, the three windmills on the East Cliff and another on the other side of the town; also the library on the eastern side of the Steine and the farm where the Royal Pavilion now stands.

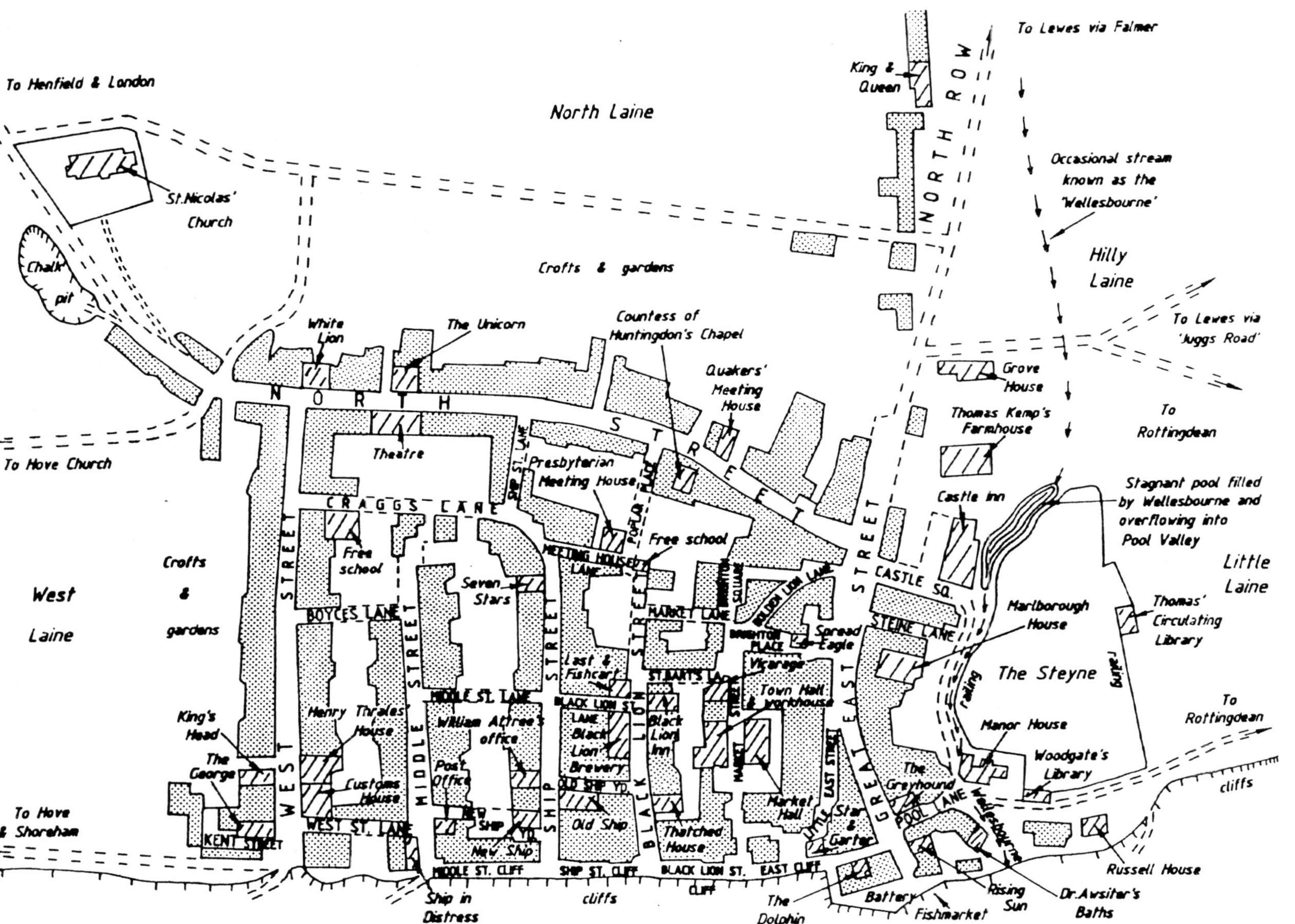

Figure 96: Brighton in 1779, based upon the survey of Yeakell and Gardner

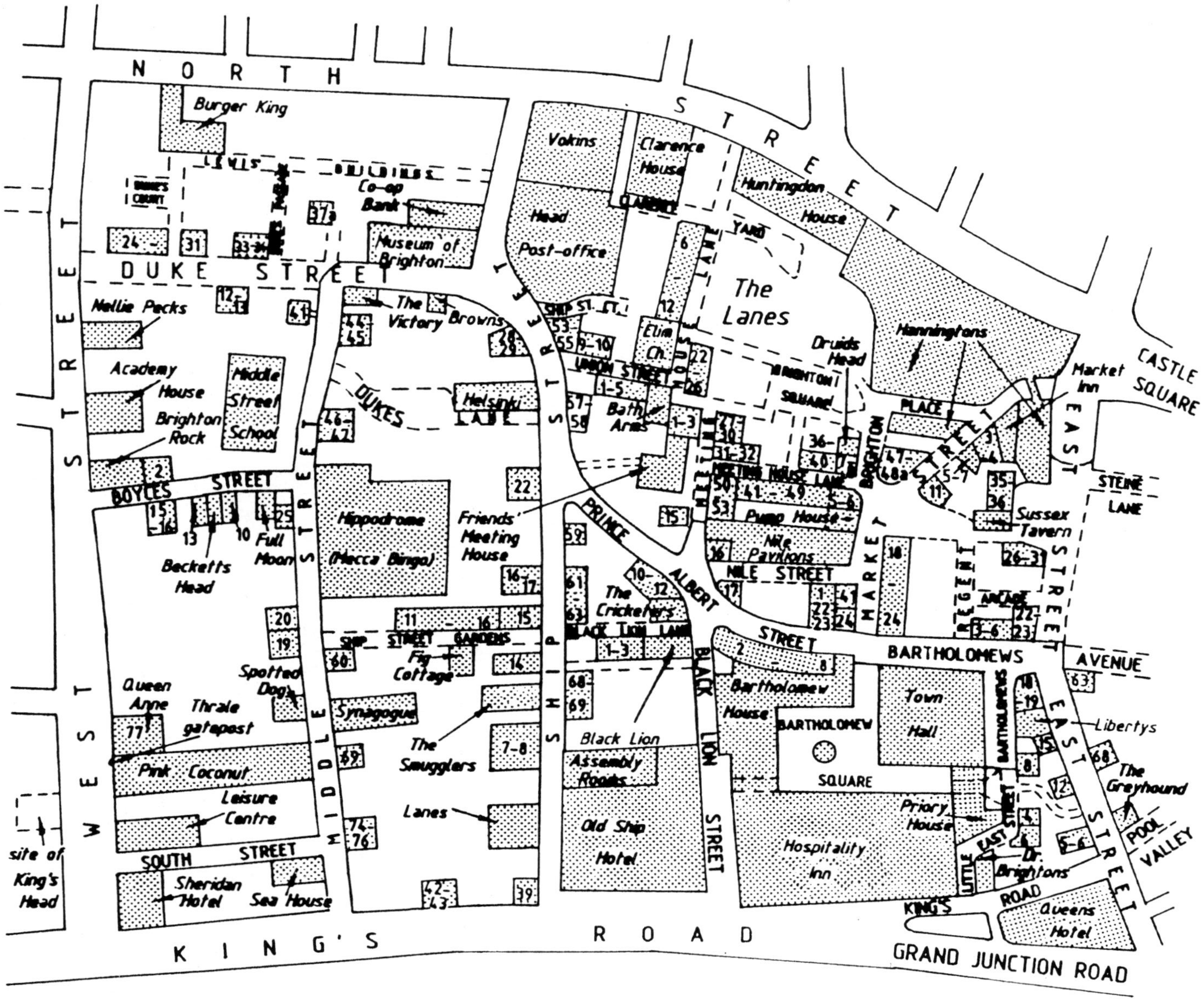

Figure 97: The Old Town, Brighton

old buildings now date from the late eighteenth and nineteenth centuries. Now chiefly commercial, the Old Town has a resident population of around 500. See also "Brighton - Early History" and "Fishing Industry". <1,10,277>

The Old Town of Brighton has been designated an outstanding conservation area, and it is to be hoped that any future development will only enhance the character of the area and that all old buildings will be respected. The streets and twittens of interest are detailed below, but see also "East Street", "Grand Junction Road", "Hospitality Inn", "King's Road", "Lower Esplanade", "North Street", "Old Ship Hotel", "Pool Valley", "Queen's Hotel", "Town Halls" and "West Street".

a) *BARTHOLOMEWS:* This road takes its name from the small Chapel and Priory of St Bartholomew that once stood on the site of Bartholomew House, just to the south-west of the junction of Market Street and Prince Albert Street. The chapel was established, possibly as a monastic farm, between 1120 and 1147 by the great Cluniac Priory of St Pancras at Lewes which supplied it with two or three monks, but little is known of its history. It was partially destroyed by French raiders in 1514, but the Prior's Lodge, a residence connected with the chapel, was spared. In 1547 the priory was dissolved under Henry VIII and some almshouses were erected on the land then known as the Bartholomews which stretched from Little East Street to Black Lion Street. In 1592 the ruinous chapel and the other buildings of the Bartholomews were purchased on behalf of the town, and the almshouses were sold to the parish in 1733 for £17. The Brighton weekly market was re-established on the Bartholomews in about 1730 and a daily market hall was built in 1774, but the land was acquired by the town commissioners in 1824 for the building of a new town hall in 1830-2. In 1774, workmen digging excavations for the market hall discovered an ancient cemetery. Downing tools in reverence. they continued on being told by the vicar, Revd Henry Michell, that the monks had been Catholics! The Prior's House, which was used as the vicarage, remained on the site of Prince Albert Street until 1790, and a small portion of an ancient flint wall which may have been part of St Bartholomew's Chapel stood to the north of the former market hall in Market Street until the area was redeveloped in the mid 1980s. <1,16,17,18,270>

In 1984-7 the Hospitality Inn (q.v.) and the municipal offices of Priory House and Bartholomew House were erected adjacent to the Town Hall to form Bartholomew Square, a civic square lined with fashionable shops and with Le Pavillon café forming an attractive centre-piece.

The road known as Bartholomews now runs along the northern and eastern sides of the Town Hall only. Nos.3-6 are early-nineteenth-century, typically Georgian-style listed buildings, no.5 in particular being an elegant four-storey house with an iron balcony; the similarly-styled buildings on the eastern side, Libertys store, are an attractive addition of 1989 which won a council planning award. No.8, The Cottage, is a charming listed house with a tarred and cobbled front, probably dating from the eighteenth century. <44>

Figure 98: Bartholomews and the Town Hall in about 1865

b) *BLACK LION LANE:* This very narrow twitten leads from Black Lion Street to Ship Street. Charles II, during his escape to France, is said to have been carried piggyback along the lane by a fisherman. On meeting a burly woman, the pair knocked the poor lady down and stepped over her! In the late eighteenth century a certain portly Mr Bullock wagered the youthful Lord Barrymore that he could outrun him, given choice of course and a ten-yard start. Choosing Black Lion Lane, Bullock merely trotted along and Barrymore, unable to pass him, lost the bet! <3,47>

There are three listed cottages on the southern side of the twitten with projecting, slate-hung upper storeys, probably on timber frames. They claim to date from c.1563; they may well date only from the seventeenth century in fact, but are probably still the oldest buildings in the Old Town. (See figure 20.) <44>

c) *BLACK LION STREET:* Developed on the Hempshares from the seventeenth century, Black Lion Street originally included what is now the southern arm of Meeting House Lane, and was considered a fashionable locality by the late eighteenth century; the eastern side, backing on to the market, was not so sought after, however <10>. It has now been almost completely redeveloped with Bartholomew House, a 200-space underground car-park and the Hospitality Inn on the eastern side, and the extensions to the Old Ship Hotel and Moore House on the western side.

One of the few remaining old buildings is the Cricketers Arms, now the oldest public house in the town centre and a listed building. It probably dates from the seventeenth century when it was known as the Last and Fishcart, a 'last' being a measure of 10,000 herrings. In 1790 a Mr Jutton became landlord and, being a keen cricketer, gave the inn its present name. The three-storey, bowed façade was added in 1824, but the cobble-fronted north wing dates from the late eighteenth century; below is the Green Yard, an area used as an animal pound as late as 1882, which still has part of a securing chain and a list of stable charges. <15,44,47>

Adjacent to the Cricketers is the Black Lion public house, a recent reconstruction of the Black Lion Brewery. Named after the Black Lion of Flanders, tradition has it that this brewery was established in about 1546, together with the Black Lion Inn, by Flemish immigrant Deryk Carver who grew hops on the Hempshares. The inn originally stood on the eastern side of the street near the cliff top, adjacent to the market place, but by 1789 it was known as the Thatched House and a new Black Lion Inn had opened to the north sometime since 1745, moving perhaps as the market was removed to the Bartholomews. It was demolished in the early nineteenth century.

It is possible that the original brewery may have also stood near the cliff top and moved to its later site opposite the second inn; certainly the buildings appeared to date from around the early eighteenth century and were considerably altered over the years, but portions of flint and rubble walls in Black Lion Lane and extensive cellars were retained which may have been from the original sixteenth century buildings. Having been used by Chapman's Brewery until 1902, the building was later used by the Rock Brewery and then by Fremlins as a store. Using water from a 54-foot well, it was said to be the oldest brewery building in the world but closed in 1968 and was demolished a few years later. In 1974 an exact facsimile of the oldest part, using many of the original flint cobbles and slates, was erected as a new Black Lion public house. The ground floor, faced in cobbles and brick, supports two upper storeys hung in slate and the original eighteenth-century black lion weather-vane; the original flint and ashlar cellars, dating perhaps from the sixteenth century, remain below ground level.
<10,18,44,123,275>

Carver himself was the first Protestant to be martyred under Mary I. He and several others were arrested in October 1554 for reading the Bible in English and was taken to Newgate Gaol in London where he was found guilty of heresy. Refusing to recant, he was sentenced to death, and on 22 July 1555 was burned in a barrel outside the Star Inn in Lewes High Street, flinging his Bible into the crowd as a final gesture; James Launder, arrested at the same time, was burnt at Chantry Green, Steyning, on the following day. A memorial to sixteen Protestant martyrs was erected on Cliffe Hill at Lewes in 1901, and this event lies behind the burning of effigies of the Pope at the annual Bonfire Night celebrations in Lewes. <3>

Figure 99: The Black Lion public house

d) *BOYCE'S STREET:* This narrow thoroughfare between Middle Street and West Street was probably developed by the mid seventeenth century, and still retains some interesting late-eighteenth- or early-nineteenth-century houses. No.2, which is on the council's local list of buildings of special interest, has two bows, glazing bars and unusual Ionic pilasters; it was the home of the Sussex and Brighton Infirmary for Diseases of the Eye from 1832 until 1846. No.10 is a very narrow house with a ground floor bow, mathematical tiles, and a steep tiled roof; no.13 also has a steep roof with a brick and cobble first floor; nos.15-16 have good fanlight doorways. Some old flint cottages on the northern side were demolished in 1875 to make room for extensions to the Middle Street Schools. <10,129,306>

e) *BRIGHTON PLACE:* Brighton Place stands on a slight eminence nearly twenty feet higher than East Street. Formerly known as the 'Knab', the ridge had buildings on it by the seventeenth century, and further development occurred from the late eighteenth century when houses were erected for the workers who serviced the prestigious developments in the East Street, Castle Square, North Street and Steine areas; the Knab also supported one of the town's wells. <10,18,47>

A few listed buildings from the later development period remain. Nos.5-6 and 7-8 retain their glazing bars, and no.6, known as Market House, bears the inscription 'God Bless George IV', probably made at the time of the coronation in 1821. The Druid's Head, faced in knapped flint with a steep tiled roof, was established as a public house in 1825 although the building is somewhat older. It is said to be haunted by the ghost of a man who died in a now blocked cellar passage <123>. The northern end of Brighton Place is dominated by the Victorian buildings of Hanningtons store. The Brighton Place roadway was pedestrianised along with Market Street in February 1989.

f) *BRIGHTON SQUARE:* A modern addition to the Lanes which opened in 1966 on a mostly derelict site. Designed by Fitzroy Robinson and Partners for a consortium headed by the Church Commissioners and Hanningtons Ltd, there are twenty-four shops and fifteen maisonettes, and use has been made of traditional materials such as flint cobbles, tiles and weather-boarding. Although it now appears dated, the development won the premier Civic Trust award of 1966, but the demolition of two cobble-fronted cottages in Brighton Place and a weather-boarded house in Meeting House Lane for the construction of the entrances led to a public outcry and to the listing of many other buildings in the Lanes. <123>

g) *DUKES LANE:* This superb development opened between Middle Street and Ship Street on 20 November 1979 on the site of an old garage. Designed by Stone Toms and Partners at a cost of £1.25 million, the colourful, intimate development has twenty-six shops and a number of maisonettes built in the style and materials of both the Lanes themselves and the best of small-scale Regency Brighton. The two and three-storey development has bow windows, ironwork balconies, tile-hung façades, Victorian-style lamps, and a central café-square; nos.9-10 and 23 even have cobble-fronted upper storeys. Note the Sun Insurance Company's firemark above the Ship Street entrance. <123>

h) *DUKE STREET:* Originally known as Cragg's Lane, Duke Street was first developed in the late seventeenth or early eighteenth century, but only a few buildings are now recognisable as dating from before the middle of the nineteenth century. No.4, Browns Restaurant, was the fire station of the Brighton Volunteer Fire-Brigade from 1875 until 1921. Nos.12-13 retain their early-nineteenth-century façades of narrow bows, while the listed no.37a, in a courtyard opposite Middle Street, is an unusual weather-boarded house of around 1780 with a bow. The town's theatre stood on the northern side of Duke Street to the west of Middle Street from 1790 until 1806 (see "Theatres"), but the present buildings on the northern side were erected

Figure 100: No.37a Duke Street

following a corporation widening scheme in 1867; nos.24-31 form a three-storey terrace with angular bays and lion head decorations. The widening also exposed the ugly southern façade of the Holy Trinity Church, now the Brighton Heritage Museum.

Duke Street was pedestrianised to the west of Middle Street in April 1983 (formally opened 10 May 1985), and now forms one of the most attractive shopping areas of the town. <10,44,108,123>

j) *KING'S ROAD:* Before the construction of the King's Road in 1821-2, traffic along the cliff top had to turn inland at Middle Street and Little East Street. The length of King's Road between Little East Street and East Street was part of the new thoroughfare, but became a quiet backwater of the Old Town when it was superseded by the Grand Junction Parade in 1829. For details on the rest of this major road, see the main entry on "King's Road".

No.6, Dolphin Cottage, is accessible only via a private passage near the corner with East Street, and is an unusual early survivor in this part of the town. The Queen's Hotel (q.v) now occupies the entire block opposite. Part of the building in King's Road, once a separate house, was designed by Amon Henry Wilds in around 1825 with four-storey bows, giant pilasters and ammonite capitals; this part is now listed. <44>

At the corner with Little East Street stands Dr Brightons. Formerly the Star and Garter Hotel, it was dubbed Dr Brightons in the nineteenth century and the name has stuck; the proprietor posted a notice on the wall giving the 'consulting hours' and listing the 'prescriptions of the finest quality' which were available inside. The hotel has played host to many famous people, including Winston Churchill, Jack Dempsey, Charlie Chaplin, Richard Burton, and the Prince of Wales (later Edward VIII), and dates back to at least 1785 when twin Irish giants were exhibited there. In front of the original bow-fronted building stood a capstan which was removed in 1827 to make way for the construction of the Grand Junction Parade. This action provoked the last major argument between the town's fishermen and other inhabitants <15,123>.

k) *THE LANES:* The attractive narrow streets and twittens which form the heart of the Old Town, principally Meeting House Lane, Union Street and the modern Brighton Square, are collectively known as the Lanes. Built on the open land in the middle of the town known as the Hempshares (see "Fishing Industry"), the Lanes were partially developed during the latter sixteenth and early seventeenth centuries as the population of the small fishing town grew with the success of the fisheries. Further building in the Lanes and on the adjacent Knab came in the late eighteenth century when the area was developed with workers houses to service the more prestigious developments nearby in the Castle Square, East Street, North Street and Steine areas. <8,10,14>

Most of the buildings now appear to date from the eighteenth or nineteenth centuries, but in some cases they may be the original houses rebuilt or refronted; the combination of narrow streets, the height of the buildings and the materials used still convey the atmosphere of a medieval town, however. Until the 1930s though, the area was considered to be shabby and unworthy of Brighton; indeed, plans advocated principally by Sir Herbert Carden were made to erect modern buildings on the site. By 1975 however, a survey showed that the Lanes, with their fascinating mixture of antique, jewellery and other specialist shops, were the most popular tourist attraction in Brighton, visited by three quarters of all visitors to the town. Recent developments on 'eyesore sites' at Brighton Square and the impressive Dukes Lane nearby have admirably enhanced the character of the area. On 31 May 1979 Queen Elizabeth II toured the Lanes. <8,14,123>

See "Brighton Square" above, and "Meeting House Lane" and "Union Street" below.

l) *LITTLE EAST STREET:* Leading from Bartholomews to the sea-front, this street was pedestrianised in 1987 and retains two interesting buildings. No.4 has a bow window and glazing bars, while nos.5-6, the Blues Brothers Café, is a listed building of about 1800 with two bow windows. In the early nineteenth century the left half was a stationer's shop and the right half an ironmongery and hardware store. In 1845 the whole building became a fishing tackle shop run by Samuel Andrew and it continued in that family until the Second World War; 'Andrew's Cottage' later became a tailor's shop. Opposite are the sweeping stairway entrances to Bartholomew Square. <44,83>

At the end of the street is Dr Brightons, an old inn that displays its 'consulting hours' on the Little East Street wall. See "King's Road" above.

m) *MARKET STREET:* This street is named from the market that was held on the Bartholomews in front of the old Town Hall from about 1730, but the northern part, once known as Golden Lion Lane, was partially developed around the seventeenth century with further growth in the latter eighteenth century; building in the southern part was stimulated by the presence of the market, and was further encouraged by the new market hall that opened in 1774. Market Street then came to be the principal street for food shops, particularly meat and dairy produce. In 1984 though, the southern half was completely obliterated by the construction of Bartholomew Square and the Hospitality Inn, but the northern part of Market Street, together with Brighton Place and Nile Street, was pedestrianised in February 1989 (formally inaugurated April 1989). <10,14>

That part to the north of Brighton Place, the former Golden Lion Lane, is lined with late-eighteenth- and early-nineteenth-century buildings. The Market Inn changed its name from the Golden Fleece in 1990. A

Figure 101: The Golden Fleece and Hanningtons store in nineteenth-century Market Street

Figure 102: The Pump House. Note the use of black glazed mathematical tiles to imitate brickwork

four-storey, listed, brick building with two first-floor bow windows, it was once known as the Three Chimneys because the owner was the Prince of Wales's chimney-sweep. Nos.3-7 are faced with mathematical tiles, and the eighteenth-century nos.48-48a are also listed. The bridge over the street linking two buildings of the Hanningtons store was constructed in 1989. <15,44>

At the junction with Brighton Place, Market Street widens out to form one of the most attractive parts of Brighton, and is lined with late-eighteenth- and early-nineteenth-century listed buildings. No.11 has a bow window and is faced with mathematical tiles with flint on the eastern side. The mid-nineteenth-century no.47, unusual in red and grey chequered brick, is also listed. The Sussex Tavern faces both Market Street and East Street, and was said to be the haunt of smugglers; it was known as the Spread Eagle until 1816. The Pump House, nos.44-46, dates from at least 1776 and possibly from much earlier. Probably named from the town well that once stood nearby on the Knab, the present façade of black mathematical tiles and bow windows dates from the early nineteenth century. Adjacent are the shops and offices of the Nile Pavilions, designed in a mixture of classical and Art Deco styles by the Robin Clayton Partnership and erected in 1987-9. <44,123>

To the south of Brighton Place, nos.18-22 Market Street are a row of rather plain buildings, but no.23 is faced in black mathematical tiles and is listed. No.24 is rather ugly, but has a good ironwork and glass canopy over the pavement and elaborate decoration above the door. On the western side, no.41 is a four-storey, early-nineteenth-century, listed building with bows and glazing bars. <44>

n) *MEETING HOUSE LANE:* This twitten is named from the former Presbyterian Meeting House in Union Street rather than the Friends' Meeting House, and until about 1790 was confined to what is now Union Street; the southern arm, widened in 1889, was part of Black Lion Street, the northern part was Poplar Place, and the eastern arm was known as Market Lane <108>.

The narrow street is lined with late-eighteenth- or early-nineteenth-century buildings, most of which now have nineteenth-century shop-fronts (although there was some development in the area around 1600 - see "Lanes" above); nos.1-12, 22-26, 27-32 and 36-53 are listed buildings. No.43, which has a projecting weather-boarded upper storey, is said to date from around 1620 and claims to be the oldest house in Brighton; it certainly looks the part and is the most evocative building in the Lanes, but it probably dates only from the eighteenth century <18>. Nos.29-30 are also weather-boarded, while no.32 has a tile-hung first-floor and no.44 is faced in yellow brick; nos.7-8 and 25 are faced with mathematical tiles. Nos.4-5 were built in 1864 as the True Briton Inn which was originally at nos.1-2, but in 1867 it became the Bath Arms and was restored to its original state in 1982. The modern weatherboarded façades at nos.16-21 were constructed as part of the Brighton Square development in 1966. (See also figure 17.)

Meeting House Lane is also said to be haunted by a nun from St Bartholomew's Priory who was walled-up alive for eloping with a soldier. Dressed in a grey habit, she has been seen at twilight gliding through a bricked-up archway into the Friends' Meeting House. Anyone who stares into her face will meet an untimely end! <18,44,83,123>

Figure 103: Meeting House Lane in 1857. The tree on the left was a poplar which gave this part of the Lanes its former name of Poplar Place.

p) *MIDDLE STREET:* Middle Street was the earliest street to be developed in the middle of the Old Town, on the area between East Street and West Street known as the Hempshares; it was built up by the sixteenth century <2>.

A number of interesting listed buildings remain in Middle Street. On the western side, no.19 has a pedimented doorway but unfortunately one bow has been removed; the passageway on the southern side once led to the ten Hayllar's Cottages, the subject of a 1937 slum clearance. The adjacent no.20, a bow-fronted, yellow-brick house with a fluted Doric porch, dates from the early nineteenth century and was the home of William Friese-Greene (1855-1921), pioneer and patentee of many cinematographic devices. He carried out many of his initial experiments there, and erected one of the first film 'studios' in the garden. He died in poverty, but has a monument by Lutyens in Highgate Cemetery and was the subject of a 1951 film tribute, *The Magic Box*.

On the eastern side, no.60 is an attractive town house probably of the eighteenth century; it was rendered with stucco in the nineteenth century, but its original knapped flint façade was restored in 1989. No.69 is a new, brick building but retains the original Doric doorway of a plain but listed eighteenth-century house, an example of nominal conservation. Nos.74-76 are four-storey, early-nineteenth-century buildings with bows and glazing bars. <44,296,311>

Brighton Synagogue, no.66, was built in 1874-5 by Thomas Lainson in Byzantine style. It was consecrated on 23 September 1875, and further improvements and enrichments were made until 1914, largely through the munificence of the Sassoon family. It was also the first synagogue to be lit by electric light. The yellow-brick building has a very large pediment with Composite pilasters, and Corinthian columns on the doors and windows. However, it is listed because of its sumptuous interior which has galleries on three sides supported by red marble columns bearing capitals of fruits mentioned in the Bible. The windows are decorated with late-nineteenth-century stained glass, and there are also splendid iron and glass railings. <44,66>

Also listed is the former Hippodrome, which opened in 1897 as the Brighton Ice-Rink but was enlarged and converted into a circus and theatre by Frank Matcham in 1901 and renamed. The Hippodrome became the town's principal variety theatre, playing host to many stars, and was enlarged again in 1939 by taking in two houses to the north. In October 1964, concerts by the Rolling Stones and the Beatles both attracted capacity audiences of 4,000, but the theatre closed the following year and after a brief period as a television film studio became the Mecca Bingo Club in 1967. The building has arched doorways, pediments and decorations above the side doors, but the exterior is otherwise rather plain, in contrast to the highly-decorated horseshoe-shaped interior. <5,44,123>

At the corner of South Street stands the former Sea House public house, originally known as the Ship-in-Distress. Until the construction of King's Road in 1822 the Sea House stood at the cliff edge, but it was rebuilt and renamed in that year. The large public room was used by the magistrates and town commissioners for several years. In September 1830 William IV visited Nelson's widow Viscountess Bronte there, and the inn became the Royal Sea House. When it was rebuilt in the 1870s, the inn business was restricted to the corner of South Street only, the southern part being converted to a toy and fancy goods repository. <15>

Other interesting buildings in Middle Street include no.25, Vesuvio's Restaurant, the home of the Brighthelmston Dispensary from 1819 until 1849, and of the Y.M.C.A. from 1854 until about 1872. Annie's Restaurant, a cobble-fronted house at the end of a passageway opposite no.43; nos.43-45, an attractive pair with glazing bars and a bow window, probably dating from the eighteenth century; nos.46-47, three-storey red-brick houses with classical doorways, date from a little later.

q) *NILE STREET:* Originally known as St Bartholomew's Lane, Nile Street was renamed following Nelson's victory over the French at the Battle of the Nile on 1 August 1798. The narrow street was pedestrianised and widened in February 1989 in conjunction with the Market Street scheme, and is now dominated by the Art Deco shops and offices of the Nile Pavilions, designed by the Robin Clayton Partnership and erected in 1987-9. No.1 is a listed building forming the rear part of nos.22-23 Prince Albert Street. <44,108,123>

r) *PRINCE ALBERT STREET:* This thoroughfare through the Old Town was completed in 1842 to link Ship Street with Black Lion Street, Market Street and Bartholomews, thereby altering the ancient pattern of streets in the area somewhat. The construction involved the demolition of the old vicarage in Market Street and several houses in Black Lion Street, but nos.10-12 Prince Albert Street and no.15 opposite are red-brick listed houses of the late eighteenth century which formerly stood in Black Lion Street. No.15 is especially elegant, and unusual in Brighton with its Georgian brick façade and Doric porch. The adjacent single-storey Victorian shops towards Ship Street, with their terracotta balustered roofs, are both unusual and attractive. Other listed buildings of the late eighteenth or nineteenth centuries include nos.16 and 17-17a at the corners of Nile Street; nos.2-8, a three-storey terrace with bows which was constructed contemporaneously with the road; and nos.22-24.
<44,112>

Approached along a path from the corner of Prince Albert Street and Ship Street, the Meeting House of the Religious Society of Friends was erected for the growing Quaker community in 1805, and was altered in 1850 and again in 1876-7 when the north wing was added. Now used as an adult-education centre, it has a large garden surrounded by a cobbled wall and is included on the borough council's local list of buildings of special interest. This building replaced an earlier meeting house in North Street which stood near the eastern corner with New Road and was converted in 1700-1 from a malt-house. At the rear was about an acre of land, the Quaker's Croft, a portion of which was used as a burial ground where the Pavilion Theatre now stands; both the meeting house and croft were sold in 1806, and shops were built on the site. Another burial ground was established at Rifle Butt Road, Black Rock, in 1855, but the interments were reburied at the Lawn Memorial Park in late 1972 before the Marina road interchange was built on the site.
<15,64a,123,306>

Figure 104: No.15 Prince Albert Street, an elegant example of a Georgian town house

s) *REGENT ARCADE:* The Regent Arcade opened in 1961 on the site of Warden's Buildings, a group of warehouses named after Francis Warden who bought land in the area in the late eighteenth century. The site was anciently known as the Mockbeggar's Croft, a field probably connected with St Bartholomew's Priory. The entrances to this select arcade in East Street, Market Street and Bartholomews have been well designed to blend in with the adjacent buildings; a new western entrance is to be built in Market Street in 1990-2. <3,123>

t) *SHIP STREET:* Named from the Old Ship Inn (q.v.), Ship Street was developed from around the start of the seventeenth century and was known as the 'street of the Hempshares' in old documents (see "Fishing Industry" for hempshares). By the mid eighteenth century it was the most prosperous street in the town, and with the economic boom that followed the establishment of the health resort, it became a centre for professionals, especially solicitors and lawyers who remain in large numbers today. With many fine examples of Georgian town architecture, Ship Street remains probably the most elegant street in Brighton and there are a large number of listed buildings along its length, mostly dating from the late eighteenth and early nineteenth centuries. <14,18>

On the western side, no.7 has two bows, a fluted Doric doorway, and a façade of mathematical tiles; no.14 dates from the early nineteenth century, as does no.15 which has a distinctive doorway and two bows; nos.16-17 are elegant buildings in red brick; no.22 is cobble-fronted; and nos.28-29, with bows, also date from the early nineteenth century.

On the eastern side, nos.53-55 have two bows and mathematical tiles; no.57 has a cobbled front with added bay windows; the three-storey nos.58 and 59 are both faced in yellow brick (or possibly mathematical tiles); nos.61-63 date from the early nineteenth century and have excellent doorways; no.64 is an elegant brick house with another good doorway; no.68 has chequered brick and bears a date of 1738; and finally no.69 is an attractive house in knapped and squared flint with brick, which bears the date c.1685 but has a façade more appropriate to the following century. <44,47,306>

The new Museum of Brighton occupies the former Holy Trinity Church. Originally erected in 1817 by A. and A.H.Wilds, in Greek Doric style with a four-column portico and square tower, it was commissioned as the Trinity Chapel for Thomas Read Kemp and his dissenting sect, but Kemp sold the freehold to Revd Robert Anderson in 1825, and it was consecrated the following year as an Anglican chapel of ease to St Nicholas's Church known as Holy Trinity. Anderson enlarged the church in 1827 and removed the portico, and the building was altered again in 1855 and 1869 when Duke Street was widened; the southern façade was thus exposed, and a chancel was also added. In 1885-7 however, the exterior was completely rebuilt in Perpendicular and Decorated styles by Somers and Micklethwaite using knapped flint as the facing material. The hexagonal lantern is topped by a weather-vane which bears the date 1886, but the interior remains largely unaltered from the original and has galleries above the north and south aisles. Holy Trinity Church closed in December 1984 and is now a listed building; it is currently being converted into a Brighton heritage museum. Holy Trinity achieved national fame through the powerful sermons of the very famous radical preacher Revd Frederick Robertson in 1847-53, and the adjacent building, now the Co-operative Bank, was built in 1930 for the parish as the Robertson Hall. <1,44,45,46,123>

The most important building in Ship Street is the Head Post-Office, which dates from 1849 at the corner of the street, but has a main façade of 1892 (see "Postal Services"). Nos.31-32 are faced with mathematical tiles, while no.70 has an unusual cobbled upper storey with a bow. No.26 is the elegant entrance to Dukes Lane, complete with Sun Insurance firemark.

The Helsinki Café-Bar is notable for its extraordinary late-Victorian architecture, with Corinthian columns and pilasters, recessed balconies, and much decoration. Until 1982 it was known as the Seven Stars, a name first recorded in 1785, and for many years the building bore the inscription 'established 1535'.

Nos.8-9 Ship Street are the offices of Howlett Clarke Cushman, the oldest solicitor's practice in the town. The firm was founded in 1773 by William Attree who acted for both the Prince of Wales and the Duke of Clarence, and was also clerk to both the town commissioners and the vestry from 1790. The firm took Somers Clarke into partnership in 1829 and then, in 1858, James Howlett. Becoming Howlett and Clarke in 1887, it was combined with the firm of Cushman in 1989. The Book of Ancient Customs (see "Ancient Customs") is preserved in the offices. <46,123,273>

Lanes Café-Bar, formerly Henekeys, is a large rendered building in Tudor style opposite the Old Ship, and was erected on the site of the New Ship Inn. The New Ship was established by 1636 (although the building says 1695) and became one of the town's principal coaching inns. On 22 October 1792 it managed

Figure 105: Georgian doorways at nos.62-63 Ship Street

to accommodate a party of thirty-seven French refugee nuns who refused to sleep two to a bed; the Prince of Wales and Mrs Fitzherbert started a public subscription to pay for their stay before they moved on to Brussels. The inn was rebuilt in the early nineteenth century with three storeys and first-floor bows, but was replaced by the present building in 1933. The older inn is commemorated by the figureheads projecting from the upper storeys. <15,18,45>

u) *SHIP STREET GARDENS:* This twitten from Ship Street to Middle Street is lined with small nineteenth-century cottages and shops. Nos.13-16 are listed buildings. Opposite are a group of houses around small gardens, where Fig Cottage does indeed have a magnificent fig tree. <44>

v) *UNION STREET:* Union Street was once known as Meeting House Lane (see above), and has several listed buildings including a plain row of early-nineteenth-century shops, nos.1-5, on the southern side, and the late-eighteenth-century cobble-fronted nos.9-10 opposite.

The former chapel at the corner of Union Street and Meeting House Lane was Brighton's first purpose-built non-conformist chapel, erected in 1698 <18,64a> as a Presbyterian meeting house. It later became an Independent chapel, and it is claimed that Dr David Livingstone married Miss Mary Moffatt there in 1844. In 1878 the chapel was taken by the Union Congregation which in 1898 joined with the Queen Square Congregational Church to form the Union Free Church. In May 1905 the chapel was sold to the Glyn Vivian Miners' Mission, and from 1927 until August 1988 was the Elim Tabernacle of the Church of the Four Square Gospel. The listed building was rebuilt and enlarged in 1825 by Charles Busby <123> in Greek Doric style, and was restored again in 1985, but the eastern façade in Meeting House Lane is faced with cobbles and dates from an earlier period, perhaps from the original construction. The interior, which can seat nearly a thousand people, is a semi-circular amphitheatre with galleries supported on Corinthian pillars. Preserved in the façade is a stone bearing the date of formation of the original congregation, 1688, following the passing of the Toleration Act. With the Elim congregation removed to Albion Street in September 1988, the building is probably to be converted into a restaurant and shops. <1,18,44,61,64a,123,311>

116. OVINGDEAN

a) *HISTORY:* Ovingdean, the 'valley of Ofa's people', is a small village in a narrow valley 2.5 miles to the east of Brighton, and just under a mile from the sea. In the Domesday Book of 1086 the manor was held by Godfrey de Pierpoint from William de Warrenne; the settlement had a small church and a population of between fifty and a hundred. Little seems to have disturbed the peaceful village since, although it may have been attacked by the French raiders who terrorised Rottingdean in 1377. It is connected with one historic event though, but only fictitiously. In 1857 novelist Harrison Ainsworth wrote *Ovingdean Grange; a Tale of the South Downs* in which he described how the fleeing King Charles II stayed overnight before escaping to France in 1651. In reality the King stayed at the George Inn in West Street, Brighton, and did not visit the village at all. <1,47,289>

Most of the western part of the parish, the East Brighton estate of 1,065 acres including the Whitehawk area, was purchased by Brighton Corporation in September 1913 for £34,100, and the whole of the parish,

Figure 106: St Wulfran's Church

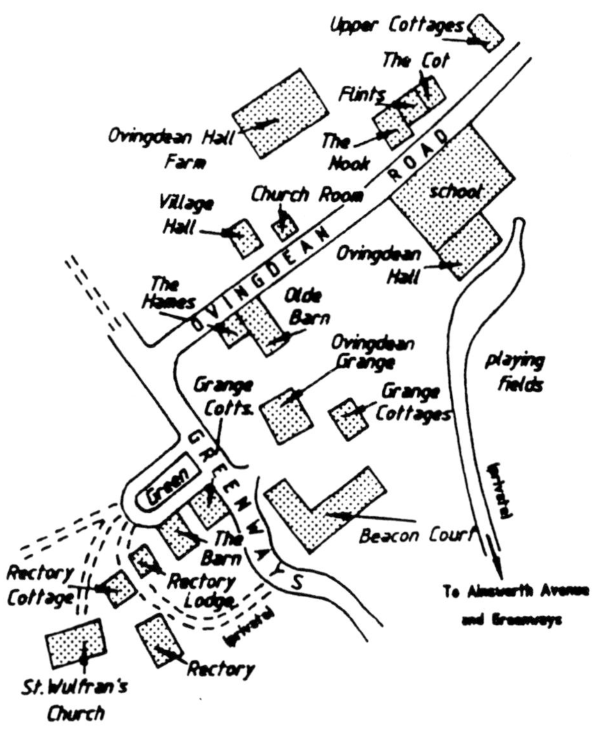

Figure 107: Ovingdean village

formerly part of the Newhaven Union and Rural District, was annexed by Brighton on 1 April 1928. Ovingdean parish had an area of 1,630 acres, stretching from Whitehawk Road to High Hill (between Rottingdean and Balsdean), and from Warren Road to Roedean Road, separated from the sea by a narrow strip of Rottingdean parish. By 1911 the population had grown to 248, but modern development started in the 1920s on the Long Hill ridge and continued in the '30s at Whitehawk, Roedean and in the New Barn area. By 1981 the population of the Ovingdean village district alone had risen to about 1,000. The village itself has been largely untouched by development and has been designated a conservation area, including the extensive grounds of Ovingdean Hall. <1,83,109,277,305>

b) *ST WULFRAN'S CHURCH:* One of only three churches in England dedicated to the eighth-century Saint Wulfran (the others are at Grantham and Dorrington in Lincolnshire), Ovingdean's charming church is built entirely of flint, the only all-flint church in the county. Although Domesday records the presence of a small church, the earliest work at St Wulfran's, the chancel and nave, appears to date from the early twelfth century; nevertheless, this makes it probably the oldest building in the whole borough. The tower, with its Sussex cap, dates from the late thirteenth century but the porch and chapel are both modern. Towards the end of the twelfth century two doors were cut in the south wall of the nave; an aisle was also built but this has been destroyed, possibly by French raiders in 1377. Now a listed building, St Wulfran's was restored in 1867.

The interior, which measures just 33 feet by 18 feet, has 125 sittings but contains no medieval monuments or memorials. However, a miniature fouteenth-century rood screen of oak remains in the chancel arch, and the chancel roof is painted with birds and foliage. Opposite the porch in the churchyard are the tombs of Charles Kempe, the renowned stained-glass artist, and the inventor Magnus Volk. Ovingdean Church Room was built in 1873 in Ovingdean Road, in flint with red-brick dressings. <1,45,64a,125>

There are a number of other listed buildings in the village, described below.

c) *OVINGDEAN GRANGE:* This house is the most historic secular building in the village and was the former manor house. The oldest part lies on the northern side and dates from the late sixteenth century; the flint walls here may be seen from the private road leading to Ovingdean Hall. The west front dates from the early nineteenth century however, and presents a disappointing plain façade in a roughcast. There is a Doric porch though, and the interior has a fine oak-beam roof.

As mentioned above, Ovingdean Grange is the title of a novel by Harrison Ainsworth about the fictitious visit of King Charles II in 1651. In 1987 the house, which was acquired as part of the East Brighton estate, was sold at auction by the council. In 1985-6 two large, nineteenth-century flint barns in the farmyard were converted into homes known as Beacon Court; there are also some eighteenth-century, flint and weather-boarded stables, now cottages. <1,44,47,125>

d) *OVINGDEAN HALL:* This fine, late-eighteenth-century mansion is approached along a private road from the New Lodge at the bottom of Ainsworth Avenue. Faced in light-yellow mathematical tiles, the house has a pediment and an impressive Doric doorway, and is now used as a voluntary residential special school for the aurally handicapped. It was erected in about 1782 for Nathaniel Kemp, the uncle of Thomas Read Kemp, who lived there until his death in 1843. He is buried in St Wulfran's churchyard along with his son, Charles Kempe (1838-1907), the stained-glass artist. <1,44,47,64a,306>

e) *OVINGDEAN RECTORY:* On the opposite side of the road from Ovingdean Grange is the village green, a small grassed area which leads up to the church. Adjacently stands Rectory Cottage, a large, three-storey, late-eighteenth-century house faced with cobbles; a single-storey, cobble-fronted building, Rectory Lodge, stands nearby. The Rectory itself beyond lies beyond the cottage and is a large, grade II*-listed house dating from 1804-7. It has a cobbled façade, Tuscan pedimented porch, and a flint coach-house on the south-eastern side. <1,44,47>

f) *OTHER LISTED BUILDINGS:* Nos.11-13 Greenways, by the green, are known as Grange Farm Cottages, knapped-flint houses of the early nineteenth century. The knapped-flint tithe barn which stands adjacently also dates from the nineteenth century and has been converted into a dwelling. In Ovingdean Road, Flints and The Cot were originally the eighteenth-

Figure 108: Ovingdean Hall

century farmhouse of Ovingdean Hall and are faced in knapped flint; the adjoining Nook dates from around 1805. <44,123>

g) *OTHER BUILDINGS:* Nos.1-3 Upper Cottages in Ovingdean Road, built in flint but mostly rendered, date from the eighteenth century and are included on the council's local list of buildings of special interest; they were extensively restored in 1976-8. The Hames, a single-storey flint cottage, stands in Ovingdean Road adjacent to the Olde Barn, a two-storey flint building converted into a residence in 1982-3. Ovingdean Hall Farm has one old knapped-and-squared-flint barn, but new flint houses were built on the farm yard in 1989. The Village Hall opened in 1986 on the site of the 1932 village club room.

At the junction of Greenways and Beacon Hill are Greenway Cottages, faced in knapped flint with red-brick dressings; they were built in 1892. The St Dunstan's building at Ovingdean Gap actually stands in the former parish of Rottingdean, but has its own entry in this text anyway. Two prominent buildings in Falmer Road also lay within the parish of Ovingdean; New Barn and Rottingdean Place are included under "Rottingdean Green (Falmer Road)". The old farm buildings in Ovingdean Road near Ovingdean Close belonged to Woodingdean Farm; see "Woodingdean". <123,306,311>

117.PALACE PIER, Madeira Drive

<44,116,126,142,143,311>

a) *CONSTRUCTION:* In 1889 the Brighton Marine Palace and Pier Company was formed to erect a new pleasure pier opposite the Old Steine, conditional upon the removal of the old Chain Pier which had been purchased for £15,000. Designed by R.St George Moore, the first screw-pile of the new Palace Pier was driven in November 1891, but progress was slow. The destruction of the Chain Pier in a storm in December 1896 avoided the need for its demolition, but the wreckage damaged not only the new adjacent structure but also both the West Pier and Volk's Railway. The consequent claims on the company for damages threatened it with liquidation, but in 1898 Sir John Howard formed a new company which purchased and then completed the Palace Pier, opening it to the public on 20 May 1899. The entrance was an illuminated archway but beyond it only the decking, adorned with delicate filigree arches, and some kiosks were initially opened. The new pier proved an instant success.

b) *DEVELOPMENT:* The first phase of the new pier was completed at a cost of £137,000 on 9 April 1901 with the opening of the landing stage and the pier-head pavilion, the actual marine palace referred to in the name of the company; the latter, decorated in oriental style with four large minaret towers, contained dining, smoking and reading rooms, and also a concert hall. In 1906 the central windscreen was erected, and further improvements were made in 1910-11 when the pavilion was remodelled as a theatre and café, a bandstand was added in the centre of the pier, and the large winter garden was erected near the shore end.

In 1930 a new entrance and clock tower replaced the three ironwork arches of the original entrance, an improvement which was inaugurated on 27 June 1930 by the mayor, Horace Aldrich, in conjunction with a widening of the promenade. The pier was extended slightly in 1938 when a 'big wheel' ride was added at the pier-head, but it was closed throughout the war and a gap was made near the middle to prevent its possible use as a landing stage by the enemy. The pier was also damaged by German bombs.

The Palace Pier reopened in the summer of 1946 and business boomed. Day-trips along the coast were operated until about 1960, a repertory company performed at the theatre until 1964, and many other attractions were introduced. However, on 19 October 1973 a seventy-ton barge, which was moored to the pier during the demolition of the derelict landing stage, broke loose during a gale and severely damaged the structure; the theatre partly collapsed and was never used again, and part of the decking was also wrecked. A replacement helter-skelter was installed the following year, but restoration of the damage was not completed until February 1976.

In 1984 the pier was purchased by the Noble Organisation which has revitalised it by introducing free admission and new attractions. Two years later, the new owners embarked upon an £8 million refurbishment and enlargement programme which will include the reconstruction of the pier-head theatre. The latter was demolished in March 1986, but will be replaced by a facsimile complete with colonnade, oriental domes and many of the original fittings; in the interim period it has been replaced by a large amusement dome. The refurbishment of the pier has included new entrance kiosks, a remodelling of the Palace of Fun, and the provision of the stylish Fish and Chip Café, Victoria's Bar and Horatio's Bar.

c) *DESCRIPTION:* The Palace Pier is generally acknowledged to be the finest pleasure pier ever built, and is also a grade II*-listed building. The peak of its popularity came in 1939 when there were two million visitors, including 45,000 on just one Bank Holiday, but it remains popular with both visitors and locals encouraged by free admission and deckchairs, and a host of new attractions. The pier retains many original features, with the refurbishment programme adding to the facilities offered.

Oriental in design, the Palace Pier now has a length of about 1,650 feet, and a width which varies from 45 feet to 189 feet at the pier-head. The entrance is flanked by two original kiosks, while two more kiosks with fish-scale roofs, originally erected at the entrance to the Chain Pier in 1872 <131>, stand either side of the former winter garden, now the Palace of Fun amusement arcade; the latter retains its fine ironwork interior, domed roof, and has many stained glass windows. Two sets of iron filigree arches remain before the circular bandstand is reached, now the Fish and Chip Café and Victoria's Bar. Near the pier-head stands a signal cannon also from the Chain Pier. The original pier-head theatre has been demolished, and the area is now occupied by a large slot-machine dome and a number of funfair rides, but the shops and bar on the eastern side retain their original minarets. A number of other original square kiosks still remain along the length of the pier, mostly marked with the initials 'BMPP' for 'Brighton Marine Palace and Pier', as the pier is still officially known.

Figure 109: One of the former toll-booths of the Chain Pier, now installed on the Palace Pier

118. PARISHES

a) *ECCLESIASTICAL PARISHES:* Parishes originated as the basic unit of ecclesiastical administration, the area served by a parson to whom dues were paid by the inhabitants. The ecclesiastical parish of Brighton (parish church St Nicholas) remained a single unit until 22 June 1873 when, with nineteen Anglican churches and chapels and a population of approximately 92,000, it was divided into several district parishes; St Peter's was designated as Brighton's new parish church, though this was only one of the seven new areas. The present area of the borough was originally divided up between nine ancient parishes (see below), but it is now split into twenty ecclesiastical parishes, all responsible to the vicar of Brighton as rural dean. (Kemp Town and Preston were also rural deaneries until the 1980s.) <57,300,314>

b) *CIVIL PARISHES:* As manorial courts gradually fell into decay and various legislation was passed, ecclesiastical parishes gradually became units of secular administration as well, particularly in the sixteenth and seventeenth centuries. Parish vestries, theoretically composed of all parish ratepayers, were authorised to levy rates for poor relief and the maintenance of highways as well as church maintenance, and they also appointed the parochial officers, the beadle, church-wardens and overseers of the poor, to conduct the parish business (see below).

In Brighton, municipal responsibilities belonged to the town commissioners from 1773 until the borough council was established in 1854. The parish, in the form of the vestry (see below), was principally responsible for poor-law administration until 1810 when the 'Directors and Guardians of the Poor' (see below) were first appointed, and for burials in the form of a burial board from 1856 until 1902. From 1825 guardians of the poor were annually elected by the parishioners, and even after incorporation they continued to be elected on a parochial rather than a borough basis. Thus Preston parish, which was partly incorporated into the borough of Brighton in 1873, continued to elect representatives to the Steyning Board of Guardians. In 1928 Brighton county borough annexed Ovingdean, Rottingdean, most of Patcham and parts of Falmer, Hove and West Blatchington parishes, and the new county borough area was constituted as a single parish. On 1 April 1930 the Brighton Board of Guardians was replaced by the county borough council, and the last secular significance of parishes in Brighton was thus extinguished. The county borough remained a parish in name until 1 April 1974 when urban parishes were abolished by the 1972 Local Government Act. See also figure 15. <14,43,115,300>

The present borough area comprises two complete 'ancient' parishes and parts of seven others. They are listed below with their areas in acres <1,39,109,279>.

Parish	Original parish area	Area now within borough	Percentage of borough (15,041 a.)
Brighton	1,640	1,637	10.9
In Steyning Union:			
Hove	778	7	0.0
Patcham	4,425	4,273	28.4
Preston	1,308	905	6.0
West Blatchington	873	131	0.9
In Newhaven Union:			
Falmer	4,393	1,985	13.2
Ovingdean	1,630	1,630	10.8
Rottingdean	3,139	3,139	20.9
Stanmer	1,341	627	4.6
Marina	-	127	0.8
Sea off marina within borough	-	567	3.8

Discrepancies in these figures are accounted for by reclaimed land. No change in parish boundaries occurred until 1894 when Preston was split into Preston and Preston Rural parishes either side of Dyke Road. In the same year the functions of the vestries in the rural parishes were transferred to elected parish councils or to parish meetings. See "Boundaries" for details of parish boundaries.

c) *THE VESTRY:* As mentioned above, parish vestries were originally closely connected with the church, but civil powers were granted over many years. The vestry was theoretically composed of all parish ratepayers, but an 'open' vestry never really developed in Brighton and decisions were taken by a select group which included the vicar, high constable, church-wardens, overseers, headboroughs and other parish officials. Town meetings were called when necessary to decide important issues however, and elections by all ratepayers were held to appoint guardians and town commissioners as detailed below.

In 1773 the town commissioners assumed responsibility for most municipal affairs, and the vestry was restricted to matters such as church maintenance, cemeteries, and poor-law, including the workhouse. Until 1804 they usually met at one of the town's many inns, but after that date, and occasionally before, the old Town Hall in Market Street was used. The 1810 Brighton Town Act transferred responsibility for the poor to the town commissioners, but it also gave the election of new commissioners to the ratepayers, and in 1825 they won the important rights to elect the 'Directors and Guardians of the Poor' and to elect sixteen new town commissioners annually. Following incorporation in 1854 however, the functions of the Brighton Vestry largely died out except for cemetery responsibility, and as an occasional body of ratepayers to discuss issues. Somers Clarke was re-appointed vestry clerk from 1830 until his death in 1892 when the post was discontinued; his bust may be found in the Town Hall.

The Brighton Vestry, under the chairmanship of the vicar, was generally Liberal, even Radical; it petitioned Parliament for an extended franchise in support of the 'People's Charter', a copy of which was even pasted into the minute book. There were notable clashes in the vestry during the incumbency of the Tory vicar of 1824-70, Revd Henry Wagner.

Vestries in the rural parishes of the area continued to function until 1894 when they were replaced either by directly elected parish councils or by parish meetings. Rural district councils were also formed that year to look after many functions in the parishes. <14,112,300>

d) *PAROCHIAL OFFICERS:* Two of the most important parochial appointments were the overseers and the church-wardens. Under the 1601 Poor Law Act, the overseers of the poor were required to levy the poor rate and to supervise its distribution; however, they lost the distributive function under the 1810 Brighton Town Act which passed that responsibility to guardians, and they then operated as collectors only. Overseers were appointed annually by the vestry until 1894, and were then appointed by the county borough council until the office was abolished by the 1925 Rating and Valuation Act.

Church-wardens, who were appointed annually by the parishioners in vestry on Easter Tuesday, had many duties and were anciently the custodians of the parish's income, using it for the maintenance of the church, parish buildings and defences. In sixteenth-century Brighton their principal income came from the 'quarter share' claimed from each fishing trip, and was mainly spent on the upkeep of St Nicholas's Church, the Townhouse and the Blockhouse. The Book of Ancient Customs of 1580 laid down strict rules for both the contributions and the expenditure, and provided for a rate from the landsmen as well. It also specified, unusually, three church-wardens for the parish of Brighton, two of which were to be fishermen and one a landsman. The parish of Brighton, now that of St Peter's Church, retains three church-wardens to this day. <14,273,300>

e) *GUARDIANS OF THE POOR:* The Poor Law Act of 1601 gave the responsibility for relief of the poor to the parish overseers, who were appointed by the parish in vestry. Under the terms of the 1810 Brighton Town Act, this responsibility was transferred to thirty 'Directors and Guardians of the Poor' to be nominated annually by the town commissioners, although the vicar, high constable, church-wardens and overseers were ex-officio guardians. They were required to set their paupers to work, to form themselves into six committees which met once a week with quarterly meetings of them all, and were authorised to borrow up to £10,000 for the construction of a new workhouse. One of their first actions was to 'improve' the workhouse diet in the interests of economy. The 1825 Brighton Town Act gave the election of guardians to the parish ratepayers, but kept the ex-officio members. From 18 March 1871 however, the Brighton Directors and Guardians were replaced by a board of 'Guardians of the Poor' responsible to the Local Government Board (replaced in 1919 by the Ministry of Health), and were required to care for both the 'outdoor' poor and those in the workhouse; conditions in the workhouse were made deliberately unpleasant to encourage inmates to go out and find work.

Initially meeting in one of several inns in the town, the guardians moved to offices in the new Town Hall in about 1832, and from 1856 occupied the present public library building. On 7 May 1895 new parochial offices were opened in Prince's Street after they had accepted a corporation offer of £7,000 to move for an enlargement to the public library (see figure 177). Following the 1894 Local Government Act, the guardians were elected on the basis of three per ward instead of by the electors in vestry, but still on a parochial rather than borough basis; thus the guardians elected for the parish of Preston, despite it being part of the borough of Brighton, sat on the board for the Steyning Union. The Brighton Guardians were increased to fifty-seven in number on the creation of 'Greater Brighton' in 1928 when the parish was extended to cover the whole of the new county borough area, but the board of guardians was dissolved on 1 April 1930 when it was replaced by the county borough council's public assistance committee under the 1929 Local Government Act. <14,95,112,115,300>

See also "Poor, The".

f) *HUNDREDS:* Another important division of the county, from Saxon times until the nineteenth century, was the 'hundred', said to be based originally upon areas containing one hundred families. Hundred courts were held at regular intervals to dispense justice and to raise taxes, and all inhabitants were required annually on Easter Tuesday to attend a 'court-leet' where certain appointments and bye-laws were made.

In most instances the hundreds were composed of two or more parishes. In 1086 Brighton was recorded as being in Welesmere Hundred with Ovingdean and Rottingdean; Falmer and Stanmer were in Falmer Hundred, and Patcham and Preston were included in Preston Hundred. Under Edward I, the Hundred of 'Whalesbone', probably a corruption of the 'Wellesbourne' stream, was created including Brighton, Hove, Patcham and West Blatchington; Falmer, Ovingdean and Rottingdean were united into Younsmere Hundred, while Preston remained a hundred in itself. Several changes occurred throughout the following centuries; Preston and Hove were united into a single hundred in the mid sixteenth century, and Patcham parish alone became the Hundred of Dean in 1724. This left Whalesbone Hundred with the parishes of Brighton and West Blatchington only. Stanmer was an 'ecclesiastical peculiar', and was usually counted in the Hundred of Ringmer. Any remaining functions of the hundreds largely died out upon the incorporation of Brighton in 1854.

The most important hundred official was the high constable, who from 1285 was appointed exclusively for the town of Brighton. He was generally chosen by the 'Society of the Twelve' in the seventeenth century, but was later appointed by the justices upon the vestry's recommendation. His duties were numerous, concerned with maintaining law and order and managing parochial affairs with the church-wardens, and for many years the appointment was considered to be an onerous burden; after incorporation in 1854 the duties consisted simply of compiling a jury list, however. The last high constable was James Martin, who was appointed on 10 April 1855 and remained in office for nearly twenty years. The constable's staff of 1828 may be seen in Brighton Museum, and a list of incumbents exists back to 1589 <6>.

Assistants to the constable known as 'headboroughs' were also appointed at the court-leet. From the earliest times Brighton had two headboroughs, a sign that it was always a place of some importance. <1,6,14,15,162,300>

119. PARKS

<126,277,306>

Brighton Council's Parks and Recreation Department is responsible for about 2,546 acres of parks, gardens, playing fields, etc., which include approximately 144 acres of allotments, 63 tennis-courts, 16 bowling-greens, 25 cricket pitches, 2 municipal golf-courses, a pitch-and-putt course, 60 football, rugby and hockey pitches, and 32 children's playgrounds. Several parks and gardens have been designated by the council as being of historic interest, and special care will be taken to preserve and restore their original layout and features; they are: the Kemp Town enclosures; Kipling Garden, Rottingdean; Park Crescent; Preston Manor grounds; Preston Park; Preston Rockery; Queen's Park; Royal Pavilion grounds; Stanmer Park; and the Victoria Gardens. Only the Royal Pavilion and Preston Manor grounds are on the English Heritage list, however, at grade II. For details of all parks, gardens and recreation grounds, consult the index entry on "parks".

120. PARK CRESCENT

a) *HISTORY and DESCRIPTION:* The houses of Park Crescent were designed by A.H.Wilds and erected over a period of several years from 1849 <83> around a private garden which was formerly the Royal Gardens cricket ground (see below). The façades of the houses are not readily viewed except from the garden, but they may be seen to have attic storeys breaking the roof line above verandahs, and form a chain of linked villas with a rear façade that resembles a plain terrace. The forty-eight houses are all listed except nos.24-26 which were erected in 1983 as facsimiles of houses that were bombed in 1942. The garden was managed by an estate agent until 1872 when the responsibility passed to a residents' committee. <44,265>

b) *ROYAL GARDENS:* The Royal Gardens themselves were laid out for James Ireland. In 1822 he purchased ten acres of the Level between the new Union Road and the future Brewer Street/Trinity Street area from T.R.Kemp, and opened his gardens to the public on 1 May 1823. From a lodge at the south-western corner, the visitor entered the cricket ground with a bowling-green and billiard-room nearby; the Hanover Arms stood at the south-eastern corner. The cricket ground was said to be the best in the entire country and staged many grand matches. One of the first was on 28 June 1823 when a Sussex XI defeated the M.C.C. by an innings and 45 runs. The Sussex County Cricket Club played their first matches on the ground, and as Sussex are the oldest formally established county club (formed 1839), this ground, which was also known as the Hanover Ground or Box's Ground, can be said to have been the first county cricket ground in England. The first match was probably Brighton versus Godalming on 2-3 June 1823, and the last was on 27-30 September 1847 when Sussex beat an All-England XI by 22 runs. It was certainly the most popular of the attractions at the gardens.

Adjacent to the cricket ground stood the assembly rooms which had reading, refreshment and dressing rooms on the ground floor, and an elegant promenade above. Beyond were the pleasure gardens including a ladies' bowling-green, an aviary, an ornamental grotto, a maze, and a small lake. However, despite numerous attractions and special events, the gardens were not a financial success and Ireland eventually sold them, but the later proprietors, including a Mr Pierpoint, Mr Brown, and Messrs Harvey and Box, also had little success. A menagerie was introduced in 1839 but lasted less than one year, and the grounds were soon allowed to fall into decay. The area was eventually developed with small terraced housing from the 1850s to the '90s, except of course at Park Crescent where the cricket ground became a private garden. However, the boundary wall of the Royal Gardens, now a listed structure, remains on the northern side of Union Road but the large lion and lioness figures on the gateposts were removed in 1987, and the wall was severely damaged by the storm of October 1987. <44,140>
<3,15,265>

c) *SALVATION ARMY:* The nearby Congress Hall of the Salvation Army in Park Crescent Terrace was completed in 1883, and was formally opened in March 1884 by Mrs Booth, the wife of the founder of the movement. Designed by E.J.Hamilton, it is a large, brick building with two flanking battlemented towers and a little terracotta decoration; it seats 1,400 people and has additions of 1925.

The army's first branch in the area was established in about 1880 at Conway Street, Hove, after General Booth's first visit in 1879. In 1891 the Salvation Army bought a former riding school in Edward Street (where the D.S.S. building, Windsor House, now stands) and established a second citadel with battlemented towers, but it was demolished in 1965 and a replacement building now stands in Carlton Hill. A goodwill centre was run in Moulsecoomb Way from the late 1930s, but an Allen West factory was built on the site in the mid '50s. There is also a Salvation Army hall at Leybourne Road, Bevendean.

During the 1880s and '90s the Salvation Army came under severe attack in Brighton as elsewhere, and police escorts were required for their marches. The windows of the Congress Hall were also smashed. <2,24,62,83,115>

d) *GAIETY THEATRE:* Park Crescent Place runs northward from Park Crescent to Trinity Street. On the western side stands a block of flats known as Devonian Court, erected on the site of the Gaiety Theatre. Opening on 31 October 1876, this theatre started life as the Royal Hippodrome, the permanent home of Ginnett's Circus with room for about 1,600 spectators; another large hall, the Grand Olympia, was erected at the rear soon afterwards. The circus proved a popular attraction, but Fred Ginnett was constantly thwarted in his attempts to obtain a dramatic licence and eventually closed the Hippodrome in 1889.

Figure 110: Circus proprietor Fred Ginnett's tomb in Woodvale Cemetery

The building reopened on 28 July 1890 under new management, but this time with a dramatic licence. It was renamed the Gaiety Theatre, offering initially music hall and melodrama, but again success was short lived and after several other proprietors had failed to make a success of the Gaiety it finally closed in March 1900 and was bought the following year by the Fryco Mineral Water Company. The building was demolished in 1930, but a special concrete floor which had been installed by Fryco was used as the foundation for Devonian Court. <3,236>

The Arcadia Theatre of Varieties also had an entrance in Park Crescent Place; see "Lewes Road".

121. PATCHAM

The former parish of Patcham was very extensive and covered an area of 4,425 acres including Moulsecoomb, Hollingbury, Tongdean and Withdean. In the Domesday Book of 1086 the manor (Patcham Court) was held by William de Warrenne, Lord of the Rape of Lewes; there was a church, and the population of between 1,000 and 1,750 made the village one of the largest settlements in the county. On 12 September 1302 King Edward I stayed the night in Patcham on his way from Beeding to Lewes. The old village has now been designated a conservation area and is fully described in the entry following this one. <1>

By 1801 the population was only 286. The first modern development in the parish was a line of villas which was built along the London Road at Withdean from the 1850s (see "London Road, Patcham"), and by 1901 the population had risen to 1,110. The first extensive development took place in the south-western-most corner of the parish at Moulsecoomb (q.v.); the South Moulsecoomb housing estate was developed by Brighton Corporation in the early 1920s, and the 94 acres of land which were used on the eastern side of Lewes Road were annexed by the county borough of Brighton and Preston parish on 1 October 1923. In 1926-7 Steyning East Rural District Council erected twenty houses at Patchdean, but on 1 April 1928 most of the parish was absorbed by Brighton; the other 152 acres to the west of Dyke Road at Tongdean Farm and Lower Tongdean Farm were added to Hove. (Tongdean Farm stood by the junction of Dyke Road Avenue and Hill Brow, but some farm cottages remain at The Spinney. Lower Tongdean Farm stood at the junction of Tongdean Road and Meadow Close. The Tongdean area remains within the ecclesiastical parish of Patcham, however.) With the integration of Patcham into Brighton development of the parish, which had been piecemeal until then, proceeded rapidly and large estates were built in the Braybon Avenue, Carden Avenue, Ladies Mile and Valley Drive areas. The Hollingbury and Westdene estates were added post-war. The Patcham, Brangwyn, Ladies Mile and Hollingbury areas have a combined population of over 13,500. <1,83,127,277,279>

Patcham was supplied with a library service by the county council prior to 1928, and this arrangement was continued for some years by agreement until the present branch library in Ladies Mile Road was opened in 1933. In 1939 a temporary church was erected at the bottom of Braybon Avenue, but the permanent Church of Christ the King, South Patcham, was built in 1958 with the old church becoming a hall. The 1963 Roman Catholic Church of St Thomas More stands adjacently. <123,124>

See also "Hollingbury", "Ladies Mile", "London Road, Patcham", "Waterhall", "Westdene" and "Withdean".

122. PATCHAM Village

The old village of Patcham is a conservation area centred around Church Hill and Old London Road. At the top of Church Hill is:

a) *PATCHAM COURT FARM:* The oldest farm in the parish and the former manorial property, Patcham Court Farm covered 733 acres and was acquired by Brighton Corporation in December 1925, having been in the Marquess of Abergavenny's family since 1439. The old farm buildings form an attractive group at the top of Church Hill, having survived a council proposal for their demolition in the 1950s when the modern Patcham Court Farm buildings were erected to the north of Vale Avenue on the road to Standean; in fact it is the 1950s farm buildings that will be demolished for the construction of the Brighton bypass with a third farm to be built higher up the Standean Road.

The large, listed farmhouse still standing in Vale Avenue is faced in knapped flint and dates from the early seventeenth century, but it has been extended and considerably restored. In its back garden alongside Church Hill stands a circular flint dovecote with walls three feet thick and 550 nesting boxes. Dating from the seventeenth century or possibly even earlier, it retains its original swinging ladder or 'potence', and is a scheduled ancient monument, the only building so designated within the borough, as well as a listed building. (See figure 42.) <1,44,123,305>

On the opposite side of Church Hill stands a magnificent, listed tithe barn, at 250 feet the longest in Sussex. Dating from the seventeenth century or earlier, it has mostly weather-boarded walls but there is some knapped flint work and also a fine beamed roof. The barn was used by agricultural merchants Levetts Ltd for many years following its reprieve in the 1950s, but in 1986-7 it was radically converted into dwellings and a church hall to form the centre-piece of the Village Barn development; the wooden interior beams have been preserved, however. A new barn-like block, built in flint and with a decorative round tower, was erected at the same time in Vale Avenue. <1,44,47,123>

See also "The Chattri" below.

Figure 111: Patcham Court Farmhouse

b) *ALL SAINTS' CHURCH:* Built principally in the Early English and Decorated styles, Patcham's parish church stands on a hill above the village and appears to date from the twelfth century; it is probably not, therefore, the same church which is mentioned in Domesday. The oldest part is the twelfth-century nave, with the chancel and tower, topped by a turret spire, probably dating from the following century. The walls are built of flint with stone dressings but unfortunately the exterior, with the exception of the north aisle, has been rendered in cement. The south porch has a fourteenth-century Gothic arch, while above the thirteenth-century chancel arch are the remains of a painting of the Last Judgement which were discovered during a restoration of 1883. Within the chancel itself is a chalk memorial to the Shelley family of Patcham Place.

All Saints' Church has room for 350 worshippers and is now a listed building. It was restored in 1825-30, 1856, 1883, in 1898 when the vestry and north aisle were added and the exterior was rendered, and 1989. It is also said to be haunted by a tall, thin lady dressed in grey who sits in the pews on frosty nights. A church hall was dedicated on 3 November 1986 in the adjacent Village Barn, formerly the barn of Patcham Court Farm (q.v.). Connected with the church are the Mackie Hall and the Church Hall of the Ascension, Westdene.

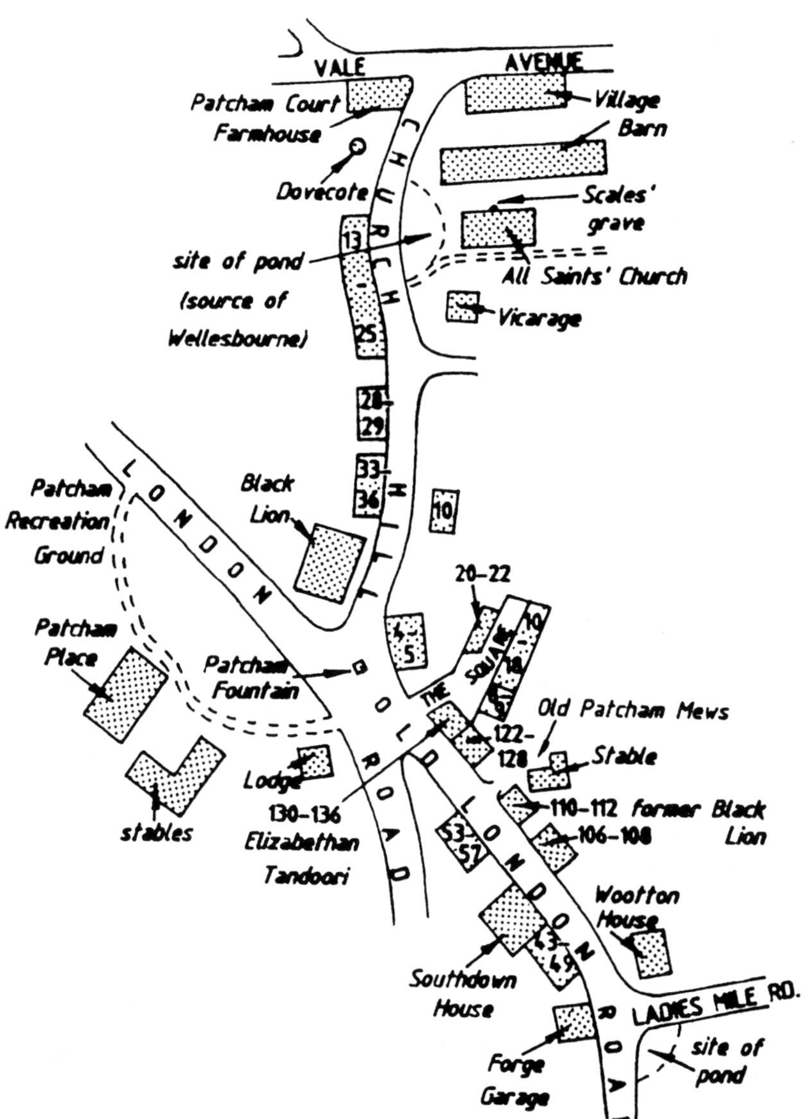

Figure 112: Patcham Village

The village war memorial stands within the churchyard, while on the northern side of the church is the grave of one Daniel Scales, shot by customs men on his way to Patcham with contraband on 7 November 1796. An eastern extension to the churchyard was consecrated in 1949.
<1,45,47,64a,128>

c) *CHURCH HILL:* The shallow depression in front of the church marks the site of a pond, one of the principal sources of the stream known as the Wellesbourne (q.v.) which ran all the way to the sea at Pool Valley. Nos.13-25 Church Hill opposite are known as Pond Cottages, plain, slate-roofed houses from the first half of the nineteenth century which were restored jointly by the corporation and the Patcham Preservation Society in about 1964. Nos.28-29, two flint cottages (originally four) on a timber frame, were probably refaced in the eighteenth century, while nos.33-36 are early-nineteenth-century flint cottages with red-brick dressings. No.10 on the eastern side, half covered by creeper, has an eighteenth-century front of knapped flint on an older timber frame. All these old cottages are listed buildings.

The large Black Lion Hotel opened in 1929. The inn originally stood at nos.110-112 Old London Road, but with the opening of the Patcham bypass in 1926 it became prudent to build a new hotel on the site of an old house by the main road.

The lowest part of Church Hill, together with part of Old London Road, was once known as Spring Street and was often flooded by the Wellesbourne in winter. Here nos.4-4a are eighteenth-century listed flint cottages, but the adjacent no.5, also listed, has been shown to date from the fifteenth century and is one of the oldest buildings in the whole borough. Patcham Fountain was erected in 1887 to commemorate the golden jubilee of Queen Victoria on the site of a donkey wheel which had supplied the village with water; the present structure is a replacement of the original which was demolished by a bus. <44,123,127a,128>

d) *PATCHAM PLACE:* Standing on the other side of the London Road, this large, grade II*-listed mansion was originally built in 1558 for Sir William West, Lord de la Warr, but it was rebuilt with the addition of the present façade of black mathematical tiles, pediment

Figure 113:
Patcham Place

and Tuscan doorway in 1764 for John Paine. In the mid sixteenth century the estate was the property of Richard Shelley, one of the commissioners for the 'Book of all the Auncient Customs' (sic) (see "Ancient Customs"), but the house is said to be haunted by one of its later owners, Anthony Stapley, who was a signatory to King Charles I's death warrant. The owner in 1840, Major Paine, fortunately insisted that the railway should pass through his land in a tunnel rather than a cutting.

At the rear of the house is a listed stable building with an unusual cobbled pediment, and there is also a lodge by the London Road. In 1926 the house and grounds were purchased by the corporation for £6,000, and since 1939 it has been leased as a youth hostel. The parkland is now known as the Patcham Recreation Ground, but the magnificent woodland on the side of Coney Hill was decimated by the storm of October 1987. <1,44,45,47,126,128,305>

e) *THE SQUARE:* Between 137 and 138 Old London Road is the entrance to the Square, an attractive group of eighteenth-century cottages. The listed nos.8-9 have weather-boarded fronts, while nos.10-20, included on the council's local list only, are built of flint although mostly rendered in cement. Nos.19-22 opposite are single-storey flint cottages. <44>

f) *OLD LONDON ROAD:* The main village street was part of the main London Road until the Patcham bypass opened in 1926 <115>. The section between Church Hill and Ladies Mile Road retains many listed buildings dating mainly from the eighteenth century, which are detailed below.

On the western side, nos.43-47 are knapped-flint cottages with very small windows. No.49, Flints, has a cobbled façade and was once the stable of the adjacent Southdown House, no.51, a handsome grade II*-listed

Figure 114:
Nos.23-24 Church Hill, flint cottages with exposed timber-framing, unusual for the area

building. An early Georgian house, it is faced in knapped and squared flint with red-brick dressings, and has a doorway with a decorated surround and pediment leading to a fine interior; the small front garden is bounded by a fine cobbled wall with an iron fence. Nos.53-57 are faced in flint, with small windows and low doors. <44>

On the eastern side, at the northern end in the part once known as Spring Street, stands the Elizabethan Cottage Tandoori Restaurant, nos.132-136 faced in knapped flint, and the adjacent nos.124-130, plain cottages with added bow windows and shutters; all these cottages may well date from before the eighteenth century. The modern development of Old Patcham Mews occupies the site of a paint works behind nos.110-112; the new houses, opened in 1989, are in traditional flint and plain cottage designs and won a R.I.B.A. award. Nos.110-112 themselves, the Old Coach House, were the Black Lion Hotel until the present large hotel was rebuilt from an older house in 1929, and have a nineteenth-century façade; they were converted together with heavily-restored flint stables at the rear at the same time as the modern development. Nos.106-108 were formerly one house built of stone. At the junction with Ladies Mile Road stands Wootton House, a late eighteenth-century house faced in black glazed mathematical tiles with a slate roof, cobble-fronted extension, and flint stables which have been converted to flats. <44>

To the south of Ladies Mile Road, Old London Road runs through some 1930s suburban development which is not included in the conservation area. Patcham House Special School occupies the former village National School building of the mid nineteenth century, while Patcham Memorial Hall was built by public subscription after the First World War in 1929. On the eastern side stand two large villas overlooking the Peace Gardens. Ashburnham House, faced in yellow brick, was built in 1888 and has a lodge by the Old London Road. Patcham Grange in Grangeways is a large, timber-framed residence of 1893, now a nursing home.

By the bend in the footpath from Grangeways to Overhill Way once stood Ballard's Mill, a squat smock-mill of around 1780 but removed just prior to 1900, although the ground floor was retained as a store until the 1920s; this was probably the site of the mill mentioned in the seventeenth and eighteenth centuries. The Mill House and some flint outbuildings remain, while nearby, at the southern end of Highview Avenue South, are the heavily-restored Mill Cottages which probably date from the same time as the mill. Old Mill Close nearby is named from this mill. <83,107,128,249a,249b,311>

Figure 115: Mill Cottages, Highview Avenue South

g) *PEACE GARDENS:* Patcham Peace Gardens cover 3.12 acres of land which were purchased from the Abergavenny estate in June 1928, chiefly through the efforts of Herbert Carden; it had been planned to build a petrol station on the site. The northern half of the gardens is a simple grassed area, but the southern half was laid out as an attractive sunken rose garden and includes a Tuscan pergola and a small Doric temple, both purchased from the 1924 Wembley Exhibition; the temple is decorated with fruit motifs and figureheads. Some statues from the Aquarium were re-sited here in 1929, but were later removed. By the roadway at the southern end is an 1897 drinking fountain which originally stood in the London Road at Home Farm, Withdean, until the road was widened. <26a,126>

h) *THE CHATTRI:* Standing 500 feet above sea-level on the Downs to the north of Patcham Court Farm, and accessed by bridleway only, is the Chattri, a memorial to the Indian soldiers who died at the Royal Pavilion when it was used as a hospital in the First World War. Now a listed building, the Chattri was erected by the India Office in conjunction with the corporation on the site of the 'ghat' (place of cremation), and was designed in white Sicilian marble by the student architect E.C.Henriques under the supervision of Sir Samuel Jacob. It is an octagonal, domed monument with pillars twenty-nine feet high on a stone plinth; three granite blocks cover the concrete crematory slabs. The memorial was unveiled by the Prince of Wales on 1 February 1921, and bears the following inscription: 'To the memory of all the Indian soldiers who gave their lives in the service of their King-Emperor this monument, erected on the site where the Hindus and Sikhs who died in hospital at Brighton passed through the fire, is in grateful admiration and brotherly affection dedicated'. Two acres around the Chattri have been laid out as a garden. <44,126,194>

123. POLICE

a) *ORIGINS:* For centuries law and order in the town was kept by the high constable and his assistants <162>, but by the nineteenth century Brighton had grown sufficiently in population and status to warrant better policing. The 1810 Brighton Town Act authorised the town commissioners to appoint eight 'watchmen' in January 1812 to patrol the town at night; another sixteen were appointed by December 1815, and were assisted by patrols of inhabitants and one special constable until 1818. In January 1821 the town was divided into eight watch districts, each with a box for the watchman; two years later the watch force consisted of sixteen men under the control of two superintendents at the old Town Hall in Market Street. The watchmen were dressed in top hats, black tail-coats and white trousers, and were armed with batons and rattles; until 1829 they also called the hours and the weather.

In 1830 a Mr Pilbeam was appointed as chief officer of the watchmen in an attempt to establish a more permanent force, but it proved to be largely ineffective and the men were eventually dismissed. They were replaced in 1838, however, by the first fully professional police force in the town, based at the new Town Hall and consisting of a chief constable, two superintendents, a night constable, three inspectors and twenty-four men. On 13 March 1844 though, the chief constable, Henry Solomon, was murdered at the Town Hall by one John Lawrence who was subsequently hanged at Lewes Prison. <112,163,164>

b) *CORPORATION CONTROL and GROWTH:* By 1854 the force comprised ten officers and fifty-one men, and in that year came under the control of the watch committee of the newly-formed Brighton Borough Council; indeed, the council's first act was to raise the force's strength by ten men, and to appoint a police surgeon and a plain-clothes detective. In 1855 the tail-coat uniforms were replaced by frock-coats, and in 1868 top hats were replaced by helmets.

By 1865 the force's strength had increased to one hundred officers and men. Further increases were made steadily over the next seventy years such that the total strength by 1901 was 150, 200 by 1921, 219 by 1938, 256 by 1956, 327 by 1961, and 424 by 1967; the first women were appointed in 1918. During the Second World War, from 1 April 1943 until 31 March 1947, a single force operated throughout Sussex. On 1 January 1968 the Brighton Police Force was combined with the East Sussex, West Sussex, Eastbourne and Hastings forces to form the Sussex Constabulary, based at Malling House, Lewes. Brighton is now a sub-division of the Central Division of the Sussex Constabulary.

The Brighton force was distinguished by its use of white helmets each summer from 1933 until 1939, and again between 1952 and 1968. It was also the first force in the world to operate with personal radios, one-way only from the central station to the constable from September 1933. <163,164>

c) *CENTRAL POLICE STATION:* The watchmen were first based at the old Town Hall in Market Street, which had a primitive lock-up known as the 'Black Hole'. A new watch station was included when the present Town Hall was erected in 1830-2 in Bartholomews. Although condemned in 1929 by the Inspectorate of Constabulary, Brighton's main police station remained in a large basement department at the Town Hall until a new station was built in John Street. Designed by borough engineer Percy Billington, the new Brighton police station was opened on 27 September 1965 by the Home Secretary, Sir Frank Soskice, but must be included amongst the ugliest of the town's public buildings. <112,123,163,164>

d) *DISTRICT POLICE STATIONS:* The first district police station was established in about 1857 at 64 St James's Street, a building with a balustered roof and urn decorations that still stands near the corner of Grafton Street; in 1885 it was replaced by no.2 Freshfield Road. Other district stations were established at the south-western end of the Level (c.1865-1919), 26 West Hill Road (1876-1919), and at Preston Circus fire station from 1903. No.18 Middle Road, Preston, was a police station by 1871, while Patcham police station was established by 1888 on a site now occupied by the Homeleigh flats in London Road. Rottingdean police station stood on the western side of the High Street by 1888, between Marine Drive and West Street, and moved to a house in West Street in 1916. There was a second station in Rottingdean parish in the 1880s and '90s at 25 Rifle Butt Road, Black Rock.

In 1928 however, most district police stations were discontinued, to be replaced by special telephone call-boxes; the Rottingdean station continued until 1931, though. A new Rottingdean station opened in 1959 at 53 Marine Drive.

In 1947 a police training school was established in some large villas at 21-27 Wellington Road. Two years later the school was converted into a police station, and the town was then divided into A and B divisional areas based at the Town Hall and Wellington Road. The Wellington Road station closed when the new John Street station opened in 1965, and the buildings were replaced by blocks of flats. <83,163,164>

e) *CHIEF CONSTABLES of the BRIGHTON POLICE FORCE 1838-1967* <164>:

1838 Henry Solomon
1844 Thomas Chase
1853 George White
1876 Owen Crowhurst
1877 Isaiah Barden
1881 James Terry
1894 Thomas Cartere
1901 William Gentle
1920 Charles Griffin
1933 William Hutchinson
1956 Charles Ridge
1957 Albert Rowsell
1963 William Carey

124. POLYTECHNIC

Brighton Polytechnic was established in April 1970 by a merger of the Colleges of Art and Technology. It expanded in September 1976 by absorbing the College of Education, and in April 1979 incorporated the East Sussex College of Higher Education at Eastbourne. The polytechnic was formally opened on 5 February 1971, but was made independent of East Sussex County Council in 1989. In 1989 the polytechnic had approximately 5,400 students on main sites at Falmer, Moulsecoomb and Grand Parade, with annexes at Bear Road, Finsbury Road, Pavilion Parade, and Eastbourne. <123>

The Faculty of Art and Design started life in 1858 as the Brighton School of Art in the great kitchen of the Royal Pavilion in Palace Place. In 1874 it became the School of Art and Science, and two years later moved to a new Italianate building by John Gibbins in Grand Parade which was opened by Princess Louise. When the corporation took control from the trustees in 1892, they removed the science departments to Richmond Terrace to form the Municipal Technical College, and then enlarged the Grand Parade building in 1910 and again from 1919. In 1947 the Municipal School of Art became the College of Arts and Crafts, but the need for further expansion was recognised in 1965 when the whole college was rebuilt in a four-storey design by Percy Billington. The major portion of the new college opened in June 1967; it has been acclaimed as one of the better 1960s buildings in the town. The Sallis Benney Theatre, named after the inter-war principal, seats an audience of 400. <83,115,123>

Brighton College of Technology opened on the site of some school playing fields in Lewes Road in 1963, and was intended for more advanced studies than those offered by the Technical College. The ten-storey Cockroft Building was followed in 1976 by the seven-storey Watts building, named after the college's first principal. Mithras House, erected at Dewe Road in 1966 as administrative offices for Allen West Ltd, has been used since 1977. (Note that the former Technical College is now known as the Brighton College of Technology.) <123>

The Falmer campus was opened in 1965 for the Brighton College of Education, a teacher-training college. In 1909 the pupil-teacher centre (for 13- to 18-year-olds) of the York Place Schools became the Municipal Training College for elementary and secondary school teachers, at 10 Richmond Terrace in a building on the northern side of the Municipal Technical College. By 1918 9-10 Hanover Crescent were also in use, but the college moved to Eastern Terrace in 1919 to release space for the technical college, and remained there until September 1965 when it moved to Falmer; it had been renamed the College of Education the previous year. From 1919 until 1961, only women were instructed at the Municipal Training College. <83,123,210>

125. POOL VALLEY

<3,10,14,15,44,289>

Referred to in a document of 1296 and again in 1497 simply as 'the Poole', Pool Valley is the natural drainage point for most of Brighton, the place where the Wellesbourne (q.v.) discharged into the sea. It is probable that there was once a small inlet or pool in the foreshore at this point, providing a small haven and easy access to the Steine onto which fishing boats could be hauled. In 1792-3 however, the Wellesbourne was culverted when a sewer to drain the Steine was constructed, and Pool Valley was bricked over. Being the town's natural drainage point, Pool Valley has often flooded or been inundated by the sea. In November 1723 a large vessel was 'cast into the Poole', and on 26 January 1795 a rapid thaw caused flooding to a depth of seven feet. It was inundated again on 23 November 1824 and on 17 July 1850.

The way from Pool Valley into East Street was via the East Gate of the town until 1760 when it was removed for the construction of the battery. Before the construction of the Grand Junction Road, Pool Valley sloped gently to the beach, but the roadway was raised to meet the main road in 1869. The southern side is now dominated by the Cannon Cinema (q.v.), but the north-western side retains some old shop fronts at nos.2 and 5, and also at no.9, the Continental Restaurant. This interesting, grade II*-listed building was erected in 1794 and is faced with black mathematical tiles; for about 150 years it was used by the Cowley family as a bun shop. The adjacent twitten, Pool Passage, leads to Old Steine and is lined with old flint walls.

The western arm of Pool Valley was pedestrianised in 1987, but the road is best known now for the inadequate coach station, formed at the rear of Royal York Buildings (q.v.) in 1929.

See also "Royal Albion Hotel".

Figure 116: Pool Valley in the storm of 17 July 1850

126. The POOR

a) *HISTORY:* In contrast to many other seaside towns, Brighton has always had more than its fair share of poverty. The parish as a whole claimed relief from taxation in 1341 on the grounds of poverty, and in 1580 the town was said to be burdened with 'the multitude of poor people, which daily are thought to increase' <273>. The first Poor Law Act was passed in 1563. requiring two officers in each parish to collect a poor rate for the relief of poverty, and by 1690 a tenement in East Street was being used as a poorhouse. The 'deserving poor', i.e. those paupers who came from the parish, were cared for in the workhouses and given useful work to do such as net-making and oakum (old rope) picking. The 'outdoor poor' remained in their own homes, but were given a weekly allowance, either in money or in kind in the form of clothes, coal, etc. Recipients of parish relief were made to wear the town badge, however. In 1690 the Lewes Justices made a rate in the neighbouring parishes for the relief of poverty in Brighton which, in 1708, was extended throughout the whole of eastern Sussex. By the mid eighteenth century only 115 out of 450 rateable properties in Brighton were not exempt from the poor rate .

Until 1810 the poor law was administered by the parish in the form of the overseers, but the Brighton Town Act of that year transferred control to thirty 'Directors and Guardians of the Poor', nominated annually by the town commissioners. One of their first actions was to 'improve' the workhouse diet in the interests of economy. The 1825 Brighton Town Act gave the election of guardians to the parish ratepayers, but the 1834 Poor Law Amendment Act reorganised the whole system of relief. Outdoor relief was abolished, and in order to obtain allowances people were forced to enter the workhouse where conditions were deliberately made harsh to discourage all but the totally destitute; the Act therefore had the desired effect of reducing the numbers claiming relief. Most parishes were amalgamated into larger unions (Patcham and Preston into Steyning Union; Falmer, Ovingdean, Rottingdean and Stanmer into Newhaven Union), but Brighton remained a separate union on its own. In 1862 the guardians opened an industrial school at Warren Farm, Woodingdean, for poor boys and girls whom it was not considered desirable to keep with adults at the workhouse.

On 18 March 1871 the Brighton Directors and Guardians were replaced by a 'Board of Guardians of the Poor', responsible to the Local Government Board (replaced in 1919 by the Ministry of Health) and continuing to administer the workhouse. Some allowances such as old-age pensions and limited unemployment benefit were introduced nationally in the 1900s and '10s, but the workhouse system remained in operation until 1 April 1930 when the local board of guardians was replaced by the county borough council's public assistance committee under the 1929 Local Government Act. In 1934 a national Unemployment Assistance Board was established, and in 1940 a general Assistance Board was created to cater for other types of relief. The years following the Second World War saw further increases in benefits with the replacement of the poor-law system by the 'Welfare State' on the so-called 'Appointed Day', 5 July 1948. In 1966 the National Assistance Board and National Insurance combined to form the Ministry of Social Security, now the D.S.S., while East Sussex County Council took over responsibility for social services from the county borough council on 1 April 1974.
<1,14,95,112,115,275a,296a,300>

See also "Parishes" and "Workhouses".

b) *NINETEENTH-CENTURY CHARITIES:* Numerous charitable and voluntary institutions were established in the nineteenth century to care for those who could not afford to care for themselves, but who did not enter the workhouse. Medical help was provided by the dispensaries (see "Hospitals and Dispensaries"), lying-in institutions, and medical missionary societies. Other societies such as the Mutual Provident Society and the Dollar Society allowed poor people to invest hard-earned money, to be returned with interest when it was most needed. Co-operatives were formed to reduce the cost of food and other essentials to the poor (see "Co-operatives"). In 1829 the first soup kitchen was established at

Figures 117 and 118: Beggars in Victorian Brighton

Spring Gardens, and permanent soup kitchens were opened at Mighell Street and Ship Street in 1839 with several others later; they lasted well into the twentieth century. Winter warmth was also provided by the Brighton and Preston Blanket Lending Society which continued until 1940. Numerous societies also tried to improve the moral welfare of the poor, including temperance societies, the Salvation Army, and the Brighton and Hove Town Mission. 'Model Dwellings for the Poor' were provided by a charitable trust in Church Street (still standing) and Clarence Yard in the 1850s. Elementary education for the poor was provided by the church and a number of charitable societies (see "Schools"), while the council built public slipper baths at North Road, Cobden Road, Ditchling Road, Park Street and the Aquarium. Similar to domestic baths, the slipper baths lasted into the 1970s and enabled the poor of the town to keep themselves clean at low cost; they were also popular social meeting places. <2,3,6,7,24,115,275a>

c) *HOUSING:* Brighton has always been a town of contrasts, and nowhere has this been more apparent than in the difference in the housing between the fashionable crescents, squares and terraces of the sea-front and central valleys, and the back-street terraces of the adjacent hillsides; physically close, but worlds apart in the conditions to be found there.

The Old Town naturally became densely populated and was infilled with small, squalid courtyards, but as the town grew outside its ancient limits in the early nineteenth century large areas of low quality housing were erected behind the fashionable terraces, particularly on the slopes of Albion Hill around Carlton Hill, Edward Street and Sussex Street; in the Russell Street area; and off Church Street. These slums were as bad as any to be found in London or the industrial north, although perhaps on a smaller scale. In 1849 the General Board of Health's inspector Edward Cresy made a detailed report on the town's sanitation with regard to the adoption of the Public Health Act. He observed that open cesspits near drinking wells were common, that the few sewers that had been built often ran above basement level, and that many families were crowded into tenements lining tiny streets and courtyards in these areas; consequently, the health of the poor was generally in a terrible state. His recommendations included the universal use of sewers for removal of privy waste, the provision of a universal pure water supply, the regulation of slaughterhouses, and the provision of an out-of-town cemetery. Another report by Dr William Kebbell in 1848 had painted a similar picture of the town's poorer districts; Kebbell himself was the chairman of the charitable trust which built the Model Dwellings for the Poor in Church Street and Clarence Yard in the 1850s. <2,14,76,284>

The 1860 adoption of the Local Government Act by Brighton Corporation allowed improvements to be made to the sewerage and the other causes for concern. The first slum clearances were made for the construction of Queen's Road in 1845, when Durham, Petty France and part of Air Street were demolished, but the first specific corporation slum clearances aimed at improving housing conditions were at Pimlico, Pym's Gardens and Orange

Figure 119: The Model Dwellings in Church Street, provided for working men by a charitable trust in about 1852

Row, which were replaced by Tichborne Street in about 1876. Further clearances and new housing followed at Little St James's Street (replaced by St James's Avenue) in 1889; Chesterfield Street, Cumberland Street, Derby Place and Thomas Street (replaced by Blaker and White Streets, inhabitants rehoused in Ewart Street) in 1896; Egremont Street and Spa Street (replaced by Tillstone Street) in 1898; and the most inappropriately named Paradise Street north of Hereford Street in 1926. <2,76,83,115,275a>.

These nineteenth-century clearances were followed by the erection of new homes by private builders. The first council-built and rented houses were erected in the late 1890s at St Helen's Road, on land given by Henry Abbey and Daniel Friend in December 1897 to mark Queen Victoria's diamond jubilee. The small yellow- and red-brick houses were first let in 1900 at 7s. 6d. (37.5p) per week, and still stand on the western side of the road. Similar housing followed at Dewe Road and at May Road (now demolished). <2,115>

In 1921 Brighton was recorded as the most densely populated county borough in the country with the sole exception of West Ham. The first large-scale council housing developments were made at Moulsecoomb (q.v.) and at the Queen's Park estate around Pankhurst Avenue in the 1920s, but it was not until the next decade, when the government made subsidies for slum clearance available for the first time, that the corporation started to tackle the housing problem on the scale required. Large clearances were made in the 1930s in the Carlton Hill, Upper Bedford Street and Upper Russell Street areas, while large housing estates were developed in the suburbs to rehouse former slum-dwellers; before the Second World War Moulsecoomb was extended, and the Whitehawk and Manor Farm estates were also laid out. However, the war brought a halt to the renewal programme, and the slums persisted until the 1950s when they were even described as the worst in Europe. <2,48a,123>

In the late '50s and '60s virtually all the Albion Hill area was cleared and redeveloped, along with large areas off Church Street, Upper Bedford Street and to the west of London Road. Now tower-block flats dominate the skyline in many areas, and there are twenty council blocks of ten storeys or more at Albion Hill; off Edward Street; Upper Hollingdean Road; Upper Bedford Street; and at north Whitehawk. The first of these blocks was Highleigh, one of four built in the phase-one Albion Hill redevelopment which was officially opened by the mayor, Alan Johnson, on 16 May 1961. The tallest council block is Theobald House which opened in Blackman Street in 1966 with 110 flats in nineteen storeys above a 310-space car-park. Large post-war council estates have also been developed at Bevendean, Coldean, Hollingbury, Hollingdean and Woodingdean, such that there are approximately 11,400 council-owned dwellings in the borough. <123>

With the obvious slum housing eradicated, the worst housing conditions are now found in the bed-sitters and flats converted from former fashionable housing, particularly in the Regency area, and also in the earliest of the council estates. With its abundant deprivation and unemployment, Brighton therefore remains, enigmatically, both one of the richest and yet one of the poorest towns in the country.

127. POPULATION

Contrary to popular belief, Brighton has been more than a 'small fishing village' since medieval times, and has always been one of the largest towns in Sussex. From 1285 the town was considered important enough to warrant its own constable, and a weekly market and fair were granted in 1313. Indeed, by the mid seventeenth century the fisheries were so prosperous that Brighton had become the largest town in Sussex, but its position and population declined with a local recession in the early eighteenth century. However, with the increasing importance of the town as a health resort from the mid eighteenth century, Brighton has prospered, and and has again been the largest town in the county since the early nineteenth century. <1>

The first official census of population was taken in 1801, and has been repeated at ten year intervals since except in 1941. Given below are estimates of the town's population at various dates based on a variety of evidence, and the census night figures since 1801. Figures relate to the parish of Brighton until 1851, and to the borough thereafter. <13,279>

1086	c.400	1831	40,634
1566	c.1,100	1841	46,661
1570	c.1,200	1851	65,569
1640	c.2,850	1861	77,693
1650	c.4,000	1871	90,011
1676	c.3,340	1881	99,091
1724	c.2,375	1891	102,716
1730	c.1,900	1901	123,478
1744	c.2,380	1911	131,327
1747	c.2,150	1921	142,430
1753	c.2,140	1931	147,427
1761	c.2,035	1941	c.127,300
1770	c.3,140	1951	156,486
1780	c.3,400	1961	163,159
1786	3,620	1968	c.164,680
1794	5,669	1971	161,351
1801	7,339	1981	149,400
1811	12,012	1989	c.143,100
1821	24,429		

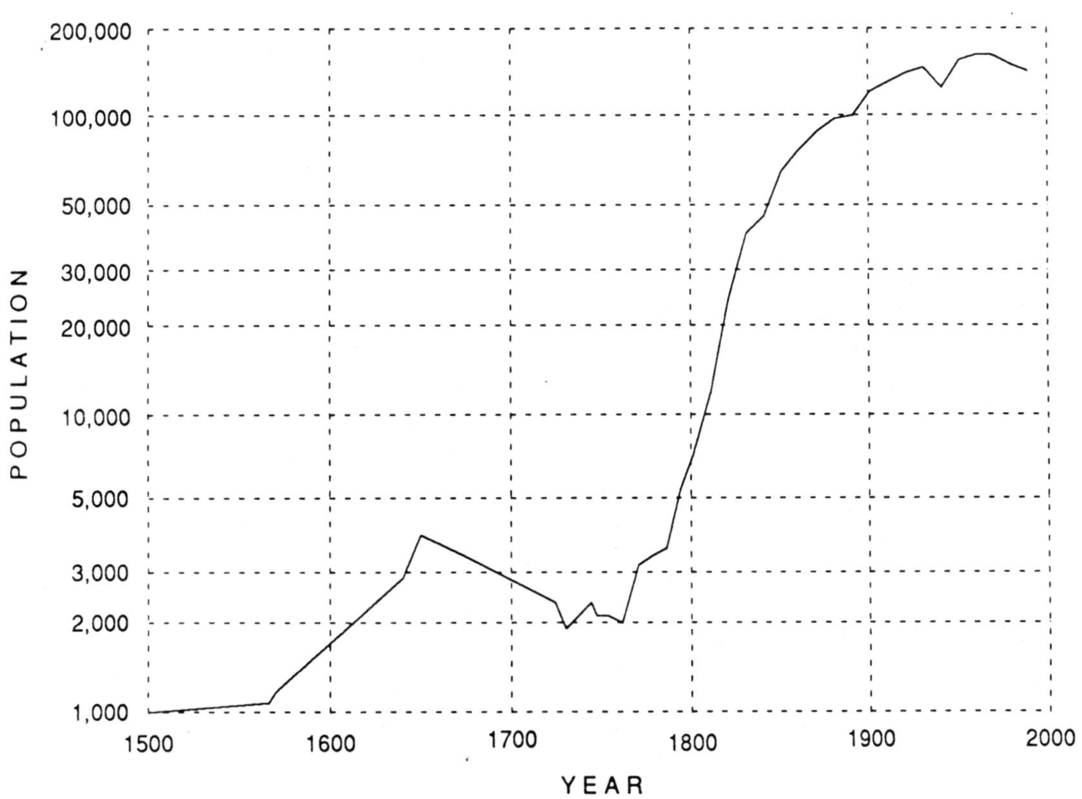

Figure 120: The growth of Brighton's population

It can be seen that the town grew considerably and then declined as the returns from the fisheries first waxed and then waned in the seventeenth and eighteenth centuries. The population rose again with the advent of the resort function, and received another large boost with the arrival of the railway in the 1840s.

Although largely a matter of definition, by 1851 Brighton was approximately the 15th largest town in England and Wales; in 1981 it was the 27th, but the population of around 280,000 of the entire built-up area from Shoreham to Saltdean is about the 17th largest conurbation; indeed one reference <299a> counts the Brighton conurbation, including Worthing and Littlehampton, as the 13th largest in the U.K. and the 10th of

England and Wales. In terms of borough and district council populations, Brighton was only the 99th largest in England and Wales in 1987. According to the Registrar General's annual figures, which are based on births and deaths, the peak population of Brighton was 164,680, attained in 1968 <294b,303>.

128. PORT of BRIGHTON

<1,2,3,10,18,112,123>

It has been suggested that a small creek once extended northwards from Pool Valley, and even that the area in East Street in front of the Sussex Tavern was the site of a wharf, but there is no direct evidence for either of these suggestions. Nevertheless, Brighton was always considered to be a port, forming part of the Port of Shoreham, and was named in the official lists of English sea-ports as early as 1301 and again in the mid sixteenth century when it was required to send ships and men for war fleets. In 1766 the limits of the Port of Brighton were officially marked for customs purposes by two four-foot-high stones set in the cliff top. The eastern stone, near the bottom of Ship Street, bore this inscription: 'This and the other pillar at a distance of 600 feet westwards were erected to ascertain the boundaries of the Port of Brighthelmstone, anno 1766 by order of Sir William Musgrave, Bart, Samuel Mead, Edward Hooper and Henry Banks Esquires, Commissioners of the Customs'; it was removed when the sea-wall was constructed, but the western stone near the bottom of West Street remained until the late nineteenth century. As late as 1860 official notices referred to the Port of Brighthelmston.

The construction of a harbour at Brighton was first suggested in 1800, if not earlier, but the idea was generally opposed by residents who did not want the town to develop as a trading port. An 1806 plan by Ralph Dodd proposed piers at East Street and West Street, but was rejected at a town meeting. In 1824 William Bush constructed a small dock near Black Rock to allow for the easy offloading of building materials for the Kemp Town estate, which were then carted through the Black Rock tunnel, but it was probably dismantled when the estate was virtually complete <46>. An 1841 scheme by Captain J.N.Taylor won vestry approval for an experiment, and three large, floating breakwaters were moored to the Chain Pier on 23 December 1844 and left for about a year, but the sections were then towed to Shoreham and no more was heard of the scheme; one section was, however, washed up on Brighton beach and the timber sold for £148. In 1842 George Wigney proposed the construction of two breakwaters from West Street and Royal Crescent around the Chain Pier, and other schemes followed in 1846, 1850, 1884 and into the twentieth century. All came to nothing though, until the construction of Brighton Marina at Black Rock in the 1970s, but even then a plan was made in April 1974 for a second marina incorporating the two piers.

The principal French port for Sussex traffic is Dieppe, which lies 72 miles distant from Brighton although both Fécamp and Boulogne are nearer at 68 miles. In 1764 a regular packet service commenced between the two towns, but following the end of the Napoleonic Wars there was a great increase in traffic such that there were nine packets on the route in 1817 and nearly 2,500 passengers were conveyed to France during that summer. The *Swift*, the first of many steam ships on the route, made its maiden journey on 25 May 1822; soon after, the General Steam Navigation Company put on two vessels which made the journey in about ten hours.

Cross-Channel passengers were usually conveyed from the beach between Ship Street and Middle Street by small rowing boats to ships moored in deeper water, but the opening of the Chain Pier in 1823 enabled passengers to disembark directly for the first time. At this time Brighton was the busiest cross-Channel port in England, and was on the quickest route between London and Paris as overland speeds were roughly the same as those at sea. Facilities were never as good as a natural harbour though, and in 1825 steam-packets started running from Newhaven, and from Shoreham in 1826. The opening of the railway to Newhaven on 8 December 1847, and the construction of ships for the Newhaven route by the London, Brighton and South Coast Railway Company, then sealed the fate of passenger traffic from Brighton.

A small revival between the wars came in the form of cross-Channel day-trips from the two piers, while Sussex coastal steamers continued to operate until about 1960. A jet hydrofoil service, the 110-ton Boeing *Flying Princess*, operated from Brighton Marina to Dieppe from 27 April 1979 until it was forced to close on 29 August 1980. Travelling at up to fifty knots, the 'Seajet' reduced the journey time to just two hours but was greatly affected by bad weather.

129. POSTAL SERVICES

<15,83,165-166>

a) *EARLY SERVICES:* The earliest reference to a Brighton mail service was in 1675, when the General Post Office established a route from Chichester to Lewes via Shoreham and Brighton. By 1788 and the arrival of fashionable society, there was a daily post from Brighton to London in the summer and four times weekly during the winter. The first Royal Mail Patent Coach from Brighton to London ran on 29 April 1791 via Lewes, and a new mail coach via Cuckfield commenced on 10 May 1810 taking eight hours, but it was replaced in 1813 by an armed rider.

b) *BRIGHTON POST-OFFICE:* The earliest known postal house in the town was sited at the Old Ship in the 1750s with the proprietor as post-master, but it moved several times before the present Ship Street premises opened. In 1777 it moved to the south-eastern side of Middle Street; to 92 North Street in about 1780; to Thomas's Library in 1781; to Crawford's Library in about 1784; to the northern end of Prince's Place in 1803; to 67 East Street in September 1822; to 149 North Street in June 1827; and to 22 New Road on 23 September 1831, a building which still stands and is decorated with fluted pilasters.

The introduction of the penny-post in 1840 brought about a large increase in mail which necessitated larger central premises. The Head Post-Office in Ship Street was therefore opened on 26 March 1849 (at the bend of the street), and was enlarged in August 1858. It was extended again in 1870 to accommodate the telegraph operation with letter-sorting removed to Brighton Station. In 1892 the Head Post-Office was expanded further northwards into adjoining premises in Ship Street where a new entrance was made, and a new sorting-office was opened at the rear on the site of the Model Dwellings. In 1926 the sorting-office was removed to a new building on the site of the Regent Foundry in North Road, extended to Gloucester Road in 1937. The former drill hall in Church Street has been used full-time for parcel-sorting since 1967.

c) *DEVELOPMENT OF THE POSTAL SERVICE:* By 1823 mail collectors ringing bells were accepting letters at the cost of one penny, and they continued collecting until 1846. In 1830 receiving houses were established at 90 St James's Street; 50 Preston Street; 17 St George's Place; and in 1832 at 2 Rock Street. Soon after, a central area of the town was defined from Cannon Place to Charlotte Street and north to Sussex Street, outside of which a surcharge of one penny was made for deliveries; this inner district was later extended to include the London Road area, but surcharges were dropped when the universal 'penny post' was introduced on 10 January 1840.

At this time the Brighton postal service had three clerks, fourteen letter carriers, and three messengers for Hove, Hurstpierpoint and Rottingdean. There were two deliveries daily and four receiving houses, with houses also at the villages of Ovingdean, Preston and Rottingdean. By 1848 further receiving houses had opened at 56 Marine Parade, 7 Belgrave Terrace (now part of Marine Parade at Belgrave Place), 66 King's Road, and at the western side of Queen's Road Quadrant.

The town's first pillar-box was erected in March 1858 in Lewes Road opposite the Percy Almshouses; another followed at the Seven Dials by July 1858, and in December another five appeared at the corners of Montpelier Road and Western Road; Old Steine and Marine Parade; Marine Parade and Marine Square; at Sussex Square; and at Holland Road, Hove. The Montpelier Road/Western Road box survives and is now listed as being of special interest. Built to the first national standard type-A design, it is thought to be the one of only four of its type remaining in service and has a distinctively shaped top <44>. (Brighton has another unusual pillar-box at the corner of Dale Crescent and Warmdene Road, Patcham, a rare Edward VIII model.)

From August 1869 there were four deliveries daily, with two a day to Preston, Patcham and Rottingdean. There were also thirty-five pillar- and wall-boxes with seven daily collections, and sixteen receiving houses with another two added in 1879-80. By 1892 there were five branch offices manned by head office staff, thirty-six receiving offices, and sixty-eight boxes with ten to twelve collections daily (!); in that year the receiving houses were redesignated sub-post-offices. Branch offices were opened at Cannon Place (1891, replacing the West Pier kiosk); Church Road, Hove (1882); College Road (1887); Western Road/Hampton Place (1973, but at Dean Street from 1890, and former Boots store 1928-66); Melville Road, Hove (1930); Oxford Street (1929, relocated 1967); St James's Street (1910); and Western Road, Hove (1885).

Brighton is now the centre of a large postal area stretching westwards past Arundel, northwards to Hurstpierpoint, and eastwards to Pevensey. The sorting office now handles over 1 million letters and packets every day.

130. PRESTON (including Preston Park Conservation Area)

a) *HISTORY:* Now a large suburb, Preston was once just a small village about 1.5 miles north-north-west of Brighton. At the time of the Domesday survey in 1086 the manor was held by the Bishop of Chichester, and a church and a mill, probably a cattle-mill or water-mill, were also recorded <18,282>; the population was less than fifty. The name is Anglo-Saxon, meaning 'priest's farmstead', and the village was often called 'Preston Episcopi' to distinguish it from similarly named settlements. The Archbishop of Canterbury himself stayed at Preston in 1230. <1>

The village was a favourite resort in the late eighteenth and early nineteenth centuries, an easy horse-ride from Brighton, and the tea gardens between Middle Road and North Road were an attraction for excursionists by 1770 until about 1815. By 1801 the population was 222.

The first Victorian developments in Preston came in the 1860s with the Prestonville (q.v.) and Clermont (see below) estates of middle-class and artisan housing. However, most of the parish formed part of the manorial estate of the Stanford family which was also sold off for development from the mid 1860s. The Stanford estate was developed with strict planning controls, and consequently remains an area of high quality housing. By 1885 a number of villa residences had been erected along the western side of Preston Road, in Stanford Avenue, and in Springfield Road, while a large area of middle-class terracing had been developed around Ditchling Rise and the area to the south now known as the St Saviour's district. By 1900 the large, attractive, residential area between Preston Park and Ditchling Road had been built, mostly in red brick and stucco, and within another ten years most of the parish had been developed including estates at Hollingdean, Tivoli Crescent, and at the area around Coombe Road known as East Preston; by 1921 the population of Preston had grown to 31,440. Only the eastern side of the Hollingdean estate has been developed since the Second World War. <45a,83>

The parish of Preston was only one mile north to south at its widest point, but it stretched 3.2 miles from Nevill Road in the west to Race Hill in the east, and covered an area of 1,308 acres. The southern boundary ran roughly along the line of Old Shoreham Road, New England Road, Viaduct Road, Ditchling Road, Hollingdean Road and Bear Road, while the northernmost point was reached at Hollingbury Rise West. On 31 October 1873, with the population over 2,500, that part of the parish to the east of Dyke Road was added to the borough of Brighton for municipal purposes only; the parochial boundary remained unaltered until 1894, when that part of the parish to the west of Dyke Road (i.e. the part not within the borough) was constituted as Preston Rural parish in Steyning East rural district, leaving the part within the borough as the new parish of Preston. On 1 October 1923 94 acres of Patcham, the South Moulsecoomb estate, were added to both Preston parish and Brighton county borough. At at the creation of 'Greater Brighton' on 1 April 1928 Preston parish was absorbed from the Steyning Union by Brighton for parochial purposes as well, while the parish and borough of Hove annexed Preston Rural. <1,38,109>

In 1970 Preston village was designated a conservation area, which was greatly extended in 1977 to include the large area of high quality, late-Victorian red-brick and stucco housing eastwards to Ditchling Road. In 1988 the conservation area was split into Preston Village and Preston Park conservation areas; the former includes the village and, confusingly, the park, while the latter covers the Victorian and Edwardian areas. For more information on Preston village refer to the following entry. <1,15,147,148>

See also "Bear Road and East Preston", "Ditchling Road", "Dyke Road", "Hollingdean", "Preston Road" and "Prestonville".

b) *CLERMONT ESTATE:* Lying to the north of the old village, the Clermont Estate was developed with middle-class housing from 1866 by Daniel Friend, and includes Clermont Road, Clermont Terrace, Lorne Villas, and Station Road, together with some larger villas in Preston Road (q.v.); Preston (later Preston Park) Station opened in 1869 to serve the new estate. Clermont United Reformed Church was erected in 1877-8 by J.G.Gibbins as a Congregational church, in Decorated style in flint and yellow brick; the church hall was built in 1880 and enlarged in 1926. <62,76,311>

c) *STANFORD AVENUE:* This wide road was developed from the 1880s on Stanford family land with large semi-detached villas; other substantial housing, including a good red-brick row at nos.97-117, was added in the 1890s and 1900s. St Augustine's Church, a large, red-brick edifice in Perpendicular style, was built in 1896 by G.E.Streatfield with a clerestoried nave and an apsidal chancel, and has stained glass by Charles Kempe of 1901-2; the church hall was built in 1901 in memory of Queen Victoria, and the parish has combined with St Saviour's. Stanford Avenue Methodist Church was built in 1897-8 in Early English Style by E.J.Hamilton, with a small lantern spire. <1,45,62,83>

d) *FLORENCE ROAD:* Florence Road has some large villas of the 1880s at its western end, with later, red-brick housing to the east. The Baptist Church is an attractive Early English design by George Baines and was erected in 1894-5. It is a large building, faced in flint with red-brick dressings, and has a spire and tower; much use has been made of stained glass. <62>

e) *PRESTON DROVE:* Preston Drove, together with Middle Road, the Drove (the steepest road in Brighton with a maximum gradient of approximately 1:4 <109>), and the Droveway, once formed an ancient trackway across the parish from Lewes to Portslade. It is now lined with substantial red-brick housing. The Blaker Recreation Ground covers 4.44 acres, the gift of Sir John Blaker in 1893, and was opened by the mayor, Sir Joseph Ewart, on 3 November 1894. Blaker also gave £1,000 for the erection of the fifty-foot-high iron clock tower which he himself inaugurated as mayor on 15 September 1896; below the cupola and dolphin weather vane is Blaker's monogram. One of Blaker's conditions on the gift was that the sale of intoxicating liquor should not be allowed. <126,147>

f) *PRESTON PARK AVENUE:* This road was developed from the 1880s with large red-brick villas, many of which still remain, but several have been replaced by blocks of flats. Whistler Court commemorates the artist Rex Whistler who was stationed in the road with the Welsh Guards during the Second World War. During his posting he decorated the wallpaper of the squadron mess at no.39, where two of his paintings were the famous 'Allegory: H.R.H. the Prince Regent awakening the Spirit of Brighton' of June 1944, and a silhouette of the Prince Regent. Whistler himself was killed during the D-Day landings, but the two pictures were presented to the town and were physically removed on the plaster-work to be framed; they now hang in the tea-room of the Royal Pavilion. Other Chinese decoration remained in the house as it was considered too difficult to remove. <3,294>

g) *OTHER BUILDINGS:* St Mary's Roman Catholic Church, Surrenden Road, was designed in Gothic style by Percy Lamb, and was built in 1910-12 in a roughened stone with a large, castellated tower. The church was completed by a 1979 extension with a large, brick cross at the rear. Florence Court on the other side of Surrenden Road stands on the site of Preston Park Baptist Church, an iron church of 1908 which was intended as the school room of a much larger church. The Elim Pentecostal Church in Balfour Road was erected in 1939. <45,62,123,311>

The former Brighton Dog Hospital of the National Canine Defence League stands at the corner of South Road and Robertson Road. It was founded in 1884 as the Sussex Temporary Home for Lost and Starving Dogs by the Misses Maria and Juliane Gregory of Withdean Lodge, in memory of their sister Caroline. The original home remains in Robertson Road, a two-storey building in red brick and knapped flint; the Modern-style building to the south was erected for the N.C.D.L. in about 1939 by Denman and Son. The home has now moved to kennels at Shoreham, but reopened in December 1988 to accept strays. <24,83,306>

131. PRESTON Village

The heart of Preston is the village, centred around North Road, Middle Road, South Road and Preston Road. The Preston Village conservation area also includes Preston Park and much of Preston Road, which have their own entries.

a) *PRESTON MANOR:* The present manor house dates largely from the eighteenth and twentieth centuries, but its origins date back to at least the thirteenth as there are the remains of a two-roomed building of that date in the basement, with two doorways from the sixteenth century. In 1738 Thomas Western had the house rebuilt above the main floor of the medieval house and small pavilions erected to flank the main block, but little now remains of the new eighteenth-century interior. The house took its present form in 1905 when Charles Peach was engaged to enlarge it; he added a dining room and a servants' wing, widened the entrance hall, and built the verandah along the north front.

As part of the manorial property, the house belonged to the bishops of Chichester until 1559 when it reverted to the crown. In 1628 the manor was leased to the Shirley family, and it then passed to the Western family in 1705. In 1794 they sold it to William Stanford, and the manor then continued in this family until the house and grounds were bequeathed to the corporation by Sir Charles and Lady Ellen Thomas-Stanford on their deaths in 1932. The house has been restored to its Edwardian heyday, and furnished with many period pieces and collections from the seventeenth, eighteenth and nineteenth centuries. Opening to the public as the Thomas-Stanford Museum in 1933, Preston Manor currently attracts some 8,000 visitors annually. Particularly impressive is the Cleves Room, lined with gilt leather which is said to have been associated with Anne of Cleves. The servants' quarters and the 'below-stairs' areas, the kitchen and laundry, have also been restored and opened to the public.

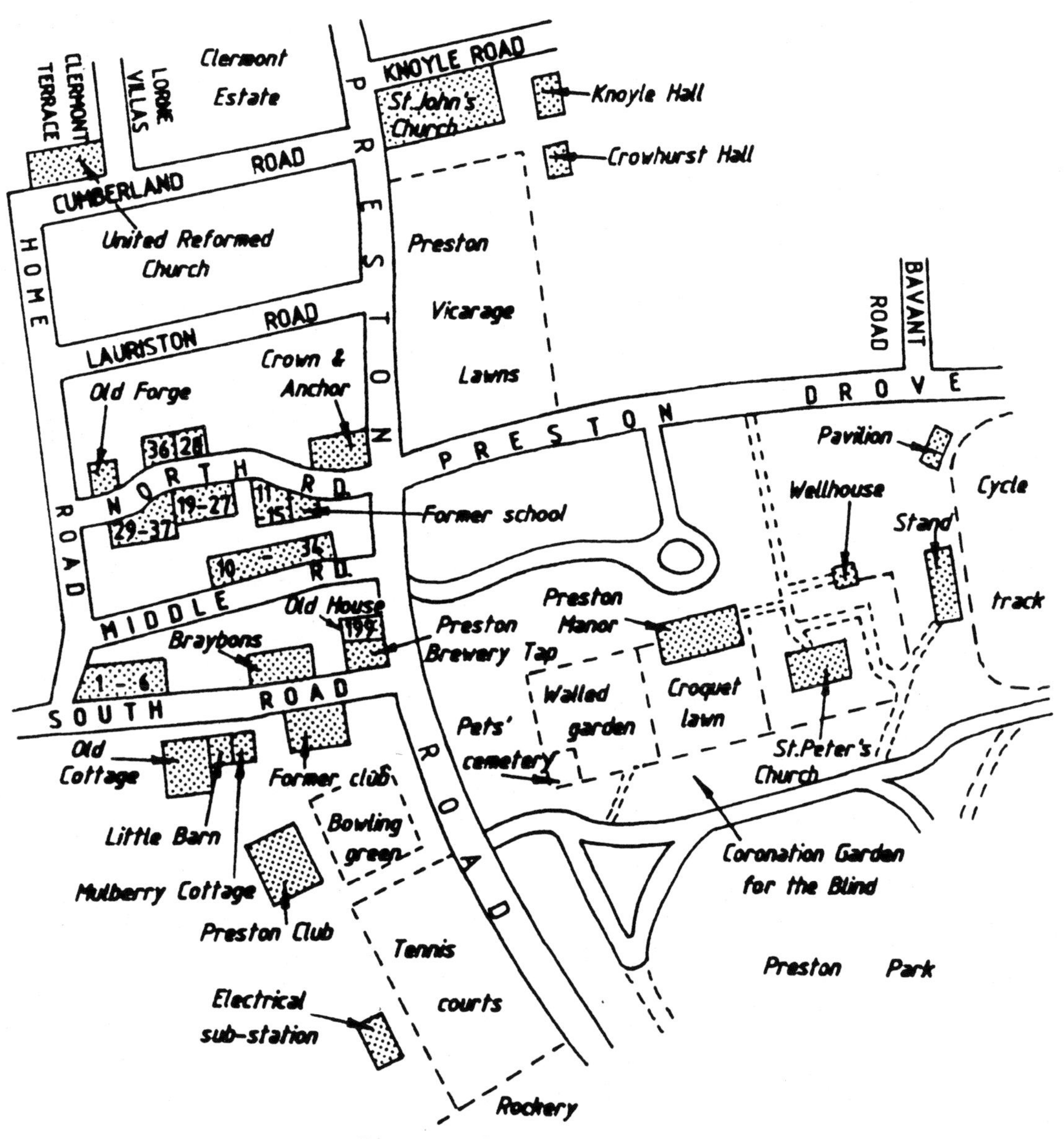

Figure 121: Preston village

A croquet lawn on the park side of the house stands adjacent to the walled garden, which has flint walls dating back to the eighteenth century and a pets' cemetery in the south-western corner. To the east of the house stands an old well-house in knapped flint which is unfortunately in a very poor condition. It dates from the 1730s and once housed an iron horse-pump and capstan. The house, garden walls, and well-house are all listed buildings, and the grounds have been designated as a garden of historic interest by English Heritage. <15,44,149>

For many years the manor house was haunted by a blonde woman dressed in white; several guests complained of unexplained happenings, and a disembodied hand was seen in the north-west bedroom. In November 1896 the spectre told a séance that she was a nun who had been wrongly expelled from the church in 1535, and that she was buried outside the house in unhallowed ground. A short time later some workmen who were clearing drains under the south terrace discovered the twisted skeleton of a woman of about fifty years of age, anything up to 400 years old. It was reburied at the edge of the churchyard, secretly after the vicar had refused on the grounds that she was a Catholic, and the ghost was not seen again. <150>

b) *ST PETER'S CHURCH:* The ancient parish church of Preston is the listed St Peter's, picturesquely situated adjacent to Preston Manor at the northern end of Preston Park and approached from Preston Drove. Dating from about 1250, the church was built in Early English style and faced in knapped flint with stone dressings; it has a nave, chancel, and a nineteenth-century porch and vestry. The tower has a Sussex cap and contains three bells, one of which is said to date from the fifteenth century. The interior, which measures only 50 feet by 26 feet, has room for 250 worshippers; it was restored in 1870 and again in 1906-7 after the building was gutted by fire on 23 June 1906. The remains of some fine mural paintings, which were discovered by Revd Charles Townsend in 1830 beneath the plaster-work, may still be seen on the walls of the nave but they were badly damaged in the fire. The principal painting depicts the murder of St Thomas Beckett, and they were possibly covered when Henry VIII ordered images of Beckett to be removed. There are also several memorials to the Stanford family of Preston Manor.

Figure 122: Preston old church, St Peter's

In 1531 the ecclesiastical parish of Preston was united with Hove, but in 1879 Preston-cum-Hove became two separate parishes once more. The Church of St John the Evangelist in Preston Road was designated Preston parish church in 1908. <1,15,18,44,45,47,64a,149>

c) *PRESTON ROAD:* At 199 Preston Road, between Middle Road and South Road, stands the Old House, an eighteenth-century listed farmhouse which has also been used as tea-rooms. Unfortunately the glazing bars of two windows have been removed, but the house remains an outstanding example of knapped and squared flint work. The Crown and Anchor was the first coaching stop outside Brighton and was rebuilt in 1894, but it dates back to at least 1711. A small parish workhouse and lock-up, known locally as the 'Black Hole', stood at the rear until 1844. <15,44>

For details on the remainder of Preston Road not within the actual village, see the separate entry on "Preston Road" itself.

d) *NORTH ROAD:* The village's northernmost road retains many old buildings, including no.28, Preston Cottage, an early-nineteenth-century cobble-fronted farmhouse, and the adjacent Garden Cottage, said to date from 1670 but with an eighteenth-century façade in knapped and squared flint; it has an impressive Doric doorway, fanlight, and broken pediment (see figure 4). Both houses are listed. Nos.19-23, a pair of cobble-fronted cottages, and nos.23-27, eighteenth-century cottages faced in knapped flint, are also listed. Other interesting buildings include nos.11-15, three cottages with bow windows, and nos.29-37, small, refronted cottages. Preston Church of England Infant School, a small Gothic building, was converted into homes in 1985-6. On the northern side at the western end stands the Old Forge, a single-storey building in brick and flint. <44,123>

e) *MIDDLE ROAD:* Part of the old drove road across the parish, Middle Road has a few old cottages, nos.10-16. No.18, a large yellow-brick building, was the village police station from at least 1871 until 1928. <83>

f) *SOUTH ROAD:* Preston Farm stood on the southern side of South Road for many years until the 1930s, but still standing is the Old Cottage, a former farmhouse faced in knapped flint with a good pedimented doorway, fanlight, and fluted Doric columns. Now a listed building, it is used by H.M.Customs and Excise, but although it bears the date 1636, the façade appears to date from the eighteenth century. The single-storey extension to the east has been divided between Mulberry Cottage and Little Barn. The large office building adjacent, Stanford House, was erected in 1908 as the original home of the Preston Club.

On the northern side, nos.1-4 are small flint cottages while nos.5-6 have bow windows, glazing bars, and shutters. To the east of these stands an old flint and brick malt-house, now occupied by Brabons but probably dating from the late eighteenth century and used by the Preston Brewery until the 1880s. <44,108,286>

Figure 123: Flint cottages at 19-27 North Road

132. PRESTON PARK, Preston Road

<24,115,124,126,311>

a) *HISTORY and DESCRIPTION:* The corporation's first public park was purchased as 67 acres of meadow land from the Bennett-Stanford family of Preston Manor in September 1883. The cost of £50,000 was taken from the 1879 bequest of £70,000 by bookmaker William Davies, who is commemorated on the pylon at the north-western entrance, but the council had previously rejected the purchase in September 1876 on the grounds of economy, when the asking price was only £30,0000.

The new park was informally opened to the public on 10 September 1883, but it was only after £22,900 had been spent on landscaping the area with trees, flower-beds, carriage drives, walks, tennis-courts and bowling-greens that it was formally opened by the mayor, Arthur Cox, on 8 November 1884. The main entrance at the southern end had a pair of handsome gates and a memorial drinking fountain, while other gates in the tall perimeter fencing were provided at Lovers Walk, and at the north-western and north-eastern corners. The chalet café in the centre of the park was opened in 1887, and housed the park police in the upper rooms.

In 1928 the park was substantially remodelled. The tall, unsightly railings and the southern entrance lodge were removed, the euonymus and other shrubs were uprooted, and more tennis-courts, bowling-greens and pavilions were provided at the southern end. The new entrances, with balustered walls and dolphin lamp-standards, were designed a little later in the 1930s.

Preston Park, covering an area of 63 acres, remains the corporation's first and largest ornamental public park. It has been the scene of many festivals, tournaments, displays and fêtes since it opened, and has numerous football pitches, tennis-courts, bowling-greens, netball-courts, etc.

An attractive rose-walk between the tennis-courts leads through the bowling-greens to a rose garden at the southern end of the park, containing a fountain and ornamental stepping-stones. Adjacent is the Rotunda Café, purchased in 1929 from the 1924 Wembley Exhibition, while the nearby southern entrance pylon commemorates the Roman villa at Preston (see "Preston Road") and the former manor of Radynden (see "Manors"). Opposite Preston Road stands the statue, unveiled in May 1987, of the Brighton-born athlete and 1980 Olympic 800-metre champion Steve Ovett, who was brought up nearby at 8 Harrington Villas and attended Varndean Grammar School for Boys. Since the 1950s the flower-beds alongside Preston Road have been used as competitive 'Gardens of Greeting' with each bed designed by another town's parks department; they present a colourful floral welcome to the town's visitors every summer.

b) *CLOCK TOWER:* The impressive red-brick and terracotta clock tower was erected at the expense of Edward White, who laid the foundation stone on 13 August 1891; it was inaugurated on 17 June 1892 by the mayor, Sir Joseph Ewart. Designed by borough surveyor Francis May, it is decorated with four broken pediments supported by Corinthian columns, and dolphin motifs with the initials EW. It bears the following delightful rhyme: 'Here I stand with all my might To tell the hour day and night. Therefore example take by me And serve thy God as I serve thee'.

c) *CORONATION GARDEN FOR THE BLIND:* Lying to the south of Preston Manor, this area of the park was laid out in Queen Elizabeth II's coronation year, 1953, as a scented garden, a gift to the blind from the corporation and their many other friends throughout the borough. The roof of the small shelter is made of 400-year-old Horsham stone from Lyminster Church.

Figure 124: The lodge entrance to Preston Park

d) *CYCLING TRACK and CRICKET GROUND:* Covering nine acres, the cricket ground was laid out in 1887 on the International Gun Polo Club grounds, and was opened on 12 May 1887 by the mayor, Edward Reeves. There is terraced seating in the north-eastern corner and the whole arena can accommodate many thousands. Indeed, regular crowds of 3,000 to 5,000 were attracted for cycle meetings after the Second World War, and a record attendance of 8,000 saw world champion Reg Harris on 4 August 1952. The simple wooden grandstand, which seats about 500, was opened on 18 October 1930 by the mayor, Horace Aldrich, and was paid for partly by a gift of Benjamin Saunders. The arena has also been used for athletics meetings, including the 1925 England v. France international, and was used by many famous international athletes for training when visiting the country. The track is now approximately 625 yards long. The cricket pavilion bears a cricketers' war memorial.

e) *THE ROCKERY:* Lying on the opposite side of Preston Road, the site of the Rockery was originally a small wood known as the Rookery; the two names are often interchanged. It was purchased along with the rest of the park, but remained in its original state, with the exception of three bowling-greens, until 1935 when the Rockery was designed by the Parks Superintendent, Captain B.MacLaren. It is the largest municipal rock garden in Britain; 1,350 tons of Cheddar stone were unloaded at the top of the railway embankment and sledded down, to be laid out below by unemployed labour.

A walk to the top of the Rockery above the artificial cascade will reward the visitor with a delightful view over the park, Preston Manor and St Peter's Church. With the tennis-courts to the north, the whole area occupies 3.5 acres. The chalet was constructed from the materials of the former police station at the Level. The large building behind the tennis-courts is an electricity substation, erected in 1924.

133. PRESTON ROAD, Preston

Preston Road runs the length of the former Preston parish, from Preston Circus to London Road (Patcham) near Clermont Road.

a) *SOUTH OF THE PARK:* The unusual terrace at the south-western end, 33-81 Preston Road, was built with a decorative brick in the 1870s as Rosneath Terrace, part of the so-called 'Dairy Estate' developed from 1871 on the site of the early-nineteenth-century dairy of the Prince of Wales; the dairy included a large private house. The estate roads were named from the family of the Marquess of Lorne, who married Princess Louise, and include Argyle and Campbell Roads <15,76>.

There is further terracing on both sides before Preston Park is reached. The College of Technology annexe by the viaduct was opened by the School Board in 1880 as the Preston Road School. It continued in use as a school until 1937, and later became the Preston Technical Institute. <83,115>

The large Endeavour garage at Springfield Road was built on the site of a Roman villa, discovered in 1876 and excavated in 1877 and 1962 when the garage was built. Several burial urns, skulls, bones, fragments of pottery, coins, figurines and an iron lamp were found, and it has been suggested that it was a temple and cemetery rather than a house. The villa is commemorated on the pylon at the southern entrance to the park. <8,151>

Branching westwards from Preston Road is Dyke Road Drive, constructed in 1878 by the local landowners in conjunction with the London, Brighton and South Coast Railway Company and the corporation to form a carriage drive from Hove to Preston Park via the Drive and the Upper Drive. Parkmore Terrace is a row of seventeen contemporary, bay-fronted houses approached through a gateway from Dyke Road Drive. Preston Road Wesleyan Chapel, a red-brick Gothic building by C.O.Ellison with a small spire, stood on the site of the London Gate office block from 1883. It closed in 1943 and became a furniture depository, but was demolished in 1974. <62,114>

b) *ALONGSIDE THE PARK:* The road alongside Preston Park was once rather narrow, hemmed in by high walls with a raised pathway along the western side. From 1874 a line of about twenty large villas was erected opposite the park, but since the 1960s they have been gradually replaced by large office blocks and now only one remains, at the corner of Lovers Walk. Before the villas were built, Preston Dairy Farm stood on the site now occupied by the General Insurance Buildings. Preston Grange, an eleven-storey block of forty-eight flats, stands on the site of a large house of that name which was originally erected in 1881 for William Stroudley, superintendent engineer of the Brighton railway works; the decorative stained-glass windows of the house, which was originally known as Bosvigo, may be seen at the Bluebell Railway's museum at Sheffield Park. <15,83,131,316>

Lovers Walk was once a hedge-lined footpath from Preston Road to Seven Dials along the lines of Stanford Road and Prestonville Road; a bridge under the railway was constructed in 1841. In 1831 the path was connected with a famous murder (see "Trunk Murders"), but with the construction of the railway's upper goods yard and Dyke Road Drive in 1878, Lovers Walk became restricted to the present cul-de-sac off Preston Road, with steps up to Dyke Road Drive. Several large villa residences were erected at this time, along with 1-4 Lovers Walk Cottages at the end of the road. These four cottages are faced in knapped flint and yellow brick, but the adjacent nos.5-6 are considerably older and date from the late eighteenth century when they probably belonged to Preston Dairy Farm. <15,108,109>

c) *PRESTON VILLAGE:* Preston Road then runs through Preston village itself, where no.199, the Old House, is an eighteenth-century listed farmhouse in knapped and squared flint. Formerly used as tea-rooms, it is one of the finest examples of flint work in the area and is illuminated at night, but the glazing bars of two windows have been unfortunately removed. The adjacent nos.201-203 have unusual large cockerel decorations in the gables. The Crown and Anchor dates back to at least 1711 when it was the first stop for coaches outside Brighton, but it was rebuilt in 1894. At the rear stood the small Preston parish workhouse until 1844, and later, from the early 1900s, a gymnasium and assembly hall used for training by famous boxers and wrestlers until about 1957. On the opposite side of the road are the Preston Vicarage Lawns, two bowling-greens laid out in 1934-5 on the site of the vicarage which stood opposite the car showroom. <15,44,123,126>

d) *NORTH OF PRESTON VILLAGE:* The area around Lauriston Road, Cumberland Road and Preston Road was badly damaged by bombing during the war. At the corner of Knoyle Road stands the Church of St John the Evangelist, built by Sir Arthur Blomfield in rough stone in 1902, in Early English style with a small turret and spire. In 1908 it was designated Preston parish church, and a clerestoried chancel was added in 1926, separated from the nave by a wooden screen. The church

Figure 125: No.199 Preston Road, a fine example of a façade of knapped and squared flint

was also damaged by a bomb. At the rear in Knoyle Road stands the Knoyle Hall, built in 1912-13 and used as a lecture theatre for the first fifty-two students of the University of Sussex in 1961-2. The single-storey Crowhurst Hall was erected by Robert Crowhurst in 1928 in memory of his wife Charlotte. <1,241,311>

A number of villas dating from the 1870s line the western side of the road to the north of the village. They were built as part of the Clermont estate (see "Preston") and the line is happily complete, although most have now been converted to flats, rest homes, etc.; nos.235-237 were used in 1961 to house the first University of Sussex students, as mentioned above. The Preston Resort Hotel opposite was the Touring Hotel from about 1969, and occupies two adjoining villas. The southern one was built in 1851 as Preston Villa, one of a group of three, semi-detached villas on the northern side of Harrington Road; the northern villa was built in the late nineteenth century. <83,109>

134. PRESTONVILLE

The Prestonville area, part of the former Preston parish, was developed by Daniel Friend as a middle-class housing estate in the mid 1860s, and originally included Brigden Street, Hamilton Road, Hamilton Terrace, Prestonville Road, Prestonville Terrace and Stanford Road; the land had originally been intended for a public abattoir. In the 1880s the Port Hall area was developed to the north, while the houses of Buxton Road, Lancaster Road and Stafford Road were added in the 1890s. On 22 February 1882 Eric Gill, the stone carver and engraver, was born at 32 Hamilton Road; he later moved as a boy to 53 Highcroft Villas. The Prestonville Arms, Hamilton Road, is said to be haunted. <76,83,123>

The parish church of Prestonville is St Luke's in Old Shoreham Road. Built in 1875 in Early English style by John Hill, it has a pleasant red-brick exterior, with a small tower and clock surmounted by a short spire at the south-east corner; it became a parish church in 1878 and the interior was enlarged in 1882 by J.G.Gibbins. St Luke's Church Hall in Exeter Street is a red-brick Gothic building of 1884, with the separate boys' and girls' entrances to the Sunday school still apparent. <1,311>

The land to the south of Old Shoreham Road, developed contemporaneously with Prestonville, belonged to New England Farm and lay within the parish of Brighton. The farm buildings stood on the site of York Grove and York Villas from the 1810s until the 1860s, but the farmhouse, with its four-column Doric doorway, attractive garden and an outbuilding, remains at 26 York Villas. The age of this house is somewhat uncertain but it is believed to date from the early nineteenth century; certainly buildings are shown on the site in maps of around 1820. In 1990 it was being converted to flats. Theatrical impresario Sir Charles Blake Cochran was born nearby at 15 Prestonville Road in 1872. <108,123,311>

135. PUBLIC HOUSES

<6,15,83,123,300>

Inns, taverns and ale-houses in Brighton have been regulated from at least 1618, and by 1800 there were 41 establishments recorded in the town. The Beer Act of 1830 permitted any ratepayer to open a beer-house on payment of two guineas; in Brighton 100 were licensed in the first week, by 1879 the number of premises had grown to 424, and in 1889 there were reported to be 774 public houses in the town, one for every 130 residents. Now, in 1990, there are still 235 public houses in the borough <124a>, one for every 600 inhabitants, but former public houses are to be seen in many streets; North Road, for instance, had 10 'pubs' in 1931. The greatest concentration is naturally in the town centre, but particularly around Brighton Station, St James's Street and the Old Town. The road with most public houses is Ditchling Road which has seven; Lewes Road has six, while Church Street, St George's Road and Southover Street all have five.

Consult the index for individual entries. See also "Breweries".

136. QUEEN SQUARE

This wide cul-de-sac was developed in the 1850s. The building at the north-eastern corner, no.12, was erected in 1856-7 as a Baptist chapel, but was taken over by the Free Church in 1904 when Gloucester Place Baptist Church was built as a replacement; in about 1948 it was converted into offices. The small (60 feet by 40 feet) Sussex Ice-Rink opened in December 1970 in a former Territorial Army drill hall. <61,62,83,123>

a) *QUEEN SQUARE HOUSE and the CENTRAL FREE CHURCH:* The large office-block on the eastern side, Queen Square House, was designed by APP Brighton and erected in 1985-7 on the site of the Central Free Church. This church, built in 1853-4 by James and Brown as a Congregational church, was a Gothic building with a small tower at the southern end, and was extensively enlarged in 1867 and refaced in 1884. In 1898 the congregation joined with that of the Union Church in Union Street to form the Union Congregational Church, which in 1973 became the Central Free Church following the amalgamation of several congregations. The church closed in September 1983, and the valuable site was then sold to fund a new church and community centre, the Brighthelm Centre (see "Church Street"). However, the pulpit of the Central Free Church may be seen in the town's museum. <61,62,83,123>

b) *AIR STREET:* Leading from Queen Square to the southern end of Queen's Road is Air Street which, as Boar's Lane, was developed by the mid eighteenth century between North Street and Church Street. Queen's Road was laid out along most of its length in 1845, but in 1849 the remaining length of Air Street was still noted as being intolerably filthy and lined with several slaughterhouses with dung accumulating in a large open cesspit in the centre; it was one of the worst slums in the town. The narrow street was improved in 1850, and now forms an attractive pedestrian shopping thoroughfare which was widened in 1985-7 when Queen Square House was erected. <14,108>

c) *ST MARY'S HOME:* Nos.1-6 and 10-11 Queen Square were once occupied by St Mary's Home for Female Penitents. In mid-nineteenth-century Brighton the many inns, taverns, beer-houses and music halls were notorious as the haunts of prostitutes; an official survey of 1860 recorded 97 brothels and 300 prostitutes with, no doubt, many others unrecorded. The most notorious areas were said to be around Edward Street and Church Street, while the nightly scenes on the beaches in front of King's Road and on the Level were said to 'beggar all description'. <2,14,23,76>

To facilitate the reform of these women, a home for female penitents (i.e. ex-prostitutes) was founded in 1853 by Revd George Wagner and Mrs Murray Vicars in a house opposite the Level, which soon moved to larger premises in Lewes Road. The routine was strict, but the girls were educated in reading, writing and scripture, and visits by mothers were encouraged. In 1855 the penitentiary was moved to houses at Queen Square and Wykeham Terrace, but following Wagner's death in 1857 it was taken over by the Community of the Virgin Mary, a convent of Anglican nuns founded by his cousin Arthur Wagner at 3-4 Queen Square. Renamed St Mary's Home, the penitentiary was enlarged to include 1-6 and 10-11 Queen Square, and 1-5 and 8-11 Wykeham Terrace. Thirty inmates from all over the country were accommodated, but the home also started to take in the aged, the disabled, the poor and the infant, and established a lying-in hospital, a nursery, an industrial school, an infirmary and a dispensary.

By 1866 the premises had become too small and part of the institution was removed to 17 Egremont Place. In 1868 a new building, the Brighton Home for Female Penitents, was opened on the eastern side of Finsbury Road where it was generally known as the Albion Hill Home. In 1917 this was taken over by the Church Army as a girls' home and school run by nuns, but in the early 1950s it was converted into a furniture factory. The Crown Hill and Westmount flats were built on the site in about 1961.

St Mary's Home remained in Queen Square and Wykeham Terrace until a new building was erected by F.T.Cawthorn at Falmer Road in Ovingdean parish in 1912. In 1938 it became St Mary's Training Home for Girls and was later an old people's home, but it was still run by the nuns. The home closed in 1977 to become St Mary's College, an international language school, and then a centre for the Scientology sect in 1980. In 1984-7 however, the buildings were converted into flats known as Rottingdean Place. The Community of the Virgin Mary is now based at 30-32 Newlands Road, Rottingdean. <65,83,123>

137. QUEEN'S HOTEL, Grand Junction Road and King's Road

Figure 126: The Queen's Hotel in Grand Junction Parade. To the left is King's Road.

The Queen's was built in 1846 on the site of the Dolphin Inn, the middle building of a row of five in Grand Junction Road; this original section still has an Ionic doorway facing the sea. The now familiar western façade, however, originally belonged to Markwell's Hotel which was erected in 1870 and absorbed by the Queen's in 1908. Part of the northern façade in King's Road is listed as being of special architectural interest. Designed by A.H.Wilds in about 1825, this section is adorned with pilasters, ammonite capitals, and four-storey bows. The Queen's Hotel can still be seen to be composed of several separate buildings of differing styles and dates.

Alterations were made to the hotel in 1978-9, including the addition of the Sake Dene Cocktail Bar, named after Sake Dene Mahomed who once ran the country's first turkish bath on the site of Markwell's Hotel (see "Bathing"). In 1983 however, the hotel was closed. It was then acquired by Cheffik Ltd, and in August 1986 the hotel, which now occupies the whole block, was reopened following a major improvement programme at a cost of £8 million. The alterations included the distinctive south-eastern corner, and the addition of a Turkish bath, appropriate to the site of Mahomed's Baths.
<2,3,44,123>

138. QUEEN'S PARK

a) *THE PARK:* The principal ornamental park of eastern Brighton covers 15.32 acres, and was first laid out in 1824 for a Mr Armstrong as a subscription pleasure garden known as Brighton Park, with entrances at Park Street and Egremont Place. It was acquired, probably the following year, by Thomas Attree who in 1829 commissioned Charles Barry to design the two formal entrance arches and a villa residence (see below). In 1836 Attree renamed the garden Queen's Park in honour of Queen Adelaide. Among the attractions provided were an aviary, and later a roller-skating rink.

In 1888 the trustees of George Duddell, the purchaser of the Attree estate, auctioned the park but it failed to sell. After prolonged negotiations it was purchased in 1890 by the Race Stand Trustees, William Burrows and Aldermen Abbey, Brigden and Ridley, for £9,504, and was presented by them to the corporation in March 1891 for use as a public park. It was then laid out for £12,000, including a further gift of £4,000 from the Race Stand Trustees, and was formally opened to the public on 10 August 1892 by the mayor, Sir Joseph Ewart. Both the Park Street gate and the more decorative Egremont gateway were rebuilt in 1890 with the names of the Race Stand Trustees added; their gift is also commemorated by the red-brick and terracotta drinking fountain to the north of the lake, a square edifice erected in 1893.

Queen's Park is perhaps the most beautiful of Brighton's ornamental parks. The central valley was used as a roller-skating rink in the latter nineteenth century, but it was converted into a delightful lake by the corporation, fed by an artificial cascade and stream running through a small rock garden. The red-brick and stone clock tower was erected from a bequest of £1,000 by William Cobley, and was dedicated by the mayor, Sir John Otter, on 24 June 1915. There are also a number of tennis-courts, a bowling-green, and a children's playground. A tree in the south-eastern corner, bearing the message 'Never again', was planted on 6 August 1985 to commemorate those killed by the atomic bombs at Hiroshima and Nagasaki forty years earlier.
<114,126,267,311>

Figure 127: Queen's Park in about 1880 with the central valley in use as a roller-skating rink

Figure 128: The Royal Spa in 1841

b) *ROYAL SPA:* At the south-western corner of the park stand the remains of an artificial spa opened in 1825 by Dr F.A.Struve, who had opened similar spas at Berlin, Dresden and Leipzig. Mineral waters chemically identical to those of many European spas were concocted with water from a well, and the spa building, which was designed by a Mr Lorraine, became very popular. Indeed, it may even have been visited by William IV and Queen Adelaide; certainly the spa was always referred to as the 'Royal' German Spa after a royal warrant was obtained in 1835. However, by the 1850s its popularity had declined so much that the pump room closed, but Hooper Struve Ltd continued the manufacture of bottled mineral waters in the building until 1965. The redundant building then became derelict and eventually passed to the corporation. The pump room at the rear was sadly demolished, but the Ionic portico and north wall were restored by T.R.Williams as an open loggia in 1978 after a long battle to save it, and the structure is now a listed building within the grounds of the Royal Spa Nursery School, a small modern building also of 1978 which was badly damaged by fire in December 1985. <123,267>

c) *ATTREE VILLA:* Thomas Attree purchased the park in about 1825 and commissioned Charles Barry (later Sir Charles, best known for the design of the Houses of Parliament and now commemorated by Barry Walk) to design a villa nearby. Standing in large grounds, the square, Italianate house, one of the earliest of its style, was completed in 1830. It had a shallow roof, broad eaves, plain walls with a loggia of three round-

Figure 129: The villa of Thomas Attree in 1835. Only the 'Pepper-Box' and the garden temple remain.

headed glass doors, and a balustered terrace. In 1863 it was purchased by George Duddell, but was vacant for about twenty years after his death until it reopened in 1909 as an Xaverian college for Catholic boys. However, when the college closed in 1966 the villa became dilapidated, and it was demolished in March 1972 despite being classed as outstanding by the Historic Buildings Council and listed grade II*.

The Attree Villa stood on the southern side of the present Attree Drive, with grounds bounded by North Drive, Queen's Park Terrace and Tower Road, but few relics remain. Some old walls and gateposts remain in Queen's Park Terrace and Attree Drive, while opposite the Carn Court flats stands the villa's garden temple, an Italianate, rectangular structure with Ionic pillars which formerly contained the statue of a seated dog; it is now listed.

The well-known 'Pepper-Box' or 'Pepper-Pot' at the junction of Queen's Park Road and Tower Road is also a relic of the Attree Villa, a ten-sided listed building sixty feet high with Corinthian pillars and a cupola. Its original purpose is uncertain, but it may have been a water or observation tower for the villa, or possibly a sewer vent. George Duddell used it for printing and publishing the *Brighton Daily Mail*, but it was part of the Queen's Park estate presented to the corporation by the Race Stand Trustees. During the Second World War the Pepper-Box was used as an observation tower, and has since been used as a scout headquarters and an artist's studio. (See also figure 173.) <3,44,45,109,123>

d) *CONSERVATION AREA:* Queen's Park is now the central feature of a conservation area which stretches from St Luke's Terrace to Edward Street, but excludes the new development on the site of the Attree Villa. Most of the high quality housing dates from the late-Victorian and Edwardian periods.

The West Drive is lined with large red-brick houses, no.18 being particularly large. No.30, the Queen's Park Villa, is a large listed building of 1851 <311> with an ironwork balcony and verandah, and was known as Pennant Lodge, the residence of Charles Freshfield after whom several nearby roads were named. Having been used as a nursing home, it was restored and refurbished as offices in 1985 with the Park View flats built in similar style to the south-west. The stable at the rear is now a cottage. <44,83>

One of the two principal approaches to Queen's Park is Park Street, which dates from the 1820s; nos.17, 23-24 and 28-29 retain cobbled fronts and are included on the council's local list of buildings of special interest. The eastern side has now been redeveloped but was once the site of the Park Street Baths. Opened by the corporation on 24 May 1888 as the Victoria Slipper Baths for the poor of the district, they closed in 1979; the inaugural tablet has been retained in the Sloane Court flats which opened on the site in 1984. <83,123>

The attractive red-brick houses of Tillstone Street were erected in 1898 on the slum clearance site of Egremont Street and Spa Street. Nos.51-61 were added later on the site of the Pilgrims Cottages, a row of almshouses built in 1852 in Spa Street by the Soames family for needy widows over sixty years of age; they remained in occupation until the mid 1960s. The chapel in nearby Park Hill has been an Evangelical Free Church since 1943, but was built in 1894 by Herbert Buckwell for the congregation of St Andrew's Presbyterian Church. This church had stood in Thomas Street, but was demolished in a slum clearance scheme when Blaker Street and White Street were constructed. <62,83,115,123>

Egremont Place forms the other approach to the park, and is lined with attractive three-storey houses of the 1810s on the western side, and of the following decade on the eastern side. Nos.8 and 10 have fluted Ionic pilasters and are listed buildings, as are nos.7, 9, 39, 41-42, 44-47 and 57-59, all dating from the early nineteenth century. The Aged Pilgrim Friend Society opened their Brighton home for elderly christians in 1879 at the yellow-brick no.35, formerly Egremont Lodge. It was enlarged in 1927, and now includes the adjacent no.36 and more recent extensions. <44,83>

In the northern part of the conservation area, St Luke's Terrace has some very attractive red-brick housing, typical of the outstanding suburban architecture of the area; nos.1-3, for instance, date from 1899-1900 and have highly decorated gables and panels. The large school building, the most prominent in the area, was erected in 1903 to the design of Thomas Simpson, the culmination of his career as architect to the Brighton and Preston School Board. The school's swimming-pool, built in red and yellow brick with wreath decorations, is included on the council's local list of buildings of special interest; the 17-metre pool was reopened in 1986 by the council as a public teaching/training pool. <45a,83>

St Luke's Church, Queen's Park Road, was built in 1881-5 by Sir Arthur Blomfield, in Early English style in flint with stone dressings and with a small octagonal tower at the south-western corner. The church hall, a red-brick building built in 1875 at the opposite corner of the junction, was used as a temporary church and mission to St Mary's prior to 1885, but was demolished following a fire in 1972 to be replaced by Sidney Tidy House. The parish of St Luke's, created in 1880, was merged into the parish of the Resurrection on 15 May 1974. <1,62,123>

Queen's Park Methodist Church, also in Queen's Park Road but not actually within the conservation area, was designed by W.S.Parnacott and opened in September 1891, but was closed in 1987. <62,123,311>

139. QUEEN'S ROAD

a) *HISTORY:* This major commercial thoroughfare was constructed in 1845 to improve access to Brighton Station from North Street and West Street; the London and Brighton Railway Company contributed £2,000 to the cost, and the improvement included the bridge over Trafalgar Street. At the southern end, several notorious slums off North Street, notably Durham and Petty France, were cleared; the new road was then laid out northwards over part of Air Street (see "Queen Square"), and between Windsor Terrace and the Hanover Chapel towards the railway station.

The road naturally became lined with hotels, public houses, shops and warehouses, and was widened in 1878, mainly at the expense of the railway company. The buildings of Queen's Road were originally continuous from Upper Gloucester Road to the bridge over Trafalgar Street; Junction Road, the link to Terminus Road and Surrey Street, was formed in 1924 by the demolition of the Terminus Hotel and the Terminus Shades in Surrey Street, and was widened again in 1935 by the removal of another two houses to form the present bus-bays. <2,15,24,26,76,115>

See also "Railways - Brighton Station" and "Clock Tower".

b) *EASTERN SIDE:* Queen's Road was widened in 1878, mainly at the expense of the railway company, and a number of large warehouses and depositories were built to the north of Gloucester Road; the last remaining one, a very distinctive Gothic design known as the 'Temple', was demolished in 1989-90. The Sergeant Yorke Casino opened in October 1971 in a building built in 1908 as a garage.

Most of the eastern side of Queen's Road is now lined with nondescript office-blocks of the 1960s and later, but Sun Dial House at the corner of North Road is an elegant, red-brick block erected in 1896 for the Brighton and Sussex Mutual Provident Society. It has a large sundial and an inscription on the southern façade: 'Our days on Earth are as a shadow and there is none abiding'. The Latin inscription translates to 'As the hours pass so does life fade away'. <24,83,311>

Queen's Road was a centre for the medical profession in the latter nineteenth century, and was at one time the location of the Brighton and Hove Dispensary; the Brighton, Hove and Preston Provident Dispensary; the Brighton, Hove and Preston Dental Hospital; the Sussex Eye Hospital; and the Sussex Throat and Ear Hospital. The sites of the two dispensaries between Church Street and North Road are now occupied by large office buildings of the 1960s and '70s. At the southern end of this block stood the large, square Oddfellows Hall, built by John Fabian and opened on 26 June 1854 for the Manchester Order. It continued as a meeting hall until required for the Second World War effort, and was later used by the Ministry of Labour before being demolished in August 1969. Its foundation stone has been placed in the south wall of 118 Queen's Road, the office-block which replaced it. The Queen's Road Rest Garden at this point is the former graveyard of the Hanover Chapel, now the Brighthelm Church and Community Centre (see "Church Street"). <83,311>

The Boots store, one of their largest in the country, was erected in 1979 to the design of Derek Sharp. It stands on the site of the Regent Cinema.

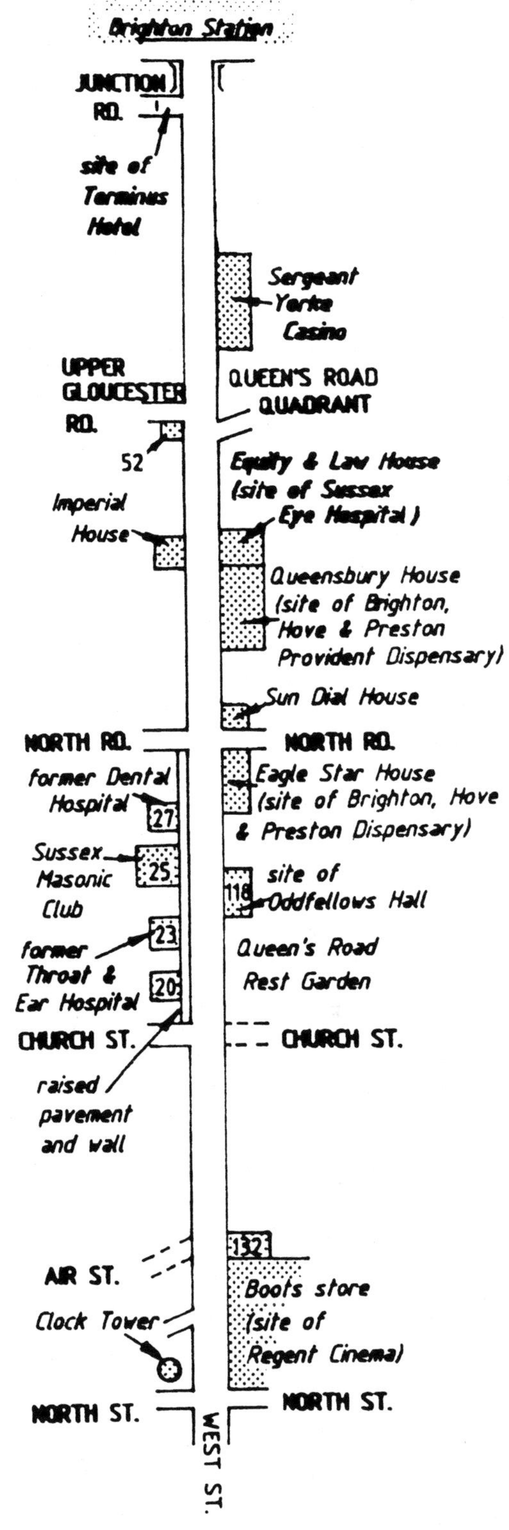

Figure 130: Queen's Road

Figure 131: The Sussex Masonic Club and the raised pavement on the western side of Queen's Road, originally Windsor Terrace

c) *REGENT CINEMA:* This spectacular cinema stood near the corner with North Street and was opened on 27 July 1921 by Provincial Cinematograph Theatres Ltd at the immense cost of over £400,000; it was built on the site of the Unicorn Inn and several other buildings. The Regent was the first of several giant Brighton cinemas, seating about 3,000 people, and indeed it was considered the most luxurious cinema in the country, the first 'super-cinema'. Designed by theatre architect Robert Atkinson, and with a classical interior by Walpole Champneys, it had spacious foyers and galleries, the Ship Café, and a Georgian-style restaurant with an orchestra. There was also a side entrance in North Street at the corner of Windsor Street.

In November 1923 the famous dance-hall or winter garden opened in the arched superstructure on the roof which had originally been intended for a roof-garden. The Regent, together with Sherrys in West Street, was then at the forefront of Brighton's night-life for many years. Late in 1928 a serious fire destroyed the stage, the organ, and the proscenium arch, but the building reopened on 1 July 1929 as Brighton's first 'talkie' cinema. The Regent was acquired by Odeon Cinemas Ltd in 1953. In 1962 a giant wide screen was installed, but the ball-room closed in July 1967 to became a full-time bingo hall, and the cinema itself closed on 14 April 1973 to be replaced by the Odeon complex at the Kingswest. The building was demolished the following year, and the site is now occupied by the Boots store. <68,68a>

d) *WESTERN SIDE:* The western side of Queen's Road has been redeveloped to a much lesser extent than the eastern side. The Queen's Head, with its typical mid-nineteenth-century façade, was restored in 1988. The block from North Road to Upper Gloucester Road retains most of a bow-fronted terrace (no.52 is listed to protect it from adjacent office development), and also contains Imperial House which was completed in 1985 in classical style on the site of the Imperial Hotel; the range is, however, spoilt by Lyndean House.

The section between Church Street and North Road on the western side predates the rest of Queen's Road. It was erected in the late 1820s or early '30s as Windsor Terrace, and was built overlooking the graveyard of the Hanover Chapel. When Queen's Road was driven through the western side of the churchyard, now the Queen's Road Rest Garden, the boundary wall was left along the western side of the new road and is now the raised pavement and railing of this section <140>. Nos.19-20 and no.27, once the dental hospital, are all elegant houses, while the listed Sussex Masonic Club remains at no.25, probably designed by Wilds and Busby in the 1820s. The adjacent Masonic Temple was opened in July 1928. <44,108,115>

140. RACE-COURSE

<2,3,15,123,266,299>

a) *ORIGINS:* Although informal challenge races were run on the springy turf of White Hawk Down, Brighton racegoers resorted to Lewes Races from 1751 where they established the Brighthelmston Plate race, valued at £50, in 1774. In 1783 however, a group of leading inhabitants including the Duke of Cumberland, Marquess of Queensberry and Earl of Egremont organised the first Brighton Races on 26-27 July. The town offered prize money of 30 guineas for three separate races, each the best of three heats of two or four miles run over White Hawk Down; this area then became known as the Race Hill.

Figure 132: Brighton races in 1790. The simple stand lasted from 1788 until 1803.

The Prince of Wales visited the second meeting on 2-3 August 1784 and became an enthusiastic follower. Brighton Races then became a very fashionable resort, and the annual meeting was increased to four days in 1786. The first stand was erected by subscription in 1788, an open-fronted structure holding about twenty-four people in four boxes. It burnt down on 23 August 1803 but was replaced the same year.

The course itself was unenclosed and stretched 1 mile 1,585 yards in a hairpin across Race Hill to Bear Road and back. The area known as the Race Ground was granted to the town on 22 April 1822 by T.R.Kemp, Charles Scrase and a number of other landowners, and in 1861 was marked with a series of boundary stones which may still be found along the course of Whitehawk Road, Haybourne Road and northwards to Bear Road; in the Bear Road cemetery wall; in the walls of the General Hospital and the adjacent reservoir in Freshfield Road; and at the northern ends of Queensway and Whitehawk Hill Road. Each stone bears the numerals '105.0.30', the area of the Race Ground being 105 acres, 0 rods and 30 poles.

b) *THE RACE STAND TRUSTEES:* Fashionable society continued to attend the race meetings until the 1840s when the railway started to bring unsavoury elements down from London during race week. The race committee, which had been established by the vestry in 1828, was short of funds to pay winners by 1848. To solve these difficulties, the 'Race Stand Trustees' were established in 1849-50. Having purchased the old stand for £360, they erected a new stand, designed by town surveyor Allan Stickney, in August 1851, made several other improvements to the course, and introduced strict regulations. The London, Brighton and South Coast Railway Company, which carried many people on excursions to the races, contributed £100 to the purchase of the old stand and also £200 annually to the race fund. The present course also became established at this time, stretching into Ovingdean parish where agreements were reached with the landowners. The reputation of Brighton Races was regained following the improvements and attendances swelled, allowing a southern wing to be added to the stand in 1866, and a northern wing by 1871.

c) *EASTER VOLUNTEER REVIEWS:* Brighton Race-Course and the Race Hill were also used for annual Easter volunteer soldier reviews for many years. The first took place in 1861 when 12,000 volunteers arrived by train to show how the railway could be used to move troops, and a number of manoeuvres were carried out on White Hawk Down, culminating in the sham 'Battle of Ovingdean' on Easter Monday, 1 April 1861; the following year, on Easter Monday 21 April 1862, the 'Battle of White Hawk Down' was fought. The reviews provided an exciting and colourful spectacle for visitors who crowded in to the race stand to watch, and they continued for many years. A rifle-range for the

Figure 133: The new race stand of 1851

volunteers was established in the 1870s at Sheepcote Valley, giving the former Rifle Butt Road its name. <3,15,115>

d) *CORPORATION TAKEOVER:* At the peak of its popularity, and under the terms of the 1884 Brighton Improvement Act, the race-course was vested in the corporation from 1 October 1888, but was leased back to the Race Stand Trustees. The trustees themselves then purchased part of the Marquess of Bristol's estate and sixteen acres of the Beard estate in Ovingdean, and presented the land to the corporation which thereby owned the whole course and race ground by 1898; the Race Stand Trustees also purchased Queen's Park on behalf of the town at this time. Two days of racing in the spring were organised for the first time, and the summer 'Sussex Fortnight' of racing at Brighton, Goodwood, Lewes and Plumpton became established. Racing was suspended during the First World War from August 1914 until September 1917, and the stand was used as an ammunition dump and food store.

e) *RACE GANGS:* By the late 1920s Brighton Races had regained an unsavoury reputation and were terrorised by London gangs running 'protection rackets' and other illicit schemes. Frequent skirmishes and razor fights horrified visitors, and trouble continued until June 1936 when the 'Hoxton Mob' were arrested at Lewes Races. The seedy underworld of Brighton and its races is described in the well-known novel ***Brighton Rock*** by Graham Greene, published in 1938. The film, starring Richard Attenborough, Hermione Baddeley and William Hartnell, was shot in 1946 and included location scenes of the Lanes, North Street, Queen's Road, Church Street, Palace Pier, Aquarium Sun Terrace and the Grand Hotel. The film crew was ordered off the race-course as corporation permission had not been given, an incident that earned the production much publicity.

f) *OTHER IMPROVEMENTS and DESCRIPTION:* In the 1930s the corporation spent some £60,000 on improvements to the race-course, including the totalisator buildings in 1930, stabling and administrative blocks in 1931, and the subway to Whitehawk in 1936. Several stands were also built, the Tattersall in 1934, two more in 1936, and a new grandstand in 1938. Racing was suspended on the outbreak of war in September 1939 until 24 August 1945, but crowds of 20,000 flocked to the races in the immediate post-war period and large profits allowed many more improvements to be made. In 1951 a new covered stand was added for 1,600 people in the north-western enclosure, followed by another covered stand in the eastern enclosure. The pulling-up ground was laid out in 1952, and the present grandstand, which holds 5,420 people including 1,445 standing, opened in May 1965 at a cost of £400,000; all the other stands, except the 1951 covered stand, were subsequently removed. The first evening races were held in June 1964. Although attendances now average about 2,000, some summer meetings still attract up to 5,000 spectators, and weekend markets and caravan pitches have helped to boost the income of the race-course in recent years. A Country Homes Garden Centre opened in 1990 to the north of the stands.

Brighton is the only race-course in the country owned and operated by a local authority, and is now controlled by the 'Race-Course Lessees' of the borough council; in 1990, however, the council decided to lease the course to private enterprise for improvements and the addition of further leisure facilities. The course itself, 1.5 miles long and downhill for much of its length, is exceptionally fast; indeed, the fastest times in the world for three-quarters of a mile and one mile were set at Brighton. The mile record of 1 minute 30.9 seconds (39.6 m.p.h.) was established by 'Chase the Door' on 26 July 1990. The race meeting on 31 May 1979 was attended by Queen Elizabeth II. A 1963 plan for housing on the Race Ground was fortunately defeated in the town council.

141. RAILWAYS

Some ninety years after Brighton was established as a fashionable resort, the arrival of the railway from London in 1841 brought great changes to the town, the effect of which can best be seen from the relevant census figures: the population rise in the period 1831-41 was 15%; in 1841-51 it was 41%. Heavy industry arrived as the London, Brighton and South Coast Railway Company established virtually all its engineering works in the town, and large areas of housing, mainly for manual workers, were developed around the station and in the Hanover area. The status of the visitor also changed somewhat as less affluent day-trippers came down from London in large numbers, and distinct seasons became established, the summer for the masses and the autumn and winter for wealthier society. Commuters to the capital used the trains from the start in 1841, and their numbers increased significantly with main line electrification in the 1930s. Only since the 1950s, with the mass availability of the motor-car and the closure of the railway works, has the importance of the railway to Brighton at all declined.

The development of the various lines and services is described in the entries following. See also "Devil's Dyke", "Kemp Town Railway", "Rottingdean Railway" and "Volk's Electric Railway".

a) *COMPANIES and GROUPINGS:* The main line to London and the branches to Shoreham and Lewes were constructed by the London and Brighton Railway Company. Mainly owing to financial considerations, the London, Brighton and South Coast Railway Company was formed under an Act of Parliament of July 1846 by amalgamating the London and Brighton; London and Croydon; Croydon and Epsom; Brighton, Lewes and Hastings; and the Brighton and Chichester railway companies. The London, Brighton and South Coast had 457 miles of track, covering most of Sussex and much of south London and Surrey, when on 1 January 1923 it was amalgamated with many other companies into the Southern Railway. This grouping lasted twenty-five years before it was nationalised as the Southern Region of British Railways on 1 January 1948. <180,181>

142. RAILWAYS - London Main Line

(N.B. London, Brighton and South Coast Railway Company abbreviated to 'L.B.S.C.R.'.)
<123,176,177,180-184>

a) *ORIGINS:* The first serious proposal for a railway from London to Brighton was made as early as 1823 when William James described a route from Waterloo to Brighton via East Grinstead, Crawley and Shoreham. In 1825 a route via Dorking was suggested, while a plan by Sir John Rennie involved a more direct route via Cuckfield. Several other proposals were made in the 1830s, but the choice eventually boiled down to either Rennie's direct route or one of three lines by Vignoles, Cundy, and Stephenson/Bidder which ran generally along the Adur valley. On 16 March 1836 a House of Commons committee commenced an examination of the four routes, advised by Captain Robert Alderson of the Royal Engineers. He recommended that a direct line, comprising portions of several different schemes, was the most suitable as the potential engineering difficulties could be overcome. Consequently the London and Brighton Railway Act was passed on 15 July 1837 authorising the London and Brighton Railway Company to construct a direct route with branches to both Shoreham and Newhaven.

The city terminus was to be London Bridge Station, which had opened on 1 December 1836. The tracks of the London and Greenwich Company were used for the first two miles, and from that point to Selhurst trains would run on the London and Croydon Company's lines which had opened on 5 June 1839; tolls were to be paid to these other companies for each passenger carried. South of Selhurst, a new line was to be constructed all the way to Brighton although the track between Coulsdon and Redhill was to be the property of the South Eastern Railway; no tolls were to be paid on this section, however.

b) *CONSTRUCTION and OPENING:* Construction of the new line commenced on 19 March 1838 under Sir John Rennie and John Rastrick, and was undertaken by a total of 6,206 men, 960 horses and 5 locomotives. The first track was laid at Hassocks in February 1839, but it was to be another thirty months, on 12 July 1841, before the line opened, and then only from London to Haywards Heath with a connecting coach service to Brighton. The line opened to Brighton itself on 21 September 1841; the first train set out for the City at 7 a.m., and the first down train arrived in the town at 2 p.m. amid scenes of great celebration. See also "Railways - Brighton Station".

c) *EARLY SERVICES:* There were initially six trains each way per day; three first-class services stopping only at East Croydon, Redhill and Reigate Road, Three Bridges, and Haywards Heath; and three stopping also at the intermediate stations at Godstone Road (now Purley), Horley, Burgess Hill, and Hassocks Gate. Within a few years a non-stop service taking 1 hour 45 minutes was running, and in 1843 third-class carriages were introduced (but they were not covered until 1852!). The first excursion tickets were issued on Easter Monday, 8 April 1844, when a train of four locomotives and some forty-five carriages left London for Brighton, with return fares priced the same as singles, i.e. 12

Figure 134: View from Rose Hill towards the New England Viaduct and Brighton Station in the 1840s; note the train entering the station. The windmill on the left is Hodson's at West Hill Road; that on the right is Lashmar's at Belmont, now Jill Mill at Clayton.

shillings (60p) first-class, 8 shillings (40p) second-class, and 5 shillings (25p) third-class. With the sudden surge of excursionists, Brighton subsequently developed the attractions of a day-tripper resort.

d) *FEATURES OF THE LINE:* The length of the line engineered by Rennie was 41 miles 59 chains from Selhurst, a total of 50 miles 46 chains from London Bridge. Five tunnels, all 25 feet wide and 25 feet high, were constructed at Merstham (1,830 yards long), Balcombe (1,133 yards), Haywards Heath (250 yards), Clayton (2,266 yards), and Patcham (488 yards); the three longest were lit by gas from their own gas-works. Trains also traverse the impressive Ouse Viaduct. Designed by David Mocatta, it is 1,475 feet long, 96 feet high, and has 37 arches each spanning 30 feet.

At Brighton, the most notable features are the huge man-made plateau cut out of the chalk hillside at the terminus, the New England Viaduct, and Patcham Tunnel. Fortunately, the owner of Patcham Place at the time, Major Paine, insisted on a tunnel through his land rather than a cutting; the final stone of the 488-yard tunnel was keyed in at an elaborate ceremony on 16 June 1841, and the north portal bears the date 1841. The original New England Viaduct (or Montpelier Bridge) is a rather elegant structure in yellow brick and may be seen whilst ascending the hill from the east. The foundation stone was laid on 27 May 1839 at a ceremony said to have been witnessed by 10,000 people. In the 1860s it was widened on the western side by the addition of a red-brick and iron structure which was rebuilt at Easter 1985.

e) *PRESTON PARK STATION, Clermont Road:* Opening on 1 November 1869 as Preston Station, it was built primarily to serve the upper- and middle-class Clermont estate. The station was rebuilt with two island platforms when the direct line to Hove, the Cliftonville Spur, was constructed, and it was renamed Preston Park when the spur opened on 1 July 1879. The modern station, rebuilt in the 1970s, now has nondescript square buildings but the original yellow-brick ticket office remains in Station Road.

f) *EXTENSIONS TO VICTORIA:* In 1858 the L.B.S.C.R. leased the West End of London and Crystal Palace Railway Company's line from Norwood, via Crystal Palace and Clapham Junction, to Battersea Wharf (called 'Pimlico') on the south bank of the Thames. Direct access to the western side of London was thus available for the first time, and two years later this line was extended to a new terminus, Victoria Station, which opened on 1 October 1860 for both Brighton and Kent traffic. A more direct line to Clapham Junction from East Croydon, via Balham and Stewart's Lane, opened on 1 February 1862; the present flyover across the Waterloo lines was added on 1 December 1867.

g) *OTHER PROPOSALS and IMPROVEMENTS:* In August 1866 an Act of Parliament was passed which authorised a line from Kent House to a terminus at the Steine via East Grinstead, Lewes, and a tunnel under the eastern town, but the plan was dropped following an agreement between the rival companies. Proposals for alternative lines continued to be made until the 1880s, but the London-to-Brighton line of today was finally established on 1 April 1900 when a new 'through route' opened to passenger traffic. Now known as the Quarry Line, it runs from Coulsdon to Earlswood, a distance of 10 miles 28 chains, and avoided the need for L.B.S.C.R. trains to run on the South-Eastern's tracks via Redhill. Two new tunnels were required, the 2,113-yard New Merstham or Quarry Tunnel, and the 649-yard Redhill Tunnel. At the same time the main line was quadrupled from Croydon to Coulsdon.

Improvements between 1903 and 1910 included the enlargement of Victoria Station, and the quadrupling of the line from Victoria to Balcombe Tunnel. Widening to Keymer Junction was authorised, but the L.B.S.C.R. concentrated on electrification instead. Services between London and Brighton also ran via East Grinstead from 1882 until 1958, via Horsham from 1867 to 1966, and via Uckfield from 1868 until 1969. In 1905 the famous Sunny South Special service started running from Liverpool and Manchester to Brighton and Eastbourne, The first scheduled 60-minute non-Pullman down train ran in 1912, but 60-minute working in both directions was not introduced until July 1928.

In 1897-8 a Bill was laid before Parliament proposing an underground railway beneath Queen's Road and West Street from the railway station to two termini in King's Road opposite Middle Street and Russell Street. The plan was opposed by the corporation though, and the Bill was in fact withdrawn before it went before the House of Lords. <183a>

h) *ELECTRIFICATION and RECENT DEVELOPMENTS:* An electric railway to London was proposed in 1901, running direct from Pimlico to Furze Hill, Hove, with a scheduled journey time of 32 minutes. The L.B.S.C.R. had electrification plans of their own though, and opened their first electric line on 1 December 1909. This overhead system, from Victoria to London Bridge, proved a success and suburban electrification was subsequently progressed.

Main-line electrification was proposed in 1920, but when the Southern Railway was formed in 1923 a third-rail, 600-volt d.c. system was chosen rather than the L.B.S.C.R. overhead system. Work on electrification between Brighton and London and West Worthing commenced in 1930, and the new electric service was inaugurated on 30 December 1932 when the Lord Mayor of London travelled to Brighton for a civic dinner. Public electric services commenced on 1 January 1933 (with steam services withdrawn at the same time), and resulted in an immediate 33% increase in traffic in the first year. Colour-light signalling was also installed, with a new powered signal-box above the carriage repair shops at Brighton replacing six small mechanical boxes.

Several lines on direct routes to Brighton were closed in the 1950s and '60s as mentioned above, while a further rationalisation in the '70s resulted in the withdrawal of non-stop trains from May 1979; all services have subsequently stopped at East Croydon. A rebuilt London Bridge Station was formally reopened on 15 December 1978, Manchester services were re-introduced via Oxford in 1979 and via Kensington in 1986, and through routes to Bedford and Scotland in 1988.

A £45 million resignalling scheme of the whole line was undertaken in 1977-85, with just two control boxes now operating at Clapham Junction and Three Bridges. The improvement resulted in the fastest ever scheduled Victoria services by 1987, run in a time of just 51 minutes, an average speed of 60 m.p.h. including the stop at East Croydon. The record time of 38 minutes 56 seconds (78.6 m.p.h.) over the 51 miles to Victoria was set in a special journey on 16 April 1988.

j) *ACCIDENTS:* Just one month after the main line opened, a train derailed to the north of Haywards Heath on 2 October 1841, killing 2 people. The worst accident on the line occurred on 25 August 1861 when two trains collided in Clayton Tunnel killing 23 and injuring 175. On 23 December 1899 6 people were killed in a collision at Wivelsfield; 7 died when a train derailed at Stoat's Nest on 29 January 1910; and on 2 October 1947 32 people were killed at South Croydon. The worst accidents of recent years, on one of the busiest lines in the world, were at Copyhold Junction on 16 December 1972 when 25 people were injured, and at Sweet Hill, Patcham, on 19 December 1978 when two trains collided killing 3 and injuring 7 passengers.

k) *BRIGHTON BELLE and OTHER LUXURY TRAINS:* The first luxury Pullman cars on the London-to-Brighton line were introduced in 1875, and the first all-Pullman train, the Pullman Luxury Limited, ran on 1 December 1881. This train included Beatrice, the first railway carriage in the world to be lit by electricity. In 1899 the train was renamed the Brighton Limited, and in a special run on 26 July 1903 made the journey in a then record time of 48 minutes 41 seconds. In 1907 another superior class train, the City Limited, was introduced to London Bridge, with a portion for Victoria detached at East Croydon until 1919, but it lost its name from the timetable in 1934.

The most famous of the luxury trains, however, was the Southern Belle, introduced at a cost of £40,000 on 1 November 1908 and dubbed 'the most luxurious train in the world'. A one-shilling supplement above the normal fare was charged, but third-class fares were introduced in September 1915. The Belle even had its own platform at Victoria, no.17 now no.19, with a greeting arch bearing the train's name. Three new five-car sets were built for the electrification of the main line in 1933, but the train was formally renamed the Brighton Belle on 29 June 1934 by the mayor, Margaret Hardy.

The three trains each way per day were run as part of the normal scheduled service, but the Belle retained its distinctive umber-and-cream livery until 1968-9 when it was refitted internally and repainted in the standard blue-and-grey livery of British Rail. The Brighton Belle was frequented by a number of famous figures in the town who considered it a most civilised mode of transport to their work in London, and in 1970 the actor Lord Olivier led a successful protest against the withdrawal of kipper breakfasts. In 1972 the train was even the subject of a BBC TV series, but it proved too expensive to maintain and was finally withdrawn on 30 April 1972. (A special trip was run on 9 May 1972 in connection with the sixth Brighton Festival.) The carriages, including the first-class cars Audrey, Doris, Gwen, Hazel, Mona and Vera, were sold for £10,000 each and were subsequently used on such trains as the London-Simplon-Venice Orient Express.

143. RAILWAYS - West Coastway

<123,176,178,180,181>

The first railway line to open at Brighton was not in fact the London main line, but rather the branch to Shoreham. It was first proposed in 1825 to provide good communication with the harbour, but it was the 1837 London and Brighton Railway Act which authorised branches to both Shoreham and Newhaven. Work on the western branch started in July 1838 under engineer John Rastrick, and the line opened at 5 p.m. on 11 May 1840, some sixteen months before the main line; an experimental service had actually been provided from 20 April 1840. Seven trains ran each way daily, taking 12 minutes, and intermediate stops were made at Hove (Holland Road), Portslade, Southwick, and Kingston-by-Sea. On the opening day a man fell to his death from a luggage van which had been fitted for passenger use.

The Shoreham line was subsequently extended westwards by the Brighton and Chichester Railway Company to Worthing on 24 November 1845; to Lyminster on 16 March 1846; to Chichester on 8 June 1846; and to Havant (and therefore Portsmouth) on 15 July 1847. Trains to Littlehampton first ran on 17 August 1863, and to Bognor Regis on 1 June 1864. The line was electrified to West Worthing at the same time as the main line from 1 January 1933, and to Havant and Portsmouth in 1938. Since 1972 it has been known as the West Coastway. Trains to the West Country were originally introduced in the 1910s and '20s, and a service to Bristol was re-established from 1981; a through service to Southampton, Bournemouth and Poole was introduced in 1990.

Locally, the major engineering features of the line are the deep cutting outside Brighton Station, and the Hove Tunnel, 231 yards long below Dyke Road, which bears the date 1839 on its eastern portal. The short but important link between Hove and the London main line, the Cliftonville spur, was opened on 1 July 1879 from Preston Park to Cliftonville Station (now Hove). It is 1 mile 34 chains long, and includes the 536-yard Cliftonville Tunnel under Dyke Road.

See also "Railways - Brighton Station".

144. RAILWAYS - East Coastway

<176,179-181,183>

The 1837 London and Brighton Railway Act authorised branches to Newhaven and Shoreham as well as the main line. The line to Lewes, which like the Shoreham branch was engineered by John Rastrick, opened on 8 June 1846 with an intermediate stop at Falmer. It was subsequently extended to Bulverhythe (near Hastings) by the Brighton, Lewes and Hastings Railway Company on 17 June 1846; to St Leonards on 7 November 1846; and to Ashford on 13 February 1851. Trains first ran on the Newhaven branch on 8 December 1847, and to Eastbourne on 14 May 1849. Electric services were formally inaugurated to Hastings, Seaford and Eastbourne on 4 July 1935, opening to the public three days later. Since 1972 the line has been known as the East Coastway and has seen a great increase in traffic since the 1960s with the establishment of the university and polytechnic at Falmer and Moulsecoomb.

One of the major features of the line is the viaduct between Brighton and London Road stations. Although known as the London Road Viaduct, this elegant structure in red and yellow brick actually crosses Preston Road and is now listed for its special architectural interest; it must have been a particularly impressive sight when it ran through open fields until the 1870s. The first stone was laid on 29 May 1845, and the viaduct was rapidly completed by 28 March 1846 with a total length of 400 yards on a strong curve; it reaches a height of 67 feet, has 27 arches, and uses approximately 10 million bricks. Opponents of the viaduct had argued that an embankment would be less costly and also less easily destroyed; they were proved correct on the second point on the afternoon of 25 May 1943 when the second pier to the west of Preston Road was destroyed by a German bomb. Repairs allowed trains to run again within a month, however.

At Moulsecoomb the Hodshrove Viaduct, or Lewes Road Bridge, is 180 feet long and 46 feet high. There are also short tunnels at Ditchling Road (63 yards long), Falmer (495 yards), and Kingston Tunnel (103 yards) under Juggs Road near Southover.

London Road Station, Shaftesbury Place, opened on 1 October 1877 57 chains from Brighton Station with four sidings and a signal-box to the west. The station building has a standard design which was also used at Hove, Kemp Town and Portslade, and was restored when the station was modernised in 1987; the footbridge dates from 1889. Nearby in Ditchling Rise stands the elegant Railway Hotel.

Moulsecoomb Station, Queensdown School Road, was opened to the public on 12 May 1980, primarily to serve Brighton Polytechnic. The first new station on Southern Region for twelve years, it was formally opened by British Rail chairman Sir Peter Parker on 10 June 1980. Designed by Jane Gray, it has a pleasing, weatherboarded building and cost £244,000.

Falmer Station opened at the same times as the line on 8 June 1846, but was originally situated on the eastern side of the village where Old Station Cottage still stands; on 1 August 1865 it was reopened at its present site off Lewes Road. Falmer Station was rebuilt in 1890 with the station-master's house integrated into the station building. There was also a single goods siding to the east, but a goods yard was opened later on the western side of the station.

See also "Railways - Brighton Station".

Figure 135: The London Road Viaduct in about 1846, seen from the Blaker's Recreation Ground area. Note the Round Hill Mill to the left

145. RAILWAYS - Brighton Station, Queen's Road

<44,123,176,180>

a) *OPENING:* Brighton's railway station stands on a huge man-made plateau 130 feet above sea-level, and opened as a very simple, open structure at the same time as the branch line to Shoreham on 11 May 1840. By the time the London line opened in September 1841, a much larger building had been completed, designed by David Mocatta in Italianate style with a saw-tooth roof 250 feet long over the platforms. The façade, although now largely obscured, remains much as originally designed with three-storey wings and a clock, but the elegant colonnade of nine arches is now merely echoed by the present arched windows and doors.

Figure 136: Brighton Station in 1842 before the construction of Queen's Road and the bridge over Trafalgar Street

b) *ENLARGEMENTS AND IMPROVEMENTS:* In 1845, when Queen's Road was constructed to provide better access to the station, the railway company built the bridge over Trafalgar Street; it was widened in 1863 and again in 1875. In 1852-4 the station itself was enlarged and the platforms extended, but the greatest change came in 1882-3 when the canopy was added over the road in front of the station and the magnificent arched roof was erected. Designed by H.E.Wallis, the roof is 590 feet long and consists of one small and two large iron and glass spans supported on slender, scrolled, iron columns. Alterations to the main building were carried out at the same time by F.D.Bannister and included the addition of the concourse clock and the extension of the eleven platforms to take two trains each.

The platforms were again extended in 1932 to accommodate twelve-car electric sets, but were renumbered one to ten when the short platform four was filled in; platform ten closed in 1971 when the adjacent car-park was opened. At one time there was also a carriage ramp running from Trafalgar Street to the former platform seven, now six. Only platform three has access to all three lines, and then only for four-car trains. On 30 September 1935 Brighton Central Station was renamed simply Brighton Station.

In 1973-5 British Rail made plans to rebuild the station completely with an office complex and hotel above, but the Department of the Environment recognised its architectural merit by listing it in April 1973 after a vigourous public campaign by opponents of the proposals; in 1988 it was included in the West Hill conservation area. Some improvements were made with the opening of a travel centre in December 1979, a new ticket office in August 1980, and a new electronic indicator board in 1987 to replace the wooden indicator which was originally used at Victoria until 1927. A restoration of the exterior also commenced in 1987, and the details of the façade and canopy are now splendidly highlighted. Always one of the busiest of provincial stations, Brighton now handles over seven million passengers per year.

c) *GOODS-YARDS and ENGINE SHEDS:* Brighton Goods-Yard, later known as the lower goods-yard, was laid out in the 1840s to the east of the passenger station and at a level thirty feet below the passenger tracks. Initially it was accessed from the Shoreham branch via a tunnel below the London line, necessitating two reversals from the main line. This arrangement was replaced in 1852-4 by a new track leaving the main line at Lovers Walk and crossing New England Road on an iron bridge to the east of the New England Viaduct. However the tunnel still exists below the station, and has since been used as a communications centre and a rifle-range. In about 1894 a large goods-shed was built to the east of the station on the site of houses in Station Street; this in turn has been replaced by the offices known as Trafalgar Place, under construction in 1990. The upper goods-yard at Lovers Walk was established in about 1870.

Further extensions to the goods facilities were made in 1905 when a coal-yard was opened on the site of Peel Place, Peel Street, Queen Street and Cavendish Place North (to the west of New England Street). The lower goods-yard was closed by British Rail in the 1970s, but it was then used by National Carriers Ltd with a few wagons daily before finally closing in October 1980. The area is now part of the huge car-park that also covers the site of the railway engineering works, and is scheduled for the massive redevelopment including New England Square; from the latter 1980s a 'giant' Sunday market has been held on the car-park. The total area covered by the station, goods-yard, engine sheds and engineering works was 44.5 acres.

The engine sheds lay to the north of the station, between the London and Shoreham lines. The main shed had fourteen roads, with an adjacent 'new shed' 483 feet long by 50 feet wide with just three roads. A combined engineering depot opened on the site on 22 April 1968 at a cost of £400,000.

See also "Railways - Engineering Works".

Figure 137: The impressive roof of Brighton Brighton Station

146. RAILWAYS - Engineering Works, New England Street

(N.B. London, Brighton and South Coast Railway Company abbreviated to 'L.B.S.C.R.'.)
<123,176,180,185,316>

a) *ESTABLISHMENT:* The Brighton Railway Works occupied a large area between the main line and Boston Street, and originated at the end of 1842 when the maintenance of London and Brighton Railway stock was concentrated in the town. Carriages were fabricated from 1848, but the main locomotive manufacturing works, and the principal maintenance and repair shops of the L.B.S.C.R. were established in 1852 by the superintendent engineer, John Chester Craven. Originally intended for Horley, these workshops were the first centre of heavy industry to be established in the town.

b) *EXPANSION:* In 1854 a new wheel shop was opened, and further additions were made in 1860 and 1870. In 1870 William Stroudley became superintendent engineer and standardised locomotive production to just six classes with interchangeable parts; a green livery was also introduced, and locomotives were given individual names. A new iron foundry was added in 1873, and the works were extended to the north of Old Shoreham Road when carriage-painting and cleaning shops were built in 1878. The Brighton works also handled marine engineering for the company's cross-Channel fleet, although the steamer workshops were moved to Newhaven in 1880.

Stroudley died in 1889 (the stained-glass windows from his villa in Preston Road are exhibited at the Bluebell Railway) and was succeeded by R.J.Billington who immediately extended the works out on columns over the lower goods-yard line. Manufacture was concentrated in the original portion and produced about twelve locomotives annually. By 1891 2,651 people were employed at the railway works; there was a railway institute and library at the works, reached from Peel Place, and a railway mission in Viaduct Road.

c) *DECLINE:* The first signs of a rundown of the Brighton works came in 1901 when all marine engineering was transferred to Newhaven, and in 1912 the carriage and wagon works were removed to Lancing. In 1914-18 the works contributed greatly to war-time production, and in April 1922 the last locomotive produced under the L.B.S.C.R., the Remembrance, was dedicated as a memorial to those who had died.

Further decline followed the formation of the Southern Railway in 1923; the workshops were partially closed in 1928 with work transferred to Ashford and Eastleigh. The locomotive maintenance shops at Highcroft Villas, known as the Lovers Walk Depot, were converted for Pullman carriage maintenance but were closed in 1963 and then used for the storage of vintage locomotives. By the mid 1930s only repair work was being performed at Brighton, and the paint shop to the north of Old Shoreham Road was converted to an electric stock maintenance centre and shed.

d) *WAR-TIME REVIVAL:* The Second World War again saw a revival and many locomotives were produced from 1942, although the works were bombed several times. After the war 850 men were still employed, and 1947 saw the 1,000th Brighton locomotive completed, the Pacific-class Battle of Britain. Following nationalisation on 1 January 1948 work was once again redistributed throughout the country, but standard British Railways steam locomotives were still turned out, and diesel-electric locomotives were produced from 1953.

e) *CLOSURE:* The rundown of the Brighton works continued however, and the last locomotive, no.80154, was produced on 20 March 1957. Locomotive maintenance continued for a while, but the works were closed completely in 1958. For a short time they were used for the assembly of imported cars, but the buildings were eventually demolished in 1969. A car-park for 900 vehicles was opened on the site in January 1972, but the vacant area, the largest in the town centre, awaits the New England Square development.

147. REFUSE

<30,112,115,123>

Under the terms of the 1810 Brighton Town Act, the town commissioners appointed 'scavengers' to collect the town's domestic rubbish and night soil. This refuse was taken to the parish dust-yard on the northern side of Hollingdean Road where it was sorted, with any useful materials sold off, but the remaining waste was then tipped at other sites, creating a considerable health problem.

In May 1886 the corporation opened a 'dust destructor' on the Hollingdean site to incinerate the refuse to ashes which were then used as material for the construction of pavements, roads and playing-fields; this policy of incineration continued until 1952. After that date household refuse was tipped at Sheepcote Valley and the Hollingdean destructor therefore became redundant; the building was subsequently demolished and the area is now used by the borough council's Technical Services Department as a depot. Since 1974 refuse collection has been the responsibility of the borough council, but disposal is now the responsibility of East Sussex County Council. Major tipping at Sheepcote continued until April 1982, by which time the valley had been significantly filled and laid out with playing-fields, but since that time most of Brighton's refuse has been carted directly to the county council's chalk-pit infill site at Beddingham; Sheepcote remains a 'household waste site' for the disposal of bulky refuse. From January 1990 the street-cleaning services in Brighton have been run by the Spanish company FOCSA.

148. REGENCY SQUARE

a) *BELLE VUE FIELD:* One of the most impressive of Brighton's grand façades, Regency Square was erected in 1818-28 on the site of the Belle Vue Field. Used for fairs, shows, military reviews, etc., this field was reputed to be haunted by 'Betsy Bedlam' in the eighteenth century <6>, and by 1744 it was also the site of the West Mill, a post-mill which may have been rebuilt in 1762. On 28 March 1797, following complaints by nearby residents, it was transported on a sledge up the Dyke Road to a site near the top of Millers Road (see "Dyke Road").

On 13 August 1793, at a time of great unrest across the Channel, the first Brighton Military Camp was established at Belle Vue Field, and about 10,000 soldiers were based there by the time it dispersed on 28 October 1793. The second camp was set up in Hove in 1794 with about 15,000 men, and they became an annual event for about ten years. The great number of men and officers in and around the town proved a natural attraction for young ladies looking for husbands or ready to sell their charms, while the regular reviews and manoeuvres provided colourful entertainment for visitors. When two men were shot and eleven others flogged for mutiny at Goldstone Bottom on 12 June 1795 however, there was an outcry amongst the townsfolk. The Brighton Camps were described by Jane Austen in *Pride and Prejudice*. <3,15,249,249b>

b) *HISTORY and DESCRIPTION of the SQUARE:* From 1818 until 1828 the new residents of Regency Square purchased individual plots from the speculative developer, Joshua Hanson, and bound themselves by covenant to complete the façades to an approved design with balconies and stuccoed ground floors. The covenants, which lasted for seventy-one years from December 1818, also required the owners to repaint the façades every three years and to contribute equally to the maintenance of the enclosure. However, faced with the prospect of the covenants expiring, the corporation assumed control of the square under the terms of the 1884 Brighton Improvement Act and extended the covenants indefinitely.

The architectural merit of the square is reflected in the grade II* listing of the entire eastern and western sides, together with nos.26-37 facing the garden along the northern side; most of the other houses, nos.21-25 and 38-46, are listed grade II. Many were probably designed by Amon Wilds and his son, Amon Henry Wilds, with the later houses by the Amon Wilds/Charles Busby partnership; most have bows and balconies, and many are faced with mathematical tiles. The houses of the eastern side are mostly adorned with Ionic doorways. The northern side is a symmetric composition of bow-fronted houses with balconies and verandahs, flanking the yellow-brick centre-piece which prominently displays the name of the square. The archway between nos.42 and 43 leads to Regency Mews (see "Regency Square Conservation Area"). Hotels now dominate Regency Square, but Dr William King, the social reformer and co-operative pioneer, lived at no.2 from 1828 until 1830. No.57 was the home of Somers Clarke, clerk to the vestry for many years until 1892.

The gardens cover 1.56 acres and now form the roof of an underground car-park for 520 cars which opened at Easter 1969 at a cost of £523,000; it was originally planned to be a surface car-park. Regency Square has now given its name to the surrounding outstanding conservation area which is detailed in the entry following. <44,46,123,126,271a,306>

c) *ST ALBANS HOUSE:* No.1 Regency Square, together with 131 King's Road, is a grade II*-listed building designed after the rest of the square in 1828-30 by A.H.Wilds; it is decorated with his familiar shell motifs. Originally known as Regency House, it was taken by the Duke and Duchess of St Albans in July 1830 and became one of the centres of Brighton society. The Duchess, formerly the actress Harriot Mellon, married first one of the richest men in England, the banker Thomas Coutts who was forty-two years her senior, but following his death she married the ninth Duke of St Albans, twenty-four years her junior. The Duchess died in 1837. <46>

d) *ROYAL SUSSEX REGIMENT WAR MEMORIAL:* Standing at the southern end of the square, this Portland stone cenotaph was erected to the 152 men of the regiment who perished in the South African or Boer War of 1900-2. It was unveiled on 29 October 1904 by the Marquess of Abergavenny, and is surmounted by a bronze bugler and four artillery shells. Now a listed structure, it also commemorates the men lost at Louisberg and Quebec in 1759, in Egypt in the 1880s, and in the two World Wars. <44,311>

Figure 138: The Royal Sussex Regiment Memorial

149. REGENCY SQUARE CONSERVATION AREA

This outstanding conservation area, which stretches westwards from the Grand Hotel to the borough boundary, was developed principally in the 1810s and '20s, and contains some of the finest examples of Brighton's famous Regency architecture. However, the district of around 2,500 people now has many housing problems with its many multiply-occupied houses and bed-sits. The streets of particular interest in the area are detailed below, but see also "Bedford Hotel", "Grand Hotel", "King's Road", "Lower Esplanade", "Metropole", "Norfolk Hotel", "West Pier", and "Western Road".

a) *BEDFORD PLACE:* A road of mostly three-storey houses, with the bow-fronted nos.2, 3, 7, 25 and 26 included on the borough council's local list of buildings of special interest. On the eastern side stands the former Christ Church School, a listed building built in 1841 for Revd James Vaughan. The original cobble-fronted building, with its Dutch gable, has a red-brick extension of the 1900s. It continued as a school until about 1948, but since about 1958 has been used by the New Venture Theatre Company. It was also a church hall until the adjacent Christ Church in Montpelier Road was destroyed. <44,45a,83,123>

b) *BEDFORD SQUARE:* The construction of this, the earliest of Brighton's squares, was commenced in about 1801. By 1814 twelve houses had been erected, and Bedford Square was completed in 1818 with forty-two houses; nos.1-3, with fluted Ionic pillars and verandahs, are now numbered 148-146 King's Road, and nos.40-42 are 145-143 King's Road, The Brighton Hotel. Designed in the main with bows, ironwork balconies and verandahs, nos.1-16, 21-26, 27-31 (the most distinguished) and 32-39 are all listed buildings; many are decorated with pilasters but have no capitals. Most of the houses were let to visitors, but no.3 was occupied for several years from 1823 by the landscape-gardener Henry Phillips, the man responsible for the Kemp Town enclosures. The Bedford Square garden covers 0.45 of an acre and became corporation property in May 1887 following the 1884 Brighton Improvement Act. <44,46,126,271a>

c) *CANNON PLACE:* Now largely redeveloped, Cannon Place was originally built from about 1813 and was named from the nearby battery on the sea-front. Nos.27-30, together with 46 Russell Square, form a listed terrace with balconies and bows. The bow-fronted nos.31-32 are also listed and form the eastern façade of the former Royal Newburgh Assembly Rooms in St Margaret's Place (see below). <14,44>

d) *CAVENDISH PLACE:* Built in about 1829 by A.H.Wilds, this cul-de-sac is lined with four- and five-storey houses adorned with balconies and Corinthian pilasters, all listed except nos.3 and 14; nos.5-6 also have bows. No.6 has a plaque to the Irish dramatist Dion Boucicault who lived there from 1862 until 1872, while no.12 was the home of writer Horace Smith from 1840 until 1849. At the top of the road stands The Curzon, a most elegant listed hotel with ironwork balconies; it was originally two separate residences known as the Cavendish Mansions. <44,46,311>

e) *CLARENCE SQUARE:* The four-storey buildings on the northern side of the square were erected in the 1800s as Clarence Place, with the shop-fronts of Western Road added later in their gardens, but the other sides were not completed until the 1820s. With most of the houses refronted in the mid nineteenth century, the square is not particularly distinguished; the only houses of especial merit were demolished in the 1960s for the widening of Cannon Place. The gardens were taken over by the corporation following the 1884 Brighton Improvement Act.

At the western end, the cottages of Clarence Gardens lead to the Studio Theatre, a small, classical building built in about 1830 as the Clarence Baptist Chapel. From about 1852 until 1884 it was the Christ Church Infant School, and was then used as a mission hall, but in 1899 it became an art school and gallery before being converted for the Brighton Little Theatre Company in 1940. It has a tiny stage and room for an audience of about eighty. <45a,62,83,123,126>

f) *MONTPELIER ROAD:* Montpelier Road once ran all the way from King's Road to Ditchling Road, but the name is now restricted to the section south of Denmark Villas. Developed from the 1820s, there are a number of listed buildings to the south of Western Road; nos.14-17 and 19 have narrow bows, while nos.21-24 were built in a late-Regency wide-bow-fronted style of about 1840. No.23 was the home of the co-operative pioneer Dr William King (1786-1865). <44,75>

Sillwood House, on the eastern side at the rear of Debenhams, dates from 1827-8; see "Sillwood Place" below. On the opposite side of the road stood Christ Church, built for Revd Henry Wagner in 1837-8 by George Cheeseman junior with a low tower and spire flanked by the entrances; see figure 181. It was consecrated on 26 April 1838 by the Bishop of Chichester, and the interior, which held 1,070, was remodelled by Edmund Scott in 1886. However, the building was was badly damaged in a fire started by vandals on 29 August 1978, and was subsequently demolished in 1982; sheltered housing was built on the site in 1985-7. The nearby pillar-box at the corner of Western Road dates from 1858 <15> and is of the first national standard type-A design; it is one of only four remaining, and is now a listed structure. <44,62,65>

For the section of Montpelier Road to the north of Western Road, see "Clifton Hill".

g) *NORFOLK SQUARE:* Developed in the 1820s, Norfolk Square is lined with three-storey houses, many with wide bows and balconies, but also includes the four-storey composition on the northern side of Western Road. The bow-fronted nos.35-45 on the eastern side, and nos.30-34 on the southern side, with their elegant façades, balconettes, and Ionic pilasters, are listed buildings, while nos.22-29 are attractive Regency villas. The flats of Norfolk Court and Dorchester Court were built on the sites of houses which were bombed in the war. The gardens were acquired by the corporation in August 1886 following the 1884 Brighton Improvement Act, while the conveniences and bus-shelters along Western Road were added in about 1950. <26,44,126,262b>

Figure 139: Grand Regency façades by A.H.Wilds in Oriental Place

h) *NORFOLK STREET:* A narrow road with some charming, early-nineteenth-century cottages. <83>

j) *ORIENTAL PLACE:* This road was originally constructed as an approach to a projected oriental garden, to be laid out by botanist and landscape-gardener Henry Phillips. The plans also included a large conservatory and cultural centre, the Athenaeum, but the project failed because of a lack of finance and was abandoned in July 1827. Oriental Place has symmetric compositions either side by A.H.Wilds, all grade II*-listed buildings. They were built from 1825 onwards, and are adorned by pilasters, ammonite capitals, shell decorations and ironwork balconies. It was also intended to erect an Oriental Terrace along King's Road either side of Oriental Place, but only three houses on the eastern side were built which were converted into King's Hotel in about 1864 by T.H.King. The hotel was badly damaged by fire in January 1967, but was subsequently restored. <3,44,46>

k) *PRESTON STREET:* Nicknamed the 'street of a thousand restaurants', there were in fact only thirty-five dining establishments in Preston Street in 1990! The phenomenon is recent as there were only two restaurants in 1956, eight in 1966, and thirteen in 1974 <83>. The street was probably named from Preston Manor, the former home of the Western family after whom Western Road is named, and retains some interesting listed buildings. No.5 has a mid-nineteenth-century shop-front of fluted Corinthian pillars, while nos.58 and 60 on the eastern side date from the early nineteenth century and have bow windows; no.58 also has Ionic pilasters. The nearby Royal Sovereign Inn has a pair of bows and dates from the 1820s, while lower down the street stands Regency Cottage, no.79, a small, bowed house with a stone balustrade roof, which was probably designed in the 1820s by Wilds and Busby. Nos.16-18, with narrow bows and verandahs, are included on the council's local list as are nos.40-44 which are decorated with fluted pilasters and ammonite capitals, a speciality of A.H.Wilds; they have been spoiled by the addition of window bays, however. <44>

l) *QUEENSBURY MEWS:* This service road for the eastern side of Regency Square is now dominated by the Metropole Exhibition Halls, but at the southern end stands the Église Prostestante Reformée Française (French Reformed Church), a very small chapel built in red brick by J.G.Gibbins and one of only two such churches in England; the other is in Soho Square, London. The congregation is said to have been founded in about 1550 by the Flemish martyr Deryk Carver, and met at a number of locations including the Union Street Chapel and, from around 1860, the Royal Newburgh Rooms until the permanent church was erected in 1887. The foundation stone was laid by a Mrs Hayes whose house, 18 Montpelier Villas, had also been used by the congregation. Services are conducted by visiting ministers. <62,64a,123>

m) *REGENCY MEWS:* Lying behind the grand façade of Regency Square, this mews is now approached only from Preston Street, although access was also via the listed archway between nos.42 and 43 Regency Square. The attractive nos.10-11 are small, bow-fronted listed houses of about 1835. <44,109>

n) *RUSSELL SQUARE:* Developed by about 1825, Russell Square has listed terraces on its western and southern sides designed by A.H.Wilds, all with ironwork balconies, verandahs and Corinthian pilasters. The gardens were taken over by the corporation in July 1887 following the 1884 Brighton Improvement Act.

The Regency Tavern, in the twitten leading to Regency Square, is said to be haunted by the ghost of a young crippled girl who lived on the first floor when it was a cobbler's shop; she unfortunately leapt to her death on smelling gas. A second ghost, that of a former landlady, roams the first floor. <44,45a,89,126,271a>

Figure 140: Detail of the façade of the Royal Newburgh Rooms, St Margaret's Place

p) *ST MARGARET'S PLACE:* Built in the 1820s as Regency Cottages, the name was changed following the erection of St Margaret's Chapel in 1824. Standing at the end of the road, this church was considered the best classical church in Brighton; it was designed by Charles Busby <64a> for Barnard Gregory, the editor of the *Brighton Gazette*, who named it after his wife Margaret. The stuccoed chapel opened on 26 December 1824, and was designed with an Ionic portico facing east and an octagonal turret tower. The large interior had wide galleries on three sides with a second gallery on the eastern side, and the 1,500 sittings were second only to St Peter's. Some alterations were made by A.H.Wilds in 1830, and as the chapel proved popular with Brighton's fashionable society it was further enlarged to include a double gallery at the western end; a chancel was added by J.Oldrid Scott in 1874. Attendances eventually dwindled though, and the last service took place on 30 September 1956. The church was demolished in June 1959 to make way for the Metropole Exhibition Halls, Sussex Heights, and a 250-space car-park (see "Metropole"). <1,3,46,62,64a,83>

Nos.2-3 on the northern side are listed buildings with Ionic pilasters, probably by Wilds and Busby. Opposite stands the grand entrance to the former Royal Newburgh Assembly Rooms, a listed building erected in about 1833 <108,140> by A.H.Wilds for Charles Wright, a bookseller and librarian. King William IV is said to have attended the opening, and the rooms were a social centre in the western town for many years. They were used by the French Reformed Church from the 1860s until 1887, but were later converted into flats. Now only the shell of the building remains, the interior being part of the Metropole Exhibition Halls. The entrance façade has two Corinthian columns either side of the doorway below a central pediment, but the ballroom which stood to the west has been demolished. <44,46,62,140>

q) *SILLWOOD PLACE:* Leads from a small gateway at Sillwood Street to Sillwood House, and was originally flanked by two terraces of about 1827-8 by A.H.Wilds. Unfortunately the western terrace, which was later used as the Hotel Montpelier until 1960 and also as the Starlight Rooms, was demolished in about 1969 and replaced by the oppressive grey bulk of Osprey House. However, the listed eastern terrace remains and is decorated with Corinthian pilasters. No.9 housed the West Cliff Catholic Mission from 1858 until St Mary Magdalene's Church opened in 1862, and has unusual, oriental ground-floor windows. <44,46,56,123>

Sillwood House itself is a mansion built in 1827-8 by A.H.Wilds for Sir David Scott who had purchased the site of the proposed Athenaeum and Oriental Garden (see "Oriental Place" above); he named the house after his family's estate at Sillwood Park, Berkshire. The three-storey building has ironwork balconies on the first and second floors, and a semi-circular portico on the western side facing Montpelier Road. In 1880 it was converted into the Sillwood Hall Hotel, but since about 1961 it has belonged to the adjacent store in Western Road, now Debenhams. A listed building, Sillwood House was derelict for many years but a restoration and conversion to flats commenced in 1989; it has a superb cast-iron staircase. An excellent model of Sillwood Place and the surrounding area may be found in Brighton Museum. <44,46,123>

r) *SILLWOOD ROAD:* Known as Western Cottages until about 1870, the name was changed when the elegant listed terrace, nos.32-47, was erected by Thomas Lainson on the western side; the three-storey houses have ironwork balconies and verandahs. Nos.13-14 on the opposite side are also listed, while nos.9-10 are decorated with Ionic pilasters. <44,83>

s) *SILLWOOD STREET:* A road of mixed development. No.5, although dilapidated, is decorated with pilasters and is included on the council's local list of buildings of special interest.

t) *WESTERN STREET:* A wide road where the bow-fronted and verandahed no.5, and no.31 with its original shop-front, are listed buildings of about 1820. Embassy Court was the first modern high-rise block of flats in the town and is listed for its architectural interest; see "King's Road". The large vacant area on the Hove side of Western Street was the site of Golden Lane and is scheduled for a mixed redevelopment. It was once a densely populated area of tenements and beershops, with the inhabitants involved principally in brickmaking. <44,262b>

150. RELIGION

Religion has always played a major part in the country's affairs and Brighton has been no exception. The medieval Priory of St Bartholomew was subject to the Dissolution of Henry VIII in 1547, and the parish church was, of course, Roman Catholic until the Reformation. In 1554 Deryk Carver of the Black Lion Brewery was the first protestant to be martyred during the reign of the Catholic 'Bloody' Mary I, and religious persecution, particularly of Catholics, Quakers and other non-conformists, continued into the late seventeenth century. In 1676 a religious census to determine the extent of dissent recorded 1,740 Anglicans in Brighton and 260 dissenters, while Preston had 64 and 1 respectively, Patcham 97 and 3, and Stanmer 43 and 0; Ovingdean and Rottingdean were not recorded. Not a single Catholic was recorded in these parishes. <3,67>

As attitudes towards opposing denominations eased so chapels for the various sects were built in the town. The dates of the first permanent chapels are: Anglican (first chapel of ease, Chapel Royal) 1795; Baptist (Bond Street) 1787; Catholic (High Street) 1806; Countess of Huntingdon (North Street) 1761; Jewish (Devonshire Place) 1826; Methodist (Dorset Gardens) 1808; Presbyterian (Union Street) 1688; and Quaker (North Street) 1701. As the nineteenth century progressed and the population increased, many proprietary chapels were built in the town, both Anglican and Independent. Many of the pews were rented to wealthy worshippers to provide an income for their ministers, however, and the poor of the town therefore had to crowd into the the old parish church and the few free sittings that were available. It was to remedy this situation that Henry and Arthur Wagner (q.v.) embarked, at great personal expense, on a massive church building scheme from the 1830s until the 1870s.

The first Catholic place of worship to be established in Brighton since the Reformation was a temporary chapel in Prospect Row (later part of St James's Street) in about 1800, but it was replaced in 1806 by a permanent chapel in High Street. As the nineteenth century progressed so the 'Anglo-Catholic' movement (variously known as 'The High Church', 'The Oxford Movement', 'Puseyism', 'Ritualism' or 'Tractarianism') became more prominent as a reaction to non-conformity; it aroused considerable passion, anger, and even violence among many Protestants. In Brighton the arguments centred chiefly around the Revd Arthur Wagner, the curate of the lavishly decorated St Paul's Church which was opened in 1848 by an ornate ceremony in marked contrast to other Brighton churches. Rituals, chanting and confessions were practised, and Wagner founded an order of Protestant nuns in Queen Square. He opened other 'High' churches at the Annunciation, St Bartholomew's and St Martin's, and was even shot at. St James's and St Michael's Churches were also involved, while some classically-designed churches were transformed into a 'more acceptable' Gothic style. It was not until the 1900s that the passionate feeling between High and Low Church in the town died down. <45a,56,62,65,115>

Brighton is now divided into twenty Anglican parishes (St Peter's is *the* Brighton Parish), and is a rural deanery within the Archdeaconry and Diocese of Chichester, Province of Canterbury. Brighton is also a Roman Catholic deanery within the Diocese of Arundel and Brighton, which was formed on 28 May 1965 in the new Province of Southwark. <123,314>

151. ROADS

a) *HISTORY:* Since at least 1285 roads were the responsibility of manorial authorities, but the Highway Act of 1555 transferred their maintenance to the parishes which were directed to appoint a surveyor, and also required able-bodied householders to contribute either money or labour towards their annual upkeep. In the eighteenth and nineteenth centuries Parliament established 'turnpike trusts' to maintain certain main highways with monies collected from tolls; the main roads into Brighton from Newhaven, Lewes, Ditchling, Cuckfield, Henfield and Old Shoreham were all turnpiked, but most were wound up in 1889 when responsibility for highways passed to the county and county borough councils. Roads within the parish of Brighton became the responsibility of the town commissioners following the 1773 Brighton Town Act, and in 1854 the corporation took over. East Sussex County Council has been responsible since 1974, but Brighton Borough Council still acts on an agency basis as the highway authority. Trunk-roads are the responsibility of the Department of Transport; as a county borough Brighton had no trunk-roads, but some short lengths of the major roads have been trunked since 1974. <29,43,300>

b) *CLASSIFIED ROADS:* Roads in the borough are grouped into five classifications, although government funding is now based on a lump sum dependent upon the total highway mileage. In 1990 the borough had approximately 1.40 miles of trunk road and 17.15 miles of principal roads (both 'A' roads); 8.55 miles of class II ('B') roads; 20.05 miles of class III roads; and about 185 miles of unclassified roads. The classified roads within the borough are <313>:

A23 (Brighton to London, Westminster Bridge Road): Old Steine; Grand Parade; Marlborough Place; Gloucester Place; York Place; London Road; Preston Road; Stanford Avenue (part); Beaconsfield Road; London Road (Patcham). Since 1980 this has been a trunk-road to the north of the Mill Road/Vale Avenue junction, the responsibility of central government.

A27 (A36 Whiteparish, Wiltshire, to A259 Pevensey): Old Shoreham Road; New England Road (part); Viaduct Road; Upper Lewes Road; Lewes Road (to Falmer boundary). Part of the Folkestone to Honiton trunk-road, but it was not trunked between Falmer and Hangleton Road. In 1984 the section from the Falmer boundary to the Southern Water Authority office became a trunk-road; the Brighton bypass, the future A27 trunk-road, will leave the Lewes Road at this point.

A27 (spur): Lewes Road from the Vogue gyratory system to Grand Parade. Lewes Road was originally part of the A26 Brighton (now Newhaven) to Maidstone road, with the A27 terminating from the west at the Upper Lewes Road junction.

A259 (A27 Havant to A20 Folkestone): King's Road; Grand Junction Road; Marine Parade; Marine Drive.

A2010: West Street; Queen's Road; Surrey Street; Terminus Road; Buckingham Place; Bath Street (part); Dyke Road (Bath Street to Old Shoreham Road).

A2038 (A23 Patcham to A27 Portslade): Mill Road.

B2066 (Old Steine to Boundary Road, Hove): Castle Square; North Street; Western Road. This was formerly the A277.

B2118: St James's Street; Upper St James's Street; Bristol Road; St George's Road; Chesham Road; Rock Place; Church Place; Bristol Gardens; Roedean Road.

B2119: Trafalgar Street.

B2121: Dyke Road (North Street to Bath Street).

B2122: New England Road (part); Chatham Place; Vernon Terrace; Denmark Villas; Montpelier Road.

B2123 (A27 Falmer to A259 Rottingdean): Falmer Road; The Green; High Street.

B2137: Arundel Road.

The class III roads in the borough are:

Bear Road.
Carden Avenue.
Coldean Lane.
Ditchling Road.
Dyke Road (north of Old Shoreham Road).
Edward Street; Eastern Road.
Elm Grove; Warren Road.
Freshfield Road.
Highcroft Villas; Dyke Road Drive.
Hollingbury Road; Upper Hollingdean Road (part); Hollingdean Road.
Millers Road; South Road.
North Road.
Ovingdean Road; Greenways.
Preston Drove.
Saddlescombe Road.
Union Road.
Vale Avenue; Winfield Avenue.
Valley Drive; Tongdean Lane (part).

c) *LONGEST ROADS:* The longest named roads within the borough are <313>:

	Road	Mileage
1.	Lewes Road	3.46
2.	Marine Drive	3.24
3.	Ditchling Road	3.20
4.	Falmer Road	2.80
5.	London Road (Patcham)	2.61
6.	Carden Avenue	2.03
7.	Warren Road	1.80
8.	Dyke Road	1.76
9.	Marine Parade	1.37
10.	Wilson Avenue	1.27
11.	Madeira Drive	1.20
12.	Coldean Lane	1.19
13.	Mill Road	1.10
14.	Preston Road	1.09
15.	Surrenden Road	1.06
16.	Eastern Road	1.01
17.	Bexhill Road	1.00

d) *TRAFFIC CONTROL:* Traffic control in Brighton probably dates from 1900 when the police started to regulate the Clock Tower junction for horse traffic. The first motor-car was seen in the town in 1895 <3>, and the rapid growth in traffic warranted the introduction of the 'gyratory system' at the Aquarium junction in 1924, with a permanent island in May 1925 said to be the first roundabout in the country; two more roundabouts appeared at Preston Circus and Seven Dials soon after. One-way traffic was introduced around the Steine and Victoria Gardens in 1926. The first parking restrictions were enforced in 1934 in East Street, and on 4 March 1963 the first of 1,180 parking meters were introduced, at a parking rate of sixpence (2.5p) per hour; they are due to be replaced by a voucher system early in 1991. The country's first pedestrian crossings, neither statutory nor marked by beacons, were painted in yellow across Madeira Drive and Marine Parade at the Aquarium in 1932.

In December 1927 a police-operated mechanical semaphore signal was installed at the junction of King's Road and West Street, said to be only the second signal of its kind in the country. It was followed by more elaborate sets at Preston Circus in 1928 and at the junction of Castle Square and Old Steine in 1929, but the semaphore signals were replaced by lights in 1933, and by 1935 there were fourteen sets operating. In October 1990 there were thirty-eight independent sets of traffic lights in Brighton, plus numerous 'pelican' pedestrian crossings. Lewes Road now has five sets, including two at the Vogue gyratory system, while Dyke Road and King's Road have four. <2,115,123,164>

e) *STREET NAME DERIVATIONS:* An explanation of the source of Brighton's street names merits a separate work. However, many may be classified into broad groups, including the following commemorative street names:

Royal forenames: Albert, Alexandra, Alfred, Charles, Charlotte, Edward, Frederick, George, Leopold, Victoria, William.

Royal dukes: Cambridge, Clarence, Cumberland, Gloucester, Sussex, York.

Royal houses: Brunswick, Hanover.

Royal residences: Carlton, Kensington, Kew, St James's, Windsor.

Dukes: Argyle, Beaufort, Bedford, Buckingham, Devonshire, Grafton, Hamilton, Manchester, Norfolk, Portland, Richmond, Somerset, Sutherland, Wellington.

Marquesses: Bath, Bristol, Bute, Exeter, Hartington, Lorne, Queensbury.

Earls: Burlington, Camden, Chatham, Chichester, Clarendon, Coventry, Egremont, Essex, Guildford, Jersey, Leicester, Liverpool, Mayo, Oxford, Powis, Shaftesbury.

Viscounts: Hereford, Sydney, Wentworth.

Barons: Chesham, Holland, Southampton, Sudeley, Tichborne, Vernon.

Peer's family surnames: Campbell, Cavendish, Compton, Grenville, Grosvenor, Hervey, Howard, Lennox, Montague, Pelham, Russell (Square), Seymour, Stanley, Wyndham.

Prime ministers: Balfour, Beaconsfield, Canning, Gladstone, Liverpool, Melbourne, Peel, Russell (Crescent), Walpole, Wellington.

United States presidents: Grant, Jackson, Lincoln, Washington.

Boer War soldiers and locations: Baden, Buller, Kimberley, Ladysmith, Mafeking, Milner, Natal, (Sir) Redvers (Buller).

Philosophers, theologians, etc: Arnold, Baxter, Bentham, Carlyle, Cobden, Cromwell, Hampden, Howard, Luther, Lynton, Milton.

Honorary freemen and women: Beatty, Carden, Churchill, Haig, Saunders, Stringer, Wolseley.

Mayors: Abbey, Aldrich, Beal, Blaker, Braybon, Brigden, Carden, Colbourne, Davey, Ewart, Galliers, Hallett, Lucraft, Pankhurst, Sadler, Southall, Stringer, Thompson.

Local landowners: Curwen, Goldsmid, Harrington, Mighell, Nevill, Stanford, Tidy, Western, Whichelo.

Topographical names are also very popular, and Sussex localities are particularly in evidence on the corporation's housing estates. Other topographical names include:

Isle of Wight: Bembridge, Bonchurch, Brading, Carisbrooke, St Helen's, Sandown, Shanklin, Totland, Whippingham.

Abbeys: Fountains, Hinton, Melrose, Romsey.

Castles: Auckland, Bamford, Bodiam, Durham, Hornby, Kenilworth, Knepp, Leybourne, Ludlow, Norwich, Taunton, Walmer.

Canadian cities: Montreal, Toronto, Quebec.

Towns of Kent: Ashford, Dover, Hythe, Sandgate.

f) *STREET NAME CHANGES:* The more significant changes are listed below. <83,108>

Barrowcliff Street - Leicester Street
Blue and Buffs - Old Steine (nos.1-4)
Boar's Lane - Air Street
Brunswick Place North - Ditchling Road (opposite Level)
Bury Street - College Place
Carlton Hill (below John St) - Kingswood Street
Chichester Street - Kingsbury Street
Church Hill Road - Dyke Road (Upper North Street to Seven Dials)
Clevedon Place - Upper Sudeley Street
Cobden Place - Prestonville Road (south)
Cragg's Lane - Duke Street
Dog Kennel Road - Hollingdean Road
Downs Road - Falmer Road (Woodingdean)
Drove Road - Peacock Lane
Falmer Close - Falmer Gardens
Fleet Street - New England Street (south of Ann Street)
Freshfield Terrace - Freshfield Street
German Place - Madeira Place
Gloucester Lane - Gloucester Road
Golden Lion Lane - Market Street (north of Brighton Place)
Grove Road - York Road
Guildford Terrace - Carlton Street
Gypsey Lane - Upper Lewes Road
Hangleton Road - Tivoli Road
Lennox Place - Richmond Terrace (nos.1-3)
Lower Rock Mews - Rock Place
Lyall Street - Chesham Place
Madeira Road - Madeira Drive
Marine Street - Wyndham Street
Mill Place - Sudeley Place
Mill Place - Vine Place
Montpelier Road East - Viaduct Road
Montpelier Road North - New England Road
Nelson Street - John Street (Carlton Hill to Sussex Street)
Newlands Road - Bishopstone Drive
New Steine Street- Wentworth Street
New Street - Bond Street
New York Street - New England Street (York Hill to Ann Street)
Norfolk Avenue - Boundary Passage
North Lane - North Road
North Parade - Old Steine (nos.6-13)
Nottingham Street - Spa Street
Park Road East - Freshfield Road
Park Road West - Queen's Park Road
Patriot Place - Tilbury Place
Peel Terrace - Dyke Road (Seven Dials to Russell Crescent)
Pelham Terrace - Pelham Square (south and west)
Prospect Place - St Peter's Place
Prospect Row - St James's Street (George Street to High Street)
Quarry Road - Greenbank Avenue (north of Mount Drive)
Queen Mary Villas - Bavant Road
Queen's Road - London Road (Brighton)
Regency Cottages - St Margaret's Place
Reservoir Road - Downland Road
Reynolds Avenue - Valley Drive (eastern end)
Richmond Road - Mighell Street
Rock Mews - Rock Place
Rottingdean Road - Roedean Road
St George's Street - Pelham Street
Saltdean Drive North - Mount Drive
South Parade - Old Steine (nos.19-34)
South Row - Old Steine (site of Royal York)
Spring Street - Church Hill and Old London Road (parts)
Suffolk Place - Cannon Street
Surrey Place - Upper Gloucester Road
Sussex Street (below wall) - Morley Street
Town Parade - Grand Parade (southern part)
Union Street - Marine Gardens
Union Street North - Oxford Place
Upper Trafalgar Street - Guildford Street
Waterloo Street North - Phoenix Place
West Drive - Rushlake Road (east of Forest Road)
Western Cottages - Sillwood Road
Wiston Close - Alan Way (Wiston Road end)
York Road North - York Hill
York Street - Eastern Road (east of Rock Street)
York Street - Camelford Street

152. ROEDEAN

Roedean Gap is a slight dip in the cliffs between Black Rock and Ovingdean Gap, and has been known as such since at least 1724. It was the site of a tollgate on the Newhaven turnpike, and Roedean Farm stood on the cliff top until the construction of the Marine Drive in the early 1930s. There was also a windmill at Roedean from around 1750 to about 1790, and the old mill-house was amongst the buildings cleared for the road construction. <108,249b,289>

Figure 141: Former coastguard cottages at Roedean Terrace

Roedean Bottom extends northwards from the gap and has been the site of a number of Roman finds. In about 1900 an isolated row of coastguard cottages now known as Roedean Terrace was erected to the west of the valley. The Roedean estate, which was developed around the terrace from the 1930s, is now one of Brighton's most exclusive residential districts with a population of around 600. The open spaces along the cliff top were acquired by the corporation in 1928-35. The miniature golf-course opened in April 1957, but was reduced to 16 holes in 1988 for the new layout of Marine Drive to cater for Marina traffic; the adjacent area to the north of Roedean Road has also been used as a pitch-and-putt course during busy periods. <83,116,123,126,277>

Roedean Road itself opened between Arundel Road and the coast road at Roedean Farm in 1897 as an alternative to the cliff-top road which had become unusable to the east of Black Rock owing to cliff erosion; seventy-five feet of land had disappeared in fifty years <26>. The new road to Rottingdean, Marine Drive, was opened on 22 July 1932 by P.J.Pybus, Minister of Transport, with the cliffs protected by the Undercliff Walk sea-wall. <112,115,116>

John Howard House at the western end of Roedean Road was opened in 1914 at the expense of Sir John Howard as a convalescent home for gentlewomen, but it was almost immediately requisitioned for use as an officers' hospital in the First World War. Since 1974 it has been a home of the Royal Hospital and Home for Incurables, which is based in Putney and run on a voluntary basis <3,123>. Opposite is a large electricity substation built by the corporation in 1924, and the Bell Tower Industrial Estate, developed in 1983 on the site of St Mark's School; the school's bell-tower is preserved as the estate's distinctive feature. <115,123>

The East Brighton Golf Club in Roedean Road is a private club, founded in 1893 as the Kemp Town Golf Club. Initially it had just a few holes alongside Roedean Road, but it was soon extended to nine holes across the Downs, and in 1897 changed its name to East Brighton with the addition of another nine holes. The small clubhouse was near the present fourth tee, but the present clubhouse was erected in 1897 and extended several times until 1912. The course itself is 6,291 yards long and was remodelled in 1903 along Wick Bottom; the land is leased from the corporation which acquired it in September 1913 as part of the East Brighton estate. Past presidents of the club include the Duke of Norfolk, Marquess of Abergavenny, Earl of Chichester and Earl Haig. <218-221,305>

153. ROEDEAN SCHOOL, Marine Drive

<203a,207,208>

This most famous of girls' schools was founded in October 1885, with ten girls and no particular name, at 25 Lewes Crescent by the Misses Dorothy, Millicent and Penelope Lawrence, in an effort to provide more than the rudimentary education that it was then customary for girls to receive. The school also took in 3 Arundel Terrace, 27 Lewes Crescent and 37 Chesham Road before moving to 35-37 Sussex Square as the Wimbledon House School; nos.34 and 29 Sussex Square were then taken in 1892 and 1893 respectively. The school had a playing-field off Roedean Road where East Brighton Park now lies.

The large school buildings at Roedean were designed by Sir John Simpson on an eighteen-acre site purchased from the Marquess of Abergavenny. Construction commenced in March 1897, the foundation stone was laid on 26 July 1897 by Mrs Henry Sidgwick, principal of Newnham College, Oxford, and Roedean School opened in January 1899. The Flemish-style main building has large gables, a clock tower, and a 500-foot frontage; the four projecting bays are the school's houses. Several new developments were added before the Second World War; twenty-four more acres were purchased in 1903 and another seventy-seven in 1930; a new chapel was dedicated in May 1906 by the Bishop of Chichester; a swimming-pool first opened in 1907; the junior school and sanatorium were opened in 1908; a new wing and a tunnel to the beach were added in 1910; Roedean House was built in the 1920s; and the Lawrence science building opened in July 1928. In 1938 Roedean School was incorporated by Royal Charter.

During the war the buildings were used by H.M.S.Vernon, a torpedo and electrical training establishment. The school itself was removed to the Keswick Hotel in Cumberland, but returned in January 1946 and now has 485 pupils, all boarders. Several further additions have included: the dining hall (1964); indoor swimming-pool (1970); Lawrence (sixth-form) House (1974); and the sports hall (1986). On 7 October 1985 a time-capsule was laid to mark the school's centenary.

154. ROTTINGDEAN

Rottingdean, 'the valley of Rota's people', is an ancient and attractive village four miles east-south-east of Brighton. In the Domesday Book of 1086 the manor was tenanted by a certain Hugh from William de Warrenne, and the village had a population of around fifty to one hundred, but by the fifteenth century the parish belonged to at least four separate manors. Despite its proximity to the sea the village remained a poor but chiefly agricultural community, suffering considerable loss of land through erosion in medieval times, and having to plead against the payments of certain taxes on the grounds of poverty. In 1377 the village was raided by the French who burnt the church with many villagers in the belfry before moving on to Lewes and holding the prior to ransom. The villagers were able to improve their lot in one way, however; Rottingdean Gap is the lowest point in the cliffs between Brighton and Newhaven, and with a natural path to the beach it was the best landing place for several miles; the smuggling trade therefore thrived at Rottingdean for centuries. <1,190,191,289>

By the beginning of the nineteenth century a horse-ride to Rottingdean was a popular outing from Brighton, and many sporting events, including bear-baiting, cricket and pugilism, were arranged as entertainment for visitors. Throughout the nineteenth century Rottingdean remained a popular but peaceful resort. There were a few lodging houses and a little development in the 1870s at Brighton Road (now Marine Drive) and West Street, while the village was a haunt of writers and artists including Kipling and Burne-Jones. The population grew from 543 in 1801 to 1,992 in 1901. Further limited development followed from the 1890s, and the Rottingdean Heights estate was developed by the Saltdean Estate Company from 1923; other first-class developments followed in the Dean Court Road area. <15,83,190,191,201>

The parish of Rottingdean, part of the Newhaven Union and Rural District, was divided into two parts which met only at a single point on High Hill. The southern part stretched along the coast from Black Rock to Longridge Avenue, an area of 1,580 acres, while the northern part, the chapelry of Balsdean, occupied 1,559 acres and stretched from the hamlet of Balsdean (q.v.) westwards to Heath Hill, Warren Road. The Woodingdean estate was developed in the Balsdean portion from the 1920s, but the entire parish was annexed by the county borough of Brighton on 1 April 1928, and with services now provided by the corporation development in the parish increased rapidly, at Saltdean (q.v.), Woodingdean (q.v.), and at Rottingdean itself. <1,83>

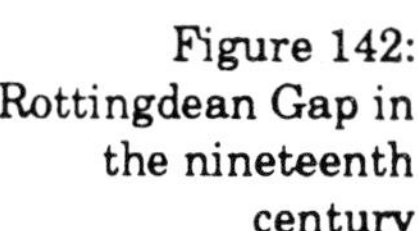

Figure 142: Rottingdean Gap in the nineteenth century

On 22 July 1932 P.J.Pybus, the Minister of Transport, opened a new sixty-foot-wide highway between Black Rock and Rottingdean, the Marine Drive; the previous cliff-top road, which was established as the Newhaven Turnpike in 1824, closed in 1897 because of coastal erosion and Roedean Road was constructed inland as an alternative route to the village. Marine Drive was constructed over two years at a cost of £105,000 in conjunction with the Undercliff Walk (q.v.) coastal protection scheme, which was itself opened to Rottingdean on 4 July 1933. The improved communication with Brighton, together with the construction of the swimming-pool and the unfortunate redevelopment of the gap, have now turned the cliff-top area into merely a busy resort suburb of Brighton, but the heart of the village, the Green and the High Street, has been well preserved and Rottingdean therefore retains much of its special village atmosphere; the village is now an outstanding conservation area. In 1981 the population of the Rottingdean village district, including the New Barn area which was formerly part of Ovingdean parish, was about 2,500. <83,112,115,116,277>

The village has two community centres. The Whiteway Centre, Whiteway Lane, was opened in April 1974. The other, Rottingdean Public Hall in Park Road, was built in 1935. The corporation's Rottingdean Library opened in December 1929 at the Church of England School on the southern side of Nevill Road. In about 1948 it moved to a house in Marine Drive between Park Road and West Street, but in 1953 the corporation purchased The Grange on the eastern side of the Green and opened it as a branch library on 29 January 1954. <83,311>

Rottingdean swimming-pool was opened by the mayor, Edward Denne, on 29 July 1935 in conjunction with the Undercliff Walk extension to Saltdean. A sea-water pool 100 feet by 35 feet, it had few facilities but occupied a wonderful location below the cliffs. In 1989 it was privately leased but damage in the storms of January and February 1990 have probably caused its permanent closure. On the eastern cliff top, behind the fence above the pool, lies the Hangman's Stone, named after the sheep-stealer who, after falling asleep at this point, was strangled by the lead he had attached to his booty. <123,190,192,201>

155. ROTTINGDEAN GREEN

<44,190-192>

The Green forms the heart of Rottingdean village, an outstanding conservation area, and is surrounded by many historic buildings. The grassed area itself, which occupies nearly half an acre, was once known as the Pump Green and was considered, for many years, to be the property of the owner of The Elms. However, the corporation started to maintain the Green in the 1930s and in 1973 registered it under the Commons Act. Standing on the Green are the parish war memorial, a simple obelisk of 1920 surmounted by a cross, and the former village well. Until mains water was introduced in 1879 this seventy-foot well was the only source of pure water in the village. The nearby pond was always a popular place for local shepherds to water their flocks, but dried up in the drought of 1976 and was found to have 'sprung a leak'. Since 1980 water from the well has been pumped to supply the pond. <83,123,126>

The many interesting buildings around the Green are now detailed below. <44,190,191>

Figure 143: The Elms, once the home of Rudyard Kipling

On the southern half of the Green stands:

a) *THE DENE:* A listed building dating from the early nineteenth century, it was previously known as Elm Lodge and Dean Court, and was used as a racing stable by Lord St Vincent. In 1877 it was acquired by E.L.J.Ridsdale who rebuilt and enlarged the house, giving it its present name. It is now a residential hotel. The garden walls and the former stables are also listed.

At the centre of the Green stands:

b) *THE ELMS:* Dating from the eighteenth century, this listed house has a broken pediment doorway and angular bays, but the rendered façade is now covered in ivy. In 1897 the writer Rudyard Kipling moved into the house, to be near his aunt Georgina Burne-Jones at North End House, and while living there wrote *Kim*, *Stalky and Co.*, many of the *Just So* stories, the poem 'Sussex', and the hymn 'Recessional'. However, he was subjected to the gaze of curious passers-by and in 1903 moved to Batemans near Burwash because of the lack of privacy.

The house's large garden, surrounded by a listed flint wall, was thankfully saved from development and opened to the public in April 1986 as the Kipling Garden; it won a council planning award in 1988. In the eastern garden wall, just south of the Dean Court Road junction and about six feet from the ground, is a face-like stone which was formerly situated in the churchyard. It is a 'wishing-stone', and anyone who wants a wish granted should stroke the nose with the right forefinger and turn around three times as the wish is made; do be wary of the traffic, though!

Figure 144: The wishing stone in the garden wall of The Elms

Starting a circular walk around the Green, actually just in Dean Court Road, we first come to:

c) *TUDOR COTTAGES and TUDOR CLOSE:* One of the timber-framed Tudor Cottages on the northern side of the road bears the convincing date of 1530, but the cottages were in fact converted from the tithe barn of Court Farm and some adjacent thatched cottages in about 1930. Tudor Close opposite is also a modern development of seven houses by the Saltdean Estate Company which incorporated two former barns and a cow-shed of Court Farm. The buildings were skilfully developed in mock-Tudor style over a period of three years, but many of the beams, timbers and tiles, which have been elaborately carved with Tudor roses and other decorations, were taken from other old barns and buildings; much of the fabric of Tudor Close and Tudor Cottages is therefore genuinely old. The Close, which was finished in about 1929, did not sell well though, and was soon converted into the Tudor Close Hotel. It was extended by architect Richard Jones in 1936-7, and became well-known for playing host to many stars of the screen and stage; film star Bette Davis stayed there for three months. However, in the 1950s Tudor Close was reconverted into twenty-nine flats. Tudor carving may also be seen at several other houses in Dean Court Road, and also at Founthill Road. <201>

Returning to the Green, the next building is:

d) *ST MARGARET'S CHURCH:* The oldest part of Rottingdean's parish church is the twelfth-century nave, but it stands on the site of an earlier Saxon church. Built in the Early English style in knapped flint, the church has an early-thirteenth-century tower with a Sussex cap which stands unusually between nave and chancel; the tower was probably rebuilt at the same time as the chancel after an earlier tower had collapsed. The west wall was rebuilt in the fourteenth century or later, but it appears that the church was once cruciform in shape as the foundations of a south transept were discovered in 1909. The present south aisle is an addition of 1855-6 by Sir George Gilbert Scott, but there is still a blocked doorway in the chancel wall that led to a former, seventeenth-century south aisle. Now a listed building, the church can hold 250 worshippers.

Figure 145: Tudor Close

In 1377 French raiders landed at Rottingdean Gap and reputedly set fire to the church with a number of villagers trapped inside the tower; some of the pillars and the western tower arch still exhibit a red hue probably caused by the heat. Seven of the stained-glass windows were designed by Sir Edward Burne-Jones to mark his daughter's wedding, and Sir Edward is buried in the churchyard along with the nineteenth-century novelist William Black. The lychgate was added in 1897 in memory of Revd Arthur Thomas, vicar for forty-seven years. During the Second World War detailed drawings were made so that an exact replica, the Church of the Recessional, could be erected at the Forest Lawn Memorial Park in Glendale, California. <1,45,64a>

e) *NORTON HOUSE:* A large, listed house of the early nineteenth century, unfortunately rendered.

f) *THE GRANGE:* A listed Georgian building with an Ionic doorway, window shutters, and an ornamental pond behind a cobbled wall. It was probably built in 1740 as a vicarage, which role it performed until 1908, but was given its present name by the artist Sir William Nicholson who lived there from 1912 until 1914. The northern wing was added in about 1800, and the house was restored in the 1920s by Sir Edward Lutyens for solicitor Sir George Lewis. In 1953 it was purchased by the corporation and now houses the Rottingdean Library, part of the National Toy Museum, a Kipling museum, a Rottingdean history room, and a number of paintings. It is also said to be haunted by the ghost of the Black Prince, who may have visited a house that once stood on the site.

Running alongside The Grange is:

g) *WHITEWAY LANE and VICARAGE TERRACE:* This lane, which becomes a bridleway as it ascends East Hill, is an ancient route to Saltdean Vale which is said to have been used by smugglers. On the northern side stands the Whiteway Centre, built of wood and flint with an unusual fish-shaped weather-vane, and opened on 20 April 1974 for social and educational activities; adjacent is the Rottingdean Primary School. On the opposite side is the Roman Catholic Church of Our Lady of Lourdes, Queen of Peace, consecrated in 1958 by the Bishop of Southwark and constructed of local flint.

The six charming cottages of Vicarage Terrace are all listed buildings. Nos.5-6 at the far end are eighteenth-century houses faced with flint. No.4 is also a rough flint cottage, believed to be the oldest in the village, while nos.1-3 have flint-cobbled fronts, glazing bars and window shutters, and date from the early nineteenth century.

Turning left out of Whiteway Lane, we come to:

h) *VICARAGE LANE:* Blacksmith Cottages date from the eighteenth century and have an underground passage, while the adjacent St John's is an early-nineteenth-century cobble-fronted house with stone dressings, tiny windows and glazing bars. Both are listed buildings, as is the adjacent K6-type telephone box.

Retracing our steps back up Vicarage Lane, we arrive at the:

j) *PLOUGH INN:* Although it was rebuilt at the turn of the century and refaced in 1937, the Plough dates from the 1840s and retains some original flint walls. The inn is the headquarters of the Rottingdean Cricket Club and was often used for training by the famous prize-fighter Tom Sayers (see "Church Street") in the 1850s. <24,26,124>

Turning left down Whipping Post Lane, just before the Plough, we arrive at:

k) *WHIPPING POST HOUSE:* A sixteenth-century listed building which was once the home of Captain Dunk, a famous Rottingdean smuggler. It has extensive

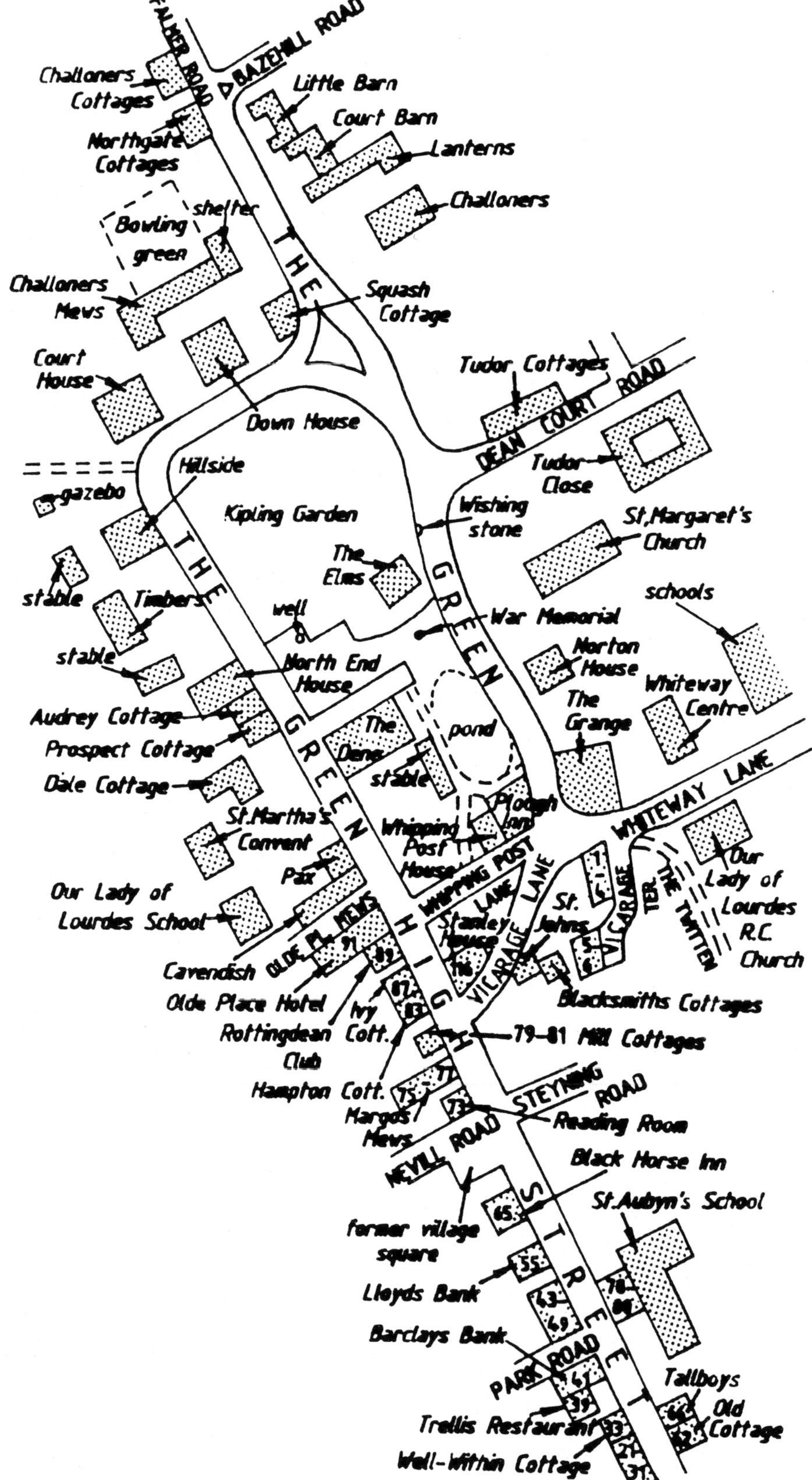

Figure 146:
Rottingdean village

cellars and tunnels underneath, and was also the village butcher's shop at one time. The chestnut tree on the small green marks the position of the former village whipping-post and stocks.

Continuing through, we meet the end of the High Street and turn right. On the left are:

l) *CAVENDISH and PAX:* A large, listed house probably dating from the eighteenth century, but refaced in the nineteenth and now divided into two houses.

m) *ST MARTHA'S CONVENT:* The order originated in France in 1643, but the Rottingdean convent was founded in 1903 and moved in 1924 to the present buildings which stand on a site formerly occupied by Rudyard Kipling's miniature rifle-range. There are a number of small flint buildings and walls in the grounds, while the R.C. Primary School of Our Lady of Lourdes, opened in 1969, stands nearby. <123,201>

n) *DALE COTTAGE:* An early-nineteenth-century listed house, with angular bays, Doric porch, and a large front garden surrounded by a cobbled wall.

p) *PROSPECT COTTAGE, AUBREY COTTAGE and NORTH END HOUSE:* In 1880 Prospect Cottage and Aubrey Cottage were purchased by the pre-Raphaelite artist Sir Edward Burne-Jones. He then merged the two into one house, which he named North End House after his London residence, and lived there until his death in 1898. In 1920 the house was bought by another artist, Sir William Nicholson, and then in 1923 by Sir Roderick Jones and his wife, the writer Enid Bagnold (1889-1981). Jones also purchased the adjacent Gothic House, and combined it with the other two to form one very large residence still known as North End House. In the 1980s the buildings were restored again into three separate houses, but Gothic House has retained the name North End House.

All three are listed buildings and date from the eighteenth century. Prospect Cottage bears a plaque to Burne-Jones, while Aubrey Cottage is an unusual building with a wooden balustrade and many windows. North End House is an elegant building with a Doric porch and is faced with black glazed mathematical tiles. <123>

q) *TIMBERS:* Formerly the main barn of West Side Farm, Timbers dates from the nineteenth century or earlier and is now a listed building with a cobbled front and steep roof. To the south are the former stables of Hillside.

r) *HILLSIDE:* An elegant, grade II*-listed house with five bays of decorative red brick and a Tuscan porch. Hillside was built in 1724 and was the farmhouse of West Side Farm. A listed gazebo at the rear looks out over the cobbled garden wall towards Falmer Road, and was built in about 1822 as a look-out for coaches from Lewes on the new Falmer Road. There is a second listed outbuilding at the rear of the house.

s) *COURT HOUSE:* Formerly the farmhouse of Court Farm, this grade II*-listed building has an eighteenth-century façade of knapped and squared flint, and has now been divided into flats including Court House Close.

t) *DOWN HOUSE:* A very attractive grade II*-listed house faced in knapped and squared flint, Down House has a broken-pediment Doric doorway and extensive cellars and passages. It dates from 1619, the date of a stone in the eastern wall of the house, and remained in the Beard family for three hundred years until it was purchased by local historian Seaburne Moens in 1909. The rear part is now known as the Old Farm House and may be glimpsed from Challoners Mews.

u) *SQUASH COTTAGE:* A single-storey listed house faced in knapped flint, formerly the stable of Down House and later fitted with a squash court. It has an unusual weather-boarded turret surmounted by a weather-vane in the shape of a hare; a pack of beagles was once kept there.

Turning left at the corner we come to:

v) *CHALLONERS MEWS:* A development of 1977 created by the conversion of the listed eighteenth-century flint barns and outbuildings of Court Farm. The adjacent farmyard was laid out in the 1950s with the Rottingdean Bowling Club's green amid great local opposition, but the result is pleasing and one old outbuilding is now used as a shelter. <126,311>

On the opposite side of the road stands:

w) *CHALLONERS:* A large, listed house faced in knapped flint which may be glimpsed over the wall from the south-west. Formerly the manor house and farmhouse of Challoners or Manor Farm, this is the oldest house in Rottingdean and was acquired by Thomas Challoner in 1456, but only the cellars date from that time as it was altered at the end of the sixteenth century. The house was the property of the Beard family for nearly 300 years. The façade now dates from the early eighteenth century with additions of about 1805 including the five-sided glass porch. In the 1980s Challoners, which had been divided into three, was restored to a single house with all period features retained. Extensive passages from the cellars once ran all the way to the beach, but they were blocked many years ago. A mulberry tree in the garden, said to be the largest in the south of England, was planted during the reign of James II. <123>

x) *LANTERNS:* A flint outbuilding of Challoners Farm, now a house.

y) *LITTLE BARN and COURT BARN:* Former barns of Court Farm, both faced in knapped flint but now converted into houses. Court Barn has a huge roof and a very low façade.

Northwards from here The Green becomes:

z) *FALMER ROAD:* Opened as a coaching road from Falmer to Rottingdean in 1822. The first group of houses on the western side are Northgate Cottages, small, cobble-fronted, listed houses of the eighteenth century with an addition of 1881. The adjacent Challoners Cottages are a group of four, late-nineteenth-century, knapped-flint and red-brick houses.

Falmer Road then continues past The Rotyngs, the site of Rottingdean School from 1893 until 1962, towards Woodingdean. It passes Court Ord Cottages at

Meadow Close, a group of late-nineteenth-century knapped-flint and red-brick houses, and also the New Barn, an eighteenth-century listed building with an adjoining stable, both in knapped flint. New Barn actually stood within the former parish of Ovingdean, as did Rottingdean Place. This development was originally erected as St Mary's Home for Female Penitents (i.e. ex-prostitutes) by F.T.Cawthorn in 1912. It later became old people's home, but closed in 1977 and was used as an international school until 1980. It was then taken by the Scientology sect, but was converted in 1984-7 into flats. (For full details on St Mary's Home see "Queen Square".) <44,65,83,108,123>

156. ROTTINGDEAN HIGH STREET

<44,190-192>

This, the main village street connecting the gap with the Green, retains many old buildings to the north of the crossroads, but has been radically redeveloped to the south. The south-eastern side near the gap was known as the 'Quarter-Deck' because of its marine outlook, but the flats of St Margarets, designed by Richard Jones, were erected in 1938 by the Saltdean Estate Company, and Highcliff Court was added in 1967; St Margarets was damaged by a bomb on 18 December 1942. Opposite stands the White Horse, formerly an important coaching inn and meeting place for the villagers, and also a centre for cock-fighting and bull-baiting in the eighteenth and nineteenth centuries. The 300-year-old inn was known as the King of Prussia for a time, but was demolished in 1934 and replaced by the present large hotel.

The first modern intrusion was the north-eastern corner of the crossroads. The car-park opposite lies on the site of a terrace of red-brick houses and the Royal Oak public house, all demolished in the 1930s. No.17 Marine Drive nearby is known as the Poet's House and was the home of poet Sir William Watson (1858-1935). <15,109,190,191,192,201>

There are many interesting buildings along the High Street to the north of West Street. The following, on the western side going northwards, are listed <44,306>.

a) *NOS.21-31:* Attractive eighteenth-century cottages, all refaced with cement except the flint no.31, which are included on the council's local list of buildings of special interest only.

b) *WELL WITHIN COTTAGE, no.33:* An eighteenth- or early-nineteenth-century cottage with an unusual façade of a cobbled ground floor with knapped flint above. Note the Sun Insurance Company's firemark.

c) *TRELLIS RESTAURANT, no.39:* Built in 1680, it was once known as Llewellyn Cottage. The façade is in knapped flint but is partly obscured by an adjoining property.

d) *BARCLAYS BANK, no.41:* A mid-nineteenth-century Gothic house in flint with stone dressings. It has been a bank since 1959.

e) *NOS.43-49:* Early-nineteenth-century cobble-fronted cottages.

f) *BLACK HORSE INN, no.65:* Dating from 1513, one of the oldest buildings in the whole borough, the Black Horse has a plaster-covered timber frame and was once known as the Black Hole; a blacksmith's forge stood where the lounge now is. It is also said to be haunted.

g) *ROTTINGDEAN READING ROOM:* The junction of the High Street and Nevill Road once formed a village square, with the village school standing on the northern side from 1859 until 1958. At the corner still stands the Reading Room, a single-storey building in knapped flint with red-brick dressings. Built in 1885, it is now used by the village club. Note that it is not a listed building. <190,191>

h) *MARGO'S MEWS, nos.75-77:* A knapped-flint terrace which started life as the late-eighteenth- or early-nineteenth-century Bunker's Barn. It was then converted into cottages for the poor, but in 1921 the building became the Sally Lunn Tea-rooms. It was restored as three houses in 1985-6. <83,123>

j) *MILL COTTAGES, nos.79-81:* Two whitewashed, flint cottages with small windows and a tiled roof, dating from the late eighteenth or early nineteenth century.

k) *HAMPTON COTTAGE, no.83:* Dates from the eighteenth century.

l) *IVY COTTAGE, no.87:* A small nineteenth-century cottage.

m) *ROTTINGDEAN CLUB, no.89:* Stands adjacent to the Olde Place Hotel of which it was once a part. Dating from the eighteenth century or earlier, it is faced in knapped flint with a tiled porch along its entire length.

n) *OLDE PLACE HOTEL, no.91:* A nineteenth-century building with a cobbled front and side walls faced in flint. A motel opened in 1977. <123>

On the eastern side of the High Street, again going northward, stand the following listed buildings.

p) *OLD COTTAGE, no.62:* A small building that claims to date from 1589.

q) *TALLBOYS, no.66:* A narrow, three-storey building with a cobble front and brick dressings. Built in 1780, it was once the customs house and has extensive cellars and passages beneath. <190,191>

r) *ST AUBYN'S SCHOOL, no.76:* An early-nineteenth-century, bowed building which was a school by 1832 and became Rottingdean School in 1887. When this school moved to the north of the village in 1894, the building became St Aubyn's Preparatory School for Boys. Tuition is provided for 115 pupils, and there is a large playing-field at the rear. <190,191,203a>

s) *NOS.78-80:* Attractive cottages dating from 1712, but refaced in the nineteenth century with window shutters and a bow. They are included on the borough council's local list only.

t) *STANLEY HOUSE, no.116:* An eighteenth-century house at the corner of Vicarage Lane, faced in knapped flint with pebble-dashed angular bays.

157. ROTTINGDEAN RAILWAY

<188,189>

The Brighton and Rottingdean Seashore Electric Railway was the brainchild of Magnus Volk, and ran from the terminus of his other electric railway at the Banjo Groyne to Rottingdean Pier, a distance of 2.93 miles.

a) *CONSTRUCTION:* An authorising Act of Parliament was obtained in July 1893, and construction of the twin tracks, which each had a gauge of 2 feet 8.5 inches, commenced the following summer. They were laid to an overall gauge of 18 feet on concrete blocks built into the chalk foreshore about 60 to 100 yards from the cliffs, but progress was slow owing to bad weather and because the line was submerged most of the time. Construction took over two years at a cost of around £30,000.

b) *ROTTINGDEAN PIER:* The Rottingdean terminus was a light, steel jetty about 100 yards long and 20 feet wide, just to the west of the gap to which it was connected by a short walkway. The pier-head was 60 feet wide and stood 30 feet clear of high water, with steps down to the landing stage. Beneath the pier-head was the railway's electric generator, a 60-kilowatt, 500-volt steam generator which powered the car via a single cable carried on poles, the return path being provided through the rails. The pier opened on 11 June 1895, and became a favourite fishing venue of Rudyard Kipling.

c) *PIONEER:* The car itself, which was named Pioneer, was built by the Gloucester Wagon Company. The elliptical deck measured 50 feet by 22 feet and had a decorated saloon with a promenade deck above; it was supported by four 24-foot legs carrying the drive and brake shafts to the wheels. The wheelbase was 28 feet, total weight was 36 tons, and Pioneer soon acquired the nickname 'Daddy-Longlegs'.

Before a licence was issued however, the Board of Trade insisted upon several conditions: that a lifeboat and individual lifebelts be provided; that no more than 150 passengers be carried; that a maximum speed limit of 8 m.p.h. be operated, with no running in bad weather; that a telephone be fitted for emergency use; and that a daily inspection of the track be carried out. The appropriate certificate was issued on the day before opening.

d) *OPERATION:* The railway opened on 28 November 1896 when Pioneer made an inaugural journey in thirty-four minutes; a celebration lunch was served at the Madeira Shelter Hall afterwards. The public service started two days later at a single fare of sixpence (2.5p), but at high tide, when the tracks were submerged by up to 15 feet of water, the speed of the vehicle fell almost to walking pace and very often only short journeys were made from the Banjo Groyne before returning for another load of passengers.

On 4-5 December 1896 however, just a week after opening, the railway was severely damaged by the storm that wrecked the Chain Pier. The car broke loose from its mooring at Rottingdean and was wrecked, and the Banjo Groyne terminal jetty collapsed, but there was little damage to either Rottingdean Pier or the track. Pioneer was subsequently reconstructed using the engines and other parts salvaged from the wreckage, and the Banjo Groyne jetty was rebuilt, although without a terminal building; the railway reopened on 20 July 1897. On 20 February 1898 the Prince of Wales made two trips on the railway in the one day, and in the same year a tall landing stage was built on the foreshore at Ovingdean Gap as a request stop.

e) *DEMISE:* After four years of operation, the railway closed temporarily for repairs in 1900 following damage caused during the construction of two new groynes. On 1 September 1900 the corporation gave Volk three months' notice to divert the line 200 feet southwards to make way for further groyne extensions at Kemp Town. Realising that was not practical, Volk suggested shortening the Rottingdean Railway by building a new terminus at Black Rock while extending his other railway from the Banjo Groyne, but this proposal was rejected by the council. Consequently, in about February 1901, the borough surveyor removed the track as necessary and thereby closed the railway. Powers were obtained to construct a viaduct along the base of the cliffs as a replacement, but this new plan failed through a lack of finance. Volk was allowed to extend his electric railway from Banjo Groyne to Black Rock as compensation, however.

Pioneer was moored to the jetty at Ovingdean until 1910, when it was scrapped along with the jetty and Rottingdean Pier was demolished. Now the only surviving relics of the former Rottingdean Railway are the concrete blocks that supported the track, still visible along the foreshore to the east of the Marina at low tide. A model of Pioneer may be found in Brighton Museum.

158. ROTTINGDEAN WINDMILL

Rottingdean Windmill stands to the west of the village on Beacon Hill, approached from Marine Drive, and is also known as the Beacon Mill. This famous smock-mill, which is said to have been used by smugglers for signalling, was erected in 1802 and continued grinding corn until 1881, but it then fell into disrepair before being renovated in 1905-6 by the Marquess of Abergavenny. In 1923 it was leased to a preservation trust, but it was not fully repaired until 1935, by Brighton Corporation some years after it had become the landowner in August 1929; by then the mill had lost its sweeps and much of its weather-boarding. Further repairs, including new sweeps and bracing against the prevailing winds, were carried out in 1966 by the Rottingdean Preservation Society with a grant from the corporation, and exterior renovation took place in 1975; the sweeps were again removed for repair in October 1988. The octagonal mill, which is weather-boarded above a stone base, is now a listed building and has become world-famous through the stylised silhouette of Sir William Nicholson which is now the trademark of publishers William Heinemann. An earlier windmill at Rottingdean stood near Bazehill Road from around the early eighteenth century until about 1817. <44,123,249a,251>

Beacon Hill itself reaches 216 feet above sea-level and was the site of a warning beacon, one of a coastal chain established by Henry VIII. There are also several archaeological sites on its slopes. In digging the foundations for the windmill in 1802 the skeleton of a warrior was found, bearing a sword which was later stolen. In 1862, during an improvement to the Rottingdean cricket pitch which was sited here until 1914, four skeletons and an urn now on exhibition in the Barbican Museum at Lewes were discovered; the long barrow is now a scheduled ancient monument. It is said that a cricketing world record score of sixty-seven runs off a single ball was established at Beacon Hill when the ball ran down the hill and was then overthrown down the opposite slope! The cricket ground is now north of Bazehill Road, but the headquarters remain at the Plough Inn. <15,17,191>

Beacon Hill and much of the cliff top to Roedean, an area of 219 acres, was acquired by the corporation in August 1929. The eighteen-hole miniature golf-course adjacent to the windmill was opened in April 1938. <123,126,305>

159. ROUND HILL

Reaching a height of about 223 feet above sea-level, Round Hill overlooks the Level from the north and was ploughed up in the eighteenth century to form a large, arable open field. Some Regency-style houses were built in the 1820s at Rose Hill, but the next development did not occur until the 1850s when the villas of Round Hill Park (now nos.68-82 on the eastern side of Ditchling Road) were erected. The rest of the area was principally developed from the 1860s with impressive middle-class housing at Richmond Road and Round Hill Crescent, with smaller dwellings in nearby streets. The Round Hill estate, between Upper Lewes and Lewes Roads, was developed from the 1860s to the 1880s, many of the houses being erected at the expense of Revd Arthur Wagner.

The curving terraces present an impressive townscape when viewed from across the Lewes Road valley, and the Round Hill area is now a conservation area which also includes the small terraces of Round Hill Road and Belton Road together with the villas of Round Hill Park. Round Hill Crescent itself has several impressive terraces on the north-western side, and nos.1-37, 69-71 and 101-113 are three-storey, listed houses with ironwork balconies, dating from the 1860s; no.101 was the Lewes Road Hospital for Women and Children in 1905-10 before moving to Ditchling Road as the Lady Chichester Hospital. <44,83,94,96,106>

The northernmost end of Belton Road was the site of a windmill until 1913. Known as the Tower Mill, Round Hill Mill or Rose Hill Mill, it was a brick structure built by John Ingledew and John Lashmar in around 1838. In about 1880 it was purchased by Charles Cuttress, founder of Forfars bakery, and a steam-engine was installed to drive the wheels with the sails fastened. <249a,249b>

160. ROYAL ALBION HOTEL, Old Steine

a) *HISTORY:* Following the demolition of Russell House in 1823 the town commissioners agreed to pay £3,000 to John Colbatch to preserve the site as an open space. However, the deal was delayed and never concluded, and so Colbatch erected the Albion Hotel on the site, opening it on 5 August 1826. Designed by A.H.Wilds, the original hotel is now the eastern wing, an exceptionally elegant four-storey building with giant Corinthian pilasters and columns, shell decorations, balconies, and a very large Doric porch. A western (now central) wing with five storeys, giant fluted Ionic columns and Doric pilasters, was added following the early success of the hotel. These two sections are now grade II*-listed buildings.

The Albion became 'Royal' in about 1847 and bears the royal arms over the entrance, but by 1900 it was in a very dilapidated condition and closed down. In 1913 it was purchased for £13,500 by the charismatic Harry Preston, the proprietor of the nearby Royal York. He restored both the fabric and the fortunes of the Royal Albion Hotel, and it became the haunt of many of the

Figure 147: The original Royal Albion Hotel, designed by A.H.Wilds

famous figures of the day, especially in art, literature, sport, and entertainment; Arnold Bennett wrote *Clayhanger* while staying there in 1910. The 115-bedroom Royal Albion was sold for £575,000 in 1978 and again in 1987; it has now taken in the entire Grand Junction Road frontage.
<3,44,45,112,123,290>

b) *ALBION ROOMS:* The Albion Rooms in the south-western wing of the hotel were originally designed as a bazaar, but they were converted into reading and lecture rooms when this venture failed. From 1841 until 1869 the rooms were a centre of the town's cultural life, playing host to the Royal Literary and Scientific Institution. Founded by John Cordy Burrows and Henry Turrell, two members of the older Brighton General Library, Literary and Scientific Institution, the society went from strength to strength with Prince Albert as patron, promoting the laudable aim of establishing a free public library in the town. A number of historical and artistic artifacts were collected as well as a fine library of books, with funds raised at scientific soirées at the Royal Pavilion. After a number of years though, these evenings lost their popularity and the institution fell heavily into debt. It was forced to close in 1869, but the collections were presented to the corporation to form the basis of the public library which had always been the principal aim of the institution.
<2,3,15,21>

c) *LION MANSION:* The present western wing of the Royal Albion was built in 1856 on the site of Williams's Baths as the Lion Mansion Hotel. Now included on the council's local list of buildings of special interest, it has an entrance on the northern side with a Doric porch surmounted by a large lion, while the façade is decorated with four giant, fluted, Corinthian pilasters. The sea-front façade has a Doric porch with two lions, and bears a plaque in memory of William Gladstone who often stayed at the Lion Mansion. It was also known as the Adelphi before being absorbed by the Royal Albion in about 1963. <67,26,306>

161. ROYAL PAVILION

This former royal palace is the best-known building in Brighton, famous throughout the world for its extraordinary architecture. It is a grade I-listed building.

a) *THE ORIGINAL MARINE PAVILION:* During his first visits to the town in 1783 and 1784 the Prince of Wales stayed at Grove House, a large residence erected on the northern part of the Steine in the previous decade and rented by his uncle, the Duke of Cumberland, from George Wyndham. In 1786 the house was rented by the Duke of Marlborough following the sale of his other Steine house, however, and he purchased it outright in 1790; the Prince of Wales therefore probably spent the 1786 season nearby at Thomas Kemp's farmhouse.

By October 1786 the Prince of Wales was looking for a permanent Brighton residence and had his Clerk of the Kitchen, Louis Weltje, acquire a lease to Kemp's farmhouse; Henry Holland was then employed to build a new marine house on the site in April to June 1787. Known initially as Brighton House, the Prince's Marine Pavilion was a classical two-storey villa in the shape of a letter 'E', timber-framed and faced with cream-coloured mathematical tiles. A domed saloon with six Ionic columns stood at the centre with bowed wings either side, while an Ionic portico provided the entrance on the western side. The interior decoration was in a brilliant French style.

Several men were killed while working on the domed roof, but the house was completed at the end of June

Figure 148: The original Marine Pavilion in 1813 with the Dome in the background

1787. The Prince took possession on 6 July 1787, but Weltje, who bought the house and grounds from Kemp in November 1787 for £5,850, charged the Prince an annual rent of £1,000 and had a house built for himself between the south-western corner and the Prince's stables. The Prince eventually purchased the Pavilion for £17,000 from Weltje's trustees in September 1807.

By 1801 the Prince was considering alterations to the house. Holland drew up a new oriental plan, but it was his nephew, P.F.Robertson, who was commissioned to add two new oval-shaped wings in 1801-2 at right-angles to the eastern façade. In 1802 also, the Prince was presented with some rolls of Chinese wallpaper which were subsequently hung in the gallery. So taken by them was the Prince that he had the whole interior redecorated in Chinese style by John Crase and Sons, and he also had plans for new Chinese-style exteriors drawn up by William Porden in 1805 and Humphrey Repton in 1806-7; neither was taken up, however. Construction of the stables (the 'Dome', q.v.) commenced in 1803, and in 1805 the grounds were laid out by Messrs Lapidge and Hooper, but few other additions or improvements were made to the Marine Pavilion in the years from 1806 until 1814. <194-198>

b) *TRANSFORMATION OF THE MARINE PAVILION:* On his elevation to the Regency in 1811 however, the Prince of Wales determined to have a palace at Brighton befitting his new status, and an estimate of £200,000 was made by the Surveyor-General, James Wyatt. Wyatt died in 1813 though, and so the Prince Regent employed architect John Nash to transform his Marine Pavilion into a new royal palace in Bath stone and stuccoed brick, the Royal Pavilion.

In 1812 Grove House was purchased by the Prince Regent and a connection was made to the Marine Pavilion, but the main alterations commenced in March 1815 with the remodelling of the interior; the ground floor corridor was enlarged, new staircases were provided, and the great kitchen was added. The new entrance hall was also finished in 1815, and a clock and water tower were erected near the south-western corner the following year. In 1817 two square wings with concave pagoda roofs were added to the north and south, and by that October the magnificent music-room had been built on the site of the adjoining Grove House; the banqueting-room was then added to the south to balance the building. A few months later the large onion-shaped Indian dome replaced the flat round dome above the saloon, with two smaller Indian domes added either side. By late 1818 most of the interior details were completed by Crase, Jones and Lambelet, and the eastern façade was virtually finished; alterations to the north front and the King's apartments continued until 1821, however. From September 1818 (although perhaps from 1816 <3>) the Royal Pavilion and grounds were lit by gas.

The cost of land and buildings acquired for the reconstruction amounted to £97,454, and Nash's alterations cost a further £148,773; the total investment in the new palace was a massive £502,797. Nash left in disgrace in 1822 over excessive costs and was succeeded as architect by Joseph Good.

The Prince Regent, now King George IV, moved into the Royal Pavilion on 2 January 1821, but he stayed in his new home only three more times, in 1823, 1824-5 and finally in 1827, mainly because of his disenchantment with prying tourists. His brother and successor William IV stayed there often though, at least once in every year of his reign, and in 1830 changed the designation from the 'Royal Pavilion' to the 'Royal Palace, Brighton'. In 1831 William had a range of new dormitories built on the southern side of the western lawns behind North Street. (See also figure 48.) <194-198>

c) *CLOSURE and PURCHASE:* William's successor in 1837, Queen Victoria, did not take to Brighton however, and made her last visit in 1845. With the Royal Pavilion now redundant as a royal palace, some of the furniture was removed to store the following year, and in 1847-8 143 van-loads of furniture were removed. The government then proposed the sale of the site to recoup money for extensions to Buckingham Palace, but the town commissioners suggested that the town might

Figure 149: A transitional view of the Pavilion in May 1818

purchase the estate and a town meeting resolved unanimously to prevent demolition; 7,406 people then signed a petition against the government's Bill.

The Bill was duly changed to allow for the sale of the estate to the town at £53,000, and the parish vestry appointed a committee of fourteen, including seven town commissioners, to effect the purchase; a contract was made out in these names. The town commissioners, however, maintained that they were the only body authorised to effect the purchase and their clerk, Lewis Slight, substituted his own name for the seven others on the contract, an action that led to great animosity in the vestry. To make matters worse, Slight announced to a vestry meeting on 20 December 1849 that he had already signed the contract the previous day, but instead of approving this contract the meeting defiantly passed an amendment rejecting purchase. A town poll was held on 21-22 December 1849 to settle the argument, and resulted in a vote for the purchase by 1,343 to 1,307, a majority of just 36 votes. The Bill was given royal assent in May 1850, and the nine-acre Royal Pavilion estate became the property of the town on 19 June 1850. It was transferred from the town commissioners to the corporation in 1855.

The remaining fittings were removed by H.M.Commissioner of Woods, Forests, Land Revenues, Works and Buildings, but £3,000 was allowed on the purchase price as the Church Commissioners claimed the former Royal Chapel and rebuilt it as St Stephen's Church in Montpelier Place (see "Clifton Hill (Montpelier Place)"). <112,194-198>

d) *OPEN TO THE PUBLIC:* In September 1850 a programme of redecoration and refurnishing was commenced by Christopher Vick, but some of the peripheral buildings, including the South Gate, were demolished in 1851. The public were admitted to the grounds for the first time in June 1850, but the building itself was formally opened at a grand ball on 21 January 1851. Ratepayers were allowed free entry on two days every month, and the Pavilion came to be used as the public assembly rooms of the town for both civic and private functions. It also housed the public art gallery, museum and library for a time until 1873. In December 1863 Queen Victoria returned some of the original fittings at the request of the custodian, F.E.de Val, and in 1898 more items were returned and the music-room was cleaned and restored. On 3 April 1883 the Pavilion banqueting-room was lit electrically for the first time by Magnus Volk who lit the rest of the building shortly after from a steam-driven dynamo. The clock tower near the South Gate was demolished in 1898. <189,194-198>

e) *FIRST WORLD WAR HOSPITAL:* During the First World War the Royal Pavilion estate, including the Dome and Corn Exchange, was offered by the corporation for use as an Indian military hospital. A high wooden fence was erected around the grounds to protect patients from prying eyes, the first of whom were admitted on 1 December 1914, and by the time the last Indian was evacuated on 15 February 1916 a total of 4,306 patients had passed through the 724-bed hospital. From 20 April 1916 until 21 July 1919 the estate was given over to the Pavilion General Hospital (for limbless men) which received 6,085 admissions. The South Gate, and also the Chattri at Patcham, were later erected as memorials to the Indian dead and wounded. On 28 August 1920 the military released control of the Royal Pavilion and the public were admitted once again. <194-196,200>

f) *RESTORATION and REGENCY EXHIBITIONS:* The buildings inevitably suffered during the war and a programme of restoration began in October 1920. In that year, and at several other times during his reign, King George V returned some of the original fittings from Windsor Castle. The first Regency Exhibition, to display

Figure 150: The Royal Pavilion from the Old Steine in 1829. Note the original position of the statue of King George IV in the Steine gardens.

the interior in its fully-furnished glory, was organised in 1946 by a private committee; original furniture was temporarily loaned by George VI from Buckingham Palace and other period pieces were exhibited. In 1948 a second Regency Exhibition was organised, and a twenty-year series of restorations were commenced under the direction of Clifford Musgrave. In October 1949 the council restricted the use of the rooms to 'appropriate' functions only, and decided also to refurnish the state apartments permanently in their original style and to keep them open throughout the year. On 9 June 1950 the Duke and Duchess of Devonshire opened the Royal Pavilion in its new state, although it attracted only a few thousand visitors initially.

A special Centenary Exhibition was held in 1950 to commemorate the town's purchase, and more Regency Exhibitions were held in 1951 and 1952. From 1954 they were continued on an annual basis by the corporation. Queen Elizabeth II returned over one hundred pieces of the original Chinese-style furniture in 1955, and many more in the following years. These returns were so successful that by the late 1960s it was indeed possible to furnish the Royal Pavilion throughout the year.

The music-room, described as 'the most beautiful room in Europe', was severely damaged by an arsonist on 2 November 1975, but reopened in January 1986 after a complete restoration. Indeed, a programme of restoration on the whole building commenced in 1982 and will continue until 1991 at a cost estimated to be in the region of £10 million. However, the music-room was considerably damaged once again, by a falling minaret during the storm of 16 October 1987. <123,194-197>

g) *BRIEF DESCRIPTION:* The Royal Pavilion is open to the public every day except Christmas Day and Boxing Day, and attracts about 320,000 visitors annually during the current restorations. Overlooking the eastern lawn are the music-room, the north (originally yellow) drawing-room, the saloon, the south (originally green) drawing-room, the banqueting-room, and the great kitchen in Palace Place. On the western side are the corridor (the long or Chinese gallery), the King's apartments, and the entrance hall. The first floor contains a tea-room and many smaller rooms, mostly bedrooms, which are currently being reopened to the public. <45,197>

Although the Royal Pavilion is now admired for its extraordinary architecture, it has not always been so and many commentators considered the building to be a gross example of bad taste. Perhaps the most famous comment was that of Sydney Smith who declared that 'the dome of St Paul's must have come down to Brighton and pupped'. It was not until the book *Brighton* by Sir Osbert Sitwell and Margaret Barton was published in 1935 that the design was generally looked at more favourably. A model of the building may be found in Brighton Museum. <47,129>

h) *GREAT KITCHEN:* Built in 1816, the kitchen, unlike the rest of the Pavilion, has a Greek Doric façade with pediment and pilasters overlooking Palace Place. Following the purchase of the estate in 1850 the great kitchen was used for art exhibitions, and from 1858 until 1876 it housed the Brighton School of Arts and Crafts which was later to become the Municipal Art College (see "Polytechnic"). The interior has now been restored and is lined with over 600 copper utensils, while the roof is supported on thin iron columns in the form of palm trees. There is also a novel roasting-spit, powered by the convection of its own fire. <194-197>

j) *PAVILION GROUNDS:* The eastern lawns of the Royal Pavilion originally formed part of the Steine, but in 1793 the Prince of Wales and Duke of Marlborough were given permission to enclose the land in front of their houses following their construction of a sewer along the western edge of the Steine. In 1805, with Great East Street now closed to the public from North Street to Church Street (see "New Road"), the grounds were laid out by Messrs Lapidge and Hooper, and were extended northwards in about 1816 when a road immediately north of Grove House was stopped up and Church Street was extended through to Grand Parade.

The western lawns were acquired by the Prince of Wales in the years from 1795 to about 1819, and included the Dairy Field of the original farm on which the Marine Pavilion was erected. The Quaker's Croft, at the rear of their former meeting house in North Street, was leased from 1806, and the Promenade Grove, the town's first pleasure garden, was also acquired. This grove, which was entered through an arched gateway in Prince's Place and stretched almost to Church Street, opened on 13 July 1793 in the presence of the Duke and Duchess of Marlborough and was described as a miniature version of the famous Vauxhall Gardens near London. There were flower-beds, shrubs, a fine avenue of elms (the only trees in the centre of the town at that time) and an elegant saloon, and many events were held including concerts, firework displays, illuminations, stage performances, dancing and pony races. On 14 August 1795 1,400 people attended a firework display in honour of the Prince's thirty-third birthday, but in August 1802 he purchased the grove in order to extend his estate, and it closed on 16 September 1802 with a grand display of Mount Vesuvius in fireworks. The Prince did allow a Mr Quartermain to reopen the gardens for one more season until September 1803, however, with the proceeds going to the poor.

Other areas were granted by the lords of the manor in 1813, 1815 and 1827, and the Pavilion grounds now cover approximately 3.5 acres. They were lit temporarily by gas in September 1818, but permanent lamp-posts were erected during the reign of William IV and nineteen of these original cast-iron standards, with copper lanterns supported by scrolls and topped by crowns, remain; they are now listed structures although some have been mutilated; see figure 63.

The Royal Pavilion grounds were first opened to the public on 29 June 1850, and bye-laws were made to prohibit smoking, intoxication, begging, games, and ragged or offensive attire. They were closed during the First World War when the estate was used as a hospital, but reopened in June 1920. In 1921-3 several improvements were made including the replacement of the tall railings by the present miniature balustrade, the levelling of the eastern lawns, and the addition of small ornamental pools. During the Second World War a bomb fell on the western lawns creating a large crater that was converted into a static water tank. In 1985-7 the western lawns were restored to their original plan, the statue of Sir John Cordy Burrows having been removed to the Old Steine. The grounds have now been designated as being of historic interest by English Heritage, but many of the fine trees were unfortunately uprooted in the great storm of October 1987. <15,126,194,199>

k) *NORTH GATE, Church Street:* The Royal Pavilion's northern entrance is an Indian-style gateway of Portland stone surmounted by a copper dome and flanked by two lodges. It is adorned with pillars and minarets, a lion and crown looking northwards, and a crown and prince of Wales's feathers looking south. It also bears the letters 'W IIII' and the date 1832, and was erected in that year for King William IV by Joseph Good. It is now a listed building. (See figure 192.) On 4 October 1837 the North Gate was decorated with flowers and turned into a triumphal arch for the first visit of Queen Victoria. The northern face has a drinking fountain of 1859. <44,141,194,195>

l) *GEORGE IV STATUE, Church Street:* (See figure 64.) Now standing to the east of the North Gate, this nine-foot bronze figure on a ten-foot granite pedestal was designed by Sir Francis Chantrey and was originally unveiled in the Steine on 9 October 1828 after a public subscription had raised 3,000 guineas. The listed statue was moved to its present position on 14 March 1922 to allow for the erection of Brighton's War Memorial. <44,124>

m) *NORTH GATE HOUSE:* Adjacent to the Royal Pavilion's North Gate stands North Gate House, a three-storey, grade II*-listed building and the only remaining house of a terrace of nine which once stood alongside the road through the Pavilion grounds. Known as Marlborough Row, this terrace was probably erected in about 1774, but nos.1-4 were demolished in 1820 and nos.5-7 in 1821. No.9 was a small blacksmith's shop whose owner refused to sell out, but it was eventually compulsorily purchased for the widening of Church Street.

North Gate House itself was presented by William IV to his sister Princess Augusta in 1830, and in 1832 was refaced with oriental windows and decorations to match the style of the new North Gate. Since 1930 it has housed the offices of the Royal Pavilion, art gallery, museum and public library, and it also housed the children's library for a time. It is hoped eventually to house the National Toy Museum in the building; see figure 192. <44,140,194>

n) *SOUTH GATE, Pavilion Buildings:* The first formal southern entrance to the Royal Pavilion was known as the South Lodge and was completed for William IV on 7 May 1831. Built in line with the other buildings of North Street, it was a scalloped Indian archway topped by oriental towers and was designed by Joseph Good; see figure 27. Following the estate purchase in 1851 the South Lodge was demolished by the town commissioners along with some other outbuildings for the erection of Pavilion Buildings, and was replaced by a new South Gate on the present site, topped by concave pagoda domes and with two large, iron gates flanked by small square archways through which pedestrians passed.

The present Indian archway stands thirty-seven feet tall and was designed by Thomas Tyrwhitt in Gujerati style with a simple dome mounted on four stone pillars. It bears the following inscription: 'This gateway is the gift of India in commemoration of her sons who, stricken in the Great War, were tended in the Pavilion in 1914 and 1915'. It was dedicated for the use of the inhabitants of Brighton by His Highness the Maharajah of Patiala on 26 October 1921. <44,194>

162. ROYAL SUSSEX COUNTY HOSPITAL, Eastern Road

a) *ESTABLISHMENT:* In February 1813 a fund was started for the establishment of a hospital in the town, but nothing came of the idea until December 1824 when a meeting at the Old Ship resolved to construct a county hospital. The lord of the manor, T.R.Kemp, provided some land to the east of the town, and architect Charles Barry was commissioned to design the new building. The foundation stone was laid by the Earl of Egremont on 16 March 1826, and the Sussex County Hospital and General Sea-Bathing Infirmary opened just over two years later on 11 June 1828 with four large and twenty-three small wards providing room for eighty patients. This original building, which is included on the borough council's local list of buildings of special interest, may still be seen to have four storeys with a projecting central bay and pediment, and bears the name and date of the hospital. Its frontal extension was opened by Prince Arthur of Connaught in April 1929.

Patients to the hospital were recommended by subscribers who could become life-governors for twenty-five guineas. As sea-water treatment was then considered very important, water was pumped through a pipe from the beach, but this practice ceased in 1876. In about 1905 the hospital received the patronage of King Edward VII and became the 'Royal' Sussex County Hospital.

b) *EXPANSION:* The hospital has been almost continually enlarged ever since its foundation; a fever block soon opened a short distance away, the Victoria Wing was added on the western side in 1839 by William Hallett, and the Adelaide Wing was built to the east in 1841 by Herbert Williams. The projecting end wings were added in 1853, and a Renaissance-style chapel was added in about 1856 by William Hallett at the expense of the Marquess of Bristol; the chapel is now listed as being of special architectural interest. The separate Jubilee Building to the east opened in 1887 to mark Queen Victoria's golden jubilee, and a pathological and bacteriological department opened in 1895 through the munificence of a Mrs Ralli. In 1901 new operating wards were added, and in 1923 the Howard Wards were opened through a fund provided by the trustees of Sir John Howard. Further additions were made in 1928, 1929, and in 1937 with the addition of the Latilla Department of Physical Medicine. In July 1948 the hospital, then still funded by subscriptions, was taken over by the National Health Service.

The 406-bed hospital is now dominated by the fourteen-storey Tower Block in Bristol Gate, opened in 1969-70 but never completed; it is to be renovated and improved in 1989-91. At the corner of Eastern Road and Bristol Gate is the Charles Hunnisett Department of Computerised Tomology, which was opened by Earl Mountbatten on 21 July 1976 and houses one of the world's first EMI body-scanners. It stands on the site of the former Blind School, but the former Female Orphan Asylum, now the Latilla Building, still stands adjacently to the west. The out-patient department was erected opposite the main block on the southern side of Eastern Road, a low, ugly building, the foundation stone of which was laid on 29 February 1896 by the Prince of Wales. <24,83,94,115,123>

Figure 151: The Sussex County Hospital in 1834

c) *SUSSEX EYE HOSPITAL:* This separate hospital was founded in August 1832 at 2 Boyce's Street as the Sussex and Brighton Infirmary for Diseases of the Eye; patients were admitted upon a subscriber's recommendation or in an emergency. On 10 November 1846 a new classical building designed by Thomas Cooper was opened at 104 Queen's Road; it had a Corinthian portico and twenty-four beds. The present 31-bed, four-storey building in Eastern Road, designed by Denman and Son, opened on 2 July 1935. The Queen's Road building then became the premises of the Royal National Institute for the Blind and the Moon Society's publishing works, but was demolished in about 1961 and replaced by Equity and Law House. <24,83,112,124>

163. ROYAL YORK BUILDINGS, 41-43 Old Steine

<15,44,115,269,290>

This site was originally occupied by the so-called 'manor house' of Brighton, a red-brick building with a slate roof which was known as Steine House and was probably erected in the first half of the eighteenth century. From 1771 it was the home of Richard Scrase, the joint lord of the manor, but in 1801 it was purchased by a Dr Hall who built three houses on the adjoining stables. In 1819 the three houses, known collectively as Steine Place, were converted into the Royal York Hotel which opened on 27 September under the managership of Charles Shepherd, ex-proprietor of the Star and Garter.

The new hotel was named after the Duke of York, brother of the Prince Regent, and was the first of the new large-scale hotels in Brighton. It had one hundred beds, and following the demise of the Castle Inn became the most fashionable venue in the town with concerts and recitals given in the public rooms; the first Tradesmen's Ball was held there in 1823. In 1827 Harry Pegg became manager, and the hotel was enlarged by taking in the two houses to the west and the house to the east, forming the building as seen today. The manor house was probably demolished at this time.

Many famous visitors stayed at the Royal York, including the Duke and Duchess of Clarence in October 1829, and Benjamin Disraeli in 1840; in 1861 Charles Dickens read *David Copperfield* to an attentive audience. However the hotel was not able to retain its popularity, and by the end of the century it was almost derelict. In 1901 the building was purchased by the flamboyant Harry Preston who did so much to revitalise Brighton in the early twentieth century and was later knighted. He restored both the building and its reputation, and the Royal York once again became the most fashionable hotel in the town. Following Preston's retirement in 1929 the corporation bought the building for £32,500 and converted it into offices known as Royal York Buildings which now include the town's registry office.

The listed building has four storeys, wide bows, and a large Doric porch with wrought-iron canopy; it also bears the date 1819. The west wing can clearly be seen to have once been separate houses, as can the east wing which has three bows. The southern façade in Pool Valley is plain and now houses the coach station which was opened in 1929, but the name 'Royal York Hotel' may still be seen on the southern wall below the royal arms, although it has been altered to 'Royal York Buildings'.

Figure 152: Royal York Buildings

164. Dr Richard RUSSELL

<1-3a,10,19a,112,123>

This doctor was instrumental in reviving the fortunes of the poor fishing town of Brighton in the mid eighteenth century. Born at Lewes in 1687 and educated at St Anne's Free Grammar School, he secretly wed a Miss Kemp of South Malling and studied medicine at the University of Leyden in Holland. He then returned to practice in Lewes and lived at South Malling Deanery following his father-in-law's death.

In 1750 Dr.Russell published a paper in Latin on the 'Glandular Diseases, or a Dissertation on the Use of Sea-Water in the Affections of the Glands' which advocated both the bathing in, and the consumption of,

Figure 153: Dr Richard Russell, by Zoffany

sea-water for numerous complaints. Although sea-bathing had been popular for many years. Russell's claims for the medicinal use of sea-water in the same way as traditional spa waters were new, and he was the foremost of several doctors to bring the sea-water cure to prominence at this time.

Perhaps in the 1730s, but certainly by the 1740s <10>, Russell was prescribing the sea-water cure for his patients at the nearest coastal town to Lewes with facilities for visitors: Brighton. As his reputation grew so the number of visitors to Brighton increased, and in 1753 Russell erected a house on the southern side of the Steine, where the Royal Albion now stands, for both his own and his patients' accommodation; a red-brick building with dormers, central gables and an elaborate, round-headed doorway, it was the largest house in Brighton at the time and had direct access to the low cliffs at the rear. Russell moved permanently into the house in 1754, and the following year published another book entitled 'The Oeconomy of Nature in Acute and Chronical Diseases of the Glands' (sic). He also prescribed the waters of the chalybeate spring at St Anne's Well in Hove, which he had enclosed in a basin.

Dr Richard Russell died on 19 December 1759 and was buried at South Malling Church where there is a small tablet to him on the eastern chancel wall; his coffin was found there in 1990. His portrait may be found in Brighton Museum, and a plaque has been erected on the southern façade of the Royal Albion, fittingly inscribed, 'If you seek his monument, look around'.

Russell's house was then let as a seasonal residence, and in September 1771 George III's brother the Duke of Cumberland took the house and returned for several years thereafter. From 1807 it was used as a boarding house by a Mrs Hill for about five years, but it was subsequently used for popular amusements including Haine's Toy Repository and Puppet Theatre. It eventually became dilapidated though, and was demolished in 1823. The town commissioners agreed to pay the then owner, John Colbatch, some £3,000 to preserve it as an open space, but a delay caused the agreement to collapse and he erected the Albion Hotel in its place.

Figure 154: Dr Russell's house in 1786 when occupied by the Duke of Cumberland

165. ST DUNSTAN'S INSTITUTE FOR THE BLIND, Kemp Town and Ovingdean Gap

<3,45,271,123>

The St Dunstan's Institute for men and women blinded on war service was founded by Sir Arthur Pearson in February 1915 at Bayswater Road, London, as the Blind Soldiers and Sailors Hostel, but such was the demand for places that it was soon removed to St Dunstan's Villa in Regent's Park (now the residence of the U.S. Ambassador) where it adopted its present title. By 1918 nearly 2,000 blinded men were being trained for work in the outside world, and other hostels and training schools were established both in this country and abroad. At the end of the war a convalescent home was opened in Brighton, at West House in St George's Road (actually 12-14 Portland Place - see "East Cliff") which was built in 1847; in 1957 it was renamed Pearson House. The façade of the listed building was preserved when the home was extensively restored and extended, reopening on 31 May 1973.

The building at Ovingdean Gap, known as Ian Fraser House, was built in 1937-9 to an International Modern design by Francis Lorne, with the foundation stone laid by Sir Arthur's widow, Lady Pearson, on 6 September 1937. The seven-storey orange-brick building, with a glass bow and square tower, was modernised in 1974-5 and had a new south wing inaugurated in April 1975. It has twice been visited by Queen Elizabeth II and Prince Philip, firstly in 1962, and again in July 1985 in connection with the Institute's seventeenth anniversary. This building is now used for training, holidays and convalescence, while Pearson House is principally for the elderly and sick.

166. ST GEORGE'S ROAD, Kemp Town

Kemp Town's main street was developed principally in the 1830s and '40s, and is named from St George's Church.

a) *CHURCH OF ST GEORGE THE MARTYR:* This attractive church was built in 1824-5 by architect Charles Busby for T.R.Kemp to serve the new estate at Kemp Town, and was consecrated on 30 December 1825, opening to the public the following day. It is an elegant, classical, listed building in yellow brick, with a recessed Ionic portico and a Grecian bell-tower surmounted by a cupola and gilt metal cross. In front of the doorway are a pair of original lamps. Considerable internal alterations were made in 1889-90 when the chancel was added and new columns were fitted to the galleries.

From 1828 until 1851 the curate was the Revd James Anderson, and Queen Adelaide was a frequent worshipper; the church's silverware was her gift. Although for a long time it was under threat (it actually closed for some years from about 1965), St George's has fortunately survived and the parish has now merged with that of the former St Anne's Church. <1,44,45,46,64a>

The former church hall stands at the corner of Paston Place and Sudeley Street, a two-storey building with Doric pilasters and large pediment. It was erected in 1864 by Frederick Mahomed, the second son of Sake Dene Mahomed, as the Royal Gymnasium and fencing rooms, these having been removed from what is now the Waggon and Horses public house in Church Street. Now used as an office, it became the church hall in 1889, but the gymnastic fittings remained in situ until 1962. <268>

b) *OTHER BUILDINGS:* At the corner of Paston Place and St George's Road stands the Bombay Bar, a low, square, listed building with oriental details and a pagoda roof. It was built in 1892 as a mausoleum for Sir Albert Sassoon. Sir Albert, who lived at 1 Eastern Terrace, was buried there in 1896, and his son Sir Edward followed in 1912, but their remains were

Figure 155: St George's Church

Figure 156: The East Mill in 1840

removed to London by the grandson, Sir Philip, when he sold it in 1933. During the war it was used as an air-raid shelter, and it became part of the adjacent Hanbury Arms public house in 1953. <3,44,45>

On the opposite side of St George's Road stood the Odeon Cinema, opened on the site of the Sassoon family's riding school on 1 February 1934. It held 900 people and also presented variety shows, but the building was badly damaged in an air raid at 3.30 p.m. on 14 September 1940 when four children and two adults were killed, and twenty others were injured. The Kemp Town Odeon closed in November 1960 and was converted into a bingo hall in 1962, but in 1983 it was used by the Bethany Fellowship as an entertainment and social centre for the needy ('The City'). The building was demolished in January 1986 to be replaced by the flats of Cavendish Court. <68,123>

Pearson House is part of the St Dunstan's Institute (q.v.), but although it stands on the northern side of St George's Road, it is actually numbered 12-14 Portland Place of which it forms the terminal view (see "East Cliff"). On the south side of the road are the modern Regency-style houses of Seymour Square, built on the site of the Kemp Town Brewery. The best nineteenth-century houses are those of the rusticated terrace at nos.29-33, dating from the 1830s.

The community centre known as the 'Kemptown Pier' was built in 1912 as a church hall for St Anne's, Burlington Street, in memory of John Nixon. <311>

Kemp Town Post-Office, just off St George's Road in College Road, is unusually decorated for such a building. It has shell motifs and opened in 1887. <15>

c) *SUDELEY PLACE and the EAST MILL:* On the western side of the attractive Sudeley Place stands the former Continentale Cinema, a small building in Renaissance style with a pitched roof and decorated façade. It originally opened in about 1891 as a Congregational chapel on the site of a temporary iron church of 1868. In 1920 the chapel was converted into the 370-seat King's Cliff Cinema, and sound was installed in 1930. In 1947 it became the Playhouse Repertory Theatre, but was taken over by Myles Byrne in 1949 as the Playhouse Cinema. In 1951 it became the Continentale, specialising in foreign films but concentrating on pornographic films from the late 1960s until it closed in December 1986. In 1990-1 it was being converted to houses. <62,68,83,123>

Opposite the bottom end of Sudeley Place once stood the East Mill, a white post-mill probably erected in the 1790s which had a round mill-house and cottage at the rear of the later no.162 Marine Parade. In the mid 1840s it was removed to Sussex Street near Windmill Street where it was then generally known as Taylor's Mill (see "Albion Hill"). Millfield Cottages, a row of small houses off Sudeley Place, probably date from the 1830s and are named from this mill. <108,249a>

167. ST JAMES'S STREET

The principal shopping street of the eastern town was first developed in the 1790s to serve the East Cliff development, and was probably named after the Royal Palace of St James as it was known as such before the chapel of that name was erected. It remains the only major shopping street in the town not to have been widened, and a large number of original buildings, many faced with mathematical tiles, remain from the early nineteenth century. The resulting congestion led to the introduction of one-way traffic in 1968. <14,108,123>

a) *NORTHERN SIDE:* Starting at the Steine, nos.1-4 on the northern side were probably designed by Wilds and Busby in the 1820s and form a bow-windowed composition decorated with shell capitals and garlands; they are included on the council's local list of buildings of special interest. No.5 was the 270-seat Imperial Picture Palace from 1912 until 1916. The narrow passage between nos.4a and 5 leads to St James's Place, a row of six early-nineteenth-century listed houses with fanlight doorways behind small front gardens. Nos.1 and 3-6 are faced in cobbles (no.5 has a bow and mathematical tiles as well), but nos.2 was refaced in Victorian times.

Figure 157: St James's Place

The Safeway supermarket opened in 1985 as Presto; its traces of Regency style, balconies, pilasters and Doric pillars, allow it to blend in rather well, particularly with the adjacent no.9, the National Westminster Bank. This building has a modern shop-front, but retains a bow-fronted upper storey adorned with fluted Ionic columns. Now a listed building, it was designed by Wilds and Busby in the 1820s and was the meeting place of the Brighton General Library, Literary and Scientific Institution from 1826 until about 1842. The Boots store was erected in 1914. Another narrow passage at no.21 leads to St James's Gardens where may be found the Brotherhood Gate Spiritualist Church and Brighton Lions Community Centre.

The Co-operative Society supermarket stands on the site of St James's Church (see below), while beyond, flanking Devonshire Place, are the flats of Devonshire Mansions and New Steine Mansions (originally the New Steine Hotel), early-nineteenth-century buildings now much restored and altered. Both are included on the borough council's local list and are decorated with Ionic pilasters, but although they were originally a symmetric pair, Devonshire Mansions has been radically refaced. No.58 is also on the council's local list. <3,44,68,306>

b) *SOUTHERN SIDE:* The southern side of St James's Street also has a number of early-nineteenth-century listed buildings. Listed grade II are: no.90; nos.95-99 which form a bow-fronted terrace, some faced with mathematical tiles; no.102, Gunn's fishmongers, which retains its original bowed shop-front with small Ionic columns; nos.120-121 which have narrow bows and mathematical tiles; no.129, a four-storey bow-fronted house faced with mathematical tiles; and no.130, decorated with composite pilasters. The council's local list includes: no.89 and the bow-fronted no.101, both faced in black mathematical tiles; a four-storey composition with bows and balconies at nos.107-111; the bow-windowed nos.116-118; and the decorated no.119. No.64, a building with a balustered roof and urn decorations near the corner of Grafton Street, was used as a district police station from around 1857 until 1885. <44,83,306>

c) *ST MARY'S CHURCH:* At the corner of Upper Rock Gardens stands St Mary's Church, originally built by A.H.Wilds in classical style in 1826-7 for Charles Elliott in the grounds of the East Lodge, the home of the Earl of Egremont. Said to be a replica of the Temple of Nemesis at Athens, it had a portico of four fluted Doric columns. Elliott's son, Revd Henry Elliott, the founder of St Mary's Hall School, was installed as curate. In June 1876 however, part of the roof and walls collapsed, and so the church was completely rebuilt in 1877-9 by Sir William Emerson in French Gothic style, in red brick with red-sandstone and terracotta dressings; a planned south-western tower was never erected. The interior of the listed church has an unusually long nave spanned by immense arches, and can hold 1,000 people. <1,3,45,64a,115>

d) *ST JAMES'S CHURCH:* This church once stood on the site of the Brighton Co-operative Society's store at the corner of Chapel Street. It was built as a chapel of ease to St Nicholas's in 1810-13 on land granted by Nathaniel Kemp. However, the proposed curate was not approved of by the Vicar of Brighton, Dr James Carr, and the chapel was used instead by Dissenters, including Kemp's nephew Thomas Read Kemp in 1816-7. In 1817 the church was purchased by Nathaniel Kemp himself and he then had it consecrated by the Anglican Church; in 1826 it finally did become a chapel of ease. In 1866 St James's was acquired by the Tractarian Revd James Purchas who reopened it with such an ornate ceremony that the Bishop of Chichester prohibited Purchas from preaching there in 1867 for a year. When Purchas died in 1872 though, the chapel was bought by the Vicar of Brighton, Dr John Hannah, and was rebuilt in 1874-5 in Early English style by Edmund Scott. Faced in flint with stone dressings, it was approached along a passageway from St James's Street but was demolished in September 1950 with some fittings removed to St Mary's. <1,3,6,62,115>

The attractive streets leading south from St James's Street are detailed under "East Cliff", but there are also some interesting streets leading northwards; a substantial amount of redevelopment has taken place, however. In topographical order from the Steine, they are:

e) *GEORGE STREET:* First developed in the 1790s for the workers servicing the high-class housing of the East Cliff, George Street retains a number of small cottages of which nos.2-10 and 17-35 are included on the borough council's local list of buildings of interest; no.20 has a cobbled front, while nos.1-8, 21-26 and 32-35 are faced with mathematical tiles. The three-storey row known as Howells Court was erected in 1987 on the site of Howell's Almshouses, ten small, stuccoed houses built in 1859 by Charles Howell 'for the benefit of the reduced inhabitants of Brighton and Hove', but they were derelict by 1965. The houses of Little George Street were erected in 1988 on the site of a group of eleven cottages of that name which were demolished in 1974. A passage between nos.1 and 2 George Street leads to St James's Court, two brick houses from around the turn of the nineteenth century. <3,6,108,123,306>

f) *DORSET GARDENS:* Lined with three- and four-storey houses of the 1790s on the eastern side. Many were refaced in the mid nineteenth century, but nos.7 and 12-18 retain their original façades and are listed buildings; nos.7 and 15 have flint-cobble fronts. The gardens cover 0.97 acres and were taken over by the corporation following the 1884 Brighton Improvement Act; in the late 1980s they were designated a 'peace park' with several trees symbolically planted. The Methodist church was built in 1808 and enlarged around 1840, but was completely rebuilt in red brick with terracotta dressings in 1884 by C.O.Ellison, with the southern extension added in 1929. It has shell capitals and an Italianate tower. The building is now used by the Dome Mission, founded at the Alhambra Music Hall in King's Road by the congregation of the Norfolk Road Methodist Church; the growing attendances necessitated a move to the Dome in 1907. <44,62,123,126>

g) *HIGH STREET:* Now dominated by the exceptionally ugly St James's House which opened in November 1966, High Street has some early council housing dating from 1910 on the western side but the surrounding area has been extensively redeveloped. The Gothic Windsor Lodge on the eastern side was originally erected in 1886 by W.S.Parnacott as a Primitive Methodist chapel. In 1898 it became the Gordon Hall, but in 1910 the building was used as a printing works, and from 1935 it was occupied by the Christian Brethren. The building was then used from 1978 until 1986 as the Greek Orthodox Church of the Holy Trinity before being converted to flats in 1987. <26,62,83,123>

Figure 158: Windsor Lodge, High Street

The town's first post-Reformation Catholic chapel also stood in High Street. A temporary mission had been established in 1798 in Prospect Row, now part of St James's Street between George Street and Dorset Gardens, but a permanent chapel was established in 1806 or 1807 at 42-43 High Street. A plain Georgian building, it was used until the Church of St John the Baptist opened at Bristol Road in 1835, and was then put to various uses including a picture gallery and garage. However, the building was demolished in 1981 and Kebbell Lodge built on the site. <56>

Figure 159: The former synagogue in Devonshire Place

h) *DEVONSHIRE PLACE:* An attractive road of large, three-storey houses in varying styles, many with balconies. The wide bow-fronted nos.42-43 are listed buildings, as are the bow-fronted nos.10-11, 16-18, 36 and 40-41 which were probably designed by Wilds and Busby in the 1820s; nos.16 and 36 have fluted Ionic pilasters, while nos.40-41 also have fluted pilasters but no capitals.

Nos.37-39, also listed, were originally built in about 1826 as a synagogue for fifty people, but the premises were enlarged in 1837 by David Mocatta to include a school room and residence. The classical building, with Doric pilasters, was used as a warehouse after the Middle Street synagogue opened in 1874, and is now the Shape Health Studio. <44,66>

j) *ST JAMES'S AVENUE:* Attractive red-brick housing erected in 1889 on the slum clearance site of Little St James's Street. <45,83>

k) *UPPER ROCK GARDENS:* The eastern side is lined with large houses built from 1879 in the grounds of the East Lodge, the home of the Earl of Egremont for many years. The western side, however, consists of early-nineteenth-century three- and four-storey houses, many with bows. The listed no.15 has a cobbled front, a bow faced in mathematical tiles, and a distinctive doorway at the side. Also listed are the two terraces, nos.16-18 which have verandahs, and nos.19-26, all dating from the 1810s. No.3, probably by Wilds and Busby, is included on the council's local list. <44,83,108>

168. ST MARY'S HALL, Eastern Road

<6,44,45a,64a,123,203a>

Opened on 1 August 1836, St Mary's Hall was founded as a school for one hundred boarding daughters of clergymen by Revd Henry Venn Elliott, the curate of St Mary's Church, and was erected on nine acres of land given by the Marquess of Bristol. Costing £4,250, Elliott himself gave £2,250 and a thousand books to the new school. St Mary's Hall is now the oldest school in Brighton with a continuous history, and the main building, which was designed by George Basevi in Early Tudor style, is now listed; it is stuccoed with mullioned windows and a cross above the central gable. The Marquess also presented other portions of land and buildings for the school's use, including a cottage and half an acre of land at the north-western corner for the establishment of an infants' school.

St Mary's Hall was extended in 1920 to admit the daughters of laymen, and in more recent times to include a new hall (1969), a classroom block and swimming-pool (1976), Venn House for sixth-formers (1981), a junior school block (1983), and a pre-preparatory block (1989). It now has over 400 pupils, both day-girls and boarders; the boarding girls are accommodated in Elliott House, and in St Hilary House at 21-22 Sussex Square.

The school's chapel and concert hall is the former St Mark's Church in Eastern Road. Commenced in about 1840, it was built for the Marquess of Bristol on land he had given to St Mary's Hall, but it was eight years before the church was completed and consecrated on 21 September 1849. Faced in a roughened stone, it was designed in Early English style by Thomas Shelbourne and has an 1860 memorial window and monument to the Marquess. Additions on the northern and southern sides were made in 1892 by W.Gilbert Scott. Originally intended for the servants and less wealthy inhabitants of the Kemp Town area, St Mark's was made Kemp

Figure 160: St Mary's Hall in 1837

Town parish church in 1873 but pew rents were not abolished until 1930. In 1985 it was made redundant and taken over by the school. St Mark's Church Institute was in the former St Mark's School in Chesham Road now used by the Nautical Training Corps. <1,45,64a,83>

169. ST NICHOLAS'S CHURCH, Church Street and Dyke Road

a) *DESCRIPTION:* St Nicholas's Church is the ancient parish church of Brighton and is dedicated to the patron saint of fishermen, St Nicholas of Myra (sometimes spelt 'Nicolas'). Built on the hill overlooking the Old Town, the site was chosen possibly as a place of refuge from raiders, or as an older sacred or pagan site, or perhaps as a landmark for fishermen. Although a church was recorded at Brighton in the Domesday Book, no structural work at St Nicholas's dates from before the fourteenth century except a few Norman stones incorporated into the tower; it was probably erected in that century to cater for the growing population of the town.

Built in the Decorated style and faced in flint, the oldest parts of the church are now the tower, the arcades of the nave, and the chancel, all of which date from the fourteenth century. The tower is forty feet tall with walls four feet thick, and has ten bells dating from 1777 but recast in 1922. The rood screen across the chancel arch also dates from the fourteenth century. St Nicholas's Church is now a listed building. <1,57,64a>

b) *NEED FOR EXPANSION:* As the population of the town grew rapidly in the early nineteenth century the church was enlarged by the addition of galleries which were accessed via steps from the outside; the galleries were packed with fishermen and other poorer townsfolk, while the pews were rented to fashionable visitors. The expanded church then held 1,300 worshippers, but although the first chapel of ease (Chapel Royal) had opened in 1795 and there were eleven other Anglican chapels in the town by 1846, St Nicholas's was too cramped to serve as the parish church of such a large town. In that year however, a town meeting rejected both the obligatory rate for the church's maintenance and also an extra rate to enlarge it; many ratepayers were not of the Church of England and so voted against the proposal. Several town polls were then held, but they all produced the same results and the impasse continued until the death of the Duke of Wellington, Arthur Wellesley, in September 1852. The vicar, the Revd Henry Wagner, suggested that the restoration of the church at which Wellington had worshipped when he was tutored in the town would be a fitting memorial to the great man. The idea was accepted by the town and a public subscription raised £4,958 for the improvements, including £1,000 from Wagner himself. <65,112>

c) *RECONSTRUCTION and ADDITIONS:* Work on the enlargement commenced on 3 June 1853 under architect Richard Cromwell Carpenter; he virtually rebuilt the church such that only the pillars and arches of the nave, the chancel arch and screen, and the tower can now be considered to be genuinely fourteenth century. The galleries were removed, the aisles widened,

Figure 161: St Nicholas's Church in 1842 before enlargement

and the north aisle was also lengthened, but when the church reopened on 8 April 1854 the number of sittings had actually been reduced to 900. Carpenter also designed the Wellington Memorial Cross, situated at the western end of the north aisle.

In 1872 a new organ was installed; it had not been possible to refit the original 1813 organ into position following the restoration. In 1877 the choir vestry and northern approach were added, and the reredos and panelling were installed around the sanctuary by George Somers Clarke. Clarke also added the north vestry and a clerestoried roof in 1892. The eastern end of the north aisle has since been consecrated as a war memorial, the Chapel of St George, while the south chapel has been restored as the Lady Chapel. The stained glass by Charles Kempe dates from around 1880, while on the south wall are two interesting tablets which record the charitable bequests to the poor of the parish. There are also memorial tablets to Dr Samuel Johnson and T.R.Kemp, and a list of incumbents. <58>

d) *The NORMAN FONT:* The church's greatest treasure, however, is the Norman font which stands in the south aisle. It was probably carved in the early twelfth century from a single block of Caen stone, and has three decorated bands; the central band has panels depicting Christ's baptism, the Last Supper and two scenes from the life of St Nicholas. The font's origin is a mystery as it predates the church, but it is possible that it came from the earlier Brighton church mentioned in Domesday. In the 1740s two church-wardens had the sculpture partly recut, and they also carved their names in the base which was replaced in the nineteenth century.

e) *PAROCHIAL HISTORY:* The ancient ecclesiastical parish of Brighton was united with West Blatchington from 1744 until 1941, but when St Peter's was designated Brighton parish church on 22 June 1873 St Nicholas's became a district parish church with John Julius Hannah, son of the Vicar of Brighton, as vicar.

St Nicholas's Parish Rooms occupied a large, red-brick building of 1880 in St Nicholas Road. At the end of World War Two it was used as an auction room, but from 1954 until 1966 the building in use as a film studio. It then became Mead's auction rooms again before being converted into flats in 1987 <123>.

f) *CHURCHYARD:* St Nicholas's churchyard is said to mark the site of a Black Death plague-pit of 1348 <18>, but by the early nineteenth century it was severely overcrowded with graves and an extension to the east was consecrated in 1818. A separate extension on the northern side of Church Street opened in 1824 and a third extension was opened across Dyke Road in 1841, but burials at the church were prohibited from 1 October 1853, necessitating the opening of the Parochial Cemetery off Lewes Road. Those buried in the churchyard include the famous actress Anna Maria Crouch, Captain Nicholas Tettersell (see "Charles II"), Martha Gunn (see "Bathing (Dippers and Bathers)"), Amon Wilds (q.v.), Sake Dene Mahomed (see "Bathing (Mahomed's Baths)"), and Phoebe Hessel (see below).

By the footpath to Dyke Road is the stump of a medieval cross on an octagonal base. It was probably destroyed at the time of the Commonwealth in the seventeenth century, but a new shaft erected in 1934 has often been vandalised. During the war a German plane fell in the north-western corner of the churchyard, which is now maintained by the corporation as a public open space.

In medieval times, it is said, the fair Lady Edona waited in the churchyard for her lover, Manfred de Warrenne, to return from the Holy Wars, but she fainted when she saw his ship sink just offshore at Brighton. Now a ghostly ship, St Nicholas's Galley, may be seen gliding into Brighton at midnight on 17 May

Figure 162: The churchyard cross. The base is medieval but the cross itself is a modern replacement.

each year. The father of Manfred, John de Warrenne, was buried in the churchyard together with his horse, and it is said that a spectre on horseback may be seen on dark nights. <6,89,123>

The 1824 extension is approached through a red-brick archway on the northern side of Church Street. Once the site of the parish stocks, it was taken over by the corporation following the 1884 Brighton Improvement Act, and in 1949 the gravestones were removed to the side walls and a children's playground built. The western extension is entered through a listed archway of 1840 on the western side of Dyke Road and was laid out by A.H.Wilds in that year. It also came under the control of the corporation following the 1884 Improvement Act and is now known as the Dyke Road Rest Garden. The gravestones line the walls, and a tree-lined pathway runs around some large Victorian tombs. Along the northern side are fourteen large burial vaults with arched entrances. The adjacent K6-style telephone box has also been listed. <1,18,45,57>

g) *PHOEBE HESSEL:* One of the most interesting graves in the old churchyard is that of Phoebe Hessel. Born Phoebe Smith at Limehouse in 1713, this venerable lady fell in love with soldier William Golding in

Figure 163: Victorian tombs in the Dyke Road Rest Garden

1728 and enlisted in the Fifth Foot Regiment to remain with him when he was posted to the West Indies. In 1745 she was wounded in the arm at the Battle of Fontenoy, but when Golding was wounded and invalided home Phoebe revealed her sex to the commanding officer's wife and was discharged after an extraordinary seventeen years service in the army. The couple were married for about twenty years and lived in Plymouth.

After Golding's death Phoebe settled in Brighton and married William Hessel in about 1769; he died in about 1792. Receiving three guineas from the parish, Phoebe bought a donkey and hawked fish and other goods in nearby villages for a living. After overhearing a conversation in a Shoreham inn one day, she provided evidence resulting in the conviction and execution at Goldstone Bottom of one Mr Rooke for robbery and murder. In about 1800, when she was eighty-seven years old, Phoebe resorted to selling ginger-bread and apples at the corner of Old Steine and Marine Parade, but not long after was taken into the workhouse. However, she discharged herself in August 1806 and in 1808 was granted a pension of a half guinea per week by the Prince of Wales. As the oldest inhabitant in the town she was entitled to sit beside the vicar at a Napoleonic celebration dinner on the Level on 12 August 1814, and, although now blind, she attended the town's coronation celebrations on 19 July 1821. Phoebe Hessel died on 12 December 1821 at the age of 108, but only one of her nine children ever reached adulthood.

Recent research <285a> has revealed evidence conflicting with Phoebe's story; indeed it was only later in her life thet she recalled her military exploits, and it has been suggested that the tale is merely a good bar-room story designed to encourage listeners to open their purses. However, the Northumberland Fusiliers, successors to Phoebe's alleged regiment, certainly believe the story as they restored the grave in the 1970s. <3,7,24,57,90,285a>

170. ST PETER'S CHURCH, Brighton

<1,45,59,64a,123,126>

Brighton's parish church stands on an island site between York Place and Richmond Place, an area once known as Richmond Green, and its construction necessitated the diversion of the Lewes and Ditchling Roads. It was built in 1824-8 as a chapel of ease to St Nicholas's Church and was consecrated by Dr James Carr, Bishop of Chichester, on 25 January 1828; the foundation stone had also been laid by Dr Carr on 8 May 1824 in his previous position as Vicar of Brighton. The church, which was designed in the Perpendicular and Decorated styles, is one of the earliest and finest Gothic revival churches in the country and is now a listed building. It was constructed to the plans of Charles Barry (later the designer of the Houses of Parliament) who had won a competition organised by the vestry in August 1823, but the original design, which had a spire atop the tower, was not adhered to. The total cost of the chapel was £20,365. On 22 June 1873 St Peter's Chapel was designated the parish church of Brighton, replacing St Nicholas's as the town was divided into several district parishes. <112>

Constructed in Portland stone, the church originally measured 150 feet by 70 feet and had a clerestoried nave of five bays with aisles, galleries, an apsidal chancel, and a fine vaulted ceiling; the 1,800 sittings were mostly free. The first curate, the Revd Thomas Cooke, served the chapel until 1873 and the font is a memorial to him. A stone reredos and organ were added in 1874-7.

In 1898-1902 major alterations were carried out by George Somers Clarke which included the extension of the nave northwards, the removal of the galleries, the addition of a muniments room underneath, and the addition of a clerestoried chancel which was consecrated by the Archbishop of Canterbury in June 1906; the new chancel's ceiling was decorated in a colourful fashion in 1967-9. Unfortunately though, Clarke's additions were made in Sussex sandstone and there is now a distinct

Figure 164: St Peter's Chapel in about 1850. In the distance is Round Hill Mill

difference in external colour. The altar window is a memorial to Queen Victoria by Charles Kempe, and the organ was added in memory of King Edward VII in 1910. A temporary parish room opened in 1903, but the church hall opened on 25 October 1927 on the York Place side as a memorial to those killed in the Great War. A new reredos was designed in 1930 by W.H.Randall Blacking, replacing the original Caen stone and alabaster reredos of 1877, but it was badly damaged along with the altar in the early hours of 4 September 1985 by an arsonist. In the porch is a list of vicars of Brighton from 1091 (see "Vicars").

St Peter's churchyard was conveyed to the corporation on 31 December 1898 for the 'free use forever of the parishioners', and the grounds were formally opened by the mayor, Alfred Hawkes, on 6 November 1899; this event is commemorated by the stone seat at the northern end <311>. The dwarf fences replaced some rather ugly high railings in about 1922, but the great storm of October 1987 destroyed virtually all the trees surrounding the church. Every year however, the churchyard is graced by an illuminated Christmas tree, the gift of the Norwegian people.

171. SALTDEAN

<44,201,202>

a) *HISTORY:* Saltdean is now a large housing estate, but for centuries it was an open area of downland and furze with a few isolated farm buildings and cottages, the oldest remaining being the mid-eighteenth-century Lower Bannings Farmhouse and barn still standing at 38-42 Bannings Vale. The area was probably named from the salty sea-spray that covered the grass after storms, and Saltdean was mentioned by name in a survey of about 1667. Saltdean Gap gave relatively easy access to the beach and was often used by smugglers, so in 1834 a row of coastguard cottages was erected near the cliff top. The cottages were demolished in 1937 but one, the post-office and store, was demolished a little later than the others and Teynham House may be seen to have been erected around it.

The history of the present estate began in 1916 when the Beard estate was acquired by speculator Charles Neville as part of his dream to develop all the land between Rottingdean and Newhaven. The area was requisitioned for agricultural use during the First World War, but in 1919 Neville sold plots in what is now Peacehaven, and he started development at Rottingdean Heights in 1923. The purchase of the Saltdean area was completed in 1922 and 1925, and in 1924 Neville established the Saltdean Estate Company in an office by the coastguard cottages. Miles of new roads were pegged out and surfaced with chalk quarried from a pit in Greenbank Avenue. A small railway was used to convey the materials along the length of Saltdean Vale.

Fortunately much stricter planning control was exercised than at nearby Peacehaven and no shacks or wooden buildings were allowed. In 1928 that part of the estate to the west of Longridge Avenue, as part of the parish of Rottingdean, was incorporated into the county borough of Brighton and development naturally proceeded more rapidly with the services now offered by the corporation. By the Second World War the Saltdean Park area and the Mount estate were largely complete, and the Estate Company had built the Lido, the Ocean Hotel, several blocks of flats, and the Smuggler's Haunt tea-rooms at the gap. Development of the Saltdean estate continued after the war until the 1970s, the Estate Company having been acquired by Homemakers Ltd. In 1981 the population of the Brighton part of Saltdean was just under 5,000 <277>.

b) *OLD BARNS:* The oldest buildings in West Saltdean (i.e. that part within the borough of Brighton) are the three barns in Saltdean Vale. At the northernmost end is Looes Barn, partly faced in knapped flint and partly rendered, which was probably erected in the early nineteenth century; it is now a virtual ruin. Newlands Barn stands at the corner of Lustrells Crescent and is faced in flint, with the Old Stable adjacent. It was used as a workshop, store, stable, and office of the Saltdean Estate Company after the development of the estate, but in 1978 the early-nineteenth-century barn was listed to save it from demolition (although the roof had already been removed) and was converted into a residence in 1983-4. The flint Saltdean Barn is also a listed building dating from the late eighteenth century, and stands in a small public garden surrounded by a flint wall at the northern end of Saltdean Park. <108>

c) *SALTDEAN PARK and LIDO:* Known also as Saltdean Oval from its shape, the park covers eighteen acres and was laid out by the Estate Company in the 1920s. In July 1961 the corporation took control and spent £45,000 on diverting the roadways which ran across the park, renovating the sixteen-hole miniature golf-course, and providing tennis-courts and swings. There is also a bowling-green and pavilion.

At the southern end of the park stands the Saltdean Lido, opened by the Estate Company on the site of some tennis-courts in 1937. The main building was designed by Richard Jones in a curvilinear Modern style, and in July 1987 it was listed as a building of special architectural interest. The pool itself measures 140 feet by 66 feet and can accommodate 500 bathers. During the war the pool was used as a water tank by the National Fire Service College which was based at the Ocean Hotel. However, when the war ended the Lido remained closed, and it was the subject of several redevelopment plans until July 1961 when it was taken over by the corporation. Saltdean Lido finally reopened in 1964 at a cost of £86,000. A new wing for community use was erected at the rear on the site of a small boating pool and includes a youth centre, clinic, and a community centre which opened in February 1965; a branch library had opened the previous month.

d) *SALTDEAN CHURCH:* St Nicholas's Church in Saltdean Vale was designed by Edward Maude and was dedicated by the Bishop of Chichester on 8 May 1965. Constructed in a grey stone with a tall tower, it was erected following a fund-raising campaign and replaced a temporary church of 1951 which is now the church hall. St Nicholas's was consecrated as Saltdean parish church in December 1970.

e) *LONGRIDGE AVENUE:* Saltdean's main shopping street was formerly a trackway known as the Droveway, and it divides Brighton from Telscombe parish for most of its length.

At the corner of Wicklands Avenue stands the Ocean Hotel, designed in Modern style by Richard Jones and erected by the Saltdean Estate Company. It could accommodate 600 guests and had all rooms either electrically- or centrally-heated and with hot and cold water. After a grand opening on 25 July 1938 however, the hotel was requisitioned in December 1939 by the Auxiliary Territorial Service; on 10 October 1941 it became the National Fire Service's training college until 1948. The hotel and its large swimming-pool then remained empty for some time, but on 3 May 1953 it was reopened on holiday-camp lines by Butlins Ltd which had acquired the building for £250,000. In 1988-9 Butlins embarked upon a major refurbishment of the hotel, which can now accommodate 750 guests.

Higher up Longridge Avenue is St Martin's United Reformed Church, designed by Peter Winton-Lewis and opened on 15 June 1957; a planned spire was never built. The adjacent church hall had opened in February 1949.

172. SCHOOLS

Brighton's schools, past and present, are too numerous to chronicle in great detail, but a brief outline of educational development in the town is given below together with the approximate opening dates of most schools. Consult the index for details of some individual schools.

a) *EARLY CHARITY SCHOOLS:* The earliest known school in the town appears to have been in existence in 1581 when William Cartwright was licensed as a schoolmaster by the Bishop of Chichester. In 1665 a 'freescoole' was recorded, and in 1702 the Revd Anthony Springett founded a free school in the Bartholomews but it ceased at an unknown date. In 1769 another free school was founded in what is now Meeting House Lane, opposite Union Street, by the bequest of William Grimmett, a former Springett pupil. Springett's School itself was revived in 1805, and these two free schools amalgamated in 1818 as a National School which moved to a new building in Church Street in 1829, the Central National Schools (see also "Church Street"). (The Church of England National Society for the Education of the Poor was formed in 1811.) <1,15,18,122,296a>

Another early school was the Union Charity School in Middle Street. The boys' school was established in 1807 by Edward Goff and was joined by a girls' school in 1809. Both were supported by public subscription and children of all denominations were taught. These schools were later taken over by the school board and then the corporation, but were demolished in February 1973 and replaced by the Middle Street Primary School. <123,206>

Many proprietary schools for the wealthy were established in the nineteenth century and Brighton was even dubbed 'School Town' <2,25>, but a minority of poor children went to charity schools such as the National and Union Schools mentioned above; also to the British and Foreign Schools Society in Eastern Road (1828); Duke Street Charity Schools (1817 for T.R.Kemp); the Puget Schools in Clarence Yard (1861); the Ragged Schools Union in Carlton Street, Dorset Street (1855), Essex Street, George Street (1853), and Spa Street; and the Wesleyan Schools in Nelson Row. <83,275a>

b) *CHURCH SCHOOLS:* Many churches also established elementary day schools for poor children in addition to Sunday schools. These included Belgrave Street Chapel (1863); Christ Church, Bedford Place (1841); St Bartholomew, Providence Place (1872); St John, Carlton Hill (1870); St John the Baptist (1907 Upper Bedford Street, 1989 Whitehawk Hill Road); St

Figure 165: The Royal British Schools in 1835. They stood in Eastern Road between Freshfield Road and Sutherland Road.

Mark (1845 Sussex Square, 1856 Chesham Road, 1896 Arundel Road, 1972 and 1982 Manor Road); St Martin (1875 St Martin's Street, 1987 Hartington Road); St Mary Magdalene (1871 Upper North Street, 1970 Hampton Street); St Paul (1877 Little Russell Street, 1924 Russell Place, 1967 St Nicholas Road); and St Stephen, Borough Street (1855). <83,123>

c) *BRIGHTON SCHOOL BOARD:* The 1870 Education Act established local 'school boards', bodies elected by the ratepayers of the district to control public elementary schools for children aged five to ten; a small weekly fee was chargeable unless the parents were very poor. Religious education was taught, but not in the views of any particular Christian denomination; there were, however, continual disagreements between the clerical and lay members of the board. Elementary education was made compulsory in 1880 and was provided free from 1891. The School Boards of Brighton and Preston were united in 1881.

Upon its foundation, the Brighton School Board immediately took control of the Puget Schools in Clarence Yard, a school in Circus Street, and schoolrooms at Belgrave Street Chapel and London Road Chapel (Belmont Street). It also took over the Middle Street Schools in 1874, and erected many new schools buildings over the next thirty years to the design of its architect, Thomas Simpson. They were: York Place (1870); Fairlight Place (1870, rebuilt 1931); Richmond Street (1873); Hanover Terrace (1873, later Secondary Technical School and now College of Technology annexe); Sussex Street (1874); Queen's Park, Freshfield Place (1880); Preston Road (1880, closed 1937, later Preston Technical Institute and now College of Technology annexe); Finsbury Road (1881, later St Luke's Secondary School and now a polytechnic annexe); Circus Street (1883, closed 1928, now a polytechnic annexe); Ditchling Road, now the Downs School (1890); Stanford Road (1893); Elm Grove (1893); and St Luke's Terrace (1903).

In addition, the board took over a disused workhouse at Chailey as an industrial school for truants in 1875, but opened a new truant school at Purley Lodge in Old London Road, Patcham, in 1882. Together with the London School Board, the Brighton and Preston United School Board built another industrial school at Mile Oak Road, Portslade, in 1902. This school was used by Brighton until 1913.
<24,83,115,296a>

d) *LOCAL AUTHORITY CONTROL:* Following the 1902 Education Act the education committee of the county borough council took over all responsibility for public elementary, secondary and technical education in the town, including the church schools, on 1 April 1903, but charges for secondary education were maintained (with one quarter of places provided free from 1907) until the 1944 Education Act was passed. Many new schools have been opened by the local education authority since 1903, including: Balfour Road (1924); Bevendean (1950); Carden (1948); Carlton Hill (1963); Coldean (1952); Coombe Road (1912); Dorothy Stringer (1955, Surrenden Pool 1972); Falmer High (1974, Stanmer Secondary 1951, Westlain Grammar 1957); Hertford Road (1931); Loder Road (1910, closed 1924); Longhill (1963); Middle Street (1974, see above); Moulsecoomb Primary (1929); Moulsecoomb Junior (1930); Patcham High (1989, formerly Patcham Fawcett (1966) & Patcham Margaret Hardy (1969, originally Patcham Secondary 1937)); Rottingdean Junior and Primary (1953); St Joseph's (1956); Saltdean (1962); Stanley Deason (1976, Whitehawk 1933, Leisure Centre 1984); Varndean Sixth Form (1931 formerly boys' grammar); Varndean High (1926 formerly girls' grammar); Westdene (1961); Whitehawk Junior (1934); Whitehawk Primary (1935); and Woodingdean Primary (1949, swimming-pool 1977).

On 1 April 1974, under the terms of the 1972 Local Government Act, East Sussex County Council became the local education authority and put into effect the county borough council's decision to change to comprehensive education over a period of several years from September 1975. Grammar schools were abolished and secondary education was concentrated on seven 'high schools', while more advanced teaching was concentrated at the new 'sixth-form colleges'. The largest school is now Falmer High which has about 1,250 pupils, followed by Dorothy Stringer High (1,170) and Stanley Deason High (1,070). <83,115,123,124,203,296a>

Michael Faraday College, a sponsored 'city technology college' for 800 eleven- to eighteen-year-olds outside the responsibility of the local education authority, was to have been established at Woodingdean in September 1991, but the proposal was dropped because of a lack of finance. <123>

e) *SPECIAL SCHOOLS:* Several special schools cater for handicapped and remedial pupils. Brighton Special School opened in 1928 at Trafalgar Court, but it used an iron building in Saunders Park from 1929 until 1955 when Woodside Special School (now renamed Queensdown School) opened at Moulsecoomb. Other council special schools are at Patcham House, Old London Road (the former village National School); and Queensdown and Uplands Schools in Lynchet Close, Hollingdean. Downsview, Coldean Lane, was built in 1962 but demolished in 1990 for bypass construction. Hamilton Lodge, Walpole Road (for the deaf 1945); St John's School, Walpole Road (1931); and Ovingdean Hall are voluntary or independent special schools. <83,123,203>

173. SEWERS AND DRAINS

<2,112,115,167,167a,169,169a>

a) *EARLY DRAINS:* Until the early nineteenth century, human waste in Brighton was either tipped into cesspits or, in the poorer areas, straight into the roadway; the few sewers that then existed were used only to drain surface rainwater. In 1792-3 a sewer was constructed to drain the Steine and carry the intermittent Wellesbourne stream to the sea, and following the inundations of the winter of 1827-8 a northern storm-water drain was laid from Preston Circus to the sea-front. Some developers did incorporate drains in new streets from the turn of the nineteenth century, but they were only intended for surface water as their use for removing foul water was prohibited under the Brighton Town Acts. The use of cesspits, regularly emptied at night by scavengers employed by the town, was preferred, although many people were in fact using the inadequate drains for sewerage.

b) *CRITICAL REPORTS:* The state of the town's sewerage was obviously a cause for great concern, especially in so fashionable a resort. In 1848 Dr William Kebbell reported on the conditions in the town, finding, among many other damning comments, that the King's Road drain was producing bad smells and that the Edward Street drain ran above basement level. In April 1849 the General Board of Health's inspector, Edward Cresy, made a detailed report on the town's sanitation with regard to the adoption of the Public Health Act <284>. He was alarmed to find several thousand cesspits cut into the porous chalk, many of them near drinking water wells, and only 32 of the 186 streets sewered. He consequently made many important recommendations to remedy the situation.

The main rainwater drain ran along the sea-front and discharged at short outfalls onto the beaches at Hove, Western Street and below the Royal Albion Hotel; the illegal use of the drains for foul waste created a considerable problem at these outfalls, however. In May 1852 the sewer was continued under Marine Parade to connect with the Kemp Town sewer, and was further extended to an outfall at the parish boundary at Black Rock in 1854. Another damning inquiry and report in 1859, when only about 4,000 houses were connected to the system and an estimated 10,000 houses retained cesspits, resulted in a scheme to drain the town into three extended outfalls at Western Street, the Albion Hotel and Black Rock in an effort to reduce the smell and effluent along the beaches; the Lewes Road sewer was also enlarged in 1866 to cope with springs along the route. The scheme was successful in reducing most of the problems on the beaches but was still far from satisfactory as patches of floating sewage could be seen on the surface and substances were sometimes washed ashore. Public agitation resulted in an examination of schemes for a new method of sewage disposal.

c) *INTERCEPTING SEWER and PORTOBELLO:* The result of the investigation, and still the basis of today's sewerage system, was the intercepting sewer engineered in 1871-4 by Sir John Hawkshaw at a cost of £105,000. It was built from Hove Street to an outfall at Portobello near Telscombe Cliffs, a distance of over seven miles, and intercepted the main sewers that previously discharged via several outfalls. The cylindrical sewer, lined with brick, has a diameter of five feet to the west of East Street, six feet to the Aquarium where the main London Road, Lewes Road and Marine Parade sewers join, and seven feet to the outfall. There were sixty ventilating shafts along its length including a 102-foot chimney erected on the cliff top to the south-east of Roedean School; a coke fire was used to produce a continuous flow of air through the sewer, but the chimney was demolished in 1933 for the construction of Marine Drive although the concrete base remains. Another ventilating shaft was built in 1885 at Rottingdean Heights disguised as an octagonal-shaped house; it was known as The Mortuary because the bodies of ship-wrecked sailors were kept there before burial, but the building was demolished following its sale in 1973. There were also ventilation flues built into the corners of the Madeira Lift shaft <261a>. The sewer then discharged untreated effluent via a short outfall at the high-water mark at Portobello. It was controlled by a body known as the Brighton Intercepting and Outfall Sewers Board.

However, severe and damaging criticism of Brighton's sanitation continued, especially in *The Lancet* <285>, and in 1882 the council commissioned Sir Joseph Bazalgette to report on the system. He considered that the sewerage was satisfactory and that there was no reason to assume that the town was unhealthy, but a few minor improvements were carried out <168>. In 1892 the outfall was extended and new trunk sewers were installed along the London Road valley. In 1928 the intercepting sewer was continued to Aldrington and a new Lewes Road sewer was constructed to prevent a repetition of serious flooding. The outfall was again extended at this time to a length of about 370 yards, well below the low-water mark, and the waste was coarse-screened. The sewer itself, which had become exposed at Black Rock, was protected in the 1930s by the construction of the Undercliff Walk.

In 1974 the Southern Water Authority replaced the Intercepting Sewer Board, and in 1977 opened a new treatment works and pumping station at Portobello which was not fully commissioned until 1983 because of technical difficulties. All solid matter over 5 mm. is extracted from the flow and removed to landfill sites; the remaining effluent, which still includes much solid human waste, is then pumped along a new outfall 2,000 yards long via diffusers, a great improvement on the old system. The old outfall is retained as a back-up, and there are also five other raw outfalls at Brighton and Hove for the rare occasions during storms when the system's capacity of four cubic metres per second is exceeded. Unfortunately raw sewage is still washed onto the beaches in such circumstances, especially from the outfall at the Albion Groyne where four main sewers converge, but Southern Water has plans to construct a parallel sewer to Portobello to eliminate this problem. The main source of sea pollution at Brighton is now from an outfall at Southwick.

Sewage takes about three hours to gravitate from Brighton to Portobello, and around 20 million gallons make the journey every day. Under an agreement with Southern Water, Brighton Council maintains the 300 or so miles of main sewers within the town.

174. SHOREHAM AIRPORT

<123,292>

The first aeroplane seen in the skies above Brighton was a Blériot monoplane which was reconstructed on the beach at Black Rock by André Beaumont, a French pioneer who had sailed over from France. With Harry Preston as his passenger, Beaumont flew low over the town and sea for forty-five minutes in 1910. On 15 February 1911 Oscar Morrison flew another Blériot monoplane from Brooklands Aerodrome near Weybridge to Brighton in one hour, landing by mistake on the beach near the Banjo Groyne; the propeller was hung as a souvenir by Harry Preston in the Royal York Hotel for many years. The Preston brothers, together with Mr Rosenthal of the Palace Pier Company, presented an £80 prize for a 'Grand Aerial Race' from Brooklands to Brighton on 6 May 1911, won on handicap by Gustav Hamel in a Blériot monoplane. Another race was flown from London to Brighton in 1913. <19,290>

As a result of these pioneering flights a permanent sea-plane station was opened in 1913 by Magnus Volk's son Herman at the Banjo Groyne, using the electric railway as the principal means of access. The venture was short-lived, however, as the small hangar was requisitioned for the war effort in 1914. A plan for a sea-plane station in front of the Kemp Town Slopes was approved by the council in 1928 but was vetoed by the Board of Trade. <189>

Meanwhile, a pioneering centre of aviation was becoming established some 6.5 miles to the west of Brighton in the parish of Lancing. The first flight was made on 10 July 1910, and the Shoreham flying ground was officially opened as Brighton Aerodrome on 20 June 1911. During the First World War the land was requisitioned by the Royal Flying Corps and after 1918 the land was returned to grazing, but the airport started again in the early 1930s with the first scheduled passenger flight made in October 1932. Services to the Isle of Wight, Croydon, Deauville and Jersey were established, and on 13 June 1936 the airfield was officially reopened as the Brighton, Hove and Worthing Municipal Airport, under the joint control of the three boroughs; a railway station also opened adjacently. The Art Deco terminal building, designed by Stavers H.Tiltman, is now listed and is often seen in television productions depicting the 1930s. The following year 6,000 passengers used the airport, but it was again requisitioned as a fighter base in the Second World War. Municipal control was re-established in 1951, but the whole airport was leased to F.G.Miles Ltd and the Beagle Aircraft Co. until 1971, with just a few scheduled flights made in the 1950s. Shoreham Airport reopened as a municipal airport in May 1971 and a 900-yard hard runway opened on 1 July 1982; this is too short for all but the smallest passenger aircraft, however. Scheduled flights to Jersey and France were resumed for a short period, but Shoreham, one of the six oldest licensed aerodromes in the country, remains the earliest still operating.

175. STANMER

a) *HISTORY:* Stanmer is an unspoilt and attractive estate village situated in the middle of Stanmer Park, and together with the park has been designated an outstanding conservation area. In 765 the manor of Stanmer was granted to the College of Benedictine Canons at South Malling and it remained their property until the Reformation, but in 1714 the estate was acquired by Henry Pelham for £7,500 and remained in the Pelham family, the earls of Chichester, until 1947. In 1086 the population was around 300 but remained at about 120 throughout the nineteenth century and into the first half of the twentieth.

In November 1947 the Stanmer estate was acquired by Brighton Corporation, 4,958 acres being purchased for £225,000 less a claim for military damage, and was bought principally to safeguard the water supply, to preserve the downland, to provide a recreational area, and to provide land for housing and educational developments. The purchase included both Stanmer and Falmer villages, six farms, and about 500 acres of commercial woodland. The estate, mansion and village of Stanmer, which had been occupied by the military for the duration of the war, were restored by the corporation and reoccupied in 1948.
<1,228,305>

The parish of Stanmer originally occupied an area of 1,341 acres including most of what is now the Coldean estate, and formed part of the Newhaven union and rural district; from 1934 it was part of Chailey rural district. In 1934 also 242 acres of land known as Patchway in the vicinity of Old Boat Corner, a detached portion of Falmer parish, were added to Stanmer. On 1 April 1952 1,028 acres of Stanmer were transferred to the county borough of Brighton under the 1951 Brighton Extension Act, the remainder of the parish being added to that part of Falmer parish not similarly transferred.

There are now a number of enjoyable signposted circular walks over the Downs as far as Ditchling Beacon and Clayton Windmills, starting at the Stanmer car-park.
<1,109,279>

b) *STANMER HOUSE:* This elegant mansion is faced in a pale yellow sandstone and has a slight, three-bay projection topped by a pediment, but a single-bay extension of 1860 spoils the symmetry. It was built near the site of an older manor house in 1721-30 for Henry Pelham junior, in Palladian style by French architect Nicholas Dubois. The Pelhams became the earls of Chichester and the house was extended in 1775 and 1860. The interior exhibits some excellent fireplaces and panelling, and has a magnificent broad oak staircase.

In 1947 the house was purchased by the corporation as part of the Stanmer estate, and although the west wing was demolished as being beyond repair the rest of the house was restored and is now listed grade I. Until January 1980 the house was leased to the university as offices, but it was then opened to the public and occupied by squatters for three weeks. Although currently unused, it is planned to restore the house fully.

To the south-west there is a large, attractive garden, while at the rear, on the site of the Jacobean manor house, is the Rural Museum of the Stanmer Preservation Society which contains many interesting exhibits. These include a seventeenth-century listed well-house with lath and plaster walls on a timber frame; the horse 'gin' (engine) is still in situ. Stanmer House's eighteenth-century stables are listed grade II* and are situated in the private Stanmer Nursery area. They are faced in knapped flint and brick, and have an archway entrance into a courtyard, the west wing of which is used as the Victoria Hall by the village. The nearby nineteenth-century, single-storey flint storage sheds, formerly cattle stalls, are also listed. <1,44,123,228-232>

The Stanmer Nurseries of the corporation's Parks and Recreation Department occupy thirty-six acres on the site of the house's kitchen garden, an orchard and two meadows. The nurseries were founded in 1875 at the Lewes Road waterworks, and later occupied three separate sites before being removed to Stanmer from 1953 where they were formally opened on 7 May 1957. Three principal operations are conducted at Stanmer: it annually provides some 70,000 trees and shrubs; 250,000 hardy plants; and thousands of flowers. A horticultural training centre was established in 1966. <45,126,228>

c) *STANMER CHURCH:* Standing on the site of a fourteenth-century church destroyed by fire, Stanmer Church was erected in 1838 but has an unknown dedication. Now listed, it was built in Early English style with a thin western tower and spire, and is faced in knapped flint with stone dressings. On the north wall of the nave is a memorial of 1580 to Sir John Pelham. The ecclesiastical parish of Stanmer has been united with Falmer since 1835, and also with Moulsecoomb from 1956 until 1976. <1,228>

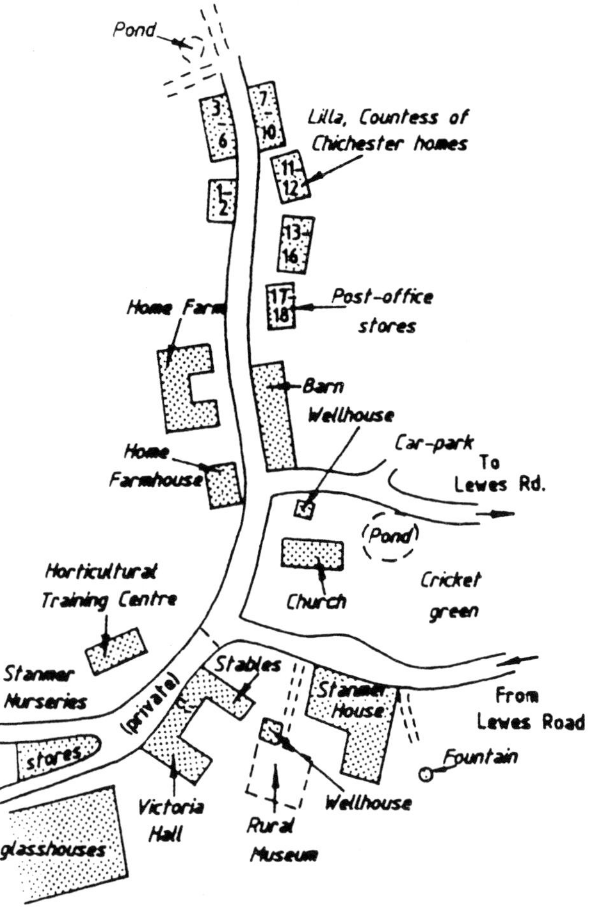

Figure 166: Stanmer village

Figure 167: Stanmer House and Park

d) *STANMER VILLAGE:* The village street is now lined with listed buildings, but the houses of the village were once sited in the paddock opposite the stores where the outlines of the foundations may still be seen. The present houses were erected in the mid eighteenth century as a new estate village by the earls of Chichester; most were severely damaged during the military occupation of the Second World War, but were subsequently restored by the corporation.

At the road junction is the Home Farmhouse, faced in knapped flint and red brick, and with flint farm buildings adjacent. Opposite stands the weather-boarded and flint Long Barn, dating from the eighteenth century or possibly earlier. Nos.1-6, 7-10 (nineteenth century) and 13-16 are all small, knapped-flint cottages, while nos.11-12 were built in 1912 in memory of Lilla, Countess of Chichester, and are not listed. Near the pond and church stands an ancient flint well-house, covered in ivy and with a slate roof. It was rebuilt in 1838 at the same time as the church, incorporating an earlier arch, and houses a thirteen-foot donkey treadmill which dates from the seventeenth century or earlier. The well itself is 252 feet deep and was dug in the sixteenth century. Stanmer pond is surrounded by large sarsen stones, probably giving the village its name which means 'stony pool'. <1,44,228,289,311>

e) *STANMER PARK:* Originally laid out by the architect of Stanmer House, Nicholas Dubois, in the 1720s, Stanmer Park was planted with trees principally in the period 1720-1800, and particularly by Thomas Pelham, the first Earl of Chichester. In November 1947 the park was purchased by the corporation as part of the Stanmer estate, and although 250 acres were set aside as a public park, 159 of them were later leased to the university. The public park is a beautiful area of gently undulating grassland and is very popular with Brightonians; in 1988 the Stanmer conservation area was extended to include the park in addition to the village. The park also includes the largest area of woodland in Brighton, Stanmer Great Wood, 45% of which was destroyed by the great storm of October 1987. The Brighton bypass, scheduled for completion in 1995, will run through the southern part of the Stanmer estate, skirting the southern edge of the Great Wood.

Standing at the Lewes Road entrance to the park are the Lower Lodges, elegant, single-storey, eighteenth-century listed houses with tall chimneys which replaced the original lodges some 400 yards further along the park road. The Upper Lodges stand at the north-western edge of the park off Ditchling Road, near the picnic area, and are plain, two-storey buildings.

Standing amidst trees to the south-west of the point where the road through the park divides is the listed Frankland monument, a three-sided obelisk in artificial Coade stone on a base of three tortoises which bears the figures of an angel, a man and a woman, with an urn at the top. It was erected in June 1775 by Thomas and Ann Pelham, the first Earl and Countess of Chichester, in memory of Ann's father Frederick Frankland, M.P., who died at the age of seventy-three on 8 March 1768. <1,44,45,123,228,229,232>

Figure 168: The Lower Lodges of Stanmer Park

176. STREET-LIGHTING

<112,115,170,189>

The streets of Brighton were originally lit by oil lamps, under no particular control until the 1773 Brighton Town Act established the town commissioners for street-lighting and for other purposes. In September 1818 the Pavilion grounds became the first area to be lit by gas, but the permanent lamp-posts which still stand (and are now listed structures) were erected in the reign of William IV. In May 1824 the Steine adopted gas-lighting, and other streets and squares followed suit such that by 1853 there were 947 gas street-lamps in the town. As late as 1939 the Lanes were still lit by gas, but the lamps were converted at the end of the war after blackouts had finished.

Figure 169: Ornate lamp-standards in King's Road

Following experiments at the Goldstone pumping station, electric street-lighting was introduced experimentally on 10 February 1881 when Charles Siemens strung a series of arc-lights along Marine Parade, with a generator installed in an arch below. Following this public experiment the corporation obtained an enabling order to light the Old Town electrically, but public electric street-lighting, as opposed to domestic lighting, was confined to the Pavilion grounds only until the 1890s. On 16 September 1893 a line of forty-one cast-iron lamp-standards with ornamental mouldings, each 28 feet high and standing 130 feet apart, were inaugurated by the mayoress, Miss Ewart, along the King's Road; a tablet to commemorate the event may still be seen on the standard by the West Pier. During the 1930s highly decorated, silver-painted, twin-pendant copper and brass lamps were added to the King's Road, Grand Junction Road, Marine Parade and Madeira Drive standards, but they were declared unsafe in October 1980 and replaced by modern angled lights. Public opinion, however, led to their replacement two years later by fibreglass replicas of the 1930s originals.

By 1896 King's Road, Grand Junction Road, Madeira Drive, Marine Parade, Western Road, North Street, St James's Street, East Street and the Valley Gardens were all lit by electricity, and the system spread into most other streets in the early twentieth century.

177. SUSSEX COUNTY CRICKET CLUB, County Ground, Hove

a) *ORIGINS AND HISTORY:* Sussex has long been a cradle of cricket, and Brighton and Rottingdean were two of the leading clubs in the mid eighteenth century when matches were an attraction for visitors and often played for prize money. The first mention of a Brighton team is on 22 July 1754 when a combined team of Bolney, Brighton and East Sussex took on Guildford, Ripley, Thursley and part of Surrey at Guildford. Brighton Cricket Club was originally formed in 1791, but was re-established in 1848 by G.King and W.Adams.

The game was played on the Steine until all ball games were banned there by the Master of Ceremonies in 1787. The Level then became the main venue with the Prince of Wales's ground being laid out in 1791, but it was replaced in 1823 by the Hanover Ground on the northern side of Union Road, now Park Crescent (q.v.). Sussex representative sides had been fielded since the mid eighteenth century, but the country's oldest county cricket club was formally established on 1 March 1839 under the presidency of Viscount Pevensey, later the second Earl of Sheffield. Infrequent fixtures were played at the Hanover Ground, but in 1848 the club moved to the Brunswick Ground in the vicinity of Third and Fourth Avenues, Hove. A final move to the County Ground was made in 1872 when nine acres were acquired from the Stanford family. The first match at the County Ground was played on 20 May 1872.

The golden ages of Sussex cricket were probably in the late 1890s and 1900s when C.B.Fry and Ranjitsinjhi dominated, and again in the 1930s with Maurice Tate to the fore. Sussex have also played at Horsham, St Leonards, Lewes, Hastings, Eastbourne, Chichester, Worthing and Arundel. However, although they are the oldest county club, Sussex have never won the county championship since it was properly established in 1890. <223-226>

b) *PLAYING RECORD (showing the championship and Sunday league positions, and rounds reached in knock-out competitions)* <227,297>:

1890	8	1904	6	1921	9
1891	7	1905	3	1922	9
1892	9	1906	10	1923	6
1893	7	1907	13	1924	10
1894	8	1908	5	1925	13
1895	11	1909	4	1926	10
1896	14	1910	7	1927	10
1897	6	1911	13	1928	7
1898	9	1912	10	1929	4
1899	5	1913	7	1930	7
1900	4	1914	6	1931	4
1901	4	1915-18	-	1932	2
1902	2	1919	11	1933	2
1903	2	1920	6	1934	2

1935	7	1939	10	1948	16	1952	13	1956	9	1960	4
1936	14	1940-45	-	1949	13	1953	2	1957	9	1961	8
1937	5	1946	17	1950	13	1954	9	1958	13	1962	12
1938	8	1947	9	1951	10	1955	4	1959	15		

	CC	Gillette/ NatWest	B & H	Sunday
1963	4	Winners	-	-
1964	9	Winners	-	-
1965	16	Q-F	-	-
1966	10	1	-	-
1967	13	S-F	-	-
1968	17	Finalist	-	-
1969	7	S-F	-	17
1970	9	Finalist	-	17
1971	11	2	-	7
1972	16	1	Q-F	15
1973	15	Finalist	Group	7
1974	13	2	Group	6
1975	17	1	Group	11
1976	10	Q-F	Group	5
1977	8	2	Q-F	4
1978	9	Winners	Q-F	8
1979	4	S-F	Group	12
1980	4	S-F	Q-F	9
1981	2	Q-F	Q-F	5
1982	8	1	S-F	1
1983	11	Q-F	Group	4
1984	6	2	Q-F	3
1985	7	2	Group	2
1986	14	Winners	Q-F	4
1987	7	2	Group	14
1988	16	1	Group	14
1989	10	Q-F	Group	11
1990	17	2	Group	13

c) *RECORDS* <297>:

Highest innings total:705-8 dec. v. Surrey, 1902.

Lowest innings total: 19 v. Notts., 1873.

Highest partnership: 490, first wicket, E.H.Bowley and John Langridge v. Middlesex, 1933.

Most appearances: 622, James Langridge, 1924-53.

Most runs in career: 34,152, John Langridge, 1928-57.

Most centuries in career: 76, John Langridge, 1928-57.

Most runs in season: 2,850, John Langridge, 1949.

Most centuries in season: 12, John Langridge, 1949.

Most runs in innings: 333, K.S.Duleepsinjhi v. Northants., 1930.

Most wickets in career: 2,211, M.W.Tate, 1912-37.

Most wickets in season: 198, M.W.Tate, 1925.

Most wickets in match: 17-106, G.R.Cox senior v. Warwicks., 1926.

Most wickets in innings: 10-48, C.H.G.Bland v. Kent, 1899, and 10-49, N.I.Thomson v. Warwicks., 1964.

178. College of TECHNOLOGY, Pelham Street and Richmond Terrace

<26,83,115,123>

Brighton College of Technology, formerly the Technical College, has its origins in the Brighton School of Art and Science which opened, as an art school only, in the great kitchen of the Royal Pavilion in 1858. In 1874 it was joined there by a new science department, but the whole school moved to a new Italianate building by John Gibbins at Grand Parade in 1876. The corporation took control of the school in 1892, and removed the science department in 1897 to a new, Renaissance-style, red-brick and terracotta building at Richmond Terrace which was formally opened as the Municipal Technical College by Princess Louise and the Duke of Fife on 8 January 1898. The new college was enlarged in 1906 by the addition of a mechanical workshop, and the adjoining teachers-training premises, which had been erected in 1909, were incorporated as a north wing in 1927. The south wing was added in 1935.

In the late 1960s the Technical College took over the York Place Schools, and a new eleven-storey block was opened at Pelham Street in January 1971. In 1984 the Technical College was renamed Brighton College of Technology. There are annexes at Francis Street, Hanover Terrace, Preston Road, Stanmer Park, and at School Road in Hove, and in 1989 there were about 1,400 full-time and 7,500 part-time students.

179. TELEGRAPHS and TELEPHONES

a) *TELEGRAPHS:* The first telegraphic message from Brighton to London was sent on 11 January 1851 by the Electric and International Telegraph Company from Brighton Station, and less than a month later, on 1 February, they opened the first telegraph-office at the Royal York Hotel. A rival service was offered by the London, Brighton and South Coast Railway Company with a system which linked their stations. In 1856 Electric and International Telegraph moved their office to 18 Old Steine, formerly Donaldson's Library, and opened a second office at the Bedford Hotel on 1 July 1865; this was removed to the eastern toll-house of the West Pier in 1867, the same year as a third office opened at Burlington Street.

In 1867 also, the British and Irish Magnetic Telegraph Company extended a wire from the South-Eastern Railway at Battle to offices at 1 Castle Square and the

Grand Hotel. On 5 February 1870, however, the two companies' plant was statutorily purchased by the General Post Office which then extended the network throughout Sussex and developed Brighton into a large telegraphic centre handling some 110,000 messages a year. The Head Post-Office in Ship Street also handled telegraphs from 1871, and it became the Head Telegraph-Office in 1877 with Old Steine reduced to a branch office. By 1880 there were eleven telegraph-offices in Brighton plus the railway stations, and nearly half a million messages were handled. Other branch offices opened at Western Road, Hove, in June 1885; College Road in August 1888; and Cannon Place in June 1891, replacing the West Pier office. In 1891, when delivery charges in large towns were abolished, over 1.5 million messages were handled, and the telegraph service continued to grow until the universal introduction of telephones in the first half of the twentieth century. <15>

b) *TELEPHONES:* Magnus Volk, the local inventor, was the first person to use telephonic communication in Brighton when he connected his house at 40 Preston Road to a friend's in nearby Springfield Road; soon after, he was appointed the local agent of the United Telephone Company. An exchange for the company was opened in 1882 at 48 West Street, the first on the south coast, and business increased rapidly when Brighton was connected to the London network in December 1884. In 1889 the principal companies throughout the country amalgamated to form the National Telephone Company, and in 1892 there were National exchanges at Brighton, West Brighton, Kemp Town, Preston, and Rottingdean. In 1896 however, all trunk-lines were statutorily transferred to the General Post Office (G.P.O.) with the National company left to operate only within specified exchange areas. By 1905 there were 3,002 National subscribers in Brighton.

The corporation was also keen to be involved in the new technology and at the end of 1903 the mayor, John Buckwell, inaugurated a municipal telephone system with an exchange in Palace Place; by March 1904 it had 750 subscribers. In 1905 the municipal system was licensed to operate over 120 square miles from Rottingdean to Shoreham and inland to Burgess Hill. However, the corporation's system, with 1,404 subscribers, was sold to the G.P.O. for £49,000 in October 1906, and when the G.P.O. also took over the National Telephone Company on 1 January 1912, their monopoly was established.

On 12 November 1927 six new, automatic exchanges opened at Brighton (above North Road sorting-office), Hove (Holland Road), Preston (Bavant Road), Rottingdean (Park Road), Portslade, and Southwick, serving a total of 6,124 subscribers. This equipment was operational until October 1959 when, with 36,000 subscribers, the Brighton Central exchange was replaced by new exchanges at Hove, Kemp Town (Freshfield Road), and at Withdean Grange in London Road which was developed as the principal exchange; the Preston exchange closed in 1968. By 1988 there were some 70,000 subscribers in the Brighton area, and in June of that year Kemp Town became the first local exchange to change to digital operation, with others following over the next few months.

The traditional red 'K6'-style telephone kiosks, designed in 1935 by Sir Giles Gilbert Scott, have been mostly replaced with nondescript new kiosks, but a number in Brighton in sensitive locations have been preserved by including them on the list of buildings of special architectural interest. These listed boxes will be found at Dyke Road (opposite St Nicholas's Church); New Road; Pelham Square; Powis Square; St Peter's Place; Upper North Street; and Vicarage Lane, Rottingdean. <44,115,123,171,189>

180. TELSCOMBE

<1,45,233>

Telscombe parish lies immediately to the east of Brighton and includes the attractive Telscombe village, East Saltdean, Telscombe Cliffs, and the large common of Telscombe Tye. At the end of the eighteenth century it was said to be inhabited almost exclusively by smugglers! Standing in an isolated position, with road access only from Southease nearly two miles away, the village has retained its appearance and peaceful character mainly through the 1933 bequest of wealthy bookmaker and lord of the manor Ambrose Gorham, who left most of the village to a trust known as 'Gorham's Gift' in the care of Brighton Council; six trustees are appointed by the council to manage the village within the strict conditions laid down by Gorham. One condition was that there should be no development. Gorham, at his own expense, had had mains electricity and water supplies laid to the flint-walled houses, and indeed Telscombe was the country's first all-electric village in 1930. In 1960 the manor house, parts of which date from the twelfth century, and fifty-four acres of the village were gifted to the National Trust by Ernest Thornton-Smith. The small, flint Church of St Lawrence dates principally from the twelfth century but has some modern additions on the northern side.

181. THEATRES

<3,15,234>

Brighton's first theatre was a barn on the northern side of Castle Square which was used by Charles Johnson's company from 7 November 1764; they returned each year until August 1770, but the seasons were necessarily short because the barn was required for the harvest.

The first permanent theatre was built by Samuel Paine in North Street with an entrance at what is now no.53, and opened on 30 August 1774 under the management of Roger Johnstone. In 1777 it was let to Joseph Fox of Covent Garden who redecorated and re-equipped it for the season. High quality productions were presented and were often attended by royalty, including the Prince of Wales, but the theatre was never a financial success and, despite a refit in 1786, closed before the end of the 1787 season owing to poor attendances. In 1789 half-price admission was introduced, but it proved to be the last season and the theatre then became Lee's printing works and later Wallis's wine and spirit vaults.

The licence was transferred to a new theatre, built by Stephen Pound in partnership with Henry Stiles, which stood in the vicinity of 32-33 Duke Street; it had a rusticated, weather-boarded exterior with a pedimented Tuscan portico. The first performances were given on 13 July 1790 under manager Joseph Fox, the former lessee of the North Street theatre, and productions were again of a high quality with the Prince of Wales a regular visitor. Fox died in 1792, but in 1794 Mrs Fox sold the freehold to Hewitt Cobb who had the theatre remodelled in the winter of 1795-6 with a new royal box. In 1804 John Brunton became manager, and after an official visit by the Prince of Wales on 12 July 1805 the name 'Theatre Royal' was adopted. After the 1806 season though, Cobb and Brunton decided to invest in a new theatre at New Road (see "Theatre Royal"), and the last performance at Duke Street was given on 1 November 1806. The building was sold the following April, but parts of the interior may still remain in Duke Street <3>.

Many other theatres have staged both variety and dramatic performances in Brighton since those described above; together with the several music halls in the town they were one of the main sources of entertainment for the mass of the population in the late nineteenth and early twentieth centuries. In the 1930s and the immediate post-war period no less than six theatres were operating at any one time. For details of other individual theatres, consult the index.

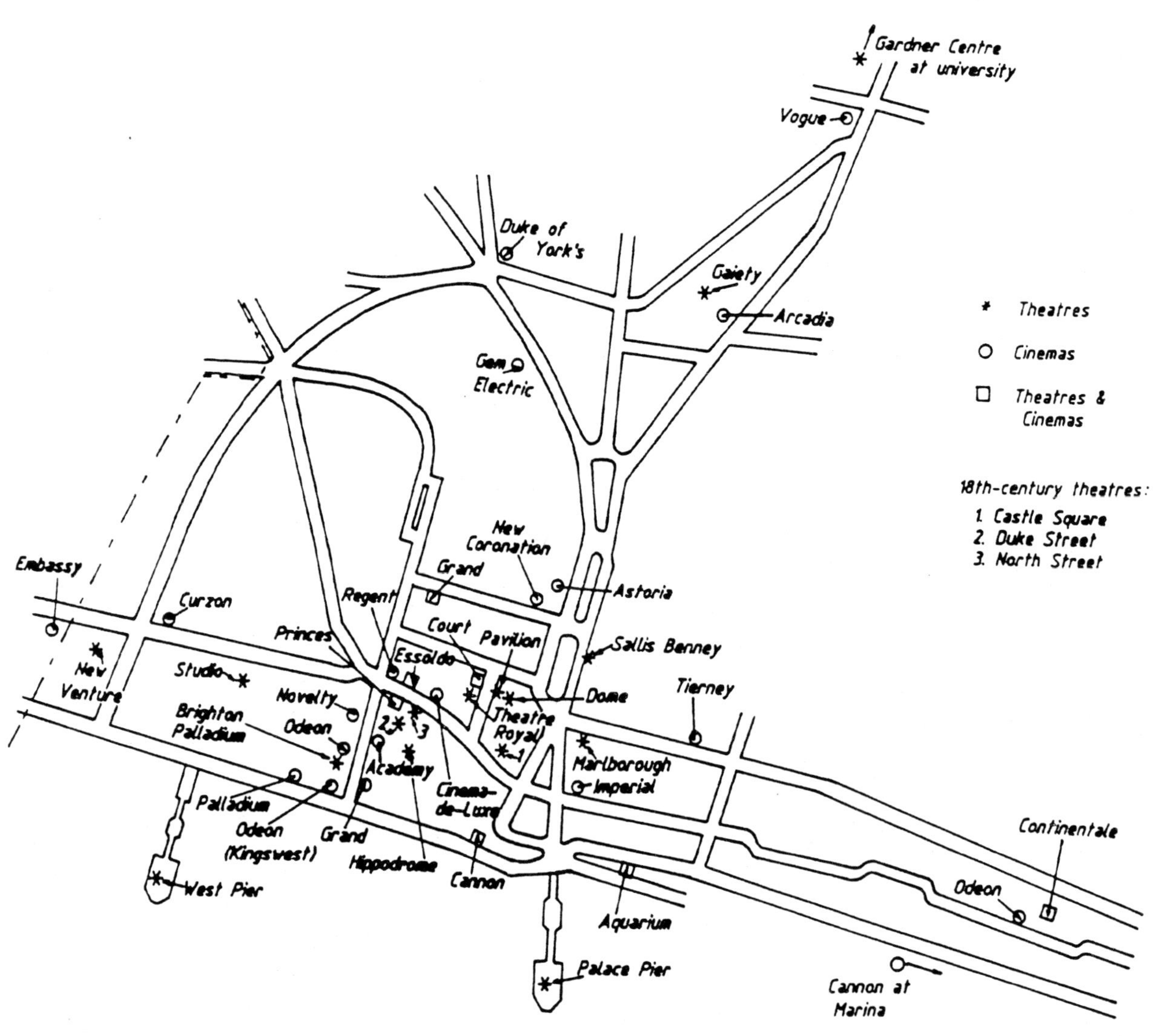

Figure 170: Theatres and cinemas in Brighton, past and present

182. THEATRE ROYAL, 9 and 11-12 New Road

<123,235>

a) *ESTABLISHMENT:* The town's principal theatre was built for Mr Hewitt Cobb at a cost of £12,000 to replace his Duke Street theatre. The foundation stone was laid on 24 September 1806 by the manager, John Brunton, and the classical building, with its three-storey façade and Doric colonnade, opened on 6 June 1807 simply as the 'new theatre'. An audience of about 1,200 could be accommodated in the highly decorated interior, which had two tiers of boxes, and the first of many quality productions they saw were *Hamlet* and *The Weather-Cock*, with the celebrated Mr and Mrs Charles Kemble in the leading roles. Gas-lighting was installed in 1819.

b) *NYE and NELLIE CHART:* A series of managers had control after Brunton left in 1811, but the theatre's fortunes waned until actor Henry 'Nye' Chart of the theatre's own company was appointed manager in 1854; he made some immediate changes to the interior with the removal of the royal box and the addition of backs to the pit benches. In 1866 Chart formed a syndicate to buy the theatre outright, and it was then rebuilt by Charles Phipps in the summer and autumn of 1866; a conservatory was built out from the first floor over the colonnade and new galleries were added, increasing the capacity to 1,900. The Theatre Royal reopened on 15 October 1866. Chart then also started to lease 9 New Road on the other side of the Colonnade Hotel for use as a property and scenery store.

Nye Chart, who died aged fifty-five on 17 June 1876, left the theatre to his wife Elizabeth 'Nellie' Chart; she assumed full control and managership, and further enhanced its reputation. Touring companies brought new productions to the town, and 'morning performances' or 'flying matinees' were introduced with a London company bringing their production down for a single daytime performance before returning to the capital for that evening. The theatre was also known for its pantomimes, and a free performance was given every Christmas for the workhouse inmates.

In 1883 Mrs Chart purchased 9 New Road for use as her own residence, and in 1889 formed the Brighton Theatre Royal Company with Henry Infield as chairman; Infield and Mrs Chart herself acted as managing directors. The company then purchased the theatre and house from Nellie for £43,000. When she died in London on 23 February 1892, the Theatre Royal's reputation as one of the leading provincial theatres was well-established.

c) *REBUILDING:* The Theatre Royal was again rebuilt in 1894 by C.E.Clayton after improvements were demanded by the corporation on safety grounds. No.9 New Road was incorporated as the principal entrance and box-office, and a dress-circle bar was added on the first floor with offices on the second. The colonnade was rebuilt outside nos.9-12, while the façade of nos.11-12, the original theatre building, was completely rebuilt above the colonnade in its present form, red brick and terracotta with two octagonal turrets at the corners. Nos.35-38 Bond Street were acquired and no.35 was converted into a new stage door, but the others were resold in 1934. With the replacement of gas-lighting by electrical, the theatre reopened on 1 September 1894 at a cost of £14,000.

The theatre operated quite profitably under managers H.Cecil Beryll and Robert Lawson Lambert, and was redecorated in 1904, 1909, and in 1912 when individual seats and a new heating system were installed. Performances continued throughout the First World War, and more seats were added and other alterations made in 1927.

d) *FALL AND RISE:* However, with the depression of the 1930s and competition from 'talkie' cinemas and other theatres, the Theatre Royal was operating at a loss by 1934 and was forced to close for four weeks. J.Baxter Somerville took over as manager in 1936 and performances continued almost throughout the war, but attendances were poor and the shoestring budget often forced Somerville to take no wages. After 1945 Somerville was again able to put on some fine productions including many pre-London runs, and the Theatre Royal's reputation was re-established. In 1961 the company was reformed with Lewis Cohen as chairman, but J.B.Somerville died on 19 January 1963 and was greatly mourned. Since that time there have been few alterations to the building, which now seats 952 people and is listed, but the Theatre Royal, which was sold for around £250,000 in December 1971, maintains its reputation as one of the country's leading provincial theatres.

For details on the Royal Colonnade and the Colonnade Bar, see "New Road".

183. TOWN COMMISSIONERS and TOWN ACTS

<14,29-32,112>

a) *1773 BRIGHTON TOWN ACT (13 George III ch.34):* With the change in the fortunes of Brighton in the latter eighteenth century, the need for proper regulation of the town, and the improvement of its facilities and streets, was paramount. In 1773 the first of the Brighton Town Acts, by which the town was to be governed for over eighty years, provided for better paving, lighting and street-cleaning; for the removal of nuisances and annoyances; for the holding and regulation of a daily market; for building and repairing groynes; and for other purposes within the town. It also named sixty-four commissioners, commonly known as the 'town commissioners' or 'improvement commissioners', to regulate these functions throughout the parish.

The commissioners, who had to meet certain financial requirements to qualify, chose their own replacements and included some of the best known names in the town such as William Attree, John Hicks, Thomas Kemp, Revd Henry Michell, Philip Mighell, Dr Anthony Relhan, Charles Scrase, Samuel Shergold, Henry Thrale, Richard Tidy and Richard Whichelo. Only a small number of commissioners were active, however. The first meeting was held at the Castle Inn on 24 May 1773, and they met at the Old Ship, the Castle Inn or the New Ship about once a month.

The Act empowered the commissioners to levy a rate of up to three shillings in the pound for the purposes of lighting, paving and cleansing the streets. They were also authorised to borrow up to £3,000 for the erection of a market building, and to charge a tax on all coal landed on the beaches to pay for sea-defences. Powers were also given to regulate the use of signs and to remove nuisances. One interesting clause of the act required inhabitants to sweep the pavements outside their houses between 8 a.m. and 10 a.m. every day except Sunday, The 'sport' of cock-throwing, the slaughtering of animals in streets, and public bonfires and fireworks, were all banned.

b) *1810 BRIGHTON TOWN ACT (50 George III ch.38):* After thirty years the commissioners found their powers limited and unsuitable for the proper regulation of the growing town, and a new Act agreed with the vestry was passed in 1810. The number of commissioners was increased to 106 plus certain ex-officio members, viz: the lords of the manors of Brighthelmston, Atlingworth, Brighthelmston-Michelham, and Old Shoreham; the M.P.s for Sussex and the Sussex boroughs; the high constable; and the vicar. The financial requirements of the commissioners were increased, but, importantly, replacements were to be elected by the parish ratepayers.

The Act additionally empowered the commissioners to appoint watchmen, beadles and constables; to widen and improve streets by compulsory purchase; to name and number streets; to regulate sewers; to inspect weights and measures; to license hackney-carriages, sedan-chairs and bathing-machines; and to build a new town hall. It also transferred the responsibility for the poor of the town from the parochial authorities to thirty 'Directors and Guardians of the Poor' who were to be appointed by the commissioners. Among other additional clauses were the requirements that new pavements should be provided at the expense of the owner of a newly-built house; no new buildings other than shops should project over pavements; no new buildings were to be thatched; no rubbish should be dumped in the streets, on the beaches, or over the cliffs; no night soil was to be tipped into the streets or sewers; and no games or other nuisances were allowed in the streets.

c) *1825 BRIGHTON TOWN ACT (6 George IV ch.179):* Still the commissioners found their powers restrictive, and a third Act was passed in 1825 which increased the number of commissioners to 116, with greater financial requirements, but abolished the ex-officio commissioners. More significantly, the Act required sixteen commissioners to retire annually from 1828, with their replacements elected by the ratepayers; the appointment of the directors and guardians of the poor was also transferred to ratepayers.

The Act empowered the commissioners to remove slaughterhouses which caused a nuisance; to remove boats if obstructing the highways; to erect a market, a town hall and a prison; to establish cattle, corn and hay markets; to water streets; to provide a fire-engine; and to require the erection or alteration of buildings to be notified to the town surveyor. The coal-tax was extended to all coal brought into the parish, with tollgates set up at the boundaries, and a schedule of roads was included for widening. Meetings were held at the Sea House in Middle Street until the completion of the new Town Hall in about 1832.

d) *INCORPORATION and DISSOLUTION:* By the 1850s many inhabitants believed that the town commissioners were too many in number, that the financial qualifications were too high, that the 1825 Act was not flexible enough to allow for change (in particular that there was no power to make bye-laws), and that the commissioners had been extravagant.

The commissioners themselves resolved to obtain a new Act in 1853, but the 'incorporationists' won the day following a Privy Council inquiry, and when the town was incorporated as a municipal borough with an elected council in 1854 the town commissioners became largely redundant. The 1855 Brighton Commissioners Transfer Act dissolved the town commissioners from 29 May 1855 and vested all their powers, privileges, liabilities and property, including the Royal Pavilion, the market and the Town Hall, in the new corporation. The last meeting was held on 28 May 1855. A bust of Lewis Slight, the clerk to the town commissioners from 1826 until 1854, may be found in the Town Hall, and his portrait in Brighton Museum.

184. TOWN HALLS

<44,45,112,115,123>

A building known as the Townhouse once stood on the cliff top between Black Lion Street and Ship Street to the east of the Blockhouse. It was mentioned in the Book of Ancient Customs of 1580, and the market was held in front of it. However, the Townhouse was gradually undermined by erosion, and the building was then either demolished or allowed to decay, probably by the early eighteenth century. <1,10>

The first building to be known as the Town Hall stood on the western side of Market Street, a small, two-storey building with gables. It was erected in 1727 and was used principally as a workhouse (see "Workhouses"), but it was also used sometimes for vestry meetings and by the superintendents of the watch, forerunners of the police; it had a small cell known locally as the 'Black Hole". Following the removal of the workhouse to Church Hill in 1822, the building was purchased by the town commissioners and was demolished in 1823 to make way for the new market building. The site is now occupied by Bartholomew Square. <14,18,112>

Figure 171: Brighton Town Hall

a) *BRIGHTON TOWN HALL, Bartholomews:* The present Town Hall was built in 1830-2 by the town commissioners on the site of the former market in Bartholomews, the foundation stone being laid in April 1830 by T.R.Kemp. The building was designed in classical style by Thomas Cooper, himself a commissioner, in the form of a Greek cross but the southern wing was never erected because the necessary land could not be purchased. The interior was a also classical design of large halls, corridors, Corinthian and Ionic columns, staircases and landings. The commissioners' debating chamber on the second floor adjoined the Great Room, which held 800 people for concerts and other performances; the central police station was also included in the new building. In 1855 the Town Hall was transferred from the now defunct commissioners to the corporation.

From late 1897 until 1899 a large reconstruction of the interior was executed at a cost of some £40,000. The Great Room was removed, the basement was converted into a larger police department, a new council chamber was provided at the southern end of the second floor, the east wing was altered considerably, and the exterior was modified by filling in the upper corners. Council meetings were held at the Royal Pavilion and petty sessions at the present public library in Church Street during the reconstruction.

The Town Hall is now a listed building of four storeys, with giant fluted Ionic columns forming porticoes above the entrances. It has proved inadequate for the purposes of modern local government, however, and municipal offices have been scattered throughout the town centre for many years. In 1936 plans were made for new offices in Market Street, and in 1958 a site to the south of Edward Street was selected. However, in 1984-7 the four-storey Bartholomew House and Priory House were erected as municipal offices around Bartholomew Square with the Hospitality Inn forming the southern façade. Ever since it was first erected the Town Hall has been criticised for being ugly and incomplete, but the opened-up vista from the civic square certainly sheds a new light on this excellent building.

185. TRAMWAYS

<237-240a>

a) *ESTABLISHMENT and ROUTES:* Schemes for tramways were suggested in 1864, 1879 and 1883, but the corporation's electric tramway system, authorised under the Brighton Corporation Act of 1900, commenced service on 25 November 1901 when the first car was ceremonially driven by the mayor, John Stafford, from the initial terminus at the southern end of Victoria Gardens along Lewes Road to Preston Barracks. Fares were charged initially at one penny for any distance.

The 9.5-mile system, completed by July 1904, was operated in a number of routes each known by the initial letter of a road or location along it, viz:

B - Beaconsfield
C - Cross-Town
D - Ditchling
E - Elm Grove
L - Lewes
M - Market
N - New England
Q - Queen's Park
S - Station
T - Tour

Special services were operated on race days, and also to Dyke Road when Brighton and Hove Albion played at home. Frequencies of four to five minutes were operated, and typical journey times from the Steine were: Station (8 minutes); Fiveways (18); Preston Barracks (15); Race Hill (18); Rock Gardens (27); and Tivoli Crescent (20).

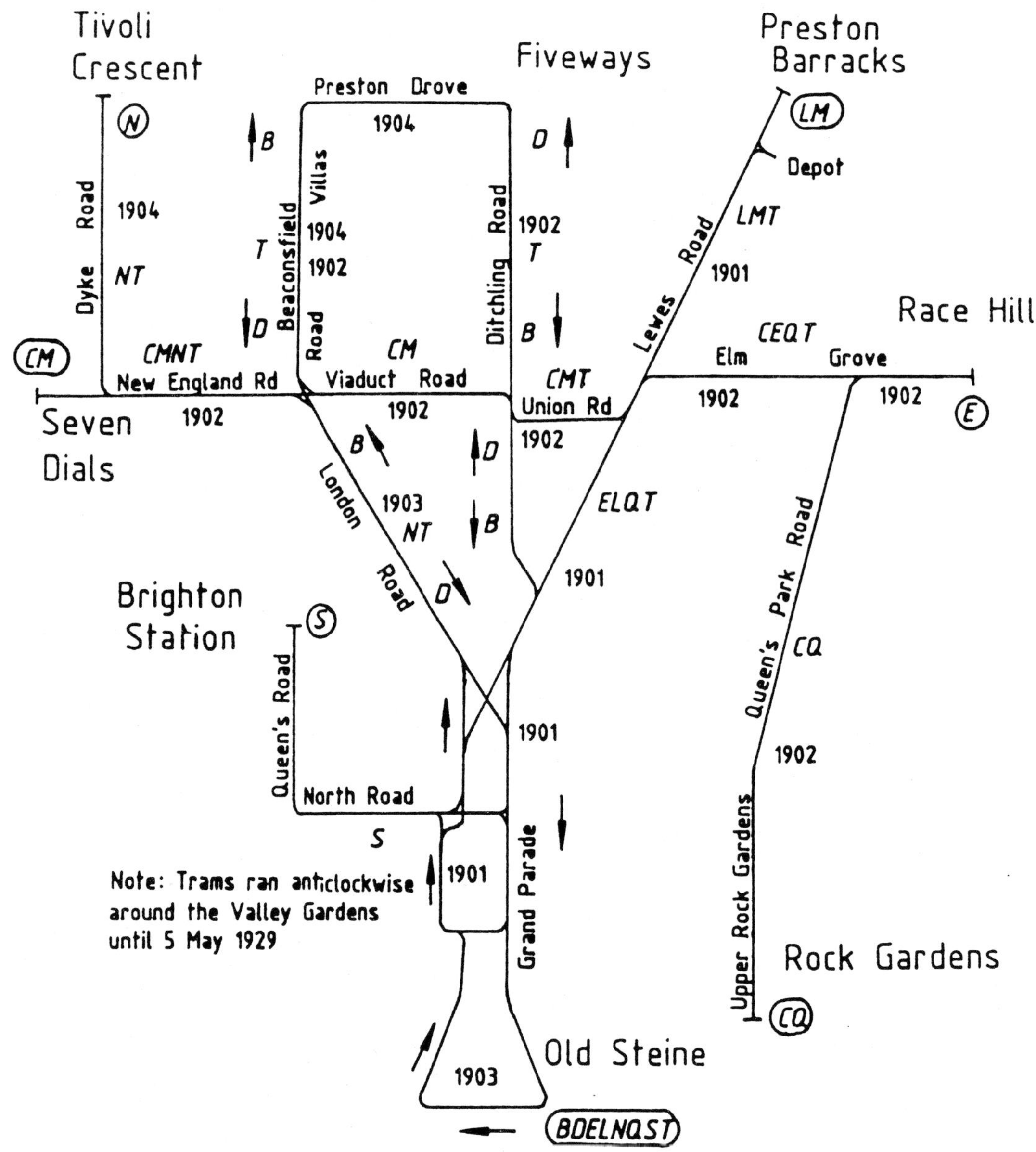

Figure 172: Brighton Corporation tramway routes 1901-39

b) *TRAM-CARS AND TRACK:* Fifty cars were initially purchased for the system, and 116 replacements were built over the years at the corporation's tramway depot in Lewes Road. All were four-wheeled, open-top, double-decker vehicles in a burgundy-and-cream livery, operating from trolley wires at 550 volts d.c. with 40-50 b.h.p. engines. The cars, several of which were illuminated with coloured bulbs, were six feet wide, nearly thirty feet long, and ran on a gauge of three feet six inches. (A model of a Brighton tram-car may be found in the town museum.) The tracks were laid in the centres of the roadways, and the road surface was then laid with wooden blocks to bring it up to the same level. Tram stops were marked by studs in the middle of the road.

c) *CLOSURE:* The increasing suburban development of the 1930s, combined with the lack of flexibility of the tramway system, prompted the corporation to opt for a new network of both trolley- and motor-buses. Tram routes were consequently withdrawn and replaced by buses from 26 April 1939 until the last Brighton tram ran from Upper Rock Gardens to the Old Steine at 2 a.m. on 1 September 1939, bringing to an end thirty-eight years of almost accident-free service. An estimated 52 million miles had been run, 629 million passengers carried, and a profit of £54,000 made by the Brighton trams.

Most of the Brighton tram-cars were scrapped for the war effort, but one does survive; no.53, dating from 1937, was discovered on a Partridge Green pig farm and awaits restoration. The other main relics of the tramways are the shelters in Ditchling Road (Florence Place), Queen's Park Road (Pepper-Box), and Dyke Road (reservoir); another has been used for the Aquarium Station of Volk's Railway, one may be found at the Stanmer Rural Museum, and two more have been removed to the Chalkpits Museum at Amberley. The tramway depot in Lewes Road is now the depot of Brighton Buses, but it retains windows etched with the

Figure 173: The former tram shelter by the 'Pepper-Box' in Queen's Park Road

words 'Brighton Corporation Tramways'; see figure 25. At the corner of Dyke Road and the Upper Drive is a standard that formerly supported the tram supply wires; it bears the initials 'BCT' and the borough arms.

d) *TRAMWAYS AND THE GENERAL STRIKE:* The General Strike of 1926 started on Monday, 3 May, and the support in Brighton was solid, the most complete of any town in the south. The railway engineering works were stopped completely, and by the Tuesday all transport services were at a standstill. Policemen were ordered to sleep at their posts, and a special reserve constabulary was sworn in to deal with possible trouble.

The strike in Brighton reached crisis point over the operation of the tramways. With the council's tramways committee considering the use of volunteer labour to take out the trams, about 2,000 strikers marched to the Town Hall to vent their feelings but were diverted away without a deputation being received. The following day a smaller crowd of about 200 gathered around the Town Hall. A woman driver, seeing the protesters, deliberately accelerated into them and injured several people. Without stopping she drove on, with police removing strikers from the car with truncheons, and she disappeared into the town.

The dispute over the trams culminated in the so-called 'Battle of Lewes Road' on Tuesday, 11 May 1926, when 4,000 strikers gathered outside the tram depot in Lewes Road determined not to allow the trams to be driven out. Unknown to them there was no intention of bringing the trams out as the volunteers were only to be trained that day. Chief Constable Charles Griffin, with 300 men on foot and 50 mounted specials, ordered the crowd to disperse, but on obtaining no response ordered his men to advance on foot and then brought up the specials on horseback. As the crowd was driven back to Hollingdean Road some fighting started and the specials charged the crowd, lashing out with batons. As the strikers hit back so a vicious struggle ensued. Eventually the crowd, in which there were many children, was driven back and dispersed, but two people were left seriously injured and many others were hurt; seventeen strikers were arrested by the police and marched through the town to the police station at the Town Hall. That night there was another disturbance outside the Brighton and District Labour Club at 93 London Road when another five people were arrested. The next day all appeared before the bench and were handed severe fines and sentences of up to six month's hard labour.

The General Strike was called off the following day by the Trades Union Congress, an act which was seen as a great betrayal by many in Brighton. The special and regular police forces were given certificates by the council with the regulars granted three days extra leave, and a 'victory' parade of mounted specials outside the Floral Hall and a celebration dinner were held. A number of strikers were not reinstated by the management of the railway works and the bus companies, but the greatest resentment was caused by the action of the police and is still keenly felt by some old folk in the town today.
<3,283>

186. TRUNK MURDERS

<3,19,124,288>

The first 'trunk murder' at Brighton occurred in 1831 when John Holloway murdered his wife near Edward Street and carried her remains in a trunk to a wood at Lovers Walk to bury her. He was hung in public at Lewes, and she was reburied at Preston Church.

The more famous Brighton Trunk Murders followed in quick succession in 1934 and led to the town being nicknamed 'the queen of slaughtering places'! On 17 June 1934 a woman's torso was found in a trunk at Brighton Station's left-luggage office by a railman, but although the legs were found at King's Cross the next day the head and arms were never recovered and the identities of the victim, a young pregnant woman, and her murderer were never discovered.

Four weeks later, on 15 July 1934, police discovered the body of 41-year-old prostitute Violet Saunders in a trunk at 52 Kemp Street, killed by a blow to the head. Toni Mancini, a man of many aliases and the dead woman's 'pimp', was soon arrested, but was acquitted after being brilliantly defended by Norman Birkett. Mancini claimed that he had found Saunders dead on his bed at 44 Park Crescent and, panicking, wheeled her in a basket to Kemp Street. However, in a newspaper article in 1976 Mancini confessed to the murder.

187. UNDERCLIFF WALK

<2,26,116,123,201>

In 1928 the parish of Rottingdean was incorporated into Brighton. In order to protect its new coastline, which had increased from 2.2 to 5.4 miles, and also to safeguard the vital intercepting sewer, the county borough council embarked on a great scheme to protect the cliffs to the east of Black Rock, a project that also enabled Marine Drive to be constructed. The result was the Undercliff Walk, a sea-wall at the base of the cliffs designed by borough engineer David Edwards. It was constructed in 1930-3 at a cost of £360,000, and used some 13,000 tons of cement, 150,000 concrete blocks, and 500 men at a time of severe depression, although there was controversy over the 'importation' of Welsh miners to do skilled rock work.

The walk was formally opened from Black Rock to Rottingdean, about 2.3 miles, on 4 July 1933 by Minister of Health Sir Hilton Young at Ovingdean Gap. The extension to Saltdean Gap was formally opened by the mayor, Edward Denne, on 29 July 1935 at the same time as the Rottingdean swimming-pool which was built to replace bathing facilities lost to the sea-wall. A sea-water pool 100 feet by 35 feet, it has few facilities but occupies a wonderful location below the cliffs. In 1989 it was privately managed, but the storms of January 1990 caused £100,000 worth of damage and the pool is in danger of permanent closure.

The last 200 yards of the sea-wall to the borough boundary opened a few months later, and a 310-yard extension by Chailey Rural District Council was opened in 1963.

The Undercliff Walk is now 3.35 miles long, part of a 7.5 mile promenade from Portslade to Saltdean. It is between 8 and 35 feet wide, 10 feet above high water, and is itself protected by about 67 groynes. Access to the beaches and rock pools may be had along its length. Access to the Undercliff Walk itself may be had at Black Rock, Roedean Café, Ovingdean Gap, Rottingdean Gap and Saltdean Gap, but care must be taken as rock falls occasionally occur, especially after heavy rain; it should not be used at all during rough weather. Great damage to the Walk was caused by the storms of February 1990, causing certain sections to be closed off, and a £7 million repair scheme has commenced.

188. UNIVERSITY of SUSSEX, Falmer

<241>

a) *IDEA AND ESTABLISHMENT:* In December 1911 a public meeting at the Royal Pavilion started a fund for the establishment of a university at Brighton, but the project was halted by the First World War and the money was used instead for books for the Municipal Technical College. However, the idea was revived in the 1950s, and in June 1958 the government approved the corporation's scheme for a university at Brighton, the first of a new generation of 'red-brick' universities. <3>

The University College of Sussex was established as a company in May 1959, and a royal charter granted on 16 August 1961 raised it to full university status, with Viscount Monckton installed as the first chancellor. The first fifty-two students were accepted in October 1961 and were temporarily accommodated at 235-237 Preston Road, with lectures given in the nearby Knoyle Hall.

b) *DEVELOPMENT OF THE NEW CAMPUS:* In the meantime a new rural campus designed in typical 1960s style by Sir Basil Spence was under construction on part of the corporation's Stanmer estate known as the Tenant Lain; the Meeting House was opened in October 1966 on the site of Tenantlain Barn, but Tenant Lain Cottages still stand by the university approach road. Falmer House, the administrative, social, and student recreational block, opened in October 1962 around a central quadrangle, a reminder of more ancient universities. It was followed in 1963 by the Physics, Arts, and Library buildings, while the residential village, Park House, was completed in 1964. Biology, Chemistry, and Applied Sciences buildings, along with Essex House and Lancaster House, were opened by 1967, but much more development occurred during the 1970s and the campus now covers an area of some 160 acres. On 13 November 1964 the new campus was visited by Queen Elizabeth II.

The Gardner Centre for the Arts was financed by the Gulbenkian Foundation and Dr Lytton Gardner, who unfortunately died before the building was completed in November 1969. The interior has a circular auditorium seating 475, with smaller units housing a foyer, studios and workshops.

c) *EDUCATIONAL AND CULTURAL DEVELOPMENT:* The new university quickly developed a reputation for radicalism and liberalism amongst its student population, but its reputation for academic excellence, research and community involvement has grown enormously since the early days. Starting in 1961-2 with just 52 students, and with 400 on-campus undergraduates the following year, the university's student population expanded rapidly to about 1,500 in 1964-5 and to 3,200 in 1967-8. The increase then slowed down until there were nearly 4,200 students in 1975-6, and it reached its present size of approximately 4,800 students and 1,750 staff in 1980-1.

A student radio station, Radio Falmer, covers the campus on a frequency of 999 kHz from an inductive loop aerial around the perimeter. It is specially licensed by the Department of Trade and Industry and has been operating since February 1976.

d) *CHANCELLORS:*

1959-65	Viscount Monckton of Brenchley
1965-85	Lord Shawcross
1985-	Earl of March and Kinrara

e) *VICE-CHANCELLORS:*

1960-7	John Fulton, later Lord Fulton
1967-76	Professor Asa Briggs
1976-87	Professor Sir Denys Wilkinson
1987-	Sir Leslie Fielding

189. VALLEY GARDENS

The twenty-three acres of gardens and lawns of the central valley, including the Old Steine, the Royal Pavilion grounds, Victoria Gardens, St Peter's Churchyard, the Level and the private Park Crescent, are collectively known as the Valley Gardens. This flat area, once known only as the Steine and the Level, probably remained undeveloped because of its swampy nature with the intermittent Wellesbourne flowing its length, and has long been used as a public open space.

Valley Gardens is also the name given to the outstanding conservation area along the valley which displays many fine examples of Regency architecture; it was extended in 1988 to include Hanover Street and Hanover Terrace, and again in 1989 to include Prince's Street, Steine Gardens, and the former court building and music library in Church Street. To facilitate an exploration of the conservation area the terraces lining the gardens from the Royal Pavilion to the Level are detailed below in clockwise order, but see also "Church Street", "Dome and Corn Exchange", "New Road", "Old Steine", "Pool Valley", "Royal Pavilion" and "Victoria Gardens", all of which lie within this conservation area.

a) *MARLBOROUGH PLACE:* The first group of buildings in Marlborough Place was erected in 1772 and known as North Row, the first development outside the limits of the old town; it was renamed in 1819. The King and Queen, however, probably dates from an earlier time and was originally a farmhouse. The inn catered for cricket and other sporting celebrations which were held on the North Steine, while at the rear was an infantry barracks (see "Church Street") which was discretely supplied through a serving-hole which may still be seen. The inn was also the venue of the town's corn market from the early nineteenth century until October 1868 when it was transferred to the Corn Exchange. The two-storey, bow-fronted Georgian building was replaced in 1931-2 by the present highly-decorated Tudor-style building, with its carved timber-framing and herring-bone brickwork, stained glass and tapestries. Despite the figures of Henry VIII and one of his queens, the inn's sign more correctly shows King George III and Queen Charlotte. Converted from three rooms in 1967, the interior matches the Tudor-style exterior and is now in the form of a spacious, medieval nobleman's hall and courtyard. <14,15,26,262a>

The southern part of Marlborough Place is lined with four-storey buildings, and no.9, which has a good doorway, is included on the council's local list of buildings of special interest. That part to the north of the inn was redeveloped in the early 1930s but no.26, a listed building at the corner of North Road, dates from the early nineteenth century and retains a cobbled front. The elegant, neo-Georgian Allied Irish Bank dates from

Figure 174: St George's Place, St Peter's Chapel and the northern end of the North Steine Enclosures in about 1860

1933 when it was designed by John Denman for the Citizens Permanent Building Society; it has decorative windows depicting different trades. <123>

The attractive early-nineteenth-century row of houses on the opposite side of North Road, 31-36 Marlborough Place, is also listed, no.33 having a cobbled front and garland decorations. Nos.37-41 were demolished in 1934 to make way for Telephone House (see "Gloucester Place" below). <44,129>

b) *GLOUCESTER PLACE:* Built in the 1800s, Gloucester Place was widened by the removal of front gardens around the turn of the century and has been somewhat rebuilt, but nos.25-26 remain, four-storey buildings with ironwork balconies and canopies. No.27, now the Gloucester night-club, was opened as the Gloucester Hotel in about 1819 in a four-storey building with bows, balconies, verandahs and a Doric doorway, but it was considerably remodelled and enlarged in 1925 when the Gloucester Mansions flats were added. <26,108,115>

Trustcard House was erected in 1985 on the site of Telephone House, an eight-storey red-brick block used as offices by the General Post Office and constructed in 1938 on the site of some Regency houses; it was found to be structurally unsafe in the early 1980s. The new building is relieved by its soft colour and use of bay windows. <123,129>

The Astoria Cinema was formally opened on 21 December 1933 by Sir Cooper Rawson, M.P., with a relatively simple interior, stage, organ, restaurant and tea-rooms, and room for 1,823 people. It was soon acquired by Associated British Cinemas Ltd and presented many long runs of epic films in the 1950s, '60s and '70s on its giant screen, but in May 1977 the cinema closed and became the Coral Social Club. <68,68a>

Lombard House was built in 1957 for the Royal Sussex Regiment. The houses that formerly stood there were destroyed by enemy bombing in the war and the site was given to the regiment on the occasion of it being granted the honorary right of entry to the borough in October 1944. The development includes flats for the benefit of all ranks, past and present. The adjacent Gloucester Place Baptist Church was damaged in the same air-raid. It was built by George Baines in 1904 to replace the former Queen Square Baptist Church which had been sold to the Union Church. <62,115,242,311>

c) *ST GEORGE'S PLACE:* A terrace of fifteen three- and four-storey bow-fronted houses, all listed buildings and probably built in yellow brick by Wilds and Busby in the 1820s. Only no.1 retains its ironwork balcony and none now have verandahs. At the rear is St George's Mews, a narrow roadway which retains its setts and has a few old cottages. <44>

d) *YORK PLACE:* Developed in the 1810s; the roadway was widened by the corporation in 1903 by the removal of the front gardens <115>. No.1 York Place is faced with black glazed mathematical tiles, as are nos.4-5 which also have bows. Nos.8-10 are included on the borough council's local list; they all have narrow bows, while nos.9-11 are faced with cobbles and no.10 has mathematical tiles as well. Nos.13-14 and 16 are also cobble-fronted while nos.17-22 have Ionic pilasters, although only nos.21-22 are unaltered above the shop-fronts. York Place is now perhaps best known for its proliferation of take-away food shops.

In 1870 the York Place Elementary Schools were established by the Brighton School Board at Trafalgar Court, and were added to in 1884 with a higher-grade school teaching technical and commercial subjects, approached through the archway at 15 York Place. Further extensions were funded by board member Daniel Hack, and in 1898 the higher-grade school was

Figure 175: Regency elegance at nos.1-6 Richmond Terrace

renamed York Place Secondary School. In 1906 annexes were provided in Trafalgar Street and Pelham Street, but when the school buildings were used as an Indian military hospital during the First World War the pupils were taught at the Technical College in Richmond Terrace. In 1926 the girls' secondary school was removed to Varndean, followed by the boys' school in 1931, and the York Place Elementary Schools then became the Fawcett School for Boys and the Margaret Hardy School for Girls. These were also removed, to Patcham in the mid 1960s, and the York Place buildings were then taken over by the Technical College, now the Brighton College of Technology. Several of the original buildings are still in use. <123,210>

e) *ST PETER'S PLACE:* A listed terrace of about 1820, possibly designed by A. and A.H.Wilds. Nos.1-3 have giant Ionic pilasters with a bowed façade in London Road, nos.4-9 have bow fronts and balconies, no.6 retains a verandah, and nos.6-9 retain their front gardens. The pair of K6-style telephone kiosks is also listed. <44,46,108>

At this point, see also "St Peter's Church", "Ditchling Road", "Level", "Park Crescent" and "Hanover".

f) *RICHMOND TERRACE:* The original terrace, nos.4-14, was built speculatively from 1818 by A. and A.H.Wilds, but it has been dominated by the Municipal Technical College since 1897 (see "Technology, College of"). All of the remaining houses are listed. Nos.4-6, large four-storey houses with ironwork Ionic pilasters and verandahs, are topped by a pediment and supported either side by gateposts with lamps bearing crowns; these mark the visits of George IV to the home of his Lord Chancellor, Lord Combermere <45a>. No.7 has the Wilds's 'trademark', ammonite capitals, while nos.11-14 are a three-storey composition with ironwork balconies and decorated gateposts.

Nos.1-3 Richmond Terrace were probably added by Wilds and Busby in the 1820s and were originally known as Lennox Place, three bow-fronted houses in yellow brick above the ground floor and with interesting chain-link decorations on the gate pillars. The bow-fronted no.15 dates from around the same time, while nos.16-18 were probably added by A.Wilds alone. <44,45,46,83>

g) *WATERLOO PLACE:* A terrace of fourteen houses with bows, balconies, verandahs and Ionic pilasters, built in about 1819 by A. and A.H.Wilds, but unfortunately only nos.1-2 survive. The rest of the terrace was demolished in 1968-70 and replaced by Wellesley House, surely one of the most lamentable planning decisions in the town. The ugly office block was actually erected around one remaining house, no.9, which was occupied by 89-year-old Miss Harriet Sylvester until she died in March 1974. A 1990 plan to redevelop the Phoenix Brewery site with housing and offices involves the demolition of this building, however. <3,44,123>

h) *RICHMOND PLACE:* Developed in the 1800s, Richmond Place has several houses which retain their front gardens. Nos.7-8, with bow windows, pilasters, mathematical tiles and good doorways, and nos.23-25, with bow windows and balconies, are particularly attractive but none are listed. A narrow twitten between nos.3 and 4 leads to Richmond Gardens, a row of charming cobble-fronted cottages of about 1826. Nos.17-19, known as St Peter's House, was completed in 1986 to a Regency Gothic design of Philip Andrews and jointly won the council's 1987 design award; it has the familiar shell motif used by A.H.Wilds. The Richmond public house was opened in 1807 by a Mr Fairs who transferred the licence from the Spotted Dog in Middle Street, but it was rebuilt in the 1960s. <15,83>

j) *GRAND PARADE:* Lined with large three- and four-storey houses, now mainly commercial, Grand

Figure 176: Cobble-fronted cottages at Richmond Gardens

Parade was developed in the late eighteenth and early nineteenth centuries. Some houses were demolished for road-widening in the 1930s and '60s, but many interesting listed buildings remain.

The northern range of buildings dates from the 1810s and '20s. Nos.9-10 and 12-13 are faced in black glazed mathematical tiles, while nos.14, and 18-19 (with giant Doric pilasters) are probably by Wilds and Busby. Nos.17, 20-23 and 26-27 are also listed. <44>

The central portion dates principally from the 1800s, and nos.30-32 and 34-35 have cobbled façades. No.47, Lancaster House, with its wide, yellow-brick bow front and ironwork balcony, is the grandest building in the whole parade and was refurbished as offices in 1989-90. It was the first home of the Brighton Grammar School and was probably designed by Charles Barry in about 1840. Nos.33, 37-38 and 40-41 are also listed. Roughly in the area of no.36 once stood the Royal Circus and Riding School, opened in August 1808 by a Mr Saunders with a billiards lounge, coffee-house and confectionery. It was not successful however, and closed in 1812, but it is commemorated by Circus Street at the rear. The Grand Parade Chapel stood at no.29 but was demolished in 1938 to provide for wider access to the new market. Built in about 1835 with a gable and small turrets, it was used by the Catholic Apostolic Church from 1853 until 1865, and in 1879 was converted into St James's Concert Hall. It then became an auction room in about 1893, but from 1913 was used by the Christian Brethren. <3,44,62,83,108>

The southernmost range of Grand Parade dates principally from the 1790s and 1800s, and was originally called Town Parade, but it is now dominated by the polytechnic (q.v.). Nos.68-72 are listed buildings, some with balconies and good doorways, but nos.78-80 were demolished for road-widening in 1931. No.68 is faced with mathematical tiles, unusually in red; it houses the Lewis Cohen Urban Studies Centre of Brighton Polytechnic. <44>

k) *PAVILION PARADE:* Built in the 1790s, this listed, elegant, four-storey terrace has ironwork balconies and now mixes bows with angular bays, but all the buildings have distinctive doorways; nos.3-4 also have cobbled fronts. Nos.10-11 are an annexe of Brighton Polytechnic. Nos.1-2 Pavilion Parade faced south on the northern side of the once narrow Edward Street, but were demolished in 1928 for road-widening. <44,116>

l) *PRINCE'S STREET:* A narrow street behind Pavilion Parade in which nos.8 and 11-12 are attractive three-storey houses, and nos.19-20 are listed buildings, refaced in Victorian times but retaining their late-eighteenth- or early-nineteenth-century doorways. The Marlborough at the corner of Pavilion Street contains the New Marlborough Theatre. Seating an audience of around fifty, the theatre was reopened on 4 March 1988.

The large red-brick building dominating Prince's Street, adorned with Corinthian pillars, an oriel window and dolphin motifs, was designed by Nunn and Hunt and was opened on 7 May 1895 as the Brighton Parochial Offices for the board of guardians and registrar; the site had once belonged to the county court which moved to Church Street in 1869. Following the dissolution of the guardians in 1930 the offices were taken by the council's public assistance committee, and from 1974 they were used by the county's social services department. In 1986-9 the offices, which are on the council's local list of buildings of interest, were used temporarily as a magistrates' court while the Edward Street building was refurbished, but the future of the building is doubtful. <44,83,115,123>

Figure 177: The former Parochial Offices in Prince's Street

190. VETERAN CAR RUN

<3,123,124,288a>

This world-famous event was first run on 14 November 1896 to celebrate the Locomotive and Highways Act of that year, which allowed vehicles to travel at up to 12 m.p.h. and removed the requirement for them to be preceded by a man carrying a red flag. Known as the 'Emancipation Day Run', the vehicles, of course, were not then veterans! Following a breakfast at London's Hotel Metropole, thirty cars set off from Hyde Park for Brighton's Hotel Metropole, the first arrival being a Bollen steam vehicle after two-and-a-half hours. Altogether seventeen vehicles finished and were stored overnight at Dupont's stables in Waterloo Street, Hove, as there were not yet any car garages in the town. A few celebration runs were held in the years following, although not always to Brighton, but in the late 1920s the Brighton run was revived, and in 1930 the Veteran Car Club was formed at the Old Ship Hotel. The rally, which has never been a race, was then made an annual event with only cars of 1905 or earlier eligible. It is run on the first Sunday in November.

The Motor-Cycle Club's annual historic rally to Brighton started in 1937, while the first historic commercial vehicle rally was run in 1962.

191. VIADUCT ROAD

Once known as Montpelier Road East, Viaduct Road marked the northern limit of the ancient parish of Brighton and also of the borough until 1873. Nos.10-32, formerly Viaduct Terrace and dating from the 1860s, are included on the council's local list of buildings of special interest and form a small classical terrace with Ionic pilasters, unusual for so late a date. Opposite, on the northern side stands the former Windsor Terrace. The Calvary Evangelical Church, a yellow-brick chapel in Early English style with some figurehead decorations, was built in 1876 by James Barnes as a Primitive Methodist chapel, the congregation of which moved to London Road in 1895. It was then taken by the Railway Mission, formerly of Peel Street, and still has some classroom buildings at the rear in Stanley Road. <62,83,306>

At the eastern end of Viaduct Road stands the Brighton Business Centre, a large listed building of knapped flint erected in Preston parish in 1854 as the Diocesan Training College for Schoolmistresses. Designed by W. and E.Habershon, it was extended in 1886 by Scott and Cawthorne. Women were trained at the college, which had originally opened in April 1842 in Black Lion Street, for two years before being appointed at Church of England National Schools. The college continued until 1939 when the building was requisitioned by the Royal Engineers. Used as the R.E. Records Office after the war, it became the Brighton Business Centre in 1987, opened officially in November 1988. <24,44,83,123>

Figure 178: The Brighton Business Centre, once the Diocesan Training College for Schoolmistresses

192. VICARS

The vicars of Brighton, who were also vicars of West Blatchington from 1744 until 1941, were appointed by St Pancras's Priory at Lewes until 1537, by the bishops of Chichester from 1615 until 1744, by the Crown from 1744 until 1824, and again by the bishops since 1824. They have always been influential figures in the town, and in the early nineteenth century the vicar was chairman of the vestry, a guardian of the poor, and an ex-officio town commissioner. He was also entitled to claim a 'half-share' after each fishing trip as a tithe payment (see "Fishing Industry"). In 1873 the parish of Brighton was divided into a number of district parishes and the Vicar of Brighton was assigned to the new parish church of St Peter's. As the vicar also holds the position of rural dean of Brighton, all parishes in the town are still responsible to him. <1,3a,63,112>

In the porch of St Peter's Church is a list of vicars of Brighton which is reproduced below:

Known pre-Reformation vicars:

1091 Ralph de Cheney
? John ?
1397 William ?
1402 John Dent
1417 Richard Robyn
? William Tupyn
1418 Robert Philpott
? Thomas Symond
1430 Thomas Wotton
1440 Thomas Maltby
1478 John Gonwaye
1490 Thomas Warde
? William Browne
1531 Peter Petersen
1535 Leonard Saville

Post-Reformation vicars:

? William Jennings
1565 Francis Cox
1575 John Drury
1614 John Hullwood
1616 Thomas Richardson
1630 Thomas Doe
? William Yeo
1646 John James
1655 Robert Evernden
1662 Edward Lowe
1681 Henry Snooke
1700 George Hay
? William Faulkner
1705 William Colbron
1744 Henry Michell
1789 Thomas Hudson
1804 Robert Carr
1824 Henry Wagner
1870 John Hannah
1888 John Julius Hannah
1902 Benedict Hoskyns
1917 Francis Pierce
1924 Frederick Hicks
1928 Alfred Rose
1935 John How
1939 Geoffrey Warde
1945 Frederick Robathan
1953 David Booth
1960 John Keeling
1975 John Hester
1985 Dominic Walker

a) *VICARAGES:* It is recorded that in 1252 a house was to be provided for the Vicar of Brighton; this may have been the so-called Prior's Lodge, an ancient building associated with St Bartholomew's Priory which stood on the site of Prince Albert Street to the west of Market Street and was acquired by the parish in 1584. It was certainly used as a vicarage in the eighteenth century, and in the 1770s and '80s Arthur Wellesley, later the Duke of Wellington, was tutored there. When it was demolished in 1790 the house was judged to date from the thirteenth century. It was replaced by a three-storey, cobble-fronted vicarage with a large garden on the same site.

However, when Prince Albert Street was planned, a new vicarage was built in June 1834 to the west of the town at the expense of the street developer. The Market Street vicarage was demolished in 1837, and the new house, designed in Tudor style by a Mr Mew with three gables and a cement rendering, was used by Revd Henry Wagner and his successors until 1922. It was then taken over by the junior school of Brighton and Hove High School and is now a listed building on the southern side of Temple Gardens where it is known as the Old Vicarage. Since 1922 the vicars of Brighton have had a number of residences; 87 London Road is currently used. <1,6,18,44,65>

193. Queen VICTORIA

<3,46,112>

Victoria's first visit to the town as Queen was on 4 October 1837 when she was greeted by a floral arch at Preston Circus and an immense floral amphitheatre at the North Gate of the Royal Pavilion. Victoria was to stay in the town several more times. During her second visit from December 1838 the Queen visited the Kemp Town esplanades and enclosures, and in February 1842 she came with her new husband, Albert. The following year she landed at the Chain Pier from France, and visited Rottingdean and Kemp Town again before embarking for Belgium.

Unlike her two predecessors however, Victoria never took to Brighton and complained that 'the people are very indiscreet and troublesome here really, which makes the place quite like a prison'. Paying her last visit to the town in February 1845, the Queen used Osborne House as her country retreat thereafter, and the Royal Pavilion was closed and emptied.

Figure 179: The Victoria Fountain, inaugurated in the Old Steine on 25 May 1846 as a tribute on the Queen's twenty-seventh birthday

194. VICTORIA GARDENS

a) *HISTORY:* These central gardens were originally a single large, flat, open space which joined the Steine and the Level, and which was usually known as the North Steine. The area was used for cricket matches, fairs and celebrations following the enclosure of the Steine in 1787, but by the 1810s it had become a 'place of shame and reproach to the town'. An improvement fund was started, to which the Prince Regent contributed £500, and the area was duly enclosed and planted with trees and shrubs, the gift of the Earl of Chichester. Known as the North Steine Enclosures, the southern part was formally opened in July 1818 and the northern part the following year, but only to local residents and subscribers.

In August 1849 the North Steine Enclosures were vested by their landowners in a body of trustees who, under the terms of the 1873 Brighton Borough Extension Act, were later appointed by the borough council. In 1883 the northern enclosure was opened to the public and an encircling path made, but the southern gardens were still reserved exclusively for subscribers until 1896. On 21 October 1896 both gardens were vested in the corporation by the trustees and were formally dedicated for public use by the mayor, Sir John Blaker, on the diamond jubilee of Queen Victoria, 22 June 1897. Many of the trees which had been planted in the 1810s were uprooted in the storm of October 1987. <7,14,15,33,36,126,311>

b) *SOUTHERN ENCLOSURE:* This part covers 2.12 acres and, until about 1922, was enclosed along the perimeter of the roadway by tall iron railings with the present pavements as interior walkways. It was then remodelled to its present form with dwarf fences along the inner edge, a layout now more ornamental than accessible. The gift of the trustees and the dedication by the mayor is recorded by a plaque at the southern end, where also stands the listed marble statue of Queen Victoria, designed by Nicoli and presented to the town by Sir John Blaker at the opening of the gardens on her diamond jubilee in 1897. In the garden also are two blind plinths which once bore allegorical figures. Originally five in number, they represented 'Morning', 'Welcome', 'Fidelity', 'Truth' and 'Night', and were presented in 1897 by Sir Edward Sassoon; one plinth went to Preston Park, one to the Wild Park and the fifth was 'lost' along with the statues.

At the northern end stands the Mazda electric fountain, given to the town in 1930 by Thomson-Houston Ltd following an exhibition. On 1 October 1987 it was switched on again following several years of disuse to delight passers-by with its multicoloured illuminated cycle and 35-foot jets of water. <44,115,123,124,126,128a,311>

c) *NORTHERN ENCLOSURE:* The northern enclosure covers 1.16 acres and was remodelled similarly to the southern enclosure in about 1925. Just beyond the northernmost end is a drinking fountain presented to the town by Frederick Chatfield for both human and animal use. Now listed, the obelisk bears the borough arms and the drinking pools are now used for floral displays. It was designed by Robert Keirle and inaugurated by the mayor, Richard Webb, in 1871; it originally stood in an isolated position in the middle of the road. <24,44,115,126>

195. Magnus VOLK

<83,189>

A famous local inventor, one of the greatest of all Brightonians, Magnus Volk was born the son of a German immigrant clockmaker on 19 October 1851 at no.40 (then no.35) Western Road. The family had been at 51 Preston Street for two years when his father died in 1869, and Magnus then became an experimenter and inventor. In 1879 he married Anna Banfield and lived at 40 Preston Road; they had seven children.

In about 1879 Volk established the first telephone link in Brighton, to his friend William Jago's house in nearby Springfield Road, and in 1880 fitted his own house with electric lights. The following year he opened a larger workshop at 25 Ditchling Rise, and demonstrated a fire-alarm which was connected to the police fire station at the Town Hall. After moving to 17 Gloucester Place in 1883, Volk used the Hammond Company's electric supply to light his new house and conceived the idea of a sea-front railway using his now redundant generator (see "Volk's Electric Railway"); he built only one other railway, a short-lived venture at Aston Hall near Birmingham. Volk also fitted the Royal Pavilion with electric lights in 1883, and the following year completed the illumination of the Dome, Corn Exchange, museum, art gallery, library, and Pavilion grounds.

By 1887 though, Volk was in debt and sold his house, renting 31 King's Road instead and moving to 71 Queen's Park Road the following year, having been declared bankrupt. In 1888 he built an electric car for H.M. Sultan Abdul Hamid of Turkey, to whom he also sold an electric launch in 1889. He then moved his family to Clapham, Halliford and Wandsworth, running electric launches on the Thames for a living before returning to Brighton in 1892. Volk took part in the Emancipation Day car rally in 1896, but in 1903 moved to Hassocks before finally residing at 128 Dyke Road from 1914 where a plaque has been erected to him.

Volk continued with his inventions, but made his last public appearance in May 1937 at the opening of his new Black Rock Station. He died on 20 May 1937 and was buried at St Wulfran's Church, Ovingdean.

See also "Volk's Railway" and "Rottingdean Railway".

Figure 180: Magnus Volk's last home at no.128 Dyke Road

196. VOLK'S RAILWAY, Madeira Drive

<123,188,188a,189>

a) *CONSTRUCTION:* This, the first public electric railway in Great Britain, was preceded only by lines at Berlin and Portrush, and opened on 4 August 1883, less than eight weeks from Magnus Volk's initial approach to the council. A car for a dozen passengers was built with mahogany sides and blue velvet curtains, and ran for about 300 yards along a two-foot gauge track which was laid on the beach from opposite the main Aquarium entrance to the Chain Pier. Using power from a 50-volt generator which Volk had previously used for lighting his house in Preston Road, the car had a maximum speed of 6 m.p.h. and the railway operated smoothly for a month until a storm on 1-3 September 1883 damaged the track. The line was quickly repaired, however.

b) *FIRST EXTENSION:* With the immediate success of the line it was not long before an extension of the railway to the Banjo Groyne was approved. Volk rented an arch below Paston Place as a workshop, and work on the new line started in January 1884. Opening on 4 April 1884, the first train on the new line was overloaded with officials and grounded on a crossing, but the railway opened to the public three days later with no problems. The completely new track, on a gauge of 2 feet 8.5 inches with transverse sleepers, was now 1,400 yards long and dived under the Chain Pier; there was also a passing loop and platform halt at the halfway point. A new car was built, nineteen feet long with sliding doors, electric lighting and room for thirty passengers, and a new generator was installed in the Paston Place arch which was initially used as a waiting room. The maximum speed was increased to 10 m.p.h., and a second car was built in 1885. In about 1886 major changes were made when a three-rail system was installed on a wooden viaduct above the shingle.

However, it was not all plain sailing for the railway as it attracted considerable opposition from cab-drivers, bus operators, boatmen, and those worried about safety and access to the beach. It was, in fact, occasionally sabotaged.

c) *DAMAGE and FURTHER EXTENSION:* On 4-5 December 1896 the wreckage of the Chain Pier caused considerable damage to the railway and £1,500 was claimed. The *Sussex Daily News* ran a public subscription to help fund repairs, and the line reopened in the spring of 1897. By 1899 five cars were operating, and Volk negotiated a 21-year lease with the council for the land occupied at six-months' notice. In February 1901 Volk received permission for an extension to Black Rock to compensate for the loss of his Rottingdean Railway; the new track, which opened the same year, was laid on a viaduct eastwards from the Banjo Groyne and then along the roadway to a terminus below the French Convalescent Home. Permission was not initially given to run cars across the Banjo Groyne however, but Volk laid the tracks anyway and through-running was allowed from January 1902 to give a maximum length of about one-and-three-quarter miles; the Paston Place terminus therefore became a through station. In 1902 also, the corporation's electricity supply was used instead of Volk's own generator.

d) *FURTHER IMPROVEMENTS:* In April 1906 the tracks were relaid with ramps and bridges following improvements to Madeira Drive, and Black Rock Station was improved and reopened on 15 April 1911. However, in May 1915 a boy fresh from bathing was electrocuted, and although no negligence was found on the railway's part Volk agreed to enclose the live rail. A new 21-year lease was granted in March 1922, but when Madeira Drive was widened in 1929-30 a new Aquarium Station was opened by the mayor, Sidney Thompson, on 27 June 1930 with the line slightly shortened. On 7 May 1937 a new Black Rock Station was opened to the west of the old station which was demolished for the new open-air swimming-pool.

e) *CORPORATION TAKEOVER:* Magnus Volk died in May 1937 and was succeeded by his son Herman, but the corporation, acting under powers granted by the 1938 Brighton Corporation (Transport) Act, took over the railway at the end of the ground lease and then leased it back to Herman Volk. On 1 April 1940 the corporation took control of the whole railway, but when the beaches were closed by the government on 2 July 1940 the railway was shut down and both termini were demolished.

Following five years of neglect the railway was restored after the war under the supervision of retired tramway engineer Mr Budd. The track was renewed, a new station was built at the Children's Playground (Peter Pan's), a redundant tram shelter was used as a new Aquarium terminus, and Black Rock station was rebuilt. Seven cars were restored, but the two original cars of 1884 and 1885 were scrapped. The line reopened on 15 April 1948, and in September 1949 the corporation converted two cars from the Southend Pier Railway (the 'toast-rack' cars, nos.8 and 9, dating from 1898).

On 11 April 1950 a second fatality occurred when a girl fell in front of a car from a ramp; from then on all crossings were fitted with warning lights with a bell also at Banjo Groyne. Since 1952 the line has been closed out of season, but has run at Christmases since 1986. The Marina terminus had to be rebuilt following an arson attack by 'mods' on 31 August 1981, and another serious fire on 27 May 1987 damaged several of the cars. In September 1977 the council's amenities committee voted against a motion to scrap the line after its centenary, celebrated in 1983, and the railway still runs happily along the sea-front with plans to extend it in both directions when finances allow.

f) *DESCRIPTION:* The line now has a length of about 1.1 miles from the Aquarium to the renamed Marina Station, with an intermediate stop at Peter Pan's Playground, also called Children's Playground or Halfway Station. In 1989 it attracted 231,000 passengers with profits going towards a maintenance fund. The railway operation is controlled by apparatus in the running sheds at the Banjo Groyne, the former Paston Place terminus; a model of the railway in this area may be found in the town museum. The oldest cars currently operating appear to be nos.3 and 4 which date from 1892.

g) *VOLK'S RAILWAY OFFICES (THE ARCH):* The building below Paston Place at the western end of the Duke's Mound was often known simply as 'The Arch' and was constructed in 1837 by the Sussex County Hospital for the purpose of pumping sea-water for medicinal use, but it was used only for storage. From 1884 the Arch was rented by Magnus Volk for use as a maintenance and storage area, and also for electrical power generation. Additionally, it was initially used as waiting and reading rooms for the new Paston Place terminus, and, until the terminus was covered, as an overnight store for the electric cars which entered via tracks laid across the roadway from a turntable; the Arch was later used solely for railway maintenance and as offices. It has an attractive weather-boarded frontage with a balcony, and is painted in the railway's brown-and-cream livery.

197. Revd Arthur WAGNER

<65>

Born at Windsor on 13 June 1824, Arthur Wagner was the son of Revd Henry Wagner (see following entry), the Vicar of Brighton, and it was his father who appointed him perpetual curate to St Paul's Church in 1850. Arthur, who was greatly influenced by the High Church ideas of Dr Edward Pusey, established at St Paul's a ritualistic ceremony which started the great public argument over 'Anglo-Catholicism' in the town during the mid to late nineteenth century. To assist with his parochial work Wagner also founded, at Queen Square, the Community of the Virgin Mary, a sect of Protestant nuns which was later connected with St Mary's Home for Female Penitents. The controversy surrounding him reached a peak in 1864 when an inmate of the home, Constance Kent, stood trial for murder; Wagner refused to reveal in court what she had told him in the confession box. He was openly assaulted in the streets of Brighton, and was even shot at.

Arthur Wagner lived with his father at the Vicarage in Temple Gardens but moved to the adjacent house, Belvedere, which was left to him by his aunt Mary, when his father died in 1870. He remained curate at St Paul's until his death on 14 January 1902 although he had been ill since about 1896. In addition to his ritualistic views Wagner is also remembered for his extraordinary generosity to the poor of the town. He had some 400 houses constructed in the Islingword Road district and the Round Hill Estate between the Lewes and Upper Lewes Roads, and also had five churches erected in the poorer parts of town mostly at his own expense, viz.: the Churches of the Annunciation; the magnificent St Bartholomew; St Martin; St Mary and St Mary Magdalene; and the Resurrection.

198. Revd Henry WAGNER

<65>

Henry Wagner, Vicar of Brighton from 1824 until 1870, was born on 16 November 1792 at 93 Pall Mall, London, the son of wealthy hatter Melchior Henry Wagner and grandson of Henry Michell, Vicar of Brighton 1744-89. In 1823 he married Elizabeth Douglas and on 30 July 1824 accepted the benefice of Brighton and West Blatchington, but his wife fell ill after giving birth to their son Arthur (see "Wagner, Revd Arthur") in the same year and eventually died in 1829. In 1830 he was appointed a royal chaplain and remarried in 1838, to Mary Watson who bore him two more sons but she died in 1840.

At the beginning of Wagner's incumbency there were just 3,000 free sittings in the town's churches, despite something in the order of 20,000 poor people living in Brighton. Both Henry and Arthur Wagner devoted much of their lives to improving this situation, and Henry Wagner himself had six churches built, namely All Saints', All Souls', Christ Church, St Anne's, St John the Evangelist's, and St Paul's; only two, St John's and St Paul's, survive however.

The strong Tory opinions of Wagner often caused friction in the Whig-dominated vestry, and he eventually stepped down from the chairmanship of that body. There was also a considerable amount of antagonism towards him in the town generally, especially over his appointments at the town's churches and over the church maintenance rates. The bad feeling reached a peak when he was convicted of assaulting a seven-year-old boy who had ridiculed him in the boy's own home in Upper North Street; the vicar was fined £2. Unlike his son Arthur though, Henry Wagner was never a follower of ritualism.

Wagner died on 7 October 1870 aged seventy-seven after forty-six years as vicar. All churches were hung in black and large crowds watched the funeral procession from St Nicholas's Church to the Parochial Cemetery. His bust may be found in Brighton Museum.

Figure 181: Christ Church, Montpelier Road, one of the six churches built for Henry Wagner

199. WATERHALL

The Waterhall estate of 737 acres was acquired by the corporation in April 1920, but only one house now remains from the late-eighteenth-century farm and hamlet in Waterhall Road. From the early 1950s until 1977 a large part of the valley was filled with 'clean' refuse and rubble, and several acres of playing fields have now been laid out on the large levelled area. <108,126,305>

Waterhall Mill is now more commonly known as Patcham Mill. A tower-mill built in 1884-5 for baker Joseph Harris, it was the last working windmill to be erected in Sussex and continued to grind corn until 1924; part of its machinery came from the old Preston Mill. It was sold for just £50 in 1928 and was converted into a house in 1936, but it was used by the Home Guard during the war before reverting to private use in 1950. The mill, which has a rendered tower forty feet tall, was completely modernised in 1975 with new sweeps, and is now a desirable residence and listed building. <44,250-253>

Waterhall Golf Club, which lies off Saddlescombe Road, was originally a private course laid out in 1922 <83> by a Mr Boddington who lived in the wooden clubhouse; it had nine holes in the valley with small greens and narrow fairways to save labour. In 1934 the course was extended to eighteen holes, absorbing a nudist camp near the seventh green in the process. Two years later the corporation acquired most of the land as part of the West Blatchington estate, and the Waterhall course, which covers 131 acres and has a length of 5,615 yards, is now maintained as a municipal golf-course; the club itself is still private, however. <126,218,221>

Mill Road runs up the slopes of Coney Hill and Red Hill with a maximum gradient of 1:9. It was once just a narrow trackway, Mill Lane and Waterhall Road, (and retains the original narrow railway bridge) but the present fifty-foot-wide highway was formally opened by the Minister of Transport on 22 July 1932 at a cost of £37,000. The open spaces by Devil's Dyke Road and on the Westdene side of Mill Road were once part of West Blatchington parish, but were annexed by Brighton in April 1928. <115,124>

Since 1989 the whole Waterhall area has been radically affected by the construction of the Brighton bypass. On 2 April 1989 Brighton Pavilion M.P. Julian Amery formally cut the first turf in the Waterhall Valley. The dual three-lane section from London Road to the Devil's Dyke Dyke Road is scheduled to be completed in 1991 and new playing fields have been laid out to compensate for those lost to the new road. Mill Road has been diverted, destroying much of the open space at the top of the hill, and will become a local road. Waterhall Road has also been diverted. <123>

Figure 182: Waterhall Mill

200. WATER SUPPLY

<123,172-175>

a) *WELLS:* Brighton's situation on the porous chalk aquifer of the South Downs provides the town with a huge natural reservoir, and the water supply has always been drawn from wells, headings and boreholes sunk into the chalk; fresh water springs can still be seen issuing from the chalk under the shingle of the beaches at low tide, particularly just east of the Palace Pier. Since medieval times regulations have existed to prevent contamination of sources, but the rapid expansion of the town in the early nineteenth century, with the consequent cutting of many cesspits into the chalk, resulted in severe public health problems throughout the century which were not alleviated until an efficient piped water supply and adequate sewerage were provided.

The main well for town use was situated at the rear of the Unicorn Inn near the top of North Street, and Richard Scrase is recorded as having erected a building over it by 1621. When the inn was rebuilt in 1892 the well was rediscovered and found to be 110 feet deep. Another town well in West Street was stopped up as being dangerous in April 1792, while the well at the Knab was completed in 1727 and was still in use in the latter half of the nineteenth century when there were also public wells by the Sussex Arms in East Street, in Market Street, and in Pool Valley. In 1858-62 a well was sunk at the Warren Farm Schools to a depth of 1,285 feet, the deepest dug well in the world.
<2,6,15,112>

b) *EARLY COMPANIES:* The first piped water supply in the town was provided to privileged houses for just two hours a day from 1834 by the Brighton, Hove and Preston Waterworks Company, from a well and pumping-station in Lewes Road, now the site of Saunders Park. This source was extended in 1853 when the first 'headings' were cut. (Headings are tunnels driven parallel to the shoreline at a depth corresponding to sea-level, thereby intercepting the fissures within the chalk strata which are the natural drainage channels.)

However the intermittent supply was considered far from satisfactory, and in the same year of 1853 the Brighton, Hove and Preston Constant Water Service Company was founded. It absorbed the older company the following year, extending the supply to 7,000 homes, and in 1866 opened a large new waterworks at Goldstone Bottom which was extended in 1876 with the addition of a second beam-engine. (The Constant Service public house in Islingword Road, despite its sign, is named after this company which owned the nearby reservoir.)

c) *CORPORATION ACQUISITION and DEVELOPMENT:* In July 1872, under the terms of the Brighton Corporation Waterworks Act, the corporation purchased the Constant Service Water Company, then supplying some 18,000 homes with 2.6 million gallons per day, for £321,000. The new undertaking covered Brighton, Falmer, Hangleton, Ovingdean, Patcham, Preston, and Rottingdean, and supplied both constant and intermittent services at different charges. By the turn of the century three other local water companies had been acquired, namely the West Brighton in 1876; Shoreham and District in 1896; and Aldrington in 1897. The purchase of the West Brighton Waterworks Company included a supply of piped sea-water to a hundred houses from tanks filled at high tide under Hove Western Lawns; it was maintained until 1939.

Increased availability of mains water necessitated several new sources and pumping-stations: at Patcham in 1889; Mile Oak in 1900; Falmer in 1904; and the first electric station at Balsdean in 1936, then the largest station of its kind and now Brighton's largest source. With the Lewes Road station closed in 1903 and demolished due to contamination of the source, the corporation took great steps over the following years to prevent further pollution of the water supply. Bye-laws eventually extending to over 30,000 acres were made and vast areas of downland were acquired to prevent turf-breaking cultivation or development over the headings.

The water obtained from the chalk is naturally clear and odourless, with no organic matter or mineral suspension, but in 1937 an ozone treatment (discontinued 1954) was introduced at the Goldstone station which had become surrounded by development, and during the Second World War chlorination of all supplies was introduced for disinfection purposes.

d) *POST-WAR DEVELOPMENTS:* The corporation undertaking was extended after the war by the acquisition of the Peacehaven Company (supplied from Saltdean, north of Looes Barn, 1922-49) in 1950, and by the amalgamation of the Lewes Company (founded 1833) in October 1958. Further development necessitated new supplies at Newmarket in 1957 and Sompting in 1963, while the older stations at Aldrington (1960), Mile Oak (1961), Patcham (1964), and Falmer (1967) were rebuilt. The Lewes Road source was reopened in 1957, and the Goldstone source in 1977. Droughts in 1976, 1989 and 1990 led to the development of further boreholes, and twenty-five sources are now on stream.

On 15 November 1967 a new headquarters building was formally opened on the site of the old Falmer pumping-station (incorporating a new electric station) to replace the offices and monitoring station at 12-13 Bond Street. By 1972 the Brighton undertaking, divided into seven pressure zones depending on elevation, was pumping some 18 million gallons per day to Brighton, Falmer, Hove, Kingston near Lewes, Lancing, Lewes, Portslade, Pyecombe, St Ann (Without), Shoreham, South Malling (Without), Southwick and Telscombe, an area of about sixty-four square miles serviced by eleven pumping stations and thirty-two reservoirs. In 1974 however, the Brighton Corporation Waterworks Department was absorbed by the new Southern Water Authority following the 1973 Water Act, and the Falmer building is now one of the main district offices. In September 1989 Southern Water became a public limited company.

Of the Victorian and Edwardian pumping-stations only one now remains, the Goldstone works in Nevill Road, Hove. Despite the efforts of Brighton Corporation to demolish it in 1972 when pumping had ceased, the building was listed to prevent its destruction and was then restored, principally by Jonathan Minns. It reopened on Good Friday 1976 as the British Engineerium, a museum of industrial history with many exhibits including the Easton & Anderson beam-engine of 1876. The boiler house, with its tall chimney, is flanked by two engine houses, and the building now forms the heart of a small conservation area.

201. WELLESBOURNE

<1,2,3,15,127a,245-246,289>

Brighton's 'lost river' was an intermittent stream known as the 'Wellesbourne' that ran from Patcham and beyond to the sea at Pool Valley, but only at those times after prolonged rainfall when the water-table within the porous chalk bedrock reached the surface along the London Road valley and water from springs was thus able to flow without repercolating, a phenomenon similar to the Winterbourne at Lewes today.

One of its principal sources was the pond in front of All Saint's Church, Patcham, now marked by a slight depression. In most winters the pond overflowed and water ran to the bottom of Church Hill (then named Spring Street) where it would be joined by water from other springs in the valley as far as Pyecombe; these included one at Brapool, which means 'pool by which bracken grew'. The stream then flowed into another pond at the corner of Old London Road and Ladies Mile Road, and along the road to Brighton where it was joined at the Level by another winter-bourne from Falmer that ran down the Lewes Road valley. The stream finally debouched into the sea at the 'pool' of Pool Valley, or perhaps slightly to the east, diverted by an artificial bank to protect the inlet <10>. The Domesday Book records the presence of a mill at Preston in 1086, possibly a water-mill powered by the stream.

The bourne often flooded the Valley Gardens in the winter and skating was occasionally possible on the frozen Steine. The swampy nature of the central valley probably prevented development upon it, but once the Steine had become a fashionable promenade with the arrival of visitors from the mid eighteenth century, such conditions were unacceptable. In 1792-3 the Prince of Wales and the Duke of Marlborough, at their own expense, laid a wooden sewer under the western edge of the Steine to carry the bourne to the sea which also drained a stagnant pool that collected in front of the Prince's Marine Pavilion; the Wellesbourne was culverted and Pool Valley was also bricked over. Following inundations in the winter of 1827-8, another drain was laid all the way from Preston Circus to the Albion Hotel.

Particularly strong flows of the Wellesbourne occurred in 1795, 1806, 1811, 1827-8, 1852, and finally in 1876 when both Lewes and London Roads were impassable, but since the construction of the Patcham Waterworks in 1889, and the consequent siphoning of water from its sources, the bourne has never flowed again. The Wellesbourne, corrupted to 'Whalesbone', may have given its name to the hundred through which it flowed, but although often referred to as an 'underground river', it is only so in the sense that spring water from Patcham may be carried under the London Road by sewer; there is no stream flowing within the chalk or Coombe deposits of the valley. After very heavy rain the water-table rises and reaches the surface in basements along the valley and occasionally at Preston Park and the Valley Gardens, giving the impression of an invisible stream. The Parks and Recreation Department uses water from the chalk along the valley for watering its gardens.

202. WEST BLATCHINGTON

<1,64a,249b,250-253,279>

Once a small village to the north of Hove, with a population of less than a hundred for many years, West Blatchington was developed as a large housing estate just before and after the Second World War, and all that now remains of the original village is the mill and church. The impressive windmill and granary is a grade II*-listed building but its age is rather uncertain; probably dating from around 1820, it certainly existed by 1823, and in 1825 was sketched by Constable. Milling ceased in 1897 and it has been open to the public since 1979.

The parish church of St Peter was rebuilt in 1890 by George Somers Clarke, but includes the Norman nave of a church which was in ruins by the eighteenth century; the position of vicar of West Blatchington was in fact united with that of Brighton from 1744 until 1941 <83>. West Blatchington also formed the Hundred of Whalesbone together with Brighton.

On 1 April 1928 most of West Blatchington became an urban parish within the borough of Hove, but 131 acres to the east of the Dyke and Saddlescombe roads, including the upper parts of the Waterhall Valley and Mill Road, were transferred to Brighton; no population or buildings were involved.

203. WEST HILL

West Hill is the name given to the eastern part of Church Hill rising westwards from Brighton Station, Queen's Road and the central valley. It was developed in the 1840s and '50s with 'working-class' and 'middle-class' terraced housing near the station, and in the 1870s with large villa residences in the grounds of the former workhouse <83>. Designated a conservation area in 1977, the streets of main interest are detailed below, but see also "Dyke Road" and "Queen's Road"; also "Railways - Brighton Station", which was added to the conservation area in 1988.

a) *ALBERT ROAD, ALEXANDRA VILLAS, ALFRED ROAD and LEOPOLD ROAD:* Developed in about 1869-75 with large, semi-detached villas in the grounds of the former workhouse. In the 1890s 13 Alexandra Villas was the home of local film pioneer Esme Collings, Brighton's first film-maker. He had a studio at 120 Western Road and made the first ever 'blue' movie. <68b,83>

b) *BUCKINGHAM PLACE:* Nos.5-19 form an attractive, Italianate listed terrace of about 1845 with balconies and verandahs. Artist Richard Henry Nibbs (1816-93) lived at no.7 from 1873 until his death, having previously resided at 8 Howard Place. He painted in Brighton from at least 1834, and was renowned for marine, architectural and topographical views. No.49, St Anne's House (formerly Compton Lodge), is a large, four-storey listed house with a fluted Doric porch and balcony, and dates from about 1820; it was once a convent and home for crippled children, and for many years had an observatory on the roof. <44,83,123,140>

Buckingham Lodge at the corner with Compton Avenue stands on the site of All Saints' Church. Designed by Richard Cromwell Carpenter in Gothic style, the church was erected by George Cheeseman in flint for Revd Henry Wagner in 1850-2. It had a small tower at the north-western end topped by a turret. All Saints' was demolished in 1957, but the altar was removed to the south chapel of St Michael and All Angels' Church; the church hall still stands at the rear of the flats. <1,45a,62,64a,65>

c) *BUCKINGHAM ROAD:* This road is lined with large villas at the southern end, erected in the 1870s in the former workhouse grounds, and some impressive terraced housing of the 1850s to the north, particularly nos.45-58 with their large square bays. No.31 was the birthplace of one of Brighton's most famous sons, Aubrey Beardsley, on 21 August 1872. A famous black-and-white illustrative artist, 'the master of line', he was educated at the nearby grammar school (corner of Upper Gloucester Road) where he illustrated a booklet for a school opera, but he later lived at 21 Lower Rock Gardens. He left Brighton at the age of fifteen to work as a clerk in a London office, but his self-taught skill as an line artist won him a major commission to illustrate an issue of Malory's ***Morte d'Arthur***. Other important commissions followed, including Wilde's *Salome* and Pope's ***Rape of the Lock***. Beardsley gained something of a notorious reputation with his grotesque and erotic art nouveau imagery, but he died of tuberculosis at Mentone, France, on 16 March 1898 aged just twenty-five. <3,296>

d) *CAMDEN TERRACE:* A narrow twitten of the 1840s with attractive cottages and some much larger houses. <108>

e) *CROWN GARDENS:* A narrow twitten, lined with bow-windowed cottages behind small gardens, which despite its location actually lies within the Clifton Hill conservation area. Dating from the 1820s, Crown Gardens is said to have been built for employees at the Royal Pavilion and royal stables. <108,123>

f) *LEOPOLD ROAD:* see "Albert Road" above.

g) *NORTH GARDENS:* An attractive road of small, bowed houses of the 1810s behind gardens. No.27, Regency Cottage, is a listed house of the early nineteenth century with two bows, an impressive doorway, and a cobbled garden wall. <44,83>

h) *TERMINUS PLACE:* An attractive little cul-de-sac of the 1840s, similar to the nearby Railway Street and Terminus Street. Nos.1-6, with bows and fanlight doorways, are included on the council's local list of buildings of special interest.

j) *TERMINUS ROAD:* The red-brick nos.20-23 have balconies and Regency-style doorways, and are included on the borough council's local list.

k) *WEST HILL ROAD:* No.26 was a police station from 1876 until 1919 <164>. Adjacent is the Providence Chapel, erected as the Nathaniel Episcopal Reformed Church in 1894-6 by Charles Hewitt; the present congregation moved from Church Street in 1965 when their former chapel was demolished <62,311>. The garages opposite stand on the site of Hodson's Black Mill, a twelve-sided smock-mill built in 1808-10 which was said to be the finest structure of its kind in the country. It was demolished in June 1866, but the original brick base remained and was used as a coal-store and garage until removed in 1966 <129,249a,249b>.

204. WEST PIER, King's Road

<25,26,123,142,143,146>

a) *CONSTRUCTION and OPENING:* This most elegant of seaside piers, the supreme example of Victorian pier-building techniques, was designed by the most famous of pier engineers and architects, Eugenius Birch, as a promenade pier for the western end of the town. Construction commenced in April 1863 using Birch's cast-iron screw piles, and took three years to complete at a cost of £27,000; the new pier was opened by the mayor, Henry Martin, on 6 October 1866. Stretching for 1,115 feet out to sea, the West Pier initially had only two square kiosks at the entrance, two octagonal kiosks with minarets in the centre, and four more octagonal kiosks at the corners of the large pier-head platform which also had some windshields; the structure was illuminated at night. Decorative ironwork features added greatly to its charm, but the pier was the subject of strong criticism by the residents of Regency Square who took a particular dislike to the square toll-houses. Among the attractions were a miniature cannon fired by the sun at midday, and the skull of a whale washed ashore in January 1882. A model of the pier at this time may be seen in Brighton Museum.

b) *ADDITIONS:* The West Pier remained largely unaltered for over twenty years until 1890 when a new company took over and immediately added the central windshield. Three years later, in 1893, the pier-head was widened and a large pavilion was erected, decorated with oriental towers and seating 1,400; a landing stage was added at the same time. In November 1896 however, the West Pier was damaged to the tune of £6,000 by wreckage from the Chain Pier. The pavilion was converted into a theatre in 1903, and further additions came with the attractive concert hall at the

Figure 183: The West Pier at the turn of the century

centre in 1916, and the raised entrance at the shore end in 1932.

Between the wars the West Pier was used by day-trippers to and from France and had resident customs officials, but in 1940 the structure was cut in two to prevent an enemy landing. When the pier reopened in 1945 the theatre, which had had its own repertory company in the 1930s, was converted into an amusement arcade. It was also used for filming *Oh! What a Lovely War* in about 1968.

c) *CLOSURE:* In 1965 the West Pier Company was taken over by AVP Industries. Four years later the owners sought permission for the demolition of the southern end; the pier was listed to protect it, but the southern part was closed in October 1970 as being dangerous. A public inquiry was then held into the pier's future in 1971, but when the council's policy committee recommended that demolition should not be opposed in December 1974 a strong protest group led by John Lloyd conducted a long campaign which, armed with a 5,000-signature petition, persuaded the council at least to postpone a decision on the pier. Meanwhile, the West Pier itself closed completely on 30 September 1975.

The council declined to buy the pier in 1976 but served a dangerous structure notice on the West Pier Company to have the section over the Lower Esplanade repaired. This action resulted in the liquidation of the company and the vesting of the pier in the Crown Estate Commissioners after the Official Receiver disclaimed it. The council also set aside a reserve fund of £300,000 in case demolition became a necessity.

d) *RENEWED HOPE:* After several abortive plans for renovation, the West Pier Trust, a registered charity established in 1978, was given the sole right to operate the pier by Act of Parliament, while the government recognised the pier's merit by changing its listing from grade II* to grade I in November 1982, the only pier to be so highly graded. In 1984 a kiosk fell into the sea, but on 23 August of the same year the West Pier Trust purchased the pier for just £100 when the Crown Estate Commissioners were satisfied that sufficient resources were available to prevent the structure becoming dangerous. Emergency works, at a cost of £55,000, were undertaken at the seaward end to prevent a collapse, and in July 1985 the Historic Buildings and Monuments Commission announced a grant of £200,000, conditional on the council matching it, with a further £300,000 in the future. The National Heritage Memorial Fund then offered an unconditional £100,000, and in October 1985 the council agreed to match the former grant from the reserve fund set up in 1977, thereby wiping out the Trust's overdraft. Further grants from English Heritage and the National Heritage Memorial Fund were forthcoming in August 1988.

In November 1988 Merlin International Ltd announced a £30 million rebuilding scheme for the pier, including an extra floor for the theatre and a new Victorian-style pavilion at the shore end. Although controversial because of the scale of the rebuilding, the plan was approved by the West Pier Trust but led to the withdrawal of the English Heritage grants. The fate of the West Pier still hangs in the balance, but essential restoration began in August 1986 and the first small section of decking was reopened on 15 September 1987 after twelve years of closure. The section over the Lower Esplanade has been removed and in March 1988 a further section of the decking was demolished to prevent further damage. Nevertheless, the intervention of Merlin has led to the best hope yet of renovation, albeit in a modified form.

205. WEST STREET

a) *HISTORY:* West Street, the western limit of the Old Town of Brighton, may well have been developed by the fishermen of the Lower Town when their growing population forced them onto the cliff top in about the thirteenth century. In 1777 it was considered the most exclusive part of the town, and a number of fine houses were built in the late eighteenth and early nineteenth centuries. During the same period much infilling took place and several small courtyards of houses were built off West Street, but all have now disappeared. See also figure 97. <1,10,14,83>

West Street was also rather narrow, only twenty-eight feet wide in places, and so the upper part was widened on the eastern side at the same time as Duke Street in 1868. The major widening was undertaken by the corporation in 1928-38 when all buildings along the western side were removed with the exception of St Paul's Church which had been built back from the road. Regency Road was then made through to Upper Russell Street, several office blocks were erected in the upper part of West Street, and the Sports Stadium and Odeon Cinema built either side of Little Russell Street. See also figures 35 and 36. <115,116>

b) *INTERESTING BUILDINGS:* West Street, on the shortest route from the railway station to the sea, has become a centre of the town's night-life and is lined with discotheques, cinemas, public houses, restaurants and amusement arcades. The western side has several office blocks in distinctive 1930s styles, while the eastern side dates principally from the late nineteenth century. However the elegant no.77, Genghis Khan's restaurant and Swifts cocktail bar, has two wide bows and dates from the early nineteenth century. Now a listed building, it was used by the local gas company as an office from 1882 until about 1967. The adjacent Booths Leisure amusement arcade occupies the ground floor of the elegant West Street Mansions, while the nearby Leisure Centre arcade at the corner of South Street

Figure 184: West Street before redevelopment

Figure 185: No.77 West Street, formerly a large residence erected in the early nineteenth century

occupies the former Chatfield's Hotel. Rebuilt in 1899, it bears the monogram 'CH' and has a highly decorated façade. The Pink Coconut is detailed under "Sherrys" below. <44,83>

Higher up the street, Academy House stands on the site of the Academy Cinema. Opened on 6 June 1911 by E.E.Lyons, the cinema was entirely rebuilt in 1913 with the capacity nearly doubled to 800 seats, and a regular programme of early 'Kinemacolour' films was presented; sound equipment was installed in October 1929. During 1931 it was briefly known as the Tatler, but the Academy closed on 24 January 1973 and was then demolished. At no.57 stands another listed building, the Nellie Peck public house with its highly decorated, late-Victorian façade adorned with coloured figures, cupola and weather-vane. Dating originally from the early nineteenth century or possibly before, it was known as the Carpenters Arms or Compasses, but became Christie's Hotel in about 1901 and The Bosun in the 1970s. It then reverted to the original name before becoming the Nellie Peck in 1986 <15>. Another cinema in West Street was the Novelty Electric Theatre which operated at no.27 for two years from 1911 in a converted bazaar but was demolished in 1934. <44,68,68b,83>

The 140-bedroom Oak Hotel, an exhibition facility and an office development are under construction on the western side of West Street at the junction with Russell Road. The northern half of the site was occupied by the Odeon Cinema, a 1,350-seat auditorium which opened in December 1937. It closed when the Kingswest Odeon complex opened in 1973 and remained empty until it was demolished in 1990. The other half of the site was occupied by the S.S.Brighton (see below), and prior to that by a number of buildings including the George Inn where Charles II stayed overnight in October 1651 during his escape to France; a branch of oak was hung out of the upper window on every anniversary of his stay. Later changing its name to the King's Head, the inn was rebuilt in the early twentieth century but was demolished in 1933. A later George Inn stood at the corner of West Street and Kent Street. <15,18,19,68,68a,123>

c) *HENRY THRALE'S HOUSE and SHERRYS:* On the pavement in front of the Pink Coconut night-club stands a small post, once one of seven chain-linked posts across the forecourt of Henry Thrale's house and now listed as being of special historical interest. The Thrale family, owners of London's Anchor Brewery, played host to many literary guests in the late eighteenth century including Dr Samuel Johnson and Fanny Burney, and their small, brick house, built in 1767, was one of the first of the new resort houses. It was demolished in 1866, but a mulberry tree from the garden was replanted in the grounds of Brighton College.

The house was replaced by the West Street Concert Hall, opened on 6 December 1867 and designed by Horatio Goulty with hotels at the West Street and Middle Street ends. A number of musical concerts and lectures were presented, including the first of the Music Festivals, but in 1877 the building was converted into a roller-skating rink. On the evening of 7 October 1882 it was virtually destroyed by a gas explosion and fire which left only the frontages standing, but the roller-skating hall was reconstructed in 1892. In 1911 the building was converted into a 2,000-seat cinema, the Grand Picture Palace which was renamed the Coliseum in 1918, but following another serious fire it reopened on 11 November 1919 as the famous Sherrys Dance Hall. Together with the Regent, Sherrys dominated Brighton's pre-war night-life, but in 1949 it was converted back into a roller-skating rink and then became the Ritz amusement arcade in the 1960s. The Italianate façade of the 1892 building was demolished in February 1969 when it was remodelled as a night-club and amusement arcade, now the Pink Coconut (opened 1983) and the Crystal Room; the plain Middle Street façade remains. <3,24,26,68,68a,115,123>

d) *ST PAUL'S CHURCH:* Designed by Richard Cromwell Carpenter, St Paul's Church was constructed in 1846-8 by George Cheeseman on the site of an 1830 Bethel chapel. It was built at a cost of £14,000 for Revd Henry Wagner, the Vicar of Brighton, and two years after it opened on 18 October 1848 Wagner's son Arthur was installed as perpetual curate. The church was consecrated on 23 October 1849. Now a listed building, the church's exterior is in a fourteenth-century Gothic style, and is faced with knapped flint and stone dressings. The tower was originally intended to have a tall spire, but the octagonal lantern was added in 1874-5 by Carpenter's son, Richard Herbert Carpenter, and is supported by four pinnacles and crowned by a short timber and lead spire; the lantern and spire were extensively restored in 1947, principally at the expense of the Emperor Haile Selassie of Ethiopia. Additions to the highly decorated interior were made in 1861 by George Bodley. The stained glass was created by William Pugin and Charles Kempe, and the triptych was decorated by Sir Edward Burne-Jones but it is presently on display in Brighton Museum. St Paul's has 1,200 sittings, 460 of which were rented until 1873, the same year in which the parish was formed. The entrance to the church is via a long corridor along the southern side so that, unlike most Brighton churches, it can be entered from the west, the liturgically correct end.

St Paul's was opened with a very ornate and ritualist ceremony, and was the first Brighton church to be so highly decorated. It was said to be the first 'Tractarian' church south of the River Thames, and in the mid nineteenth century was at the centre of the ritualist movement led by Arthur Wagner (q.v.), a movement which led to much anger within the town. Wagner also had a reading-room built to the west of the church, but it was not used by the fishing community for whom it was intended and was converted into a vestry. <1,44,45,62,64a,66,83>

A new church hall, the Wagner Hall, was erected in Regency Road in conjunction with the Churchill Square development on the site of the 1834 Baptist Tabernacle. <62,123>

e) *SPORTS STADIUM or S.S.BRIGHTON:* This popular centre was opened by Commodore Earl Howe on 29 June 1934 as the S.S.Brighton swimming-pool, a square building faced with cream tiles which was erected at the corner of Russell Road on the site of many small tenements and other buildings at a cost of £80,000. The interior was decorated in the style of an ocean liner (hence S.S.) and housed the largest covered sea-water swimming-pool in the world, 165 feet long by 60 feet wide. Swimming championships and bathing-beauty contests were held, but after only one year the pool was converted into an ice-skating rink, reopening on 16 October 1935 as the Brighton Sports Stadium but still also known as S.S.Brighton.

The first of the many ice-shows opened on New Year's Eve 1936 and was followed in the summer by a sensational show called *Marina*. After the war many other attractions were staged including judo, wrestling, basketball and professional tennis, but in September 1959 the stadium was relaunched as the Brighton Palladium, staging Sunday variety shows, musical concerts and party political conferences as well as sporting events. After a takeover by Top Rank in February 1962 though, the building reverted to its original name.

Top Rank threw their investment into a new, adjacent entertainment centre (Kingswest Boulevard) however, and the Sports Stadium was closed in October 1965 and subsequently demolished. The site was originally intended for a restaurant, car-park and cinema extension to the Top Rank Centre, but it remained vacant until 1990 when construction of the Oak Hotel commenced. One of the town's most popular entertainments for over thirty years has yet to be adequately replaced, however. <3,115,123>

The Sports Stadium was also famous as the home of the Brighton Tigers ice-hockey team. Formed in 1935, they played to packed crowds after the war under the management and coaching of star player Bobby Lee, and won the British League in seasons 1946-7, 1947-8 and 1957-8, and the Autumn Cup in 1946-7, 1950-1, 1956-7 and 1958-9. In December 1957 the Soviet Union national team were beaten 6-3. When the post-war boom subsided the star Canadian players left and the club went into intermediate-grade hockey in 1960, although attendances actually rose. However, the Tigers were doomed as Top Rank refused them a lease on the new ice-rink next door, and they played their final home match on 23 May 1965; the team then continued to play away matches only until 1967. <19,123,302>

206. WESTDENE

This housing estate, centred around Mill Rise, Bankside and Barn Rise, was developed principally in the 1950s on the slopes of Coney Hill and Red Hill, although there was some development in the Barn Rise and Eldred Avenue areas in the 1930s. Westdene Woods occupy over eight acres between Eldred Avenue and Fairview Rise, and were acquired by the corporation in May 1939. Westdene Library was opened on 13 March 1964 by the mayor, Stanley Deason, while the Church Hall of the Ascension in Mill Rise was designed by John Wells-Thorpe and dedicated in February 1958 in connection with All Saints' Church, Patcham. Coppercliff in Redhill Drive, the former home of the Braybon family that developed much of the area, became a cancer hospice in 1965. <83,123,126>

At the lower end of the greensward enclosed by Barn Rise and Dene Vale is an old flint wall surrounding a children's play area, all that remains of a former farmyard which was demolished in the late 1950s. Newmans Barn, which stood adjacently, probably dated from the late eighteenth century but was removed in the early 1960s. Bowling-greens were then laid out following meetings with residents, but they proved a failure and were removed although the wooden pavilion remains <126>.

207. WESTERN ROAD

a) *HISTORY:* Now the town's principal shopping street, Western Road was originally a narrow trackway running through the West Laine from North Street to Hove Church. In the early nineteenth century a number of large houses were built with their gardens backing onto the road, terraces known as Regent's Place, Clarence Place and Western Place, but by 1830 Western Road itself (which was named after the land-owning Western family <47>) was developed as far as Montpelier Road and was the principal access to Brunswick Town. There were also some shops by the 1830s, and the development of high-class residential areas on either side ensured the prosperity of Western Road as a service road and shopping street for the area. Many more shops were then built in the gardens of the large houses, and by the 1860s virtually the entire length was lined with shops. <14,15,83,108>

The roadway became very narrow as the building line was brought forward. The corporation started to acquire properties on the northern side of Western Road in 1906, and between 1926 and 1936 a major widening scheme between Hampton Place and North Street was carried out with many of the present large stores erected (the leases of which generate considerable income for the corporation). Further redevelopment came in the late 1960s when Churchill Square (q.v.) was constructed, and the Western Road area is now one of the largest provincial shopping centres in the country. Private car access has been restricted since 28 January 1974. <26,116,123>

b) *BUILDINGS OF INTEREST:* The buildings of Western Road are rather drab compared with many streets in the town, but the bow-fronted nos.103, 105 and 108, and also no.104, are listed buildings of the 1820s; nos.117-122, including the Temple Bar, form a much-altered composition with some bow-windows and pilasters, and are included on the council's local list of buildings of special interest. Some older buildings of the 1810s and '20s with bows remain on the southern side, a few faced with mathematical tiles; no.40 was the birthplace of famous local inventor Magnus Volk (q.v.) in 1851. Nos.87-93 form an impressive, decorated, four-stroey composition, formerly Sillwood Terrace, while the four-storey composition facing Norfolk Square is actually numbered as part of the square. No.115, the last building in Brighton on the northern side, has a very wide bow front.

Hampton Lodge may be seen to the west of Hampton Place, behind the single-storey shops which were erected in its garden in 1903. Formerly a single house, it was built in about 1823 and was the home in the 1830s of Admiral Sir Edward Codrington, the victor of the Battle of Navarino in 1827 <83,108>. The adjacent Hampton Place post-office is splendidly decorated with lion-head figures and was formerly a bank. The pillar-box at the corner of Montpelier Road dates from 1858 <15> and is one of only four of its type still in service; it has a most unusual top and is listed as being of special architectural and historic interest. <24,44>

Figure 186: Western Road in the early years of the century. The road on the right leads to Clarence Square.

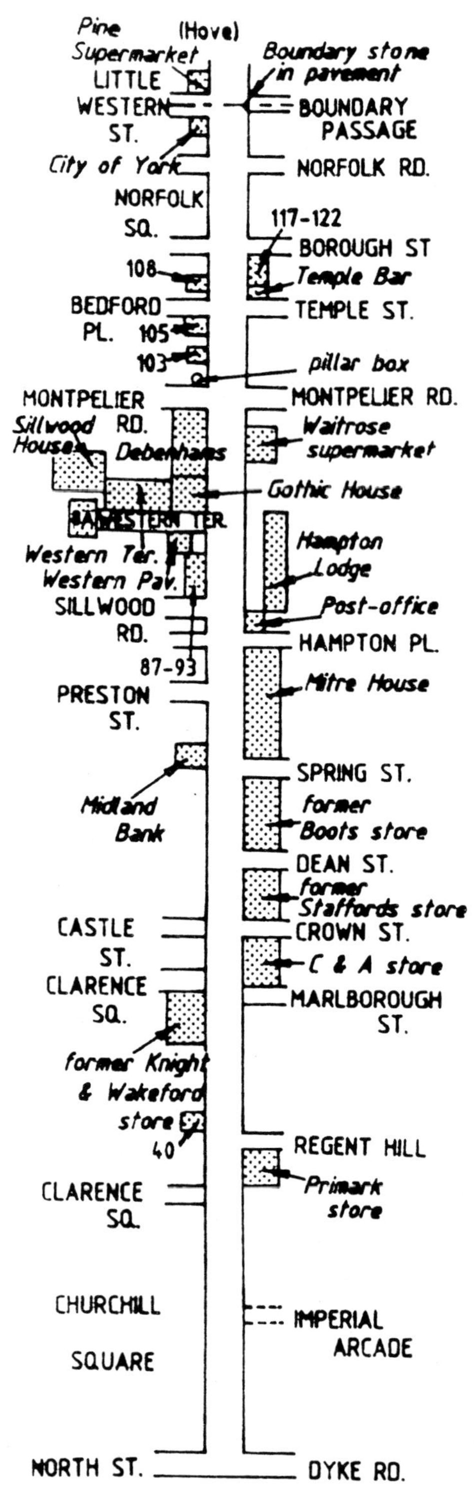

Figure 187: Western Road

The best of the large store buildings are the domed and decorated CJ's, nos.49-55 at the corner of Clarence Square, which was built in 1903 for Knight & Wakeford's drapery <83>; the 1931 C & A building (originally British Home Stores) and the Primark (originally Wades) store of 1928, both with Art Deco façades; the Seeboard showroom, etc., between Dean Street and Crown Street, formerly Staffords store of about 1930 which has some elegant decoration; and the Virgin Megastore, formerly Boots which opened on 29 November 1928 in neo-classical style and is decorated with Ionic columns (it had a popular restaurant and orchestra until the war, and also one of the country's busiest post-offices until 1966). The heavily decorated Midland Bank, built of golden sandstone in 1905, enlivens the street with its Edwardian Baroque design; the nearby National Westminster Bank, also built in stone, dates from 1925. <26,45a,123>

Mitre House, a six-storey block of flats and offices designed by J.Stanley Beard and Bennett, was built in 1935 by International Stores Ltd (whose trademark is a mitre) with the largest grocery store on the south coast on the ground floor (now Halfords). Imperial Arcade was originally built in 1923 on the site of the North Street Brewery, but was rebuilt in 1934 with the adjoining buildings added in the style of the day, resembling the prow of a ship. <26,130>

The Pine Supermarket, just over the borough boundary in Hove, was a cinema from around 1912 until 1981. Originally the Hove Cinematograph Theatre, it became the Tivoli in 1922 and the Embassy in 1948. <68a>

c) *DEBENHAMS and WESTERN TERRACE:* However, the most interesting building in the whole road is the Gothic House, a listed building of about 1823 by Wilds and Busby with crocketed turrets and spires, their only venture into Georgian Gothic architecture. It was also known as The Priory or Priory Lodge, but was converted into a shop in 1898 for Sharmars drapery. Now forming part of the Debenhams store, it was extended westwards in 1880 by W.H.Stevens, while part of its eastern façade is unfortunately hidden by an extension for Plummer Rodis Ltd of 1920.

The adjacent road leads to Western Terrace, a small, stuccoed, listed terrace with ammonite pilasters built in about 1827 by A.H.Wilds but used since 1920 by the adjacent store. Opposite the terrace is the grade II*-listed Western Pavilion, built in Oriental style in 1831 also by A.H.Wilds as his own residence. The house has a large Indian dome and Hindu details, and was used an office and confectionery from 1931. It was later acquired by Debenhams but has now been restored as a house; the dome contains a large bathroom. No.8a at the end of the road was probably a coaching lodge for Sillwood House, the mansion adjoining Western Terrace (see "Regency Square Conservation Area (Sillwood Place)"). An excellent model of the whole area around Western Terrace may be found in Brighton Museum. <44,46,123>

d) *CURZON CINEMA:* The Waitrose supermarket's western extension stands on the site of the Curzon Cinema, which was opened by Harold Speer as the Electric Bioscope on 13 January 1909 in a converted shop with about fifty seats. The following year it was enlarged to 250 seats by taking in the adjacent shop and became the Queen's Electric, the first authentic cinema in the town with a pit orchestra, drawn curtains, dimming lights, and continuous performances. The name changed in 1915 to the Queen's Picture Theatre, to the Picturedrome in 1919, the Scala in 1922, the Regal in 1932, and, following a remodelling in Art Deco style, to the Curzon in 1936. Sound was eventually introduced in March 1930 after a brief stand against the new films, with the cinema advertising 'No talkies here! Orchestra!'; there were also 'lover's seats' without armrests in the circle. The Curzon was substantially redecorated in May 1958 and was taken over by Classic Cinemas Ltd in September 1965, the name being changed to the Classic in 1975 when it showed specialist films, but it finally closed on 31 August 1979 to make way for the supermarket extension. <68,68a,123>

Figure 188: Western Pavilion

e) *SIDE STREETS:* Western Road runs between the Regency Square and Clifton Hill outstanding conservation areas, and the roads leading northwards from it are worth exploring. Regent Hill, Marlborough Street, Crown Street, Dean Street and Spring Street, the first five side streets from Dyke Road, all retain small, attractive artisan cottages of the 1820s, many with bowed façades or windows and balconies. Nos.18-20 Regent Hill have narrow bows and are listed buildings, while nos.14, 15, 19, 22 and 23 Crown Street are included on the borough council's local list of buildings of special interest.

Hampton Place was developed in the 1820s and has an attractive terrace with balconies and Ionic pilasters on the eastern side of which nos.8-28 and 32-34 are listed. The western side is lined with bowed houses, with nos.15, 19-21, 25 and 29-39 listed.

Temple Street was laid out in the next decade, the 1830s, with attractive three-storey terraces. Nos.2, 29, 31, 37 and 42, all with narrow bows, are listed buildings, while no.7 is included on the local list.

Borough Street commemorates the creation of the Parliamentary Borough of Brighton in 1832, and is lined with attractive terraced housing with those on the western side mostly having bows; nos.3, 8-13, 16, 20-22, 24 and 26 are listed buildings. St Stephen's House was built in 1855 as St Stephen's School and was enlarged in 1895. The listed building is faced in knapped flint and was used as a warehouse from 1931 until 1990.

Figure 189: Bow-fronted houses of around 1832 in Borough Street

Norfolk Road is lined with attractive three-storey houses dating from the 1830s, with the large double-bowed no.3 probably built by Wilds and Busby. It is a listed building, along with the bow-fronted nos.1-2, 18, 24-26, 37-39, 41-44 and 47. Norfolk Road Methodist Church was built in 1865 by C.O.Ellison, a Gothic building of flint with stone dressings and a south-eastern turret, but it was demolished in 1965 and Braemar House now occupies the site. It was the congregation of this chapel that founded the famous Dome Mission, originally at the Alhambra in King's Road. The growing attendances at the services necessitated a move to the Dome in 1907, but it later found a home at the Dorset Gardens Methodist Church <62,123>. <44,83,108>

208. WHITEHAWK

a) *WHITEHAWK HILL CAMP:* 'White Hawke Hill', which reaches 396 feet above sea-level, was recorded as such in 1587, but has the earliest known inhabited site in Brighton at the Neolithic Camp, one of twelve known causewayed camps of the Neolithic 'Windmill Hill' culture in Britain. Inhabited circa 2700 B.C., the camp, which is a scheduled ancient monument, covers twelve acres and was excavated by the Brighton and Hove Archaeological Club in January 1929, 1932-3, and again in 1935 when Manor Hill was laid out over the site. The whole camp measures 950 feet north to south and 700 feet east to west, and has four concentric ditches, the innermost three feet deep and the outermost seven feet deep, which are interrupted by numerous causeways. Among the finds were decorated pots, flint instruments and human skeletons, now exhibited in Brighton Museum, but found amongst the animal bones were some charred human bones, suggesting that the inhabitants may have been cannibals. The ditches of the camp may still be seen, centred on the junction of Manor Hill and Whitehawk Hill Road. <247,248>

b) *HISTORY and DEVELOPMENT:* From the late eighteenth century the main attractions of the area were the races run on Whitehawk Down (renamed Race Hill), and the associated White Hawk Fair which was held from 1791 for some years. It was after visiting the fair one day that Editha Elmore, daughter of the squire of Woodingdean, disappeared. She was later said to haunt the area as the 'White Hawk Lady' leaving a cloven footprint behind, but her spirit was not seen again after 1807 when a woman's bones were found <6>. Whitehawk Hill was also the site of a telegraphic station from at least the early nineteenth century, and is now the site of the town's main television and radio transmitter (see "Broadcasting") <108>.

Whitehawk Bottom formed the eastern limit of the parish of Brighton, the boundary running along the former course of Whitehawk Road (including Haybourne Road), but when the East Brighton estate was purchased in September 1913 the area now occupied by the Whitehawk housing estate became corporation property and it became part of the county borough itself on 1 April 1928 when Ovingdean parish was annexed. The south-westernmost part of Whitehawk Road was developed in the early 1880s, but Whitehawk Bottom contained only a few farm buildings, piggeries, allotments and playing fields until the late 1920s when the corporation erected houses along the western side of Whitehawk Road and in Hervey Road and Whitehawk Crescent. The large council estate was then developed in 1933-7 with nearly 1,200 houses, all with large gardens for growing vegetables but none with garages. Private housing was added near Wilson Avenue post-war, and the corporation's Swanborough flats opened in 1967. In 1981 the population of Whitehawk (together with Manor Farm) was nearly 8,000. <2,83,109,277,305>

In 1975 the rebuilding of Whitehawk and its drab housing began. By radically altering road alignments, many small cul-de-sacs have been created in the Whitehawk Crescent and Whitehawk Avenue areas, increasing the number of houses but making the estate more attractive; the scheme involved 1,440 new houses. By 1988 redevelopment south of Lintott Avenue was complete and work was proceeding on large areas to the north, but financial restrictions had slowed down the project somewhat. A major new road, Whitehawk Way, has been constructed along the line of Whitehawk Avenue and Fletching Road, and a new park has been laid out over Lintott Avenue. <123>

c) *BUILDINGS:* St Cuthman's Church was originally erected in Lintott Avenue in 1937, but was destroyed on 16 August 1943 by a German bomb with a churchwarden buried alive. The new church was built in 1951-2 <83,311>. The church hall was sold to the community association in 1982 to become the Valley Social Centre. St David's Mission Hall, still standing at the junction of Whitehawk Road and Whitehawk Way, was used before the church opened, and was later used by the Whitehawk and Manor Farm Boys' Club <83>. The Catholic Church of St Louis, King of France, opened on 20 December 1964 in Modern style at Henley Road, but as it was constructed of high-alumina cement it was later declared unsafe and closed in October 1982 to be replaced by a block of flats, Henley Court, in 1985-6 <56,123>.

Whitehawk Library opened in 1934 in a building in front of Whitehawk Primary School in Whitehawk Road, but it was eventually required for classrooms and a temporary library was established at Rugby House, Rugby Place, in August 1969. A new community centre and library, the largest of the town' s branches, was opened by Princess Alexandra on 9 November 1973 in Whitehawk Road; the toy 'library' was opened by Dame Flora Robson three weeks later. <123,311>

Stanley Deason School opened in Wilson Avenue in 1976; the community sports hall and squash courts were added in 1984. <123>

For details of Roedean Road see "Roedean".

d) *EAST BRIGHTON PARK and SHEEPCOTE VALLEY:* Whitehawk has the advantage of lying between the open spaces of the Race Hill and East Brighton Park off Wilson Avenue. Covering 60.67 acres in the

Black Rock Valley, the land occupied by East Brighton Park was acquired by the corporation in September 1913 as part of the East Brighton estate of 1,065 acres, then part of Ovingdean parish. The southernmost part alongside Roedean Road was once the playing field of the forerunner of Roedean School and was later used by East Brighton Golf Club, but in 1925 the park was excavated, levelled, and laid out with ornamental plantings, tennis courts, football pitches and a cricket square. From September 1923 about twenty-five acres were leased to Brighton College, but financial problems caused much of this area to be returned and in 1947 the Enclosed Football Ground, the home of Whitehawk Football Club (see below), was hedged in on part of the former college playing fields. A large children's playground was constructed in 1987. <126,204,208,305>

To the north of the park lies the Municipal Camping and Caravan Ground, the first municipal ground in the country, which was opened by the mayor, Herbert Hone, on 14 May 1938. It incorporates the buildings of the former Newhouse Farm; the farmhouse is used as the warden's residence, the flint barn as a hall, and the stables as a toilet block; they probably date from the late eighteenth century. However, the caravan park is to close by March 1991 to make way for a large leisure development. <108,123,124,126>

The northern part of the Black Rock Valley is known as Sheepcote Valley, and from the 1870s was the site of a rifle-range laid out for volunteer soldiers, giving the former Rifle Butt Road its name. In 1916 the tipping of scavengings commenced, and in 1928 household refuse from Rottingdean was dumped at Sheepcote; in 1952 large scale tipping by Brighton Corporation commenced and continued until April 1982. The valley has now been significantly filled and levelled for use as playing fields, but a 'household waste site' remains for bulky household rubbish. A golf driving-range was operated in 1982-4, but the whole area is scheduled for a large leisure development including dry ski-slopes, a boating lake, riding stables, a sports hall, a wildlife park, a hotel and a swimming-pool. In about 1968 the desolate area was used as a battlefield in the filming of *Oh! What a Lovely War*. <114,123>

e) *WHITEHAWK FOOTBALL CLUB:* The premier football club actually playing within the boundaries of Brighton was founded in 1945 as Whitehawk and Manor Farm Old Boys F.C. and initially competed in the Brighton League, but after winning the Sussex Senior Cup in 1951 the club was elevated to the Sussex County League (SCL) in 1952. The team achieved consistent success in the 1950s and early '60s, finishing out of the top six only once from 1953 until 1964, but they have been relegated twice since, in 1967 and 1977, although promotion was gained after one year and four years respectively. Many trophies have been won, and there have been several successes at junior, intermediate and youth levels as well. In 1960 the club became simply Whitehawk Football Club and opened a new clubhouse in September 1980. <123,216,217>

The club has achieved the following honours:

1949	Sussex Junior Cup winners
1950	Sussex Intermediate Cup winners
1951	Sussex Senior Cup winners
	Brighton Charity Cup winners
1952	Sussex Junior Cup winners
1955	Sussex RUR Cup winners
1959	Sussex RUR Cup winners
	Brighton Charity Cup winners
1961	SCL Div.1 Invitation Cup winners
	Brighton Charity Cup winners
1962	Sussex Senior Cup winners
	SCL champions
1964	SCL champions
1968	SCL Div.2 champions
1970	SCL Div.1 Invitation Cup winners
1981	SCL Div.2 champions
	SCL Div.2 Cup winners
1982	Brighton Charity Cup winners
1983	SCL Challenge Cup winners
	Worthing Charity Cup winners
	Brighton Charity Cup winners
	Norman Wingate Trophy winners
1984	SCL champions
1987	Norman Wingate Trophy winners
1988	Brighton Charity Cup winners
1990	Brighton Charity Cup winners

209. Amon and Amon Henry WILDS

<45a,46,311>

Two of the leading architects and builders of Regency Brighton. Born in 1762, Amon Wilds established his building firm at Lewes with his son Amon Henry (born c.1790), but in about 1815 they moved to Lewes Road, Brighton. Their first major work in the town was the Trinity Chapel in Ship Street in 1817 for Thomas Read Kemp, and two years later they were commissioned by Kemp again to build him a new residence, The Temple, off Montpelier Road. The Wilds partnership also developed Richmond Terrace.

It appears that the son did most of the architectural design work, and that Wilds senior was principally a builder. In 1822 however, Amon Wilds, who lived at 9 Richmond Terrace, entered into partnership with architect Charles Busby while his son established his own business. Wilds and Busby then proceeded to build both the Kemp Town and Brunswick estates, and many of the other finest houses in the town, particularly on the East Cliff. Again, Wilds was concerned with building and Busby with design. Other Wilds and Busby work probably includes the Gothic House (Debenhams) in Western Road; 87 London Road; the former Elim Church in Union Street; and many houses in Marine Parade, Marine Square, Portland Place, Regency Square and St George's Place.

Amon Wilds died on 12 September 1833 aged 71 and is buried in the eastern part of St Nicholas's churchyard, his prominent tomb being decorated with shell motifs and probably designed by his son. Charles Busby, who was born in 1788, published several books of architec-

Figure 190: The tomb of Amon Wilds in St Nicholas's churchyard

tural designs and spent seven years in the U.S.A. He lived at 11 Waterloo Place before moving to Lansdowne Place, Hove, in 1830, but he died on 18 September 1834 and is buried at St Andrew's Church, Hove.

Amon Henry Wilds continued to design many of the finest buildings to be seen in the town today, including the Western Pavilion for his own residence in about 1828. He later moved to 8 Western Terrace, to the nearby Gothic House (Debenhams), to 5 Western Terrace, and in 1848 to the Western Pavilion again. He retired in the 1850s and died in 1857 at Shoreham. Among his many works may be numbered Cavendish Place; Park Crescent; Sillwood Place; Waterloo Place; the Royal Albion Hotel; St Alban's House; Sillwood House; the Unitarian Church; the Royal Newburgh Assembly Rooms; and the Victoria Fountain.

Distinctive features of A.H.Wilds's work are shell motifs and the spiral 'ammonite' capitals which were probably a pun on the name 'Amon'. They were first used by the Wilds partnership at Castle Place, 166 High Street, Lewes. In Brighton they may be found at Hanover Crescent; Montpelier Crescent; 53-56 Montpelier Road; 26 Old Steine; Oriental Place; 40-44 Preston Street; on the northern side of the Queen's Hotel; 7 Richmond Terrace; Western Terrace; and also as an exhibit in Brighton Museum.

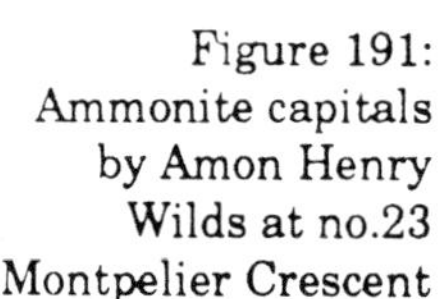

Figure 191: Ammonite capitals by Amon Henry Wilds at no.23 Montpelier Crescent

210. King WILLIAM IV

<3,194>

George IV's brother William visited Brighton many times as the Duke of Clarence before succeeding to the throne in 1830, but he made his first official visit as King on 30 August 1830 when a triumphal floral arch fifty feet high was erected at the northern entrance to the Royal Pavilion. William IV enjoyed Brighton very much, staying in the town every year during his reign, and with Queen Adelaide would often stroll along the Chain Pier, ride to Rottingdean, and walk through the Kemp Town gardens and slopes. He also further developed the Royal Pavilion and grounds, officially redesignating it the 'Royal Palace, Brighton'.

Figure 192: The North Gate of the Royal Pavilion, built in 1832 for William IV. On the left is North Gate House.

211. WINDMILLS

<10,249-253>

Brighton has had many windmills over the centuries, but now only two survive and the locations and dates of many others are far from certain. The first known were the two mills that stood on Church Hill (the Dyke Road ridge) and were recorded in a drawing of the town of 1545, but they may not be the two town mills referred to in the Book of Ancient Customs of 1580, one of which was 'utterly decayed'. By the late 1570s another mill was described in the Little Laine near the cliff top to the east of the town, and by the late seventeenth century there were still two town mills plus three mills in the Little Laine. Two mills were known to have been destroyed by the great storm of 1703, and although three mills remained in the Little Laine for most of the eighteenth century, by 1801 a survey listed only two windmills at Brighton. Now only Rottingdean and Waterhall windmills stand within the borough, but Jill Mill at Clayton was removed from Belmont (which was situated in the parish of Hove at that time) in the 1850s.

For details of individual mills consult the index entry on "windmills". See also figure 193.

212. WITHDEAN

a) *HISTORY:* The first record of Withdean, 'Wihta's valley', dates from the early twelfth century when it was referred to as 'Wictedene'. The hamlet by the London Road formed part of the parish of Patcham, but by the eighteenth century enclosures and the concentration of land had resulted in its depopulation and the establishment of a single farm. The manor of Withdean was the property of St Pancras's Priory at Lewes until 1537 and was granted to Anne of Cleves in 1541, but in 1794 the manorial estates of Withdean Kayliffe and Withdean Court were purchased from the Western family by William Roe. Over the next fifty years or so Roe and his family planted many of the trees that today give Withdean its attractive wooded prospect, in addition to plantations at Varndean that existed by 1750. (Withdean Woods, 6.62 acres between Wayland Avenue and Withdean Road, were acquired by the corporation in December 1938 to limit housing development <126>, but many of the area's trees were uprooted by the storm of October 1987.) <1,76,254,255,289>

By the middle of the nineteenth century the hamlet consisted of Withdean Farm, Withdean Court, and a number of farm houses and outbuildings grouped

Figure 193: View from Race Hill in about 1850, showing three windmills on Albion Hill, three more on the Dyke Road ridge, and the Hanover Mill in the near distance. See "Windmills".

around the bottom of Peacock Lane and Tongdean Lane, but the only remaining buildings now are Home Farmhouse, and Karibu and Tabora. The latter stand on the western side of London Road, listed farm houses of around 1800 faced in flint and now divided into two cottages with the single-storey Tabora Forge nearby. Home Farmhouse, almost opposite, is also an early-nineteenth-century listed building, faced in knapped and squared flint. (See also "London Road, Patcham".) <44>

The manor house was known as Withdean Court and stood on the site of the present bog-garden of Withdean Park in Peacock Lane. In the 1860s the name was transferred to a large new residence on the other side of London Road where Regency Court now stands and the older house then became known as the Old Court House, but it was demolished in 1936. Withdean Court is now the name of five blocks of flats erected in 1937 at Varndean Road with tennis-courts, ornamental pond, rockery and cascade. The site of Withdean Farm, demolished in about 1934, is now occupied by Bourne Court. <76,254,255>

From 1853, William Roe's heiress Elizabeth Ogle began to sell land in London Road to the south of Withdean for development, encouraged by the removal in May 1854 of the turnpike tollgate from Preston to a hundred yards north of Withdean. A number of large Victorian and Edwardian villas were erected, only three of which now survive: at Towergate; St Bernadette's School; and at Withdean Hall, Varndean Road; see "London Road, Patcham" for details. Withdean Baptist Chapel stood on a site to the south of Tongdean Lane, between London Road and the railway, during the late nineteenth and early twentieth centuries. <83,109,254>

Surrenden Road, exceptionally wide and beautifully lined with trees, was laid out in 1875 (although the Preston part was not completed until 1894) as an equestrian ride from Preston Park to Ditchling Road, but only one nineteenth century house was built in the road, Mount Harry on the site of Surrenden Holt. In Edwardian times several large villa residences were erected of which only no.66 remains, but other large houses were erected in the same period at Dyke Road Avenue and Withdean Road. <109,126,254>

The Withdean area on both sides of the valley was greatly developed in the late 1920s and '30s with suburban semi-detached and detached housing. Since then a number of blocks of flats have been built on the sites of many large residences, with small scale housing at the Varndean Park estate and on the eastern side of Surrenden Road. <83,254,255>

There were also two other settlements that formed part of the Withdean estate:

b) *ROEDALE:* Probably named from William Roe himself, Roedale Cottages stand in the woods opposite Hollingbury Copse adjacent to a latter-nineteenth-century, restored flint barn. Lower Roedale was once known as the Roedale Model Dairy Farm and still has two early-nineteenth-century flint cottages at the northern end of Stanmer Villas; they are now used by the Parks and Recreation Department and an associated mid-nineteenth-century house stands nearby; the corporation's Roedale Nursery lay to the east until the 1950s. Upper Roedale, along the road to the golf clubhouse opposite Woodbourne Avenue, was established at about the same time and is now used as a storage and maintenance area with one old building remaining. <107,123,126>

c) *VARNDEAN:* The other small farm established in the early nineteenth century was Varndean, although the name dates from the thirteenth century <76,289> and the plantations of trees date from around 1750. A flint barn, now partly restored in brick and used as a maintenance store, remains along with three cottages in Stringer Way; no.2 Varndean Cottages retains its flint façade. The late-nineteenth-century brick and flint farmhouse, Varndean Holt, stands in the woods to the west. <109>

Figure 194: Home Farmhouse, Peacock Lane, Withdean

The land around Varndean was purchased by Brighton County Borough Council's Education Committee in about 1909, and the area is now known for the five schools in the vicinity. Varndean High School was opened in 1926 by the Duchess of Atholl to replace the York Place Girls' School, while Varndean Sixth-Form College was the boys' municipal secondary school, opened on 2 March 1931 by Viscount Hailsham to replace the Pelham Street Boys' School; both later became grammar schools. The other schools are Dorothy Stringer High (opened 1955), Balfour Road Junior (opened 1924), and Balfour Primary. The Surrenden Pool opened in 1972. <123,124,210,305>

d) *WITHDEAN PARK:* Covering thirty-eight acres, Withdean Park is one of the most beautiful of Brighton's parks, carefully laid out with ornamental shrubs and flowers. Originally farm land, the park site was acquired by the corporation in July 1933 to prevent its development, chiefly through the efforts of Sir Herbert Carden. The buildings at the bottom of Peacock Lane, including the old manor house, were demolished in 1936, but the new park was kept in an informal state until the Second World War when it was given over for food production. After the war it was initially used as allotments before reverting to parkland, and a long debate followed over its future use with suggestions that a school should be built. However, from 1960 Withdean Park has been developed as a horticultural exhibit of specific genera, especially *Berberis*, *Cotoneaster*, *Viburnum*, and floribunda roses, with new varieties added as they become available. The park is also famous for its collection of lilacs, the second largest in the world with over 250 types, and has been designated by the National Council for the Conservation of Plants and Gardens as the National Reference Collection for the species and cultivars of the genus *Syringa* (lilacs).

A delightful bog-garden with two lily-ponds has been laid out in a natural bowl near the south-western corner, on the site of the manor house. However, the great storm of October 1987 devastated the park's trees, and virtually wiped out the neighbouring woodland which had stood since at least the mid nineteenth century when it was planted by the Roe family of Withdean.
<76,123,124,126>

213. WITHDEAN STADIUM, Tongdean Lane

<26,27,123,126>

Brighton's premier sporting venue occupies the site of the Marshall's Playing Fields which were used for many years by Brighton Technical College. The stadium was originally developed as a tennis centre by the Lawn Tennis Association. The centre court was laid out between an open seating area and the grandstand, which had room for over 2,000 spectators. Beyond this were many other tennis-courts, and the development also included four squash-courts and a small zoo <123>. Opening in 1936, it was recognised as the finest tennis centre outside Wimbledon and was set to host the South of England Championships until the war intervened. The Davis Cup match between Great Britain and New Zealand was held at Withdean in the spring of 1939.

During the war the stadium was used as a mortuary, but on 22 May 1947 it was relaunched as the Brighton Olympic Stadium, still principally concerned with tennis but with the zoo expanded and a miniature railway installed. However, this venture proved to be unprofitable and closed in 1952. Brighton Council opted to convert the stadium into an athletics arena at a cost of £28,000, and on 14 May 1955 the mayor, Walter Dudeney, formally opened the Brighton Sports Arena;

floodlights were added in August 1956. The stadium has now played host to numerous different events and sports including athletics, circuses, floodlit cricket, regular horse shows until 1962, scout jamborees, displays, and football (association, rugby and American). In October 1962 an England athletics international was held there.

Withdean Stadium covers an area of 15.15 acres and has its own public house, the Withdean Sportsman, which is owned by the corporation. The grandstand is now unfortunately dilapidated but the words 'Withdean Zoo' may still just be made out on the façade. Extra squash-courts were added in the 1970s, and on 20 September 1980 Olympic champion Steve Ovett inaugurated an all-weather running track. On 1 April 1988 an indoor tennis centre was opened which it is hoped will make Withdean a major centre for the sport once more; several outdoor courts have also been added. The record attendance for any event at the stadium was established on 8 December 1985 when 12,000 people saw an American football match between the Brighton B52s and the City College of San Francisco.

214. WOODINGDEAN

a) *HISTORY and BUILDINGS:* The original Woodingdean House stood on the northern side of Ovingdean Road from at least the late eighteenth century until the 1950s when it was replaced by the houses of Ovingdean Close, but several flint cottages and outbuildings of the farm remain which were converted in 1985-6 into housing known rather anonymously as Meadow Vale. <83,108,109,123>

The Woodingdean housing estate, known as the Downs Estate until about 1927, occupies an area to the north-east of the old farm. Prior to the 1920s the Warren Farm Schools (see below) and Wick Farm in Falmer Road (recorded in 1296 <289>), together with a few isolated houses and barns, were the only buildings in the area, but from the mid '20s plots were sold piecemeal and developed with shacks, bungalows and detached houses. The farm and estate were located in the Balsdean chapelry of Rottingdean parish.

When the area became part of Brighton county borough on 1 April 1928, local services and planning regulation improved and brought about a rapid increase in building. That part of the estate to the north of Warren Road on Wick Farm land was completed in the 1930s, but piecemeal development to the east of Falmer Road continued into the '60s. The corporation also developed housing estates, at South Woodingdean in the early '50s and the North Woodingdean estate later in the decade, such that the population of the district is now something just over 10,000. Woodingdean industrial estate opened from 1961. <83,108,277>

The Church of the Holy Cross, Warren Road, is a single-storey building in yellow brick which was erected in 1968 on the site of a simple structure completed in 1941. A second Anglican chapel, the Church of the Resurrection, was designed by John Wells-Thorpe and dedicated on 15 June 1959. However, it was later taken over by the Roman Catholic Church and is now St Patrick's R.C.Church, Broad Green. Woodingdean Methodist Church, The Ridgway, dates from 1953 but was greatly extended in 1986. The Downs Free Church, Downsway, was built in about 1932 with a more recent extension at the rear. <83,123,311>

Woodingdean Library first opened at 48 Warren Road on 2 May 1940 and moved to the Warren Farm School building in about 1952. The permanent library was opened on 10 July 1959 by the mayor, Ernest

Figure 195: St Patrick's Roman Catholic Church, Broad Green, opened in 1959 as the Anglican Church of the Resurrection

Kippin. The swimming-pool at the adjacent school opened in 1977. Central Woodingdean Park covers 5.7 acres off Lockwood Crescent and was grassed in 1970, with the bowling-green and tennis-courts following in 1972-3, and the pavilion and car-park in 1974. The Happy Valley Park in Falmer Road has 11.37 acres of woods and playing fields which were levelled in the 1950s and '60s. <123,124,126>

Part of the land of Warren Farm was later used for the Lawn Memorial Park, developed in 1962 on 9.5 acres off Warren Road. The gravestones are laid flat to preserve the external appearance as a park and to allow for easy mowing. Opened on 1 January 1963, this is now the principal cemetery in Brighton for new burials. It includes 311 interments removed from the Quaker's burial ground in Rifle Butt Road in 1972. <126>

Laughton Road, on the north-eastern edge of the estate, is the highest road in Brighton at 575 feet above sea-level; 13-15 Laughton Road are the highest houses. Falmer Road is the borough's highest main road at 535 feet, and also has the highest numbered house, no.576. <83,109>

b) *WARREN FARM SCHOOLS:* The most historic building remaining in Woodingdean is the former school building in Warren Road. It was originally erected on twenty acres of Rottingdean parish by the Brighton Board of Guardians as an industrial school for poor children whom it was not considered appropriate to keep in the workhouse with adults. Known as the Warren Farm Industrial Schools, construction commenced in March 1859 to the design of parish surveyor George Maynard, and the building was completed on 1 December 1859 with accommodation for 300 children. In March 1858 a well was started, but water was not reached until 16 March 1862 by which time a depth of 1,285 feet had been reached, the deepest dug well in the world. It was only when the water supply was ready that the buildings were opened, and on 14 August 1862 seventy-seven boys and sixty-five girls marched in procession from the Dyke Road workhouse to Warren Farm. In 1878, however, the well was abandoned in favour of the corporation's piped water supply.

The boy inmates were taught skills in gardening, tailoring and bootmaking, etc., while girls were instructed in domestic service. The Warren Farm Industrial Schools continued until the replacement of the workhouse system in 1930 and then continued as a children's home until the early '50s. In 1937 infant and junior schools were also opened in the buildings. After the children left, the buildings were used for miscellaneous purposes including civil defence, the branch library and manufacturing, but in about 1955 they were taken by the St John the Baptist Roman Catholic School which moved from Upper Bedford Street, and were later renamed the Fitzherbert R.C.Secondary School; the school closed in 1987.

The main building, which is a rather plain edifice, is now included on the council's local list of buildings of interest. In 1989 the conversion of the building to a sponsored 'city technology college' for around 800 11- to 18-year-olds outside the authority of the county council commenced. Michael Faraday College, which was to be one of the first of its kind in the country, teaching subjects according to the Steiner principles and with an emphasis on environmental issues, was, however, abandoned in April 1990 because of a lack of finance, leaving the buildings' future in some doubt. The four blocks of houses to the east were built in 1911-12 by the guardians and are now used as offices and clinics. <6,24,83,115,123>

215. WORKHOUSES

a) *EAST STREET:* The first record of a poor-house at Brighton dates from 1690 when a tenement in East Street was set aside for the purpose, as required by the Poor Law Act. Nothing else is known of its history, though. <7>

b) *MARKET STREET:* Encouraged by Knatchbull's 1723 Workhouse Act authorising the enforcement of labour on the poor in return for relief, the Brighton parochial officers erected a new poor-house on the western side of Market Street in 1727, a building that came to be known as the Town Hall. It took in the sick, the aged, and poor children, and the inmates were expected to make their own clothes and prepare their own food. The building could accommodate about thirty-five people and included a kitchen, workroom, pantry, brew-house, two cellars and bedrooms; it also housed the town scales and a dungeon for wrong-doers. In 1733 a portion of the adjoining almshouses, which were built at the Reformation on the site of St Bartholomew's Chapel, was added to the workhouse.

As the town grew so the number of poor increased, and the workhouse was enlarged again in 1800 to accommodate 150 inmates, all of whom were given brown uniforms to wear. The 1810 Brighton Town Act passed responsibility for poor-law to thirty 'Directors and Guardians of the Poor' and they soon made certain 'improvements' to the workhouse diet in the interest of economy. However, by the 1820s the building was too small for its purpose and it was demolished in 1823 by the town commissioners. <6,7,14,112>

c) *CHURCH HILL:* A larger workhouse was built in 1821-2 on a fourteen-acre site to the north of St Nicholas's Church. Designed by William Mackie, it had accommodation for 600 inmates and cost £11,400. The building had a frontage of 191 feet, and included a kitchen, wash-house, brew-house, bake-house, laundry, a separate infirmary, and large garden; over the doorway a tablet proclaimed 'Brighthelmstone Poor House erected A.D. 1821'. It was opened in September 1822 with a procession of ninety-five inmates from the old workhouse.

The 1834 Poor Law Amendment Act abolished 'outdoor relief' in an effort to cut the number of poor-law dependents, and introduced extremely harsh regimes in the workhouse to discourage all but the totally destitute from applying for relief. Brighton was otherwise largely unaffected by the Act and was not united with any other parish. However, the numbers of poor in the town grew steadily and by 1851 there were 440 inmates. It was obvious that another building would be required, and when the new workhouse opened at Elm Grove in 1867 the Church Hill site was sold for development and the large villas of Albert Road, Alexandra Villas, Alfred Road, Buckingham Road, Dyke Road and Leopold Road were erected. <6,7,14,112>

In August 1862 an industrial school opened at Warren Farm for the workhouse children. See "Woodingdean (Warren Farm Schools)".

d) *ELM GROVE:* The new parish workhouse and infirmary was built by George Maynard on seven acres of land purchased in 1854, but the cost of construction, £41,118, was mostly offset by the sale of the Church Hill workhouse and grounds. The foundation stone was laid on 11 May 1865 by Lieutenant-Colonel Robert Moorsom, chairman of the local board of guardians, but the buildings were not finished until June 1867 after considerable delay. The principal building, facing north-west above Elm Grove, has a frontage of 318 feet and stands 50 feet high with a central clock tower which bears the date 1866. At the rear was the infirmary with a chapel on the top floor.

The first inmates were accepted on 12 September 1867 and the change-over took ten days. Accommodation for 861 people was available, and the facilities included the workhouse proper, an infirmary with several wards, a chapel, laundry, and casual wards for temporary relief. Water was taken from the Warren Farm well until 1878, and a cesspit was used until the building was connected to the Lewes Road sewer in about 1876. The workhouse was extended when new casual wards opened in April 1887, and two new infirmary blocks (now facing Pankhurst Avenue) opened in July 1891 with a third block opening at the rear in 1898. Professional nurses were introduced by 1902, but did not have a permanent home until 1929.

From March 1871 regulations were issued by the national Poor Law Board and the workhouse was inspected weekly by the guardians' visiting committee. A harsh regime was maintained in order to discourage people from applying for parish relief, and those that did were made to wear the workhouse uniform; men were issued with grey suits and were set to work breaking stones, while the women wore blue and white striped dresses, and picked oakum (tarred rope). The inmates were allowed one outing during the summer, and one at Christmas to visit a pantomime.

In early 1914 Brighton Workhouse was renamed the Brighton Poor Law Institution, but shortly afterwards the building was offered to the military as a hospital and the 1,050 inmates were evacuated to large houses in Brighton and Hove, and to other institutions in the county. The 'Kitchener Hospital' opened in January 1915 and was used until April 1916 for wounded Indian soldiers and then for British troops. It was handed back to the guardians in July 1920, reopening as the Poor Law Institution, but on 1 April 1930 the Brighton Board of Guardians was replaced by the county borough council's public assistance committee as the workhouse system was brought to an end and a more liberal regime was introduced to dispel the old workhouse atmosphere; only the aged and infirm were then accommodated in the Poor Law Institution which became known as the Elm Grove Home. On 1 November 1935 the Brighton Municipal Hospital was established and took over most of the buildings, and it took over the whole site in 1939-40 with the remaining dependents evacuated once again to various establishments in the county. In 1948 the buildings became Brighton General Hospital upon the establishment of the National Health Service (see "General Hospital"). <95,296a>

216. WORLD WARS

a) *FIRST WORLD WAR:* Although the U.K. entered the Great War on 4 August 1914, the summer season at Brighton continued in full swing and it was not until the first casualties arrived in the town about a month later that the reality of the conflict hit the inhabitants. The Royal Pavilion estate, the Poor Law Institution and several schools were then given over to the military for use as hospitals, and the town was also filled by many Londoners who left the city to avoid possible zeppelin raids. Women played a major part in keeping the town running while the men were at the front, but Brighton was largely unaffected otherwise and the holiday seasons continued relatively normally. On 7 October 1922 Earl Beatty unveiled the Brighton War Memorial in Old Steine. It bears the names of 2,597 men and 3 women of the town who fell in the Great War. <3,115>

b) *SECOND WORLD WAR:* The war of 1939-45 had a much greater effect on Brighton than that of 1914-18, and air-raid precautions began before war was declared on 3 September; a general blackout was enforced over the south of England in August 1939 and shelters were dug in school playgrounds and parks. Brighton's art and museum treasures were removed to the safety of the countryside. In an uneasy initial period all entertainments were stopped for a couple of weeks but were later allowed to continue with suitable precautions taken. Anti-aircraft guns and searchlights were set up along the sea-front, but there was no sign at Brighton of the impending 'Battle of Britain' until 10 May 1940 when a badly shot-up sea-plane made a forced landing on the beach. With the threat of a German invasion looming, the beaches were closed at 5 p.m. on 2 July 1940, and were duly mined and guarded with barbed-wire; the two piers had sections demolished to prevent their use as enemy landing stages. Brighton was declared to be no longer a 'safe area' and the 30,000 evacuees in the town were then re-evacuated to other areas, together with local children. <123>

The first raid on Brighton came on 15 July 1940 when Kemp Town was bombed, and was followed by several others that month, mainly over Whitehawk and Kemp Town. At 3.30 p.m. on 14 September 1940 twenty bombs fell on Kemp Town; four children and two adults were killed when the Odeon Cinema in St George's Road received a direct hit and another forty-nine died in the surrounding area.

On 26 March 1941 the south coast was declared a 'defence zone' and no visitors were allowed into the area. That summer the whole conurbation was surrounded by barbed-wire fences in order to prevent a mass panic 'escape' of the population in the event of intensive bombing or invasion, thereby avoiding the resulting undermining of military operations. However, although facilities such as the Kemp Town tunnel were available on a temporary basis, an acute shortage of suitable air-raid shelters eventually persuaded the War Cabinet to allow the inhabitants to evacuate to London in such circumstances which mercifully never transpired. <123>

Daytime raids continued throughout 1941 and into 1942, and eight people were killed by German fighter-bombers in late 1942. From 17 December 1942 a 9.30 p.m. bus curfew was operated except for night workers, but the following day Rottingdean was hit and the Steyning Road vicarage was destroyed. A direct hit on the Black Rock gas-works resulted in a 300-foot orange flame. The heaviest raid occurred on 25 May 1943 when the town was dive-bombed by German fighters. Twenty-four people were killed and fifty-one seriously injured as the planes strafed pedestrians in the streets, and the London Road viaduct was seriously damaged. In a night raid in September 1943 thousands of incendiary bombs were dropped, destroying part of the railway works and a gas main in London Road. Another raid saw bombs fall in the Pavilion grounds, shaking the Dome walls out of the vertical, but the crater was put to use as a static water tank.

With the course of the war swinging in the Allies' favour the ban on visitors was lifted by 1943, but was reimposed in August and September 1943 and prior to D-Day, 6 June 1944. The last raid on the town was on 22 March 1944, but from 1939 until 1945 Brighton suffered from 1,058 siren warnings; 685 local alarms and 56 actual raids; 381 high explosive bombs were dropped along with numerous incendiary bombs; 198 people were killed, 357 seriously injured and 433 slightly injured; over 200 houses were destroyed, 894 seriously damaged and 14,232 slightly damaged. The worst hit areas were Albion Hill; the area between Carlton Hill and Edward Street; Essex, Hereford and Montague Streets; the Chichester Place area; Bennett Road and Rugby Place; and Preston village. Fortunately, few of the architecturally distinguished buildings were destroyed, these being three houses in Park Crescent, three in the upper part of Chichester Place and two in Norfolk Square.

Brighton greeted Victory in Europe Day, 8 May 1945, with great celebration. The mayor read a proclamation of victory from the Town Hall balcony to a large and enthusiastic crowd, bonfires were lit on the Downs and beaches, and street parties were held all over the town. Further celebrations were held on Victory in Japan Day, 15 August 1945. <2,242-244>

SOURCES AND BIBLIOGRAPHY

It is impractical to document in the text every single reference for a work of this nature, but the sources (books, manuscripts, etc.) are listed for each entry in the encyclopaedia in angular brackets thus <...>. The following list of sources also serves as a bibliography for the study of the history, geography and functions of the Borough of Brighton; most are available through East Sussex County Libraries, principally Brighton Reference and Lending Libraries, and Lewes Lending Library.

GENERAL:

1. *The Victoria History of the Counties of England - A History of Sussex:* vol. vii *Lewes Rape (*1940). (The most scholarly work, particularly strong on early history, the principal source on outlying parishes, manors and churches.)
2. E.Gilbert *Brighton, Old Ocean's Bauble* (1954). (Very thorough, tracing development of Brighton and health resorts in general.)
3. Clifford Musgrave *Life in Brighton (*1970 and 1980). (Covering all aspects, especially fashionable society.)

HISTORIES:

(The early histories should not be taken as entirely accurate.)

3a. T.Horsfield *The History, Antiquities and Topology of the County of Sussex* Part One (1835). (A thorough work on each each parish.)

3b. J.R.Armstrong *A History of Sussex* (1961).

4. P.Dunvan *Ancient and Modern History of Lewes and Brighthelmston* (1795). (Commonly known as "Lee's History". Contains much on the medieval town which cannot now be substantiated.)
5. A.Relhan *A Short History of Brighthelmston* (1761). (The earliest history and guide.)
6. J.Erredge *History of Brighthelmston* (1862), and:
7. H.Martin *The History of Brighton and Environs* (1871). (Both useful but not entirely accurate.)
8. E.Underwood *Brighton* (1978), and:
9. R.Flower *The Old Ship: A Prospect of Brighton* (1986). (Strong on the town's social life.)
10. J. and S.Farrant *Aspects of Brighton 1650-1800* (1978), and:
11. J. and S.Farrant 'Brighton 1580-1820: Tudor Town to Regency Resort' *Sussex Archaeological Collections. no.118*, and:
12. J.Farrant 'The Rise and Decline of a South Coast Seafaring Town: Brighton 1555-1750' *The Mariner's Mirror* vol. 71 no.1, and:
13. S.Farrant *Brighton before Dr.Russell* (1976), and:
14. S.Farrant *Georgian Brighton 1740-1820* (1981). (Five works by the Farrants which provide a thorough insight into the seventeenth and eighteenth century town, its trade and economy, and its subsequent rise into a fashionable resort.)

'SPECIFIC' HISTORIES:

(The following books contain chapters and articles on specific aspects of the town's history:)

15. J.G.Bishop *A Peep into the Past: Brighton in the Olden Time* (1880 and 1892).
16. G.Aitchison *Unknown Brighton* (1926).
17. F.Harrison *The Story of Brighton, Hove and Neighbourhood* (1931). (Reprinted from the *Brighton Gazette.*)
18. F.Harrison and J.North *Old Brighton, Old Hove, Old Preston* (1937).
19. *The Argus 100: A Century of News* presented with the *Evening Argus* 31 March 1980.

19a. James Walvin *Beside the Seaside* (1978). (A social history of seaside holidays.)

GUIDE BOOKS:

(Many guide books to Brighton have been published since the early nineteenth century. The following are particularly useful.)

20. R.Sicklemore *An Epitome of Brighton* (1815).
21. W.Saunders *The Stranger's Guide to Brighton* (1838).
22. W.Fleet *An Illustrated Handbook of Brighton and its Environs with some account of the Fishery* (1847).
23. 'A graduate of the University of London' *Brighton as it is...* (1860). (Contains, in addition to the usual descriptions, details on the town's 'low-life' and social deprivation.)
24. *W.E.Nash's Guide to Brighton* (1886). (The best Victorian guide book, with detailed perambulations of the town.)
25. *D.B.Friend's (Brighton) Almanack* (1884-1895).
26. Harold P.Clunn *The Capital by the Sea* (1953). (Much detail on the twentieth-century buildings and improvements; the best post-war guide.)

26a. Harold P.Clunn *Famous South Coast Pleasure Resorts, Past and Present* (1929). (The best 1920s guide.)

27. Brighton Corporation Guide Books. (Published from at least 1913, they contain information principally on the resort facilities.)
28. The Brighton Society *Children's Brighton: A Guide for all the Family* (1977).

ACTS OF PARLIAMENT:

(The following important Acts have proved useful, but there have been many other local Acts.)

29. 1773 'Brighton Town' Act.
30. 1810 'Brighton Town' Act.
31. 1825 'Brighton Town' Act.
32. 1855 Brighton Commissioners Transfer Act.
33. 1873 Brighton Borough Extension Act.
34. 1884 Brighton Improvement Act.
35. 1888 Local Government Act.
36. 1896 Brighton Corporation Act.
37. 1900 Brighton Corporation Act.
38. 1923 Ministry of Housing Provisional Order Confirmation (Brighton Extension) Act.
39. 1927 Brighton Corporation Act.
40. 1938 Brighton Corporation (Transport) Act.
41. 1951 Brighton Extension Act.
42. 1968 Brighton Marina Act.
43. 1972 Local Government Act.

ARCHITECTURE AND BUILDINGS:

44. Department of the Environment *List of Buildings of Special Architectural or Historic Interest: Brighton (*August 1971, with numerous amendments). (Great architectural and usually brief historical detail of all listed buildings.)
45. I.Nairn and N.Pevsner *The Buildings of England: Sussex* (1965). (The 'Bible' for all interested in buildings, with architectural detail and information on all interesting examples, including modern.)

45a. Brighton Polytechnic *A Guide to the Buildings of Brighton* (1987). (A valuable introduction to the history and architecture of many public buildings in Brighton, Hove, Lewes and Shoreham. Chapters on the town's development, A. and A.H.Wilds and Busby, and the Wagners.)

45b. Stewart Ullyott *Brighton Rocks* (1986 for the Booth Museum). (Geological details of the stonework on many Brighton buildings.)

46. A.Dale *Fashionable Brighton 1820-1860* (1947). (The best book on the Regency buildings, architects and developers.)

47. A.Dale *About Brighton* (1951 and 1965). (Small but useful guide to the town's architecture, including the outlying parishes.)

48. A.Dale *The History and Architecture of Brighton* (1950).

48a. *Backyard Brighton* Queenspark book no.20 (1988). (A description and recollections of the houses demolished in the slum clearances of the 1930s.)

48b. *Back Street Brighton* Queenspark book no.22 (1989).

49. Brighton Museum *The Buildings of Brighton* (1984-85). (Four cardboard brochures with details of the most interesting buildings.)

BUSES:

50. A.Peasgood *The Horse Buses of Brighton and Hove* (1985).

51. J.Roberts *British Bus and Trolley-Bus Systems: Brighton, Hove and District* (1984). (History of all services within the Brighton area.)

52. *The Southdown Story* (1965).

52a. C.Morris *British Bus Systems: Southdown* (1985).

53. Brighton Corporation *Corporation Passenger Transport 1901-51*.

53a. Alan J.Piatt *Commemorative Brochure celebrating 85 years of Borough Transport Services to the Community of Brighton* (1986).

54. R.Knight (ed.) *Brighton Corporation Transport: Fleet History* (1971). (Details of every tramcar, bus and route operated by the Corporation Transport Department.)

55. D.Kaye and M.Nimmo *The Trolley Buses of Brighton and Hove* (1968).

CHURCHES AND RELIGION:

(The Victoria County History provides details on individual churches, particularly the ancient parish churches. Directories also give much information in their introductory sections. Most churches have published at least brochures, but those listed below have proved most useful.)

56. T.Pugh *The Church of St.John the Baptist, Brighton 1835-1985*. (Includes details on early Catholic missions.)

57. A.F.Day *The Church of St.Nicolas of Myra, Dyke Road, Brighton: A History with some diversions*. (Comprehensive guide to Brighton's mother church and those who are buried there.)

58. S.Clarke 'Restoration of St.Nicholas's Church' *Sussex Archaeological Collections* no.32.

59. *Brighton Parish Church (St.Peter's) Guide*.

60. M.Webb *The History of the Chapel Royal, Brighton* (1977).

61. A.Carson *Union Church, Brighton: A Short History* (1954). (History of the Union Street chapel and the Free Church in Queen Square.)

62. R.Elleray *Victorian Churches of Sussex* (1981). (A comprehensive book with a check-list of all churches from the eighteenth century to the First World War, a description of religious development in Sussex, particularly Anglo-Catholicism, and many photographs.)

62a. R.F.Chambers *The Strict Baptist Chapels of England* Vol.II: *The Chapels of Sussex* (c.1955).

63. F.Harrison 'An Ecclesiastical History of Brighton' *Sussex Archaeological Collections* no.29. (Includes a list of variations of the name 'Brighthelmston'.)

64. J.Sawyer *The Churches of Brighton* (three volumes).

64a. A.Dale *Brighton Churches* (1989).

65. Sir A.Wagner and A.Dale *The Wagners of Brighton* (1983). (Much information on the Wagnerian churches and institutions, and Anglo-Catholicism.)

66. D.SPector *The Jews of Brighton 1700-1900*.

67. 'A Religious Census of Sussex, 1676' *Sussex Archaeological Collections* no.45.

CINEMAS:

68. J.Montgomery 'The Lost Cinemas of Brighton' (1980). (Manuscript in Brighton Reference Library.)

68a. D.Robert Elleray *A Refuge from Reality - The Cinemas of Brighton and Hove (1989).*

68b. 'Hove to Hollywood', exhibition at Hove Museum (1989).

CLIMATE:

(The Corporation has records from the town's weather station, but no modern works have been published.)

71. A.Relhan *A Short History of Brighthelmston, with remarks on its air and analysis of its waters* (1761).

72. W.Kebbell *The Climate of Brighton* (1859).

73. F.Sawyer *The Climate of Brighton* (1877).

COACHING:

69. W.Blew *Brighton and its Coaches: A History of the London and Brighton Road* (1894).

70. S.Farrant 'The Development of Coaching Services from Brighton to London c.1750-1822' *The Sussex Genealogist and Local Historian* March 1986.

CONSERVATION:

70a. Brighton Borough Council Planning Dept. *Conservation Facts* (1989).

CO-OPERATIVES:

74. W.Brown *Brighton's Co-operative Advance 1828-98 with the Jubilee History of the Brighton Equitable Co-operative Society* (1938). (Information on early co-operatives.)

75. Sir William Richardson *The People's Business* (1985). (History of Brighton Co-operative Society and earlier co-operatives.)

DEVELOPMENT:

76. S.Farrant, A.Peasgood and K.Fossey *The Growth of Brighton and Hove 1840-1939* (1981). (Excellent content, especially on the Stanford Estate, public transport and slum housing.)

77. Lewis Cohen Urban Studies Unit *How Brighton Grew*. (Leaflet with map of development periods.)

78. Lewis Cohen Urban Studies Centre *Development of the North Laine area 1770-1820*. (Leaflet.)

DEVIL'S DYKE:

79. E.Ryman *The Devil's Dyke - A Guide* (1984).

80. *The Legend of the Devil's Dyke*. (Cardboard souvenir.)

81. P.Clark *Railways of the Devil's Dyke"* (1976).

82. East Sussex County Library *On the Track of the Devil*. (Leaflet on Dyke Railway footpath.)

DIRECTORIES AND REGISTERS:

83. (Classified street directories are a valuable source of information although they should not be taken as absolutely accurate, especially with regard to dates. The introductory sections are also useful. The following have been used:)

Cobby: 1799.
Button: 1805.
Wright: 1818.
Baxter: 1822.
Swayland and Gill: 1832.
Leppard: 1839; 1843; 1845.
Folthorp: 1848; 1850; 1852; 1854; 1856; 1859; 1861; 1862; 1864.
Taylor: 1854.
Page: 1865; 1866; 1867; 1869-95.
Pike: 1887-1939.
Kelly: 1893-1906; 1913-20; 1922-40; 1947; 1951; 1954; 1956; 1958; 1960; 1962; 1964; 1966; 1968-74.

(Sussex directories are listed in J.Farrant *Sussex Directories 1784 to 1940* (1975).)

83a. Electoral registers of the Borough of Brighton.

FALMER:

84. D.Williams *Falmer Parish Reflections* (1985).

MRS FITZHERBERT:

85. W.Wilkins *Mrs Fitzherbert and George IV* (1905).

86. A.Leslie *Mrs Fitzherbert* (1960).

87. G.Sampson *The Uncrowned Queen: The Story of Maria Fitzherbert* (1971).

88. R.Bogan *Three Wedding Rings for Mrs Fitzherbert of Brighton* (1980).

GHOSTS, LEGENDS AND FOLKLORE:

89. R.Moore *Sussex Ghosts* (1976), and:

90. J.Moore *Sussex Legend and Folklore* (1976). (Both in the *Viewing Sussex* series.)

91. 'The Haunting Tale of Old Strike-a-Light' *The Sussex Genealogist and Local Historian* March 1986.

92. *The Spectre of the (Preston) Manor* (1984).

HOLLINGDEAN:

93. R.Carter *A History of Hollingdean* (1987).

HOSPITALS AND DISPENSARIES:

94. L.Lauste 'The Development of the Hospitals in Brighton and Hove' *Proceedings of the Royal Society of Medicine* vol.65 February 1972. (Principally the dispensaries, the Royal Sussex, and the New Sussex/ Lady Chichester.)

95. J.Gooch *A History of Brighton General Hospital* (1980).

96. *The New Sussex Hospital for Women and Children* (1938).

97. *The New Borough Isolation Hospital* (1898 souvenir brochure).

98. *The Royal Alexandra Hospital for Sick Children 1868-1964: A Short History*.

99. J.Wright 'Hospital for the Indian War Wounded at Brighton' *Sussex Life* November 1968.

HOVE:

100. J.Middleton *The History of Hove" by J.Middleton* (1979).

100a. H.C.Porter *The History of Hove, Ancient and Modern* (1897).

101. K.Hamer *Hove's Architectural Heritage* (1987). (Description of conservation areas.)

101a. Hove Borough Council *Hove: The Official Guide* (1990).

102. Hove Civic Society *Walking about Hove: Brunswick Town*. (Cardboard brochure.)

103. Hove Planning Dept. *Brunswick Town Trail* (1982). (Cardboard brochure.)

LABOUR MOVEMENT:

104. M.Carritt *Brighton, Hove and District Trades Council 1890-1950*.

105. A.Durr *A History of Brighton Trades Council and Labour Movement 1890-1970* (1974).

MAPS AND TERRIERS:

(The oldest known sketch of the town is in the Cotton MSS in the British Museum, depicting the town in 1514 although drawn in 1545. See references 2, 3 and 18.)

106. Budgen's Terrier (1792). (Shows the landholdings in Brighton, the laines and furlongs. See reference 18.)

107. (Tithe maps showing landholdings are held at Lewes by East Sussex County Record Office, and are the most detailed early maps of the outlying parishes:)

Brighton: 1851 (incomplete).
Falmer: 1838.
Hove: 1839.
Ovingdean: 1839.
Preston: 1838.
Patcham: 1841.
Rottingdean: 1838.
Stanmer: 1840.
West Blatchington: 1829.

108. (The following early maps and street plans have proved useful.)

1665: modern sketch by Farrant (see reference 10).
1779: Yeakell and Gardner - street plan of Brighton (2,3,14).
Yeakell and Gardner- survey of Sussex
1788: Budgen (14).
1799: Cobby (14,15,18,141).
1808: Marchant (2,14).

1822: Baxter (14).
1824: Sicklemore (213).
1824-25: Pigott-Smith.
1827: Bruce (2).
1830: Saunders.
1835: Lewis (2).
1841: Wallis.
1852: Saunders.
1854: Taylor.
1856: Saunders.
1867: Pike and Ivimy.

109. Ordnance Survey plans are usually highly accurate, and are held at Brighton Reference Library and the County Record Office. The first edition of the 1-inch map dates from 1811 while 6-inch and 25-inch surveys have been made in c.1875 (also 1:500), c.1900, c.1930 and c.1963.

109a. Map of wards in the Borough of Brighton, in Brighton Reference Library.

MOULSECOOMB:

110. *Moulsecoomb Diamond Jubilee Souvenir* (1981).

110a. Ruby Dunn *Moulsecoomb Days* Queenspark book no.23 (1990).

111. F.Harrison 'Moulsecoomb Place: Historical Notes'. (Typescript in Brighton Reference Library.)

MUNICIPAL ACTIVITIES:

112. A.Dale *Brighton Town and Brighton People* (1976). (Activities of the Vestry and Town Commissioners, taken directly from minute books.)

113. F.May *The Development of Brighton* (1899).

114. W.Attwick *Jubilee of the Brighton Corporation: Review of Fifty Years' Municipal Work* (1904).

115. W.Attwick *Brighton Since the Grant of the Charter, 1854-1929*. (Valuable information on all aspects of municipal enterprise.)

116. R.Baxter and D.Howe 'Municipal activities in Brighton during the past twelve years' *Proceedings of the Institute of Municipal and Corporate Engineers* vol.63 pp.31-76 (1936). (Details on many important municipal projects.)

MUSEUMS AND ART GALLERIES:

117. *Illustrated Guide and Introduction to the Collections in the Art Gallery and Museum, Brighton* (1975).

118. Booth Museum of Natural History Information Sheet No.1.

119. E.J.Bedford 'The Booth Museum of British Birds' *Sussex County Magazine* vol.2 pp.32-35.

120. A.Griffith 'The Booth Collection of British Birds' *Sussex County Magazine* vol.7 pp.730-733 & 802-806.

121. 'E.T.Booth and his Birds' *Sussex County Magazine* vol.8 pp.167-170.

122. 'Booth's Bird Museum at Brighton' *The Lady* 18 August 1968.

122a. English Life Publications Ltd *The Booth Museum of Natural History, Brighton* (1990).

NEWSPAPERS:

(Much information has been taken from contemporary articles in the following newspapers:)

123. *Evening Argus* published 1880 to date.

124. *Sussex Daily News* published 1868-1956.

124a. *Brighton Line* the official newspaper of Brighton Borough Council.

OVINGDEAN:

125. M.Walker *Ovingdean and its Church* (1977).

PARKS:

126. 'Parks and Gardens Department 1975'. (Typescript in Brighton Reference Library with history of all parks and open spaces.)

PATCHAM:

127. S.Farrant *Changes in Brighton and Hove's Suburbs: Preston and Patcham 1841-1871* (1985).

127a. J.E.G.Geddes *Patcham Past and Present*.

128. *South Patcham Parish Magazine* June-August 1986. (Miscellaneous information.)

PHOTOGRAPHS and PRINTS:

128a. Brighton Library collection.

(Many books have been published including the following:)

129. J.Betjeman and J.Gray *Victorian and Edwardian Brighton from old photographs* (1972).

130. J.Gray *Brighton between the Wars* (1976).

131. East Sussex County Library *Brighton in Retrospect* (1974).

132. A.Dale and J.Gray *Brighton Old and New* (1976).

133. J.Montgomery *Brighton Past and Present* (1986).

134. M.John *Bygone Brighton Volume One: Places* (1980).

135. M.John *Bygone Brighton Volume Two: Events* (1980).

135a. D.Robert Elleray *Brighton: A Pictorial History* (1987).

136. A.Elliott *A Portrait of Brighton circa 1911 and Today* (1980).

137. A.Elliott *A Second Portrait of Portslade and Brighton* (1981).

138. A.Elliott *An Early Portrait of the Villages and Hamlets of Brighton and Hove* (1984).

139. E.Scott and A.Payne *Rottingdean in Old Picture Postcards* (1985).

140. J. and J.Ford *Images of Brighton* (1981). (1,217 prints reproduced in miniature with explanatory text.)

141. E.Hollingdale *Old Brighton* (1979). (Prints.)

PIERS:

142. S.Adamson *Seaside Piers* (1977). (The definitive work on British piers.)

142a. C.Bainbridge *Pavilions on the Sea* (1986).

143. T.Mickleburgh *Guide to British Piers* (1979).

144. S.Simes *Description of the Brighthelmston Chain Pier* (1830).

145. J.Bishop *The Brighton Chain Pier: In Memoriam* (1896).

146. *West Pier Trust*. (Leaflet.)

PRESTON:
147. J. and S.Farrant *Preston in the 17th and 18th Centuries* (1975).
148. S.Farrant *Changes in Brighton and Hove's Suburbs: Preston and Patcham 1841-1871* (1985).
149. Preston Manor Guidebook (1985).
150. *The Spectre of the Manor* (1984).
151. 'A Roman Villa at Preston' *Brighton and Hove Archaeologist* 1926.

PRINCE REGENT:
152. R.Fulford *George IV* (1949).
152a. Joanna Richardson *George IV: A Portrait* (1966).

PUBLIC SERVICES AND UTILITIES:
153. R.Hennessey 'Brighton: The Electrical Pioneer' *Sussex Life* no.10.
154. W.Clinch *Brighton's Electricity Supply Municipal Review vol.3* pp.101-103 1932.
155. C.E.G.B. South-East Region *Brighton 'A' Power Station 1904-76: A Souvenir.*
156. E.Hollingdale and J.Thomas 'Brighton Fire-Brigade: A History' (1974). (Typescript in Brighton Reference Library.)
157. Brighton Fire-Brigade *A History and Handbook* (1969).
157a. Preston Circus Fire Station Open Day leaflet (1989).
158. Brighton, Hove and Worthing Gas Company *Portslade Works* (1936).
159. Brighton, Hove and Worthing Gas Company *Co-Partnership Magazine* 1923-49 (quarterly).
160. J.Middleton *Lifeboats and Shipwrecks at Victorian Brighton* (1982).
160a. Jeff Morris *An Illustrated Guide to our Lifeboat Stations* part 3: *Sheerness to Poole* (1988).
161. 'Brighton Lifeboats' *Sussex Life* June 1974.
162. F.Harrison 'Constables and Headboroughs' *Brighton and Hove Archaeologist* 1926.
163. *Brighton Police Centenary 1838-1938.*
164. G.Baines *History of the Brighton Police* (1967).
164a. N.Poulsom, M.Rumble and K.Smith *Sussex Police Forces: A Pictorial History 1836-1986* (c.1987).
165. E.Trory *A Postal History of Brighton 1673-1783* (1953).
165a. 'Brighton Postal History' *Sussex County Magazine* vol.27 pg.466.
166. J.Greenwood *The Posts of Sussex: The Chichester Branch 1250-1840* (1973).
167. J.Carter *History of the Brighton Intercepting and Outfall Sewers Board* (1935).
167a. S.Farrant 'The Drainage of Brighton: Sewerage and Outfall Provision as an Issue in a Famous Seaside Resort c.1840-80' *Sussex Archaeological Collections* no.124.
168. Sir J.Bazalgette 'Report on Brighton Sewerage' (1882).
169. Southern Water Authority *Portobello Long Sea Outfall and Pumping Station*. (Publicity leaflet.)
169a. Southern Water *Brighton Sewers*. (Information brochure provided on sewer visits)
170. J.Middleton *The Lights of Brighton and Hove* (1982).
171. 'Brighton Telephone Service: The First 90 Years' (1972). (Article in Brighton Reference Library.)
172. J.Minns *The Engineerium: A History and Guide* (1980).
173. F.N.Green *The Development of Brighton's Water Supply* (1950).
174. Brighton Corporation Water Dept. *Your Water Supply* (1964).
175. Brighton Corporation Water Dept. *Brighton Water 1872-1972* (1972).

RAILWAYS:
176. B.Cooper *Rail Centres: Brighton* (1981). (Information on stations, branches and the engineering works.)
177. V.Mitchell and K.Smith *Southern Main Lines: Three Bridges to Brighton* (1986), and:
178. V.Mitchell and K.Smith *South Coast Railways: Brighton to Worthing* (1983), and:
179. V.Mitchell and K.Smith *South Coast Railways: Brighton to Eastbourne* (1985). (Principally photographic but with accompanying text and plans.)
180. J.Turner *London, Brighton and South Coast Railway* (1977-79 three volumes).
181. C.Marshall and P.Kidner *A History of the Southern Railway* (1963).
182. A.Gray *The London to Brighton Line 1841-1977.*
182a. Michael Baker *London to Brighton* (1989).
183. M.Searle *Down the Line to Brighton* (1986).
183a. *Sussex History* Vol.1 no.3 Spring 1977.
184. N.Owen *The Brighton Belle* (1972).
185. J.Gairns 'Brighton Locomotive Works' *Railway Magazine* vol.32 (1913).
186. P.Clark *Railways of the Devil's Dyke* (1976).
187. East Sussex County Library *On the Track of the Devil*. (Leaflet about former railway.)
187a. Leslie Oppitz *Sussex Railways Remembered* (1987).
188. A.Jackson *Volk's Railway, Brighton* (1968).
188a. *Volk's Railway, Brighton* - 1883-1983 centenary brochure.
189. C.Volk *Magnus Volk of Brighton* (1971).

ROTTINGDEAN AND BALSDEAN:
190. S.Moens *Rottingdean: The Story of a Village* (1952).
190a. Lewis Cohen Urban Studies Centre *Rottingdean.* (1988 leaflet.)
191. H.Blyth *Smugglers' Village: The Story of Rottingdean.*
192. E.Scott and A.Payne *Rottingdean in Old Picture Postcards* (1985).
193. N.Norris and E.Hockings 'Balsdean Chapel' *Sussex Archaeological Collections* no.91.

ROYAL PAVILION:
194. H.Roberts *The History of the Royal Pavilion, Brighton* (1939). (The definitive work.)
195. C.Musgrave *The Royal Pavilion, Brighton: An Episode in the Romantic* (1959).
196. C.Musgrave *The Royal Pavilion* (1954).
196a. J.Dinkel *The Royal Pavilion, Brighton* (1983).
197. Royal Pavilion Guidebook.
198. J.Bishop *Brighton Pavilion and its Royal Associations* (1884).

199. S.Farrant 'Physical Development of the Pavilion Estate and its Influence on the Town 1785-1823' *Sussex Archaeological Collections* no.120.
200. J.Wright 'Hospital for the Indian War Wounded at Brighton' *Sussex Life* November 1968.

SALTDEAN:
201. D.d'Enno *The Saltdean Story* (1985). (A major work.)
202. K.White *Saltdean* (1984).

SCHOOLS:
(Many schools have produced brochures: the following have proved useful.)
203. East Sussex Education Authority Handbooks
203a. Independent Schools Yearbooks.
204. G.Burstow and M.Whittaker *A History of Brighton College* (1957).
204a. Martin Jones *A Short History of Brighton College* (1986).
205. *Brighton and Hove High School 1876-1952.*
206. G.Haffenden *The Middle Street School, Brighton 1805-1905*
207. D.de Zouche *Roedean School 1885-1955.*
208. *1885-1985 History of Roedean School.*
209. N.Caplan 'Swan Downer's School' *Sussex Notes and Queries* no.17.
210. J.Miller *The York Place - Varndean Story 1884-1984.*
211. J.Farrant 'The Brighton Free School' *Sussex Archaeological Collections* no.122.

SOCIAL LIFE IN BRIGHTON:
(The following books deal mainly with the fashionable social life of the town.)
212. L.Melville *Brighton* (1909).
213. O.Sitwell and M.Barton *Brighton* (1935).

SPORT:
214. J.Vinicombe *Albion* (1978).
215. Brighton and Hove Albion Club Handbooks, numerous editions.
216. P.Willis *A Sussex Non-League Football Annual 1983-84.*
217. Whitehawk Football Club programmes.
218. R.Browning *Golf in Sussex.*
219. P.Smartt *Sussex Golf: The Nineteenth-Century Clubs* (1977).
220. 'East Brighton Golf Club' *Sussex County Magazine* vol.28 pg.71.
221. *The AA Golf Course Guide* (1986).
222. 'Brighton Rugby Club' *Sussex County Magazine* vol.5 pg.106.
223. Sir Home Gordon *Sussex Cricket Club* (1948).
224. G.Washer *A Complete Record of Sussex Cricket Club 1728-1957.*
225. J.Marshall *Sussex Cricket: A History* (1959).
226. *Sussex County Cricket Club, Hove 1872-1972.*
226a. Christopher Lee *From the Sea End: The Official History of Sussex County Cricket Club* (1989).
227. Sussex County Cricket Club handbooks.

STANMER:
228. Stanmer Preservation Society *Stanmer* (1981).
229. C.Yeates *Hovel in the Wood* (1986).
230. 'Stanmer House' *Country Life* vol.71 pp.14-20 2 January 1932.
231. 'Stanmer House' *Sussex County Magazine* vol.4 pg.349.
232. S.Farrant 'The Building of Stanmer House ...' *Sussex Archaeological Collections* no.117.

TELSCOMBE:
233. D.Hardman *Telscombe: A Village in Sussex.*

THEATRES:
234. H.Porter *The History of the Theatre in Brighton from 1774-1885* (1886).
235. A.Dale *The Theatre Royal, Brighton* (1980).
236. R.Gunnell 'The Brighton Gaiety Theatre' *Sussex County Magazine* September 1954.

TRAMWAYS:
237. R.Warmer 'The Brighton Corporation Tramways' *Tramway Review* vol.6 nos.44-47.
238. A.Elliott *A Portrait of the Brighton Trams 1901-39* (1979).
239. *Corporation Passenger Transport 1901-51.*
240. R.Knight (ed.) *Brighton Corporation Transport: Fleet History* (1971). (Details of every tram-car and route.)
240a. Leslie Oppitz *Tramways Remembered - South and South-East England* (1988).

UNIVERSITY:
241. University of Sussex Annual Reports.

WARS:
242. Brighton and Hove Herald *Brighton and Hove in Battledress* (1945). (Includes a map showing the locations of bombs which fell on Brighton and Hove.)
242a. A.Saunders and P.Burgess *Battle over Sussex 1940* (1990).
243. L.Cluett *Brighton and Hove under Fire 1940-44* (1945), and:
244. Brighton and Hove Gazette *Brighton and Hove at War* (1945). (Mainly pictorial.)

WELLESBOURNE:
245. E.Martin 'Brighton's Lost River' *South-Eastern Naturalist* (1915).
246. H.Toms 'The Welesmere Quest' *Sussex County Magazine* no.9 pp.366-368.

WHITEHAWK:
247. E.C.Curwen 'Whitehawk Camp' *Sussex Archaeological Collections* no.71.
248. N.Norris and E.Hoskings 'Whitehwak Camp' *Sussex Archaeological Collections* no.77.

WINDMILLS:
249. F.Bramwell 'The Windmills of Brighton' *Brighton Herald* 6-13 August 1938. (Details of former windmills.)
249a. H.Simmons 'Sussex Windmills' (c.1934 typescript in five volumes in Brighton Reference Library). (Much detail on individual mills with sources.)

249b. H.T.Dawes 'The Windmills and Millers of Brighton' *Sussex Industrial History* no.18 (1989).

250. P.Hemming *Windmills in Sussex.*

251. M.Brunnarius *The Windmills of Sussex* (1979).

252. B.Austen *Windmills of Sussex* (1968).

253. R. and R.McDermott *The Standing Windmills of East Sussex* (1978).

WITHDEAN:

254. S.Farrant *Changes in Brighton and Hove's Suburbs: Preston and Patcham 1841-1871* (1985).

255. S.Farrant 'William Roe of Withdean' *Sussex Archaeological Collections* no.119. (The owner of the Withdean estate from the late eighteenth century.)

MISCELLANEOUS BRIGHTON LOCATIONS:

255a. K.Eastaugh *Havergal Brian: The Making of a Composer* (1976).

256. J.Garratt *Brighton Aquarium 1872-1972.*

257. J.Bishop *Strolls in the Extra-Mural Cemetery* (c.1880 several editions).

258. 'The Story of Hanningtons' *Brighton and Hove Gazette* 29 October 1965.

259. D.Ranger 'Hanover Crescent' (1977 typescript in Brighton Reference Library.)

260. Brighton Museum *Hollingbury Camp* (1983).

261. A.Dale *History of the Kemp Town Gardens* (1964).

261a. Lewis Cohen Urban Studies Centre *Madeira Lift 1890-1990* (1990).

262. L.Robinson *The Lanes of Brighton* (1966).

262a. S.Farrant *The Development of the North Laine.* (One of many useful leaflets published by the Lewis Cohen Urban Studies Centre, 68 Grand Parade.)

262b. G.Mead *Trades of the Black Lands - Norfolk Square, Brighton.* (1989 leaflet from Lewis Cohen Urban Studies Centre.)

263. *A Short Social History of the North Road Slipper Baths* (1985).

263a. Alan F.Hill *Barclays Bank, North Street, Brighton - An Informal History* (1988).

264. C.Musgrave *The Crown, the Ship and the Queen of Watering Places* (1953). (The royal escape, the Old Ship and Nicholas Tettersell.)

265. R.Cooke *The Park Crescent Story* (1983).

266. 'Historical Notes on Brighton Race-Course' (typescript in Brighton Reference Library).

267. B.Pointon *The Royal German Spa at Brighton* (1978).

268. R.Thornburgh *Mahomed's Royal Gymnasium* (1980).

269. H.Walbrook *One Hundred Years of the Royal York* (1919).

270. 'St.Bartholomew's Priory' *Brighton and Hove Archaeologist* 1926.

271. Lord Fraser of Lonsdale *My Story of St.Dunstans.*

271a. Lewis Cohen Urban Studies Centre *Building on Brighton's West Laine c.1779-c.1830.* (Leaflet.)

OTHER MISCELLANEOUS PUBLICATIONS:

272. *The Allen West Story* (1960).

273. C.Webb and A.Wilson *Elizabethan Brighton: The Ancient Customs of Brighthelmston 1580* (1952).

274. B.Austen *Athina B, Brighton* (1980).

275. H.Simmons 'Brighton Breweries' (typescript in Brighton Reference Library).

275a. B.Bannier *Into the Streets and Lanes - A History of the Brighton and Hove Town Mission 1849-1989* (1989).

276. Brighton and Hove Gazette Yearbooks, 1940s and 1950s.

277. Brighton Borough Planning Dept. *Brighton Towards 2000: Draft Borough Plan* (1987). (Miscellaneous information.)

278. L.Laughton 'The Burning of Brighton by the French' *Transactions of the Royal Historical Society* 1916.

279. Census Returns for Sussex 1801-1981.

280. 'The Escape of Charles II' *Sussex Archaeological Collections* no.32.

281. *Who was Harry Cowley?* Queenspark book no.13 (1984).

282. J.Morris (ed.) *Domesday Book: Sussex* (1976).

282a. *A Description of England and Wales* (1770).

283. E.Trory *Brighton and the General Strike* (1975).

283a. British Geological Survey *Geology of the country around Brighton and Worthing* (1988).

284. E.Cresy 'Report to the General Board of Health ...' (1849).

285. 'Report on the Sanitary Condition of the Borough of Brighton' *The Lancet* no.4 pp.747-763 1882.

285a. *Sussex History* no.26 Autumn 1988.

285b. *Sussex History* no.21 May 1986.

286. *Sussex Industrial Archaeology: A Field Guide* (1985).

287. J.Montgomery 'Mods v. Rockers: The Battle of Brighton Beach' (typescript in Brighton Reference Library).

288. Charles Hindley *The Brighton Murder* (1885).

288a. Lord Montagu of Beaulieu *The Brighton Run* (1990).

289. A.Mawer and F.Stenton *The Place Names of Sussex* part 2 (1929).

290. H.Preston *Memories* (1928).

291. N.Griffiths *Shops Book, Brighton 1900-30* Queenspark book no.6 (1978). (Personal recollections with information on street markets.)

292. R.Almond 'Shoreham Airport' *Sussex Industrial History* no.14.

293. I.Margary 'The Development of Turnpike Roads in Sussex' *Sussex Notes and Queries* no.13.

294. L.Whistler *Laughter and the Urn: The Life of Rex Whistler* (1985).

294a. F.Harrison *Historical and Literary Associations of Brighton and Hove.*

REFERENCE BOOKS:

294b. Brian Mitchell *British Historical Statistics* (1988).

295. Brigadier P.Young *A Dictionary of Battles 1816-1976.*

296. *The Dictionary of National Biography.*

296a. Revd W.D.Parish *A Dictionary of the Sussex Dialect* (1875 and 1957).

296a. R.Cootes and L.Snellgrove *Britain Since 1700* Longman Secondary History Series (1968).

297. C.Martin-Jenkins *Wisden's Book of County Cricket* (1981).

298. F.H.S.Craig *British Parliamentary Election Results* (1977 five volumes).

299. *The Guinness Book of Records* (several editions).

299a. *The Guinness Book of Answers* (1990 edition).

300. J.Richardson *The Local Historian's Encyclopaedia* (1974).

301. British Library *Catalogue of the Newspaper Library, Colindale* (1975).

301a. Eilert Ekwall *Concise Oxford Dictionary of English Place Names* (1936 and 1960).

302. C.Harvey (ed.) *The Encyclopaedia of Sport* (1959).

303. Whittaker's Almanack (numerous editions).

303a. Various national gazetteers and atlases.

UNPUBLISHED and OTHER SOURCES:

304. Ex-inf. Department of Transport.

305. Ex-inf. Brighton Borough Estates Surveyor Department.

306. Ex-inf. Brighton Borough Planning Department and Plan Registry.

307. Ex-inf. Brighton Borough Secretary Department.

308. Ex-inf. Brighton Borough Tourism and Resort Services Department.

309. Ex-inf. British Broadcasting Corporation.

310. Placard in Brighton Town Hall Council Chamber.

311. Foundation stones, memorial tablets, plaques and other visual evidence.

312. Author's personal records.

313. Ex-inf. Brighton Borough Technical Services Department.

314. Ex-inf. Diocese of Chichester.

315. Minutes of Brighton Borough Council.

316. Exhibits at Bluebell Railway Museum, Sheffield Park Station.

GENERAL INDEX

This index references buildings, roads, places and other topographical features, and also general topics; there is a separate index for people. The numbers refer to the encyclopaedia entry numbers. Principal entries are shown in **bold** type.

abattoir, Hollingdean Road: **76**
Abbey Road: 58
Abbotts, King's Road: **83c**
ABC Cinema:
see: Cannon Cinema.
Academy Cinema, West Street: **205b**
Ace Cinema, Hollingdean Road: **87d**
Acts of Parliament:
see: Borough Extension Act; Commissioners Transfer Act; Improvement Act; Town Acts.
Adelphi Hotel, Grand Junction Road: **160c**
Adullam Chapel, Windsor Street: **36c**
Advision studios, St George's Terrace: **23**
aerodromes & airports: **174**
Aged Pilgrim Friend Society, Egremont Place: **138d**
air-raids: **216b**
also: 1a,12,69b,87d,112b,117b,133d,144, 146d,156,161j,166b,169f,189b,208c
Air Street: **136b**
Al Forno's Restaurant, East Street: 57
Albert Road: **203a**
Albion Brewery, Albion Street: **14a**
Albion Groyne: **43b**
also: 95d
Albion Hill: **1**
(development of area): **49(ix)**
Albion Hill Home, Finsbury Road: **136c**
Albion Hotel:
see: Royal Albion Hotel.
Albion Street:
(breweries): **14**
(Elim Church): **1a**
aldermen: 47a,b
Alexandra Villas: **203a**
Alfred Road: **203a**
Alhambra Opera House, King's Road: **83b**
see also: Dome Mission.
All Saints' Church, Compton Road: **203b**
All Saints' Church, Patcham: **122b**
All Souls' Church, Eastern Road: **58**
Allenwest Ltd, Moulsecoomb: **105d**
Alliance & Leicester Building Society, North Street & Hove: **112a**
allotments: 119
almshouses:
(Bartholomews): 115a
(George Street): 167e
(Lewes Road): 87b
(Tillstone Street): 138d
Amber Ale Brewery, Preston Circus: **14b**
ambulance station, Elm Grove: **70**
American Express Corporation, Edward Street: **60**
ammonite capitals: **209**
'Ancient Customs': **2**
(fishing fares): 67b
ancient monuments: **45b**
Anglo-Catholicism: **150**
Ann Street: **91c**
(St Bartholomew's Church): **91d**
also: 53b
Annunciation Church, Washington Street: **74c**
Aquarium and Dolphinarium, Madeira Drive: **3**
(Dolphinarium): **3e**
(fittings): 21,122g
also: 104,140e
Aquarium traffic roundabout: **151d**
Arcadia Cinema, Lewes Road: **87d**
architecture: **4**
areas of borough & parishes: **13**,**118b**
Argus newspaper:
see: Evening Argus.
Argyle Road: 96,133a
arms of the borough: **47c**
Art College:
see: Polytechnic.
Art Gallery, Church Street: **106**
(evacuation): 216b
(lighting): 195
(offices): 161m
Artillery Baths, King's Road: **7h**
Artillery Place, King's Road: 7h,8e,72
Artillery Street: **8e**,**37**
Arts Information Centre, Church Street: **36a**
Arundel & Brighton R.C. diocese: 150
Arundel Road: 172b
(Bush Hotel): 81b
Arundel Street: 99h
Arundel Terrace: **81b**
(garden): **81f**
(Roedean School): 153
Ascension Church Hall, Westdene: **206**
Asda superstores:
(Hollingbury): **75d**
also: 75c
(Marina): **98e**
assembly rooms:
see: Castle Inn; Old Ship Hotel; Royal Gardens; Royal Newburgh; Royal Pavilion.
Astoria Cinema, Gloucester Place: **189b**
Athenaeum, Oriental Place: 149j
Athenaeum Hall, North Street: **112d**
Athina B shipwreck: **95d**
Atlingworth manor: **96**
also: 183b
Atlingworth Street: **56j**
attacks:
(on Brighton): **17d**
(on Ovingdean): 116a,b
(on Rottingdean): **154**,**155d**
Attree Drive: 138c
Attree Villa, Queen's Park: **138c**
Augustinian Convent, Manor Road: **97**
Avenue: 6
Avenue, The, Moulsecoomb: **105b**
aviation: **174**
AVP Industries:
see: Bedford Hotel; Metropole Hotel; Norfolk Resort Hotel; West Pier.
Awsiter's Baths, Pool Valley: **7e**
Baker Street: 91c
see also: Brighton Co-operative Society (London Road).
Baker's Library, Old Steine: **89a**
Balfour Road:
(Elim Church): 130g
(schools): 212c
ball-rooms & dance halls:
see: Aquarium; Castle Inn; Kingswest Boulevard; Old Ship Hotel; Palace Pier; Regent Cinema; Royal Newburgh Assembly Rooms; Royal Pavilion; Royal York Hotel; Sherrys; West Pier.
Ballard's Mill, Patcham: **122f**
Balsdean: **5**
(pumping station): **200c**
B & Q superstore, Lewes Road: 87f
bandstands:
see: Aquarium; King's Road; Madeira Lawns; Old Steine; Palace Pier.
Banjo Groyne: **43b**
(sea-plane base): 174
see also: Rottingdean Railway; Volk's Railway.
banks: **6**
Bannings Vale, Saltdean: 171a
Bannister's Baths, Old Steine: **7g**
Baptist Tabernacle, Montpelier Place & West Street: **39q**
Barclays Bank: **6**
(London Road/St Peter's Place): **189e**
(North Street): **6**
(Rottingdean): **156d**
Barn Rise, Westdene: **206**
Barrack Yard: 36a
barracks:
see: Church Street; Corn Exchange; Dome; Preston Barracks.
see also: drill halls.
Barry Walk: 138c
Bartholomew Square: **115a**
see also: Hospitality Inn.
Bartholomews: **115a**
see also: markets; Regent Arcade; Springett's School; Town Hall.
Bat & Ball, Ditchling Road: 86
Bates Estate, Moulsecoomb: **105b**
baths and bathing: **7**
(corporation slipper baths): **126b**
see: Aquarium; Cobden Road; Ditchling Road; North Road; Park Street (Victoria).
(machines): **7c**,**183b**
(pools):
see: Black Rock; Brill's Baths; Lower Esplanade (paddling-pool); North Road Baths; Prince Regent Swimming Complex; Rottingdean; St Lukes Terrace; Saltdean Lido; S.S.Brighton; Surrenden Pool; Woodingdean School.
(proprietary establishments): **7d**
B.A.T.S.: **26m,p**
batteries: **8**
Battery Baths, King's Road: **7h**
'Battles':
(of Brighton): **104**
(of Lewes Road): **185d**
(of Ovingdean): 140c
(of White Hawk Down): 140c
see also: attacks.
Bavant Road: 179b
Bazehill, Rottingdean: 5,96,158
Beach Deck: 93
beaches: **43**
also: 45a,136c
see also: bathing; cross-channel traffic; flints (building material); Lower town.
Beacon Court, Ovingdean: **116c**
Beacon Hill, Rottingdean: **158**
also: 45b
Beacon Mill, Rottingdean: **158**
Beaconsfield Villas: 4h
see also: trolley-buses.
bear-baiting: 9,154
Bear Inn, Lewes Road: 9
Bear Mill: **9**
Bear Road: **9**
(boundary stones): 13a,140a
(development of area): **49(xiv)**
see also: Bevendean Hospital; Downs Crematorium; Race Hill; Woodvale Cemetery.
Bedford Hotel, King's Road: **10**
(telegraph office): 179
Bedford Place: **149a**
Bedford Square: **149b**
Bedford Street: **56p**
Belgrave Place: **56v**
Belgrave Street: 74d,172b,c
Bell Tower Industrial Estate, Black Rock: **152**
Belle Vue Field: **148a**
Belle Vue Gardens: 58
Belmont: **55c**
Belmont Street: 172c
Belton Road: 159
Belvedere, Montpelier Road: **39h**
Belvedere Terrace: **39a**
also: 39h
'bending in': **67d**
Bennett Road: 216b
Bentham Road: 74d
Bernard Road: 63
Bethel Chapels: 67c,205d
Bethsaida Chapel, Windsor Street: 36c
Bevendean: **11**
(development of area): **49(xxviii)**
(school): 172d
also: 24f,120c
Bevendean Hospital, Bevendean Road: **78d**
Bevendean Road: 11,33b
see also: Bevendean Hospital.
BHASVIC, Dyke Road: **22**
Bijou cinema, North Street: **112d**
bingo halls: 54,87d,112d,115p,139c,166b,189b
Black Horse Inn, Rottingdean: **156f**
Black Lion Brewery, Black Lion Street: **115c**
Black Lion Hotel, Patcham: **122c**
Black Lion Inn, Black Lion Street: **115c**
Black Lion Lane: **115b**
Black Lion Street: **115c**
(and Prince Albert Street): 115r
see also: Bartholomew House; Diocesan Training College; Floral Hall; Hospitality Inn; markets; Old Ship Hotel.
Black Mill, Preston: **55d**
Black Rock: **12**
(antiquities): 17a,106b
(dock): **128**
(gas-works): **69**
(groyne): **43b**
(laines): **53b**
(sewage outfall): 173b
(swimming-pool): **12**
(tunnel): **12**
also: 174
see also: French Convalescent Home; Marina; Rifle Butt Road; Undercliff Walk; Volk's

Railway.
Black Rock Valley: 208d
Blackman Street: 91c,126c
Blaker Recreation Ground, Preston: **130e**
Blaker Street: **60**
Blenheim Hotel, Church Street: **36a**
also: 24b
Blenheim Place: **110b**
Blind School, Eastern Road: **58a**
Blockhouse: **8a**
also: 2c
Bloomsbury Place: **56s**
Blucher Place: 37
Blue & Buffs, Old Steine: **114g**
Boer War: 9,68(ii),68(ix),148d
Bombay Bar, Paston Place: **166b**
Bond Street: **110a**
(market): 100f
(Theatre Royal): 182c
(Water Department H.Q.): 200d
Books of Ancient Customs:
see: Ancient Customs.
Booth's Museum of Natural History, Dyke Road: **55e**
Boots stores:
(London Road): 91a
(North Street): **112b**
(St James's Street): 167a
(Western Road): **207b**
Borough Cemeteries, Lewes Road & Bear Road: **33b**
Borough Extension Act 1873: 13,86,114b,194a
Borough Hospital, Bevendean Road: **78d**
Borough of Brighton:
(arms & motto): **47c**
(boundaries & area): **13**
(freedom): **68**
(municipal incorporation): **47a**
(Parliamentary): **61**
also: 207e
(population): **127**
see also: corporation & council.
Borough Street: **207e**
boundaries: **13**
(at Black Rock): 12
(stones): **13a**
Boundary Passage: 13a
Boundary Road, Black Rock: 13
see also: Black Rock gas-works.
Bowen's Library, Old Steine: **89b**
bowling:
(greens): 114a,119
(tenpin): 84
Box's Cricket Ground, Union Road: 120b
Boyces Street: **115d**
boys' clubs:
(Brighton): **60**
(Central Brighton): 110u
(Whitehawk & Manor Farm): 208c
Brangwyn Estate, Patcham: **92e**
Brapool, Patcham: **92e**
also: 201
Braybon Avenue, Patcham: 121
Bread Street: 36d
'Breeze into Brighton': 15
breweries: **14**
Brigden Street: 134
Brighthelm U.R. Church & Community Centre, Church Street & North Road: **36e**
see also: Central Free Church.
Brighthelmston: **16a**
also: 128
Brighthelmston Bank: **6**
Brighthelmston Circulating Library, Old Steine: **89a**
Brighthelmston Dispensary: **78a**
Brighton:
(boundaries): **13**
(development): **49**
also: 15,53b
(early history): **17**
(employment): **15**
(etymology): **16a**
(functions): **15**
(location): **15,17b**
(Lower Town): **94**
(name variations): **16a**
(nicknames): **16c**,172a
(other Brightons): **16b**
(parish): **13,118**
(population): **127**
(street patterns): **53b**
also: 115
Brighton Area Transport Services: **26m,p**
Brighton Belle (luxury train): **142k**
'Brighton Bombing': **72**
Brighton Buses: **26p**
(Lewes Road depot): 185c
see also: Brighton Corporation Transport.
Brighton Business Centre, Viaduct Road & Ditchling Road: **191**
Brighton bypass: **27**
Brighton camps: **148a**
Brighton Centre, King's Road: **18**
(TVS studio): 24f
Brighton & Chichester Railway Co.: 141a,143
Brighton College, Eastern Road: **19**
(conservation area): **19c**
also: 14e,205c,208d
Brighton Co-operative Society: **46b**
(London Road store): **91b**
(St James' Street store): 167a
Brighton Corporation:
see: Corporation & council.
Brighton Corporation Transport:
(buses): **26g-p**
(Lewes Road depot): 185c
(tramways): **185**
Brighton Cricket Club: 86,120,177
Brighton Daily Mail: 138c
Brighton & Dyke Railway Co.: 50b
Brighton Festival: **15**
also: 24e,67d,142k
Brighton Film Theatre, North Street: **112d**
Brighton Gas Light & Coke Company: **69**
Brighton Gazette: **108b**
also: 112d
Brighton General Library, Literary & Scientific Institution, St James's Street: 167a
Brighton Grammar School: **22**
also: 29,203c
Brighton Herald: **108c**
Brighton Heritage Museum: 115t
Brighton Home for Female Penitents: **136c**
Brighton & Hove Albion Football Club: **20**
also: 55f,185b
Brighton & Hove Bus & Coach Co.: **26p**
Brighton & Hove Dispensary: **78a**
Brighton, Hove & District Omnibus Co.: **26f,k,l,n**
Brighton, Hove & District Transport: **26g**
Brighton & Hove Gazette:
see: Brighton Gazette
Brighton & Hove General Gas Company: **69b**
Brighton & Hove Golf Club: **50c**
Brighton & Hove Herald:
see: Brighton Herald
Brighton & Hove High School, Temple Gardens: **39q**
Brighton and Hove Leader: 108b
Brighton, Hove & Preston Dental Hospital: **78e**
Brighton, Hove & Preston Dispensary: **78a**
Brighton, Hove & Preston Provident Dispensary: **78b**
Brighton, Hove & Preston United Omnibus Co.: **26a-e**
Brighton & Hove Stadium, Hove: **21**
Brighton, Hove & Sussex Sixth Form College, Dyke Road: **22**
Brighton & Hove Women's Hospital, West Street: **78f**
Brighton, Hove & Worthing Gas Company: **69**
Brighton, Hove & Worthing Municipal Airport, Lancing: **174**
Brighton Intercepting & Outfall Sewers Board: 173c
Brighton, Lewes & Hastings Railway Co.: 141a,144
Brighton Limited (luxury train): **142k**
Brighton Lions:
(carnival): **64**
(community centre, St James's Street): 167a
Brighton Marine Palace & Pier:
see: Palace Pier.
Brighton Palladium, West Street: **205e**
Brighton Park:
see: Queen's Park.
Brighton Park Mill: **1b**
Brighton Place: **115e**
Brighton & Preston Cemetery, Hartington Road: **33c**
Brighton & Preston United School Board: **172c**
see also: Marlborough House.
Brighton Provident & Self-supporting Dispensary: **78b**
Brighton Railway Station:
see: Brighton Station.
Brighton Rock: **140e**
Brighton & Rottingdean Seashore Electric Railway: **157**
Brighton School of Music, North Street: 112d
Brighton Square: **115f**
Brighton Standard: **108d**
Brighton Station: **145**
(postal sorting office): 129b
(telegraphs): 179a
(underground railway): **142g**
also: 135
see also: horse-buses; Queen's Road; railway engineering works; tramways; trolley-buses; Trunk Murders.
Brighton & Sussex Bank, St James's Street: 6
Brighton & Sussex Equitable Permanent Benefit Building Society, North Street: 112a
Brighton Tigers (ice-hockey): **205e**
Brighton Union Bank, North Street: **6**
Brighton Youth Centre, Edward Street: **60**
Brill's Baths, East Street: **7j**
also: 57
Brill's Lane: 7j
Bristol Brewery, Kemp Town: **14e**
Bristol Estate: 81e,97
Bristol Gardens, Kemp Town: 58
Bristol Gate: 58a,162b
Bristol Place, Kemp Town: 81e
Bristol Road: **23**
British Engineerium, Hove:
see: Goldstone Pumping Station.
British Schools, Eastern Road: 172a
Broad Street: **56c**
Broadcasting: **24**
Bromley Road: 51
Brotherhood Gate Spiritualist Church, St James's Street: 167a
Brunswick Baths, Western Street: 83c
Brunswick Court, Oxford Street: 91c
Brunswick Cricket Ground, Hove: 177a
Brunswick Place, Hove: **25**
(Lady Chichester Hospital): 39x
Brunswick Town, Hove: **25**
Buckingham Place: **203b**
Buckingham Road: **203c**
see also: Brighton Grammar School; Dental Hospital; Sussex Maternity Hospital.
Bullock Hill, Woodingdean: **53d**
B.U.P.A., Freshfield Road: 26p
Burger King Restaurant, North Street: 112d
burial responsibility: 33b
see also: cemeteries.
Burlington Street: **56q**
(telegraph office): 179a
buses: **26**
see also: coaching.
Bute Mission Hall, Sutherland Road: **19c**
Butlins Ocean Hotel, Saltdean: **171e**
by-elections: **61**
bypass:
(Brighton): **27**
also: 44,50c,51,55f,75d,85,92a,92e,122a,199
(Patcham): 92a
cable television: **24h**
Calvary Evangelical Church, Viaduct Road: **191**
Camden Terrace: **203d**
Camelford Street: **56e**
Campbell Road: 133a
camping & caravan ground, Sheepcote Valley: **208d**
Cannon Brewery, Russell Street: **14d**
also: 100l
Cannon cinemas:
(East Street & Grand Junction Road): **28**
also: 104
(Marina): **98e**
Cannon Place: **149c**
(post office): 129c
(telegraph office): 179a
see also: Churchill Square.
Cannon Street: 37

Carden Avenue, Patcham: 51,75d
Carden Community Centre, Patcham: **75c**
Carden Park, Patcham: **75c**
Carden School: 172d
Carlton Hill: **30**
(Salvation Army): 120c
(schools): 172b,d
also: 53b
Carlton Street: 172a
Carn Court, Queen's Park: 138c
carnival: **64**
Castle Hill, Balsdean: **5**
Castle Inn, Castle Square: **31**
also: 57,71b
see also: Master of Ceromonies; St Stephen's Church; town commissioners.
Castle Square: **32**
(banks): **6**
(telegraph offices): 179a
(theatre): **181**
(traffic lights): 151d
see also: buses; Castle Inn; coaching.
Catholic Apostolic Churches:
(Grand Parade): **189j**
(Kingswood Street/Sussex Street): **30**
cattle market: 100h
Cavendish Place: **149d**
CD 1 number plate: 66c
cemeteries & crematoria:
(burial responsibility): 33b
see: Bartholomews; Brighton & Preston; Downs Crematorium; Extra-Mural; Jewish; Lawn Memorial Park; Pets' Cemetery; Quakers; St Nicholas's Churchyard; Woodvale (Borough, Parochial).
Centenary Industrial Estate, Hughes Road: 82
Central Free Church, Queen Square: **136a**
see also: Brighthelm U.R Church.
Central National Schools, Church Street: **36b,172a**
(Blind Asylum): 58a
(infant school, Upper Gardner Street): 110u
Central Spiritualist Church, North Street: 112d
Central Woodingdean Park: **214a**
Chailey Road:
(dispensary): 78b
see also: Moulsecoomb.
Chain Pier: **34**
also: 101b,128
see also: Palace Pier.
chalk pits: 55a,171a
Challoners, Rottingdean: **155w**
Challoners Cottages, Rottingdean: **155z**
Challoners Mews, Rottingdean: **155v**
Chapel Royal, North Street: **112e**
Chapmans Brewery, Black Lion Street: 115c
charities: **126b**
charity schools: **172a**
Charles Street: **56b**
Charlotte Street: **56m**
charters of incorporation: **47a,b**
Chartwell Court, Cannon Place: **37**
Chates Farm Court, Albion Hill: **1a**
Chatfield's Fountain, Victoria Gardens: **194c**
Chattri, Patcham: **122h**
Cheapside: 53b
Cheltenham Place: **110c**
Chesham Place: **56x**
Chesham Road: 153,168,172b
Chest clinic, Morley Street: **1a**
Chesterfield Street: 60
Chichester Place: **56y**
Chichester Terrace: **81c**
(garden): **81f**
Chief Constables: **123e**
Chief Fire Officers: **66d**
Children's Hospital, Dyke Road: **55b**
Children's Library, Church Street: **88d**
Christ Church Evangelical Chapel, New England Road: **91c**
Christ Church, Montpelier Road: **149f**
(infant school, Clarence Gardens): 149e
(school, Bedford Place): **149a**
Christ Church (Unitarian), New Road: **107**
Christ, Church of, Oxford Street: **91c**
Christ the King, Church of, South Patcham: **121**
Christ Scientist, First Church of, Montpelier Road: **39h**
Christian Bretheren chapels:
(Grand Parade): **189j**
(High Street): **167g**
Church Army homes:
(Albion Hill): **136c**
(Miles Court): 58
Church Hill, Brighton:
see: cattle market; Clifton Hill; Dyke Road; West Hill; windmills; workhouse.
Church Hill, Patcham: **122a-c**
church schools: **172b**
Church Street: **36**
(barracks): **36a**
also: 135,140e
see also: Art Gallery; Brighton Gazette; Corn Exchange; Dome; fire-stations; George IV statue; Library (Brighton); Museum (Brighton); Music Library; North Gate House; Royal Pavilion (North Gate); Prince Regent Swimming Complex; St Nicholas's Church; Sussex Throat & Ear Hospital.
church-wardens: **118d**
churches & chapels: **150**
(Domesday): **17c**
(organisation): 118a,150
(schools): **172b**
(Anglican):
(pre-Reformation - originally Catholic):
see: All Saints, Patcham; Balsdean; St Andrew, Hove; St Bartholomew's Chapel; St Laurence, Falmer; St Lawrence, Telscombe; St Margaret, Rottingdean; St Nicholas, Brighton; St Peter, Preston; St Peter, West Blatchington; St Wulfran, Ovingdean; Stanmer.
(post-Reformation):
see: All Saints, Brighton; All Souls; Annunciation; Ascension, Westdene; Chapel Royal; Christ Church; Christ the King, South Patcham; Good Shepherd, Preston; Holy Cross, Woodingdean; Holy Nativity, Bevendean; Holy Trinity; Mackie Hall, Patcham; Resurrection, Brighton; Resurrection, Woodingdean; Royal Chapel; St Alban, East Preston; St Andrew, Brunswick Town; St Andrew, Moulsecoomb; St Anne; St Augustine, Preston; St Bartholomew; St Cuthman, Whitehawk; St David's Hall, Whitehawk; St Francis's Hall, Moulsecoomb; St George, Kemp Town; St George's Hall, Whitehawk; St James; St John, Brunswick Town; St John the Evangelist, Carlton Hill; St John the Evangelist, Preston; St Luke, Prestonville; St Luke, Queen's Park; St Margaret, Brighton; St Mark, Kemp Town; St Martin; St Mary; St Mary Magdalen, Coldean; St Mary & St Mary Magdalen; St Matthew; St Matthias; St Michael; St Nicholas, Saltdean; St Paul; St Peter, Brighton; St Richard, Hollingdean; St Saviour, Preston;St Stephen; St Wilfrid.
see also: cemeteries (for mortuary chapels)
(Baptist):
see: Baptist Tabernacle; Clarence; Ebenezer; Florence Road; Galeed Strict; Gloucester Place; Islingword Road; Mighell Street; Moulsecoomb; Pavilion; Preston Park; Queen Square; Salem; Withdean.
(Catholic): (note that the pre-Reformation churches and chapels were originally Roman Catholic - see 'Anglican' above.)
see: Catholic Apostolic Church, Grand Parade; Catholic Apostolic Church, Kingswood Street; High Street; Our Lady of Lourdes, Rottingdean; St Francis of Assisi, Moulsecoomb; St John the Baptist; St Joseph; St Louis King of France, Whitehawk; St Mary, Preston; St Mary Magdalen; St Patrick, Woddingdean; St Thomas More, Patcham; West Cliff Catholic Mission.
(Christian Bretheren):
see: Grand Parade; High Street.
(Congregational):
see: Belgrave Street; Bentham Road; Dials; London Road Chapel; Queen Square; Sudeley Place; Union; Union Street.
see also below: United Reformed Churches.
(Countess of Huntingdon's Connexion):
see: London Road Chapel; North Street.
(Elim Church):
see: Albion Street; Balfour Road; New England Road; Union Street.
(Methodist):
see: Bristol Road; Dorset Gardens; High Street; Hollingbury; Islingword Road; London Road; Norfolk Road; Patcham; Preston Road Wesleyan; Queen's Park; Stanford Avenue; Sussex Street; Viaduct Road; Woodingdean.
(Presbyterian):
see: Hanover Chapel; Presbyterian Meeting House; St Andrew; Trinity Independent.
see also below: United Reformed Churches.
(Spiritualist):
see: Brotherhood Gate; Central Spritualist; Mighell Street; National Spiritualist.
(Synagogues):
see: Devonshire Place; Jew Street; Middle Street; Poune's Court.
(United Reformed - a union of Congregational and Presbyterian Churches):
see: Brighthelm; Central Free; Clermont; Lewes Road; St Martin.
(other churches & chapels):
see: Adullam Chapel; Bentham Road; Bethel Chapels; Bethsaida Hall; Calvary Evangelical; Central Free Church; Christ Church Evangelical, New England Road; Christ Church (Unitarian); Christ, Church of (Oxford Street); Connaught Institute; Downs Free Church; Emmanuel Episcopal Reformed; Emmanuel Full Gospel; First Church of Christ Scientist; French Reformed; Friends' Meeting House; Gloucester Rooms; Gordon Hall; Grand Parade; Greek Orthodox Churches; Hanover Chapel; Hollingbury Gospel Hall; Islingword Road; Jireh Chapel; Latter Day Saints, Church of Jesus Christ of (Mormon); Nathaniel Episcopal Reformed; Oxford Street; New Life Centre; Park Hill; Providence Chapel, Church Street; Providence Chapel, West Hill Road; Railway Mission; Salvation Army; Trinity Chapel; Union Free Church; Unitarian; University Meeting House; West Hill Road; Windsor Street Chapel; Zion Chapel; Zoar Chapel.
Churchill House, Queen's Road: **78a**
Churchill Square: **37**
Cinema-de-Luxe, North Street: **112d**
cinemas: **38**
see: Academy; Aquarium; Arcadia; Astoria; Cannon; Cinema-de-Luxe; Continentale; Court; Curzon; Duke of York's; Embassy; Essoldo; Gem Electric; Grand; Grand Picture Palace; Imperial Picture Palace; New Coronation; Novelty; Odeon, Kemp Town; Odeon, Kingswest Boulevard; Odeon, West Street; Palladium; Prince's; Regent; Tierney Royal Picture Theatre; Vogue.
Cinescene Cinema, North Street: **112d**
Circus Street:
(circus): 189j
(market): **100e**
also: 189j
(schools): 172c
City Limited (luxury train): **142k**
city technology college, Woodingdean: **214b**
Clarence Baptist Chapel, Clarence Gardens: **149e**
Clarence Gardens: **149e**
Clarence House, North Street: **112c**
see also: courts.
Clarence Square: **149e**
Clarence Yard:
see: Model Dwellings; Puget Schools.
Clarendon Mansions, East Street & Grand Junction Road: **57**
Clarendon Terrace: **99f**
Classic Cinema, Hollingdean Road: **87d**
Classic Cinema, Western Road: **207d**
Clayton:
(tunnel): **142d**,142j
(windmills): **55c**

Clermont Estate: **130b**
(Preston Road): 133d
(U.R.Church): **130b**
see also: Preston Park Station.
cliffs: **43**
(antiquities): 17a
(Black Rock SSSI): **12**
(defensive wall): **8b**
(lifts): **3e**,**95**
(Saltdean SSSI): 45b
Clifton Gardens: **39d**
Clifton Hill:
(conservation area): **39**
(development of area): **49(iii)**
(road): **39b**
see also: Vine's Mill.
see also: Crown Gardens; Dyke Road; Montpelier Road; St Nicholas's Church; Western Road.
Clifton Mill: **1b**,**39d**
Clifton Place: 39w
Clifton Road: **39c**
(Homelees House): 55a
Clifton Terrace: **39d**
Cliftonville, Hove: **79**
(buses): 26a
(railway spur & tunnel): **143**
also: 142e
climate: **40**
Clock Tower, North Street: **41**
clock towers:
see: Aquarium; Blaker's Recreation Ground; Clock Tower, North Street; Palace Pier; Patcham; Preston Park; Queen's Park; Royal Pavilion.
Clowns Café, Madeira Drive:
see: Madeira Shelter Hall.
coach stations:
(Pool Valley): **125**
(Steine Street): **26d**
coaching: **42**
coal tax: **43b**
also: 69a
coastline: **43**
cobbles (building material): **4b**
Cobden Road Baths, Hanover: **74d**
Coldean: **44**
(boundary stone): 13a
(development of area): **49(xxix)**
(Parkway): **105f**
(school): 172d
(TV transmitter): 24g
(Wild Park): **105f**
Coldean Lane: 51,27
Coliseum Cinema, West Street: **205c**
Coliseum Theatre of Varieties, New Road: **107**
College Conservation Area: **19c**
College of Art:
see: Polytechnic.
College of Education:
see: Polytechnic.
College of Technology:
(formerly at Moulsecoomb):
see: Polytechnic.
(now at Pelham Street, Richmond Terrace, etc.):
see: Technology, College of.
College Place: **56**
College Road: 166b,**179a**
College Terrace: **19c**
Colonnade Bar, New Road: **107**
Colonnade, Royal, New Road: **107**
Comet retail warehouse, Lewes Road: **87f**
Commercial Vehicles Rally: **190**
Commissioners, Improvement:
see: Town Commissioners.
Commissioners Transfer Act: **183d**
Community of the Virgin Mary, Queen Square: **136c**
commuters: 42b,141
Compton Avenue: 203b
Compton Road, Preston: 4h
concert halls:
see: Aquarium; Brighton Centre; Dome; Kingswest Boulevard; Palace Pier; West Pier; West Street.
see also: assembly rooms.
conferences & exhibitions: **15**,**18**
(centres):
see: Brighton Centre; Dome; Kingswest Boulevard; Metropole; S.S.Brighton.
Congress Hall, Park Crescent Terrace: **120c**
Connaught Institute, Lewes Road: **87d**
conservation: **45**
conservation areas:
(Brighton): **45a**
(Hove): **79c**
constables: **118f**
also: 2,183b
Constables, Chief: **123e**
Constant Service, Islingword Road: 200b
constituencies: **61**
Continentale Cinema, Sudeley Place: **166c**
Coombe Road, East Preston: **9**
(school): 172d
also: 24f
coombe rock: 12,43d,53a
co-operatives: **46**
(Brighton Co-operative Society): **46b**
Coppercliff hospice, Westdene: **203**
Corals Social Club, Gloucester Place: **189b**
Corals Stadium, Hove: **21**
cork shop, Gardner Street: **110e**
Corn Exchange, Church Street: **52d**
(lighting): 195
also: 66c
corn market: **100j**
Coronation Cinema, North Road: **111**
corporation and council: **47**
(ambulance service): 70
(bathing restrictions): 7a
(buses): **26c**,**g**,**k**,**p**
(cemeteries): 33b
(clearances): **126c**
also: 1,37,36d,58f
(education): **172d**
(electricity supply): **62**
(fire-brigade): **66d**
(functions): **47b**
(hospitals): **78c**
(housing): **126c**
(housing estates):
see: Bevendean; Coldean; Hollingbury; Hollingdean; Manor Farm; Moulsecoomb; Queen's Park; Whitehawk; Woodingdean.
(planning awards): **4m**
(police): **123b**
(political composition): **47d**
(property, purchases & acquisitions): **47f**
see also many individual entries.
(race-course): **140d**,**f**
(refuse): **147**
(roads): 151a
(street widening): 60,111,112a,115n,205a,207a
(telephones): **179b**
(tramways): **185**
(water supply): **200c**
(Wilson report): **4l**
see also: Aquarium; bathing; Brighton Centre; Carden, Sir Herbert; manors; parks; Volk's Railway.
council:
see: corporation & council.
council housing: **126c**
Country Homes Garden Centre, Brighton Race-course: 140f
county courts: **48**
County Ground, Hove: **177a**
(Brighton and Hove Albion): 20a
Court Barn, Rottingdean **164y**
Court Cinema & Theatre, New Road: **107**
also: 108a
Court Farm, Rottingdean: 155c,g,v,y
Court House, Rottingdean: **155s**
Court Ord Cottages, Falmer Road: **155z**
courts: **48**
(brewsters): 91a
(Church Street): **36a**
(Edward Street): **48**
(hundreds): 118f
(manors): **96**
Cox's Pill Factory, Lewes Road: 87d
Crawford's Library, Old Steine: **89b**
crazy golf: **93**
Creak's Baths, Pool Valley: **7e**
crematoria: **33b**,**c**
Crescent Place: **56r**
cricket: **177**
(grounds): **177a**
see also: Brighton College; Hanover; Level; Lillywhite's; North Steine; Preston Park; Prince of Wales's; Rottingdean.
Cricketers Arms, Black Lion Street: **115c**
cross-Channel traffic: **128**
Crowhurst Hall, Knoyle Road: **133d**
Crowhurst Road, Hollingbury: **75d**
Crown & Anchor, Preston: **133c**
crown courts: **48**
Crown Gardens: **203e**
Crown Street: **207e**
also: 97
Cumberland Place: 60
Cumberland Road, Preston: 133d
'Cure, The': **164**
also: 7,71b
see also: Royal Spa; St Anne's Well.
Curzon Cinema, Western Road: **207d**
Curzon, Hotel, Cavendish Place: **149d**
Customs, Ancient: **2**
(fishing fares): **67b**
customs (revenue):
17e,122b,128,131f,156q,204b
'Daddy Longlegs' railway: **157**
Dairy Estate, Preston: **133a**
Dale Crescent, Patcham: 129c
dance halls:
see: ballrooms.
D'Aubigny Road: 82
Davis Cup tennis: 18,213
De Courcel Road: **99g**
De Montfort Road: 63
Deaf & Dumb School, Eastern Road: **58a**
see also: Hamilton Lodge School.
Deaf, Diocesan Centre for the, Carlton Hill: **30a**
see also: First Base Day Centre.
Dean Court Road, Rottingdean: 155c
Dean Hundred: **118f**
Dean Street: **207e**
(post-office): 129c
Debenhams store, Western Road: **207c**
(Sillwood House): **149q**
also: 209
defences:
(sea): **43**
(town): **8**
Dene, The, Rottingdean: **155a**
Denmark Terrace: **39e**
Dental Hospital: **78e**
Dentsply Ltd, Coombe Road: 9
Department of Social Security: **60**,**126a**
also: 120c
Derby Place: 60
Devil's Dyke: **50**
also: 24f,81b
Devil's Dyke Road: 55f,199
see also: Brighton & Hove Golf Club.
Devonshire Cinema, Edward Street: **60**
Devonshire Place: **167h**
Dewe Road: 126c
(Mithras House, Polytechnic): **105d**
Dials Congregational Church, Dyke Road: **55a**
Dieppe, France: **128**
Diocesan Centres for the Deaf: **30a**,39g
Diocesan Training Centre, Viaduct Road: 191
dippers: **7b**
Directors & Guardians of the Poor: **118e**
dispensaries: **78a**,**b**
see also: Lewes Road Hospital & Dispensary; Lying-In Institution & Dispensary; St Mary's Home.
Ditchling Beacon: **51**
also: 40
Ditchling Rise: 130a
see also: London Road Railway Station; Volk, Magnus.
Ditchling Road: **51**
(public houses): 135
(railway tunnel): **144**
also: 53d,170
see also: Bat & Ball; Brighton Business Centre; Brighton, Hove & Preston Dispensary; Downs School; Hollingbury; Lady Chichester Hospital; Level; Roedale; Round Hill; tramways; trolley-buses; Upper Lodges; Varndean High School.
'Doctor Brighton': 16c
Doctor Brightons, King's Road: **115j**

Dog Hospital, Robertson Road: **130g**
Dolphin Theatre, New Road: **107**
Dolphinarium, Madeira Drive: **3e**
Dome, Church Street: **52**
(air-raid): 216b
(lighting): 195
also: 98b
Dome Mission, Dorset Gardens: **167f,207e**
Domesday Book: **17c,96**
Donaldson's Library, Old Steine: **89a**
also: 108b,179a
Dorothy Stringer School, Loder Road: 212c
Dorset Gardens: **167f**
(Methodist Church): 167f
also: 27
Dorset Street: 172a
Down House, Rottingdean: **155t**
Downs, South: **53**
see also: Black Rock; cliffs; Devil's Dyke.
Downs Crematorium, Bear Road: **33c**
Downs Estate, Woodingdean: **214a**
Downs Free Church, Woodingdean: 214a
Downs School, Ditchling Road: 172c
Downsview School, Coldean: 172e
drains: **173**
also: 43b
'Dr Brighton': 16c
Dr Brightons, King's Road: **115j**
drill halls:
(Church Street): **36c**
(Dyke Road): **55d**
(Gloucester Road): **110f**
(Prince's Place): 112a
(Queen Square): 136
(Somme T.A. Centre, Lewes Road): **87f**
see also: military camps & manoeuvres.
Drove, The, Preston: **130e**
Drove Road, Woodingdean: 87a
Druid's Head, Brighton Place: **115e**
D.S.S.: **60,126a**
also: 120c
Dudlow's Library, Old Steine: **89a**
Duke of York's Cinema, Preston Circus: **54**
Duke Street: **115h**
(Brighton Co-operative Society): 46b
(school): 172a
(theatre): **181**
see also: Holy Trinity Church; Volunteer Fire-Brigade.
Dukes Lane: **115g**
Duke's Mound: **81d**
see also: Volk's Railway (offices).
Dulot & Gregory's Library, Old Steine: **89a**
Dunns store, North Street: **112b**
Durham, North Street: 112a
dust destructor, Hollingdean: **147**
Dutch Elm disease: 40a
Dyke Golf Club: **50c**
Dyke railways: **50a,b**
Dyke Road: **55**
(boundary stone): 13a
(Burial Grounds): **169f**
(radio mast): 24a
(Rest Garden): **169f**
(traffic lights): 151d
also: 4h
see also: Brighton, Hove & Sussex Sixth Form College; St Nicholas's Church; tramways; windmills.
Dyke Road Avenue: **55,55f**
(Tongdean Farm): **121**
Dyke Road Drive: **133a**
Dyke Road Park: **55d**
Eagle Hotel, Gloucester Road: 103,110f
Eagle Iron Foundry, Gloucester Road: 110f,114e
Eagle Star Insurance, Queen's Road: 78a
East Battery: **8d**
East Brighton estate: **116a**
East Brighton Golf Club, Roedean Road: **152**
East Brighton Park, Wilson Avenue: **208d**
(Whitehawk F.C.): **208e**
East Cliff: **56**
(battery): **8d**
(conservation area): **56**
(sea-wall): **43c**
(windmills): 211
see also: Bristol Road; Kemp Town; Marine Parade; St George's Road; St James's Road.
East Coastway: **144**
(abattoir siding): 76
(Kemp Town Junction signal-box): 82
East Gate: **8b**
East Laine: **53b**
East Lodge, Upper Rock Gardens: 167c,k
East Mill: **166c**
East Preston: **9**
(development of area): **49(xiv)**
East Street: **57**
(car-parking): 151d
(lighting): 69a,176
(post-office): 129b
(wells): 200a
see also: Brill's Baths; Cannon Cinema; Queen's Hotel; workhouse.
East Street Groyne: **43b**
East Sussex County Council: **47b**
Easter volunteer reviews: **140c**
Eastern Road: **58**
also: 53b
see also: Brighton College; British Schools; Kemp Town; Kemp Town Brewery; Royal Sussex County Hospital; St Mark's Church; St Mary's Hall; Sussex Eye Hospital.
Eastern Terrace: **99e**
(Training College): 124
Eastwick Barn, Patcham: **85**
(earthworks): 45b
Eaton Place: **56w**
Ebenezer Baptist Chapel, Richmond Parade: **1a**
Edburton Avenue: 4h
Eden Theatre, North Road: **111**
education: **172**
(importance to Brighton): **15**
(offices): 114k
Education, College of:
see: Polytechnic.
Edward Street: **60**
(prostitution): 136c
(sewer): 173b
(trunk murder): 186
also: 4a,53b,184a,189k
see also: courts; Globe Music Hall; Salvation Army; Southdown Motors Ltd.
Egremont Place: **138d**
(Queen's Park gateway): **138a**
see also: Deaf & Dumb School; St Joseph's Convent of Mercy; St Mary's Home.
Egremont Street: 138d
Egyptian Campaign Memorial, Old Steine: **114f**
elections:
(Parliamentary): **61**
(council): **47a-c**
Electric Bioscope, Western Road: **207d**
electric buses: **26c**
see also: trolley-buses.
Electric House, Castle Square: **62e**
Electric & International Telegraph Co.: **179a**
Electric Light Company: **62**
electricity supply: **62**
(and trolley-buses): 26k
see also: street-lighting.
electrification of railways:
(East Coastway): **144**
(London main-line): **142h**
(West Coastway): **143**
Elim Churches:
(Albion Street): **1a**
(Balfour Road): **130g**
(New England Road): 91c
(Union Street): **115v**
Elm Court, Port Hall Avenue: 55e
Elm Grove: **63**
(development of area): **49(xii)**
(school): 82,172c
see also: ambulance service; General Hospital; workhouse.
Elm Grove Home: **70,215d**
Elms, The, Rottingdean: **155b**
also: 155
Embassy Cinema, Western Road, Hove: **207b**
Embassy Court, King's Road: **83c**
Emmanuel Episcopal Reformed Church, Montpelier Place: **39g**
Emmanuel Full Gospel Church, De Montfort Road: **63**
Empire Theatre, New Road: **107**
employment: **15**
Engineerium, Hove:
see: Goldstone pumping station.
Enterprise Estate, Hollingbury: 75d
Equity & Law House, Queen's Road: 162c
erosion: **43**
see also: Lower Town; Roedean Road.
esplanades:
see: promenades.
Essex Street: 58,172a
Essoldo Cinema/Theatre, North Road: **112d**
Eurovision Song Contest: **52c**
Evangelical Free Church, Park Hill: **138d**
Evening Argus: **108**
Ewart Street: 126c
Ewe Bottom, Patcham: 45b
Exeter Street: 134
Extra-Mural Cemetery, Lewes Road: **33a**
also: 33b
Eye Hospital, Eastern Road: **162c**
Fairlight Schools, Fairlight Place: 172c
fairs: **64**
Fairway Retail Park, Moulsecoomb: **105d**
Falmer: **65**
(boundary stone): 13a
(ecclesiastical parish): 175c
(hundreds): **118f**
(manors): **96**
(pumping station & Southern Water): **200c,d**
(railway station): **144**
(railway tunnel): **144**
also: 62e,200c
see also: Coldean; Moulsecoomb; Polytechnic; University of Sussex.
Falmer High School, Lewes Road: 65,172d
Falmer Road: **155z**
also: 155r,214a
see also: Downs Free Church; Wick Farm.
Farm Green, Bevendean: 11
Farm Yard: 37
Fawcett School, York Place: **189d**
Female Orphan Asylum, Eastern Road: **58a**
Female Penitents, Brighton Home for, Finsbury Road: **136c**
Festivals:
(Brighton Arts): **15**
(fishing customs): 67d
(Brighton Belle): 142k
(Festival Radio): **24e**
(Britain 1951): 93
(Brighton Film): 38
Festival Radio: **24e**
film studios: 79a,115p,169e
Film Theatre, North Street: **112d**
Finsbury Road: 136c,172c
fire-brigades: **66**
(stations): **66**
(Wyndham Street): **56l**
see also: Ocean Hotel; Saltdean Lido.
First Base Day Centre, Montpelier Place: **39g**
First Church of Christ Scientist, Montpelier Road: **39h**
Fish Market: **67e**
Fisher's Library, Old Steine: **89b**
fishing industry: **67**
see also: ancient customs; Jugg's Road; Lower Town; Old Steine; Resurrection, Church of the.
Fitzherbert R.C. Secondary School, Woodingdean: **214b**
flats:
(council 'tower-blocks'): **126c**
(tallest): 103,126c
see also: Embassy Court; Milner Flats; Model Dwellings; *and many other individual blocks.*
flints (as building material): **4b**
Floral Hall, Market Street & Black Lion Street: **100d**
Florence Place: 13,51,76
Florence Road, Preston: **130d**
Florida Rooms, Madeira Drive: **3e**
Forfars bakery: 159
fortifications: **8**
Foundry Street: 111
fountains:
see: Chatfield's Fountain; Mazda Fountain; Victoria Fountain.
Fonthill Road, Saltdean: 155c

Francis Street: 178
Franklin Road: 63
Franklin Tavern: 87d
Frederick Gardens: **110d**
Frederick Place: 4m
Free Butts, Phoenix Place: 14g
free schools: **172a**
Freedom of the Borough: **68**
Freehold Burial Ground, Florence Place: **51**
Fremlins Brewery, Black Lion Street: 115c
French Convalescent Home, De Courcel Road: **99g**
French Reformed Church, Queensbury Mews: **149l**
Freshfield Industrial Estate: 82
Freshfield Place: 172c
Freshfield Road:
(B.U.P.A.): 26p
(police station): 123d
(race-ground boundary stone): 140a
(Southdown buses): 26d,l,p
(telephone exchange): 179b
see also: General Hospital; race-course.
Friends' Meeting House, Prince Albert Street: **115r**
(ghost): **115n**
Fryco Mineral Water Company, Park Crescent Place: 120d
furlongs: **53b**
Gaiety Cinema, Hollingdean Road: **87d**
Gaiety Theatre, Park Crescent Place: **120d**
Galeed Baptist Chapel, Gloucester Road: **110f**
Gardner Centre for the Arts, University of Sussex: **188b**
Gardner Street: **110e**
(market): 100f
gas:
(buses): **26j**
(lighting): **176**
also: 69a,b
(supply): **69**
see also: Black Rock gas-works.
gates, defensive: **8b**
Gateway superstore, Brighton Marina: **98e**
Gazette newspaper:
see: Brighton Gazette
Gem Electric Cinema, London Road: **91a**
General Hospital, Elm Grove: **70**
also: 140a
General Library, Literary & Scientific Institute, St James's Street: **167a**
General Strike: **185d**
geology: 12,43d,45b,53a
George Beard, Gloucester Road: 103,110f
George Humphrey Park, Coldean: **44**
George Inn, West Street: **35,205b**
George Street: **167e**
Georgian architecture: **4d**
German Spa:
see: Royal Spa.
ghosts:
see: All Saints' Church, Patcham; Belle Vue Field; Bevendean Hospital; Black Horse Inn; Druid's Head; Grange, The; Meeting House Lane; Moulsecoomb Place; 'Old Strike-a-Light'; Patcham Place; Port Hall; Preston Manor; Prestonville Arms; Regency Tavern; St Nicholas's Churchyard; 'White Hawk Lady'.
Ginnett's Circuses:
(Park Crescent Place): **120d**
(North Road): 111
Girls' Club: **30b**
girls' homes:
see: Albion Hill Home; girls' orphanage; St Mary's Home.
girls' orphanage, Eastern Road: 58a
Gladstone Place: 87d
Gladstone Terrace, Lewes Road: **87d**
Globe Music Hall, Edward Street: 30c
Gloucester Place: **189b**
(horse-buses): 26a
(Magnus Volk): 195
Gloucester Road: **110f**
(postal sorting office): **129b**
see also: Eagle Hotel.
Gloucester Rooms, Gloucester Street: 110g
Gloucester Street: **110g**
(Female Orphan Asylum): 58a
Golden Fleece, Market Street: **115m**
Goldsmid Road, Hove: 13(iii)
Goldstone Bottom, Hove: 148a,169g
Goldstone Football Ground, Hove: **20a**
Goldstone pumping station, Hove: **200b-d**
also: 176
Golf Club railway halt: **50b**
golf courses:
see: Brighton & Hove; crazy golf; Dyke; East Brighton; Hollingbury Park; Lower Esplanade (putting greens); Roedean miniature; Rottingdean
Windmill miniature; Saltdean miniature; Sheepcote Valley (driving range); Waterhall.
Good Shepherd, Church of the, Dyke Road: **55f**
goods yards:
see: Brighton Station; Kemp Town Railway.
Gothic House, Western Road: **207c**
also: 209
Gothic revival architecture: **4f**
also: 87b
Grafton Street: **56k**
Grammar School: **22**
also: 29,203c
Grand Cinema, North Road: **111**
Grand Hotel, King's Road: **72**
(telegraph office): 179a
also: 140e
see also: Artillery Place.
Grand Junction Road: **73**
(lighting): 176
(and Pool Valley): 125
see also: Aquarium roundabout; Brill's Baths; Cannon Cinema; Fish Market; Queen's Hotel; Royal Albion Hotel.
Grand Olympia, Park Crescent Place: **120d**
Grand Parade: **189j**
see also: Grammar School; Polytechnic.
Grand Picture Palace, West Street: **205c**
Grand Theatre, North Road: **111**
Grange, The, Rottingdean: **155f**
Grange Farm Cottages, Ovingdean: 116f
'Greater Brighton': **13(iii)**
see also: Pylons.
Greek Orthodox Churches:
(Carlton Hill): **30a**
(Church Street): 36e
(High Street): 167g
Green, The, Rottingdean: **155**
Grenville Place: 37,78g
Greyhound, East Street: **57**
greyhound stadium, Hove: **21**
Grimmett's School: **172a**
Grove House: **161a,b**
groynes: **43b**
see also: Albion Groyne; Banjo Groyne.
Guardians of the Poor: **118e**
see also: Parochial Offices; Warren Farm Schools; workhouses.
Halfords:
(Western Road store): 207b
(Lewes Road superstore): 87f
Hamilton Lodge School, Walpole Road: 172e
Hamilton Road: 134
Hamilton Terrace: 134
Hammond Electric Light & Power Co.: **62a**
Hampton Place: **207e**
(Hampton Lodge): **207b**
(post-office): 207b
Hampton Street: 172b
Hand in Hand, Upper St James's Street: 14e
Hangman's Stone, Rottingdean: **154**
Hanningtons store, North Street: **112b**
(East Street): **57**
see also: Brighton Square.
Hanover: **74**
(development of area): **49(x)**
Hanover Chapel, Church Street: **36e**
Hanover Cricket Ground, Union Road: **120b**
Hanover Crescent: **74b**
(Training College): 124
Hanover Mill: **74d**
Hanover Place:
(almshouses): **87b**
(Brighton Co-operative Society): 46b
Hanover Street: **74b**
Hanover Terrace School: 172c
Happy Valley Park, Woodingdean: **214a**
harbours: **128**
see also: Marina.
Hare & Hounds, Preston Circus: **91a**
Harrington Farm, Hollingdean: **76**
Harrington Road, Preston: 4h,133d
Harrington Villas, Preston: 132a
Hartington Place: 33
Hartington Road: 63
(Brighton & Preston Cemetery): **33c**
(railway halt & viaduct): **82**
(St Martin's School): 87c,172b
(Scabe's Castle): 33,53b
Hartington Terrace: 33
Harveys store, Lewes Road: **87f**
Haybourne Road, Whitehawk: 13,13a(v)
Hayllar's Cottages, Middle Street: 115p
headboroughs: **118f**
health:
see: dispensaries; hospitals; poor; sewers; water supply.
Helsinki Café-Bar, Ship Street: **115t**
Hempshares: **67a**
Henley Road: 208c
Her Majesty's Theatre, New Road: **107**
Herald newspaper:
see: Brighton Herald.
Hereford Street: 56q,58,126c
Hertford Road, Hollingdean: 76
High church: **150**
high constables:
see: constables.
High Street, Brighton: **167g**
(Lying-In Institution): **78b**
High Street, Rottingdean: **156**
(police station): 123d
Highcroft, Dyke Road: **55d**
Highcroft Villas: 55d,134
see also: Lovers Walk Depot.
highest:
(hill): **53d**
(house number): 214a
(roads): **53d**
Highfields, Coldean: 13a
Highleigh, Albion Hill: **1a**
Highview Avenue South, Patcham: 122f
hill-forts: 17a,50a,51,75a,208a
hills: **53d**
(steepest): 1a,130e
Hillside, Rottingdean: **155r**
Hilly Laine: 53b
Hippodrome, Middle Street: **115p**
Hippodrome Circus, North Road: 111
Historic Commercial Vehicles Rally: 190
Hobden's Baths, King's Road: **7h**
Hodshrove, Moulsecoomb: **105e**
(railway viaduct): **144**
Hodson's Black Mill: **203k**
hogboats: **67d**
Holiday World, Madeira Drive: 3e
Hollingbury: **75**
also: 68(viii)
(housing estate): **75c**
(development of area): **49(xxvi)**
also: 24f
Hollingbury Castle Camp: **75a**
Hollingbury Gospel Hall, Hollingdean: **76**
Hollingbury Industrial Estate: **75d**
also: 4k,108a
Hollingbury Park: **75b**
see also: Roedale.
Hollingbury Park Avenue: 4h
Hollingbury Road: 76
Hollingdean: **76**
(development of area): **49(xix)**
see also: dust destructor; Hollingbury; St Joseph's School.
Hollingdean Road: **76**
(electrical sub-station): 62d
see also: Centenary Industrial Estate; dust destructor; Lewes Road waterworks; Saunders Park; Vogue gyratory system.
Hollingdean Terrace: 76
Holy Cross, Church of the, Woodingdean: **214a**
Holy Nativity, Church of the, Bevendean: 11
Holy Trinity Church, Ship Street: **115t**
Home Farm, Moulsecoomb: **105a**
(Business Centre): **105b**
Home Farm, Stanmer: **175d**
Home Farm, Withdean: **92d**

also: 92e
Homelees House, Dyke Road: 55a
Homeleigh, London Road: 123d
Homemakers Ltd:
see: Saltdean Estate Company.
Hooper Struve Ltd, Queen's Park: 138b
Horsdean Recreation Ground, Patcham: 85
horse-buses: **26a,b**
Hospitality Inn, King's Road: **77**
hospitals & clinics: **78c**
(and Queen's Road): 139b
see: Bevendean; Brighton, Hove & Preston Dental; Chest Clinic; French Convalescent Home; General; Hove General; Lady Chichester; New Sussex; Preston Barracks; Royal Alexandra; Royal Hospital & Home for Incurables; Royal Sussex County; St Francis, Haywards Heath; St Mary's Home (lying-in hospital & dispensary); School & Maternity Clinic; Sussex Eye; Sussex General Infirmary; Sussex Maternity; Sussex Throat & Ear.
see also: military hospitals.
house number (highest): 214a
housing: **126c**
Hove: **79**
(Amber Cup): **106b**
(constituency): 61
(and Edward VII): 59
(flax-growing): 67a
(hundreds): 118f
(and Preston): 131b
(promenades): 79c
(railway station): 79b,143,144
(railway tunnel): **143**
(town commissioners): 25
(Town Hall): **25**
also: 38
also: 7j,17d
see also: boundaries; Brighton & Hove Albion; Brighton & Hove Golf Club; Brighton & Hove Stadium; Brighton, Hove & Sussex Sixth Form College; British Engineerium; Brunswick Town; buses; dispensaries; Dyke Railway; Dyke Road Park; postal services; Sussex County Cricket Club; telegraphs; telephones; water supply; West Blatchington; West Coastway.
Hove Mill, Dyke Road: **55c**
Hove Villa, Dyke Road: **55c**
Howard Place: 203b
Howell's Almshouses, George Street: **167e**
Howlett Clarke Cushman (solicitors): **115t**
hundreds: **118f**
Huntingdon's Connexion, Countess of:
(North Street church): **112f**
(London Road chapel): 91c
Hyde, The, Bevendean: **11**
ice hockey: **205e**
ice skating:
see: skating (ice).
Imperial Arcade, Western Road/Dyke Road: **207b**
Imperial Picture Palace, St James's Street: **167a**
Imperial Theatre/Cinema, North Street: **112d**
Improvement Act 1884: **36e**,39m,47b,56g,74b, 95b,99c,d,140d,148b,149b,e,g,n,167f,169f
Improvement Commissioners:
see: Town Commissioners.
incorporation: **47a**
(and hundreds): 118f
(and town commissioners): 183
(and vestry): 118c
In Deo Fidemus: **47c**
industrial estates:
see: Bell Tower; Centenary; Coombe Road; Freshfield; Hollingbury; Home Farm; Hyde, The; Moulsecoomb; Woodingdean.
industrial schools, Woodingdean: **214b**
also: 136c,172c
Intercepting Sewer: **173c**
Inwood Crescent, Preston: 4h
Ireland's Gardens:
see: Royal Gardens.
I.R.A. bomb at Grand Hotel: **72**
Islingword Road: **74d**
(Constant Service): 200b
(Lewes Road Dispensary): 39x
also: 197
isolation hospitals: **78c,d**
Jacey Cinema, North Street: **112d**
Jack & Jill Windmills, Clayton: **55c**
Jesus Christ of Latter Day Saints, Church of, Coldean: **44**
jetfoil: **128**
Jew Street: **36c**
Jewish Cemeteries: 33b,51
Jill Mill, Clayton: **55c**
Jireh Chapel, Robert Street: **110p**
John Howard House, Roedean Road: **152**
John Street:
(boys' club): 60
(Chates Farm Court): **1a**
(courts): **48**
(police station): **123c**
Jubilee Street: **36b**
Junction Road: **139a**
Jugg's Road: **87a**
Kemp Street: **110h**
Kemp Town: 81
(air-raids): 216b
(constituency): **61**
(development of area): **49(viii)**
(and King's Cliff): 59
(pillar box): 129c
(post-office): **166b**,179a
(railway, station & tunnel): **82**
also: 87f
(St George's Road): **166**
(telephone exchange): 179b
also: 118a
see also: Kemp Town Estate
Kemp Town Brewery, Seymour Street: **14e**
Kemp Town Estate: **81**
(conservation area): **81**
(dock): **128**
(enclosures): **81f**
(esplanades): **81g**
(slopes): **81g**
also: 173b
see also: Black Rock (tunnel); St George's Church; St Mark's Church.
Kemp Town Golf Club, Roedean Road: **152**
Kemp Town Pier, St George's Road: **166b**
Kemp Town Place: **81c**
Kensington Gardens: **110j**
Kensington Place: 110k
Kent Street: **84**
King & Queen, Marlborough Place: **189a**
King Street: 36c
King's Cliff: **59**
see also: East Cliff; Marine Parade; Kemp Town.
King's Cliff Cinema, Sudeley Place: **166c**
King's Hotel, King's Road: **83b**
King's Road: **83**
(Bandstand): **83b**
(cliffs): **43d**
(lighting): 176
(planning award): 4m
(postal services): 129c
(sewers): 173b
(traffic lights): 151d
(underground railway): **142g**
also: 38,136c,195
see also: Bedford Hotel; Brighton Centre; Brighton Hotel; Grand Hotel; Hospitality Inn; King's Hotel; Kingswest Boulevard; Lower Esplanade; Mahomed's Baths; Metropole, Hotel; Norfolk Hotel; Old Ship Hotel; Queen's Hotel; St Alban's House; War Memorial (Regency Square); West Battery; West Pier.
King's Road Arches: **93**
also: 67c
see also: Fishmarket; lifeboats.
Kingswest Boulevard, King's Road & West Street: **84**
also: 18
Kingswood flats: **1a**
Kingswood Street: **30**
Kipling Garden, Rottingdean: **155b**
Kitchener Hospital, Elm Grove: **215d**
Knab: **115e**
Knight's Baths:
(King's Road): 7f
(Old Steine): 7g
Knoyle Hall, Knoyle Road: **133d**
Knoyle Road: 133d
Labour Clubs: 87d,185d
Ladies Mile Estate, Patcham: **85**
(development of area): **49(xxv)**
see also: Eastwick Barn earthworks.
Ladies Mile Road, Patcham: **85**
see also: Patcham High School; Patcham Library; Patcham Schools.
also: 24g
Lady Chichester Hospital, Ditchling Road & Hove: **39x**
Ladysmith Road, East Preston: 9
laines: **53b**
also: 76,188
Lamprell's Baths, East Street: **7j**
Lanes, The: **115k**
(lighting): 176
also: 140e
Lanes Café-Bar, Ship Street: **115t**
Lashmar's Windmill, Belmont: **55c**
Latter Day Saints, Church of Jesus Christ of, Coldean: **44**
Laughton Road, Woodingdean: 214a
Lauriston Road, Preston: 133d
Lawn Memorial Park, Woodingdean: **33d**
Leader newspaper: 108b
leakways: **53b**
Lee's Trap Cricket Ground: 39f
Lennox Street: 1b
Leopold Road: **203a**
Level, The: **86**
(police staion): **86**,66a
also: 42d,67d,136c
Lewes: **87a**
(Kemp family): 80
(martyrs): 115c
(races): 140a,e
(water supply): 200d
also: 6,42a,48,177a
see also: East Coastway; Russell, Dr Richard; St Pancras's Priory; Wilds, Amon.
Lewes Crescent, Kemp Town: **81d**
(Brighton College): 19a
(enclosures): **81f**
(Roedean School): 153
Lewes Road: **87**
('Battle of'): **185d**
(Co-operative store): 46b
(Falmer diversion): 65
(pillar boxes): 129c
(public houses): 135
(schools):
see: Fairlight Schools.
(railway station & viaduct): **82**
(sewer): 173b
(stream): 201
(traffic lights): 151d
(U.R.Church): **87d**
(waterworks): **200b-d**
also: 87e,175b
also: 151b,170,197
see also: Allenwest Ltd; Bear Inn; Extra-Mural Cemetery; Falmer High School; Falmer pumping station; Falmer (railway station); Hodshrove; Hodshrove Viaduct; Level; Moulsecoomb; Moulsecoomb Place; Moulsecoomb (railway station); Parkway; Polytechnic; St Mary's Home; sewers; Southern Water; Stanmer Park; Sussex Daily News; tramways; trolley-buses; University of Sussex; Wild Park; Wilds, Amon; Woodvale Cemetery.
Lewes Road Borough Cemetery:
see: Woodvale Cemetery.
Lewes Road Hospital & Dispensary for Women & Children, Round Hill Crescent: **39x**
Lewis Cohen Urban Studies Centre, Grand Parade: 189j
Leybourne Road, Bevendean: 120c
Libertys store, East Street: 57,115a
libraries:
(proprietary): **89**
(public):
(Brighton Library, Church Street): **88**
(children's library): **88d**
(lighting): 195
(music library): **36a,88d**
also: 161m

see also: Coldean; Hollingbury; Moulsecoomb; Patcham; Rottingdean; Saltdean; Westdene; Whitehawk; Woodingdean.
lifeboats: **90**
Lillywhite's Cricket Ground: 39f
Lincoln Street, Hanover: 74d
Lion Mansion Hotel, Grand Junction Road: **160c**
listed buildings: **45c**
literary & scientific institutions: 114g,160b,167a
Little East Street: **115l**
Little George Street: 167e
Little Laine: 53b
(windmills): 211
Little Russell Street: 172b
Little St James's Street: 167j
Little Theatre Company, Clarence Gardens: **149e**
Lloyds Bank, Rottingdean: **6**
local government:
see: corporation; parishes; town commissioners.
Loder Road Schools: 172d
London:
see: coaching; railways.
'London to Brighton in four minutes': **142h**
London & Brighton Railway Company: **141a,142a**
(and Queen's Road): 139a
(engineering works, New England Street): 146a
London to Brighton rallies: **190**
London to Brighton road: 42a,92a
London, Brighton & South Coast Railway Co.: **141a**
(engineering works, New England Street): **146**
(London main-line): **142**
(and Newhaven): 128
(and Queen's Road): 139a
(and races): 140b
see also: Dyke Road Drive; Kemp Town Railway; telegraphs.
London railway line: **142**
London Road (Brighton): **91**
(air-raids): 216b
(banks): 6
(carpark): **91c**
(development of area): **49(vi)**
also: 185d
see also: trolley-buses; Wellesbourne.
London Road (Patcham): **92**
(police station): 123d
also: 85
see also: Black Lion Hotel; Patcham Place; Patcham village; Wellesbourne; Withdean; Withdean Grange; Withdean Park.
London Road Chapel, Ann Street: **91c**,172c
London Road Railway Station, Shaftesbury Place: **144**
London Road Viaduct: **144**
also: 36d
London Street: 46a
longest roads: **151c**
Longhill School, Ovingdean: 172d
Longhursts Brewery, Preston Circus: **14b**
Longridge Avenue, Saltdean: **171e**
Lorne Villas, Preston: **130b**
Lourdes:
see: Our Lady of Lourdes.
Lovers Walk, Preston: **133b**
(railway depot & sidings): **145c,146c**
(trunk murder): 186
Low church: **150**
Lower Esplanade: **93**
(Aquarium subway): 3e
(and West Pier): 204c
see also: groynes; Fish Market; lifeboats.
Lower Rock Gardens: **56h**
also: 203c
Lower Roedale: **212b**
(former golf clubhouse): **75b**
Lower Tongdean Farm, Hove: 121
Lower Town: **94**
Luccombe's Library, Old Steine: **89a**
lunatic asylum, Haywards Heath: 78c
Lying-In Institute & Dispensary, High Street: **78f**
see also: St Mary's Home.
Mackie Avenue Recreation Ground, Patcham: **85**
Mackie Hall, Patcham: **85**
Madeira Drive: **95**
(buses): 26d
(coaches): 42d
(lighting): 176
see also: Aquarium; Aquarium roundabout; Banjo Groyne; Chain Pier; Kemp Town Estate Slopes; Palace Pier; sea-walls; Volk's Railway.
Madeira Lawns, Madeira Drive: **95c**
Madeira Lift, Madeira Drive & Marine Parade: **95b**
also: 173c
Madeira Place: **56d**
Madeira Shelter Hall, Madeira Drive: **95b**
also: 157d
Madeira Terrace, Madeira Drive: **95b**
Madeira Walk, Madeira Drive: **95b**
magistrates: **48**
Mahomed's Baths, King's Road: **7f**
also: 137
Mahomed's Royal Gymnasium, Paston Place: **166a**
Majestic Cinema, Edward Street: **60**
Manchester Street: **56a**
(boys' club): 60
Manor Farm Estate: **97**
(development of area): **49(xxx)**
see also: St David's Hall; Whitehawk F.C.
also: 19a
Manor Hill: **208a**
Manor Road: **97**
(St Mark's School): 172b
manors: **96**
(manor house, Brighton): **163**
(Saxon history): **17b**
also: 183b
Maresfield Road: 97
Margaret Hardy School: 189d
Margo's Mews, Rottingdean: **156h**
Marina: **98**
(borough boundary): **13(v)**
(fishing boats): 67c
see also: boundaries; lifeboats; Rifle Butt Road; Seajet; Volk's Railway.
Marine Drive: **154**
(boundary stones): 13a
(police station): 123d
(Rottingdean Library): 154
also: 156
see also: Intercepting Sewer; Marine Gate; Roedean; Roedean School; Rottingdean Windmill; St Dunstan's Institute; Saltdean; White Horse Hotel.
Marine Gardens: **56n**
Marine Gate, Marine Drive: **12**
Marine Parade: **99**
(Aquarium lift): 3e
(lighting): 176
(planning award): 4m
(postal services & pillar boxes): 129c
(storm): 40a
see also: Carden, Sir Herbert; cliff lifts; East Cliff Battery; East Mill; Kemp Town Estate; Royal Escape; sewers.
Marine Pavilion: **161a**
Marine Square: **99d**
(pillar box): 129c
Marine Terrace Mews: 99b
Market Inn, Market Street: **115m**
Market Street: **115m**
(wells): 200a
see also: markets; Regent Arcade; town halls; vicarages; workhouse.
markets: **100**
also: 2c,140f,145c,183d
see also: Brunswick Town.
Markwell's Hotel, King's Road: **137**
also: **8c**
Marlborough House, Old Steine: **114k**
Marlborough Place: **189a**
(Dental Hospital): **78e**
(Radio Sussex): **24b**
Marlborough Row: **161m**
also: 71c,f
Marlborough Street: 207e
Marlborough Theatre, Pavilion Street: **189l**
Marshall's Row: 91c
Martha Gunn winch: 67c
martyrs: 115c
Masonic Temple, Queen's Road: **139d**
Master of Ceremonies: **101**
Maternity Hospital, Buckingham Road: 78e
mathematical tiles: **4c**
'Matins & Muttons': **83b**
May Road: 126c
mayors: **102**
(car number-plate CD 1): 66c
also: 48
Mazda Fountain, Victoria Gardens: **194b**
Meadow Vale, Ovingdean Road: 214a
meat markets: **100l**
Mecca bingo hall, Middle Street: **115p**
medieval history: **17d**
Meeting House Lane: **115n**
(free school): 172a
Melbourne Street: 82,87d
Melville Road: 13(iii),129c
Members of Parliament: **61**
also: 183b
Menagerie, Coldean: 44
meteorology: **40**
Metropole, Hotel: **103**
(exhibition halls): **103**,149p
also: 190,27
MFI superstore, Hollingbury: 75d
Michael Faraday College, Woodingdean: **214b**
Middle Road, Preston: **131e**
Middle Street: **115p**
(post-office): 129b
(schools): **172a,c**
also: 115d
see also: Brighthelmston Dispensary; Brighton Herald; Brighton Provident & Self-Supporting Dispensary; Dukes Lane; Sherrys; Y.M.C.A.
Midhurst Rise: 75c
Midland Banks:
(Western Road): **207b**
(North Street): 112a
Mighell Street: **30c**
(soup kitchen): 126b
Mile End Cottages, Patcham: **85**
military camps & manouevres: **140c,148a**
military hospitals: 22,75b,81d,152,189d,215d
(Royal Pavilion): 161e
see also: Chattri; Royal Pavilion South Gate.
Mill Cottages, Patcham: **122f**
Mill Cottages, Rottingdean: **156j**
Mill House, Patcham: 122f
Mill Road, Patcham: **199**
see also: bypass (Brighton); Patcham pumping station.
Millers Road, Preston: 55d
Millfield Cottages, Sudeley Place: **166c**
Milner Flats: **1a**
Mithras House, Dewe Road: **105d**
Model Dwellings, Church Street & Clarence Place: **36c**
Mods & Rockers: **104**,196e
Montagu Motor Museum, Madeira Drive: **3e**
Montague Place: 26c,e
(Bristol Road Methodist Church): 23
Montpelier Crescent: **39f**
(Brighton and Hove High School): 39q
Montpelier Hotel, Sillwood Place: 149q
Montpelier Place: **39g**
Montpelier Road: **39h,149f**
see also: Brighton & Hove High School; Sillwood House.
Montpelier Street: **39j**
Montpelier Terrace: **39k**
Montpelier Villas: **39l**
also: 149l
Morley Street: **1a**
Mormon Church, Coldean: **44**
Morning Argus: **108a**
mortuary: **33a**
Motor Cycle Rally: 190
Motor Museum, Madeira Drive: **3e**
Motor Race Week: **95b**
motto (*In Deo Fidemus*): **47c**
Moulsecoomb: **105**
(Baptist church): 105c
(community leisure centre): **105c**
(development of area): **49(xxvii)**
(dispensary): 78b
(industrial estate): **105d**,4k
(railway station): **144**
(schools): 172d
(Wild Park): **105f**
also: 24g

see also: Polytechnic; Queensdown School.
Moulsecoomb Place, Lewes Road: **105a**
Moulsecoomb Way: 105
(bus garage): 26l
(churches): 105c
(community leisure centre): **105c**
(industrial estate): **105d**,4k
(Salvation Army): 120c
Municipal Hospital, Elm Grove: **70**
municipal incorporation: 47a
museums:
(Brighton, Church Street): **106**
(exhibits): **106b**,216b
also: 29,34c,41,47b,55a,67d,110e,118f, 149q,157e,161g,164,183d,185b,196f,198, 204a,205d,207c,208a,209
(lighting): **195**
(offices): 161m
see also: Booth's Natural History; Grange, Rottingdean; Motor Museum; Museum of Brighton; Preston Manor (Thomas-Stanford Museum); Slot Machine Museum; Stanmer Rural Museum; Toy Museum.
Museum of Brighton, Ship Street: **115t**
also: 106b
music library, Church Street: **36a**,**88d**
Muttons Hotel & Restaurant, King's Road: 83b
Nathaniel Episcopal Reformed Church, West Hill Road: **203k**
National Bus Company: **26n**
National Canine Defence League, Robertson Road: **130g**
National Fire Service: **66d**
see also: Saltdean Lido.
National Lilac Collection, Withdean Park: **212d**
National Museum of Penny Slot Machines, King's Road Arches: **93**
national nature reserve (Castle Hill, Balsdean): **5**
National Schools: **172a**
National Speed Trials, Madeira Drive: **95b**
National Spiritualist Church, Edward Street: **60**
National Telephone Company: **179b**
(Rottingdean exchange): 6
National Toy Museum: 106b
National Westminster Banks:
(London Road): 6
(North Street): 112a
(Pavilion Buildings): 32
(St James's Street): **167a**
(Western Road): 207b
naturist beach: **7a**
Nelson Row: 1b,30b,172a
Nevill Road, Rottingdean: 154,156g
New Barn, Falmer Road: **155z**
(flooding): 40a
New Coronation Cinema, North Road: **111**
New England Farm: **134**
New England House: **91c**
New England Square: 91c
New England Road:
(boundaries): 13,13a
(Christ Church Evangelical Chapel): **91c**
(Elim Chapel): **91c**
(railway bridge, lower): 145c
(railway viaduct, upper): **142d**
(boundary stone): **13a**
see also: trolley-buses.
New England Street: 91c,d
(goods yard): 145c
(London Road carpark): **91c**
(Railway Enginering Works): **146**
New Inn:
see: Clarence House.
New Life Centre, Lewes Road: **87d**
New Oxford Music Hall, New Road: 107
New Road: **107**
(Chapel Royal hall): 112e
(fire-station): 66b
(Pavilion Theatre): **52c**
(post-office): 129b
see also: Theatre Royal; Volunteer.
New Ship Inn, Ship Street: **115t**
also: 183a
New Steine: **56g**
also: 34a,43c
New Steine Mansions, St James's Street: 167a
New Sussex Hospital, Windlesham Road: **39x**
New Venture Theatre, Bedford Place: **149a**
Newhaven:
(port): 128,146b,c
(railway): 144
(turnpike): 249319a
Newhouse Farm, Sheepcote Valley: 208d
Newlands Road, Rottingdean: 136c
newspapers: **108**
nicknames for Brighton: **16c**,172a
Nile River Expedition: **114f**,148d
also: 68(i)
Nile Street: **115q**
also: 78a
Norfolk Buildings, Sillwood Street: 109
Norfolk Groyne: **43b**
Norfolk Resort Hotel, King's Road: **109**
Norfolk Road: **207e**
Norfolk Square: **149g**
Norfolk Street: **149h**
Norfolk Terrace: 39a
(Brighton & Hove High School): 39q
Norman history: **17c**
North Drive, Queen's Park: 138c
North End House, Rottingdean: **155p**
North Gardens: **203g**
North Gate House: **161m**
North Laine: **110**
(development of area): **49(v)**
see also: North Road.
North Moulsecoomb: **105b**
North Place: 110
North Road, Brighton: **111**
(postal sorting office): **129b**
(power station): **62**
(public baths): **111**
(telephone exchange): 179b
see also: Brighthelm Community Centre; Brighton Co-operative Society; Evening Argus; Sun Dial House.
North Road, Preston: **131d**
North Row: 189a
North Steine:
see: Victoria Gardens.
North Street: **112**
(banks): 6
(Chapel Royal): **112e**
(coaching): 42a
(Countess of Huntingdon's Church): **112f**
(courts): 48
(lighting): 176
(post-office): 129b
(theatre): **181**
also: 140d
see also: Brighthelmston Dispensary; Clock Tower; Friends' Meeting House; newspapers; Regent Cinema; Royal Colonnade.
North Street Brewery: **14f**
Northgate Cottages, Rottingdean: **155z**
Norton Farm, Balsdean: 5
Novelty Cinema, West Street: **205b**
nude bathing: **7a**
Oak Hotel, West Street: **205b**
Ocean Hotel, Saltdean: **171e**
Oddfellows Hall, Queen's Road: **139b**
Odeon Cinemas:
(Kemp Town): **166b**
(King's Road): **83b**
(Kingswest Boulevard): **84**
(West Street): **205b**
Old Bank, North Street: **6**
Old Boat Corner: **51**
'Old Crocks' rally: **190**
Old Farm House, Rottingdean: **155t**
Old Fashioned Penny Palace, Lower Esplanade: **93**
Old London Road, Patcham: **122f**
(Wellesbourne): 201
see also: Patcham House School; Purley Lodge; Square, The.
Old Mill Close, Patcham: 122f
"Old Ocean's Bauble": 16c
Old Ship Hotel: **113**
(coaching): 42a
(Master of Ceremonies): 101
(post-office): 129b
also: 162a,190
see also: corn market; courts.
Old Shoreham Road:
(boundaries): 13(iii),13a,130a
(railway works): 146b,c
also: 4g
see also: Brighton & Hove Albion F.C; Prestonville.
Old Steine: **114**
(pillar-boxes): 129c
(and Prince of Wales): 71b
(traffic lights): 151d
also: 31c,34a,177a
see also: Baker's Library; Donaldson's Library; North Steine; Royal Pavilion Grounds; Royal Albion Hotel; Royal York Buildings; Russell House; telegraphs; Wellesbourne; Williams's Baths; Woodgate's Library.
'Old Strike-a-Light': **57**
Old Town: **115**
(development of area): **49(i)**
(lighting): 62c,176
(Lower Town): 94
also: 126c,135
see also: Brighton (early history).
Old Vicarage, Temple Gardens: **39q**,**192a**
Olde Place Hotel, Rottingdean: **156n**
Olde Place Mews, Rottingdean: **155l**
oldest buildings: 105a,115b,115c,115n,116b, 122c,155g,156f
Olympic Stadium:
see: Withdean Stadium
'On a clear day you can see forever': 81f
Open Market: **91c**
Orange Row: **36d**
orchestra (municipal): 3d
Oriana's nightclub, King's Road: **84**
Oriental Place: **149j**
orphanage: **58a**
Osprey House, Sillwood Place & Montpelier Road: 149q
Our Lady of Lourdes:
(Convent, London Road): 92c
(R.C. Church, Rottingdean): **155g**
(R.C. School, Rottingdean): **155m**
Overhill Way, Patcham: 122f
Overseers of the Poor: **118d**
also: 17e
Over Street: **110l**
Ovingdean: **116**
('Battle of'): 140c
(boundary stones): 13a
(development of area): **49(xxxii)**
(hundreds): 118f
(postal service): 129c
(TV transmitter): **24g**
also: 17e,200c
see also: New Barn; Race-course; Rottingdean Place.
Ovingdean Close: 214a
Ovingdean Gap: 43d
(Rottingdean Railway): 157d
(St Dunstan's Institute): **165**
(Undercliff Walk): 187
Ovingdean Grange: **116c**
(novel): 81b,116a
Ovingdean Hall: **116d**
(farm): 116g
Ovingdean Road: **116f,g**
(Church Room): 116b
(Meadow Vale): **214a**
(Woodingdean Farm): **214a**
Oxford Street: **91c**
(post-office): 129c
paddling pools: **93**
Palace Pier: **117**
also: 128,140e
Palace Place: 31a,179b
see also: Royal Pavilion Great Kitchen.
Palladium, West Street: **205e**
Palladium Cinema, King's Road: **83b**
Pankhurst Avenue: 126c
see also: General Hospital.
Paradise Street: 126c
Paris Cinema & Theatre, New Road: **107**
parishes: **118**
(boundaries): **13**
Park, The, Lewes Road, Coldean:
see: Parkway, The.
Park Crescent: **120**
(Trunk murder): **186**
Park Crescent Place: 87d,120d
Park Crescent Terrace: 120c

Park Hill: 138d
see also: Royal Spa.
Park Road, Coldean: 44
Park Road, Rottingdean: 154,179b
Park Road Terrace: 1b
Park Street: **138d**
(Queen's Park gateway): **138a**
parking meters: 151d
Parkmore Terrace, Dyke Road Drive: **133a**
parks: **119**
(parks, recreation grounds & playing fields):
see: Avenue, Moulsecoomb; Barn Rise; Blaker Rec.; Brapool; Carden; Central Woodingdean; Dyke Road Park; East Brighton; Farm Green; George Humphrey Park; Happy Valley; Hollingbury; Horsdean; Level; Mackie Avenue Rec.; Parkway; Patcham Rec.; Plainfields; Preston; Preston Vicarage Lawns; Queen's; St Anne's Wells Gardens; Saltdean; Saunders; Stanmer; Surrenden Field; Tarner Rec.; Vale Avenue; Waterhall; Whitehawk; Wild Park; William Clarke Park; Withdean.
(gardens):
see: Bedford Square; Chattri; Clarence Square; Clifton Gardens; Dorset Gardens; Dyke Road Rest Garden; Extra-Mural Cemetery; Hanover Crescent; Kemp Town Estate Enclosures; Kipling Garden; Marine Square; Montpelier Crescent; New Steine; Norfolk Square; Old Steine; Park Crescent; Peace Gardens; Pelham Square; Powis Square; Preston Rockery; Queen Mother's Garden; Queen's Road Rest Garden; Regency Square; Rottingdean Green; Royal Pavilion Grounds; Russell Square; St Nicholas's Churchyard; St Peter's Churchyard; Victoria Gardens; Western Lawns.
see also: golf courses.
Parks and Recreation Department: **119**
(nurseries): **175b**
also: 86,87e,105a,201,212b
Parkway, The, Lewes Road, Coldean: **105f**
also: 61
parliamentary borough: **61**
also: 207e
Parochial Cemetery:
see: Woodvale Cemetery.
Parochial Offices, Prince's Street: **118e**,189l
Paston Place: **56u**,**166a**,**166b**
Paston Place Groyne:
see: Banjo Groyne
Paston Place Station:
see: Volk's Railway.
Patcham: **121**
(bypass): 92a
(Clock Tower, Mackie Avenue): 85
(development of area): **49(xxiii)**,**49(xxiv)**
(fountain): **122c**
(hundreds): 118f
(library, Ladies Mile Road): **121**
(manors): 96
(Memorial Hall, Old London Road): 122f
(Methodist Church, Ladies Mile Road): 85
(police station, London Road): 123d
(postal services): **129c**
(pumping station, Mill Road): **200c,d**
also: 201
(railway tunnel): **142d**
(schools): 122f,172d,189d
(TV transmitter): **24g**
(village): **122**
(windmills):
(Waterhall): **199**
(Ballard's): **122f**
also: 17e,150,200
see also: Brangwyn Estate; Chattri; Hollingbury; Horsdean Recreation Ground; Ladies Mile; London Road (Patcham); Moulsecoomb; Peace Gardens; Wellesbourne; Westdene; Withdean.
Patcham Court Farm, Vale Avenue: **122a**
also: 121
Patcham High School: 172d
Patcham House School, Old London Road: **122f**
Patcham Place, London Road: **122d**
Patcham Recreation Ground, London Road: **122d**
Patchdean, Patcham: 121
Patchway: 65,96
paul-pieces: **53b**
Pavilion Baptist Chapel, Church Street: **36a**
Pavilion Buildings: **32**
see also: Royal Pavilion South Gate.
Pavilion constituency: **61**
Pavilion Centre, Lewes Road: **87f**
Pavilion Parade: **189k**
Pavilion, Royal:
see: Royal Pavilion.
Pavilion Street: 189l
Pavilion Theatre, New Road: **52d**
also: 66b,115r
Peace Gardens, Patcham: **122g**
Peace Memorial, King's Road: **83b**
Peacock Lane, Withdean: 92d
see also: Withdean Park.
Pearson House, St George's Road: **56t**,**165**
also: **19a**
pedestrian crossings: 151d
Peel Place: 145c,146b
Peel Street: 145c,191
Pelham Institute, Upper Bedford Street: **58**
Pelham Square: **110m**
Pelham Street:
(schools): **189d**
(College of Technology): **178**
'Pepper-Box', Queen's Park Road: **138c**
Percival Terrace: **99f**
Percy & Wagner Almshouses, Lewes Road: **87b**
Peter Pan's Leisure Park, Madeira Drive: **95c**
see also: Volk's Railway.
pets' cemetery, Preston Manor: 131a
Petty France, North Street: 112a
Petty Sessions: **48**
Phoenix Brewery, Albion Street: **14g**
also: 14a
Phoenix Place: 14g
Picton Street: 82
Picturedrome Cinema, Edward Street: **60**
Picturedrome Cinema, Western Road: **207d**
piers:
see: Chain Pier; Palace Pier; Rottingdean Pier; West Pier.
Pilgrims Cottages, Tillstone Street: **138d**
pillar boxes: 129c
Pimlico, Church Street: 36d
Pirates Deep, Madeira Drive: 3e
pitch & putt courses:
see: Roedean; Rottingdean Windmill; Saltdean.
Plainfields, Patcham: 85
planning:
(awards): **4m**
(controls): 47b,183
Playhouse Cinema & Theatre, Sudeley Place: **166c**
pleasure gardens:
see: Promenade Grove; Queen's Park; Royal Gardens; Tivoli Gardens.
Plough Inn, Rottingdean: **155j**
Plymouth Bretheren: 110g
police: **123**
(police fire-brigade): **66c**
(police stations): **123c,d**
see also: ambulance service; General Strike; Mods & Rockers; Saturday morning market; traffic control.
Polytechnic: **124**
(Bear Road annexe): **9**
(Circus Street annexe): 172c
(Falmer (former College of Education)): **124**
also: **55d**
(Finsbury Road annexe): 172c
(Grand Parade (former College of Art)): **124**
also: **30**
(Lewis Cohen Urban Studies Centre): 189j
(Mithras House, Dewe Road): **105d**
(Moulsecoomb (former College of Technology)): **124**
(Pavilion Parade annexe): 189k
Pool Valley: **125**
(wells): 200a
see also: Awsiter's Baths; Brill's Baths; Cannon Cinema; Greyhound; Lion Mansion Hotel; Royal York Buildings; Wellesbourne.
poor: **126**
(bequests): 169c
(charities): **126b**
(history): **126a**
(housing): **126c**
see also: Guardians of the Poor; Overseers; Warren Farm Schools; workhouses.
Poor Law Institution, Elm Grove: **215d**
Poplar Place: 115n
population: **127**
also: 17e,141
Port Hall, Dyke Road: **55d**
(mill): **55d**
Port Hall Avenue:
see: Elm Court.
Port Hall Road: 26a,55d
Port of Brighton: **128**
Portland House, Portland Place/St George's Road: **56t**
see also: Brighton College.
Portland Place: **56t**
see also: Portland House.
Portland Street: 36c
Portman Building Society, North Street: **112c**
Portobello Sewage Treatment Works, Telscombe Cliffs: **173c**
Portslade:
(annexation by Hove): 79b
(conservation area): 79c
(gas-works): **69**
(industrial school): 172c
(railway station): 143
(telephone exchange): 179b
also: 38,62e,78b,96,97,111,200d
see also: Southern Sound Radio.
postal services: **129**
(administrative offices): 37,189b
(General Post-Office):
see also: telegraphs; telephones.
(head post-office): **129b**
see also: telegraphs.
(post-offices): **129c**
also: 166b,207b
(sorting offices): 129b,c
(parcels): 36c
also: 62c
Poune's Court, West Street: 36c
poverty of town: 17d,e,f
(the poor): **126**
(Rottingdean): 154
power stations: **62**
Powis Grove: **39w**
Powis Square: **39m**
Powis Villas: **39n**
Presbyterian Meeting House, Union Street: **115v**
Presbyterian Church, Church Street: **36e**
Preston: **130**
(boundary stones): 13a
(buses): 26a
(constituencies): 61
(development of area): **49(xv)**,**(xvi)**,**(xvii)**
(Guardians of the Poor): 118e
(hundreds): 118f
(infant school): 131d
(mills):
see: Bear Mill; Port Hall; Preston Mill.
(old church): **131b**
also: 131a,186
(postal services): 129c
(Roman Villa): **133a**
(telephone exchange, Bavant Road): 179b
(toll-gate): 92b
(village): **131**
also: 118a,150,200c
see also: Bear Road; Coombe Road; Ditchling Road; Dyke Road; Dyke Road Drive; East Preston; fairs; Hollingdean; horse-buses; markets; Prestonville; Radynden Manor.
Preston Barracks, Lewes Road: **87f**
also: 61
see also: Saunders Park.
Preston Brewery Tap, Preston Road: 14h,131f
Preston Circus: **91a**
(fire station): **66c,d**
(roundabout): 151d
(traffic lights): 151d
also: 193
see also: Duke of York's Cinema; police stations.

Preston Club, South Road/Preston Road: 131f
Preston Dairy Farm, Preston Road: **133b**
Preston Drove: **130e**
see also: Preston Manor; Preston Park; St Peter's Church; trolley-buses.
Preston Farm, South Road: 131f
Preston Grange, Preston Road: 133b
Preston Manor, Preston Drove: **131a**
(exhibits): 55d,106
also: 149k
see also: Preston Park.
Preston Mill, Dyke Road: **55d**
Preston Park: **132**
(carnival): 64
(conservation area): **130**
(cycle track & cricket ground): **132d**
also: 87e
also: 194b,201
Preston Park Avenue: **130f**
Preston Park Baptist Church, Surrenden Road: **130g**
Preston Park Railway Station, Clermont Road: **142e**
Preston Resort Hotel, Preston Road: **133d**
Preston Road: **133**
(Roman Villa): **133a**
(Wesleyan Chapel, Dyke Road Avenue): **133a**
see also: London Road Viaduct; Preston Brewery Tap; Preston Park; Preston Rockery; Volk, Magnus.
Preston Rockery, Preston Road: **132e**
Preston Rural parish: **130a**
(annexation by Hove): 79b
(constituencies): 61
(Dyke Road Park): 55d
(Grammar School): 22
Preston Street: **149k**
(postal services): 129c
see also: Volk, Magnus.
Preston Vicarage Lawns, Preston Road: **133c**
Prestonville: **134**
(development of area): **49(xviii)**
also: 4g
Prestonville Arms, Hamilton Road: 134
Prestonville Court, Dyke Road: 55c
Prestonville Road: 133b,134
Prince Albert Street: **115r**
(vicarage): 192a
(Y.M.C.A.): 111
Prince of Wales's Cricket Ground, The Level: **86**
Prince of Wales's Dairy, Preston: **133a**,96
Prince Regent Swimming Complex, North Road/Church Street: **111**
Prince's Cinema, North Street: **112d**
Prince's Hall, Madeira Drive: **3e**
Prince's Hotel, Grand Junction Road: **73**
Prince's Place: **112a**
(post-office): 129b
see also: Brighton Herald; Chapel Royal; Promenade Grove.
Prince's Street: **189l**
Prior's Lodge: **192a**,115a
Priory House, Bartholomew Square: 115a,184a
promenades:
see: Grand Junction Road; Hove; Kemp Town Esplanades; King's Road; Lower Esplanade; Madeira Drive; Madeira Terrace; Madeira Walk; Marine Parade; Old Steine; Undercliff Walk.
see also: piers.
Promenade Grove: **161j**
prostitution: **136c**
also: 107,**148a**
Protestant martyrs: **115c**
Providence chapels:
(Church Street): **36d**
(West Hill Road): **203k**
Providence Place: 91d,172b
(London Road Carpark): **91c**
Public Assistance Committee: 118e,126a,189l,215d
public houses: **135**
Puget Schools, Clarence Yard: 172
Pullman trains: **142k**
also: 146c
Pump House, Brighton Place: **115m**
Purley Lodge, Patcham: 172c
putting greens: **93**
Pylons, The, London Road: **92e**
Pym's Gardens, Church Street: **36d**
Quakers: **115r**
also: 35
Quarter Sessions: **48**
Queen Mother's Garden, Pelham Square: **110m**
'Queen of watering places': 16c
Queen Square: **136**
Queen Street: 145c
Queen's Electric Cinema, Western Road: **207d**
Queen's Gardens: **110n**
Queen's Hotel, King's Road & Grand Junction Road: **137**
Queen's Nurses' Home, Wellington Road: **63**
Queen's Park: **138**
(conservation area): **138d**
(development of area): **49(xi)**
(housing estate): 4j,126c
(Methodist Church): **138d**
(school): 172c
Queen's Park Rise: 4h
Queen's Park Road: **138d**
(Pepper-Box): **138c**
also: 185c,195
Queen's Park Terrace: 4h,138c
Queen's Picture Theatre, Western Road: **207d**
Queen's Place: **91c**
also: 46a
Queen's Regiment: 68(ix)
Queen's Road: **139**
(lighting): 62a
(postal sevices): 129c
(Rest Garden): **36e**
(underground railway): **142g**
also: 4k,140e
see also: Boots store; Brighton, Hove & Preston Dispensary; Brighton, Hove & Preston Provident Dispensary; Brighton Station; Clock Tower; Dental Hospital; Sussex Eye Hospital; Sussex Throat & Ear Hospital; tramways; White Lion Inn.
Queensbury Mews: **149l**
see also: Metropole.
Queensdown School, Moulsecoomb & Hollingdean: 172e
Queensway: 140a
Race-course: **140**
(gangs): 140e
(Race Stand Trustees): **140b,d**
see also: Queen's Park.
also: 7b,185b
Race Hill: **140a**
(boundary stones): 13a,140a
(fairs): 64,208b
(windmill): **9**
also: 53d,185b
see also: Bear Road.
radio stations: **24a-e**
Radio Sussex: **24a**
Radynden Manor, Preston: **96**
Ragged Schools: 172a
Railwayland, King's Road Arches: 67e
Railway Mission, Viaduct Road: **191**,146b
Railway Street: 203h
railways:
(accidents): **142j**,143
(Brighton Belle): **142k**
(companies & groupings): **141a**
(effects of railway): **141**
(Brighton as a port): 43a,128
(coaching): 42c
(London Road area): 91c
(Master of Ceremonies): 101c
(military transport): 140c
(races): 140b
(electrification): **142h,143,144**
(engineering works): **146**
also: 185d
(goods yards): **82,145c**,144
(lines):
(Cliftonville Spur): **143**
also: 142e
(Devil's Dyke Railway): **50b**
(Dyke Suspension Railway): **50a**
(Dyke Steep-Grade Railway): **50a**
(East Coastway): **144**
also: 76,82
(Kemp Town Railway): **82**
also: 87d
(London main-line): **142**
(Rottingdean Railway): **157**
(Saltdean): 171a
(underground railway): **142g**
(Volk's Railway): **196**
also: 174,195
(West Coastway): **143**
(Withdean Stadium): 213
(luxury trains): **142k**
(services): 142g,h
(stations):
(Aldrington Halt): **50b**
(Brighton):
see: Brighton Station.
(Dyke): **50b**
(Falmer): **144**
(Golf Club Halt): **50b**
('Hangleton Halt'): 50b
(Hartington Road Halt): **82**
(Hove): **79b**,143,144
(Kemp Town): **82**
(Lewes Road): **82**
(London Bridge): **142b,n**
(London Road): **144**
(Moulsecoomb): **144**
(Portslade): 82,143
(Preston Park): **142e**
(Rowan Halt): **50b**
(Victoria): **142b,g,k**
also: 145b
see also: Rottingdean Railway; Volk's Railway.
(tunnels):
(Balcombe): **142d**
(Brighton Goods): **145c**
(Clayton): **142d,j**
(Cliftonville): **143**
(Ditchling Road): **144**
(Falmer): **144**
(Haywards Heath): **142d**
(Hove): **143**
(Kemp Town): **82**
(Kingston): **144**
(Merstham): **142d**
(New Merstham (Quarry line)): **142g**
(Patcham): **142d**
(Redhill): **142g**
(viaducts):
(Hartington Road): **82**
(Hodshrove): **144**
(Lewes Road): **82**
(London Road): **144**
also: 36d
(New England): **142d**
also: 13a
(Ouse Valley): **142d**
(widening): 142g
rainfall: **40**
Ramada Renaissance Hotel:
see: Hospitality Inn.
ratepayers:
see: vestry.
'red-brick architecture': **4h**
Refuge Assurance House, North Street: 108j
refuse: **147**
see also: Waterhall.
Regal Cinema, Western Road: **207d**
Regency, The: **71e**
Regency architecture: **4e**
Regency Exhibitions, Royal Pavilion: 161f
Regency Mews: **149m**
Regency Road: 205a
see also: Wagner Hall.
Regency Society: 25
Regency Square: **148**
(conservation area): **149**
(development of area): **49(ii)**
(planning award): 4m
also: **204a**
see also: Abbotts; Regency Mews; Regency Tavern.
Regency Tavern, Russell Square/ Regency Square: **149n**
Regent Arcade: **115s**
Regent Cinema, Queen's Road: **139c**
Regent Hill: **207e**
see also: North Street Brewery.
Regent Iron Foundry, North Road: **111**
also: 62
Regent Row: **55a**
registry offices: 163,189l

religion: **150**
see also: parishes.
Resurrection, Church of the, Russell Street: **100l**
Resurrection, Church of the, Woodingdean: **214a**
Resurrection, Parish of the: 9,87c,138d
Rex Cinema, North Road: **111**
Richmond Gardens: **189h**
Richmond Green: 170
Richmond Parade: 1a
Richmond Place: **189h**
see also: St Peter's Church.
Richmond Road: 159
Richmond Street: **1a**
(school): 172c
Richmond Terrace: **189f**
see also: Brighton & Hove Women's Hospital; College of Education; Level; Technology, College of; Wilds, Amon.
Rifle Butt Road, Black Rock: **12**
(police station): 123d
(Quakers): 115r
also: 78b,208d
rifle-ranges: 3e,140c,145c,155m
Ringmer Road, Moulsecoomb: 105c
ritualism: **150**
also: 205d
R.N.L.I.: **90**
roads: **151**
(classified): **151b**
(development): **49**
(highest): 53d
(history): **151a**
(longest): **151c**
(name changes): **151f**
(name derivations): **151e**
(steepest): 1a,130e
(turnpikes): **151a**
also: 183b
Robert Street: 108j,110p
Robertson Road, Preston: 130g
Rock Brewery: **14j**
see also: Black Lion Brewery.
Rock Grove, Kemp Town: 81c
Rock Street, Kemp Town: 129c
rockeries:
(Preston Park): **132e**
(Queen's Park): 138a
rockers & mods: **104**
Roedale, Ditchling Road: **212b**
Roedale Road, Hollingdean: 75c,76
Roedean: **152**
(development of area): **49(xxxi)**
(fire-station, Roedean Road): **66d**
(miniature golf-course): **152**
(sewer chimney): 173c
(Undercliff Walk): 187
(windmill): **152**
Roedean Road: **152**
see also: East Brighton Park; Roedean fire-station.
Roedean School, Marine Drive: **153**
roller-skating:
see: skating (roller).
Roman history: **17a**
Roman villa, Preston: **133a**
Rookery, Preston: **132e**
Rose Hill: 159
Rottingdean: **154**
(air-raids): 156
(bowling club): 155v
(cricket club): **158**
(development of area): **49(xxxiii)**
(Gap): **154,156**
(Rottingdean Railway & Pier): **157b**
(floods): 40a
(Green): **155**
(High Street): **156**
(hundreds): 118f
(library): 154
(manors): 96
(miniature golf-course, Marine Drive): 158
(pier): **157b,e**
(pond): **155**
(postal services): 129c
(Public Hall, Park Road): **154**
(railway to Brighton): **157**
(Reading Room): **156g**
(refuse): 208d
(royalty): 193,210
(schools): 154,155g,156g,172d
(swimming-pool): **187**
(telephone exchanges): 6,179b
(Undercliff Walk): **187**
(village schools): 154,156g
(village square): **156g**
(war memorial): **155**
(windmill): **158**
also: 24f,85,200c
see also: Balsdean; Beacon Hill; Falmer Road; fire stations; Marine Drive; police stations.
Rottingdean Green: **155**
Rottingdean Heights: 154,173c
Rottingdean High Street: **156**
Rottingdean Place, Falmer Road: **155z**
Rottingdean School: 155z,156r
Rottingdean Railway: **157**
Rottingdean Windmill: **158**
Rotyngs, The: 155z
Round Hill: **159**
(development of area): **49(xiii)**
also: 61
Round Hill Crescent: **159**
(Lewes Road Hospital): **39x**
roundabouts: **151d**
Royal Albion Hotel, Old Steine: **160**
also: 73,164
Royal Alexandra Hospital, Dyke Road: **55b**
Royal Bank of Scotland, Castle Square: **32**
Royal Chapel: **31c**
(St Stephen's Church): **39g**
Royal Circus & Riding School, Grand Parade: **189j**
Royal Colonnade, New Road: **107**
Royal Crescent: **99c**
Royal Crescent Hotel, Marine Parade: **99b**
Royal Escape, Marine Parade: 35
Royal Gardens, Union Road: **120b**
Royal German Spa, Queen's Park: **138b**
also: **36e**
Royal Gymnasium, Paston Place: **166a**
Royal Hippodrome, Park Crescent Place: **120d**
Royal Hospital & Home for Incurables, Roedean Road: **152**
Royal Literary & Scientific Institution: **160b**
also: 114g
Royal National Institute for the Blind, Queen's Road: 162c
Royal National Lifeboat Institution: 90
Royal Newburgh Assembly Rooms, St Margaret's Place: **149p**
Royal Pavilion: **161**
(chapel): **31c**
(St Stephen's Church): 39g
(clock tower): 161d
(dormitories): **32**
also: 108b
(great kitchen): **161h**
(grounds): **161j**
(air-raids): 216b
(Burrows Statue): 114d
(library, museum & art gallery): 88a,106a
(military hospital): **161e**
see also: Chattri; Royal Pavilion South Gate.
(North Gate): **161k**
also: 193
(offices): 161m
(paintings): 7b,130f
(purchase): **161c**
(Regency Exhibitions): **161f**
(riding school):
see: Corn Exchange.
(South Gate): **161n**
(stables):
see: Dome.
also: 18,24f,29,160b,184a
see also: Crown Gardens; William IV.
Royal Pavilion Tavern, Castle Square: **32**
Royal Spa, Queen's Park: **138b**
also: **36e**
Royal Sussex County Hospital, Eastern Road: **162**
(maternity): 78f
(throats & ears): 78g
also: 112b,196g
Royal Sussex Regiment: **68(ix)**
also: 36c,114f,148d,189b
Royal York Buildings/Hotel, Old Steine: **163**
(telegraphs): 179a
also: 174
royalty: 71b
Rugby Place, Whitehawk: 208c,216b
Russell Crescent: **55c**
Russell House, Old Steine: **164**
Russell Place: 172b
Russell Square: **149n**
Russell Street:
(Cannon Brewery): **14d**
(clearances): 37
(market): 100l
(Church of the Resurrection): **100l**
also: 18,67c,126c
Saddlescombe: **50d**
Saddlescombe Road: 42a,199
Sainsbury superstore, Lewes Road: **87d**
St Alban's Church, Coombe Road: **9**
St Albans House, King's Road/Regency Square: **148c**
St Andrew's Church, Brunswick Town: 25
St Andrew's Church, Hove: 79c,209
St Andrew's Church, Moulsecoomb: **105c**
St Andrew's Church, Park Hill: **138d**
St Anne's Church, Burlington Street: **56q**
St Anne's Well Gardens, Hove: **79a**
St Aubyn's School, Rottingdean: **156r**
St Augustine's Church, Preston: **130c**
St Bartholomew's Chapel & Priory: **115a**
also: 115n,115s
St Bartholomew's Church, Ann Street: **91d**
also: 91a
(school): 91d,172b
St Bartholomew's Day Fair: **64**
St Bernadette's School, London Road: 92c
St Cuthman's Church, Whitehawk: 208c
St David's Mission Hall, Whitehawk: 208c
St Dunstan's Institute, St George's Road & Greenways: **165**
also: 33b
St Francis of Assisi R.C.Church, Moulsecoomb: **105c**
St Francis's Hall, Moulsecoomb:
see: St Francis of Assisi R.C.Church.
St Francis's Hospital, Haywards Heath: 78c
St George's Church, Kemp Town: **166a**
St George's Hall, North Moulsecoomb: **105c**
St George's Place: **189c**
also: 129c
St George's Road, Kemp Town: **166**
also: 99e,135
see also: Bristol Road Methodist Church.
St George's Terrace:
see: Bristol Road Methodiat Church.
St Helen's Road: **126c**
St James's Avenue: **167j**
St James's Church, St James's Street: **167d**
see also: Blind Asylum; Deaf & Dumb School.
St James's Concert Hall, Grand Parade: **189j**
St James's Court, George Street: **167e**
St James's Gardens: 167a
St James's Mansions, Old Steine: 89a
St James's Place: **167a**
St James's Street: **167**
(development of area): **49(vii)**
(lighting): 176
(post-offices): 129c
also: 53b,135
see also: fire stations; police stations; Rock Brewery; Brighton & Sussex Bank.
St John's Church, Brunswick Town: 25
St John's Church, Carlton Hill: **30a**
(church halls): 30a,30c
(school): 172b
St John's Church, Preston: **133d**
St John's Special Residential School, Walpole Road: **172e**
St John the Baptist R.C. Church, Bristol Road: **23**
(school): 172b,214b
St Joseph's Convent of Mercy, Bristol Road: **23**
St Joseph's R.C.Church, Elm Grove: **63**
St Joseph's School, Hollingdean: 172d
St Laurence's Church, Falmer: **65**
St Lawrence's Church, Telscombe: **180**
St Louis King of France R.C. Church, Whitehawk: **208c**
St Luke's Church, Prestonville: **134**
St Luke's Church, Queen's Park: **138d**
St Luke's Road: 4h
St Luke's Secondary School, Finsbury Road:

172c
St Luke's Terrace: **138d**
(swimming-pool): **138d**
St Margaret's Church, St Margaret's Place: **149p**
(Circus Street Mission): 100e
St Margaret's Church, Rottingdean: **155d**
St Margaret's Place: **149p**
see also: Sussex Heights.
St Mark's Church, Kemp Town: **168**
(school): 152,172b
also: 19c
St Martha's Convent, Rottingdean: **155m**
St Martin's Church, Lewes Road: **87c**
also: 63,150
St Martin's School, St Martin's Street: 87c,172b
St Martin's Street: 87c,172b
St Martin's U.R. Church, Saltdean: **171e**
St Mary's Church, St James's Street: **167c**
(school): 74d
also: 23,58,138d,167d
St Mary's Hall, Eastern Road: **168**
also: 56y
St Mary's Home, Queen Square & Falmer Road: **136c**
also: 197
St Mary's Place: 14j
St Mary's R.C. Church, Preston: **130g**
St Mary's Square, Kemp Town: **56y**
St Mary Magdalen's Church, Coldean: **44**
St Mary Magdalen's R.C.Church, Upper North Street: **39r**
(school): 39r,172b
St Mary & St Mary Magdalen's Church, Bread Street: **36d**
St Matthew's Church, Sutherland Road: **19c**
St Matthias's Church, Ditchling Road: **51**
also: 76
St Michael's Church,Victoria Road: **39u**
also: 150,203b
St Michael's Place: **39p**
St Nicholas's Church, Dyke Road/ Church Street: **169**
(chapels-of-ease): **169b**
also: 112e,115t,167d,170,125889c
(churchyard): **169f**
also: 7b
(Kemp family): 80
(storm damage): 40a
also: 2a,17d,36f,74c,118d
St Nicholas's Church, Saltdean: **171d**
St Nicholas Court, Church Street: **36f**
St Nicholas Road: 169e,172b
St Pancras's Priory, Lewes: 57,65,87a,154,192a,212a
St Patrick's R.C.Church, Woodingdean: 214a
St Paul's Church, West Street: **205d**
also: 74c,100l,197
St Paul's School, St Nicholas Road: 172b
St Peter's Church, Brighton: **170**
(parish): 112e,118a,118d
(vicarage): 91a
also: 80
St Peter's Church, Preston: **131b**
also: 131a,186
St Peter's Church, West Blatchington: **202**
St Peter's Place: **189e**
St Richard's Church Hall, Hollingdean: **76**
St Saviour's Church, Ditchling Road: **51**
(mission hall): 91c
St Saviour's (district): 51
also: 4g
St Stephen's Church, Montpelier Place: **39g**
(school, Borough Street): **207e**
St Thomas More R.C. Church, Patcham: 121
St Wilfrid's Church, Elm Grove: **63**
St Wulfran's Church, Ovingdean: **116b**
also: 116d
Salem Baptist Chapel, Bond Street: **110a**
Sallis Benney Theatre, Grand Parade: 124
Saltdean: **171**
(community centre): **171c**
(development of area): **49(xxxv)**
(cliffs): 17a,**45b**
(gap): **171a**
(library): 171c
(lido): **171c**
(miniature golf course): 171c
(pumping station): 200d
(railway): 171a
(school): 172d
(TV transmitter): 24g
(Undercliff Walk): 187
also: 17a
Saltdean Drive: 4j
Saltdean Estate Co.: **171a**
also: 154,155c,156
Saltdean Lido: **171c**
Saltdean Park: **171c**
(barn): **171b**
Salvation Army: **120c**
sanatorium, Bevendean Road: **78d**
Saturday morning market: **100f**
Saunders Park, Lewes Road: **87e**
(school): 172e
(waterworks): **200b-d**
Savoy Cinema-Theatre, East Street/Grand Junction Road: **28**
also: 104
Saxon history: **17b**
Scabe's Castle: **33**,53b
Scala Cinema, Western Road: **207d**
scavenging: 147,173a
School Board: **172c**
see also: Marlborough House.
School Clinic, Morley Street: **1a**
schools: **172**
see also: Blind School; Brighton College; Brighton Grammar; Brighton & Hove High; Brighton, Hove & Sussex Sixth Form; Central National Schools; Christ Church; Deaf & Dumb; Female Orphan Asylum; Fitzherbert R.C; Hertford Road; Jew Street; Michael Faraday College; Our Lady of Lourdes R.C; Patcham House; Pelham Street; Preston Infants; Prestonville; Roedean; Rottingdean; Royal Spa; St Aubyn's; St Bartholomew's; St Bernadette's; St John's; St Luke's Terrace; St Mark's; St Martin's; St Mary's Hall; St Stephen's; Swan Downer; Varndean High; Varndean Sixth Form; Warren Farm; Xaverian College; York Place.
sea-bathing:
see: bathing.
sea defences: **43**
sea-front: 29
see also: batteries & fortifications; beaches; piers; promenades; sea defences.
Sea House, Middle Street: **115p**
sea-walls: **43c**
see also: Undercliff Walk.
sea-water cure:
see: bathing; Russell, Dr.Richard.
also: 71b
Seajet: **128**
seasons: 59,141
Seeboard: **62e,f**
(Western Road store): 207b
also: 36d
Segas: **69c**
Seven Dials:
(boundaries): 13(iii)
(pillar-box): 129c
(roundabout): 151d
also: 133b
Seven Stars, Ship Street: **115t**
sewers & drains: **173**
also: 43b
see also: Pepper-Box.
Seymour Square: 14e
Seymour Street: 14e
Shades Bar, Steine Lane: **32**
Shaftesbury Place: 144
Shaw's Library, Old Steine: **89b**
sheep fair: 64
Sheepcote Valley: **208d**
see also: refuse.
Shelter Halls:
see: Madeira; West Street.
Sheridan Hotel, King's Road/West Street: **83b**
Sherrys Dance Hall, West Street: **205c**
Ship Street: **115t**
(head post-office): **129b**
(soup kitchen): 126b
see also: Old Ship Hotel; Vokins store.
Ship Street Gardens: **115u**
shipwrecks: 12,40a,85,95d,125
shopping: **15**
Shoreham:
(airport): **174**
(harbour): 12,67c,95d,128
see also: gas supply; power stations.
also: 35,42a,200c,200d,209
see also: West Coastway.
Sillwood House, Sillwood Place: **149p**
also: 207c
Sillwood Place: **149q**
Sillwood Road: **149r**
Sillwood Street: **149s**
sites of special scientific interest: **45b**
skating:
(ice): 84,115p,136,201,205e
(roller): 3b,95c,138a,205c
slaughterhouses: 76,91c,134,139b,183a,183c
slot machine museum, King's Road Arches: 93
slums: **126c**
smallpox hospitals: 78c,d
Smithers Breweries: **14b,f,k**
smuggling: 57,122b,154,155g,155k,171a,180,158
see also: customs (revenue).
Society of the Twelve: **2**
soup kitchens: **126b**
South Downs: **53**
South-Eastern Electricity Board:
see: Seeboard.
South-Eastern Gas Board:
see: Segas.
South Moulsecoomb: **105b**
South Patcham: 121
(development of area): **49(xxiv)**
South Road, Preston: **131f**
(Dog Hospital): **130f**
Southdown Avenue: 4h
Southdown Cable Vision: **24h**
Southdown House, Freshfield Road: **26l,p**
Southdown Motor Services: **26e,g,l,n,p**
also: 3d,56b,185d
Southern Belle (luxury train): **142k**
Southern Publishing Co.: **108j**
also: 112d
Southern Railway Co.: **141a**
also: 142h,146c
Southern Region B.R.: **141a**
Southern Sound Radio, Portslade: **24c**
Southern Water: 173c,200d
Southern Weekly News: **108e**
Southover Street, Hanover: **74b,d**
(Phoenix Brewery): 14g
also: 135
Southwick:
(Tamplins Brewery): 14a
(power station): **62**
(railway station): 143
also: 62e,179b,200d
Spa Street: 138d,172a
Special Schools: **172e**
Speed Trials: 95b
'Spirit of Brighton' (painting): **130f**
Spiritualist churches:
(Brotherhood Gate, St James's Street): 167a
(Central, North Street): 112d
(Edward Street): **60**
(Mighell Street): 30c
sports pitches: 119
Sports Stadium, West Street: **205e**
Sports Stadium, Withdean: **213**
Springett's School, Bartholomews: **172a**
Springfield Road: 78b,130a,195
(Roman Villa): 133a
Spring Gardens: 108a,126b
Spring Street, Brighton: **207e**
Spring Street, Patcham: 122c
Square, The, Patcham: **122e**
S.S.Brighton, West Street: **205e**
S.S.S.I.s: **45b**
Stanford Avenue, Preston: **130c**
also: 26a,96
Stanford Road, Preston: 133b,134
(school): 172c
Stanley Deason School and Leisure Centre, Whitehawk: **208c**
Stanley Road: 191
Stanmer: **175**
(boundary stone): 13a
(church): **175c**
(Coldean): 44

(constituencies): 61
(hundreds): 118f
(nurseries): **175b**
(Rural Museum): **175b**
also: 51,185c
also: 150
see also: University of Sussex.
Stanmer House: **175b**
Stanmer Park: **175e**
also: 85,178
Stanmer School, Lewes Road: 172d
Stanmer Villas, Hollingdean: 212b
Star & Garter, King's Road: **83b**
Starlight Rooms, Sillwood Place: 149q
Station Road, Preston & Withdean: 92b,130b
(Preston Park Station): 142e
Station Street: 145c
statues:
see: Burrows, Sir John Cordy; George IV; Ovett, Steve; Peace Gardens; Royal Crescent; Victoria, Queen; Victoria Gardens.
steamers: **128**
steepest roads: 1a,130e
Steine, The:
see: Old Steine.
Steine Gardens: 60
Steine House (former manor house): **163**
Steine House (Y.M.C.A.): **114l**
also: 32
Steine Lane: **32**
also: 6
Steine Street: 26d
Stevenson Road: 82
storms: **40a**
also: 8a,8c,196a
streams: **201**
also: 79a
streets:
(cleaning): 183a
also: 147
(lighting): **176**
also: 161j
(name changes): **151f**
(names): **151e**,183b
(paving): 183a
Streeter's Mill, Preston: **55d**
Stringer Way, Withdean: 212c
stucco: **4e**
students: **15**
see also: College of Technology; Polytechnic; University of Sussex.
Studio Theatre, Clarence Gardens: **149e**
Sudeley Place, Kemp Town: **166c**
Sun Dial House, Queen's Road/North Road: **139b**
Sun Terrace (Aquarium): **3**
also: 34c,104,140e
Sunday Schools: 19c,90,114c
Sunny South Special (train): 142g
sunshine: **40**
Surrenden Crescent, Withdean: 92d
Surrenden Field, Withdean: **92d**
Surrenden Holt, Withdean: 212a
Surrenden Pool, Withdean: 212c
Surrenden Road, Preston & Withdean: **212a**
(St Mary's R.C. Church): 130g
see also: Varndean.
Surrey Street: **139a**
Sussex Advertiser: **108f**
Sussex Constabulary: 123b
Sussex County Cricket Club: **177**
also: 39f,120b
see also: County Ground.
Sussex County Hospital:
see: Royal Sussex County Hospital.
Sussex Daily News: **108g**
also: 92e,196c
Sussex Downs: **53a**
Sussex Eye Hospital, Eastern Road: **162c**
'Sussex Fortnight': 140d
Sussex General Infirmary, Middle Street: **78a**
Sussex Heights, St Margaret's Place: **103**
Sussex Ice Rink, Queen Square: 136
Sussex Masonic Club, Queen's Road: **139d**
Sussex Maternity Hospital, Buckingham Road: **78f**
Sussex, Radio, Marlborough Place: **24b**
Sussex Square, Kemp Town: **81e**
(pillar-box): 129c
(Roedean School): 153
(St Mark's School): 172b
(St Mary's Hall): 168
Sussex Street: **1a**
(Millers Arms): 1b
(school): 172c
(slums): 126c
(Tarnerland Nursery): 30b
(Tarner Recreation Ground): **30b**
also: 53b
Sussex Temporary Home for Lost or Starving Dogs, Robertson Road: **130g**
Sussex Throat & Ear Hospital, Church Street: **78g**
Sutherland Road: **19c**
also: 14e
Sutton Farm, Balsdean: 5
Swan Downer Schools: **55a**,**110e**
Swanborough estate, Whitehawk: **208b**
swimming-pools:
see: Baths.
Sydney Street: **110q**
Sylvan Hall, Ditchling Road: **51**
synagogues:
see: Devonshire Place; Jew Street; Middle Street; Poune's Court.
Tallboys, Rottingdean: **156q**
tallest buildings: 72,103
Tamplins Brewery, Albion Street: **14g**
Tarner Recreation Ground, Sussex Street: **30b**
Tarnerland Estate: 1a
Tatler Cinema, West Street: **205b**
Taylor's Mill: **1b**
teacher training colleges:
(Diocesan): **191**
(Municipal):
see: Polytechnic (Falmer).
Technical College:
see: Technology, College of.
Technology, College of: **178**
(Lewes Road, now Polytechnic): **124**
(formerly Technical College): **178**
(Belgrave Street annexe): 74d
(Hanover Terrace annexe): 172c
(Pelham Street): **178**,189d
(Preston Road annexe): 133a
(Richmond Terrace): **178**,189d
(York Place): **189d**
also: 188a,213
telegraphs: **179a**
Telephone House, Gloucester Place: **189b**,189a
telephones: **179b**
also: 6,62c
television: **24f,g**
(cable): **24h**
Telscombe: **180**
(boundary stone): 13a
also: 62e,200d
see also: Portobello.
temperature: **40**
Temple, Temple Gardens: **39q**
Temple Fields: 39f
Temple Gardens: **39q**
(boundary stone): 13a
see also: New Sussex Hospital.
Temple Street: **207e**
Tenant Lain: 188b
Tenantry Down Road: 53c
tenantry downs: **53c**
tenantry laines: 53b
Terminus Place: **203h**
Terminus Road: **203j**
Terminus Street: **203h**
Territorial Army:
(Dyke Road): **55d**
(Somme Centre, Lewes Road): **87f**
see also: drill halls.
Texas Homecare superstore, Moulsecoomb: **105d**
Thatched House, Black Lion Street: 100c,115c
The Event nightclub, King's Road: **84**
Theatre Royal, Duke Street: **181**
Theatre Royal, New Road: **182**
see also: Royal Colonnade.
theatres & music halls: **181**
see also: Alhambra Opera House; Aquarium; Arcadia Cinema; Brighton Palladium; Castle Square; Court; Dome; Duke Street; Essoldo; Gaiety; Gardner Centre for the Arts; Globe Music Hall; Grand; Grand Olympia; Hippodrome; Marlborough; New Oxford Music Ha ll; New Venture; North Street; Palace Pier; Pavilion; Playhouse; Sallis Benney; Savoy; Studio; Theatre Royal; West Pier.
Theobald House, Blackman Street: **126c**
also: 24g,91c
Thomas-Stanford Museum, Preston: **131a**
Thomas Street: 60,138d
Thomas's Library, Old Steine: **89a**
(post-office): 129b
Throat & Ear Hospital, Church Streeet: **78g**
Tichborne Street: **36d**
Tidy Street: **110r**
Tierney Royal Picture Theatre, Edward Street: **60**
Tilbury Place: **30b**
Tilley's horse-buses: 26b,87d
Tillings buses: **26e,26f,26l**
Tillstone Street: **138d**
Tivoli Cinema, Western Road, Hove: **207b**
Tivoli Estate, Preston: 92b,130a
Tivoli Gardens, Withdean: **92b**
toll gates & houses: 43b,51,66a,87a,92a-c,99a
Tongdean: 79b,121
(farm): **121**
also: 92d
Tongdean Lane: 92d
see also: Withdean Stadium.
Top Rank Bingo Hall, North Street: **112d**
Top Rank Centre:
see: Kingswest Boulevard.
see also: S.S.Brighton.
Toronto Terrace: 1b
tourism: **15**
(Lanes): 115k
tourist information centres:
(King's Road): **83b**
(Old Steine): **114k**
'tower blocks': **126c**
Tower Gate, Withdean: **92b**
Tower Mill: 159
Tower Road: **138c**
Town Acts: **183**
(fire-engines): 66
(police): 123a
(sea-defences): 43b
(sewers): 173a
Town Books:
see: Ancient Customs.
Town Commissioners: **183**
(clerks): 115t,161c,183d
(New Road/Bond Street): 107,110a
(Old Steine): 114b
(Royal Albion Hotel): 160
(Royal Pavilion purchase): 161c
also: 6,12,16,36
see also: fire brigade; Guardians of the Poor; incorporation; markets; refuse; roads; sewers & drains; streets; sea-defences; town halls; watchmen.
Town Halls: **184**
(Bartholomews): **184a**
also: 18,183d,185d
see also: courts; fire-brigade; Guardians of the Poor; police stations; vestry.
(Brunswick Town): **25**
(Hove): **25**
also: 38
(Market Street): **184**
see also: courts; police stations; vestry; workhouses.
town polls: 26h,47a,98b,161c,169b
Townhouse: **184**
also: 118d
Toy Museum: 106b
Trades Council: **103**
Trades & Labour Club, Lewes Road: 87d
Trafalgar Street: **110s**
(Brighton Special School): 172e
(co-operatives): 46a
see also: Brighton Station; York Place Schools.
Trafalgar Terrace: **110t**
traffic:
(Commissioners): 26e,26l
(congestion): 15
(control): **151d**
(lights): **151d**

Training Colleges:
see: Diocesan Training College: Polytechnic (Falmer).
tramways: **185**
also: 91a
trees: 40,40a,45d
Trinity Chapel, Ship Street:
see: Holy Trinity Church.
Trinity Independent Presbyterian Chapel, Church Street: **36a**
trolley-buses: **26c,h,k**
Troxy Cinema, North Road: **111**
'Trunk Murders': **186**
Trusler's Mill, Preston: **55d**
Trustcard House, Gloucester Place: **189b**
Tudor Close, Rottingdean: **155c**
Tudor Cottages, Rottingdean: **155c**
turnpike roads: **151a**
Tussaud's Waxworks, Grand Junction Road: **73**
T.V.S.: 24f
Twelve, Society of the: **2**
Undercliff Walk: **187**
underground railway: **142g**
'underground river': **201**
Unemployed Centre, Tilbury Place: **30b**
Unicorn Inn, North Street: 112c
Union Bank, North Street: **6**
Union Charity Schools, Middle Street: **172a**
Union Congregational Churches:
(Queen Square): **136a**
(Union Street): **115v**
Union Free Church, Queen Square: **136a**
Union Road: 86,120b
Union Street: **115v**
(chapel): **115v**
also: 149l
Unitarian Church, New Road: **107**
United Telephone Co.: 179b
University of Sussex, Falmer: **188**
also: 175b,e
Uplands School, Hollingdean: 172e
Upper Bedford Street: **58**
(St John's School): 172b
Upper Bevendean Farm: **11**
Upper Gardner Street: **110u**
Upper Hollingdean Road: 76,100l,147
Upper Lodges, Stanmer: 175e
Upper North Street: **39r**
also: 46a,55a,172b
Upper Rock Gardens: **167k**
see also: St Mary's Church.
Upper Roedale, Ditchling Road: **212b**
also: 75b
Upper Russell Street: 37,66b,126c
Upper St James's Street: 14e,26a
Upper Wellington Road: 82
Vale, The, Ovingdean:
see: Longhill School.
Vale Avenue, Patcham: 85
see also: Chattri; Horsdean Recreation Ground; Patcham Clock Tower; Patcham Court Farm.
Vallance & Catt Brewery, West Street: **14k**
Valley Drive, Withdean: **4j**
Valley Gardens: **189**
(conservation area): **189**
(lighting): 176
also: 40a,151d,201
see also: Level; Old Steine; Park Crescent; Royal Pavilion Grounds; St Peter's Churchyard; tramways; Victoria Gardens.
Varndean: **212c**
(High School, Balfour Road): **212c**
(Sixth-Form College, Surrenden Road): **212c**
also: 132a
Varndean Gardens, Withdean: 92c
Varndean Park, Withdean: 18,92c,212a
Varndean Road, Withdean: 92c,212a
Vernon Terrace: **39s**
Vestry: **118c**
(bathing restrictions): 7a
(cemeteries): 33b
(clerks): 115t,148b
(Royal Pavilion purchase): 161c
(and Town Commissioners): 183b,c
also: 128,140b,170
see also: Guardians of the Poor.
Veteran Car Run: **190**
Viaduct Road: **191**
see also: Preston Circus.
vicarages: **192a**
(Brighton): **91a**
(Preston): 133c
(Rottingdean): 155f
Vicarage Lane, Rottingdean: **155h**
Vicarage Terrace, Rottingdean: **155g**
vicars of Brighton: **192**
also: 2b
see also: Wagner, Henry.
Victoria Fountain, Old Steine: **114e**
Victoria Gardens: **194**
(one-way traffic): 151d
(trams): 185a
Victoria Lending Library, Church Street: **88b**
Victoria Place: **39t**
Victoria Road: **39u**
Victoria Slipper Baths, Park Street: **138d**
Victoria Railway Station, London: **142f,g,k**
also: 145b
Victoria Street: **39v**
Victorian architecture: **4g**
Village Barn, Patcham: **122a**
Vine Place: **39w**
Vine's Mill: **39w**,39b
Vogue Cinema, Hollingdean Road: **87d**
Vogue 'gyratory system': 87d
Vokins store, North Street/Ship Street: **112b**
Volk's Railway, Madeira Drive: **196**
(offices): **196g**
also: 12,95d,174,195
see also: Rottingdean Railway.
Volunteer, Church Street: 36a
Volunteer Fire-Brigade: **66b**
volunteer soldiers: 36a,140c
see also: drill halls.
Waggon & Horses, Church Street: 36a
Wagner Hall, Regency Road: **205d**
also: 27
Waitrose supermarket, Western Road: 207d
Walpole Lodge, Eastern Road: 19a,58
Walpole Road: 19c,58,172e
Walpole Terrace: 19c
war memorials:
(Brighton Old Steine): **114f**
(Chattri): **122h**
(Egyptian Campaign): **114f**
(Patcham): 122b
(Regency Square): **148d**
(Rottingdean): **155**
(South African War): **148d**
see also: Brighton College; Good Shepherd, Church of the; Patcham Memorial Hall; Preston Park Cricket Ground; Railway Engineering Works; Royal Pavilion (South Gate); St Martin's Church; St Nicholas's Church; St Peter's Church.
wards: **47e**
Warmdene Road, Patcham: 129c
Warren Avenue, Woodingdean: 11
Warren Farm Schools, Woddingdean: **214b**
also: 1b,214a
Warren Road, Woodingdean: **214**
Warwick Street: 14j
Washington Street, Hanover: 74c
watchmen: 123a
Water Department: **200**
also: 40
water supply: **200**
Waterhall: **199**
Waterloo Place: **189g**
also: 209
Watneys Ltd: 14g
waxworks, Grand Junction Road: **73**
weather: **40**
weather-boarding: **4a**
weekly market: **100a**
Welesmere Hundred: **118f**
Wellesbourne stream: **201**
Wellington Road: **63**
(dispensary): 78f
(flats): 91c
(police station): 123d
wells: **200a**
(St Anne's Well, Hove): 79a
also: 94,115c,122c,131a,138b,155,175b,175d, 214b
Wentworth Street: **56f**
Wesleyan Schools, Nelson Row: 172a
West Battery: **8e**
West Blatchington: **202**
(hundreds): 118f
(windmill): **202**
also: 17e,62e
West Brighton: **79b**
also: 179b,200c
West Cliff Catholic Mission, Sillwood Place: 149q
West Coastway: **143**
West Drive, Queen's Park: **138d**
West Hill: **203**
(development of area): **49(iv)**
West Hill, Newtimber: 53d
West Hill Road: **203k**
West Laine: **53b**
West Mill: **148a**
West Pier: **204**
(steamers): 128
(post-office): 129c
(telegraphs): 179a
also: 34c
West Street, Brighton: **205**
(co-operatives): 46a
(telephone exchange): 179b
(Concert Hall): **205c**
(Shelter Hall): **83b,93**
(synagogue): 36c
(traffic lights): 151d
(underground railway): **142g**
(well): 200a
see also: Baptist Tabernacle; Brighton & Hove Women's Hospital; Kingswest Boulevard; Poune's Court; Sheridan Hotel.
West Street, Rottingdean: 66d,123d,154,156
West Street Brewery: **14k**
Westdene: **206**
(development of area): **49(xxii)**
(school): 172d
see also: Waterhall Mill.
Western Bathing Pavilion: **93**
Western Lawns: **93**
Western Pavilion, Western Terrace: **207c**
(and A.H.Wilds): 209
Western Road: **207**
(boundary stone): 13a
(lighting): 62a,176
(post-offices): 207b
(telegraphs): 179a
(toll-house): 66a
also: 195,203a
see also: Children's Hospital; Churchill Square; Female Orphan Asylum; Norfolk Square.
Western Street: **149t**
see also: Embassy Court.
Western Terrace: **207c**
(and A.H.Wilds): 209
Westlain School, Moulsecoomb: 172d
Whalesbone Hundred: **118f**
Whipping Post House, Rottingdean: **156k**
Whippingham Road: 63
'White Hawk Lady': **208b**
White Horse Hotel, Rottingdean: **156**
White Lion Inn, North Street: **112c**
also: 112f
White Street: **60**
Whitecross Street: 91c
Whitehawk: **208**
(air-raids): 208c
(bus garage): 26e
(development of area): **49(xxx)**
(fair): 208b
(ghost): **208b**
(library): **208c**
(park): 208b
(schools): 172d,208c
Whitehawk Avenue: 78b,78f,208b
Whitehawk Down:
('Battle of'): 140c
see also: Race Hill; Whitehawk Hill.
Whitehawk Football Club, East Brighton Park: **208e**
(Enclosed Ground): **208d**
Whitehawk Hill: **208a**
(Neolithic camp): **208a**
(TV & radio transmitter): **24g**
also: **53b**
Whitehawk Hill Road: 140a,208a
Whitehawk Road: **208b**
(boundary stones): 13a,140a

(bus garage): 26e
see also: Stanley Deason School.
Whiteway Centre, Rottingdean: **155g**
Whiteway Lane, Rottingdean: **155g**
wholesale market: **100**
also: 189j
Widgett's Library, Old Steine: **89b**
Wigney's Bank: **6**
Wild Park, Lewes Road: **105f**
William Clarke Park, Picton Street: **82**
William Street: 48
Williams's Baths, Old Steine: **7g**
Wilson Avenue: 208b
see also: East Brighton Park; Sheepcote Valley; Stanley Deason School.
Wincombe Road: 55f
Windlesham Avenue: 13a
Windlesham Road: **39x**
Windmill, Upper North Street: 39r
Windmill Street: 1b
Windmill Terrace: **1a**
windmills: **211**
see also: Albion Hill; Ballard's; Bear; Clifton; East Mill; Hanover; Hodson's Black; 'Jack & Jill'; Lashmar's; Port Hall; Preston; Race Hill; Roedean; Rottingdean; Round Hill; Vine's; Taylor's; Waterhall; West Mill; West Blatchington.
Windsor House, Edward Street: **60**
also: 120c
Windsor Street: **36c**
also: 55a
winter gardens:
see: Aquarium; Kingswest Boulevard; Metropole; Palace Pier; Regent Cinema.
wishing stone, Rottingdean: **155b**
Withdean: **212**
(Baptist chapel): 212a
(development of area): **49(xx),49(xxi)**
see also: London Road (Patcham).
Withdean Grange, London Road: 179b
Withdean Hall, Varndean Gardens: **92c**
Withdean Lodge, London Road: 92c,130g
Withdean Park: **212d**
Withdean Stadium, Tongdean Lane: **213**
Withdean Woods: **212a**
Women's Hospital, West Street: **78f**
Woodgate's Library, Old Steine: **89b**
Woodingdean: **214**
(buses): 26e
(development of area): **49(xxxiv)**
(farm): **214a**
also: 208b
(school): 172d
also: 24f
see also: Bullock Hill.
Wood's Baths, Pool Valley: **7e**
Woodside Avenue, Preston: 92b
Woodside School:
see: Queensdown School.
Woodvale Cemetery & Crematorium: **33b**
also: 81e,120d,140a,198
Woollards Nursery, Lewes Road: 105f
Workhouses:
(Church Hill): **215c**
also: 100h
(East Street): **215a**
(Elm Grove): **215d**
also: 66a,182b
(Market Street): **215b**
also: 100b
(Preston): 133c
see also: Warren Farm Schools.
World War One: **216a**
(closures): 20a,82,140d,174
(railway engineering works): 146c
(Shoreham Airport): 174
also: 56d,68,75b,171a,188a
see also: military hospitals, war memorials.
World War Two: **216b**
(Allenwest Ltd.): 105d
(buses): 26j
(closures): 43a,117b,140f,177a,196e,204b
(Evening Argus): 108a
(fire-brigades): 66d,171c,e
(police): 123b
(railway engineering works): 146d
(requisitions): 3e,5,81f,81g,103,138c,153,166b,174,175a,199,212d,213
also: 19a,62d,68
see also: air-raids; Whistler, Rex.
Wykeham Terrace,Dyke Road: **55a**
Wyndham Street: **56l**
Xaverian College, Tower Road: **138c**
yardlands: **53b**
Y.M.C.A.: **111**
(North Road): **111**
(Old Steine): **114l**
York Grove: 134
York Hill: 53b
York Place: **189d**
(schools): **189d**
also: 110m
see also: St Peter's Church.
York Villas: 4g,134
Young Men's Christian Association:
see: Y.M.C.A.
Younsmere Hundred: **118f**
Youth Centre, Edward Street: **60**
Youth Hostel, Patcham: 122d
Zion Chapel, Upper Bedford Street: 58
Zoar Chapel, Windsor Street: 36c
zoos, menageries & aviaries:
see: Aquarium; Queen's Park; Royal Gardens; Withdean Stadium.

INDEX TO PEOPLE

This index references people; there is a separate general index. The numbers refer to the entry numbers of the encyclopaedia. Principal entries are given in **bold** type.

Abbey family: 14e,58,126c,138a
Abergavenny, Marquesses of:
122a,122g,77,148d,152,153,158
Adam, Robert: 114k
Adelaide, Queen:
(Queen's Park): 138a
(stables): 52a
(visits): 34b,79a,81f,138b,163,166a,210
Ainsworth, William Harrison: **81b**,113c,116a
Albert, Prince: 41,81f,160b,193
Alexandra, Princess: 55b,208c
Alexandra, Queen: 41,55b
Amelia, Princess: 8c
Anderson, Revd James: 81a,166a
architects & builders:
see: Adam, Robert; Barry, Sir Charles; Birch, Eugenius; Blomfield, Sir Arthur; Busby, Charles; Carpenter, Richard Cromwell; Cheeseman & Son, George; Clarke, George Somers; Cooper, Thomas; Cubitt, Thomas; Hallett, William; Holland, Henry; Nash, John; Porden, William; Scott, Edmund; Scott, Sir George Gilbert; Scott, Sir Giles Gilbert; Spence, Sir Basil; Waterhouse, Alfred; Wilds, Amon; Wilds, Amon Henry.
also:
Andrews, Philip: 189h
Anscombe, Parker: 91c
APP Brighton: 36d,75d,136a
Ariba, Richard Melhuish: 11
Atkinson, Robert: 52c,52d,139c
Baines, George: 130d,189b
Bannister, F.D.: 145b
Barnes, James: 191
Basevi, George: 79c,168
Beard & Bennett: 207b
Bethell & Swannell: 91b
Billington, Percy: 48,123c,124
Bloom, Maurice: 12
Blount, Gilbert: 39r
Bodley, George: 36d,39u,205d
Boxall, T.: 3b,30c
Brodo, W.K.: 63
Brown, Capt.Samuel: 34
Buckler, Charles: 23
Buckwell, Herbert: 138d
Burges, William: 39u
Burton, Decimus: 25
Carpenter, Richard H.: 51,100l,205d
Cawthorn, F.T.: 51,74c,136c,191
Chapple, John: 39u
Clayton, Black & Daviel: 76,99g,111,112a
Clayton,C.E.: 54,182c
Coates, Wells: 83c
Cooper & Lynn: 107
Crunden, John: 31a
Dancy, William: 74c
Denman, John, & Son:
32,92e,130g,162c,189a
Diplock, Russell: 18,37,84
Dubois, Nicholas: 175b,e
Edwards, David: 3e,187
Ellison, C.O.: 133a,167f,207e
Emerson, Sir William: 167c
Fabian, John: 139b
Ferrey, Benjamin: 56q
Fitzroy Robinson & Partners: 32,115f
Gibbins, J.G.: 91c,124,130b,134,149l
Gibbs, Peter: 85
Glen, William: 28
Golden, Robert: 7e,113b
Gollins Melvin Ward Partnership: 60
Good, Joseph: 161b,k,n
Goodhart-Rendel, H.S.: 63,112a
Goulty, Horatio: 109,205c
Gray, Jane: 144
Habershon, W & E: 191
Hamilton, E.J.: 120c,130c
Hansom, J.S.: 63
Harford, A.: 87d
Henriques, E.C.: 122h
Hewitt, Charles: 203k
Highet, Graeme: 66d
Hill, John: 134
Hodges, David: 98c
Horton, John: 19c
Hunter, Stuart: 111
Jackson, Sir Thomas: 19a
Jacob, Sir Samuel: 122h
James & Brown: 136a
Johnson, John: 41
Jones, Richard: 155c,156,171c,171e
Keirle, Robert: 194c
Kendall, William: 81g
Lainson, Thomas: 23,55b,115p,149r
Lamb, Percy: 130g
Lockwood, Philip: 52b,88a,95b,106a
Lorne, Francis: 165
Lutyens, Sir Edward: 155f
Mackie, William: 215c
Mackintosh, L.A.: 30a
Matcham, Frank: 83b,111,115p
Maude, Edward: 171d
May, Francis: 60,78d,100d,132b
Maynard, George: 70,214b,215d
Mew, Mr: 39q
Mew, Messrs: 58
Michael Lyell & Associates: 77
Miller Bourne: 107
Mocatta, David: 142d,145a,167h
Moore, R.St George: 117a
Nunn, Benjamin: 110f
Nunn and Hunt: 189l
Overton & Partners: 60,98a
Parnacott, W.S.: 138d,167g
Peach, Charles: 131a
Phipps, Charles: 182b
Ridge, Lacy W.: 9,51
Robinson, Malcolm: 111
Robertson, P.F.: 161a
Robin Clayton Partnership: 115q
Russell, S.B.: 22
Saunders, Thomas: 112e
Scott, J.Oldrid: 149p
Scott, W.Gilbert: 168
Seifert & Partners: 10,103
Sharp, Derek: 112b
Shelbourne, Thomas: 168
Simpson, Sir John: 114f,153
Simpson, Thomas:
55a,74d,100c,110a,138d,172c
Simpson, William: 91c
Somers & Micklethwaite: 115t
Stevens, W.H.: 207c
Stickney, Allan: 140b
Stone Toms & Partners: 115g
Streatfield, G.E.: 130c
Stroud & Mew: 36b
Tiltman, Stavers H.: 174
Trent, Newbury: 83b
Tyrwhitt, Thomas: 161n
Wallis, H.E.: 145b
Walters, F.A.: 63
Warren, E.P.: 55f
Weir, James: 91a
Wells-Thorpe, John: 36e,206,214a
Whichcord, John: 72
Williams, Herbert: 78a,162b
Williams, T.R.: 138b
Wimble, John: 112f
Winton-Lewis, Peter: 171e
Wood, C.J.: 1a
Arthur of Connaught, Princes: 3a,162a
artists:
see: Beardsley, Aubrey; Brangwyn, Sir Frank; Burne-Jones, Sir Edward; Constable, John; Feibusch, Hans; Nibbs, Richard Henry; Nicholson, Sir William; Russell, John; Turner, Joseph; Whistler, Rex.
Attree, Thomas: 99d,138a,136129d
(Queen's Park villa): 138c
Attree, William: 96,115t,183a
Augusta, Princess: 161m
Austen, Jane: 148a
Awsiter, Dr John: **7e**
Bagnold, Enid: 155p
Barry, Sir Charles:
25,56k,138a,138c,162a,170,189j
Barrymore, Lord: 114l,115b
Barton, Margaret: 4e,161g
Beardsley, Aubrey: **203c**
Beatty, Earl: **68(iv)**
Bede, Cuthbert: 83b
Bennett, Arnold: 160a
Birch, Eugenius: 3a,34c,204
Black, Hugh Milner: **68(xi)**
also: 1a,55d,87e
Black, William: 56u,155d
Blomfield, Sir Arthur: 39g,112e,133d,138d
Boucicault, Dion: 149d
Boxall, William Percival: 58,99f
Brangwyn, Sir Frank: 92e
Brian, William Havergal: **105c**
Brigden, John: 102,138a
Bristol, Marquess of: **81e**
also: 33a,33b,87b,99b,140c,162b,168
Brown, Captain Samuel: **34**
Buckhurst, Lord: 2
Burne-Jones, Sir Edward: **155d,p**
also: 74c,155b,205d
Burney, Fanny: 205c
Burrows, Sir John Cordy: **114d**
also: 3a,114e
Busby, Charles: **209**
also: 56t,91a,149p,166a
see also: Wilds & Busby.
Byron, Lady: 46a
Canning, George: 99b
Carden, Sir Herbert: **29**
also: 50a,92e,122g,212d
Caroline of Brunswick, Princess: **71d,f**
also: 112e,114k
Carpenter, Richard Cromwell: 169c,203b,205d
Carr, Dr James: 30a,167d,170
Carroll, Lewis: 81e
Carver, Deryk: **115c**
also: 149l
Carver, Thomas: **35**
Charles II, King: **35**
also: 47a,115b,116a,205b
Charles, Prince of Wales: 93
Charlotte, Princess: **71d**,99b
Chart, Nye & Nellie: **182b**
Cheeseman & Son, George:
30a,39g,50a,52b,58a,99f,149f,203b,205d
Chichester, Bishops of:
(consecrations):
56q,58,300569,112e,149f,149p,170,171d
(and Preston): 64,100a,130a,131a
also: 19a,55b,153,167d,172a,192
Chichester, Earls of: 19a,39x,65,86,152,194a
see also: Stanmer.
Churchill, Sir Winston: **68(x)**
also: 83b
Clarence, Duke of:
see: William IV.
Clarke, George Somers:
55a,58a,87c,169c,170,202
Clarke, Somers: 115t,148b,118c
Clements, Sir John: 99c
Clifton, Major General Sir Arthur: 114j
Cobb, Hewitt: 181,182
Cochran, Sir Charles: 134
Codrington, Admiral Sir Edward: 207b
Cohen, Levi Emmanuel: 108h
Collings, Esme: **203a**
Colwell, Maria: **97**
Combermere, Lord: 189f
Constable, John: 34b,202
Cooper, Thomas: 10,36a,162c,184a
Coppard, Alfred: **87d**
Cowley, Harry: **100f**
Cresy, Edward: 173b,126c
Crouch, Anna-Maria: 169f
Cubitt, Thomas: 56v,56w,80,81a,c,d,99f
Cumberland, Duke of: 71b,140a,161a,164
Cuttress, Charles: 159
Defoe, Daniel: 43a
Devonshire, Dukes of: 81d,161f
Dickens, Charles: 10,163
Disraeli, Benjamin: 163
Dodd, William: **68(xiii)**
Duddell, George: 138a,c
Edward I, King: 121
Edward VII, King: **59**
also: 162a,170
(Peace Memorial): 83b
(as Prince of Wales): 41,59,157d,162b
(Queen's Nurses' Home): 63
Edward VIII, King:
(as Duke of Windsor): 72
(post-box): 129c
(as Prince of Wales): 60,83b,122h
Egremont, Earl of: 140a,162a,167c,167k
Eld, Lieutenant-Colonel John: **101c**
Elizabeth II, Queen:

19a,21,55b,98d,115k,132c,140f,161f,165,188b
Elwyn-Jones, Lord Frederick: **81d**
Fawcett, Lieutenant-Colonel John: 102
Feibusch, Hans: 63
Fife, Duke of: 81d
Fitzherbert, Mrs Maria: **71c,d,e**
also: 52d,115t
see also: Shades Bar; Steine House.
Forth, William: **101b**
French, Sir John: **68(ii)**
Friend, Daniel: 126c,130b,134
Friese-Greene, William: **115p**
George IV, King: **71f**
(statue): **161l**
also: 83a,115e,189f
(as Prince of Wales): **71**
(bathing): 7a
(and Chapel Royal): 112e
(cricket ground): **86**
(dairy): **133a**,96
(Old Steine): 114b,g
(and races): 140a
(statue): **99c**
also: 47a,78a,89a,105a,115t,169g,181
(as Prince Regent): **71e**
also: 194a
see also: Castle Inn; Dome; Fitzherbert, Mrs Maria; Gunn, Martha; Hessel, Phoebe; Mahomed, Sake Dene; Miles, Smoaker; New Road; Promenade Grove; Royal Pavilion; Whistler, Rex.
George V, King: 161f
George VI, King: 161f
(as Duke of York): 3e,50a,55b,60,92e
Gill, Eric: 134
Gladstone, William: 160c
Gloucester, Dukes of: 60,71b
Greene, Graham: 140e
Gunn, Martha: **7b**
also: 67c
Haig, Earl: **68(iii)**
also: 152
Hall, Sir Edward Marshall: 114g
Hallett, William: 14e,23,97,99b,162b
Hamilton, 'Single-speech': 114k
Harding, Gilbert: 39l
Hardy, Margaret: 102,142k
Hawkshaw, Sir John: 173c
Helen, Princess, of Romania: 36f
Hessel, Phoebe: **169g**
Hicks, John: 113b,183a
Hill, Sir Rowland: 74b
Hobden, Dennis: 61
Holland, Henry: 161a
Holyoake, George Jacob: **56e**
Howard, Sir John: 39x,117a,152,162b
Hudson, Revd Thomas: 112e
Infield, Henry John: 51,108g,108j,182b
Johnson, Dr Samuel: 7a,169c,205c
Kebbell, Dr William: 36c,126c,173b
Kemp, Nathaniel: 53c,116d,167d
Kemp, Thomas: **80**,**183a**
Kemp, Thomas Read: **80**
(Kemp Town): **81**
(St George's Church): **166a**
(Temple): **39q**
also: 51,172a,184a
see also: Level; Old Steine; Race-course; Royal Sussex County Hospital; tenantry downs; Trinity Chapel.
Kempe, Charles: **116d**
also: 58,116b,130c,169c,170,205d
King, Dr William: 46a,78b,148b,149f
Kipling, Rudyard: 155b,f,m,157b
Knowles, Sir James: 99f
La Croix, Inspector Victor: 66b,c
Lambert, William: 43c
Livingstone, Dr David: 115v
Louise, Princess: 81d,124,133a,178
Mahomed, Sake Dene: **7f**
Mantell, Dr Gideon: **114g**
Marlborough, Duke of: 114b,114k,161a,161j
Mary, Queen: 75b
Melville, Alan: 39d,v
Michell, Revd Henry: 115a,183a,198
Miles, John 'Smoaker': **7b**
Miller, Max: **56q**
Moens, Seaburne: 155t
Mountbatten of Burma, Earl: 162b
Murray, D.L.: 81c
Nash, John: 81a,161b
Neagle, Anna: 81d
Neville, Charles: 171a
Newman, Cardinal John: 99d
Nibbs, Richard Henry: **203b**
Nicholson, Sir William: 155f,p,158
Noble, Ray: 39k
Norfolk, Dukes of: 83b,91c,100e,152
Olivier, Lord Laurence: 99c,142k
Ovett, Steve: 132a,213
Pelham family:
see: Chichester, Earls of.
Phillips, Henry: 81f,86,149b,j
Pickles, Wilfred: 99h
Porden, William: 52,107,114l,161a
Preston, Sir Harry: 160a,163,174
Prince Regent:
see: George IV.
Princes of Wales:
see: Charles; Edward VII; Edward VIII; George IV.
Rastrick, John: 142b,143,144
Rawson, Sir Cooper: 61,189b
Relhan, Dr Anthony: 40,183a
Rennie, Sir John: 142a,b
Robertson, Revd F.W.: 39h,39k,115t
Robson, Dame Flora: 55a,56n,208c
Roe family: 212a
royalty: 71b
see also: Adelaide, Queen; Albert, Prince; Alexandra, Princess; Alexandra, Queen; Amelia, Princess; Arthur, Princes; Augusta, Princess; Caroline of Brunswick, Princess; Charles II; Charles, Prince of Wales; Charlotte, Princess; Cumberland, Duke of; Edward I; Edward VII; Edward VIII; Elizabeth II; George IV; George V; George VI; Gloucester, Dukes of; Helen, Princess; Louise, Princess; Mary, Queen; Mountbatten of Burma, Earl; Victoria; William IV; York, Dukes of.
Russell, John: 7b
Russell, Dr Richard: **164**
St Alban's, Duke & Duchess of: **148c**
Sala, George Augustus: 99e
Sassoon family: 59,99e,115p,166b,194b
Saunders, Arthur: 75b,87e
Saunders, Benjamin: **68(viii)**
also: 75b,87e
Sayers, Tom: **36d**
Scott, Sir David: 149q
Scott, Edmund: 36c,51,58,74c,91d,149f,167d,191
Scott, Sir George Gilbert: 7j,19a,155d
Scott, Sir Giles Gilbert: 179b
Shelley, Richard: 2a,122d
Shergold, Samuel: 6,31,114k,183a
Shirley, Sir Thomas: 2a
Sitwell, Sir Osbert: 4e,161g
Slight, Lewis: 161c,183d
Smith, George Albert: 79a
Smith, Horace: 16c,74b,149d
Somerville, J.Baxter: 107,182d
Spence, Sir Basil: 188b
Spencer, Herbert: 99f
Stanford family:
68(v),68(vi),79b,130a,131a,b,132a,177a
statues:
see: Burrows, Sir John Cordy; George IV; Ovett, Steve; Royal Crescent; Victoria, Queen.
Stringer, Dorothy: **68(xii)**
Stroudley, William: **146b**,133b
Struve, Dr F.A.: 36e,138b
Sudeley, Lord: 99e
Surrey, Earls of:
see: Warrenne family.
Talleyrand, Charles: 114g
Tettersell, Nicholas: **35**
(Old Ship): 113a
Thackeray, William: 16c,113c
Thomas-Stanford family:
see: Stanford family.
Thrale, Henry: 183a,205c
Tilt, Thomas: 31b
Tryon, Major George: 55f,61
Turner, Joseph: 34b
Victoria, Queen: **193**
(fountain): **114e**
(jubilees): 41,122c,126c,162b,194a
(memorials): 130c,170
(and Royal Pavilion): 161c,d
(statue): **194b**
(visits): 34b,50a,81f,161k
also: 31c,86,112b
Volk, Herman: 174,196e
Volk, Magnus: **195**
also: 12,41,179b
see also: Rottingdean Railway.
Wade, Captain William: **101a**
Wagner, Revd Arthur: **197**
(ritualism): 150
(St Mary's Home): 136c
also: 198
Wagner, Revd George: 39g,136c
Wagner, Revd Henry: **198**
(and St Nicholas's Church): 169b
also: 87b,c
Wagner, Mary: 39a,g,h,87b
Warrenne family: 11,17c,64,87a,96,100a,169f
Waterhouse, Alfred: 25,103,112a
Watson, Sir William: 156
Wellington, Duke of: 169b,192a
Weltje, Louis: 161a
Western family: 131a,149j,207a,212a
Whistler, Rex: **130f**
Wigney, Isaac: 6,61
Wilcox, Herbert: 81d
Wilds, Amon: **209**
also: 107,189f
(with Charles Busby): **209**
also: 32,39c,h,56p,q,r,83b,99b,d,114g,139d,148b,149k,p,167a,h,k,189c,f,j,207c,e
(with Amon Henry Wilds): **209**
also: 148b,189e,f,g
Wilds, Amon Henry: **209**
also: 32,33a,39f,h,51,74b,83a,86,107,114e,g,137,148c,149d,j,k,n,p,q,167c,169f,207 c
see also: Wilds, Amon (with Amon Henry Wilds)
William IV, King: **210**
(as Duke of Clarence):
34b,71d,112c,115t,163,210
(Royal Pavilion): 161b,k,n
(visits): 50a,81f,115p,138b,149p
also: 31c,71e,161m
see also: Mahomed, Sake Dene.
Wilson, Sir Hugh: 4l
Windsor, Duke of:
see: Edward VIII.
Wolseley, Viscount: **68(i)**
writers & poets:
see: Ainsworth, William Harrison; Austen, Jane; Bagnold, Enid; Barton, Margaret; Bede, Cuthbert; Bennett, Arnold; Black, William; Boucicault, Dion; Burney, Fanny; Carroll, Lewis; Coppard, Alfred; Defoe, Daniel; Dickens, Charles; Greene, Graham; Johnson, Dr Samuel; Kipling, Rudyard; Knowles, Sir James; Melville, Alan; Murray, D.L; Sitwell, Sir Osbert; Smith, Horace; Thackeray, William; Watson, Sir William.
York, Dukes of: 71b,86,163
York, Duke of (later George VI):
see: George VI.